Encyclopedia of
AFRICAN HISTORY AND CULTURE

Encyclopedia of
AFRICAN HISTORY
AND CULTURE

VOLUME III

FROM CONQUEST TO COLONIZATION

(1500 TO 1850)

Willie F. Page, Editor

Revised edition by R. Hunt Davis, Jr., Editor

A Learning Source Book

☑®
Facts On File, Inc.

Encyclopedia of African History and Culture,
Volume 3: From Conquest to Colonization (1500 to 1850)

A Learning Source Book
Editorial: Brian Ableman, Edward C. Haggerty, Bertram Knight,
Christopher Roberts, Bodine Schwerin (revised edition),
Ismail Soyugenc (revised edition), Anthony Yearwood
Consultant: Emilyn Brown

Facts On File, Inc.
132 West 31st Street
New York NY 10001

Library of Congress Cataloging-in-Publication Data

Page, Willie F., 1929–
  Encyclopedia of African history and culture / edited by Willie F. Page; revised edition edited by R. Hunt
Davis, Jr.—Rev. ed.
      p. cm.
  "A Learning Source Book."
  Includes bibliographical references and index.
  ISBN 0-8160-5199-2 ((set ISBN) hardcover)
  ISBN 0-8160-5269-7 (vol. I)–ISBN 0-8160-5270-0 (vol. II)–
  ISBN 0-8160-5271-9 (vol. III)–ISBN 0-8160-5200-X (vol. IV)–
  ISBN 0-8160-5201-8 (vol. V)

  1. Africa—Encyclopedias. I. Davis, R. Hunt. II. Title.
  DT3.P27 2005
  960'.03-—dc22
                                  2004022929

Facts On File books are available at special discounts when purchased in bulk quantities for businesses, associations, institutions or sales promotions. Please call our
Special Sales Department in New York at (212) 967-8800 or (800) 322-8755.

You can find Facts On File on the World Wide Web at
http://www.factsonfile.com
Design: Joan Toro, Joseph Mauro III
Illustrations: Pam Faessler
Maps: Sholto Ainslie, Dale Williams
Printed in the United States of America

VB PKG 10 9 8 7 6 5 4 3 2 1

This book is printed on acid-free paper.

For my wife, Grace,
and my sons, Ed and Chris

CONTRIBUTORS

Editor of First Edition

Willie F. Page is professor emeritus (retired) of Africana studies at Brooklyn College, in Brooklyn, New York. He is the author of numerous reviews and journal articles. His published works include *The Dutch Triangle: The Netherlands and the Atlantic Slave Trade 1621–1664*.

General Editor of Revised Edition

R. Hunt Davis, Jr., Ph.D., is professor emeritus of history and African studies at the University of Florida. He received a Ph.D. in African studies from the University of Wisconsin, Madison. Dr. Davis is an expert on the history of South Africa, African agricultural history, and the history of education in Africa. His published works include *Mandela, Tambo, and the African National Congress* (1991) and *Apartheid Unravels* (1991), along with numerous articles and book chapters. He served as director at the University of Florida Center for African Studies and is also a past editor of the *African Studies Review*.

Contributing Editors of Revised Edition

Agnes Ngoma Leslie, Ph.D., outreach director, Center for African Studies, University of Florida

Dianne White Oyler, Ph.D., associate professor of history, Fayetteville State University

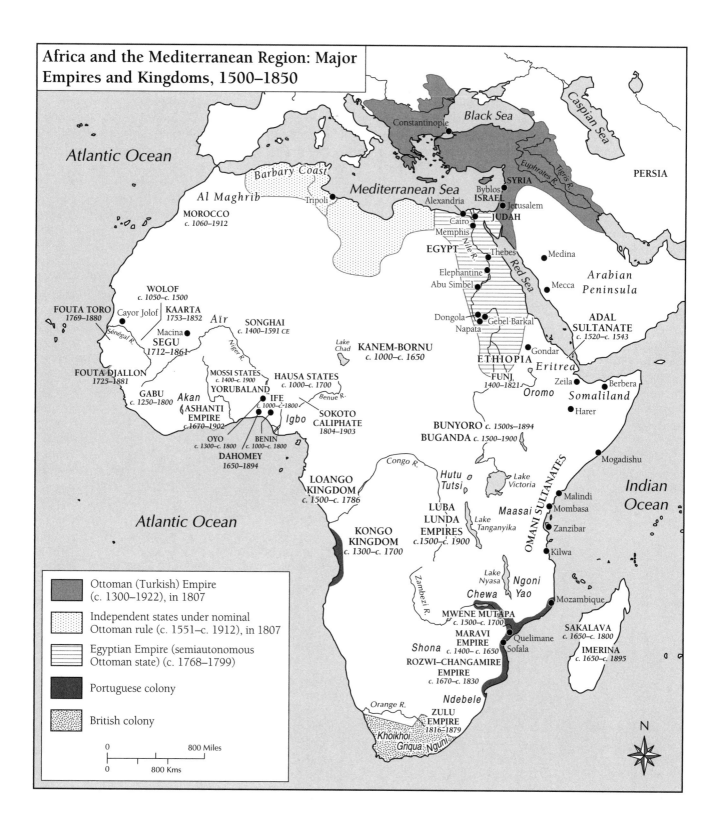

Africa and the Mediterranean Region: Major Empires and Kingdoms, 1500–1850

Atlantic Ocean

Black Sea

Caspian Sea

PERSIA

Constantinople

Barbary Coast

Mediterranean Sea

Euphrates R.

Tigris R.

SYRIA

Byblos
ISRAEL
Alexandria

Al Maghrib

Tripoli

Jerusalem
JUDAH

Cairo

MOROCCO
c. 1060–1912

Memphis

EGYPT

Thebes

Medina

Nile R.

WOLOF
c. 1050–c. 1500

Elephantine
Abu Simbel

Mecca

Arabian
Peninsula

Red Sea

FOUTA TORO
1769–1880

Cayor Jolof

KAARTA
1753–1852

Aïr

SONGHAI
c. 1400–1591 CE

Dongola

Napata

Gebel-Barkal

ADAL
SULTANATE
c. 1520–c. 1543

Sénégal R.

Macina

SEGU
1712–1861

Niger R.

Lake
Chad

KANEM-BORNU
c. 1000–c. 1650

Gondar

ETHIOPIA

Eritrea

Zeila

Berbera

FOUTA DJALLON
1725–1881

MOSSI STATES
c. 1400–c. 1900

HAUSA STATES
c. 1000–c. 1700

FUNJ
1400–1821

Oromo

Somaliland

GABU
c. 1250–1800

YORUBALAND

Akan

IFE
c. 1000–c. 1800

Benue R.

Harer

(ASHANTI
EMPIRE
c. 1670–1902

Igbo

SOKOTO
CALIPHATE
1804–1903

BUNYORO c. 1500s–1894

BUGANDA c. 1500–1900

OYO
c. 1300–c. 1800

BENIN
c. 1000–c. 1800

Mogadishu

DAHOMEY
1650–1894

Hutu
Tutsi

Lake
Victoria

Indian
Ocean

Congo R.

LOANGO
KINGDOM
c. 1500–c. 1786

LUBA
LUNDA
EMPIRES
c.1500–c. 1900

Maasai

Malindi

Mombasa

Atlantic Ocean

Lake
Tanganyika

Zanzibar

KONGO
KINGDOM
c. 1300–c. 1700

Kilwa

Zambezi R.

Lake
Nyasa

Ngoni
Yao

Chewa

Mozambique

MWENE MUTAPA
c. 1500–c. 1700

MARAVI
EMPIRE
c. 1400–c. 1650

Quelimane

Sofala

SAKALAVA
c. 1650–c. 1800

IMERINA
c. 1650–c. 1895

Shona

ROZWI–CHANGAMIRE
EMPIRE
c. 1670–c. 1830

Ndebele

Orange R.

ZULU
EMPIRE
1816–1879

Khoikhoi

Griqua

Nguni

N

Ottoman (Turkish) Empire
(c. 1300–1922), in 1807

Independent states under nominal
Ottoman rule (c. 1551–c. 1912), in 1807

Egyptian Empire (semiautonomous
Ottoman state) (c. 1768–1799)

Portuguese colony

British colony

0   800 Miles

0   800 Kms

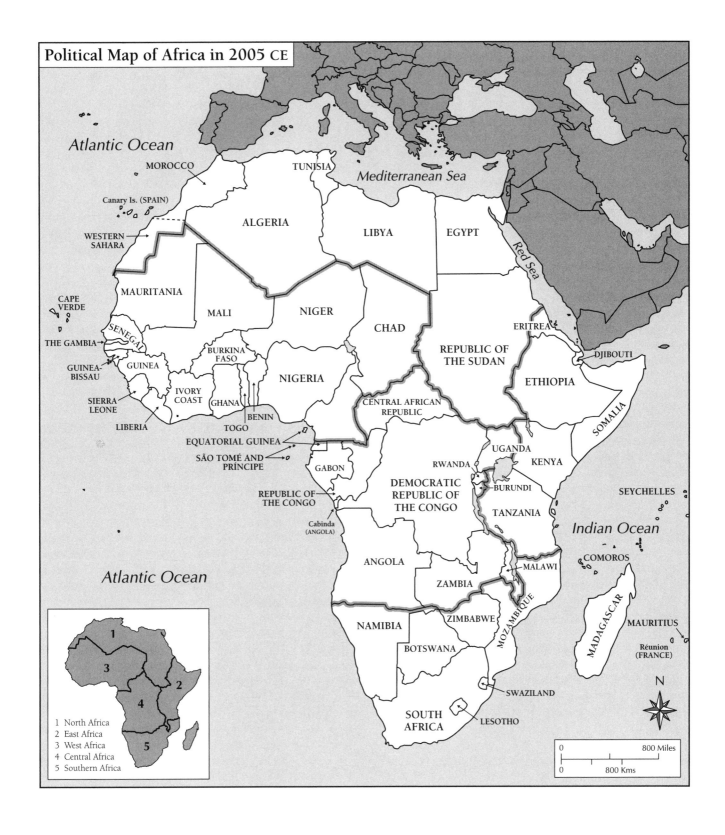

Political Map of Africa in 2005 CE

Atlantic Ocean

MOROCCO

Canary Is. (SPAIN)

WESTERN SAHARA

CAPE VERDE

MAURITANIA

SENEGAL

THE GAMBIA

GUINEA-BISSAU

GUINEA

SIERRA LEONE

LIBERIA

IVORY COAST

GHANA

TOGO

EQUATORIAL GUINEA

SÃO TOMÉ AND PRÍNCIPE

MALI

BURKINA FASO

NIGERIA

BENIN

TUNISIA

ALGERIA

LIBYA

NIGER

CHAD

Mediterranean Sea

EGYPT

Red Sea

ERITREA

DJIBOUTI

REPUBLIC OF THE SUDAN

ETHIOPIA

SOMALIA

CENTRAL AFRICAN REPUBLIC

GABON

REPUBLIC OF THE CONGO

Cabinda (ANGOLA)

DEMOCRATIC REPUBLIC OF THE CONGO

RWANDA

BURUNDI

UGANDA

KENYA

TANZANIA

ANGOLA

ZAMBIA

MALAWI

MOZAMBIQUE

NAMIBIA

ZIMBABWE

BOTSWANA

SWAZILAND

SOUTH AFRICA

LESOTHO

SEYCHELLES

Indian Ocean

COMOROS

MADAGASCAR

MAURITIUS

Réunion (FRANCE)

Atlantic Ocean

1 North Africa
2 East Africa
3 West Africa
4 Central Africa
5 Southern Africa

N

0   800 Miles

0   800 Kms

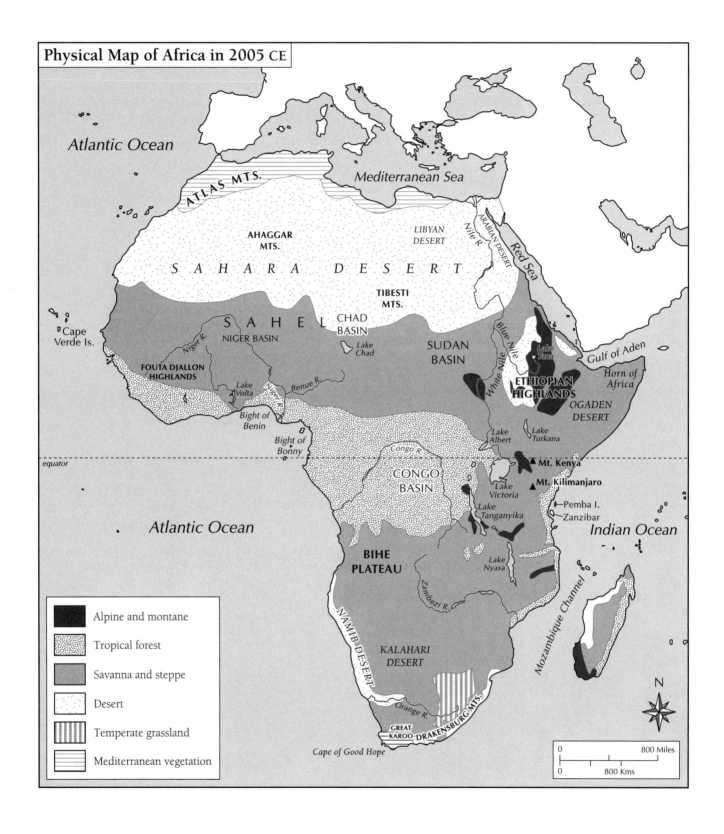

Physical Map of Africa in 2005 CE

Atlantic Ocean

Mediterranean Sea

ATLAS MTS.

AHAGGAR MTS.

LIBYAN DESERT

S A H A R A   D E S E R T

Nile R.

Arabian Desert

Red Sea

TIBESTI MTS.

S A H E L

CHAD BASIN

NIGER BASIN

Lake Chad

SUDAN BASIN

White Nile

Blue Nile

Lake Tana

Gulf of Aden

Horn of Africa

Niger R.

FOUTA DJALLON HIGHLANDS

Lake Volta

Niger R.

Benue R.

ETHIOPIAN HIGHLANDS

OGADEN DESERT

Bight of Benin

Lake Albert

Lake Turkana

Cape Verde Is.

Bight of Bonny

Congo R.

▲ Mt. Kenya

equator

CONGO BASIN

Lake Victoria

▲ Mt. Kilimanjaro

Atlantic Ocean

Lake Tanganyika

Pemba I.

Zanzibar

Indian Ocean

BIHE PLATEAU

Lake Nyasa

Zambezi R.

NAMIB DESERT

KALAHARI DESERT

Mozambique Channel

Orange R.

DRAKENSBURG MTS.

GREAT KAROO

Cape of Good Hope

N

Legend

- Alpine and montane
- Tropical forest
- Savanna and steppe
- Desert
- Temperate grassland
- Mediterranean vegetation

0		800 Miles
0		800 Kms

CONTENTS

LIST OF ENTRIES

HOW TO USE THIS ENCYCLOPEDIA

This encyclopedia is organized chronologically, dividing the African past into five major eras. This division serves to make it easier to study the vastness and complexity of African history and culture. It also allows students and general readers to go directly to the volume or volumes they wish to consult.

Volume I, *Ancient Africa*, deals with Africa up to approximately 500 CE (roughly, in terms of classical European history, to the Fall of the Roman Empire and the dissolution of the Ancient World on the eve of the emergence of Islam). The volume also includes articles on the continent's key geographical features and major language families. In addition you will find articles that deal with certain basic aspects of African life that, in essential ways, remain relatively constant throughout time. For example, rites of passage, funeral customs, the payment of bride-wealth, and rituals related to spirit possession are features common to many African societies. Although these features can evolve in different cultures in radically different ways, their basic purpose remains constant. Accordingly, rather than try to cover the evolution of these cultural features in each volume, we offer a more general explanation in Volume I, with the understanding that the details of these cultural touchstones can vary widely from people to people and change over time.

On the other hand there are entries related to key cultural and social dimensions whose changes are easier to observe over time. Such entries appear in each of the volumes and include architecture, art, clothing and dress, economics, family, music, religion, warfare, and the role of women.

Volume II, *African Kingdoms*, focuses on what may be loosely termed "medieval Africa," from the sixth century to the beginning of the 16th century. This is the period that witnessed the rise and spread of Islam and, to a lesser degree, Arab expansion throughout much of the northern and eastern regions of the continent. It also saw the flowering of some of Africa's greatest indigenous kingdoms and empires. Other Africans, such as the Maasai and Kikuyu living in and around present-day Kenya, did not live in powerful states during this time yet developed their own dynamic cultures.

Volume III, *From Conquest to Colonization,* continues Africa's story from roughly 1500 to 1850. During this era Africa became increasingly involved with the Atlantic world due to European maritime exploration and subsequent interaction through trade and cultural exchanges. This period also included the rise of the transatlantic slave trade, which in turn created the African Diaspora, and the beginnings of European colonization. As a result, it marks a period when the dynamics shaping African culture and society began to shift.

Volume IV, *The Colonial Era,* covers Africa during the years 1850–1960. This historical period begins with Europe's conquest of the continent, leading to the era of colonial rule. Political control enabled Europe to extend its economic control as well, turning Africa into a vast supply depot of raw materials. Volume IV also covers the rise of nationalist movements and the great struggle Africans undertook to regain their independence.

Volume V, *Independent Africa,* deals with the continent since 1960, when Africans began regaining their independence and started to once again live in sovereign states. (This process, of course, took longer in the southern portion of the continent than in other parts.) In common with the rest of the world's people, however, Africans have faced a host of new and challenging problems, some of which are specific to Africa, while others are of a more global nature.

In addition to the aforementioned cultural entries that appear in all five volumes, there are entries for each of the present-day countries of the continent as identified on the Political Map found at the front of each volume. Readers can thus learn about the key developments in a given country within a given time period or across the entire span of African history. There are also articles on individual ethnic groups of Africa in each of the volumes. Since there are more than a thousand identifiable groups, it has been necessary to limit coverage to the major or key groups within a given period. Thus, a group that might be historically important in one period may not be sufficiently important, or may not even have existed, in a period covered by one or more other volumes. Likewise, there are entries on the major cities of the continent for given time periods, including, in Volume V, all the present national capitals. Another key set of entries common to all volumes concerns historically important persons. In general, historians are more readily able to identify these individuals for recent periods than for earlier times. As a result the latter volumes contain more individual biographical entries. An exception here is the case of Ancient Egypt, where historical records have enabled us to learn about the roles of prominent individuals.

In preparing these volumes, every attempt has been made to make this encyclopedia as accessible and easy to use as possible. At the front of each volume, readers will find an introduction and a timeline specific to the historical era covered in the volume. There are also three full-page maps, two of which appear in all five volumes (the current political map and a physical map), and one that is specific to the volume's time period. In addition the front of each volume contains a volume-specific list of the photographs, illustrations, and maps found therein. The List of Entries at the front of each volume is the same in all volumes and enables the reader to quickly get an overview of the entries within the individual volumes, as well as for the five-volume set. Entries are arranged alphabetically, letter-by-letter within each volume.

Entry headwords use the most commonly found spelling or representation of that spelling, with other frequently used spellings in parentheses. The question of spelling, of course, is always a major issue when dealing with languages utilizing an alphabet or a script different than that used for English. Changes in orthography and the challenges of transliteration can produce several variants of a word. Where there are important variants in spelling, this encyclopedia presents as many as possible, but only within the entries themselves. For easy access to variant and alternate spelling, readers should consult the index at the end of each volume, which lists and cross-references the alternate spellings that appear in the text.

Each volume contains an index that has references to subjects in the specific volume, and the cumulative index at the end of Volume V provides easy access across the volumes. A cumulative glossary appears in each volume and provides additional assistance.

The entries serve to provide the reader with basic rather than exhaustive information regarding the subject at hand. To help those who wish to read further, each entry is linked with other entries in that volume via cross-references indicated by SMALL CAPITALS. In addition the majority of entries are followed by a **See also** section, which provides cross-references to relevant entries in the other four volumes. The reader may find it useful to begin with one of the general articles—such as the ones dealing with archaeology, dance, oral traditions, or women—or to start with an entry on a specific country or an historically important state and follow the cross-references to discover more detailed information. Readers should be aware that cross-references, both those embedded in the text and those in the **See also** section, use only entry headword spellings and not variant spellings. For those readers who wish to research a topic beyond the material provided in individual and cross-referenced entries, there is also a **Further reading** section at the end of many entries. Bibliographical references listed here guide readers to more in-depth resources in a particular area.

Finally, readers can consult the **Suggested Readings** in the back of each volume. These volume-specific bibliographies contain general studies—such as atlases, histories of the continent, and broad works on culture, society, and people—as well as specialized studies that typically cover specific topics or regions. For the most part, these two bibliographic aids contain those recently published works that are most likely to be available in libraries, especially well-stocked city and college libraries. Readers should also be aware that a growing number of sources are available online in the form of e-books and other formats. The World Wide Web is also a good place to look for current events and developments that have occurred since the publication of this encyclopedia.

LIST OF IMAGES AND MAPS IN THIS VOLUME

Photographs and Illustrations

Maps

INTRODUCTION TO THIS VOLUME

The history of Africa has been as dramatic as its culture has been rich. But few periods in that history have been as turbulent as the one covered in this volume, from 1500 to 1850. Kingdoms and empires—some of the most famous in all of African history—rose and fell. In West Africa, the great Songhai Empire flourished, reached the pinnacle of its economic and military power, and then eventually collapsed, a victim of both internal forces and pressure from more powerful Moroccan invaders. Its fall, however, after a turbulent period of religious and civil unrest, led to the formation of another great empire, the Sokoto Caliphate.

In Ethiopia, Christians and Muslims battled in an era of civil war known as the Age of Princes. Further south, in what is now the present-day country of Zimbabwe, Mwene Mutapa emerged as a military and commercial force, and elsewhere, the Omani Sultanate assumed dominance of the Swahili coast. The Akan and Hausa states, the Kongo kingdom, Kanem-Bornu, Oyo, Kuba, the Ashanti Empire—these names all evoke stories that figure prominently in the era's history.

Some of the most fascinating personalities in African history walked the stage during this period. Few, of course, were more famous than the storied Shaka, the ruthless military genius who transformed a culture and forged a Zulu nation. But, beyond this, there were figures such as Osei Tutu, the brilliant ruler of the Ashanti Empire, and Shamba Bolongongo, whose administrative skills helped create the Kuba kingdom. There was the astonishing Queen Nzinga, who ruled over the Mbundu people, in present-day Angola, and held the Portuguese at bay during her long reign. And there was also the Omani sultan Sayyid Said, who ruled over much of the Swahili Coast; Usman dan Fodio, who inspired the Fulani jihads that transformed the politics and history of West Africa; and Agaja, who conquered several disparate states to expand the kingdom of Dahomey. In Egypt, Muhammad Ali began the process of transforming the country from a province of the Ottoman Empire into a modern nation state.

History, of course, is not always a matter of individual personalities. During these same years massive migra-

tions—like those of the Tutsi, who moved into Rwanda and Burundi; and the Luo, who migrated from the Sudan into the Great Lakes region—reshaped the ethnographic landscape. Sometimes brought on by natural causes and, at other times, by political religious, or social upheaval, these population movements played an important role during the period.

Also important were rivalries between ethnic groups, as these groups vied for land and access to trade routes. Conflicts between Hutu and Tutsi, Mijikenda and Somalis, and Tunjur—like the conflicts between many others—marked the period's history with everything from simple competition to complex social interactions, from trading rivalries to bloodshed.

These years, of course, also mark an event that changed the face of Africa for all time—the transatlantic slave trade. When the peoples of West Africa opened their shores to the Portuguese in the mid-15th century, little did they imagine that it would initiate four centuries of rape, plunder, and genocide, the magnitude of which is virtually unfathomable even today. At first it was gold that spurred on the Europeans. Then, when the need arose for labor in Europe's New World colonies, attention turned to the extraction of humans, or "black gold," in what became a system of chattel slavery.

Slavery, of course, had been known virtually everywhere in the world and throughout history. It was even well known among Europeans, who had practiced it, in various forms, from classical times through the Middle Ages. Similarly, a system of domestic servitude, or slavery, had traditionally existed within Africa itself. There, for example, an individual could be reduced to the condition of slavery as a prisoner of war, for violating a custom, for committing a crime, or even for being unable or unwilling to settle a debt. In general, however, this slavery functioned within prescribed customs that, in effect, amounted to limits or boundaries. The enslaved, for instance, generally could be ransomed to their kinfolk through the efforts of slave merchants. Further, while the treatment of slaves varied from one ethnic group or region to another, the conditions of slaves held in this traditional African system did not begin to approach the brutality and inhumanity that came to be known when the transatlantic slave trade arose. In West African cultures, for example, enslaved families could not be separated. In addition, in most parts of Africa, enslavement was not perpetual. In fact, children whose parents were enslaved frequently became members of the master kinship group, often marrying members of their masters' families or even rising to prestigious positions in society.

During the early years of the transatlantic slave trade it is possible that some of the Africans sold to the Europeans were already in slavery. But, as the years passed, the vast majority of the millions of Africans transported abroad was not living as slaves. They usually were citizens of some small state or village that was raided or attacked, not because of inter-ethnic warfare, but as a well-planned system of abduction in which men, women, and children were kidnapped or killed. Those who survived the raids were now captives, hostages. But unlike conventional victims of kidnapping, these could not be ransomed by their families and kin. Instead they were swiftly removed from the vicinity of their homelands and eventually transported to new, alien lands.

Clearly the massive abduction of millions of Africans could not have taken place without the cooperation of some Africans—merchants or leaders willing to engage in the trade in human flesh. But why, many ask, would Africans sell other Africans? This, however, is not quite the right question to pose. Except for a few individuals, Africans of this time had little sense of their African identity. In fact, the sense of being Africans vis-à-vis people from other continents emerged out of the experiences of slavery in the Western Hemisphere, conquest by Europeans in the late 19th century, and a period of colonial rule that lasted nearly a century. Even after a sense of African identity did emerge, it has not stopped some Africans from committing dreadful acts against other Africans. The 1994 Rwandan genocide, while clearly an African event, is also an example of a human—rather than particularly African—phenomenon. In Cambodia in the late 1970s, some 1.7 million people

died as a result of a deliberate government policy; the 1992–95 conflict in Bosnia led to so-called ethnic cleansing that resulted in the death of thousands of Muslims at the hands of the Serbs.

The proper phrasing of the question, then, is why did some people living in Africa participate in selling other people living in Africa? In some cases the answer was simple greed. The chiefs, merchants, and warlords who plundered villages, kidnapped innocent victims, and sold them were power-seekers who simply attacked their weaker neighbors for gain and profit. In other instances the chiefs were settling accounts with traditional enemies. However, the most common scenario appears to have been different. In truth, many ethnic groups found themselves in the throes of a dilemma: either agree to participate in the trade or be subjected to it themselves, either raid or be raided, either be drawn into the trade in human cargo or become subject to it themselves.

It is for these and other reasons that, in this volume, we have chosen, when speaking of the transatlantic slave trade, to use terms such as "Africans," "hostages," and "captives," instead of the simple term "slaves." For, in truth, while the trade might be referred to as the "slave trade," few of the people who made up the cargo ever accepted their status as slaves. Both individual attempts at escape and larger-scale rebellions were more than common; they were frequent. Indeed North American slaveholders recognized this fact so much that they preferred to receive Africans who had been "seasoned" or "broken" in the Caribbean—often with branding irons, floggings, and other forms of physical punishment—before accepting them for work on their plantations.

What emerges from this period, 1500 to 1850, is a history of remarkable richness and depth, a tapestry of memorable people, events, and issues that engages the minds and spirits of everyone from scholars to casual readers. Above all, it is with an appreciation of this richness and depth—as well as of the facts of African history and culture—with which we would like to leave those who read and use this volume.

TIME LINE (1470–1860)

1470	Elmina, first European fort in tropical Africa, built by Portuguese in southern Ghana
	Mwene Mutapa emerges as an active trading kingdom, monopolizing region's trade in ivory, gold, salt, and captives
1472	Ngazargamu established as capital of Kanem-Bornu Empire by Mai Ali Gaji
1481–1504	Ozolua, warrior king of Benin, uses alliance with Portuguese to extend Benin's borders from southwestern Nigeria to Lagos
1490–1590	Changamire dynasty rises to power in present-day Zimbabwe
1493	Askia dynasty takes power in Songhai
1498	Vasco da Gama lands at Malindi
c. 1500	Buganda, in present-day Uganda, emerges as independent kingdom
	In present-day Tanzania, Haya and Zinza peoples combine with Hinda caste members from the north to found Hinda States
	Kebbi flourishes among the Hausa States in present-day northwestern Nigeria

c. 1500	Luo people migrate from the Sudan into the Great Lakes region, leading to the demise of the Chwezi dynasty of Kitara
1500–1530	Tengella and his son Koly Tengella lay the foundations of the Fulani Denianke dynasty, in present-day northern Senegal
1500–1800	Mozambique becomes center of Portuguese activity in East Africa
1505	Afonso I takes throne in Kongo kingdom
1515	Swahili coast traders begin selling Turkish-made firearms
1516	Barbarossa brothers capture Algiers, giving control to Ottoman Turks
1517	Ottoman Turks take control of Egypt
1520	Francisco Alvares travels through Ethiopia
1525	Kanem-Bornu dominates present-day Chad
1525–1625	Rise of Dyula trading network
1533	Ahmad Grañ dominates Ethiopia
1543	Ahmad Grañ defeated by Ethiopian Christians and their Portuguese allies, in part due to the effects of firearms

1549–1582	Askia Daud rules Songhai Empire
	Oyo plundered by Nupe and Borgu
1556	Ndongo people win independence from Kongo kingdom and hold off Portuguese until 1671
1550–1575	Gonja, in present-day northern Ghana, founded by invading Mandinka cavalry from Songhai Empire
1559–1776	Denianke dynasty rules Fouta Toro state, in West Africa
1570–1603	Idris Alawma rules in Kanem-Bornu
1575	Akan state of Denkyira founded in present-day Ghana
1591	Moroccan forces of Abd al-Mansur, led by Judar Pasha, defeat Songhai army at Battle of Tondibi and go on to take Timbuktu; leads to eventual collapse of Songhai Empire
1593–1698	Portugal and Oman vie for control of Mombasa
c. 1600	Gorée Island, off the coast of Senegal, becomes important center for the transatlantic trade in African captives
1600–1620	Shamba Bolongongo rules Kuba kingdom, strengthening the central government, and encouraging the arts
1600–1730	Akan state of Akwamu flourishes in modern-day Ghana
	European trade in African captives develops in Angola
1600–1650	Kalonga Masula rules Maravi federation, stretching south from Lake Malawi

1600–1807	Ashanti Empire rises and flourishes in present-day Ghana
1610–1640	Tunjur people, who had inhabited Darfur since the 14th century, are driven out by the Muslim Maba; Tunjur settle in Bulala-controlled Kanem, where they are eventually conquered by Sefuwa-led Bornu
1624	Death of Gatsi Rusere, whose confiscation of Portuguese assets set off decades of conflict within the Mwene Mutapa kingdom
1630	Matamba, in present-day Angola, becomes kingdom, later ruled by Queen Nzinga
1631–1702	Muradid dynasty rules in Tunisia
1640	Suliman Solong establishes Kayra dynasty in Darfur
1650	Height of Hausa States power, with territory stretching from central Nigeria to Bornu. near lake Chad
	Bambara king Massa founds kingdom of Kaarta, with capital at Sounsan
1650–1673	Dutch, Danish, and British build forts and trading posts near Accra, in present-day Ghana
1650–1700	Sakalava Empire rises to prominence on Madagascar
1650–1750	Height of power for Yoruba Oyo Empire, in Nigeria
1650s	Dutch East India Company establishes outpost at Cape of Good Hope
1650–1717	Osei Tutu builds Ashanti Empire into major power in the region of present-day Ghana

1659–1677	Attempt by Nasir al-Din, a Muslim cleric, to curb European influence and establish orthodox Muslim rule in Senegambia leads to Marabout War
1662–1663	Queen Nzinga rules over the Mbundu people, helping hold off Portuguese power
c. 1665	Kongo kingdom begins to disintegrate
1666	Mawlay al-Rashid founds Alawi dynasty in Morocco
1666–1681	Ouagadougou, in the central region of modern-day Burkina Faso, reaches the height of its power under Waraga.
1680–1690	Changamire Dombo rises to power in the region south of the Zambezi River, marking the beginning of the Rozwi dynasty.
1683	Rozwi kings take control of Butua gold fields
1700	In Burundi, Ntare Rushatsi becomes first king
1700–1725	Igbo defeat Ibibio people and establish a confederation of Igbo-Ibibio towns in West Africa
1700–1750	Opokuware II creates the Great Oath of the Ashanti
1705	Husseinid dynasty comes to power in Tunisia
1706	Tekla Haymonot engineers the assassination of his father, Iyasu I, and becomes king of Ethiopia
1717	Akyem groups defeat Ashanti ruler Osei Tutu
1720–1750	Opoku Ware II adds Banda, Dagomba, Gonja, and Akyem to Ashanti Empire
1711–1835	Karamanli dynasty rules in Libya
1712	Mamari Kulibali becomes first official king of the long-standing state of Segu
1724–1727	Agaja conquers Abomey, Allada, and Whydah to expeand kingdom of Dahomey
1725	Karamoko Alfa proclaims jihad, or holy war, to convert Fouta Djallon to Islam
1730	Mombasa comes under the control of Zanzibar
1730–1750	Oyo regains power and prominence through slave trade
1740	Dissenters from Lunda establish Kazembe, in Central Africa
1741	Busaidi dynasty comes to power in Mombasa, vying for dominance with the rival Masrui family
1750–1790	Mandara kingdom flourishes south of Lake Chad
1754	Forces from Segu demolish Kaarta kingdom, which is reestablished near Kumbi by Sey Bamana Kulibali
1759	Ngwaketse state established in southeastern Botswana
1766	Ngolo Diarra forms Segu kingdom in present-day Mali
1769–1855	Zemene Mesafint, or Age of Princes, with unrest and civil war in Ethiopia
1775	Independent Fante states in coastal region of present-day Ghana unify under a high king, or *brafo*
1776	Tukulor establish theocratic Muslim state in Fouta Toro

1781–1800	Peak of transatlantic slave trade
1782–1810	Andrianampoinimerina rules Merina kingdom in Madagascar
1794	Monson Diarra defeats Kaarta and establishes Segu as the predominant Bambara kingdom
1795–1805	Mungo Park explores Gambia and Niger rivers in West Africa
1800	Chagga empire formed on eastern slopes of Kilimanjaro by Orombo
1800–1895	Tutsi rise to power in East Africa
1803–1825	Ras Gugsa rules in Yejju, in north-central Ethiopia
1804	Usman dan Fodio launches Fulani jihad, seeking to convert Hausa States to Islam; leads to formation of Sokoto Caliphate
1804–1856	Sayyid Said leads Omani Sultanate to its peak of wealth and power along the Indian Ocean coast of East Africa
1806	Great Britain establishes Cape Colony in present-day South Africa
1807	Great Britain outlaws the trade in human beings in its colonies around the world; trade continues unabated in some areas
1816	Shaka assumes power within the Zulu clan
1817–1840	Mfecane ("the crushing") leads to mass death, migration, and breakdown of traditional clan structures across southern Africa
1817–1860	Mshweshwe founds Sotho kingdom in wake of Mfecane

A

Abd al-Mansur (Ahmad al-Mansur) (c. 1549–1603)
Moroccan sultan

Al-Mansur's father, Muhammad al-Shaykh, founded the SADIAN DYNASTY, under whose rule MOROCCO attained international status unknown since the rule of the Almohads in the 12th and 13th centuries. The most successful ruler of the dynasty, al-Mansur assumed power when his brother Abd al-Malik died in 1578 while defending Morocco against Portuguese invasion.

From his capital in MARRAKECH, al-Mansur consolidated Morocco's power through royal trade monopolies and by creating a slave army to defend against invasion by Ottoman Turks from ALGERIA. He also created an alliance with Britain, which was fast becoming a world power and with which Morocco had a mutual enemy in Spain. Even though the Ottoman Empire controlled all of the other coastal regions of northern Africa by the end of the 16th century, Morocco was able to stay independent, largely because of al-Mansur's foresight.

In 1590 al-Mansur sought to contain the expansion of the SONGHAI Empire, which threatened Morocco from the south. He sent his commander, JUDAR PASHA (fl. 1590s), with about 4,000 well-armed and experienced soldiers across the Sahara to confront the Songhai cavalry of Askia Ishaq II (r. 1588–1591). The soldiers on the Moroccan side, some of them Christian and Turkish mercenaries, had vastly superior firearms and training, and they decisively routed the Songhai at Tondibi, a town outside the trading center of Gao.

Within a few years, al-Mansur was able to take the former Songhai cities of Gao, TIMBUKTU, and JENNE, carrying plunder back to Marrakech and levying heavy taxes that further enriched al-Mansur's coffers. Ultimately, the occupation of the southern cities so far from his capital proved to be too costly, and he abandoned the territory.

Al-Mansur's successors could not maintain the central authority that he had established, and within a few years of his death in 1603, Morocco was divided between rival Sadian princes from Marrakech and FEZ.

Abeokuta
Capital of Ogun State in present-day southwestern NIGERIA; founded by Yoruba refugees in the 19th century. Its name means "refuge among rocks." Abeokuta was founded in 1830 among rocky outcroppings that dotted the savanna regions along the Ogun River. Sodeke, a hunter, banded together EGBA refugees from the decaying OYO EMPIRE and established Abeokuta as the new Egba capital.

Early Abeokuta was a confederation of four Egba subgroups, the Ake, Gbagura, Oke-Ona, and Owu. As these subgroups grew they eventually formed a single confederation that became Abeokuta. Although the city was ruled in the traditional Yoruba style by kings called *obas,* it was actually the town's war chiefs who had the final authority.

The British Church Missionary Society established its Yoruba mission at Abeokuta, 10 years after Sodeke established the city, in response to requests from freed captives who had returned to YORUBALAND from SIERRA LEONE. The founding members of the mission were an Englishman, Henry Townsend (1815–1886), and an ex-captive, Samuel Ajayi Crowther (1808–1891). Prior to their arrival Abeokuta was primarily an agrarian society. The MISSIONARIES, along with Krios from Sierra Leone, were largely responsible for transforming Abeokuta into a key trading town along the trade routes that connected LAGOS with Ibadan. By the end of the 19th century PALM OIL was Abeokuta's most valuable trade commodity.

See also: CHURCH MISSIONARY SOCIETY (Vol. IV); CROWTHER, SAMUEL AJAYI (Vol. IV); OGUN (Vol. I).

Abidjan Former capital city of present-day IVORY COAST. Located on the Ebrie Lagoon of the Gulf of Guinea, Abidjan was first inhabited during the 16th century. By the end of the 1500s, three Ebrie fishing villages had been established in the area. The villages of Locodjo, Anoumabo, and Cocody would later merge and become Abidjan.

Although Portuguese explorers arrived in Abidjan in the 17th century, Europeans showed little interest in the area until 200 years later, at which time the town began to grow into an important trade city.

See also: ABIDJAN (Vols. IV, V).

Abo (Toposa) Nomadic, Nilotic-speaking people of West Africa. Much of what is known about the early history of the Abo has been handed down orally. The Abo believe their founder was a ruler named Esumaiukwu. Esumaiukwu's father, the ruler of the kingdom of BENIN, Oba OZOLUA (r. 1481–1504), was a cruel leader who oppressed his people in order to build a powerful empire. He levied heavy taxes and executed those who rebelled against him. The resulting turmoil sparked the migration of a large group of Abo people.

Esumaiukwu led a group to find a new, more peaceful homeland. His brothers Oputa, Exoma, Akilini, Osimili, Etim, and Chima Ukwu accompanied him. They split into two groups at Agbor, in the southeastern part of what is now NIGERIA. The first group, led by Chima Ukwu, settled in the Agbor-Assaba region. Esumaiukwu led the second group toward Ukwuani to Ologwu. After many months, Esumaiukwu and his siblings moved on, his brothers eventually settling and forming the kingdoms of Usoro, Ashaka, Afor, and Osissa.

Esumaiukwu and his remaining followers finally settled at Ugboko Ukwa, an area inhabited by the Akiri people. The Akiri were unwilling to integrate peacefully with the Abo, so Esumaiukwu and his people subdued them. A kingdom was established, and Esumaiukwu became the ruler, or *oba,* of the Abo people. His children inherited the throne upon his death, and throughout the 16th and 17th centuries, the Abo gradually gained control over much of the lower NIGER region.

Abomey Principal city in the 17th-century kingdom of the same name and later the capital of the kingdom of DAHOMEY. Located in present-day Republic of BENIN, in West Africa, Abomey was established around 1625 by a prince named Do-Aklin, who fled there from ALLADA after losing a power struggle with his two brothers.

Abomey flourished under Do-Aklin and his grandson WEGBAJA (c. 1645–1680). At some time during the reign of Wegbaja some of the FON people of Abomey began referring to their kingdom as "Dahomey." Thereafter, the two kingdoms became synonymous, though the city of Abomey retained its name. A long line of shrewd rulers, including AGAJA (c. 1673–1740) and TEGBESU (r. 1740–1774), led Abomey-Dahomey in dominating trade along the West African coast.

Abomey was long dominated by remarkable royal palaces. Created by a succession of rulers starting in the late 17th century, the palaces contained luxurious residences that had walls adorned with numerous works of ART. The palace complex was especially noteworthy for a series of sculpted earthen murals that depicted important events, customs, and myths associated with the history of the city and its people. Unfortunately, the palace was destroyed by fire in the late 19th century during a period of French occupation, and many of its treasures were destroyed.

Until the reign of GEZU (1818–1858), the main source of Abomey's wealth was the sale of captive Africans, although prior to his reign Britain had abolished the TRANSATLANTIC SLAVE TRADE. Eventually, however, the commercial demand for humans abated, and the emphasis in Abomey shifted to the exportation of PALM OIL.

See also: PORTO NOVO (Vol. III); WHYDAH (Vol. III).

Further reading: Francesca Piqué and Leslie H. Rainer, *Palace Sculptures of Abomey: History Told on Walls* (Los Angeles: Getty Conservation Institute and the J. Paul Getty Museum, 1999).

Accra Capital of present-day GHANA. The city of Accra emerged as trade increased at three neighboring European trading posts along what was known as the GOLD COAST. Prior to the arrival of Europeans, the inhabitants of the region were the GA-DANGME people, who began settling there in the 15th century. Portuguese explorers discovered the Ga-Dangme villages as early as 1482 but expressed little interest in the area. In 1650 Dutch explorers, too, arrived on the Gold Coast, and they built a trading post called Fort Crèvecoeur. In 1661 the Dutch were joined by Danish traders, who built their own fort, Christiansborg Castle, in the nearby Ga-Dangme town of OSU.

The Dutch also established a coastal town they called both Accra and Ussher Town. By 1673 British merchants had also joined the fray, building a trading post known as Fort James.

The rival Danish, Dutch, and British trading posts eventually merged into one large town known as Accra. As the town grew, the primary interior Ga-Dangme village of AYAWASO deteriorated, and most of its inhabitants migrated south to Accra. Although Accra was an important European trading center, its society remained heavily influenced by Ga-Dangme culture.

Accra's lucrative trade in GOLD and human captives attracted African rivals from the north, as well. For example, by the end of the 17th century, Accra was made a vassal state of AKWAMU, an AKAN state. By the middle of the 18th century, however, the Ashanti, also an Akan group, had gained control of the coast. In 1826 the Ga-Dangme and other coastal African groups, including the FANTE, joined with the British to defeat the Ashanti, driving them from the area. Although the victory relieved the Ga-Dangme of oppressive Ashanti rule, Britain soon monopolized power along the coast. By 1877 Accra was the new capital of the British Gold Coast colony.

See also: ACCRA (Vols. II, IV, V); ASHANTI (Vol. II); ASHANTI EMPIRE (Vols. III, IV); ENGLAND AND AFRICA (Vols. III, IV); GOLD COAST COLONY (Vol. IV).

Further reading: I. van Kessel, ed., *Merchants, Missionaries and Migrants: 300 Years of Dutch-Ghanaian Relations* (Amsterdam: KIT Publishers, 2002); John Parker, *Making the Town: Ga State and Society in Early Colonial Accra* (Portsmouth, N.H.: Heinemann, 2000).

Acholi (Shuli, Gang, Acoli) Nilotic people who inhabited regions of present-day UGANDA and southern Republic of the SUDAN. The Acholi are probably descended from several groups of LUO peoples who settled in central Uganda and KENYA during the southern migration of Nilotic peoples from the region of Sudan starting in the early 16th century. About the middle of the 17th century the ancestors of the Jie and Lango peoples (long time rivals of the Acholi) conducted a series of raids against the Luo and Madi groups. These raids, which lasted well into the 18th century, contributed to the assimilation of the Luo and Madi into Acholi. Though the Lango and Acholi lived side-by-side and shared a common language and other cultural traditions, the Lango generally refused to acknowledge any historical ties to the Luo.

Acholi society is based on patrilineal descent. The people live in small chiefdoms. Traditionally the Acholi were hunters, but they also participated in both pastoral and agricultural activities. They still herd sheep and cattle, and they produce nuts, vegetables, and grains such as millet and sorghum.

See also: ACHOLI (Vol. II).

Further reading: Ronald R. Atkinson, *The Roots of Ethnicity: The Origins of the Acholi of Uganda before 1800* (Philadelphia: University of Pennsylvania Press, 1994).

Adal (Adel, Adaiel, Adela, Adem) Muslim state situated near the Gulf of Aden, on the Horn of Africa. Fleeing the tyranny of Ethiopian emperor Amda Siyon (r. 1314–1344), the Walashma came to Adal in the 14th century and formed an independent kingdom. From 1415 until the end of the 15th century, the Walashma dynasty monopolized Adal's government.

Adal was involved in a series of disputes with its Ethiopian neighbors throughout the 14th and 15th centuries. By the 16th century these petty conflicts turned into a full-blown battle for religious and political superiority and, more significantly, control of trade routes. In the last decade of the 15th century, Muhfuz (d. c. 1517), the Muslim governor of nearby ZEILA, designated himself imam, or ruler, and became the religious and military authority of Adal. Muhfuz waged a jihad against the Christian Ethiopian state, usually attacking just after Lent, when the Christians were weak from their fasting. Muhfuz carried out these raids for nearly 25 years. After each of these missions, Muhfuz returned home with a large number of captives and a great amount of plunder, which won him the support of his fellow Muslims. Muhfuz fell in 1517 when Ethiopian emperor LEBNA DENGEL (r. c. 1508–1540) and his army hunted down the renowned Islamic leader. He was slain by a monk named Gabra Endreyas, and his soldiers returned to Adal shortly after his death.

Like Muhfuz before him, AHMAD GRAÑ (c. 1506–1543) declared himself the imam of Adal and renewed the jihad against the Christian state. Ahmad was a charismatic warrior and leader who led his Muslim army to countless victories over the Christians and forced Lebna Dengel to become a fugitive in his own land. By 1533 Ahmad had taken most of central ETHIOPIA. He appeared to be unstoppable until 1543, when the Christians, with the help of the Portuguese, defeated the Adal army and killed their celebrated leader. After Ahmad's death his army fled and the Ethiopians took back their territory.

In the latter half of the 16th century the OROMO proved to be a greater threat to Adal than the Christians had ever been. Through a series of invasions, Oromo migrants managed to take away all the power and territory that Adal had acquired earlier in the century.

See also: ADAL (Vol. II); AMDA SIYON (Vol. II); JIHAD (Vols. II, IV).

Further reading: Harold G. Marcus, *A History of Ethiopia* (Berkeley, Calif.: University of California Press, 2002).

Adamawa (Fumbina) Emirate encompassing parts of present-day eastern NIGERIA and northern CAMEROON; established by Adama (r. 1806–1848), a commander of the early 19th-century FULANI JIHADS. Prior to the founding of Adamawa in 1806, Fulani chiefs ruled in the region, but little evidence exists of a distinct kingdom. Migratory patterns show, however, that the Jukun, Chamba, Bata, and other peoples preceded the Fulani but did not remain in the area for long before they were either displaced or continued their migrations to another region.

In 1804 the Muslim Fulani cleric USMAN DAN FODIO (1754–1817) began a holy war in an effort to convert the people of the HAUSA STATES and the surrounding regions to the Islamic faith. In the campaign throughout portions of today's northern Nigeria, his forces were led by Adama, who carried the Muslim title *modibbo,* or "learned one." In 1806 Adama was rewarded for his efforts in the jihad when he was made emir of a region located south of Bauchi and KANEM-BORNU that came to be called *Adamawa* in his honor. The title *lamido,* meaning "governor" or "ruler," was also bestowed on Adama, but he preferred to keep his original title and was therefore known as Modibbo Adama.

The Adamawa Emirate grew as Adama continued his jihad, overthrowing nearby kingdoms such as Demsa, in 1810; MANDARA, in 1820; and Malabu, during the 1830s. Adama chose the city of Gurin as his first capital but was forced to move to the more strategically placed town of Ribadu, in 1830. In 1839 the capital was moved again to Jobolio before it was finally decided the city of Yola should be the seat of Adama's emirate. The swamps and marshes of Yola offered excellent protection from groups that were hostile to the Fulani, including the Bata and Verre peoples.

> Beginning in the mid-19th century Adamawa was also known as the kingdom of Fumbina.

Adama's reign as emir ended in 1848 but Adamawa, by then a sizeable Fulani kingdom, continued to grow for some time through the conquests of later emirs—four of whom were sons of Adama.

Adangme See GA-DANGME.

Adansi (Adanse) Early AKAN trading state established in present-day GHANA at the beginning of the 16th century. According to oral tradition, Adansi was founded by a chief named Opun Enim. Located between the Oda and Fum branches of the Pra River, Adansi is considered the homeland of the AKAN and Adansi people, as well as many subgroups of the Ashanti and Akem. The importance of Adansi is reflected in its name, which means "beginning of change" or "house building."

The Adansi state was located on a busy north-south GOLD-trading route. In Adansi's early years the town of Adansimanso served as the first capital. It was located near present-day Mansia, where the Adansi people lived in the surrounding hills of Kwisa and Moinsi. About 1657 Adansimanso was destroyed in a battle with the DENKYIRA, and the capital of the kingdom was briefly moved to Dompoase and finally to Fomena.

See also: ASHANTI (Vol. II); ASHANTI EMPIRE (Vol. III).

Afar (Denkel, Danakil, Adalis) Ethnic group known as Danakil by the AMHARA and Arabs and as Adalis by the Somalis and Harari. The Afar people reside in present-day ERITREA, ETHIOPIA, SOMALIA, and DJIBOUTI, as well as in the desert region of the Danakil Depression. They speak an Eastern Cushitic language similar to that spoken by their Somali and Saho neighbors, although they consider themselves to be ethnically distinct.

There are two major Afar groups, Asaimara (the red "aristocratic" house) and Adoimara (the white "commoner" house), which consist of loosely organized clans and kinship groups. Many of these groups embraced Islam and banded together during war. Aussa, founded in the 16th century, was the capital for Afars settled in the southern area. The northern groups, including Afar peoples from Eritrea, were at various times subject to Tigray rule and the Naibs of Semar while the southern groups were tributary to SHOA. In the 16th century, after converting to Islam, Afars and Somalis took part in the jihad of AHMAD GRAÑ (c. 1506–1543) against the Christians of Ethiopia. After the famed military leader perished in action, the Afars turned on their Somali cohorts and continued the campaign against their AMHARA and OROMO enemies.

Early in the 18th century an Asaimara group, the Mudaito, overthrew the Harari imams who had occupied the southern Afar region since 1577. The Mudaito chief Kedafu (r. c. 1734–1749) established a sultanate in Aussa and enjoyed a reign that was mostly peaceful and prosperous. At the end of the 18th century, after the death of Sultan Ijdahis (r. c. 1779–1801), Aussa fell into a decline from which it did not recover. In 1810 the Wema invaded and gave the sultan Anfari (c. 1802–1862) no choice but to share his power with the Adoimaras. The Asaimaras eventually lost everything to their Adoimara rivals, including their salt deposits and trade routes.

See also: AFAR (Vols. I, II); DANAKIL DEPRESSION (Vol. I).

Further reading: I. M. Lewis, *Peoples of the Horn of Africa: Somali, Afar, and Saho* (Lawrenceville, N.J.: Red Sea Press, 1998).

Afonso I (Alphonse I, Nzinga Mbemba) (c. 1461–1543) *Christian king of the Kongo kingdom*

Afonso's father, NZINGA NKUWU (d. c. 1506), distrusted the Portuguese and limited his contact with them. He renounced the Christianity that he had earlier accepted and turned his back on the Catholic Church. Afonso, on the other hand, refused to give up his Christian beliefs and for this was exiled to the Kongo district of Nsuri, beginning about 1495.

About 1505 Afonso succeeded his father as *manikongo* (king). His half-brother Mpanzu challenged him to a battle for the title, which Afonso won with the assistance of Portuguese troops.

King Afonso openly embraced the Portuguese and their religion. He was responsible for building churches and made Christianity the official state religion. He tried to rid his kingdom of nonbelievers, sentencing many to death or banishment from the kingdom. He cultivated a trading partnership with the Portuguese and welcomed visiting clergymen and scholars, who educated the members of Afonso's royal court. Afonso set out to modernize his country by establishing elite schools, remodeling Mbanza, the capital city, and teaching his subjects to use western European weaponry. In exchange for the gifts from the Portuguese Afonso sent them goods, including captives.

The Portuguese issued a *regimento,* or royal order, in 1512 proclaiming that the KONGO KINGDOM was to supply them with natural resources and captives. Through written letters, Afonso pleaded with King John of Portugal to cease the practice of trading in human beings, but was ignored. In 1539 he survived an attempt on his life by Portuguese traders. By 1540 the Portuguese were export-

King Afonso I (c. 1461–1543) of the Kongo kingdom. In this 1650 print he is dressed in the trappings of a European monarch and sits on a European-style throne to receive European soldiers and their commander. © *Corbis*

ing more than 7,000 Africans annually, causing Afonso to call again for a ban on the trade in humans. Forced to bow to Portuguese pressure and to the superiority of European weapons, Afonso had to repeal his order, and the trade continued unabated. Afonso died in 1543.

See also: CHRISTIANITY, INFLUENCE OF (Vols. II, III, IV, V); PORTUGAL AND AFRICA (Vol. III).

Further reading: Anne Hilton, *The Kingdom of Kongo* (New York: Oxford University Press, 1985).

Afrikaans (Cape Dutch) An official language of SOUTH AFRICA that was developed from a dialect of Netherlandic Dutch in the late 18th century. Afrikaans is a combination of numerous linguistic influences. The language was derived through the mixing of the colonial Netherlandic dialect with the languages of non-Dutch Europeans, native Khoisan speakers, and peoples brought into the area as captives and forced laborers.

Afrikaans was adopted as a literary language in the 19th century. It gradually began to be used in newspapers, and by the early 1900s Afrikaans was integrated into schools and the Dutch Reformed Church.

See also: AFRIKAANS (Vols. IV, V); CAPE COLONY (Vols. III, IV); NETHERLANDS AND AFRICA (Vol. III).

Agades (Agadez) Historical trading city located in present-day NIGER. The city of Agades was known for being an important trading center from the 16th through the 19th centuries due to its strategic location along a major trans-Saharan trade route stretching from Lake CHAD and north to LIBYA and EGYPT. While trade—including copper and salt mined from the area—made the city prosperous, Agades also became known in the surrounding regions for being a place of Islamic scholarship.

Established about the 11th century at the southern end of the AÏR MASSIF, Agades and its trade routes were controlled by a succession of kingdoms. The kingdom of Mali reigned over the city in the 14th century; it became the capital of the TUAREGS in the 15th century. The SONGHAI Empire then conquered and ruled Agades in the early 16th century until the trading empire of KANEM-BORNU overtook the city sometime near beginning of the 17th century. Agades remained a part of Kanem-Bornu until the 19th-century FULANI JIHADS led by the Muslim leader USMAN DAN FODIO (1754–1817) led to FULANI rule.

See also: MALI EMPIRE (Vol. II).

Agaja (Agadja) (c. 1673–1740) *Third ruler of the West African kingdom of Dahomey*

Agaja was a powerful ruler who was able to greatly expand the kingdom of DAHOMEY through military conquest. Between 1708 and 1727 he conquered many neigh-

boring peoples, culminating with the takeover of the kingdom of ALLADA in 1724 and the coastal state of WHYDAH in 1727. These last two conquests provided landlocked Dahomey with access to the lucrative sea trade.

Agaja also instituted administrative reforms that centralized his power and allowed Dahomey to become one of the most powerful kingdoms in West Africa. He began the practice of maintaining an elite female militia, expanded the kingdom's army, and gathered information about neighboring peoples through a network of spies.

The transatlantic trade in humans became increasingly profitable during Agaja's reign. Despite the wealth to be gained from this trade, Agaja tried to create a plantation society based on forced LABOR. Agaja's plans created tension with the powerful OYO EMPIRE, which sought to curb Agaja's ambition. Dahomey was forced to surrender to Oyo in 1730. As a result, Agaja relented on his opposition to the trade in humans. He did, however, insist on a royal monopoly, leading to internal unrest among Dahomey's merchant class. Eventually Agaja was compelled to participate in the trade of humans and Dahomey became a major supplier of captives for many years to come.

See also: OYO (Vol. II); SLAVE TRADE, THE TRANSATLANTIC (Vol. III).

Further reading: Edna G. Bay, *Wives of the Leopard: Gender, Politics, and Culture in the Kingdom of Dahomey* (Charlottesville, Va.: University of Virginia Press, 1998).

Age of Princes *See* ZEMENE MESAFINT.

agriculture As of the beginning of the agricultural revolution, between 9,500 and 7,000 years ago, farming throughout Africa was done to sustain small groups of people. But in areas where states emerged and as kingdoms grew to become empires, African agriculture evolved to become more than a subsistence activity. The products of African farming still fed local populations, but by the beginning of the 16th century they also were used to pay tribute to more powerful kingdoms and to make exchanges with other merchants, thereby creating wealth.

In East Africa, for instance, the main crops included millet, sorghum, bananas, and yams. By the late 15th century, however, Portuguese traders brought new types of FOOD products to the continent, among them MAIZE, cassava, and peas. All of these grew well in the climate and were successfully cultivated by African farmers. Groups such as the GANDA, living in what is now UGANDA, were soon profiting from the new and different agricultural products that they grew. By the 18th century they also were tending such crops as bananas, coffee, and plantains and soon were using a neighboring group of peoples—the NYAMWEZI of present-day TANZANIA—to broker their produce and other items with the Europeans stationed along the coastline. Some of these crops were considered "cash crops," desirable items that were grown in order to be traded for other needed items. Many agricultural peoples produced one or more cash crops, and examples of these included coffee, TOBACCO, PALM OIL, sugarcane, and COTTON, which were sold to the Europeans for such items as weapons or cloth; they were also sold or traded to other, nonagrarian African groups for cattle, salt, or metals. Cash-crop agriculture grew steadily in importance over the course of the 19th century.

Of the new crops brought into and then produced in Africa, one of the most important was maize, also known as corn. Introduced during the 16th century, maize was produced in conjunction with other, indigenous cereal grains, such as sorghum and millet. For example, from the late 16th century onward the AJA people, who lived in what is now the Republic of BENIN, were bringing in maize harvests twice a year and using the grain both for consumption and trade. By the 18th century maize had taken over as one of the leading crops in the LUNDA EMPIRE, which covered areas in present-day ZAMBIA, the Democratic Republic of the CONGO, and ANGOLA. Other cereal grains, including wheat, which was introduced by the Moroccans, were of great importance to northern Sudan areas such as present-day EGYPT. During the 17th and 18th centuries North African wheat was so abundantly produced that large quantities of it were sold both on the caravan routes and to Europeans at coastal trading markets.

In the kingdoms of the Lunda empire and in the HAUSA STATES of northern NIGERIA, the peoples most often relegated to the tending and harvesting of agricultural crops were captives. The Lunda, who lived in a sparsely populated area, conducted raids on other states in order to capture people who could carry out the agricultural duties of their kingdoms. Elsewhere, agricultural duties were carried out by free people. Among these agricultural peoples, however, the workers often sought out other occupations during the months when the ground was too dry or in the periods between harvests. Among the more common secondary occupations were mining GOLD and engaging in trading activities.

See also: AGRICULTURE (Vols. I, II, IV, V); AGRICULTURAL REVOLUTION (Vol. I); CASH CROPS (Vols. IV, V); FARMING TECHNIQUES (Vol. I).

Ahmad Grañ (Ahmad ibn Ibrahim al Ghazi, Ahmed al-Ghazali Ibrahim, Ahmed Gragn) (c. 1506–1543) *Warrior and political leader from the Muslim state of Adal*

Ahmad was known to his Muslim followers as *Sahib al-Fath* (the conqueror) and as *Grañ* (the left-handed) by Christians. Between 1525 and 1527 he headed a series of military operations that substantially weakened Christian defenses in ETHIOPIA and strengthened Muslim control of Bali, HADYA, Kembata, and SIDAMO. His ADAL army, comprised of newly converted Somali and AFAR people, was trained in military tactics and weaponry by Turks from the Ottoman Empire. With promises of wealth and religious domination, Ahmad's troops were not only physically equipped but were ripe with enthusiasm by the time Ahmad declared his jihad in 1528. In the Battle of Shimbra Kure the Ethiopian emperor, LEBNA DENGEL (r. 1508–1540), lost much of his territory to the Muslims. These lost territories included AMHARA, Dawaro, Lasta, and SHOA.

Within a decade of the beginning of the holy war, Ahmad had conquered and converted most of south and central Ethiopia. He also had started to penetrate the mountainous region to the north. His army tore through the country burning churches and destroying all traces of Christian culture. Lebna Dengel took refuge in the highlands that had yet to be conquered. From there he sent a message to the Portuguese asking for their assistance. But Portuguese assistance did not arrive until 1541, by which time Ahmad had enlisted the Ottomans in his cause. As a result Ahmad continued to dominate the Christians in battle.

Under Lebna Dengel's successor Galawdewos (r. 1540–1559), the Portuguese helped retrain the Ethiopian army. In 1543 it defeated Ahmad's army in a battle during which Ahmad was killed. After Ahmad's death, his army, which relied heavily on his dynamic leadership, dispersed, allowing the Ethiopians to reclaim their land.

See also: CHRISTIANITY, INFLUENCE OF (Vol. III); ISLAM, INFLUENCE OF (Vols. II, III, IV, V).

Aïr Massif Mountainous region in the southern Sahara desert in north-central NIGER that is the homeland of the southern TUAREGS, a seminomadic group of herders and traders. Beginning in the 1400s the area was also the site of the sultanate of Aïr. The Tuareg capital of AGADES is located south of the highest peaks on the Aïr Massif.

Early in the 1500s, prior to the rise of the SONGHAI Empire, Songhai settlers pushed east into Aïr, displacing some of the Tuaregs around Agades. When Songhai soldiers set out later in the 16th century to conquer the region, their domination was facilitated by the presence of the earlier settlers. Later, in the 17th century, warriors from KANEM-BORNU in the Lake CHAD region fought with the Songhai and ultimately occupied much of the Aïr Massif, including Agades and Takedda. Though Kanem-Bornu ruled the region into the 19th century, by the end of the 1700s the Tuaregs had reestablished their dominance along most of the trade routes that passed through it. Many Tuareg nomads still inhabit the Aïr Massif.

See also: AÏR MASSIF (Vol. II).

Aja (Adja) West African ethno-linguistic group inhabiting southern parts of present-day Republic of BENIN and TOGO. Their language belongs to the Kwa group of the Niger-Congo language family. The Aja are tied ethnically, culturally, and linguistically to their EWE, Mina, and FON neighbors, all of whom are descended from the Aja kingdom, which reached the height of its power in the 16th century.

The Aja were part of a secondary migration into the region that divided the earlier Yoruba settlers in two. Large segments of the Aja and the Yoruba, who shared many religious beliefs and practices, were at times under the authority of the same rulers.

It is believed that the Aja were originally from Old Oyo in NIGERIA and that they fled this war-torn region between the 13th and 15th centuries. They first migrated to KETU and then to Nuatja or Watchi in Tado (present-day Togo), where they mixed with the indigenous people and formed the Ewe.

By the 15th century a group of Aja had settled in ALLADA, which later became the capital of the Great Ardra kingdom. In 1625 the kingdom fragmented when three princes vied for the throne. In the end, Prince Kokpon stayed in Great Ardra, Prince Do-Aklin established ABOMEY, and Prince Te-Agdanlin founded Little Ardra (PORTO NOVO).

Abomey grew to become a powerful kingdom. The new Aja settlers assimilated with the Abomey people and together they formed a new group who came to be known as the Fon or DAHOMEY. The Dahomey became heavily involved in trade and their kingdom was strong and wealthy until they were conquered by the Oyo in 1738.

Because of linguistic peculiarities, the Aja are sometimes classified as a Ewe subgroup, rather than vice versa. Modern historians might refer to the Aja settlers of Allada, Abomey, and WHYDAH as "Ewe-speaking" peoples, thereby making them members of Ewe subgroups. More precisely, though, the Ewe were originally a southern branch of the Aja who migrated from Oyo.

Because their lands were situated close to the coast, the Aja fell under the sway of various European influences. The Dutch first encountered the Aja around 1595 and placed representatives in Assim, located in the Allada kingdom. In 1640 French Capuchin missionaries arrived but failed to win converts. The French established a trading station at Whydah, in 1671, and before the end of the century other European nations followed suit. These incursions weakened the traditional bonds that united the Aja people, and economic rivalry replaced the traditions of consultation and cooperation that had once united them.

Traders played active roles in installing kings who would favor the economic interests of the Europeans. The rivalry between brothers that led to the foundation of Dahomey is one of the earliest examples of this breakdown. The war between the Aja kingdoms of Allada and Whydah that lasted from 1712 to 1722 was precipitated by rivalries between the Dutch and the Portuguese along the coast. The war ultimately led to the fall of both Allada and Whydah.

See also: AJA (Vol. II); FRANCE AND AFRICA (Vol. III); OLD OYO (Vol. II).

Akan People, region, and language of West Africa. The Akan are concentrated along the Guinea Coast in the present-day countries of GHANA and TOGO and in IVORY COAST between the Komoé and Volta rivers. The Akan migrated to their present-day location between the 11th and 18th centuries. During these migrations, they mixed with indigenous peoples and settled small villages, which evolved into a trade network that spread Akan influence from Ivory Coast to Benin. The sprawling trade economy helped forge the social organization of the Akan people, who organized themselves into a number of highly developed states, including the northern state of BONO and the southern states of DENKYIRA, AKWAMU, FANTE, and Ashanti.

The northern Akan state of Bono was established about 1450 in the present-day Brong-Ahafo region of Ghana. Bono quickly became a major participant in the trans-Saharan GOLD trade because of its proximity to BEGHO, a major trading city of the Muslim DYULA traders, some 40 miles (64 km) away. The Akan gold fields became major sources of gold, which was extracted by the labor of captives and by farmers, who worked in the gold fields in the dry season when the fields lay fallow. Much of the gold was then shipped by caravan across the Sahara to the North African coast and from there to Europe and the Near East. Bono became a powerful state that frequently warred with neighboring peoples. In 1722 the rival ASHANTI EMPIRE conquered Bono.

The southern Denkyira state, founded in the late 16th century, had a diverse economy based on AGRICULTURE, MINING, and trade. Its powerful status enabled the Denkyira to exercise control over the smaller southern Akan states. From about 1698 to 1701, however, the Denkyira were subjugated by the expanding Ashanti state led by its famous king OSEI TUTU (d. 1712). One of the purposes of this conquest was to gain direct contact with Europeans along the coast. Many Akan states, including the Ashanti, the Denkyira, and the Fante, served as intermediaries between the Europeans and the inland peoples.

The Akwamu established their state at the beginning of the 17th century in present-day Ghana. As they grew wealthy through agriculture and the gold trade, the Akwamu expanded their territory by conquering the states of Ladoku, Agona, and WHYDAH. In 1731 the Akwamu state collapsed after its conquest by the AKYEM people.

The Fante states formed an alliance at the end of the 17th century to defend against the growing Ashanti kingdom. Due to their location on the Gulf of Guinea, the Fante served as intermediaries between the Ashanti and European merchants. In order to gain control over this strategic territory, the Ashanti conquered the Fante in 1806.

The Ashanti kingdom rose to prominence under the leadership of the OYOKO clan. By 1750 the Ashanti had established the most powerful empire along the GOLD COAST, having conquered Denkyira, Akyem, Akwapim, and Akwamu. The Ashanti remained the most powerful state in the region until the mid-19th century, when the British colonial presence became more important.

Because of their location along the coast, the Akan states became involved in the slave trade. Both the Fante and the Ashanti for example, acted as intermediaries between the African traders on the interior and the European traders operating on the coast.

See also: AKAN (Vols. I, II, IV); VOLTA RIVER (Vol. II).

Further reading: Ivor Wilks, *Forests of Gold: Essays on the Akan and the Kingdom of Asante* (Athens, Ohio: Ohio University Press, 1993).

Akwamu Early AKAN state that flourished from 1600 to 1730 in the AKYEM Abuakwa region along the GOLD COAST, in West Africa. Founded in the late 16th century by the Akan people of Twifo Heman, Akwamu quickly became a wealthy GOLD trading state. Gold from the Birim River district enabled the people of Akwamu to establish political authority to the south and southeast. Between 1677 and 1681 the king of Akwamu, ANSA SASRAKU (d. c. 1689), conquered GA-DANGME and FANTE coastal settlements, as well as Ladoku to the east.

After Ansa Sasraku's death, circa 1689, Akwamu captured Agona, a Fante state to the west, and WHYDAH along the DAHOMEY coast. By 1710 they had encroached upon Ho, a region occupied by the EWE people. Akwamu's dominance was short-lived, however, and by 1731 it had been destroyed by the neighboring state of Ashanti. Akwamu survivors of the Ashanti wars traveled across the Volta River where they established a small community.

See also: ASHANTI (Vol. II); ASHANTI EMPIRE (Vols. III, IV); VOLTA RIVER (Vols. I, II).

Akyem Ethnic group located mostly in what is now southern GHANA. The Akyem descended from the forest-dwelling AKAN peoples by the 16th century and retained close ties with their fellow Akan, the ADANSI, Ashanti, and DENKYIRA, into the first part of the 17th century. During that time the emerging Akyem state was known as "Great Akanny," in reference to the important role it still played in the Akan state. This was due in large part to GOLD, which was mined and worked by the Akyem and traded at the coastal city of ACCRA. During the 17th century, though, the Akyem were forced to migrate to the east as the Denkyira expanded their territory. The Akyem relocated to establish a new state in the mountainous region near the Birim River. The Akyem state developed rapidly due to its well-structured political system in which power was centralized by its chief, and the state became prosperous by trading gold, kola nuts, and ivory. By the mid-17th century Akyem was a powerful state, and it became even stronger when merchants began trading for European weapons.

Although known for being gold traders, the Akyem probably derive their name from the Twi word for "salt trader."

Despite its success, as the Akyem state grew its governing system weakened. By 1715 multiple head chiefs were claiming to be the Akyem leader. This loss of centralized authority eventually led the Akyem to break into three distinctive groups: Akyem Abuakwa, Akyem Kotoku, and Akyem Bosume. Despite the split, the Akyem subgroups continued to cooperate with one another to their economic and political benefit. One of their most important group efforts came in 1717 during a battle against the ASHANTI EMPIRE. During this clash the Akyem groups banded together to repel Ashanti invaders and killed the famed Ashanti ruler OSEI TUTU (r. c. 1650–1717) in the process. The Akyem groups again collaborated to resist invasion in 1730 against the Akwamu people and, in 1742, against yet another group of Ashanti forces.

See also: AKYEM (Vol. II); GOLD COAST (Vol. III); IVORY TRADE (Vols. III, IV); SLAVERY (Vols. I, II, III, IV).

Further reading: Kofi Affrifah, *The Akyem Factor in Ghana's History, 1700–1875* (Accra, Ghana: Ghana University Press, 2000).

Algeria Large North African country covering approximately 919,600 square miles (2,381,800 sq km). Today Algeria is bordered by the Mediterranean Sea to the north, TUNISIA and LIBYA to the east, NIGER and Republic of MALI to the south, MAURITANIA and WESTERN SAHARA to the southwest, and MOROCCO to the northwest. Once part of the Berber Almoravid and Almohad empires, Algeria was the first country of the MAGHRIB to be ruled by the Ottoman Empire. The city of TLEMCEN had been the eastern capital of Almohad Algeria, and the seaports of ALGIERS, Annaba, and Bijaya were important centers of trade with European markets.

The Almohad empire fell when the Marinids, a group of nomadic Zanatah BERBERS, migrated northward in search of better pasture land and captured MARRAKECH in Morocco in 1269. The Zayyanids, a rival Zanatah Berber clan, captured Tlemcen and held it until the early 1500s, although the Marinid dynasty gained occasional possession of that city throughout the 13th and 14th centuries. Most of western Algeria was nominally under control of the Zayyanid dynasty.

The regional instability created by the fall of the Almohads led to a dramatic rise in piracy along the Mediterranean coast. As Spanish and Portuguese merchants vied with the Ottoman Turks for control of trade in the western Mediterranean, CORSAIRS based in TANGIER, TRIPOLI, Algiers, and Tunis raided Christian merchant ships. This state of affairs led the Spanish to blockade ports that were known as pirate dens and force them to pay tribute. Algeria and other cities were occupied by Spanish ground forces. The Muslims felt forced to seek the help of the Ottoman Empire, which dispatched a fleet to expel the Spanish. The driving force behind the call for Ottoman assistance were the two Barbarossa brothers, Aruj (d. 1518) and Khayr ad-Din (d. 1546), who captured Algiers in 1516 and used it as a base against the Spanish. In 1518 Khayr ad-Din Barbarossa swore allegiance to the Ottoman sultan. With Ottoman military help, Khayr ad-Din was able to dominate the Maghrib, and Algeria became the first country in that region to fall under Ottoman rule.

At first Algeria was ruled by Ottoman governors sent from Istanbul. In 1689, however, Ottoman troops

French forces capturing the city of Algiers on July 5, 1830. Under control of the Ottoman Empire, Algiers was a major base of the Barbary pirates for 300 years until it fell to the French. © *Bettmann/Corbis*

in Algeria revolted against the governor and set up military rule. These troops, members of the elite corps of Janissaries, functioned as a Turkish military caste in Algerian society. Thereafter, until the French captured Algeria in 1830, a series of military commanders chosen from among the Janissaries were the de facto rulers of the country. They assumed the title *dey* (from Turkish *dayi,* literally, "maternal uncle") and governed Algeria as a semiautonomous province of the Ottoman Empire. The *deys* maintained a connection with the empire by recognizing the authority of the sultan as caliph, a ruler descended from the prophet Muhammad, and by following the same Hanafite school of Muslim law as the empire followed. Most of the revenue of the state through the mid-1700s was generated from piracy, the ransoming of Christian captives, and tribute paid by European countries.

As European power in the Mediterranean grew, Algerian piracy—and revenue from piracy—began to diminish. High taxes caused unrest and rebellion among the common people. As an emerging United States entered Mediterranean trade, it too paid tribute to the so-called Barbary PIRATES in exchange for immunity from attack. In 1815, however, an American squadron of warships commanded by Stephen Decatur (1779–1820) attacked Algiers and forced the governor to accept a treaty that protected American vessels from piracy. In 1816 a combined British and Dutch fleet all but destroyed the Algerian navy. The stage was set for the French invasion of Algiers in 1830.

The campaign against the Barbary pirates is immortalized in the opening line of the United States Marine Corps hymn: "From the halls of Montezuma, to the shores of Tripoli." Tripoli in Libya was a pirate stronghold. Montezuma, now more properly spelled Moctezuma (1466–c. 1520), was the Aztec emperor of Mexico. The reference in the song is to the capture of the Castle of Chapultepec, a fortress in Mexico City, during the U.S.–Mexican War (1846–1848).

See also: ALGERIA (Vols. I, II, IV, V); ALMOHADS (Vol. II); ALMORAVIDS (Vol. II); ISLAM, INFLUENCE OF (Vols. II, III, IV, V); OTTOMAN EMPIRE AND AFRICA (Vols. III, IV).

Further reading: Cyril E. Black and L. Carl Brown, eds., *Modernization in the Middle East: The Ottoman Empire and its Afro-Asian Successors* (Princeton, N.J.: Darwin Press, 1992); Julia Clancy-Smith, ed., *North Africa, Islam, and the Mediterranean World: From the Almoravids to the Algerian War* (Portland, Oreg.: Frank Cass, 2001).

Algiers Capital and port city located on the northern coast of ALGERIA. After its destruction by Vandals in the fifth century, Algiers was rejuvenated by the BERBERS, and by the 10th century it had become a Mediterranean trade center. In the early 16th century the city became a refuge for Moors escaping persecution in Christian Spain. These Moors began to threaten Spanish maritime trade, and in 1511 Spain fortified the neighboring island of Peñón. Spain fought for control of the strategic port city for five years. However, in 1516 the Ottoman Empire gained control, and Algiers became an independent city under Ottoman rule. The city soon became a base for the CORSAIRS of the BARBARY COAST, and Algiers thrived as a commercial center for the next 300 years. In 1830 France captured the city, and it served as headquarters for the French occupation until Algerian independence in 1962.

See also: ALGIERS (Vols. IV, V) FRANCE AND AFRICA (Vol. III); OTTOMAN EMPIRE AND AFRICA (Vols. III, IV).

Allada (Alladah, Arda, Ardah) Kingdom centered near the present-day town of Cotonou, in southern Republic of BENIN. Allada was the most powerful kingdom in the region until about 1625, when rivalry among princes split it into three parts. The original village of Allada was established around 1575 by AJA immigrants. The Aja originally came from Tado on the Mono River, which rises near modern Benin's border with TOGO and empties into the Bight of BENIN. About 1625 a dispute among three princes who staked claims to the Allada throne culminated in the establishment of two new villages, Little Arda and ABOMEY. Prince Kokpon remained in the diminished Allada and became its new king, while Te-Agdanlin set himself up as the ruler of Little Arda, later called PORTO NOVO by the Portuguese merchants who controlled the trading center. The third prince, Do-Aklin, founded Abomey. Although all of the kingdoms paid tribute to the OYO EMPIRE, after the split Abomey became the most powerful of the three, maintaining a strong centralized government and a standing army.

The Aja founders of Abomey intermarried with the local groups to form the FON people. In 1724 AGAJA (c. 1673–1740) reunited the Fon with what remained of Allada. Soon thereafter, about 1727, Agaja conquered the neighboring kingdom of WHYDAH using firearms he had acquired from European merchants along the Gulf of Guinea. His victory led to the unification of Abomey, Allada, and Whydah into the new kingdom of DAHOMEY, with Allada then becoming one of Dahomey's three provinces. One of the key towns in Allada was Arda, the name by which the kingdom of Allada was known to most Europeans.

Allada, Abomey, and Whydah were all involved in the transatlantic SLAVE TRADE and became prosperous as intermediaries between the suppliers on the interior and

European traders in their trading forts at Porto Novo and Whydah on a stretch of the Gulf of Guinea often called the SLAVE COAST.

See also: ALLADA (Vol. II); SLAVERY (Vol. III); WARFARE AND WEAPONS (Vol. III).

Further reading: Robin Law, *The Oyo Empire 1600–1836 A West African Imperialism in the Era of the Atlantic Slave Trade* (Oxford, U.K.: Claredon Press, 1977).

Alvares, Francisco (fl. c. 1520) *Portuguese priest who wrote about his journeys through Ethiopia*

Father Francisco Alvares was sent to ETHIOPIA in 1520 as part of a diplomatic mission to locate the gold-rich kingdom of a legendary priest named Prester John. His purpose during this mission was to gather information on the conditions in Africa. Alvares's account of this journey, published by 1540, was the first foreign work to describe the kingdom of Ethiopia, including some of its history and descriptions of places of interest, such as the churches of Lalibela.

See also: GOLD (Vol. III); LALIBELA, CHURCHES OF (Vol. II).

Amhara Ethnic group present in ETHIOPIA, especially in the central highlands. Like their Tigray neighbors, the Amhara subscribe to a Monophysite form of Christianity. They speak a Semitic language called Amharic that is similar to Tigrinya and has roots in Ge'ez, the traditional language of the Ethiopian Orthodox Church. Throughout the centuries the Amhara have practiced AGRICULTURE, cultivating mostly grains such as millet, wheat, sorghum, *teff*, and a cereal known as *Eragrostis abyssinica*.

Amhara province was located east of the Blue Nile River in the region between present-day GOJJAM and Welo. Between about the 13th and 16th centuries, Amhara was the center of the Ethiopian state.

From the 13th to the 20th centuries all but one of Ethiopia's emperors were from Amhara. This political dominance was a main point of contention between the Amhara and other groups in Ethiopia, such as the Tigray and the OROMO. By the 15th century Amhara language, culture, and political control had infiltrated the regions of Begemdir, Gojjam, SHOA, DAMOT, Wegera, Dembya, SIMIEN, and Welo. The primary goal of the Amhara missionaries at this time was to squelch all traces of traditional beliefs and practices of the neighboring peoples and to impose on them their own brand of Christianity.

The Ethiopian state under Amhara rule reached its zenith during the 15th and the 16th centuries. After that time its vast territory was substantially reduced by Muslim forces, especially during the time of AHMAD GRAÑ (c. 1506–1543), the celebrated Islamic warrior and political leader. Under the Christian emperor Galawdewos (r. 1540–1559), Ethiopia gradually began to rebuild. However, the Oromo expansion over the following two centuries proved to be even more destabilizing to the Amhara monarchy than the Muslims had ever been. Eventually, the Oromo adopted the culture and RELIGION of the regions they dominated, including Amhara culture.

See also: AMHARA (Vols. I, IV); AMHARIC (Vols. I, II); BLUE NILE (Vol. I); GE'EZ (Vol. I); MONOPHYSITE (Vol. I); TIGRAY (Vols. I, IV, V); TIGRINYA (Vol. I).

Amina, Queen *Hausa warrior queen and heroine*

Most of what is known about Amina comes from Hausa oral traditions and the *Kano Chronicle*, a history of the Hausa state of KANO written in the 19th century. Although it was long thought that she lived during the 16th century, recent investigations have found that it was probable that Amina lived in the 15th century and possibly even earlier.

Andrianampoinimerina (Nampoina) (c. 1745–1810) *Brilliant general, political leader, and unifier of the Merina people of the central highlands of Madagascar*

In 1780 Andrianampoinimerina was a chief at Ambohimanga, a province of the MERINA kingdom. Around 1782 he led a successful coup against the Hova Merina ruler with the support of a small but disciplined and well-organized army. After gaining control he established his capital at the fortified city of TANANARIVE (today called Antananarivo).

By the beginning of the 19th century Andrianampoinimerina had reorganized the administration of the Merina kingdom. He was viewed by his people as an energetic and effective leader, and his radical changes affected practically every layer of Merina society, even the relations between FAMILY members. Under his direction, the Merina adopted an organized and codified law that is still in use to a large degree. He changed laws regarding trade and taxation that greatly increased the resources of his centralized authority. He also installed a corps of peasant workers who performed public works, including the development of extensive canals and irrigation for the cultivation of rice. Andrianampoinimerina further cemented his absolute authority and inspired loyalty from conquered peoples by establishing a system of land administration that appointed members of the indigenous groups as the local authorities.

The ECONOMY of the Merina kingdom under Andrianampoinimerina relied heavily on the trading of slaves to the French, who needed laborers to work their sugar plantations in the MASCARENE ISLANDS. Captives, rice, and cattle were traded for French arms and other manufactured goods that served to maintain Merina superiority throughout the 19th century. Despite trade with the French, Andrianampoinimerina made laws that prohibited the European powers from establishing too much influence in Tananarive.

Andrianampoinimerina's hand-picked successor was his son, Radama I (r. 1810–1828), who continued the state-building tradition. During Radama's reign the Merina also established closer relations with European powers, especially the British, who sent MISSIONARIES to the island.

Further reading: Pier M. Larson, *History and Memory in the Age of Enslavement: Becoming Merina in Highland Madagascar, 1770–1822* (Portsmouth, N.H.: Heinemann, 2000).

Angola Southwest African country measuring approximately 476,200 square miles (1,233,400 sq km) in size. Angola is bordered by the Democratic Republic of the CONGO to the north, ZAMBIA to the east, and NAMIBIA to the south. Its capital is the coastal city of LUANDA. Angola was a major trading region beginning in the 16th century.

The region that is now Angola gets its name from the title given to MBUNDU kings. Subgroups of the Mbundu included the NDONGO, MATAMBA, PENDE, SONGO, and LIBOLO, whose kings were called *Ngola*.

Shortly after it began exploring the region in the 15th century, Portugal sent traders back to the coastal land in search of captives, who were used primarily to colonize parts of Brazil. Some captives were also sent back to Portugal, however, where they were used to fill the gap in the LABOR market. Others were traded for GOLD dust on the GOLD COAST. Initially almost two-thirds of these captives were men, but the demand for fertile women increased over time.

Later, in the 16th century, the Dutch began to trade for captives as well, and as the demand grew, Mbundu kings became eager to expand their kingdoms. The manufactured goods that the kings received for the captives—including cheap European firearms—augmented their power and wealth.

As the ECONOMY grew, several mercantilist states emerged within Angola. One of these was Ndongo, which was formed by a Mbundu group from Luanda in the early 16th century. Ndongo prospered throughout the 16th century, but trade relations with Portugal were not always amicable. On several occasions, Ndongo's rulers detained Portuguese ambassadors for no apparent reason. In addi-

tion, Jesuit MISSIONARIES, frustrated by their unsuccessful attempts to convert the local people to Christianity, pressured Portugal to replace the local government with a Christian infrastructure. The culmination of these conflicts came in the late 16th century, when Portugal initiated a military conquest of Angola.

Over the next few years Angola and Portugal engaged in periods of both war and trade, during which several months of war would frequently be followed by periods devoted to trade. Eventually, the Portuguese defeated the Angolans and forced NZINGA (1582–1663), the queen of Ndongo, into exile in neighboring Matamba, where she built a powerful new state. Without local Angolan support, the Portuguese quickly lost their economic advantage and were forced to make peace with the queen in order to establish a new trading partner. With Portuguese support, Matamba became one of the most important markets in the 17th century, which it remained until the 18th century.

Although the trade in captives was economically successful for the Europeans, the long-term effects for the people of Angola itself certainly were less positive. Pressured to provide FOOD for the Europeans' ships, regions like Angola shifted their agricultural production from food crops for local consumption to cheap food for captured Africans. The loss of agricultural labor into the slave trade further compounded the disruption of the economy. The African economy never recovered from this shift in agricultural focus.

See also: ANGOLA (Vols. I, II, IV, V); BENGUELA (Vol. III); PORTUGAL AND AFRICA (Vols. III, IV, V); SÃO SALVADOR (Vol. III); SLAVE TRADE, THE TRANSATLANTIC (Vol. III); WARFARE AND WEAPONS (Vol. III).

Further reading: David Birmingham, *Portugal and Africa* (New York: St. Martin's Press, 1999); Joseph C. Miller, *Kings and Kinsmen: Early Mbundu States in Angola* (Oxford, U.K.: Clarendon Press, 1976); Joseph C. Miller, *Way of Death: Merchant Capitalism and the Angolan Slave Trade, 1730–1830* (Madison, Wisc.: University of Wisconsin Press, 1988).

Anlo (Awuna) A subgroup of the EWE people who live between the coast of modern GHANA and the Volta River. The Anlo speak Ewe, a Kwa subgroup of the Niger-Congo languages. According to oral history, the founders of the Anlo people migrated to present-day Ghana from Notsie (in what is now TOGO) during the mid-17th century. A settlement supposedly was founded by the Anlo forefathers Sri and Wenya. After establishing their kingdom the Anlo were in continuous battle with the neighboring Ada people over fishing, salt-mining, and trade rights. By 1776 more than half of the Anlo population had been killed in battle. The Anlo were forced to surrender when the Ada aligned with Denmark in the 1780s.

The British defeated the Danish in 1850 and used military force to suppress the Anlo. The Anlo submitted to Britain in 1874 under the Treaty of Dzelukofe and remained British subjects for more than 80 years. In 1956 the Anlo joined the neighboring Ewe territories as part of the new autonomous country of Ghana.

The Anlo were made up of patrilineal clans divided into two groups. The first group was associated with the sky gods. These people were believed to be Anlo and were granted greater property rights than those in the second group, the migrant Anlo not indigenous to the area. Anlo women played a significant role in village life prior to the 17th century. Not only were they able to inherit and bequeath land, but they were actually involved in the commercial endeavors of the community. Young women were allowed to select their marital partners, and female elders became respected advisers within the community.

By the late 19th century European influence altered the status of Anlo women in society. Property ownership decreased among women, and the increasing international flavor of trade pushed them out of commercial industries. The influx of foreign settlers made the Anlo cautious about property dispersal. Therefore, marriages were soon arranged in order to keep property within the clan. To avoid arranged marriages, Anlo women began adopting foreign religious practices.

As the slave trade grew throughout the 18th century, economic status became increasingly important. Some of the Anlo became involved in raiding neighboring villages and selling the captives. Wealthy classes developed in Anlo society, resulting in deep divisions among the clans. By the end of the 18th century, European influence had virtually erased traditional Anlo society.

See also: DENMARK AND AFRICA (Vol. III); ENGLAND AND AFRICA (Vol. III); KETA (Vols. II, III).

Further reading: Sandra E. Greene, *Gender, Ethnicity, and Social Change on the Upper Slave Coast: A History of the Anlo-Ewe* (Portsmouth, N.H.: Heinemann, 1996).

Ansa Sasraku (unknown–c. 1689) *Ruler, or akwamuhene, of Akwamu, an Akan state in southern Ghana*

About 1600 the AKAN state of AKWAMU began to gain importance as a major GOLD-trading power along the GOLD COAST, in present-day southern GHANA. Ansa Sasraku was the sixth ruler of Akwamu, and by the time he had become *akwamuhene*, the trading town of Nyanoase was firmly established as the Akwamu capital. From Nyanoase, Ansa Sasraku and his army were able to control important gold trade routes from ACCRA, on the Ghana coast, to the thickly forested inland regions around the Volta River. Due to his success in controlling trade, he also became known as the first *akwamuhene* to exercise power over the coastal EUROPEAN TRADING STATIONS.

By mid-17th century the Akwamu state was collaborating with the rulers of the ASHANTI EMPIRE, located in the forest regions of present-day Ghana, in a political alliance against the DENKYIRA and AKYEM peoples. Ansa Sasraku allied himself with a young Ashanti prince named OSEI TUTU (c. 1680–1717), who eventually reigned as *asantehene,* or Ashanti king, from about 1650 to 1717. When Osei Tutu had an affair with the princess of the Denkyira kingdom and was forced to flee for his life, Ansa Sasraku gave him shelter within the Akwamu state and then offered him the protection of the Akyem army when Tutu left to return to Ashanti territory.

By 1677 Ansa Sasraku had successfully conquered the GA-DANGME peoples of southeastern Ghana, forcing many Ga-Dangme groups to migrate east. By 1681 his army had overcome the state of Ladoku, in the east, and the coastal state of WHYDAH. When Ansa Sasraku died in 1689, he was the leader of a powerful state that covered the territory between the Pra and Volta rivers, from the coastal state of Agona to the inland Kwahu Plateau.

Antalaotra Muslim peoples of Arabic, Bantu, and Persian descent who inhabit various islands in the western Indian Ocean, especially the large island of MADAGASCAR, off the southern coast of East Africa. The Antalaotra, whose name means "people of the sea" in Malagasy, originally spoke a KISWAHILI dialect that took on many Malagasy words as it evolved on the island. For hundreds of years after their arrival in Madagascar, the Antalaotra were one of the few groups who knew the art of writing, and their scribes, called *kitabi,* wrote in the Arabic alphabet.

It is theorized that the Antalaotra migrated from the COMOROS and began settling in northern parts of Madagascar about the year 1000. (Ruins of some of the oldest Antalaotra trading posts still exist.) About the end of the 15th century the ANTEMORO, a subgroup of the Anta-laotra, migrated by sea to the southeastern region of Madagascar. There, among their nonliterate Malagasy neighbors, they were respected for their ability to read and write, and for their extensive knowledge of MEDICINE and the supernatural.

When Portuguese traders first came to northern Madagascar in the 16th century, Antalaotra trading towns were flourishing. Their trading activities diminished throughout the 17th and 18th centuries, though, as European merchants came to the island in greater numbers.

See also: TANANARIVE (Vol. III).

Further reading: Mervyn Brown, *Madagascar Rediscovered: A History from Early Times to Independence* (Hamden, Conn.: Archon Books, 1979); Raymond K. Kent, *Early Kingdoms in Madagascar, 1500–1700* (New York: Holt, Rinehart and Winston, 1970); Pierre Verin, *The History of Civilisation in North Madagascar,* David Smith, trans. (Boston: A. A. Balkema, 1986).

Antankarana (Ankara) Muslim people located on the northern tip of MADAGASCAR, an island located off the southern coast of East Africa. The Antankarana are related to various Muslim-influenced groups throughout the island, including the ANTALAOTRA and ANTEMORO.

Antankarana means "people of the rocks" in Malagasy, the language of Madagascar, although the source of this name is unclear.

In the 16th and 17th centuries trade had created a measure of wealth in Antankarana territory, especially in the important east-coast port towns of Vohemar (formerly Iharana) and Antsiranana (formerly Diego Suarez). Evidence indicates that successful Antankarana traders also occupied the island of Nosy-Be.

Excavations of royal tombs at Vohemar revealed African ivory, Chinese pottery, and Persian glass and jewelry, indicating that the Antankarana were active in the Indian Ocean trade from an early date. It is known from the records left by Antankarana scribes that they maintained commercial ties to the sultans of ZANZIBAR, on the SWAHILI COAST of Africa, and with the ruling powers in the COMOROS islands.

By the middle of the 18th century the Antankarana had come under the dominion of the Boina kings of the SAKALAVA empire, who had managed to unify most of the western half of Madagascar.

Further reading: Mervyn Brown, *Madagascar Rediscovered: A History from Early Times to Independence* (Hamden, Conn.: Archon Books, 1979); Pierre Verin (trans. David Smith), *The History of Civilisation in North Madagascar* (Boston: A. A. Balkema, 1986).

Antemoro (Antaimoro) Ethnic group that emerged late in the 15th century from the mixing of traders from MALINDI, on the coast of present-day KENYA, and indigenous peoples in the southeastern region of MADAGASCAR. The Antemoro are considered a southeastern subgroup of the northern ANTALAOTRA, peoples of mixed Arabic, African, and Malagasy descent.

Antemoro tradition traces their history to an ancestor named Ramakararube, an Antalaotra chief, who arrived in southern Madagascar during the late 1400s. He married into the local ruling lineage and began a royal dynasty that ruled the Antemoro into the 18th century.

Like many cultures that were influenced by Islam, the Antemoro maintained an aristocratic class of intellectuals that occupied the top level of society. These learned men were one of the few groups on Madagascar to know the art of writing. Although they spoke Malagasy, they wrote in the Arabic alphabet, keeping relatively detailed records of their early history and ancient beliefs. Related to their writing, the Antemoro were also one of the few groups on Madagascar to know how to produce paper. The oldest of the Antemoro manuscripts, of which hundreds still survive, date back to the late 1500s.

Antemoro means "people of the shore" in the Malagasy language spoken on Madagascar.

Early in the 16th century the Portuguese failed in their attempts to establish a trading factory in Matitana, in Antemoro territory. By the middle of the century the Antemoro had established an insular Muslim theocratic state that ruled the east coast of the island between Mananjary, to the north, and Farafangana. Although the Antemoro did not become a regional power like the SAKALAVA and MERINA, their holy men became influential in areas inhabited by other Malagasy-speaking people. Antemoro priests, called *ombiasses,* were widely respected throughout Madagascar for their knowledge of traditional MEDICINE and the supernatural.

The Antemoro maintained trade relations with French colonists, who arrived in southern Madagascar in 1638. About 1659, however, they clashed with French soldiers, who came north from their colony at Fort Dauphin. Ultimately, diseases and the difficulties that the French had in trading with the Antemoro—and other southern groups, including the Antanosy—eventually drove them from the region. During the 18th and into the 19th centuries, the Antemoro continued to trade with other Europeans, including the Dutch and Portuguese, and maintained their influence by counseling political and religious leaders of other Malagasy groups.

Further reading: Mervyn Brown, *Madagascar Rediscovered: A History from Early Times to Independence* (Hamden, Conn.: Archon Books, 1979); Pierre Verin, *The History of Civilisation in North Madagascar,* David Smith, trans. (Boston: A. A. Balkema, 1986).

Arabs, influence of See ARABIC (Vols. I, II); ARABS (Vol. II); ARABS, INFLUENCE OF (Vol. II); ARAB WORLD AND AFRICA (Vol. V); OMANI SULTANATE (Vol. III); SLAVE TRADE ON THE SWAHILI COAST (Vol. III); SLAVERY, CULTURAL AND HISTORICAL ATTITUDES TOWARD (Vol. III); SWAHILI COAST (Vols. II, III).

architecture In general, between the 16th and 19th centuries traditional indigenous African architecture changed

A thatched house, built in a traditional Zulu beehive style. The photograph was taken sometime between 1984 and 1997. © O. Alamany & E. Vicens/Corbis

very little. Throughout sub-Saharan Africa, homes, shrines, and royal palaces continued to be built using the same designs and materials that had been used for thousands of years. Similarly, Islamic North African architecture, like the Muslim religion itself, tended to stay true to established tradition. Nevertheless, architectural styles did evolve, especially in places where disparate cultures came together. Hence, the most notable architectural innovations that occurred during the period took place in EGYPT, West Africa, and coastal regions of sub-Saharan Africa.

Islamic Architecture in North and East Africa
Egyptian architecture during the period reflected a subtle foreign influence, first by the Turkish MAMLUKS, and later by Ottoman Turks. The Mamluks were Muslim Turkish slaves who successfully rebelled and gained control of Egypt from about 1170 to 1517. The markets and residential buildings that they constructed for both rich and poor were usually of uniform height, no more than two stories high, so the minarets and towers of mosques could easily be seen from anywhere in town. When the Turks from the Ottoman Empire seized Egypt from the Mamluks in the early 16th century, they generally followed the building traditions of their fellow Muslims.

Architects note, however, that the Ottomans influenced North African architecture by incorporating a typically Turkish style of simple and clean lines into the usually ornate and intricate Arabian designs. By the middle of the 18th century the Ottoman Turks also controlled many of the cities on North Africa's Mediterranean coast, influencing architectural styles there, as well.

In the MAGHRIB, a region covering the modern North African countries of MOROCCO, ALGERIA, TUNISIA, and LIBYA, building design and construction continued to be dominated by the Arabian-influenced Islamic style of architecture. Muslim builders constructed *casbahs*—multistory, baked-mud brick residential complexes—to which rooms could be added as families grew. The casbahs were often built with interior courtyards for privacy and had strategically placed openings in ceilings and walls for the circulation of air. Construction materials included earth, bricks, mortar, stone, and timber. Walls of the casbahs needed to be replastered often, especially after heavy rains, and the structures were usually whitewashed in order to reflect some of the intense sunlight that punishes the region throughout the year.

Soninke dried-mud house, with the traditional flat roof and perforated walls. This house, located on the banks of the Senegal River, was photographed in 1988. © *Margaret Courtney-Clarke/Corbis*

Along East Africa's SWAHILI COAST, Muslim master builders constructed Islamic-style administrative buildings and residential palaces for wealthy Swahili merchants. Swahili architecture, like the culture itself, was a mixture of African styles with Indian, Persian, and Arabian elements. The buildings on Africa's Indian Ocean coast, therefore, reflected the heavy Asian influence in their intricate design elements and building materials. Swahili Coast palaces had elaborate arched entrances, domes, vaults, and plastered walls decorated with Arabic script. The builders used coral limestone blocks to create impressive geometrical buildings, the most impressive of which was the 100-room Husuni Kubwa Palace, built in the late 13th or early 14th century on the island of KILWA.

Islamic Architecture in the Western Sudan
Wealthy Muslim traders from North Africa were present in the western Sudan, in what is now West Africa, as early as the 10th century, spreading their religion and building mosques as they extended their trade routes to the south and west. As practiced in this region, Islam was unique in that it incorporated elements from local, traditional beliefs, resulting in a combination of different religious forms that is known as *syncretism*. This syncretism of northern and local influences was even reflected in the architectural features of the mosques. Naturally, the designers of the structures were influenced by what they had seen in their native North Africa. Mosques there were built out of stone or baked-mud brick, and featured straight, geometrical lines and tall, slender minarets. The mosques in the western Sudan, however, were sometimes made of packed red clay and often featured squat, conical minarets.

By the 14th century there were mosques at JENNE and TIMBUKTU, near the Niger bend, and by the middle of the 16th century, mosques had also been built in KANO and KATSINA, in present-day northern NIGERIA. By the end of the 1500s, mosques were common features of the landscape all the way to the Gulf of Guinea. By the middle of the 18th century syncretic mosques could be found as far west as the SENEGAMBIA region too. One of the more interesting examples was a mosque in FOUTA DJALLON built in the 1730s that was constructed in a shape typical of the local houses, like a beehive, with a circular base and bulging walls that met at the top of the structure. This beehive style of traditional architecture is found, with local variations, in many parts of Africa, as far distant as Zululand on Africa's southeastern coast.

European Architecture in Sub-Saharan Africa

The first example of European architecture in sub-Saharan Africa was the Portuguese fort built between 1480 and 1482 at ELMINA, on modern Ghana's GOLD COAST. Under Commander Diogo Azumbuja, a work force of more than 500 Portuguese—architects, laborers, builders, and stone masons—worked on the construction of the building that began a period of Portuguese trading prowess in West Africa.

Portuguese records of the construction of their forts and castles from the period are incomplete. Hence, many of the architects and master builders who designed the Portuguese structures on the Atlantic coast remain anonymous.

By the 18th century, Europeans had built nearly 30 other trading outposts on the Gold Coast, though few were as large as Elmina. The architecture of the fort reflected a medieval European mentality that paralleled the function of the structure: high, turreted towers and thick defensive walls projected an attitude of strength and indominability that probably contributed to the Portuguese traders' commercial success. The geometrical fort was designed with living and sleeping quarters, large storage spaces for provisions, and holding rooms that were used to house captives before they were exported to labor on Portuguese plantations in the Americas. The Portuguese used many of the same techniques when they built Fort São Sebastian on MOZAMBIQUE ISLAND, in 1522, and the trade outpost in MAPUTO, in the 1540s.

In western Central Africa, Kongo king AFONSO I (c. 1451–1543) was converted to Christianity by Jesuit MISSIONARIES in the late 15th century. Afonso maintained close ties to Portugal, and in the early 16th century he had a palace and Catholic churches built in the European style, thereby bringing new architectural ideas to the area.

Other notable European structures in the area were the cathedral built at LUANDA, in 1628, and Fort São Miguel, built on a small island off of the coast of Luanda, in 1641. The fort was built to facilitate the trading of captives on the southern coast and was basically a fortified town built in medieval European style. Its geometrical design was anthropomorphic, similar to Fort Jesus, with fortified buildings that extended like arms and legs from a central "trunk." The "head" of the structure was the fort's administrative center.

In the 17th century the Portuguese were joined on Africa's Atlantic coast by trading companies and missionaries from Holland, Germany, Britain, France, and Denmark, all of which erected structures that were modeled after examples from their homelands. The Dutch built a trading lodge on the Gold Coast in 1642, the Swedes completed Fort Carolusborg on Ghana's CAPE COAST in 1655, and a German trading company built Ft. Fredericksburg in the region in 1683. European architecture, however, was rarely *purely* European in design. Builders often had to use whatever local materials were available and also adapted their designs to include features from indigenous buildings, which usually were organically designed to withstand the particular climatic and environmental stresses of the region. For example, European builders imitated the local technique of building on stilts in areas where seasonal flooding was common.

The most significant European architectural presence prior to 1850 was in SOUTH AFRICA. CAPE TOWN emerged from the start as a Dutch city. Its most notable building was the massive stone fort known as "the Castle," which the DUTCH EAST INDIA COMPANY had begun constructing in the 1660s. Another landmark was the Dutch Reformed Church, which was notable for its tall spire. Gradually a series of public buildings and private homes, many with the gabled style that came to symbolize the Cape Dutch style of architecture, were built. The expansion of Dutch settlement into the interior led to the spread of this architectural style, especially in the CAPE COLONY. The second British occupation of the cape, in 1806, introduced English architectural styles, particularly the Georgian, which added a new dimension to the appearance of Cape Town. In the eastern cape and Natal, the emergence of new towns occupied by European settlers assumed a very English appearance.

The architectural character of the FREETOWN colony in SIERRA LEONE was an interesting mixture of American, Brazilian, and West Indian influences. Founded in the late 1700s, Freetown was populated by repatriated freed slaves from the Americas, whose architectural knowledge was informed by the British and Portuguese colonial styles there.

See also: ARCHITECTURE (Vols. I, II, IV, V); BATAMMALIBA BUILDING TRADITIONS (Vol. III).

Further reading: Nnamdi Elleh, *African Architecture: Evolution and Transformation* (New York: McGraw-Hill, 1996).

Ardra   See ALLADA.

Arochukwu oracle (Arochuku)   Traditional shrine controlled by the Aro people, an IGBO subgroup of southeastern NIGERIA. Named in honor of the supreme deity Chukwu, the oracle was established before the arrival of European traders in the late 15th century. The Aro frequently invoked the oracle to achieve economic and political gain.

The Aro exploited the power of the Arochukwu oracle primarily because members of neighboring clans believed enough in his pronouncements to pay large fees for his services. By the early 19th century the shrine had become a nexus for trade as well as a means of solving political problems, helping the Aro people to become some of the most powerful traders in the region.

See also: AROCHUKWU ORACLE (Vol. II); DIVINATION (Vol. I); ORACLE (Vol. I).

art The artistic creativity of indigenous Africans has been expressed for thousands of years in diverse forms ranging from rock art, paintings, jewelry, and pottery to woodcarvings, masks, sculptures, and woven items. Although it would be difficult to describe a typically "African" aesthetic style, tradition usually dictates the acceptable forms of artistic expression among the people of a certain group. Hence, the styles of art in many regions of the African continent have changed little over thousands of years. Nevertheless it is apparent that from the 16th to the 19th centuries, African art reflected the influence of Europeans in sub-Saharan Africa and the Turks of the Ottoman Empire in North Africa.

Beginning about the turn of the 15th century the art forms from sub-Saharan regions of Africa were largely rejected by a European culture that derided them as "primitive" and didn't recognize their unique aesthetic qualities. During the late 19th century, however, the cultural elite of Europe became fascinated by African art objects as they began to appreciate their deep cultural and spiritual significance.

Many of the groups inhabiting regions of West Africa were heavily involved in the MINING and working of metals, which they formed into elaborate sculptures and jewelry pieces. The AKAN people of present-day GHANA were one of the most notable groups who consistently produced artistic objects out of GOLD and prospered from the trade of the precious metal in the centuries prior to the era of European colonization. For more than a thousand years bronze had been worked in the Yoruba kingdom of Ife in modern NIGERIA, and the region and its artisans

Ndebele Zulu baskets bearing traditional designs. They were photographed in 1996. © *Lindsay Hebberd/Corbis*

were praised by visiting European traders for the intricately cast bronze sculptures. Since the Muslim RELIGION rejected iconic art—art that elevates an image—during this period West Africa was influenced by Islamic North Africa. Sculptures were produced less prolifically, and other forms of art, especially cloth making and architectural design, began to flourish.

East Africa also reflected a wide range of artistic forms and styles. In arid areas of present-day KENYA, TANZANIA, and UGANDA, for instance, painted designs decorated everything from rocks to the human body. By the 16th century, ARCHITECTURE had become a high-art form in the Great Lakes region and along the Indian Ocean coast, where Islamic Arab, Persian, and Indian culture greatly influenced the building styles. Large clay and wood sculptures were produced in present-day MOZAMBIQUE and MALAWI, while funeral pieces, including intricately adorned burial chambers, have been found in Kenya, ETHIOPIA, and on the island of MADAGASCAR, located in the Indian Ocean off the coast of Mozambique.

Ethiopia became a hotbed for artistic expression for more than 100 years beginning about 1632. During this era, known as the GONDAR Period after the splendid capital city founded by Emperor FASILIDAS (r. 1632–1667), Ethiopian culture was expressed in a flourish of religious and scholarly activity. Elaborate palaces and libraries were built and adorned by paintings, frescoes, and murals that commonly depicted symbols and images related to the Coptic Christian faith. The architectural styles of the Gondar Period reflected the Portuguese and Indian origins of the architects who were brought to Ethiopia to erect the castle-like palaces and other buildings.

The influence of Europeans—notably the Dutch and the English—could be seen in the architecture and stone masonry of their buildings in parts of southern and Central Africa, especially on the coast. The artistic creations of the people of West Africa were seen in the African-American arts produced in the New World after the mid-17th century. The trading of both commodities and African captives brought African influences to other countries as well. Many European countries also continued to adopt features of the Islamic artistic style of North Africa. European architects and furniture-makers were especially fascinated by the intricate curves and repeated patterns that typify the Islamic art of MOROCCO and EGYPT.

The arts that came out of North Africa are often left out of descriptions concerning African art due to the notion that works produced in North Africa more closely resembled those of the Muslim and Christian cultures that flourished around the Mediterranean Sea. Therefore, the various arts that originated in North Africa are commonly referred to as *oikoumenical* (from the Greek *oikoumenikos,* or "the whole world"). From the 16th century through the 19th century North African art in LIBYA, TUNISIA, and ALGERIA reflected the aesthetic influence of the Turks from the Ottoman Empire, who dominated their coastal territories. Although later ruled by the Ottomans as well, Egypt retained the styles credited to the MAMLUKS, Turkish slaves who came to rule the country. Mamluk arts survived in Egypt's culture until around the 19th century, but thereafter began to develop the same European characteristics as many other African arts throughout the continent.

See also: ART (Vols. I, II, IV, V); BEADS AND JEWELRY (Vol. II); MASKS (Vol. I); POTTERY (Vols. I, II); ROCK ART (Vol. I); SCARIFICATION (Vol. I); SCULPTURE (Vol. I).

Further reading: Jan Vansina, *Art History in Africa: An Introduction to Method* (New York: Longman Group Limited, 1984).

Asaba (Ahaba) City located in the Igboland region of present-day NIGERIA known for its 17th-century foundation legend. The people of Asaba claim a figure named Nnebisi as their official founder. Legend states Nnebisi was born to a woman from the Anambra region of Nteje in western Igboland, probably in the early 17th century. He soon realized he was treated differently from others and was told it was because Nteje was not his homeland. Nnebisi then traveled the NIGER RIVER in search of his native home armed with only a charmed MEDICINE pot, which he was told to wear on his head as it would fall at the site of his true home. The pot was said to have fallen on the western shores of the Niger at the shrine to the goddess Onishe of Ahaba—and it was there Nnebisi staked claim to the land.

The name *Ahaba* came from the IGBO expression *ahabam*, which translates to, "I have appropriately chosen."

Even though he was of slave descent himself, Nnebisi became rich in Ahaba as an agriculturalist who used slaves to tend his lands. He was also a skilled hunter who increased his wealth by hunting elephants for their ivory tusks. Once he gained wealth and power he then proclaimed himself king. It was during his reign that the Asaba instituted the practice of human sacrifice. Nnebisi married two wives, producing two sons and a daughter with his first wife and one son with the second wife. Later, it was the five grandsons of Nnebisi (all from the offspring of his first wife) who took over the original communities left by the earliest settlers of Ahaba and formed five districts within the city that still remain to the present day. It was only during the British occupation of the area in the 19th century when the city's name of Ahaba was anglicized to Asaba.

See also: IVORY TRADE (Vol. III).

Ashanti Empire (Asante) Vast territory that was controlled by the Ashanti, a subgroup of the AKAN people in present-day GHANA, beginning in the 17th century. The roots of the Ashanti Empire lay in the expansion of trade that began during the 14th century, as Dyula traders made their way across the savanna. The Akan of the forest regions, who had long maintained trade in both GOLD and KOLA NUTS, seized on the opportunities this offered, and they soon were using slave labor to both mine additional gold and clear land for more farms. By the 15th century, permanent Akan settlements were developing in the forest that, when the Portuguese arrived in the latter part of the century, engaged in a lively trade with the Europeans. Gold was exchanged for cotton cloth, metals, and even captives from the area of BENIN, and in time the Akan even began farming MAIZE and other crops introduced to them by the Portuguese. By the 16th century several important and rival Akan states—including Denkyira, Akwamu, Fante, and Ashanti—had developed, and by the end of the century the competition between them began to give way to unification. And, it was the Ashanti who seized the opportunity to draw the groups together.

By the time they reached the West African coast, about 1600, the Ashanti had formed a kingdom around Lake Bosumtwe. This kingdom grew as neighboring peoples intermixed with the Ashanti. The Ashanti united under the leadership of their first three OYOKO chiefs: OBIRI YEBOA (d. c. 1660), OSEI TUTU (c. 1680–1717), and OPOKUWARE II (c. 1700–1750). These leaders cultivated the loyalty of local kings by including them in the new Ashanti government as commanders of the Ashanti army or as members of the king's advisory council. New soldiers for the growing Ashanti army were provided by these individual kingdoms as well. Despite the centralized political system, village kings retained their power over everyday village affairs.

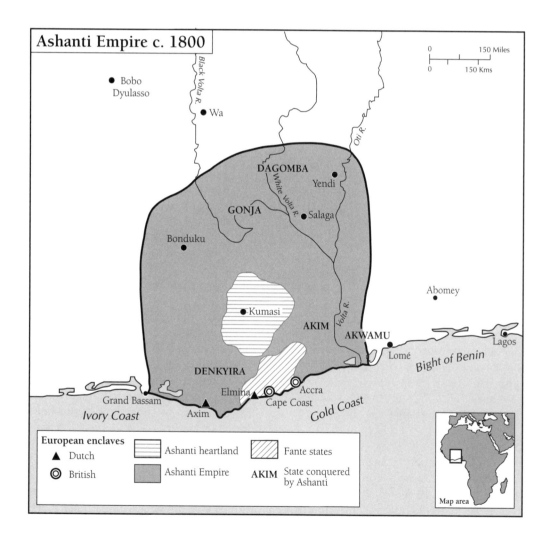

When Osei Tutu took the throne in the late 17th century, he was called the *asantehene,* or "king of the Ashanti." His nation rapidly increased its power by forming alliances with the neighboring peoples, leading to the formation of the Ashanti Union, around 1700. Tutu also established his capital at KUMASI, located inland, in the central forests of present-day Ghana. During his reign he started the tradition of the GOLDEN STOOL. According to legend a golden stool fell into Tutu's lap, thus establishing a divine royal lineage. The throne became the symbol of Ashanti authority.

In the 18th century the Ashanti conquered the neighboring kingdoms of DENKYIRA, Assin, Aowin, Amanahia, WASSAW, Twifo, and Wenchi. By 1740 they had added TEKYIMAN, BANDA, Gyama, and western GONJA to their territory. By the 19th century the Ashanti had conquered all of the neighboring kingdoms except the Fante. The Fante were spared only because they were under British protection. By this time the Ashanti kingdom had become the most powerful force on the GOLD COAST.

The Ashanti kingdom went into a decline about 1807 primarily because of conflict arose with British merchants and expeditionary forces, who were coming to the region in increasing numbers in hopes of monopolizing coastal trade. The Ashanti simultaneously were expanding their own trade networks from the interior. The two powers soon set to open warfare.

The situation was complicated by the continued efforts of the British to make allies of the smaller kingdoms, such as Fante and Denkyira, that were being dominated by the Ashanti during their campaigns of territorial expansion. A series of conflicts with the British, known as the Anglo-Ashanti Wars, included a crucial loss at Katamanso, in 1826. In the aftermath of their defeat at Katamanso, the Ashanti were forced to renounce claims of sovereignty over those groups that had allied with Britain. The Anglo-Ashanti Wars would continue throughout the 19th century.

See also: AKAN (Vol. II); ANGLO-ASHANTI WARS (Vol. IV); ASHANTI (Vol. II); ASHANTI EMPIRE (Vol. IV); TWIFO (Vol. II).

Further reading: T. C. McCaskie, *State and Society in Pre-colonial Asante* (New York: Cambridge University Press, 1995); Ivor Wilks, *Asante in the Nineteenth Century: The Structure and Evolution of a Political Order* (New York: Cambridge University Press, 1989); Ivor Wilks, *Forests of Gold: Essays on the Akan and the Kingdom of Asante* (Athens, Ohio: Ohio University Press, 1993).

asiento The monopoly granted by the government of Spain to sell captives and other people in its territories. According to the terms of the Treaty of Tordesillas, signed by Spain and Portugal in 1494, Portugal was granted a monopoly on trade and territorial claims in Africa. Spain was granted a similar monopoly in the Americas, except for a small portion of eastern Brazil, which was placed in Portuguese hands. Thus, in the early 1500s, when Spain decided to import Africans to supplement and later replace Native American forced laborers in the Caribbean, Spain had to rely on outside suppliers. These suppliers worked under contract (in Spanish, *asiento*) with the Spanish government and purchased the exclusive right to supply a specified number of African slaves for a given period of time.

The first *asiento* on record was granted to a company from Genoa, Italy, in 1517. The company agreed to supply 1,000 captives between 1517 and 1525. In 1528 the *asiento* then passed to a company from the state of Brandenburg in eastern Germany. Subsequently, individual Spaniards and Portuguese held the contract. In 1701 the Guyana Company, chartered by the French government, received the *asiento* from Spain but lost it in 1713 to Britain as one of the provisions of the Treaty of Utrecht, which was formally ratified the following year. By that agreement Britain owned the right to sell captives for the next 30 years.

The Treaty of Utrecht resolved a series of disputes among the major European powers that had exploded into the War of the Spanish Succession (1701–1714). As a result of this treaty Britain became a major political force in Europe and a major trading power in the world of commerce. Britain dominated the slave trade until the British Parliament banned it in 1807.

See also: SLAVE TRADE, THE TRANSATLANTIC (Vol. III).

Askia dynasty Line of Muslim rulers who led the SONGHAI Empire from 1493 to 1592. In total there were 10 rulers who took the name *Askia,* all but one lineal descendants of Askia MUHAMMAD TOURÉ (r. 1493–1528), also known as Askia the Great. Muhammad Touré started the dynasty when he overthrew the son and successor of Sunni Ali (d. 1492), the Songhai founder. Upon taking his position as head of the Songhai, Muhammad Touré designated himself *Askia Muhammad.* His pilgrimage to Mecca as well as his myriad accomplishments in the political, religious, cultural, and educational spheres made him a popular ruler. Not only did he consolidate the vast territory accumulated by Sunni Ali but he extended it and completely reorganized its administration as well. During Askia Muhammad's reign the empire was at its height in both power and prosperity. In a state of ill health and vulnerability, Askia Muhammad was deposed in 1528 by a rebellion led by his eldest son, Musa (r. 1528–1531).

Askia Musa's reign, like that of all of the *askias* that followed him, met with fear and suspicion of those in line for the throne. Askia Muhammad had 34 sons, all as ambitious and ruthless as Musa himself. The sons split into groups and formed allegiances with one another. Those who did not support Musa fled, but Musa went after them and had them killed. Eventually the remaining brothers banded together in a revolt against the tyrannical Musa and assassinated him.

The name *Askia* is a family name that pre-dated Askia Muhammad Touré, but it has come to be used as a generic term, when in lower case, to mean the "emperor of Songhai."

Askia Muhammad's nephew Muhammad Benkan (r. 1531–1537) became the third *askia*. He was deposed, however, in 1537, by a group of Songhai nobles who felt he had usurped the throne. This group succeeded in restoring the leadership to Ismail (r. 1537–1539), one of Askia Touré's sons, who then became the fourth *askia*. Ismail brought his father back from exile, but after only three years as the head of the Songhai Empire, Ismail died of natural causes.

Ismail's brother Ishaq I (r. 1539–1549) enjoyed a peaceful succession to the throne. This peace did not last long, however, as Ishaq was every bit as afraid of deposition and disloyalty as the *askias* before him had been.

Ishaq's brother Askia DAUD (r. 1549–1582) became the sixth *askia*. Of all the *askias* who followed Askia Muhammad, Daud had the longest and most successful reign. He was remembered for being a devout Muslim, for his support of ART, ARCHITECTURE, and education, and for helping the poor. The empire's economy flourished under Daud's leadership. Frequently he led expeditions against the MOSSI STATES, but his major threat was Sultan ABD AL-MANSUR (r. 1578–1603) of MOROCCO, whose occupation of the Taghaza salt mines became an increasing concern of the empire. Daud was the last son of Askia Muhammad to rule Songhai. After Daud's death all the succeeding rulers of Songhai were Daud's sons and were no less ruthless in trying to occupy the throne than his brothers had been.

Al-Hajj Muhammad (r. 1582–1586) became the seventh *askia* of the Songhai Empire. He ruled violently and harshly and lived in fear of being overthrown, a fate that was realized in 1586 when his brother, Askia MUHAMMAD BANO (r. 1586–1588), was elected the eighth Songhai king. During his short reign Bano had to deal with the unruly western provinces that had attempted several times to rebel against him. He died on the same day he began an expedition to attend to the civil war that had broken out and was replaced by his brother Ishaq II (r. 1588–1591).

Immediately upon taking the throne Ishaq killed al-Sadduk, the leader of the western revolt, and managed to maintain some sense of control, though the empire had been substantially weakened.

The Moroccans, using the political instability of the Songhai Empire to their advantage, invaded in 1591. The Songhai forces were so badly defeated that Ishaq submitted to the Moroccan leader Mawlay ABD AL-MANSUR (r. 1578–1603), but his offer to pay tribute was rejected, and the sultan proceeded to lay siege to the Songhai.

The defeated Songhai army deposed Ishaq and designated Muhammad Gao the tenth *askia* in 1591. His rule didn't last long, and he was killed by al-Mansur the same year he assumed his title. Having lost most of its power, the former ruling dynasty was reduced to the leadership of a small independent state in Dendi, over which a son of Askia Daud reigned.

See also: DENDI (Vol. II); SUNNI ALI (Vol. II).

Further reading: David Conrad, *The Songhay Empire* (New York: F. Watts, 1998).

Ayawaso (Ayaso) Town located near the coast of present-day GHANA. Founded during the 15th century by the GA-DANGME people, Ayawaso is situated on the Nsachi River, north of ACCRA. Ayawaso became the Ga-Dangme capital during the 16th century. Ruled early on by priests, the Ga-Dangme changed to monarchical rule by the early 17th century. The most notable Ga-Dangme *mantse*, or king, was Okai Akwei (r. c. 1640–1677), who reigned in Ayawaso when the Ga-Dangme kingdom reached its peak. As early as the 1660s, however, Ayawaso was coming under pressure by the AKAN state of AKWAMU, and some of the Ga-Dangme people were forced to migrate south to Accra, which was in the process of becoming a major trading center for European merchants.

In 1677, under the leadership of the *akwamuhene* (ruler) ANSA SASRAKU (d. c. 1689), Akwamu attacked and conquered Ayawaso, burning the city to the ground and making it a tributary state. Despite being devastated, Ayawaso continued to function as the Ga-Dangme capital until 1680, when the seat of the Ga-Dangme kingdom was moved to Accra.

Azande (Zande, Nzakara, Niam-Niam) Ethnic group of present-day Republic of the SUDAN, the Democratic Republic of the CONGO, and the CENTRAL AFRICAN REPUBLIC. During the 18th century the Ambomu people of the Mbomu River region in north-central Democratic Republic of the Congo began conquering other Sudanic peoples to the south and east; the Azande emerged from the assimilation of these groups.

The Azande speak a Sudanic dialect of the ADAMAWA-Ubangi branch of the Niger-Congo family of languages. Organized into scattered villages, the Azande were traditionally agriculturalists. However, they also engaged in hunting, fishing, and limited trade. Azande RELIGION reflects a unique and complex worldview. They call their Supreme Being *Mbori,* who is considered to be the creator of all things. According to some sources, the Azande believe that Mbori lived in the headwaters of streams. This seems to be supported by Azande origin myths that talk about the ancient times when human beings were sealed inside a canoe and had not yet populated the earth. The sons of Mbori—the sun, moon, stars, and the night sky—tried to open the seal, but only the sun's hot rays succeeded.

The NGBANDI, a Sudanic group of the upper Ubangi River in the Central African Republic, mixed with the Azande in the 18th century, adopting their language and culture. The Bandia—who are one of the most important aristocratic Azande clans along with the Vungara—are descended from the Ngbandi.

The Azande honored their ancestors and stressed the importance of traditional knowledge, which was considered an important spiritual gift. Traditional knowledge of medicines, for instance, was limited to a select group of men who were to become *abinza,* or traditional healers. The apprenticeship of future *abinza* could begin as early as age five.

As part of their education in the medicinal arts, young men and boys apprenticed themselves to older, recognized healers. In the initial phase of their training, these youngsters were provided with special MEDICINE that conferred on them the powers of prophecy. The trainees were then given public funerals that symbolically buried their pasts. At that point their education about healing herbs and medicinal bark from certain trees officially began. While completing their training, which often took many years, the students had to observe many taboos, including those against sexual activity.

Successful practitioners often organized themselves into ritual clans or associations. Among the practitioners, one of the most powerful responsibilities was to forewarn their rulers, or even their society as a whole, of potential dangers. This usually was done through divination. The *abinza* also acted as oracles, making predictions and offering advice to those who consulted them.

Any misfortune or bad luck that befell any member of the Azande usually was blamed on witchcraft. It was believed that when used in a certain way, witchcraft could cause the loss of crops or bring about illness, accidents, or fires. The belief in witchcraft has remained strong among the Azande over many centuries.

Another important responsibility of Azande medicine men involved detecting of individuals suspected of crimes or other violations of the community's mores. Medicine men knew how to identify a substance known as *mangu,* which was believed to be found in the stomach of those suspected of witchcraft. The *abinza* also used a combination of medicinal herbs and tree bark known as *beng* to make a form of poison that they believed could be used to identify those practicing witchcraft or similar crimes. Medicine men were not only obligated to identify supposed witches in these ways but were also required to cure or reverse the ill effects they caused. The *abinza* also prevented the ill effects from recurring again. Suspected and proven witches were required to undergo a rite of cleansing, which often included offering a blessing to their victims.

Anthropologists who have studied the Azande point to the prevalence of witchcraft and methods of detection as part of a religious belief system in which everything has an underlying cause. Once these causes are identified they become the basis for controlling social behavior.

The Azande homeland was rather inaccessible to Africa's Muslim and Christian populations as well as to the European colonial powers, so they were able to escape the direct pressures of foreign influence until the late 19th century, when the French began to infiltrate the area north of the Ubangi River.

See also: HEALERS AND DIVINERS (Vol. I); RELIGION, TRADITIONAL (Vol. I); WITCHCRAFT (Vols. I, IV).

Further reading: Benjamin C. Ray, *African Religions: Symbol, Ritual, and Community,* 2nd ed. (Upper Saddle River, N.J.: Prentice Hall, 2000).

Azemmour (Azamor) City in present-day MOROCCO located along the coast at the estuary of the Oum Rbia River. Established possibly as early as the fifth century BCE, Azemmour was conquered in 1513 by Portugal under the leadership of King Manuel I (r. 1495–1521). By 1514 the city was known as a haven for Portuguese Jews who had been forced to flee their homeland.

Azemmour was the birthplace of the famous Moroccan slave Estevanico. Born in 1503, Estevanico was sold to a Spaniard named Andres de Dorantes about 1520. In 1527 he then traveled with Dorantes and the explorer Alvar Núñez Cabeza de Vaca (c. 1490–1557) to the Americas, where he traversed parts of what are now Florida, Arizona, New Mexico, and Texas before crossing into the present-day country of Mexico. Estevanico was killed in 1539 by the Zuni in what is now New Mexico.

Although the Portuguese erected large defensive walls at Azemmour, some of which still stand today, they were not able to hold sway over the city for long. They were forced to abandon the city after less than 30 years of rule. In 1542 the Portuguese relinquished control of the city as Moroccan forces, led by Muhammad al-Shaykh (d. 1557), captured the Portuguese-ruled port of Agadir, threatening Portuguese dominance in Azemmour and the neighboring coastal city of Safi.

In the centuries that followed, Azemmour continued to be a productive city under Moroccan rule, but it was often surpassed in importance by other cities along the coast, such as MAZAGAN, which boasted superior ports.

See also: PORTUGAL AND AFRICA (Vols. III, IV, V).

B

Baganda See GANDA.

Bagirmi (Baguirmi) Kingdom that emerged in the Lake CHAD region of present-day CHAD early in the 16th century. Though the original Bagirmi kingdom was non-Muslim, under Abdullah IV (r. c. 1568–1598) the kingdom adopted Islam, ultimately turning their state into a sultanate, with its capital at Massenya. Later, in the early 17th century, Bagirmi was absorbed into KANEM-BORNU, to the north, but gained a measure of independence during the latter part of the century.

By the beginning of the 18th century Bagirmi was profiting from the Arab trade in human captives. Although it was under the control of Kanem-Bornu, Bagirmi managed to maintain its power through its own tributary states. By the mid-1700s Bagirmi had returned to paying tribute to Kanem-Bornu. In the early 1800s Bagirmi suffered from attacks by the TUNJUR peoples of the neighboring WADAI kingdom and fell into decline.

Further reading: S. P. Reyna, *Wars Without End: The Political Economy of a Precolonial African State* (Hanover, N.H.: University Press of New England, 1990).

Bahinda See HINDA.

Bakele Ethnic group inhabiting coastal regions of present-day GABON. Known as successful hunters and traders, the Bakele, under pressure from migrating Fang peoples, eventually dispersed from their long-time homeland in the region of the Como and Remboué rivers.

Prior to the emergence of large-scale trading in captives in what is now Gabon, the Bakele exchanged items such as ivory and EBONY with their coastal neighbors, including the Fang and the Seke peoples. The Bakele also controlled part of the river waterways that transported goods to both African and European trading outposts.

During the late 18th century the Bakele became highly involved in the trade in captives and were known to have been one of the few groups to conduct trade both locally and over long distances to obtain captives to satisfy the European demand. After the decline of this trade early in the 19th century, the Bakele continued to trade with the Europeans in ebony and other woods and were also prominent in the trade of rubber.

See also: FANG (Vol. II); IVORY TRADE (Vol. III); SLAVERY (Vols. I, III, IV).

Bakongo See KONGO.

Bakuba See KUBA.

Bamako Ancient trading city located on the NIGER RIVER, near SEGU, in present-day southwestern Republic of MALI. From the 11th to 15th centuries Bamako was a trading port and a center for Islamic education within the Mali Empire. Then, during the mid-18th century, Bamako was ruled by the BAMBARA kingdom of Segu after Mamari KULIBALI (r. 1712–1755) extended his territory to points along the Niger River.

Bamako's name comes from words meaning "crocodile river" in the Bambara language.

Little is known of its history thereafter until 1806, when Scottish explorer Mungo PARK (1771–1806) described Bamako as a small trading village inhabited by the Bozo people. Prior to Bamako's occupation by the French in 1883, the city was subjugated for a short time by the forces of Muslim warrior Samori Touré (c. 1830–1900). In 1908 Bamako became the capital of Mali—then called French Soudan—and remained the capital after Mali declared its independence in 1960.

See also: BAMAKO (Vols. II, IV, V); FRANCE AND AFRICA (Vols. III, IV, V); FRENCH SOUDAN (Vol. IV); ISLAMIC CENTERS OF LEARNING (Vol. II); MALI EMPIRE (Vol. II)

Bambara (Bamana) Mande-speaking agrarian people originally from the Niger Valley; the Bambara, who emerged as a people during the 17th century, inhabit present-day MALI and speak Bamana, a language related to Mandinka. Under its early ruler, Kaladian Kulibali (r. 1652–1682), the Bambara kingdom of SEGU expanded, eventually becoming a small empire. The empire grew larger still under Mamari KULIBALI (1712–1755), who, aided by a professional army and navy, succeeded in unifying the Bambara peoples between Bamako, to the southwest, and JENNE and TIMBUKTU, to the northeast. In the years that followed, the empire prospered and grew until, in 1818, it was overthrown by Shekhu Ahmadu Lobbo of MACINA. KAARTA, too, expanded, eventually covering most of Middle Niger. Kaarta fell in 1854 to the Tukulor warrior al-Hajj Umar Tal (c. 1797–1864).

According to oral tradition, the Bambara originated with two brothers who crossed the NIGER RIVER on the back of a giant catfish named *Kulibali* ("no boat"). The tradition goes on to say that Barama Ngolo, who was the "good" brother of the pair, eventually founded the kingdom of Segu. The other, or "bad" brother, who was named Nia Ngolo, founded Kaarta. In truth, the most likely origin for the Bambara kingdoms was an invasion of FULANI cavalry who came to the area at about the time of the collapse of the SONGHAI Empire. The Fulani apparently unified the various Bambara groups and established the kingdoms of Segu and Kaarta.

Bambara society traditionally was organized according to clans, each of which was made up of several families descended from a common ancestor. The clan leaders, in turn, were under the authority of a village leader, or chief, who, according to tradition, descended from the original founder of the village. As both political and spiritual leader of the village, he was responsible not only for the cultivation of the lands of the village but also for its religious activities.

In addition to clans, Bambara society traditionally was based upon age groups, to which Bambara men invariably belonged. The smallest of these groups, known as a *flambolo,* was made up of the individuals who had participated in the same circumcision ceremony. Beyond this was a *flanton,* which was made up of three *flambolos.* As a result of this intricate system, the entire Bambara male population was unified by the bonds of age and the memories of common ceremonies.

Traditional Bambara RELIGION involved ceremonies undertaken by various secret religious societies. These utilized striking masks and statues, which played important and, because of the secretive nature of the societies, often mysterious roles in the various rituals undertaken.

In 1799 Segu was visited by the Scottish explorer Mungo PARK (1771–1806), who wrote in glowing terms of the empire's magnificent capital. It was made up, he noted, of four separate towns, each surrounded with high mud fortifications and filled with square, flat-roofed mud-brick houses. Mosques, according to Park, were common, and the city's streets were wide enough for wheeled carriages to pass through. According to Park the rich and crowded capital was inhabited by more than 30,000 people.

See also: AGE SETS (Vol. I); BAMANA (Vol. I); BAMBARA (Vol. II); SECRET SOCIETIES (Vol. I).

Further reading: Sundiata A. Djata, *The Bamana Empire by the Niger: Kingdom, Jihad, and Colonization, 1712–1920* (Princeton, N.J.: Markus Wiener, 1997).

Banda Traditional AKAN state located in present-day GHANA. Dating back as far as the 13th century, Banda was known to have been highly active in both the MINING and trading of GOLD. Along with the state of BONO, Banda was one of the earliest Akan states, formed in response to the rise of trans-Saharan trade. Banda quickly became a main point of contact for Mande and DYULA traders, who purchased goods such as kola nuts, spices, and gold to sell at the market center of JENNE in present-day southern Republic of MALI. This relationship between Banda and the Mande was apparently prosperous and continued well into the 18th century or later. In the early 18th century, however, the Ashanti had begun to take over much of the Akan regions in an effort to gain control of the trading routes. By 1730 Banda and its profitable gold mines had been effectively taken over by the forces of the Ashanti ruler, OPOKUWARE II (r. 1720–1750), and brought into the realm of the ASHANTI EMPIRE.

See also: MANDE (Vols. I, II, IV).

Banjul (Bathurst) Island and capital city of present-day The GAMBIA, in West Africa. Situated near the entrance to the Gambia River, the island of Banjul was an ideal location for the British to establish a trading port in the SENEGAMBIA region. Once the slave trade was outlawed by the British in 1807, Banjul also served as an observation point from which the British could check the illegal activities of slave traders from other countries.

In 1816 Banjul Island was transferred to the British captain Alexander Grant for an annual sum of 25 pounds sterling. Grant renamed the island St. Mary's and right away started construction on civilian houses, barracks, and a trading station. Once his settlement was complete, he renamed the town Bathurst, after Lord Henry Bathurst, the British secretary of state.

> In 1973, eight years after The Gambia became independent, President Jawara officially changed Bathurst's name back to Banjul.

Within a few years, the population of Bathurst nearly tripled, as the settlement attracted Wolof traders and recently freed Jola, Mandinka, and Aku slaves from SIERRA LEONE, as well as British merchants.

See also: BANJUL (Vols. III, V); MANDINKA (Vol. II).

Bara Ethnic group inhabiting the inland savanna regions of southern MADAGASCAR, an island off of the southern coast of East Africa. The Bara kingdom was made up of a group of decentralized pastoralist chiefdoms that unified in times of war to present a formidable challenge to the SAKALAVA and MERINA empires that attempted to subjugate them.

Of all the groups in Madagascar, the Bara most closely resemble Bantu-speaking people in physical appearance, and they share many religious customs and linguistic similarities with ethnic groups from the African continent. Some modern anthropologists even classify the Bara as a directly related subgroup of the Mbara, a group from the Lake Nyasa region in MALAWI. The denomination "Bara" only came into use at the beginning of the 19th century. Until that time the Bara were referred to by their clan names, including Zafimanely, Iansantsa, Imamono, and Vinda.

As described by the few European explorers bold enough to enter Ibara, as Bara territory is called, the Bara were fierce warriors and difficult traders. As a result, for a long time there was little definitive information about the Bara found in European texts.

> Bara oral traditions refer to Rabiby, a chief of the Zafimanely clan, as the founder of the Bara. According to these traditions, Rabiby came to Madagascar from the African continent around the middle of the 18th century, bringing with him African concepts of political organization that were previously unknown on the island. Although this tradition is helpful in explaining why the Bara have certain affinities with Bantu-speaking Africans more than other Madagascar groups, it does not account for the mystery of why they speak a dialect that is obviously Malagasy.

In the latter half of the 18th century the Bara maintained their pastoralist culture by raiding cattle from neighboring groups, including the Mahafaly and Sakalava, and by trading with those same groups for agricultural products and weapons. For the most part the Bara managed to maintain their independence from the Sakalava empire, which flourished in the region east of Ibara during the 17th century. The also remained largely independent as the Merina came to dominate southern Madagascar in the 19th century.

See also: BANTU EXPANSION (Vols. I, II); BANTU LANGUAGES (Vol. I).

Further reading: Raymond K. Kent, *Early Kingdoms in Madagascar, 1500–1700* (New York: Holt, Rinehart and Winston, 1970).

Barbary Coast During the 16th century, under Ottoman rule, the coastal region of North Africa became known as the Barbary Coast. Its center was at Tunis, which served as the base for piracy against European ships in the Mediterranean. The term was derived from the name of the BERBERS, the ancient inhabitants of the region.

Man from the Barbary Coast, which was then under the control of the Ottoman Empire. The print is from an engraving by the French artist Le Hay made in 1713–14. © Historical Picture Archive/Corbis

See also: OTTOMAN EMPIRE AND AFRICA (Vols. II, III); PIRATES (Vol. III); TUNIS (Vols. II, V).

Barbot, Jean (1655–1712) *French writer who described the transatlantic slave trade*

Between 1678 and 1682 Jean Barbot visited the West African coast, near present-day Republic of BENIN, as an agent of the French Royal African Company. Barbot's most widely read book was *A Description of the Coasts of North and South Guinea,* written in 1682, which included detailed descriptions of the inhabitants, coastal settlements, and even wildlife and flora from the region. The book also included Barbot's illustrations of the people, places, and things that he described. Barbot's often graphic descriptions of the condition of the peoples taken captive and sold into bondage make for startling reading even today. No early abolitionist, however, Barbot generally expressed the prejudices of the Europeans of the day, taking the view that the captives were far better off in European, rather than African, hands.

See also: SLAVE TRADE, THE TRANSATLANTIC (Vol. III).

Basotho See SOTHO.

Batammaliba building traditions The Batammaliba (a name meaning "those who are the real architects of the earth") inhabit the mountainous grasslands in the border region of today's TOGO and the Republic of BENIN. The dominant feature of this region is the Atacora Mountains. The Batammaliba are thought to have migrated to the area in the 17th or 18th century. They were probably drawn to the region because of its frequent rainfall and fertile soil.

Batammaliba ARCHITECTURE is deeply rooted in religious belief. Each house serves not only as a self-sustaining compound but also as a sanctuary. According to oral history, Batammaliba architecture originated at the village of Linaba. It was there that Kuiye, the all-powerful solar god, created the first humans. Kuiye lived on Earth with these first humans and provided for their every need. There was no hunger, no rain, no cold, and no need for LABOR. Therefore, the first Batammaliba structures were simple, open-sided shelters (*kufiku*) made with forked posts holding up a thatched roof. Because of their role at Linaba, *kufiku* are among the first structures built in newly founded Batammaliba villages today. These shelters are always placed to the west of Batammaliba houses in deference to Linaba and Kuiye's house in the western sky. They act as shady resting places, drying areas for crops, and even allow for storage atop the flat roof.

According to tradition Kuiye became more annoyed with humans, he fled Earth, leaving humans to fend for themselves. Humans were now subjected to darkness, seasonal changes, inclement weather, hunger, birth, and death. They had to learn to hunt, fish, farm, and protect themselves from the elements. Therefore, the original shelter was no longer sufficient. Humans needed a larger structure with cooking facilities, storage areas, and secure sleeping rooms for pregnant women and infants, while providing adequate protection from the elements.

The Batammaliba developed a new architectural structure in the form of a three-room earthen compound (*kucuku*). Two rooms were covered with straw roofs while the kitchen was covered with an earthen terrace roof. Several important characteristics were evident in this new architectural form: the west-facing placement of the compound, the presence of a sacred fire in the compound's front room, a womb-like front portal hole, and earthen shrines placed in front of the compound portal. The westward orientation of the compound was out of reverence to Kuiye and his house in the western heavens. The earthen shrines also paid homage to Kuiye. The sacred fire and womb-like portal represented Kuiye's separation from humans and the role they now had to play in the reproduction and maintenance of the human race. These characteristics reinforced the house's role as a religious sanctuary and are still seen in Batammaliba houses today.

When the Batammaliba migrated to the Atacora region, a new multilevel architectural style developed that coupled the Batammaliba's own terrace style with the two-story form used by many people indigenous to the Atacora. This multistory style resulted in larger compounds with more storage area for the animals and foodstuffs supported by the fertile soil and pasturelands. It is still the predominant form of Batammaliba architecture seen today.

Batammaliba compounds are built on the sites of previous residences. These sites have good soil from past fertilization and are thought to be free of evil spirits. Houses are constructed with the rich clay common to the Atacora region. The clay is covered with a plaster made of silt, fruit, manure, and oils that protect the walls from rain. Each house is a grouping of circular rooms constructed within a small yard. Since these compounds are built to serve as self-sufficient facilities, they contain areas for the sheltering of animals, drying crops, and storing grain. Houses are symmetrically divided into male and female sides. The north side of the house contains the women's granaries and shrines, and the south side of the house contains the men's granaries and shrines.

Because Batammaliba houses serve not only as a residence for humans but also as a residence for the gods and ancestral spirits, these compounds incorporate many features symbolic of the ideological and religious beliefs of the Batammaliba. Compounds are built facing west out of deference to Kuiye. Shrines within the house and its yard are oriented along an east-west axis to parallel the path of the sun. These shrines honor Kuiye, lesser deities, and deceased FAMILY members. The most prominent feature of the Batammaliba house is the two-story structure. The verticality of this style represents Kuiye's position as the highest of all deities. It is from Kuiye that all things flow, and the house is the ultimate shrine and testament to his greatness. The Batammaliba believe that any modification to these traditional styles may incur the wrath of the gods.

Further reading: Suzanne Preston Blier, *The Anatomy of Architecture: Ontology and Metaphor in Batammaliba Architectural Expression* (New York: Cambridge University Press, 1987).

Baule (Baol, Baoule)

AKAN people concentrated in IVORY COAST. The Baule are mainly a farming people with yams as their most important crop. In fact, at harvest time the first yam is presented as a gift to the ancestors.

After refusing to be incorporated into the ASHANTI EMPIRE, the Baule migrated to their present-day location in the mid-18th century. Under the rule of Queen Pokou (fl. late 1700s), they expanded their control over the majority of what is presently Ivory Coast. The Baule successfully fended off continuous European attempts to conquer their kingdom. In the mid-19th century, however, they were finally conquered by the French and fell under colonial rule.

Beatrix, Doña (Doña Beatriz, Kimpa Vita) (c. 1684–1706) *Kongo spiritual leader*

Doña Beatrix was born to a noble family in a small town east of the old Kongo capital of SÃO SALVADOR. From an early age, she was recognized by her people as a medium between the natural and supernatural worlds, or *nganga,* the same title given by the Kongo to Catholic priests. Endowed with *kindoki,* or religious power, she became a charismatic leader who claimed possession by the spirit of St. Anthony. She was said to have healed the sick and brought fertility to sterile women.

Doña Beatrix amassed a huge following as she traveled the country, spreading an alternative version of Christian history. In her sermons, she preached that Jesus was born to an African woman in São Salvador. Also known by her Kongo name, Kimpa Vita, Doña Beatrix challenged the European Church by criticizing its refusal to recognize African saints. In turn, the Catholic priests in the region denounced her as a witch and urged the Kongo king to silence her.

Dona Beatrix moved to São Salvador and recruited MISSIONARIES, whom she called "Little Anthonies." They were dispatched throughout the country to disseminate her teachings and build support for the coming of a new king who would reunite the KONGO KINGDOM. Her message threatened the sovereignty of the Christianized Kongo king, Pedro IV, and some of his rivals exploited the situation by declaring their support for Dona Beatrix and her Antonian movement. In 1706 she was captured by the king's allies and burned at the stake.

See also: WOMEN IN PRECOLONIAL AFRICA (Vol. III).

Further reading: John Thornton, *The Kongo Saint Anthony: Dona Beatriz Kimpa Vita and the Antonian Movement, 1684–1706* (New York: Cambridge University Press, 1998).

Begho (Nsoko)

Historic trading city, most notably of textiles and GOLD, of what was known as the northern AKAN region of Brong-Ahafo, located west of the Volta River of present-day GHANA. The city of Begho probably developed as early as the 11th century but did not begin to prosper as an influential market center until the 15th through the late 18th centuries. Due to its strategic location at the edge of the Volta River forest, Begho effectively controlled the trade between the adjoining savanna and forest regions by serving as a link between the two zones and providing a place where the resources of each region could be easily exchanged. Begho was also a center frequented by European traders as well as DYULA, Muslim merchants from the NIGER RIVER regions and other trading cities, such as JENNE and TIMBUKTU in present-day Republic of MALI.

Begho itself was divided into three main sectors called Kramo, BONO (Brong), and Dwinfour, which were inhabited by ethnic groups such as the Mande, Numu, and Nsoko peoples. Dwinfour was especially important, as it was known to be the area that housed the artisans who produced trade items made from ivory, brass, copper, iron, GOLD, and cloth.

European and southern Akan traders often referred to Begho as Nsoko—possibly in reference to the Nsokohene, who ruled the Nsoko area and were known to protect the southern Akan who brought their wares to trade in Begho.

The bulk of trade within Begho's region of dominance came from the sale of gold and textile goods. The Begho region was known to have an abundance of mines from which gold was extracted and used to trade for items produced in the southern regions of present-day Ghana. By the 16th century Begho was also maintaining relations with the nearby gold-producing and gold-trading state of Bono. Cloth produced in Begho was probably the best-known export, however. The Muslim inhabitants dominated the dyeing industry, and their fine, woven clothing items were sought after by African and European traders alike.

By the start of the 18th century Begho had begun relations with the Ashanti peoples. While the relationship was at first fruitful, the Ashanti overran the city of Begho around 1723 and made it part of their kingdom. In 1764 Begho attempted to regain its independence but was quickly defeated by the Ashanti forces. It appears Begho went into a state of decline after this point, as the gold mines came under Ashanti control and severely weakened Begho's trade. From 1798 to 1800 civil war between the Akan and Muslims brought further strife to the region, and Begho was abandoned at that time or shortly thereafter.

Further reading: Timothy F. Garrard, *Akan Weights and the Gold Trade* (London: Longman Group Ltd., 1980).

Beira Trading center in MOZAMBIQUE. Although modern-day Beira was not founded until 1891, the Portuguese explorer Pêro da Covilhã (c. 1460–c. 1526) discovered the site in 1487. Located at the intersection of the Pungue and Buzi rivers, the town would later become an important Indian Ocean trading port for ZIMBABWE and MALAWI.

See also: INDIAN OCEAN TRADE (Vol. II).

Bemba Bantu-speaking people of northeastern ZAMBIA as well as parts of the Democratic Republic of the CONGO and ZIMBABWE. Although a human skull dating back 125,000 years has been found in the area, the Bemba apparently have only lived in their home region since the 18th century. In the closing years of that century, the Bemba formed a centralized government under a supreme chief known as the *chitimukulu,* who was descended from a matrilineal royal clan. Royal income came, for the most part, from tribute and from taxes on the trade in captives, in which the Bemba were heavily involved.

Traditionally, Bemba society was made up of about 40 matrilineal clans, each of which was led by a headman. The people lived in villages made up of about 30 huts. In the past Bemba men saw themselves primarily as warriors and hunters, leaving most agricultural work to women. Due to the poor soil in the area, villages were forced to move or relocate their fields every four or five years.

As the Lunda kingdom of KAZEMBE expanded during the 18th and 19th centuries, the Bemba increasingly focused on raiding the Bisa traders who served as intermediaries in the rich trading network that moved through Bisa territory. The riches from their raids helped make the Bemba a major power in the region during the 19th century.

See also: BISA TRADING NETWORK (Vol. III); KINGDOMS AND EMPIRES OF EASTERN AFRICA AND THE INTERIOR (Vol. III); LUNDA EMPIRE (Vol. III).

Further reading: Andrew D. Roberts, *A History of the Bemba: Political Growth and Change in North Eastern Zambia before 1900* (Harlow, U.K.: Longman, 1973).

Benadir Coast Name given to a stretch of Indian Ocean coastline on the Horn of Africa. The port town of MOGADISHU marked the northern end of the Benadir Coast, while the mouth of the Juba River marked its southern end. Besides Mogadishu, other port towns on the Benadir Coast included the Swahili trading centers of Marca and BRAVA. Between the 16th and 19th centuries the ports on the Benadir Coast were the termini of several important caravan routes that brought trade items, including ivory, wood, and gums, among other items, from the hinterlands in exchange for firearms and other goods.

See also: INDIAN OCEAN TRADE (Vol. II); IVORY TRADE (Vol. III); SLAVE TRADE ON THE SWAHILI COAST (Vol. III).

Further reading: Ahmed Dualeh Jama, *The Origins and Development of Mogadishu AD 1000 to 1850: A Study of the Urban Growth Along the Benadir Coast of Southern Somalia* (Uppsala, Sweden: Uppsala University, 1996).

Benguela Major port on the west coast of southern Africa in what is now ANGOLA; founded in 1617 as part of the Portuguese colony of Angola. During the 16th century the Portuguese began trading for salt, ivory, copper, dried fish, and other foods along the southern coast of Angola. During the next century they established a settlement at Benguela with the hope of finding copper and other valuable minerals in the area. Since no mineral wealth was found and the land was generally swampy and unproductive, the settlement never grew very large. Dutch seamen captured the port in 1623, but the Portuguese retook it soon after. Benguela was attacked sporadically by the Dutch and later the French, but was generally under Portuguese control.

High mountains separated Benguela from the interior highlands, and it was not until the late 1600s that the Portuguese began to penetrate the region east of the port. Portuguese-sponsored traders, or POMBEIROS, built fortified trading stations to facilitate trade across the highlands with the OVIMBUNDU. Salt was plentiful near Benguela and was mined and traded for ivory and skins from the interior.

During the 18th century the Portuguese coerced the Ovimbundu to help them in the trade in human captives, and Benguela quickly rivaled the northern Angolan port town of LUANDA in the number of captives it exported. By 1800, almost one-half of the Africans shipped from Angola left from the port of Benguela.

See also: IVORY TRADE (Vol. III); PORTUGAL AND AFRICA (Vol. III); SALT TRADE (Vol. II); SLAVE TRADE, THE TRANSATLANTIC (Vol. III).

Benin, Bight of A 550-mile-wide (885-km) bay, the northern arm of Gulf of Guinea on the Atlantic Ocean played a strategic role during the slave trade between the 16th and 19th centuries. Located on the West African coast, the Bight of Benin is situated within the Gulf of Guinea and is adjacent to TOGO, the Republic of BENIN, southeastern GHANA, and southwestern NIGERIA. The Bight is fed by the NIGER RIVER and several other bordering rivers. Its major ports are Cotonou in Benin, LAGOS in Nigeria, and Lomé in Togo. The Bight's location and its accessibility to neighboring ports made it a popular waterway for the trade and TRANSPORTATION of captives between the 16th and 19th centuries. Due to the heavy volume of this trade, the area of coastal lagoons west of the Niger Delta became recognized as the SLAVE COAST. After the abolition of SLAVERY in the 1830's, trade in PALM OIL became the main source of commerce in that region.

Benin City (Edo) Capital city of the ancient kingdom of BENIN. Located in the Edo state, which lies in present-day southern NIGERIA, it is a port city on the Benin River. Benin City was the capital of the kingdom of Benin since its founding in the 13th century and was home to the *oba*, or king, and his palace. During the latter part of the 15th

century it served as the center of trade in ivory, cloth, and pepper to the Europeans. The city is also famous for its numerous works of ART, which date as far back as the 13th century. Carvings in ivory and wood and figures cast in iron and brass, which were once believed to be of bronze, are some of the finest works of art in Africa. Although the city lost its importance during the kingdom's decline in the 18th century, during the 1800s the expansion of trade in palm products with the Europeans helped reestablish Benin as a significant trading post.

Benin, kingdom of Edo kingdom that occupied present-day southern NIGERIA between the 13th and 19th centuries; this kingdom is not to be confused with the modern republic of the same name. In the 15th century the warrior-king Ewuare (c. 1440–1480) took control of the small Edo state of Benin and turned it into a thriving and prosperous kingdom. Under Ewuare's leadership, Benin secured the area between YORUBALAND and the NIGER RIVER and revamped its government. As a great supporter of the arts, Ewuare also made substantial cultural reforms that impacted the kingdom long after his rule.

Ewuare was succeeded by his son OZOLUA (r. 1481–1504) and then his grandson Esigie (r. c. 1504–1550). During their reigns, both Ozolua and Esigie continued to nurture the relationship with Portuguese traders that had commenced during Ewuare's reign. In return for facilitating coastal trade, the Portuguese provided the kingdom with firearms—weaponry much more powerful than that of the indigenous Africans in surrounding areas—and assisted in times of military crisis. After an era of great territorial expansion Benin's ECONOMY expanded rapidly, and the kingdom became the leading Atlantic coast exporter of cloth, pepper, PALM OIL, and ivory. As Benin grew more prosperous, the monarchy took a greater interest in the arts, and it is from this period that Benin artisans produced some of the empire's most celebrated bronze work and wood carvings.

Although much of Benin's economy was dependent on the trade in captured people, the kingdom was also concerned about maintaining its own healthy population. During most of the 16th and 17th centuries Benin imposed a ban on the export of its own male captives. In response the Portuguese and other European traders moved their business elsewhere. This embargo of Benin eventually isolated the kingdom from the trade in human captives, which became one of the most profitable forms of commerce along the Atlantic coast over the next three centuries.

Benin declined during the 18th and 19th centuries. The kings, or *obas*, withdrew from politics, ushering in a period of civil unrest. When the British abolished the slave trade, in 1807, like that of most of West Africa, Benin's economy plummeted. NUPE, Ibadan, and European traders moved in on Benin territory, taking advantage of the kingdom's vulnerable state.

See also: BENIN, KINGDOM OF (Vol. II, IV); BENIN, BIGHT OF (Vol. III); BENIN CITY (Vols. III, IV, V); EWUARE (Vol. II); IVORY TRADE (Vol. III); WARFARE AND WEAPONS (Vol. III).

Benin, Republic of Country in coastal West Africa measuring approximately 43,500 square miles (112,700 sq km) that shares borders with NIGER and BURKINA FASO to the north, TOGO to the east, the Atlantic Ocean to the south, and NIGERIA to the west.

In the years following the appearance of Europeans along West Africa, northern Benin and the neighboring region of Nigeria saw the emergence of BORGU. It was centered on Nikki, one of the major chiefdoms that made up Borgu. Two lesser Borgu chiefdoms, Parakou and Kandi, both founded about 1700, were also located in northern Benin. About 1625 internal political turmoil in the AJA kingdom of ALLADA within southern Benin, led to the founding of ABOMEY. Its inhabitants were the FON, and they came to call their state DAHOMEY. By the early 18th century Dahomey was emerging as the strongest state in southern Benin. In 1724 it conquered Allada and, a few years later, the rival coastal trading state of WHYDAH. In 1730, however, the OYO EMPIRE, located in the YORUBA-LAND area of western Nigeria, made Dahomey a tributary state without destroying its political structure. This relationship was to last throughout the remainder of the century until Oyo was weakened by internal strife. Oyo had also established hegemony over Borgu, which it also lost in the late 18th century.

Tragically, for the people of Benin, the emergence of Dahomey was linked to the growing transatlantic SLAVE TRADE. Its ECONOMY and society became deeply implicated in the trade in human captives, and its rulers used their armies to this end. The king became the largest slave trader, and he added to the state's revenues by taxing the other slave dealers. Indeed, the availability of large numbers of captives for purchase led the Europeans to name this portion of the Atlantic coast the "SLAVE COAST." While the state structure of Dahomey was centered on the trade in human captives, they nearly all came from beyond its own borders. Thus, the general populace was not directly affected and continued with its agricultural pursuits. The state did tax the people very heavily, however. This eventually helped promote the production of PALM OIL for export to Europe as a source of income, once the trade in human captives began to decline as the practice became abolished in the early 19th century.

See also: BENIN, REPUBLIC OF (Vols. I, II, IV, V).

Further reading: Edna G. Bay, *Wives of the Leopard: Gender, Politics, and Culture in the Kingdom of Dahomey* (Charlottesville, Va.: Univ. of Virginia Press, 1998); Robert B. Edgerton, *Warrior Women: The Amazons of Dahomey and the Nature of War* (Boulder, Colo.: Westview Press, 2000); Patrick Manning, *Slavery, Colonialism, and Economic Growth in Dahomey, 1640–1960* (New York: Cambridge Univ. Press, 1982).

Berbera Port city located in present-day SOMALIA, east of DJIBOUTI on the Gulf of Aden. Along with the city of ZEILA to the northwest, Berbera was one of the busiest Arab trading ports on the Gulf of Aden. When the Portuguese sacked and occupied Zeila, in 1516, Berbera became the northern hub of Arab-controlled trade in the region. Its glory was short-lived, though, as Berbera itself was attacked by Portuguese soldiers in 1518.

During the 17th century Berbera was controlled by the sharifs of the Yemeni emirate of Mocha, across the Gulf of Aden, then sank into relative obscurity until the colonial era in the late 19th century.

Early Arab geographers referred to the northern regions of the Horn of Africa as the Bilad al-Barbar (Land of the Barbarians). The town of Berbera retained the name that once described the whole northern coastline.

See also: INDIAN OCEAN TRADE (Vol. II); PORTUGAL AND AFRICA (Vols. III, IV, V); SLAVE TRADE ON THE SWAHILI COAST (Vol. III).

Berbers Non-Arabic group that inhabits regions of North Africa, especially MOROCCO and the central Sahara. The all-encompassing term *Berber* refers to several heterogeneous groups, including the Sanhaja and TUAREGS, all of whom practice Islam and speak the Berber language. Berber history from the 14th century until modern times is characterized by a movement from greatness to relative isolation.

The glory of former Sanhaja Berber dynasties such as the Almoravids and Almohads had disappeared by the end of the 13th century. Then, around the beginning of the 16th century, the teachings of Sanhaja Berber scholars in TIMBUKTU became influential, as they were spread throughout North Africa by the students who attended the Islamic Sankore University.

Also in the 16th century the Ottoman Empire came to conquer most of the coastal regions of North Africa. The interior regions of Morocco resisted, however, under the Berber leadership of the SADIAN DYNASTY, a line of ZAWAYA sheiks who traced their ancestry to the prophet Mu-hammad. Recognizing the strength of the Ottoman navy—and allied by virtue of their shared Islamic RELIGION—some of Morocco's Berbers made peace with the invading Turks and even fought as mercenaries in their armies against the European Christians who were vying for superiority on the Mediterranean Sea.

The Ottoman Turks, in turn, allowed Zawaya clerics to perform limited administrative duties in their government. On the whole, though, the Berbers were without any real political power during the period of Turkish occupation in North Africa.

In the 18th century Berber clerics and traders of the KUNTA clans monopolized the salt trade north of Timbuktu, in present-day Republic of MALI. Over the latter half of the 18th century the Kunta were led by Sidi Mukhtar (1729–1811), a writer and a learned Muslim cleric of the QADIRIYYA brotherhood who resolved disputes between rival Tuareg factions and brought stability to the region.

The Kunta monopoly on this salt trade allowed other Berber groups, including the Tuaregs, to continue a successful trans-Saharan slave trade. Salt from the western Sahara was mined by forced laborers and vassals and brought south via caravan. At the southern market towns, the salt was traded for grains, cloth, and captives. Many of these captives were then brought north to be traded with merchants from LIBYA and ALGERIA for jewelry, metals, and other luxury items. The Tuaregs did keep some of the captives, however, and used them to tend to their camels, protect their camps, and cultivate their oases.

See also: BERBERS (Vols. I, II, IV, V); OTTOMAN EMPIRE AND AFRICA (Vols. III, IV); SLAVE TRADE, EXPANSION OF EUROPEAN INVOLVEMENT IN (Vol. (III).

Further reading: Michael Brett and Elizabeth Fentress, *The Berbers* (Cambridge, Mass.: Blackwell Publishers, 1996).

Beta Israel (Falasha) People of ETHIOPIA who inhabited the GONDAR region north of Lake Tana, as well as Begemder, SIMIEN, and Dembiya. The Beta Israel pray in Ge'ez and participate in Ethiopian rituals such as male and female circumcision. There are various traditions as to the origin of the Beta Israel. Some hold that they are the descendants of a Jewish migration from EGYPT that took place early in the common era. Others believe that they are an Agaw people who were converted to Judaism before Christianity reached Ethiopia and who managed to hold on to their RELIGION despite fervent attempts by the Christians to convert them.

Despite the continuous movement against them by the Ethiopian monarchy, the Beta Israel formed a united front under the leadership of a warrior and chieftain named Radai (fl. 1550). For a few years Radai held back the forces of the monarchy, succeeding, even, in defeating an invasion led by King Menas Wanag Sagad II (r. 1559–1563). Radai was eventually defeated, however, by King Sarsa Dengel Malak Sagad I (r. 1563–1597) in a battle that took place at Mashaka, near the Marek River. A rebellion by Radai's brother Kaleb also ended in defeat for the forces of the Beta Israel.

The Beta Israel were persecuted by Ethiopia's Christian rulers for centuries. Christian campaigns in the 14th and 15th centuries forced the Beta Israel into Wegera and into the mountainous regions of Begemder, Sagade, Salamt, and Simien, where they were subsequently pressured into conversion by the tireless efforts of both Tigray and AMHARA clerics. In an attempt to put an end to Beta Israel resistance, Bahr Negash YISHAQ (r. 1413–1430) made a law by which only those baptized in the Christian faith were allowed to inherit land.

Leadership of the Beta Israel passed to Gideon (Gedewon), in 1616, but he, too, suffered a serious loss, this time at the hands of King Susenyos (r. 1605–1632) and was killed in 1626 during a vicious battle in the Simien Mountains. Soon after, the Beta Israel were forced from Simien and the Lake Tana area during an aggressive mission in which King Susenyos ordered the death of all those who refused to convert to Christianity. The Beta Israel eventually settled in northwestern Ethiopia and by the 18th century had established their own monarchy.

See also: AGAW (Vols. I, II); BETA ISRAEL (Vols. I, II, IV, V); GE'EZ (Vols. I, II).

Further reading: Steven Kaplan, *The Beta Israel (Falasha) in Ethiopia: From Earliest Times to the Twentieth Century* (New York: New York University Press, 1992).

Betsileo A Malagasy people from the southern central highlands of MADAGASCAR. The Betsileo originated in the southeastern coastlands and moved to the central plateau, probably between the 13th and 14th centuries. Compared to other southern Malagasy groups, the Betsileo were mobile and culturally advanced. They were cattle herders and rice farmers who had mastered the irrigation techniques required to cultivate the terraced paddies of their difficult, mountainous habitat. The four subgroups of the Betsileo—the Lalangina, Anindrano, Isandra, and Menandriana—were all organized under central chiefs, who relied on village elders to help them govern.

The Betsileo were one of several Malagasy groups who maintained a snake-worship tradition, or "*fanany* cult," as part of their religious practices. When a Betsileo prince died, his body was tightly wrapped in cloth and strapped to a post. A small outrigger, or canoe, was placed underneath. Mourners would gather around and wait, sometimes for a week, for the body to decompose. Eventually, a putrid substance began to drip from the body and collect in the outrigger, and worms would appear in the substance soon thereafter. The believers thought that the spirit of the departed prince was contained in the largest worm. At that point the body was buried and the outrigger set afloat on a pond that was reserved for just such an occasion. The Betsileo believed that the worm eventually grew into a large snake, or *fanany*, and slipped into the pond. For this reason, they believed that the snakes in their land were the reincarnations of their departed leaders.

Relatively isolated in the central plateau, the Betsileo had little interaction with the other Malagasy groups that surrounded them: the BARA, to the south; the SAKALAVA, to the west; the BETSIMISARAKA and ANTEMORO, to the east; and the MERINA, to the north. Early in the 19th century, though, the Betsileo were subjugated by the Merina, who expanded into their territory from the north. By 1830, the Merina had established the city of Fianarantsoa as the capital of the Betsileo province. In Fianarantsoa (whose name means "good learning"), Betsileo culture and traditional arts flourished, and they became known for their exceptional woven textiles, wood carvings, MUSIC, and poetry.

Further reading: Sandra J. T. M. Evers, *Constructing History, Culture and Inequality: The Betsileo in the Extreme Southern Highlands of Madagascar* (Boston: Brill, 2002).

Betsimisaraka Ethnic group inhabiting the eastern regions of the island of MADAGASCAR. The Betsimisaraka emerged in the 18th century from a confederation of coastal states and came to control much of the east coast of Madagascar by the end of the century. Their first leader, Ratsimilaho (d. 1751), was allegedly the son of a British pirate and a Malagasy princess named Antavaratra Rahena.

The Betsimisaraka, whose name means "numerous and inseparable" in the Malagasy language, have tradition-ally been traders, fishers, and farmers. The important east coast ports of Toamasina and Île Ste-Marie are located in what was Betsimisaraka territory.

See also: BETSIMISARAKA (Vol. II).

Bijago (Bissagos, Bidyogo) West African ethnic group inhabiting the Bijago Islands, located just off the coast of present-day GUINEA-BISSAU. The major islands include Bubaque, Carache, Caravela, Formosa, Orango, Orangozinho, Roxa, and Uno. The Bijago are believed to be descended from the Papeis and the Nalus people who came to the area between 900 and 1300. During the era of the transatlantic SLAVE TRADE, from the late 15th into the early 19th centuries, the Bijago earned a fierce reputation among European slave traders. Bijago warriors in large canoes that held up to 70 people attacked European slave ships and trading posts along the Guinea Coast, and the few Bijago who were captured often committed suicide rather than live a life in bondage.

Traditionally the Bijago sustained themselves through fishing and AGRICULTURE, producing primarily rice and PALM OIL. Their traditional RELIGION was animistic.

Birnin Kebbi Capital of the Hausa state of KEBBI from 1700 to 1805. Birnin Kebbi is located in present-day NIGERIA, along the Sokoto River. Originally a small kingdom of the Kebbawa (a Hausa subgroup), Birnin Kebbi rose to prominence in the early 16th century when it became part of the Kebbi kingdom. In 1516 Kebbi's founder, Muhammadu Kanta (r. c. 1515), captured Birnin Kebbi, beginning a century of Kebbi dominance over the six neighboring HAUSA STATES. By 1620 the Kebbi state stretched over much of present-day western Nigeria. Later in the 17th century Kebbi's power began to decline.

About 1700, Tomo (r. 1700–1717), the king of Kebbi, named Birnin Kebbi the new capital of his state. It remained the capital city until 1805, when FULANI invaders burned Birnin Kebbi. Birnin Kebbi was subsequently rebuilt as part of the Fulani empire. Prior to its decline Birnin Kebbi served as a river port and market center for local items, including millet, fish, cattle, and COTTON.

Bisa trading network System of transporting goods for trade between Bantu-speaking peoples from the southeastern African interior and Arabs, Europeans, Indians, and Swahili peoples on the Indian Ocean coast. During the 18th and 19th centuries Bisa traders acted as intermediaries in the trade of iron, copper, salt, captives, and ivory. They exchanged these goods for cloth, guns, beads, and luxury goods from abroad, which they brought back to the interior. Bisa merchants were widely admired for their commercial prowess.

The Bisa people themselves originated in the Lunda-Luba empire of southern Central Africa. When land became scarce there, in the 17th century, they migrated southeast to new territory in the Luangwa Valley, in what is now northeastern ZAMBIA. Their new lands lay along a major trade route that cut through Zambia to the coast of MOZAMBIQUE. The BEMBA kingdom lay to the north, and the YAO lived to the east. The Bisa traded with the Yao, the LUNDA EMPIRE, and other neighboring groups, as well as with the Portuguese at SENA and TETE, along the ZAMBEZI RIVER.

The Bisa were skilled hunters who established guilds to organize the pursuit of elephants, hippopotamuses, rhinoceroses, buffalos, lions, and ant bears. The elephant hunters, or *nkombalume,* were the most highly regarded. They killed their prey with traps, bows and arrows, axes, and spears, which were often tipped with poison. One hunting method involved having some members of the hunting party climb trees overhanging elephant paths, while other members herded the animals toward the trees. When the elephants passed under the trees, the men threw their heavy, poisoned spears between the animals' shoulder blades. The Bisa also cast spells and carried charms to aid them in their ritual hunt.

See also: IVORY TRADE (Vol. III); LUBA (Vol. II); LUBA EMPIRE (Vol. III).

Bissau Capital of the present-day country of GUINEA-BISSAU. The town gained prominence in the 17th century as a major port in the transatlantic SLAVE TRADE. Originally inhabited by the Papei people, Bissau was controlled by the Mali Empire until the 15th century. Its people grew relatively prosperous through a combination of farming, hunting, and cattle herding.

Toward the end of the 15th century Portuguese explorers landed at the Geba River estuary and discovered the port. European interest was limited for the next 200 years, although a small Portuguese settlement was established there by the end of the 15th century. There, Portuguese merchants and peoples of mixed indigenous and European blood traded everything from manufactured goods, horses, and firearms for PALM OIL, GOLD, and captives. Since the nearby kingdom of GABU had long been a part of trans-Saharan trade, Bissau's role as a center for the trading of captives grew quickly, despite the resistance of groups such as the Balanta, Nalu, Felupe, and Manjaca.

By the latter half of the 17th century the Portuguese established a second settlement, and the area had become a major link in the transatlantic slave trade. It is believed that as many as 600,000 people passed through it on their way to the Americas.

In 1696 Bissau was placed under the control of a series of Portuguese captain-majors. Other ports in the area became more important to the Portuguese in the early 18th century, and, in 1707, Bissau was closed. It reopened in 1753, when a revival of the slave trade sparked a renewed interest in this strategically located port. This revival, which was led by the Grão-Pará Company, renewed Bissau, and the town eventually became more important to the Portuguese than their long-time chief port of CACHEU. Captives, PALM OIL, and GROUNDNUTS (peanuts) were the primary exports. Spain, France, Holland, and Britain all attempted to thwart Portuguese dominance, but to no avail. Internal conflict was prevalent as captives were procured by coercing local indigenous groups to engage in warfare. The losing group was sold abroad.

Although conflict between the indigenous groups was continuous, this did not lead to Bissau's decline in the early 1800s. The abrupt end of the European slave trade virtually destroyed Bissau's ECONOMY. In the late 19th century only a small colony of less than 600 people remained.

See also: BISSAU (Vols. II, V); PORTUGAL AND AFRICA (Vol. III); SLAVERY (Vol. III).

Further reading: Walter Hawthorne, *Planting Rice and Harvesting Slaves: Transformations Along the Guinea-Bissau Coast, 1400–1900* (Portsmouth, N.H.: Heinemann, 2003).

Bito (Babito, Biito) Ruling clans in BUGANDA, BUNYORO, BUSOGA, and TORO in the GREAT LAKES REGION of East Africa, in what is now UGANDA. The Bito were the aristocrats among LUO pastoralists who, by the first decades of the 15th century, had seized control of many kingdoms and smaller chiefdoms in the region.

According to Nyoro oral tradition, the Bito are so named because their clan progenitors conceived their offspring under a bito tree, a scrub tree native to dry regions of Africa and Asia. According to the same tradition, the first true Bito king was Rukidi (fl. 15th century), who established the Nyoro monarchy, called *mukama.* Rukidi's brothers left Bunyoro to found the kingdoms of BUSOGA and BUGANDA, to the east. (GANDA traditions tell a different story, however.)

From the 16th to the 18th centuries the Bito *mukama* of Nyoro conducted frequent invasions into neighboring kingdoms to the south and to the east, including Buganda. According to Bunyoro traditions, a plague infected Nyoro's cattle during the reign of Cwa I (1731–1782), who was also known as Duhaga I. So many cows had to be destroyed to prevent the plague's spread that the king ordered major raids into RWANDA and NKOLE, kingdoms ruled by HINDA clan leaders, to replenish Nyoro herds. Cwa I succeeded in obtaining more cattle and in occupying Nkole for some time. He captured the Hinda king's royal cattle and cut the royal drum, an act that was the ultimate symbol of Nkole's defeat. However, the *mukama* did not permanently secure the territory. He later died during an attack on rival Buganda.

Elsewhere, however, the Bito conquests were successful. At its greatest extent, about 1700, Bito-controlled territory stretched from the top of Lake Albert in the north, past Nkole to the south, and into Busoga to the east. The Bito continued to be the most powerful clan in the region into the 18th century.

See also: BITO (Vol. II); HAYA (Vol. III).

Boers People of Dutch and Huguenot descent who originated in the CAPE COLONY in the latter half of the 17th century. In the mid-19th century they settled in the Transvaal and the Orange Free State. Boer descendants are referred to as Afrikaners.

The DUTCH EAST INDIA COMPANY established a shipping depot in 1652 that became the site of CAPE TOWN. The company encouraged immigration to support its various endeavors. The Cape Colony resulted and quickly grew, with African slaves becoming the primary LABOR force.

There was little, however, to entice all of the white settlers to remain in the western cape. Many spread out into the countryside to become subsistence farmers and pastoralists. These settlers became known as *Trekboers,* meaning "migratory farmers," in Dutch. As they did this, the Trekboers encroached upon the lands of the region's indigenous peoples, and, as a result, became embroiled in constant frontier warfare with the Africans. The Boers organized themselves into wandering patriarchal communities. They were staunch Calvinists and felt that they had a divine right to rule over the land and its native inhabitants.

With the end of the Napoleonic Wars, the Cape Colony fell under British control in 1806. The Boers opposed the British policies regarding the southern African frontier. As a result, between 1835 and 1840, several thousand Boers fled the colony for the interior highveld and regions in southern Natal. The journey, which became known as the GREAT BOER TREK, was dangerous. For instance, the ZULU, with their strong military force, controlled much of the pasture land in Natal and had no desire to share their land with the Boers. Eventually, however, the Boers defeated the Zulus by using guerrilla tactics and establishing fortified camps.

The Boers quickly settled into their new homelands, but peace was short-lived. The Zulu continued to apply military pressure on the Boers, as did other African groups who opposed them. Britain, too, viewed the Boers as a threat to their coastal trade, and British policies resulted in further Boer migrations in the middle of the 19th century. These eventually led to the establishment of the independent Boer republics of Transvaal (1852) and the Orange Free State (1854).

See also: AFRIKAANS (Vols. III, IV, V); AFRIKANERS (Vols. IV, V); AFRIKANER REPUBLICS (Vols. IV, V); BOERS (Vol. IV); NETHERLANDS AND AFRICA (Vol. III).

Further reading: Norman Etherington, *The Great Treks: The Transformation of Southern Africa, 1815–1854* (New York: Longman, 2001); Hermann Giliomee, *The Afrikaners: Biography of a People* (London: C. Hurst, 2003); G. H. L. Le May, *The Afrikaners: An Historical Interpretation* (Cambridge, Mass.: Blackwell, 1995).

Bondu Region located in West Africa just south of the middle Senegal River, near KAYOR, between FOUTA TORO and FOUTA DJALLON. Bondu was the site of the first of the FULANI JIHADS that took place in the latter half of the 17th and early decades of the 18th centuries.

In the 1680s the Muslim ruler, Malik Si (fl. 1675), from Fouta Toro occupied Bondu with the consent of the *tunka* (king) of Gadiago. Eventually he established the Islamic state of Haalpularen, which was occupied by both FULANI and TUKULOR people. As Malik Si's religious, economic, and political importance grew, the *tunka* of Gadiago began to feel threatened. During an expansion campaign, Malik Si perished at the hands of the Gadiago army. He was succeeded by his son Bubu Malik Si (fl. 1700), who allied with the Fulani from Fouta Djallon to force Gadiago to withdraw from Bondu. Bubu Malik Si moved his forces across the Faleme River to Bambuk, where he, too, was killed in action. Soon after, the Malinke of Bambuk made their way to Bondu and drove Malik Si's descendants, the Sisibe people, into nearby Fouta Toro. Eventually, with the help of the Fulani from both Fouta Djallon and Fouta Toro, the Sisibe reestablished their authority in Bondu.

Bubu Malik Si's son Maka Jiba (fl. 1730–1740) assumed the rule of Bondu and continued in the fight against the Sisibe's Malinke enemies in Bambuk. His outstanding military achievements increased his political authority and aroused the distrust of Sule Ndyaye (fl. 1730), the ruler of Fouta Toro, who felt that he should have power over the Sisibe people. After an unsuccessful campaign against Maka Jiba, Sule Ndyaye agreed to a peace treaty, circa 1740, in which he acknowledged the Bondu as autonomous.

In 1796 Abd al-Qadir (fl. 1775–1796), who had been proclaimed the first *almamy,* or imam, of Bondu in 1775–1776, conquered Bondu and designated a puppet ruler to replace the existing *almamy,* Sega Gaye (fl. 1796).

Al-Qadir's control of Bondu was eventually challenged by Sega Gaye's brother Ahmadi Issata (fl. 1800–1810), who joined forces with the BAMBARA of KAARTA to defeat al-Qadir in 1807.

Bonny Port in southern NIGERIA located along the Bonny River, near the Bight of Bonny, formerly known as the Bight of Biafra. Before the arrival of Europeans, the port traded in PALM OIL, salt, and fish. Then, beginning in the 15th century, the trade in human captives became the focal point of Bonny's ECONOMY. More than 20,000 people were shipped off to the Americas by its traders in the year 1790 alone.

During the 400-year period between 1500 and 1900, the port grew in size and power, becoming the capital of the Bonny state and a major commercial center of the IJO people. Bonny reached its zenith under the Pepple dynasty during the 18th and 19th centuries. Although this dynasty tried to resist Britain's abolition of the transatlantic SLAVE TRADE, the end of this trade forced Bonny to reemphasize other exports, especially palm oil and palm kernels. The port proved successful in this transition and remained powerful until the arrival of the railroad in the early 20th century.

See also: BONNY (Vol. II).

Bono West African people and state located in the central region of present-day GHANA. The people of Bono were a subgroup of the AKAN peoples, and the state of Bono was probably established in response to the GOLD trade that had developed during the 13th through the 15th centuries in the Mali Empire. Bono's royal household dates to about 1450, although members of that royal family frequently claimed that their lineage went back 200 years further. The royal household converted to Islam after being influenced by Muslim traders from Mali.

Until the 18th century Bono and its influential rulers were highly active in the gold trade and were also known to have instituted new methods of MINING in the area. Early in the 18th century, however, Bono's clashes with both the kingdom of GONJA and the ASHANTI EMPIRE ended in Bono's eventual downfall.

See also: BONO (Vol. II).

Borgu State located in the northern regions of the present-day countries of NIGERIA and the Republic of BENIN. Borgu had a long history of trading, especially in kola nuts, cattle, GOLD, and copper. The region's inhabitants were known as fierce warriors and caravan raiders.

By the 16th century there were three main kingdoms flourishing within the territory of Borgu—Illo, Nikki, and BUSA—each of which was ruled by kings claiming descent from the legendary seventh-century Arabian leader, Kisra.

Kisra figures in the legends of not only Borgu, but of several neighboring peoples as well, including the Yoruba, the Guruma, and the Bedde. Borgu oral tradition states that Kisra, who resided near Mecca, clashed with the prophet Mohammed (c. 570–632) when he refused to convert to the Muslim faith. When Mohammed declared war on Kisra, Kisra fled, eventually settling on the western side of the NIGER RIVER. There he—or perhaps his descendants—established Nikki, Busa, and Illo. According to Borgu traditions, a dynasty established by Kisra held sway in Nikki, Busa, and Illo even after the British and French colonized the area in the late 19th century.

The 16th century saw disputes between Borgu and the forces of such West African states as the SONGHAI Empire, the OYO EMPIRE, KANEM-BORNU, and the HAUSA STATES. Borgu was able to successfully defend itself against all of these attackers except Oyo, which conquered Borgu in the mid-16th century. Oyo continued to rule over Borgu until the latter part of the 18th century, when revolts against the dictatorial Oyo ruler, Gaha (r. 1745–1765), led to the decline of the Oyo empire. Ultimately Borgu asserted its independence from Oyo in 1783, although it continued to make tributary payments to the empire until 1818.

Borgu was inhabited by many different ethnic groups. The two most important, however, were the Bariba and the Dendi, a Bariba subgroup who converted to Islam. The Bariba, however, continued to practice their traditional RELIGION. The Bariba also were noted for being traders, and they were famous for encouraging trade at their outposts but also for fiercely attacking and looting caravans that came into their territory.

For many centuries the inhabitants of Borgu were known as skilled artisans who made pieces out of brass and copper by an intricate procedure called *ciré perdue*, or "lost wax." The process involved the use of clay and beeswax to form casts that give shape to the molten metals. When the cast was heated, the wax melted, leaving a clay mold capable of containing the extremely hot, liquefied metal without breaking or cracking.

See also: BARIBA (Vol. II); CARAVANS (Vol. II); COPPER (Vol. I); DENDI (Vol. II); ISLAM (Vol. II).

Further reading: Marjorie H. Stewart, *Borgu and Its Kingdoms: A Reconstruction of a Western Sudanese Polity* (Lewiston, N.Y.: Edwin Mellen Press, 2004).

Bornu See KANEM-BORNU.

Bosman, Willem (1672–unknown) *Dutch writer who described the trade in humans on the Guinea Coast*

Willem Bosman was a merchant and agent employed by the DUTCH WEST INDIA COMPANY at ELMINA. His work, *A New and Accurate Description of the Coast of Guinea Divided into the Gold, the Slave, and the Ivory Coasts*, was published in 1701 and translated into English in 1705. Bosman's descriptions emphasized not only the lives of the various peoples of the areas, but also the commercial realities of the transatlantic SLAVE TRADE and the role of the West African kings in the states engaging in that trade.

See also: NETHERLANDS AND AFRICA (Vol. III).

Botswana Landlocked country covering approximately 231,800 square miles (600,400 sq km) in southern Africa. The country is bordered by NAMIBIA, ZAMBIA, ZIMBABWE, and SOUTH AFRICA. Botswana is made up mainly of desert (Kalahari), with better-watered grasslands on its eastern borders and the Okavango wetlands in the north.

Botswana had been inhabited by Khoisan-speaking people from about 17,000 BCE until the middle of the 17th century. During the early 18th century the TSWANA dynasties of the Hurutshe, Kwena, and Kgatla migrated into present-day Botswana from what is now the western Transvaal. Archaeological evidence suggests that competition for cattle, hunting and MINING resources, and coastal trade drove these people from their homelands to the desert lands of Botswana.

About 1759 Kwena and Hurutshe migrants established the NGWAKETSE state in the southeastern region of the country. This state developed into a powerful military kingdom that controlled much of the hunting, cattle raiding, and copper production in the Kalahari west of Kanye.

See also: BOTSWANA (Vols. I, II, IV, V); KALAHARI DESERT (Vol. II); OKAVANGO RIVER (Vol. I).

Further reading: Thomas Tlou and Alec Campbell, *History of Botswana* (Gaborone, Botswana: Macmillan Botswana, 1984).

Brava (Barawa, Baraawe) Port town located south of MOGADISHU on the Indian Ocean coast of SOMALIA. Unlike Mogadishu, which was involved in Arab and Persian coastal trade almost exclusively, Brava had extensive contact with Swahili cities further south on the East African coast.

Historically, Brava's ECONOMY was based on Indian Ocean trade, which was dependent on the commercial interaction between the townspeople and from these interior regions, or hinterlands. Caravans directed by Somali and OROMO traders brought animal hides, ivory, and wood to trade for Arabic and Persian cloth and pottery. Bantu-speaking farmers also frequented the town to trade their grains, onions, and garlic, and these farmers and nomadic pastoralists sometimes sought relief in the town during droughts.

Accounts from the late 15th century described Brava as a cosmopolitan town with well-heeled traders and large stone houses, mosques, and a lighthouse tower. In 1503 Brava's sea merchants were threatened by Portuguese PIRATES and agreed to pay tribute to them in exchange for safe passage along the Indian Ocean coast. Three years later the town was sacked by Portuguese naval forces led by Tristão da Cunha (c. 1460–1514).

The people of Brava spoke a unique dialect of KISWAHILI called *Kimbalawi*. It was more heavily influenced by the Bantu language than most Kiswahili dialects, probably because the Bantu agriculturalists who inhabited the Brava hinterland did not entirely abandon the area when they were displaced by Somali and Oromo peoples.

In 1585 Turkish forces invaded the coastal towns of East Africa. The rulers of Brava readily swore their allegiance to the Ottoman sultan, as they were tired of what they believed were the unreasonable demands of Portuguese captains. Brava enjoyed a peaceful interim until the middle of the 17th century, when Arabs from Muscat in the OMANI SULTANATE rose to take MOMBASA and conquer most of the northern East African coast. Omani sultans ruled Brava into the 19th century, when Brava became a busy slave-exporting center.

See also: BENADIR COAST (Vol. III); INDIAN OCEAN TRADE (Vol. II); PORTUGAL AND AFRICA (Vol. III); OTTOMAN EMPIRE AND AFRICA (Vols. III, IV).

Buduma Kanuri subgroup located on the islands and around the shores of Lake CHAD in what is now the country of CHAD. The Buduma were a group within the trading empire of KANEM-BORNU (fl. 14th–19th centuries). Buduma traditions trace the group's origins back to the 15th century, when a Kanembu man named Boulou supposedly married a woman of the neighboring Sao people. This pair then left the mainland to reside on the lake islands, starting a new ethnic group in the process.

By the 16th century the Buduma were known mostly for being skilled boatmen, fishermen, cattle-herders, and traders of salt, slaves, and whips made from hippopotamus hides. They were active slave traders, often working with the TUAREGS of the AÏR MASSIF, northwest of Lake Chad. Although aspects of Islam were adopted by the Buduma, their isolationist nature led them to remain mostly free of the influences of their Muslim neighbors.

See also: SALT TRADE (Vol. II); SAO (Vol. II); SLAVERY (Vols. I, III, IV).

Buganda Kingdom of the GREAT LAKES REGION of East Africa in what is now UGANDA. Buganda began to seriously challenge BUNYORO as the most powerful kingdom in the region by the end of the 18th century. Buganda emerged as an independent kingdom northwest of Lake Victoria by 1500. According to the traditions of its Bantu-speaking people, the GANDA, their kingdom existed before the BITO clan founded Bunyoro. Because the two kingdoms were rivals, however, each claimed an earlier origin than the other. Nyoro traditions claimed that Buganda was, in fact, founded after Bunyoro by Kato, the twin brother of the first Bito king, Rukidi (fl. 15th century).

Bunyoro was the stronger kingdom in the 1500s and invaded Buganda during the second half of the century. The Ganda *kabaka*, or king, Nakinge was slain during the war, although Buganda managed to retain its independence. The kingdom grew stronger throughout the 1600s, and it began to compete with Bunyoro for dominance in the region.

Buganda was an agricultural society, with bananas as the principal crop. It featured a patron-client system that revolved around farmland rather than cattle, as in other pastoral kingdoms of the region, such as RWANDA. The Ganda *kabaka* had ultimate power over all the land. He usually controlled it through appointed chiefs, or *bakungu*, who administered specific territories. They were responsible for collecting tribute in the form of FOOD, timber, bark cloth, and beer from the common people who cultivated the land.

During the 17th and 18th centuries Buganda developed a highly centralized government that centered on the king. The Ganda *kabakas* steadily increased the number and influence of appointed chiefs while curtailing the power of chiefs who inherited their positions. The kings also fully incorporated conquered territory into the kingdom's government by installing new leaders, who were often military men, rather than retaining the defeated rulers and merely exacting tribute from them. These policies had the effect of unifying Buganda to a much greater extent than other kingdoms in the region.

By the end of the 18th century Buganda had expanded to more than twice its original size. The kingdom annexed the Bunyoro tributary of Buddu, to the southwest, as well as parts of BUSOGA, to the northeast. The expansion of Buganda brought the kingdom into contact with new coastal-based trade routes in what is now TANZANIA, to the south and east. This conveyed additional power and wealth to the *kabaka*. The developing regional trade networks further increased competition between Buganda and Bunyoro during the late 1800s.

See also: BUNYORO-KITARA (Vol. II); BUGANDA (Vols. II, IV, V); NYORO (Vol. II).

Further reading: Richard J. Reid, *Political Power in Pre-colonial Buganda: Economy, Society & Warfare in the Nineteenth Century* (Athens, Ohio: Ohio University Press, 2002); Christopher Wrigley, *Kingship and State: The Buganda Dynasty* (New York: Cambridge University Press, 1996).

Bulala (Boulala) Ethnic group traditionally linked to the kingdom of Kanem (c. 800–1200) in the Lake CHAD region. Known as pastoral nomads, during the 14th century the Bulala battled extensively with the KANURI people who originally inhabited the Kanem kingdom. The Bulala were successful in initially displacing the Kanuri and killing several *mais,* or kings, in the process. This forced the Kanuri under Mai Umar ibn Idris (r. c. 1382–1387) to relinquish the capital at Njimi and move southwest to the Bornu region. The kingdom of Kanem became stronger under Bulala rule over the next two centuries, in part due to the establishment of trade relations with Egyptians. It was only during the late 16th-century rule of Mai IDRIS ALAWMA (r. c. 1570–1603) that the Kanuri were able to conquer the Bulala peoples and regain power in Kanem, effectively creating the kingdom of KANEM-BORNU. The Bulala, however, were granted permission to remain in Kanem and govern the area in a tributary fashion.

See also: BORNU (Vol. II); KANEM (Vol. II).

Bullom (Sherbro, Bulom) Ethnic group living in the West African region of SIERRA LEONE. Believed to be among the first inhabitants in the area, the Bullom settled along the coastal regions of the present-day island republic of CAPE VERDE to the mainland town of Cape Mount. By the latter half of the 16th century the northern Bullom were joined by the Temne, SUSU, and Baga peoples, with whom they eventually assimilated. The southern Bullom are commonly called *Sherbro,* a name adopted from a MANE chief. The Bullom social and political systems are based on matrilineal descent. They have secret societies such as the Poro (male), Bundu (female), Tuntu (male and female), and Thoma (male and female). In addition to fishing, the Bullom produced rice, cassava, PALM OIL, and salt.

The Bullom began trading with the Portuguese in the middle of the 15th century, exchanging captives and ivory for manufactured goods. A century later the Portuguese benefited from the wars between the Mane people and the coastal inhabitants. As the Mane plundered their way to the coast, the Portuguese followed in their wake, gathering up Bullom, Temne, and Loko refugees and turning them into captives. According to some sources, the Mane were so fierce that the Bullom king chose to submit to the Portuguese rather than face what the Mane might have had in store for him.

By the 17th century the British had set up trading posts in the Sherbro region. They paid the local kings for trading rights and established a monopoly. Wood & Co. and the ROYAL AFRICAN COMPANY were among the earliest and most successful trading companies. By the 18th century the MENDE had penetrated into the region and were slowly displacing the area's inhabitants.

See also: PORTUGAL AND AFRICA (Vol. III).

Bunyoro Kingdom of the GREAT LAKES REGION of East Africa that flourished from the 16th to the 19th centuries in what is now UGANDA. Bunyoro was founded by Nilotic-speaking LUO people, who took over much of the Chwezi-ruled kingdom of Kitara by 1500.

The Bantu-speaking people of Bunyoro, called the *Nyoro* or *Banyoro,* were farmers and cattle herders of combined Bantu and Nilotic origin. According to Bunyoro tradition, the first Bito clan king of Bunyoro was Rukidi (fl. 15th century), who divided Kitara among his brothers. He ruled the northwest territory and sent his twin, Kato, to rule the southeast territory. Soon after, Kato was said to have declared his independence and founded the separate kingdom of BUGANDA. The two kingdoms became rivals and frequently waged war against one another during the 17th and 18th centuries.

According to the Nyoro, when Kato founded the kingdom of Buganda, he adopted the name Kimera, which means "branch." Kimera took this name when he declared his territory's independence in order to signify his branching off from the parent tree of the Nyoro people. According to tradition, Kimera declared: "I have taken root here and will not move. No man shall transplant me."

Bunyoro controlled valuable iron and salt deposits, which helped develop regional trade. The kingdom maintained a strong military, which was crucial to acquiring new territory. During the 1600s and 1700s, Bunyoro's armies launched major campaigns, raiding the kingdoms of Buganda and BUSOGA to the east, and NKOLE and RWANDA to the south. By 1700 Bunyoro was by far the largest kingdom in the Great Lakes region.

Bunyoro's control over newly conquered territory generally meant only that tribute was exacted from defeated local rulers. Because the BITO *mukama,* or king, did not always install a member of his clan to govern these territories, Bunyoro's rule was frequently challenged. Tributary kingdoms, including Nkole, were inspired to develop stronger central governments in part to resist Bunyoro power, and they took advantage of Bunyoro's frequent military engagements elsewhere to rebel. The kings of Bunyoro were not ideally equipped to counter these rebellions because the kingdom was ruled locally by hereditary chiefs, who held authority independent of the *mukama.*

At the end of the 18th century Bunyoro's regional supremacy began to be seriously challenged by other kingdoms, especially by Buganda, which annexed tributary states previously under Bunyoro's control. Other Bunyoro tributaries seceded, including Toro. By the early 19th century Bunyoro was much reduced in size, although it remained among the most powerful kingdoms in the region.

See also: BUNYORO (Vol. IV); BUNYORO-KITARA (Vol. II); CHWEZI KINGDOM (Vol. II); KITARA (Vol. II); NYORO (Vol. II).

Burkina Faso Landlocked present-day country located south of the Sahara desert. The country covers approximately 105,900 square miles (274,300 sq km) and is bordered by Republic of MALI, NIGER, Republic of BENIN, TOGO, GHANA, and IVORY COAST.

By the 16th century the MOSSI STATES were flourishing within both the eastern and central regions of Burkina Faso and parts of Ghana. These states, including OUAGADOUGOU, Tenkodogo, YATENGA, and FADA-N-GURMA remained important and prosperous well into the 19th century. Most of the success attributed to the Mossi States came from the people's trading skills. It also came from their use of a highly trained cavalry that could defend the state's territories against attacks from such opponents as the SONGHAI Empire.

Much of Burkina Faso's history is centered around the Mossi. However, there were other important ethnic groups in the region, too, including the Gurunsi, Bobo, and LOBI, the latter being an agrarian people who migrated into Burkina Faso during the late 18th century. European exploration in the area began with the German explorer Gottlob Adolph Krause, in 1886, and the French army officer Louis-Gustav Binger, in 1888. A French protectorate was established in 1895, with French control lasting into the mid-20th century.

See also: BURKINA FASO (Vols, I, II, IV, V); FRANCE AND AFRICA (Vols. III, IV, V).

Buruli State of the Ruli people that once belonged to the East African kingdom of BUNYORO, in present-day UGANDA. During the 18th century some parts of the Bunyoro kingdom broke off to form independent states. Initially, these states, which included Buruli, RWANDA, BURUNDI, Karagwe, Kooki, Igala, NKOLE, Mpororo, BUGANDA, and later Toro, paid tribute to the Bunyoro. Later, however, they declared their independence, leading the Bunyoro to wage several unsuccessful military campaigns against the rebel kingdoms. In the late 19th century Buganda welcomed the British as allies against the Nyoro, eventually helping the newcomers defeat the long-time regional power. As a reward Britain gave Buganda control over a number of states, including Buruli.

See also: BUNYORO-KITARA (Vol. II).

Burundi Present-day country of approximately 10,700 square miles (27,700 sq km) in the southern GREAT LAKES REGION of East Africa. Located directly south of RWANDA, Burundi also borders TANZANIA and the Democratic Republic of the CONGO. During the precolonial period, Burundi was a densely populated kingdom covering roughly the same area as the present-day country. Its partly mountainous high plateau region was occupied by Bantu-speaking HUTU and TUTSI peoples and Twa peoples.

The kingdom of Burundi emerged in the 1600s under the leadership of members of the HINDA clan, which had probably been pushed southward because of the invasion of the Nilotic LUO people from the north. The first king of Burundi was Ntare Rushatsi (c. 1675–1705), whose name means "rock." Ntare expanded the kingdom by launching military campaigns into neighboring lands.

The kingdom of Burundi was considerably less centralized than that of Rwanda. In Burundi, four ruling dynasties competed for control of the monarchy. Moreover, the authority of the MWAMI, or king, was shared by his sons, or *ganwa*. Each prince ruled a territory that was of more or less value depending on his place in the line of succession. Each *ganwa* had the power to appoint subchiefs, raise armies, and collect tribute independently of the *mwami*. The offspring of a particular king generally retained power until another king ascended the throne, but by then their power was so firmly established that bitter disputes often broke out with each new succession.

A separation of LABOR similar to Rwanda's also developed in Burundi. Under this system the Tutsi raised cattle and the Hutu farmed the land. Burundi also had a feudalistic patron-client system, called *bugabire,* but it was entirely separate from the political system and less rigorous and more limited than its counterpart in Rwanda. Because political authority was primarily in the hands of the *ganwa*, who were considered a distinct ethnic group, neither Tutsi nor Hutu were the ruling class. Power struggles between *ganwa* caused them to seek the allegiance of both Hutu and Tutsi peoples, so that neither group necessarily held more political power than the other. In addition, both Hutu and Tutsi recognized rank according to lineage, which often superseded rank according to ethnic group.

Burundi's military was relatively weak, and it was less successful than Rwanda's at acquiring new lands. Burundi remained a relatively small kingdom until the late 18th and early 19th centuries, when the army of Mwami Ntare Rugaamba (1795–1852) conquered areas of what are now Rwanda and Tanzania.

See also: BURUNDI (Vols. I, II, IV, V); GANWA (Vol. II); TWA (Vol. II).

Further reading: Jean-Pierre Chrétien, *The Great Lakes of Africa: Two Thousand Years of History* (Cambridge, Mass: MIT Press, 2003).

Busa (Bussa, Bussangi) Mande-speaking Muslim people concentrated in present-day NIGERIA and BURKINA FASO. The Busa established their own kingdom within the BORGU region in the middle of the 18th century. Eventually, the Busa state became powerful enough to force neighboring kingdoms such as Kaiama and Illo to pay tribute. In the late 19th century, however, Britain conquered the Busa, and the their kingdom ultimately endured only as an emirate.

Busaidi (Busa Idi, Al Bu Sa'idi) Omani dynasty influential in the politics and history of both the OMANI SULTANATE and East Africa. In 1741 Ahmad ibn Said (fl. 1740–1749), a member of the Busaidi family, overthrew the Persian Yarubid (Yorubi) dynasty and seized the Omani throne. By 1744 the Busaidis were taking a far more active interest in East African affairs than their predecessors in the Omani sultanate had ever done.

In reaction to this, the MASRUI family, which ruled in MOMBASA, rebelled and declared Mombasa's independence from Oman. The two families, the Busaidis and the Masruis, vied for power throughout East Africa until the Busaidis, under SAYYID SAID (1791–1856), took control of Mombasa, in 1837. The Busaidis also remained powerful in Oman, retaining control there into the 21st century.

See also: BUSAIDI (Vol. IV).

Bushongo Large subgroup of the KUBA people, in present-day Democratic Republic of the CONGO. Since the early 17th century the Bushongo have been the ruling class of the Kuba people, also called Bakuba. Beginning with the *nyim,* or king, SHAMBA BOLONGONGO (r. 1600–1620), Bushongo kings ruled the Kuba with the support of an administration representative of the subgroups and a royal army. Each subgroup also had its own traditional chief who inherited the throne by divine right. Several councils made up of local ruling-class villagers supported each chiefdom.

During early Bushongo rule the Kuba kingdom flourished. New crops with high yields were introduced, and the villagers capitalized on the surplus by establishing long-distance trade. By the middle of the 18th century the Kuba were suppliers in the IVORY TRADE. This made them a commercial force in coastal Central Africa and encouraged migration to the area.

Busoga (Soga) Kingdom of the northeast GREAT LAKES REGION of East Africa in what is now UGANDA. Busoga was frequently under the control of Nyoro and BUGANDA during the precolonial period.

Busoga lay east of the Nile River, sandwiched between Lake Victoria in the south and Lake Kyoga in the north, and was settled by Bantu-speaking and Nilotic peoples. Busoga oral traditions, like those of the GANDA, trace their origins to Kintu, the legendary first man and ancestor-hero of the Ganda, who reportedly came from the east and founded settlements throughout the northern Great Lakes region.

Migrating LUO moved into the area during the 1500s. The BITO clan, which ruled Nyoro to the west, also established subdynasties in Busoga, where they established the *mukama* kingship. The Luo settled mainly in the northern cattle country and continued to immigrate to Busoga through the 1600s.

The people of the Busoga kingdoms, called the Basoga, were primarily farmers, and bananas were their staple FOOD. They also cultivated millet, cassava, sweet potatoes, peas, beans, and nuts. Their agricultural way of life is expressed in the Basoga saying, "The hoe is my mother." Around the lakes, which surround most of Busoga, fishing with nets as well as hooks and lines was an important activity. Fish were a valuable source of food, and were also traded to neighboring groups who lived in the interior. The Basoga also hunted wild animals and raised cattle, especially in the northern regions that were less suitable for farming and had fewer tsetse flies, which carry diseases fatal to cattle.

The territory encompassed at least 40 separate chiefdoms. These were led by no central authority but instead by many local rulers who belonged to the most powerful clans. Each clan (*ekika*) had at least one *butaka,* or piece of land, where the ancestors were buried. In theory the king controlled all *butakas* in his kingdom, and dispensed plots that then became hereditary to his princes and to other favored disciples. Chiefs administered the non-hereditary lands, called *kisoko,* which anyone could settle on and farm as long as he paid tribute to the *kisoko* chief.

The king appointed both commoners and royal kinsmen to government positions. The highest officeholders under the king were *bakungu,* who, depending on the size of the kingdom, ruled over large territories or small villages. Succession wars and the secession of territories were common in Busoga. Other larger kingdoms in the region took advantage of internal wars by forming alliances with struggling Busoga rulers in exchange for tribute.

Nyoro influence over the territory continued throughout this period. By the 18th century, however, the kingdom of Buganda to the south had established dominion over much of Busoga.

Butua (Butwa, Guruhuswa) Region in present-day southwestern ZIMBABWE, ruled at various times by TOGWA and ROZWI kings, as well as by the Portuguese. According to records maintained by Portuguese merchants as far back as the early 16th century, the Butua region was ruled by the kings of the Togwa dynasty of the SHONA KINGDOMS. In the middle of the 17th century these kings forged a treaty with Portuguese traders. Their goal was to thwart the efforts of Muslim traders from the coast, who were penetrating their territory and taking over the GOLD and ivory trades in the region. With the help of the Portuguese, Butua's rulers expelled the Muslim traders and regained control of the region. In 1683 Butua was annexed by the powerful CHANGAMIRE DYNASTY of the Rozwi kingdom. Near the end of the 17th century the Rozwi in turn expelled the Portuguese traders, who had previously been welcome at the trading fairs along the SABI RIVER and in the Butua highlands.

During the 18th century the Butua region was closely guarded by the Rozwi kings, who rejected any foreign influence and spent most of their resources glorifying their courts with profits from both the ivory and gold trades.

See also: IVORY TRADE (Vol. III); PORTUGAL AND AFRICA (Vols. III).

Cabinda (Kabinda) Region north of the mouth of the Congo River between the present-day Republic of the CONGO and northern ANGOLA, on Africa's west coast. The region was the home of the Bantu-speaking kingdoms related to the KONGO KINGDOM: Kakongo, LOANGO, and NGOYO. In the 15th century Cabinda was dominated by an expanding Ngoyo kingdom, which became wealthy by selling African captives to European traders. In 1783 the Portuguese began to build a trading fort at Cabinda, in an effort to monopolize the trade of human captives in western Africa. Before the fort could be completed, however, it was destroyed by the combined forces of Ngoyo and KONGO people, who were also aided by the French.

See also: CABINDA (Vol. V); PORTUGAL AND AFRICA (Vol. III); SLAVE TRADE, THE TRANSATLANTIC (Vol. III).

Cacheu Trading center near the mouth of the Cacheu River in present-day northwestern GUINEA-BISSAU. The town's location made it an ideal post for African traders bringing goods to the Atlantic coast and for European traders looking for accessible trade routes into the West African interior. The Portuguese, who had been trading in the area for a century, were the first Europeans to settle in Cacheu, assigning trade captain to the town in 1588.

Merchants in Cacheu traded kola nuts, PALM OIL, grains, and livestock in exchange for manufactured European goods. The peace and prosperity enjoyed by Cacheu made it an important center for the transatlantic SLAVE TRADE during the 17th and 18th centuries. However, its importance diminished greatly during the 19th century, with the British prohibition of the slave trade and the subsequent decline of the West African slave trade.

Further reading: George E. Brooks, *Landlords and Strangers: Ecology, Society, and Trade in Western Africa, 1000–1630* (Boulder, Colo.: Westview Press, 1993).

Cairo Capital of EGYPT and largest city in Africa. Although the city dates back to ancient Egypt, the origins of modern Cairo date to about 640, with the founding of the town of al-Fustat by Islamic Arabs. From 969 to 1161 Cairo was the capital of the Fatimids, a Shiite dynasty from the MAGHRIB region of North Africa. The city truly flourished, however, under the famous sultan Saladin (c. 1137–1193), founder of the Ayyubid dynasty, who claimed Cairo as his capital.

After several hundred years of power and prosperity, the city began to decline during the rule of the MAMLUKS, a dynasty of former Ottoman slaves who rebelled to take control of Egypt. For almost 1,000 years Cairo had been able to profit from its location on the strip of land that separates the Mediterranean Sea from the Red Sea. Because of its strategic position, Cairo grew as a commercial center, filled with bazaars and merchants who acted as intermediaries in the lucrative European-Asian cloth and spice trades. In the early 1500s, however, Portuguese explorers found an alternate sea route to India around the southern tip of Africa, bypassing Cairo, and the city began to slip into relative obscurity.

In 1517 the Turks of the Ottoman Empire invaded from the north, seized Cairo from the Mamluks, and made it a provincial capital of their vast North African territory. Under the Ottomans, Cairo remained semi-autonomous and maintained some of its former prestige thanks to al-Azhar University, a great Islamic center of learning. But the city's population declined steadily over the next 200 years. Ottoman Turks ruled Cairo uncontested until 1798, when French general Napoleon Bonaparte (1769–1821) seized the city for a short time; by 1801 the Ottoman Turks had retaken Cairo.

In 1805 MUHAMMAD ALI (1769–1849) was appointed *pasha*, or ranking official, of Ottoman Egypt and enacted sweeping administrative reforms that allowed the country to become practically independent of Ottoman rule. The dynasty begun by Muhammad Ali ruled Egypt from Cairo into the 20th century.

See also: CAIRO (Vols. I, II, IV, V); ISLAMIC CENTERS OF LEARNING (Vol. II); OTTOMAN EMPIRE AND AFRICA (Vols. III, IV); SALADIN (Vol. II).

Further reading: André Raymond, *Arab Cities in the Ottoman Period: Cairo, Syria, and the Maghreb* (Burlington, Vt.: Ashgate/Variorum, 2002); André Raymond, *Cairo* (Cambridge, Mass.: Harvard University Press, 2000).

Calabar See OLD CALABAR.

Cameroon Western Central African country covering about 183,600 square miles (475,500 sq km) and located on the Gulf of Guinea. By the 16th century the northern region of present-day Cameroon was dominated by two kingdoms, Kotoko and MANDARA. At its height the Kotoko kingdom, extending into what is now NIGERIA, had gained strength after it conquered the Sao peoples in the 15th century. The Kotoko remained influential in this region until they were overtaken in the 19th century by KANEM-BORNU. The Mandara kingdom was also established in the 15th century and was at its most powerful during the late 18th to mid-19th centuries. While Mandara was able to fend off attacks from Kanem-Bornu, it was defeated by the FULANI during their extensive jihads in the late 19th century.

During the 17th century the central region of what is now Cameroon was controlled by the Mum kingdom, which was governed by kings of the Tikar ethnic group. In the 18th century Mum was invaded, but not conquered, by the Muslim Fulani.

Europeans were familiar with the Cameroon shoreline since the Portuguese explorer Fernão do Pó landed off the coast in 1472. Other groups, including the Spanish, Dutch, and French, began trading in the area as early as the mid-16th century. Local commerce was generally regulated by treaties that gave the Europeans the right to trade in the area, usually in exchange for protection from attack by indigenous people. Although various groups were active traders, the Mileke and Duala were especially successful in controlling the trade of ivory, PALM OIL, nuts, salt, metals, and human captives in Cameroon. Stationed at coastal posts around the mouth of the Wouri River, European traders came to rely on Duala intermediaries to acquire captives destined for servitude.

The name *Cameroon* came from the Portuguese word *camarões,* meaning "prawn," and referred to the multitude of crayfish, mistaken for prawns, located in a local river the Portuguese called Rio de Camarões.

After the practice of SLAVERY was abolished by Britain in 1807, the trade in humans began to decline in the area and, as a result, trade in ivory, rubber, and palm oil began to increase. Even though the Portuguese and Dutch began to withdraw from Cameroon, the British and Germans maintained a strong presence into the 19th century, at which time Germany claimed the region of Cameroon as a territory of imperial Germany.

See also: CAMEROON (Vols. I, II, IV, V); CAMEROON GRASS FIELDS (Vol. I); KOTOKO (Vol. II); SAO (Vol. II).

Further reading: Ralph A. Austen and Jonathan Derrick, *Middlemen of the Cameroons Rivers: The Duala and Their Hinterland, c.1600–c.1960* (New York: Cambridge University Press, 1999); Mario Azevedo, ed., *Cameroon and Chad in Historical and Contemporary Perspectives* (Lewiston, Me.: E. Mellen Press, 1988).

Cape Coast (Cabo Corso) Port city that was originally a trading station located on the coast of present-day GHANA in West Africa; its history reflects the violence and armed confrontation that characterized the battles fought by the European powers in their attempts to monopolize trade with Africa. Originally the site of a 15th-century Portuguese trading lodge, the Cape Coast trading station was taken by armed Swedish traders in the middle of the 17th century. By 1655 the Swedes had expanded the outpost into a substantial fort and renamed it Carolusborg Castle, around which a substantial town developed. The British took the castle from the Swedes in 1664. By the middle of the 18th century the British turned it into one of the busiest centers for trading human captives in West Africa. It continued to serve as the British commercial and political capital of the GOLD COAST until the late 19th century.

See also: CAPE COAST (Vol. IV); ENGLAND AND AFRICA (Vol. III); PORTUGAL AND AFRICA (Vol. III).

Cape Colony (Colony of the Cape of Good Hope) Dutch colony established in 1652, and then taken over by the British in 1806, located in present-day SOUTH

AFRICA. The indigenous SAN and KHOIKHOI inhabitants of the region were primarily hunter-gatherers and cattle herders, respectively. The first European arrival at the cape region of southern Africa came in 1488, when Bartholomeu Dias touched down at Mossel Bay. In 1497 Vasco da Gama rounded the CAPE OF GOOD HOPE en route to India. The region lay halfway between India and Europe, so for the next 150 years Europeans would stop along the cape to replenish their stores and repair their ships.

It wasn't until 1647 that a more permanent European presence began to emerge in the region. That year, the Dutch ship *Haarlem* was grounded at Table Bay. Its crew was forced to wait for the next year's trading fleet. Upon their return they suggested a supply post be placed along the Cape Coast. In 1652 The DUTCH EAST INDIA COMPANY arrived at Table Bay to establish a provisioning station. The settlement would become known as CAPE TOWN.

To procure an adequate food supply for their trading fleet, the Dutch imported Indian and East African servants to work on their farms. They also bought the cattle reserves of the Khoikhoi herders. However, the supply of beef proved inadequate, so the Dutch East India Company began to raise its own cattle and expected its settlers to do the same. Soon Dutch cattle, as well as grain, wine, and fruit farms, were prevalent in the mountainous area around Table Bay.

Although the purpose of the settlement at Cape Town was to supply provisions to passing Dutch merchant vessels, it quickly became headquarters for an expanding colony. In order to supplement their own production, the Dutch settlers traded with the indigenous Khoikhoi peoples. By 1657, however, it became necessary for the settlers to cultivate lands further inland, as they had outstripped the coastlands. In order to achieve this, a group was released from their service to the company, granted land rights, and allowed to farm independently.

In the 18th century, as these settlers searched for new land, they encroached upon the territory of the Khoikhoi. Early Dutch-European settlers known as BOERS gradually forced the Khoikhoi to leave their mountain homelands or enlist as Boer shepherds or guides. Relations between the indigenous people and the colonists quickly soured, and conflict broke out in 1659. By 1677 the Khoikhoi had been decimated by the more powerful Boer forces. Between exposure to smallpox and being a target of raids for human captives, the Khoikhoi had practically disappeared by 1713. Those who remained intermarried with the Afrikaners to produce a new racial category known as *Cape Coloureds,* or simply Coloureds.

Dutch, as well as other European settlers, immigrated to the Cape in waves during the 18th century. The Dutch East India Company encouraged these immigrants to settle new lands beyond the coast. Many settlers took up a nomadic lifestyle and moved into the northern reaches of the colony. These settlers, known as Trekboers, encroached upon XHOSA territory in search of new grazing lands. This invasion created a strained relationship between the colonists and the Xhosa.

By 1750 Europeans had established a series of garrisons to protect themselves from the unknown number of indigenous peoples who inhabited the interior. A colonial border was established at the Great Fish River in 1780 to separate the settlers from the Xhosa. However, those Xhosa living west of the river were forcibly removed by the Europeans. The heightened tensions between the groups led to nearly a century of wars. These CAPE FRONTIER WARS lasted until the late 1800s, by which time all Xhosa lands had been incorporated into the colony.

In 1795 Britain conquered CAPE COLONY in an effort to keep it out of the hands of the French. In 1803 it was returned to the Dutch for a brief interlude, only to be returned to British rule in 1806. Discontentment over British rule resulted in the GREAT BOER TREK of the late 1830s, during which more than 10,000 Boers migrated to the Transvaal. In the mid-19th century the discovery of GOLD caused a renewed rush of British immigrants to the cape, thus solidifying British dominance for many years to come.

See also: CAPE COLONY (Vol. IV); DIAS, BARTOLOMEU (Vol. II); NETHERLANDS AND AFRICA (Vol. III); ENGLAND AND AFRICA (Vol. III); PORTUGAL AND AFRICA (Vol. III).

Further reading: Richard Elphick and Hermann Giliomee, eds., *The Shaping of South African Society, 1652–1840* (Middletown, Conn.: Wesleyan University Press, 1988).

Cape Frontier Wars (Kaffir Wars, Kafir Wars)

Series of nine wars, the first of which occurred in 1779, between European colonists and the XHOSA people of the eastern CAPE COLONY of SOUTH AFRICA. These wars are sometimes called Kaffir Wars, from a disparaging Arabic word meaning "infidel" used by the enemies of the Xhosa to refer to their foes. Continuing into the late 19th century, the Cape Frontier Wars resulted in the incorporation of the Xhosa and their lands into the Cape Colony.

From 1779 to 1801 Dutch colonists waged three wars against a faction of Xhosa peoples who had migrated into the Zuurveld region. These conflicts were initiated by differences regarding land use and the trading of cattle. During the third war KHOIKHOI slaves, bearing stolen guns and riding stolen horses, joined the Xhosa to help defeat the Dutch. However, British forces expelled the Xhosa from the Zuurveld in 1811, as Britain became more involved in the region. Later Cape Frontier Wars in the 19th century pitted the Xhosa against the British, with the British ultimately solidifying control of the region.

Cape Town, in what is now South Africa, shown in a 1676 map. The colony originated as a supply stop for Dutch ships sailing to the Far East. Table Mountain is in the center; Lion's Head and the Cape of Good Hope are to the right. © *Corbis*

The British decision to restore land to the Xhosa led to discontent among the BOERS of the eastern cape, and helped launch the GREAT BOER TREK.

See also: AFRIKANER REPUBLICS (Vols. III, IV); ENGLAND AND AFRICA (Vol. III); NETHERLANDS AND AFRICA (Vol. III); WARFARE AND WEAPONS (Vol. III).

Cape Town Port city that was the first European settlement in the region that is present-day SOUTH AFRICA. Cape Town was founded in 1652 by the DUTCH EAST INDIA COMPANY as a resupply station for its ships rounding the CAPE OF GOOD HOPE. When Dutch settlers arrived on the Cape, they found the region inhabited by SAN hunter-gatherers and KHOIKHOI pastoralists. These native peoples provided the Dutch with much-needed foodstuffs, but they did not supply them with any LABOR. Because of this, by the 1660s the Dutch were importing laborers from India and East Africa.

Although the Dutch depended upon the Khoikhoi for cattle, they attempted to seize Khoikhoi grazing lands. The Khoikhoi resisted, but they were no match for European firearms and military might, and the Khoikhoi population was decimated. During the 18th century a new population began to emerge from the mixing of Khoikhoi, Europeans, Indians, and Africans. This mixed race became known as the *Cape Coloured* people.

The Dutch used the term *Bushmen* to refer to the San and coined the term *HOTTENTOT* to refer to the Khoikhoi. Although both terms were commonly used by European historians and anthropologists until the 20th century, they are now generally considered derogatory.

By the late 1700s numerous European powers were struggling for control of the strategic cape region. The Dutch and French constructed a fort in 1781 in an effort to repel British advances on Cape Town. Despite this effort, by 1806 the British had gained control of Cape Town and its surrounding areas.

See also: CAPE TOWN (Vols. IV, V); ENGLAND AND AFRICA (Vol. III); FRANCE AND AFRICA (Vol. III); NETHERLANDS AND AFRICA (Vol. III).

Cape Verde, Republic of Present-day nation made up of a group of ten islands and five islets located in the Atlantic Ocean off the coast of SENEGAL. The Barlavento Islands include Santo Antao, São Vicente, São Nicolau, Santa Luzia, Sal, and Boa Vista. The Sotavento Islands include São Tiago, Brava, Fogo, and Maio. The capital city is Praia and is located on São Tiago.

In the late 15th century Portuguese colonists established settlements in the Cape Verde Islands, and the region soon became a holding station for captives and supplies for the transatlantic SLAVE TRADE. Some Portuguese men married indigenous women, with whom they produced mixed-race offspring called *lançados*. The *lançados* became successful trade intermediaries by virtue of being familiar with the commercial cultures of both Europeans and Africans.

By the 16th century Cape Verde was not only the administrative center for Portugal's coastal activities but it also served as a place of exile for DEGREDADOS, people convicted of civil or political crimes in Portugal. Because of their location on the Atlantic, the islands became vulnerable to attacks by French, Dutch, and British PIRATES, who were well aware of the many valuable commodities, including rum, cloth, and enslaved Africans, that passed through the ports. The Portuguese hold on the islands' trade steadily decreased throughout the 17th and 18th centuries as these European countries further encroached on Portugal's territory.

When the Portuguese trade in humans came to a close in 1876, the Cape Verde Islands suffered severe economic hardships that were further aggravated by the recurrent droughts and famine that plagued the islands during most of the 19th century.

See also: CAPE VERDE ISLANDS (Vol. IV); CAPE VERDE, REPUBLIC OF (Vols. I, II, IV, V); PORTUGAL AND AFRICA (Vol. III).

Further reading: Laura Bigman, *History and Hunger in West Africa: Food Production and Entitlement in Guinea-Bissau and Cape Verde* (Westport, Conn.: Greenwood Press, 1993); Richard A. Lobban, Jr., *Cape Verde: Crioulo Colony to Independent Nation* (Boulder, Colo.: Westview Press, 1995); Deirdre Meintel, *Race, Culture, and Portuguese Colonialism in Cabo Verde* (Syracuse, N.Y.: Syracuse University, 1984).

Central African Republic Present-day country covering approximately 240,300 square miles (622,400 sq km) in the center of Africa. The Central African Republic is bordered by CHAD to the north, the Republic of the SUDAN to the east, the Republic of the CONGO and the Democratic Republic of the CONGO to the south, and CAMEROON to the west.

Large, organized states did not exist in the region until the 16th and 17th centuries, when the Islamic kingdoms of BAGIRMI, DARFUR, and WADAI emerged. These groups all launched campaigns to expand their kingdoms, taking captives from the smaller villages they dominated. The captives were either assembled into slave armies or sold to Muslim slave traders who brought them east to Red Sea ports.

Later, during the 18th century, the AZANDE people established chiefdoms around the Ubangi River and in the eastern part of the region. They cultivated crops, including maize and cassava, and were unified by a complex system of religious beliefs. The leaders of these chiefdoms descended from the NGBANDI, whose aristocratic clans originated in the northeast.

See also: CENTRAL AFRICAN REPUBLIC (Vols. I, II, IV, V); SLAVERY (Vol. III).

Further reading: Dennis D. Cordell, *Dar al-Kuti and the Last Years of the Trans-Saharan Slave Trade* (Madison, Wisc.: University of Wisconsin Press, 1985); Tamara Giles-Vernick, *Cutting the Vines of the Past: Environmental Histories of the Central African Rain Forest* (Charlottesville, Va.: University Press of Virginia, 2002).

Ceuta Port city and military outpost on the Mediterranean coast of MOROCCO, at the entrance to the Strait of Gibraltar. Ceuta has a long history, serving as a colony of Carthage, Greece, and Rome. When it fell to Muslims in 711, Ceuta was the last outpost of the Byzantine Empire in the west. Coveting Cueta's strategic location near the narrow eastern opening of the Mediterranean Sea, the Portuguese seized the city from the Moors in 1415 during their military campaign along the Moroccan coast. During the 16th century Ceuta was one of the few port cities, Melilla being another, that was not recaptured by the Moors. Ceuta was seized by Spain in 1580, and the Treaty of Lisbon officially designated Ceuta a Spanish territory in 1688. Although attached to Morocco, Ceuta has been governed by Spain for nearly 500 years.

See also: SPAIN AND AFRICA (Vols. III, IV).

Chad Landlocked present-day country covering approximately 496,000 square miles (1,284,600 sq km) in the central Sudan. The region was the site of KANEM-BORNU, WADAI, and BAGIRMI, three Islamic states that flourished between the 16th and 19th centuries.

In the early 16th century Kanem-Bornu, located around Lake CHAD, was at the height of its expansion and occupied much of the western region of what is now Chad as well as parts of both present-day NIGER and NIGERIA. Like many African kingdoms, Kanem-Bornu had an economy based on trade. Its wares, including ivory, foodstuffs, and human captives, were transported along its caravan routes to the Mediterranean trading port of TRIPOLI, in LIBYA.

The KANURI people, who were converted to Islam in the 11th century, were the dominant group within the population of what had once been the separate states of Kanem and Bornu. The Kanuri were formed by the intermarriage of two groups, the SAO and the KANEMBU, who were located mostly in Chad. Although Kanem-Bornu was in slow decline through the 17th and 18th centuries, it continued to dominate the Lake Chad region, including the HAUSA STATES to the west of Lake Chad. In the early 19th century the FULANI states founded during the jihads of the cleric USMAN DAN FODIO (1754–1817) disputed Kanem-Bornu's control over the Hausa States and dethroned its leader, Mai (King) Ahmad, in 1808. Although Ahmad soon regained his throne, disputes with the Fulani continued until mid-century.

While Kanem-Bornu was at its peak during the 16th century, the foundations of two new kingdoms were being laid to the east and southeast. The first, called WADAI, was a vassal kingdom of DARFUR established by the TUNJUR people. About 1630, after a period of resistance, they converted to Islam and established a Muslim dynasty in Wadai. Wadai was located along the present-day border between Chad and the Republic of the SUDAN, at the crossroads of two important trade routes. One led from the upper Nile and Darfur to Bornu and KANO, and the second ran across the Sahara to Banghazi, in Tripoli, on the Mediterranean coast. Despite clashes with Darfur, the Wadai sultanate prospered until the French colonized the area in the latter half of the 19th century.

Founded by the Barma people, Bagirmi, to the southeast of Lake Chad, was the second new kingdom in the region. The kingdom officially converted to Islam under the rule of Abdullah IV (1568–1598), and the city of Massenya was chosen as the capital. Bagirmi was highly active in the slave trade, raiding smaller states for captives to send to the Ottoman Empire. For a large part of its history, Bagirmi was a vassal state of Kanem-Bornu and became independent only for a short period between the late 17th and mid-18th centuries. Throughout the 18th century Bagirmi repeatedly fended off attacks from the Wadai sultanate until political decline and internal strife forced the kingdom to become a tributary state of Wadai in the 19th century.

See also: BORNU (Vol. II); CHAD (Vols. I, II, IV, V); FULANI JIHADS (Vol. III); KANEM (Vol. II); SUDAN, THE (Vol. II); TRANS-SAHARAN TRADE ROUTES (Vol. II).

Further reading: Mario Azevedo, ed., *Cameroon and Chad in Historical and Contemporary Perspectives* (Lewiston, Me.: E. Mellen Press, 1988); Dennis Cordell, *Dar al-Kuti and the Last Years of the Trans-Saharan Slave Trade* (Madison, Wisc.: University of Wisconsin Press, 1985).

Chad, Lake Freshwater lake situated in the central Sudan, on the southern edge of the Sahara. Present-day countries that border the lake include NIGER, NIGERIA, CAMEROON, and CHAD. Once a part of a vast ancient sea, Lake Chad is fairly shallow, and its surface area, dependent on climatic conditions, averages about 6,875 square miles (17,800 sq km). Fed by the southward-flowing Chari-Logone River, Lake Chad is the largest lake in Central Africa as well as a historic region around which important kingdoms prospered, some beginning as early as the sixth century. Many of the groups living on and around the lake's shores took advantage of the established TRANS-SAHARAN TRADE ROUTES that passed through the region. The caravans carried commodities such as EBONY, PALM OIL, ivory, and horses.

The most influential empire to emerge from the Lake Chad region was KANEM-BORNU. Established in the area possibly as early as the 11th century and ruled by kings from the SEFUWA dynasty of the KANURI people, Kanem-Bornu was at its peak during the reign of Mai (King) IDRIS ALAWMA (r. 1571–1603). By the time of his reign the empire literally surrounded Lake Chad, and Kanuri people could be found in portions of present-day Nigeria, Niger, and Chad. The Kanuri flourished by using caravan routes to transport goods, including human captives, up and down the lake's western shore to sell at European trading outposts.

Other kingdoms situated near Lake Chad also became successful trading states. These include the HAUSA STATES of present-day Nigeria and BAGIRMI and WADAI of what is now Chad.

Chagga Bantu-speaking people of present-day TANZANIA. One of the largest ethnic groups in Tanzania, the Chagga have lived for centuries on the slopes of Mount Kilimanjaro. There they have inhabited land that, through a sophisticated irrigation system, has become particularly well suited to AGRICULTURE. By 1300 the Chagga had developed a monarchic system. Beneath the monarch were numerous chiefs, at times more than 20. Disputes among these lesser chiefs were common, and there were frequent battles and even full-scale wars, leading to shifts in power from one chief to another.

One of the best-known of the Chagga chieftains was Orombo, who, beginning about 1800, created a minor empire on the eastern slopes of Kilimanjaro. After assembling a supply of spears and other weapons, which he acquired primarily from the PARE people, Orombo led his age set on a series of raids against other chiefdoms, eventually amassing large numbers of both human captives and cattle. With the forced LABOR of his captives, Orombo then built a stone fort, from which he was able to dominate nearby clans and chiefdoms. Orombo's empire was short-lived, however, as he was killed in a battle with the MAASAI. Without his leadership, the empire collapsed.

Primarily agriculturalists, the Chagga developed only minor trading systems, the most notable being an iron-ore trade dating back to the 16th century.

In the 16th century one Chagga chiefdom, Mamba, established and maintained extensive trade in iron ore and weapons. Mamba blacksmiths traveled as far away as Ugweno, where they traded their cattle for iron. The smiths then created iron weapons, which they exchanged at markets on the eastern slopes of Kilimanjaro and other places.

Changamire dynasty Ruling dynasty during the 16th through 18th centuries that controlled the ivory- and GOLD-producing region between the ZAMBEZI and Limpopo rivers in present-day ZIMBABWE. Changamire (fl. c. 1490), probably a relative of Matope (d. c. 1480), the ruler of the MWENE MUTAPA kingdom, founded the dynasty near the end of the 15th century. After Matope appointed him a provincial governor, Changamire defected from the empire to establish the ROZWI kingdom, which is sometimes called the Changamire kingdom; Rozwi rulers after him also were called *Changamire*.

The Changamire dynasty developed strong relations with Arab traders and Portuguese coastal settlers. However, from 1693 to 1695 the Rozwi drove the Portuguese from their settlements in the African interior. During this period of conquest they were also able to virtually eliminate the Mwene Mutapa as a regional trading power. In this manner the Changamire dynasty seized control of the lucrative international gold trade in southern East Africa.

The Changamire dynasty reigned supreme on Zimbabwe's central plateau for more than 100 years but was finally destroyed during the MFECANE, a forced migration

that took place early in the 19th century as ZULU peoples ransacked the region during their campaigns of territorial expansion.

See also: CHANGAMIRE (Vol. II); LIMPOPO RIVER (Vol. II); MATOPE (Vol. II).

Further reading: Innocent Pikirayi, *The Zimbabwe Culture: Origins and Decline in Southern Zambezian States* (Walnut Creek, Calif.: AltaMira Press, 2001).

Charles V, Emperor (1500–1558) *Holy Roman Emperor, king of Spain (as Charles I), and archduke of Austria who inherited the vast Spanish and Hapsburg Empire*

In 1517 young King Charles I of Spain signed an edict that sanctioned the beginning of the abduction and subsequent enslavement of millions of Africans in what was to become known as the transatlantic SLAVE TRADE.

Later, as Holy Roman Emperor, Charles endeavored to conquer North Africa, an undertaking first imagined by his grandfather, Ferdinand of Aragon. His primary goal was to take control of Mediterranean maritime trade away from the Muslims. As part of this effort he led a military campaign against Tunis in order to retake the port that had been seized a few years earlier by the Turkish Barbarossa brother Khayr al-Din (d. 1546).

The mission was a success. Tunis and the coastal fortress of La Goletta, as well as much of the Ottoman naval fleet, fell to Charles's 30,000-man expedition. Charles planned successive attacks on ALGIERS and Constantinople the following year, but the plan was foiled due to increasing conflicts with France. In 1541 Charles led another force to Algiers, but the campaign failed.

See also: OTTOMAN EMPIRE AND AFRICA (Vols. III, IV); SPAIN AND AFRICA (Vol. III).

Chewa (Cewa, Chipeta) Ethnic group indigenous to southern MALAWI, in East Africa, that was incorporated into the MARAVI confederation in the 16th and 17th centuries. The Chewa were hunters, pastoralists, agriculturalists, and traders, and they thrived by maintaining peaceful relations with neighboring peoples. They spoke a Bantu language known as chiChewa, which today is one of the official languages of Malawi.

The word *Malawi*, meaning "people of the fire," most likely comes from the chiChewa language. It is the name that the Chewa called the members of the Phiri clan, the group that produced the leader, or *KALONGA*, of the Maravi confederation.

The Katanga, a Bantu-speaking group from eastern ZAMBIA, are often considered the ancestors of the Chewa. After 1200, Katanga people migrated east toward Lake Malawi, establishing both the Banda and Zimba chiefdoms, which are considered early Chewa groups. These groups are sometimes called *Kalimanjira*, or "path makers," in Chewa oral tradition, referring to the fact that they cleared the land for the later migrating Chewa groups.

Chewa oral history cannot explain the dynamics that turned these groups into a defined Chewa chiefdom. What is relatively certain is that two major chiChewa-speaking subgroups, the Manganja and the Nyanja, inhabited the area to the south and southwest of Lake Malawi, north of the ZAMBEZI RIVER, by the end of the 15th century. From there they moved to the highlands, escarpments, and the shore areas southwest of Lake Malawi.

Late in the 16th cenntury the movement of Maravi peoples into Chewa territory forced some Chewa groups to migrate north, where they mixed with the indigenous Tumbuka people. The new group these two groups created, the Tonga, founded the chiefdoms of Kabunduli and Kaluluma, among others. The Chewa who remained in their original homeland south of Lake Malawi were integrated into the loosely defined Maravi confederacy, which had begun to dominate trade in the area in the beginning of the century.

Chewa oral tradition says that their chiefs agreed to let the outside Maravi leadership have political authority as long as the Chewa could continue to work their land. Peaceful relations ensued, and by the middle of the 17th century, the Chewa leaders even participated in Maravi government. The Chewa resisted full assimilation into Maravi culture by continuing to use their own language and religious practices. They maintained group ties, especially through secret societies like the *Nyau* society, which performed important religious rituals and encouraged identification among Chewa peoples.

Like the other groups in the region, during the 17th and 18th centuries the Chewa participated in the IVORY TRADE, which dominated the local ECONOMY. About the same time, the demand for slaves from East Africa increased, and by the end of the 19th century the peaceful Chewa were subject to constant raids by the well-armed YAO and Arab slave traders, who invaded their territory from the east, as well as by the NGONI, from the south.

Chico Rei (Galanga) (1717–1774) *Kongo prince who was abducted by the Portuguese and sent to work in the gold mines of Brazil in the 18th century*

Galanga (as he was then called) was a KONGO prince from Kibongo, located in modern-day Democratic Republic of the CONGO. According to tradition he was widely respected as a fierce warrior and a just leader of his peo-

ple. At the same time, the Portuguese discovered GOLD in their Brazil colony and needed slave LABOR to work the mines. The Portuguese regularly contracted slave raiders to abduct Africans in ANGOLA and Congo to sell into slavery, and Galanga happened to be unfortunate enough to be captured in such a raid. In 1739 he, his wife Djalo, his son Muzinga, and the others in their village were shackled, brought to the coast, and taken aboard the slave ship *Madalena*.

In 1740 Galanga, by then known as Chico Rei, and the rest of the captives reached Brazil; only 112 of the original 191 people survived the crossing. They were taken to the town of Ouro Preto (Portuguese for "black gold") and sold to a mine owner named Major Augusto.

Over the years Augusto was impressed not only by Chico's ability to learn and speak Portuguese but also by his regal bearing and his concern and care for his people. Eventually Major Augusto granted Chico his freedom. When Augusto became gravely ill, Augusto even loaned his former slave money to buy the mine. Under Chico's leadership, gold production at the mine increased, and Chico eventually was able to purchase the freedom of his former subjects. Chico Rei spent the rest of his life striving to improve the lives of the Africans who had been forced to work in the Brazilian gold mines. After Chico's death in 1774, the mine once again declined, eventually falling into disuse.

Before setting sail across the Atlantic, the members of Galanga's village were baptized by a Portuguese priest. The men were all forced to take the Christian name Francisco and the women were made to take the name Maria. The name Chico is a nickname for Francisco, and the word *rei* means "king" in Portuguese. Galanga was given the name Chico Rei by the Portuguese, who recognized how greatly he was respected by the others who came from his village.

See also: PORTUGAL AND AFRICA (Vol. III); SLAVE TRADE, THE TRANSATLANTIC (Vol. III).

Chokwe (Cokwe, Tshokwe) Subgroup of the Mbuti people in what is now northeastern ANGOLA. The Chokwe were ruled by disinherited princes from the ruling clans of the LUNDA EMPIRE who settled between the lower Kwango and Kasai rivers starting about 1500.

The Chokwe were primarily elephant hunters and wax gatherers, although some of them were also farmers. They were skilled sculptors, weavers, ironworkers, and pottery and mask makers. The Chokwe were especially noted for ceremonial objects made to honor their rulers, including royal portrait statues and finely carved scepters, staffs, and thrones. Their arts and crafts were influential in the Lunda courts and throughout the Kwango Valley.

In the late 18th century the Chokwe began to grow wealthy from the ivory trade and expanded to conquer neighboring territories in Central Africa. Their success was short-lived, though, as internal disputes and European colonizing activities disrupted Chokwe rule in the 19th century.

Christianity, influence of

Christianity, influence of Between the 15th and the 19th centuries Islam continued to be the dominant world religious presence in Africa in terms of conversions; social, political, and cultural influence; and territorial control. Two of the most ancient Christian churches in Africa, the Coptic Church in EGYPT and the Coptic Church in ETHIOPIA, were small islands of Christianity in an ever more Muslim continent. North Africa, once an important center of Christianity in the Roman world and the third major center of Christianity in Africa, remained fervently Muslim; the last indigenous Christians in North Africa outside of Egypt disappeared in the 12th century. Islam continued to spread in West Africa, sometimes peaceably along the trade routes and sometimes by jihad, or holy war. Islam was also strong in East Africa, along the SWAHILI COAST. Christian MISSIONARIES who accompanied Portuguese explorers in their sea voyages along the coast of Africa made some small inroads in West Africa, as did missionaries of the Dutch Reformed Church in SOUTH AFRICA. However, large-scale Protestant and Catholic missionary efforts did not begin until the start of the 19th century. Traditional African religions maintained their hold on the peoples of the interior of eastern and southern Africa and at times coexisted with Islam in West African societies.

The Christian Church at Large A *patriarch* is the bishop of an important see who has authority over other bishops in the region. Of the five major patriarchates into which the early Church organized itself, only Rome and Byzantium (Constantinople) remained independent at the start of the 15th century.

Derived from the Latin word *sedes*, meaning "seat," the English word *see*, as in a bishop's see or the Holy See (a Roman Catholic term for Rome), refers to the site of the bishop's throne. Symbolically, the episcopal throne is the center of his jurisdiction or authority.

The patriarchates of Alexandria in Egypt, Antioch in present-day Turkey, and Jerusalem in the Holy Land were in territory under Muslim control. The Great Schism of 1053, which was the result of acrimonious doctrinal and jurisdictional disputes between Rome and Constantinople, had further divided Christianity into separate parts: the Roman Catholic Church and the Eastern Orthodox Church. In 1453, when Constantinople fell to the forces of the Ottoman sultan, Mehmed II (1451–1481), the Eastern Orthodox Church came under Muslim domination and had its freedom and rights restricted. The Coptic Church of Egypt and the Ethiopian Coptic Church, which received its bishops from the Coptic patriarch of Alexandria, were effectively cut off from the church in the West and the church in Constantinople and consequently turned their attention inward.

Meanwhile, the Roman Catholic Church was undergoing a series of transformations. The Protestant Reformation, led by the German theologian Martin Luther (1483–1546) and the French reformer John Calvin (1507–1574), was a reaction to abuses in the Church, theological disputes over the issues of redemption and grace, the authority of Scripture over tradition, and a rejection of the authority of the pope. The Reformation formally began on October 31, 1517, when Luther publicly nailed his Ninety-five Theses to the door of the University Church in Wittenberg, Germany. This local reform movement touched off other reform movements in Germany and in other countries in Europe and led to the establishment of Protestantism as the third major branch of Christianity, along with Catholicism and Eastern Orthodoxy. Of the countries of Europe that had a direct effect on Africa, Spain, Portugal, and France remained largely Roman Catholic; Britain, The Netherlands, and many of the German states became Protestant. Religious reformers rather than missionaries, the Protestant churches did not begin their well-known, wide-scale missionary activities in Africa until the 1800s.

Meanwhile, in response to the Reformation, the Roman Catholic Church was undergoing its own transformation. The Council of Trent, a meeting of important church leaders held from 1545 to 1563 in the city of Trent in northern Italy, began what became know as the church's Counter-Reformation period. The council clarified many church doctrines and rules, reformed many abuses, revitalized religious practices, and reaffirmed the authority of the pope. The Council of Trent turned the Roman Catholic Church's direction outward.

Indicative of the new spirit in the Church was the founding of the Society of Jesus (Jesuits) in 1534, a religious order dedicated to education and missionary work. A Spanish Jesuit missionary, Francis Xavier (1506–1552), was one of the original Jesuits and the most important Roman Catholic missionary of modern times. He established the Church in Portuguese India, Japan, and the

Malay Peninsula. Another early Jesuit, the Italian Matteo Ricci (1552–1610), introduced Christianity to the imperial court in Beijing, China. The Italian Jesuit Roberto de Nobili (1577–1656) sought to reconcile Hinduism and Christianity in India. Jesuit Peter Claver (1581–1654) became prominent as a missionary among the indigenous peoples and enslaved Africans in South America. The Jesuit *reducciones,* or missionary settlements, in Brazil, Paraguay, and elsewhere on the continent, some housing as many as 20,000 people, offered indigenous people some measure of protection from Spanish slave raids. However, Africa did not become the focus of Roman Catholic missionary activity until the 19th century.

In 1622 the Roman Catholic Church established the Sacred Congregation for the Propagation of the Faith, a bureau of the Roman Curia, the administrative body of the church. The purpose of this group was to take the organization of missionary activities out of the hands of the religious orders and impose Roman control over them.

Christianity in Sub-Saharan Africa Although India and the Americas were considered important missionary areas in the 16th, 17th, and 18th centuries, Africa did not receive equivalent attention from Catholic missionaries during those centuries. Their activities were generally restricted to the west coast and only slightly inland and failed to leave a lasting imprint on Africa. Missionaries followed in the footsteps of Portuguese explorers and entered the KONGO KINGDOM in 1491 for the purposes of converting the king and controlling commerce in the region. Efforts eventually met with success when the Portuguese installed a new king, who was baptized and ruled under the name AFONSO I (c. 1461–1543). Afonso made Christianity the state religion and encouraged the Portuguese to convert his people. A bishop was named. In the early 1500s, however, missionary activities faltered in Kongo, as they soon did in the kingdom of BENIN. By the 1560s Christian missionary activity was also slowing down in East Africa and in the MWENE MUTAPA kingdom, which covered parts of present-day MOZAMBIQUE and ZIMBABWE. At the same time, Muslim missionaries were making strong inroads in the interior.

South Africa The Protestant Dutch brought the Dutch Reformed Church (Nederduitse Gereformeerde Kerk) with them when the DUTCH EAST INDIA COMPANY established the provisioning station at the CAPE OF GOOD HOPE, at the southernmost tip of Africa, which grew into the CAPE COLONY. The Nederduitse Gereformeerde Kerk, founded in 1652, was almost exclusively white.

The first African Christians came from the population of people held in bondage in the region, although masters often forbade them baptism for fear that they would have to be released. The 19th-century GRIQUA, a people of mixed KHOIKHOI and European ancestry who lived north of the Orange River in southern Africa, were among the first Africans to convert to Christianity when

Protestant missionaries arrived at the start of the 19th century. Before that, little missionary activity among Africans is recorded.

Christianity in Egypt For the first four centuries after the Arab conquest of Egypt (c. 639), Coptic Christians were free to practice their religion. They remained autonomous, although they were subject to a special tax, called *gezya,* leveled on nonbelievers, that qualified them as *al-zemma* (protected). By the 11th century, however, Arabic was replacing Coptic as the language of the people, and by the end of the 12th century Egypt was a primarily Muslim country. The Coptic Church became ever more subject to restrictions on repairing old churches and building new ones, on testifying in court, on public behavior, on inheritance, and on public religious display. While the Ottoman Empire ruled Egypt during the years 1517 to 1798, the caliphs did not interfere much in the internal affairs of the church. Although there was occasional persecution and periodic outbreaks of hostility, the Coptic Church maintained its identity and remained internally stable. The position of the Coptic Orthodox Church did not improve until the 19th century and the accession of MUHAMMAD ALI (1769–1849). By 1855 the *gezya* was lifted, and Christians were allowed into mainstream Egyptian life.

Roman Catholic missionaries were first active among the Copts in the 17th century. The Capuchins, a branch of the Franciscans, established a mission in Cairo in 1630; in 1675 the Jesuits also began missionary activity in Egypt. During the 1600s a number of theological dialogues between Rome and the Coptic Church took place but were fruitless. Then, in 1741, a Coptic bishop in Jerusalem named Amba Athanasius (fl. 1740s) renounced the traditional Orthodox Coptic belief in the single divine nature of Christ and became a Roman Catholic. Pope Benedict XIV (1675–1758) made Amba Athanasius the Vicar Apostolic, or titular bishop, of the small community of Egyptian Coptic Catholics (numbering not more than 2,000), and thus established the Egyptian Catholic Church, in union with Rome. Athanasius eventually returned to the Coptic Orthodox Church, and the two vicars apostolic named as his successors were unable to travel to Europe to be ordained bishops. In 1824 Rome mistook the intent of the Egypt's Ottoman viceroy and established a patriarchate at Alexandria for the Coptic Catholic Church. This position remained unfilled until 1898, when an actual patriarch, Cyril II, was named. The Ottoman Empire allowed the Coptic Catholic Church to build its own churches beginning in 1829.

Christianity in Ethiopia The Ethiopian Orthodox Church traces its roots back to the fourth century, when Athanasius (296–373), the patriarch of Alexandria, appointed Frumentius (d. c. 383) the first *abuna* (meaning "our father," or bishop) of Aksum. Through Frumentius's efforts, ancient Aksum, under the rule of Emperor Ezana

(r. c. 320–350), became a Christian kingdom. From then until the 20th century the patriarch of Alexandria named the bishops of Ethiopia. Like their Egyptian preceptors, the Ethiopian Orthodox Church adhered to the traditional Monophysite beliefs regarding the nature of Christ, a doctrine condemned by the Council of Chalcedon of 451, a formal assembly of the leaders of the entire church.

During the seventh century the spread of Islam cut the Ethiopian Church off from the rest of the Christian world except for the Ethiopian monastery in Jerusalem and with the Coptic Church in Egypt. Although originally protected by Muslims, as the Copts were also "people of the Book," relations between Muslims and Ethiopian Christians deteriorated. The Ethiopians retreated into their mountain strongholds, where they could maintain their independence and their culture.

Christian Europe was aware of the existence of Ethiopia, along the Red Sea on the Horn of Africa. It was thought of in a vague way, however, as the putative kingdom of the legendary though mythical Christian king Prester (from Greek *presbyteros,* "priest") John, reports of whose existence had filtered through Europe for generations. Some Europeans hoped to ally themselves with this Christian kingdom and circumvent Muslim control of the region's trade.

In 1516 the Ottoman Empire conquered Egypt and set up a major trading station for human captives on the Dahlak Islands in the Red Sea. In 1531 the Muslim general and religious reformer AHMAD GRAÑ (c. 1506–1543), from the kingdom of ADAL, became a threat. He led a jihad against the people of the Ethiopian Highlands in an attempt to eradicate Christianity. His army consisted of Somalis and AFAR people from the Denakil Plain on the Ethiopian-Eritrean border. Ahmad Grañ was initially victorious against the armies from the SHOA kingdom and pushed his way toward Tigray and ERITREA, along the Red Sea coast, conquering almost three-quarters of Ethiopia and converting the majority of people to Islam.

The Portuguese, however, felt that their interests in the Red Sea region were threatened by Ahmad Grañ's jihad. They answered Ethiopia's request for assistance and landed 400 musketeers at Massawa, in Eritrea. After gaining the support of Tigrayan soldiers, the Christian army trained in European tactics and defeated Ahmad Grañ and his Ottoman reinforcements at the Battle of Wayna Daga, near Lake Tana, in 1543. Grañ was killed by a Portuguese musket ball. The Muslim threat waned temporarily, but the Muslims seized Massawa again in 1560 and maintained their foothold there for 300 years.

During Ahmad Grañ's jihad a Portuguese adventurer named John Bermudez claimed that the dying *abuna* had named him his successor as head of the church in Ethiopia and that the pope had confirmed this appointment. Although no evidence existed to back his claim, the Portuguese in Ethiopia believed him and urged the emperor, Galawdewos (r. 1540–1559), to become a Roman Catholic. A group of Jesuit missionaries was sent to assist in the conversion of the Ethiopian Orthodox believers to Catholicism, but to no avail.

In the following century, Jesuit missionaries led by Spaniard Pedro Páez (1564–1622) arrived in Ethiopia, converted the emperor, Susenyos (r. 1607–1632), to Roman Catholicism, and for a time most of Ethiopia was in communion with Rome. Susenyos's motivations were political rather than theological; he sought a military alliance with Portugal.

During Susenyos's reign, Alfonsus Mendes, the patriarch-designate sent from Rome, demanded that all Ethiopians be rebaptized and all priests reordained—clear affronts to the validity of the Ethiopian Coptic Church's sacraments. He outlawed the practice of circumcision and demanded that the church celebrate the sabbath on Sunday, instead of the traditional Saturday sabbath of Ethiopian custom. Missionary efforts prospered for a time, but rivalries soon developed with the Ethiopian Orthodox Church. These differences led to bloody conflicts between Christian factions. All missionaries were expelled by Susenyos's successor, and Ethiopia entered a period of isolationism.

See also: AKSUM (Vol. I); CHRISTIANITY (Vols. I, II); CHRISTIANITY, INFLUENCE OF (Vols. II, IV, V); FULANI JIHADS (Vol. III); ISLAM (Vol. II); ISLAM, INFLUENCE OF (Vols. II, III); JIHAD (Vols. II, IV); MONOPHYSITE (Vol. I).

Further reading: John Baur, *2000 Years of Christianity in Africa: An African History, 62–1992* (Nairobi, Kenya: Paulines, 1994); Peter B Clarke, *West Africa and Christianity* (London: E. Arnold, 1986); Elizabeth Allo Isichei, *A History of Christianity in Africa: From Antiquity to the Present* (Lawrenceville, N.J.: Africa World Press, 1995); Adrian Hastings, *The Church in Africa: 1450–1950* (New York: Oxford University Press, 1994).

cloth and textiles Throughout African history, cloth has been seen not only as a utilitarian object but has also played important political, religious, cultural, and economic roles within the diverse and ever-changing African societies. As with any artistic craft, African cloth making has changed in its design and style over time. For example, before the 1600s Ashanti cloth was usually blue and white. But increased trade and demand caused craftspeople to begin to incorporate a variety of colorful fabrics into their textiles. Cloth was also used for ceremonial and ritual purposes, such as wrapping a corpse or adorning a bride. Other textiles were created in order to record a people's history. Ashanti *adinkra* cloth was designed with symbolic figures that were stamped into patterns that represented people and events in Ashanti history. In this way cloth design could facilitate the keeping of oral history.

Traditionally cloth was viewed as a symbol of wealth, and it was the members of the royalty who demanded luxury cloths and fabrics. In many cities where commercial textile production thrived, such as the HAUSA city-state of KANO, the weavers and dyers usually received their business only from those of the upper strata of society. The ceremonial *kente* cloth of the Ashanti, made with silk that the court imported from Europe through trans-Saharan and coastal trade, was worn exclusively by some local monarchs. As early as the 17th century the Ashanti were unraveling fine imported cloth and working the yarn into their own textiles.

At times in African history, cloth was used as a form of MONEY AND CURRENCY for bride-wealth, tributes, and taxes. In the Congo and in coastal West Africa, certain cloths could be used to pay court fines. In the southern and eastern parts of the Congo, a 24-by-16-inch (61-by-41-cm) piece of raffia cloth called *madiba* was used for tribute. The people of the Congo also used books of cloth strips as an early form of money. Congolese Kwango-Kwilu society esteemed the weavers who created the cloth money bundles.

In the 16th century the Portuguese colonists on the CAPE VERDE ISLANDS used forced labor to cultivate indigo, a plant from which a deep blue cloth dye was collected and later exported to Europe. In Europe in the 1500s, indigo was, weight for weight, as valuable as GOLD.

In both precolonial and colonial times, cloth served as a valuable item of trade in West Africa, along the sudanic belt, and along the SWAHILI COAST. European garments and fabrics were sometimes brought in through North African ports and exchanged for human captives. The Islamic state of KANEM-BORNU, near Lake CHAD, imported garments from TUNIS, and the ZAGHAWA king of the central Sudan adorned himself with imported European wool and silk. On East Africa's Indian Ocean coast, Arabic, Persian, and Indian traders brought great amounts of COTTON and silk cloth to Swahili commercial ports—including ZANZIBAR, MOMBASA, MOGADISHU, and ZEILA—where it was exchanged for gold, ivory, and human captives.

In the 17th century elaborate raffia textiles made by KUBA weavers were popular throughout the Congo region. During the same era the town of KETA, in present-day southeastern GHANA, was the center for the intricately woven cloth appropriately known as Keta cloth.

By the 18th century the cloth industry prospered in many parts of the continent as cotton, raffia, and bark-cloth all continued to be manufactured by African craftspeople using traditional weaving and dyeing processes. Magenta silk from Italy and France was imported by KANO in the 19th century and processed in the same traditional way as cotton, wool, and wild silk.

See also: CLOTH AND TEXTILES (Vols. I, II, IV, V).

Further reading: Duncan Clarke, *The Art of African Textiles* (San Diego, Calif.: Thunder Bay Press, 1997); John Picton and John Mack, *African Textiles* (London: British Museum, 1989); Irmtraud Reswick, *Traditional Textiles of Tunisia and Related North African Weavings* (Seattle, Wash.: University of Washington Press, 1985).

Comoros (Comoro Islands) Volcanic archipelago in the western Indian Ocean, located between the island of MADAGASCAR and the southern East African country of MOZAMBIQUE. Today officially called the Federal Islamic Republic of the Comoros, the islands were a major center of trade from the 15th to the 18th centuries. Because of its location along the popular Indian Ocean trade network between Asia and the African continent, the culture of the Comoros reflected a unique blend of Arab, African, and Asian influences. The earliest settlers were of Malay-Polynesian descent, followed by Arabic- and Bantu-speaking peoples from the Middle East and the African continent, respectively.

One of the products exported from the Comoro Islands was ambergris, a pale blue substance used in perfumes and lamp oil. Ambergris washed up on the island shore in solid egg-like form after being excreted from the stomachs of the sperm whales living in the surrounding Indian Ocean.

Because of its origins and value, Swahili peoples called it "treasure of the sea." The Chinese especially prized ambergris, believing it to be a potent aphrodisiac. Not knowing where it came from, they called it "dragon's spittle."

When Portuguese merchants arrived about 1505, Comoro trade expanded to Europe and eventually to the Americas. Local sultans warred with each other to supply the new traders, who increasingly demanded captives from the African coast. By the 18th century captives had become the islands' primary export. In the late 1700s other peoples, including the SAKALAVA of Madagascar, raided the Comoros for laborers, whom they sold to the owners of French sugar plantations on the other Indian Ocean islands of Madagascar, MAURITIUS, and RÉUNION.

See also: COMOROS (Vols. I, II, IV, V); INDIAN OCEAN TRADE (Vol. II); SHIRAZI ARABS (Vol. II).

Congo   Large region of Central Africa that is drained by the CONGO RIVER. Today the region is made up of the Democratic Republic of the CONGO and the Republic of the CONGO. The Congo encompassed the precolonial African states of the KONGO KINGDOM, the LUBA EMPIRE, and the LUNDA EMPIRE, as well as the smaller kingdoms of MBUNDU, LOANGO, TEKE, and Kuba.

At the end of the 19th century Congo was divided into the two European colonies of the French Congo, or "Middle Congo," and the Belgian "Congo Free State." In 1960 the Congo colonies declared their independence, eventually becoming the two nations of the People's Republic of the Congo and the Democratic Republic of the Congo.

From the 16th to the 18th centuries the Congo region underwent an explosion of regional and international trade. New technologies involving the mining of iron, copper, and other metals encouraged the development of new commercial markets. Cloth and salt were also important local commodities.

The international demand for ivory and captive LABOR forces increased trade between Africans and Europeans on the west coast, near the mouth of the Congo River, as well as between peoples living on the African coasts and those living in the interior regions. Greater wealth and the logistical demands of long-distance commerce created centralized kingdoms of Bantu-speaking peoples, including the Lunda and Luba empires. The trading networks of these states stretched across the continent. Most Africans continued to live in small villages, but large urban areas also began to emerg, including SÃO SALVADOR, the Portuguese name for Mbanza Kongo, the capital of the Kongo kingdom.

While expanding trade created wealth and new political systems in the Congo, the trade in human captives ravaged the local population and upset the balance of power between Africans and Europeans. The Dutch, French, Portuguese, and British all used a combination of military force, economic coercion, and Christian conversion to expand their presence in the region. By 1800 most of the great Congo kingdoms were declining and struggling to retain their sovereignty.

See also: CONGO BASIN (Vols. I, II); CONGO RIVER (Vol. I); MBANZA KONGO (Vol. II); SLAVE TRADE, THE TRANSATLANTIC (Vol. III).

Congo, Democratic Republic of the (DRC; Congo-Kinshasa; formerly Zaïre)   Western Central African country, approximately 905,400 square miles (2,345,000 sq km) in size and occupying the larger portion of the CONGO region. Today the DRC is the continent's third-largest country and is crucial because of its central location. To the north are the CENTRAL AFRICAN REPUBLIC and the Republic of the SUDAN, and to the east lie UGANDA, RWANDA, BURUNDI, and TANZANIA. ZAMBIA lies to the southeast and ANGOLA to the southwest. Congo has a narrow outlet to the Atlantic at the mouth of the CONGO RIVER, which, along with the UBANGI RIVER, constitutes its eastern border with the Republic of the CONGO, which is the other part of the Congo region.

The extensive river system in the DRC has facilitated transportation and the movement of peoples and goods for several millennia. Approximately half of Africa's tropical forests are in the Congo, and they constitute its principal ecological feature. Transitional woodlands lie to the north and south of the rain forest, while the southernmost area consists of savanna grasslands and light woodlands. The Mitumba mountain range runs along the country's eastern edge, bordering the RIFT VALLEY.

From the 16th to the middle of the 19th centuries the peoples of the Congo underwent dramatic changes that set the stage for the perhaps even more dramatic changes of the following 100 or so years. The KONGO KINGDOM, located along the lower reaches of the Congo River, was at its peak in the 16th century, when it developed strong diplomatic and trade relations with Portugal. The Portuguese interest was predominantly in the transatlantic SLAVE TRADE, however, and in 1575 Portugal founded a colony to the south, at LUANDA, in what is today Angola. This then became the focal point of Portuguese trade with the African interior. In 1568 invaders inflicted a severe defeat on the kingdom, and it took Portuguese military assistance to reestablish royal authority. A century later Portugal went to war with Kongo, touching off the disintegration of the kingdom.

In the Katanga region of the interior southern savanna, the political and economic developments that had led to the emergence of the Luba kingdom also led to the expanded LUBA EMPIRE and the closely associated LUNDA EMPIRE, also called the Lunda "Commonwealth." Portuguese-African traders based in Luanda and BENGUELA managed to penetrate into the deep interior and trade with the Luba and Lunda states. However, in contrast to states on or near the coast, such as Kongo, the transatlantic slave trade did not play much of a role in the political events of the interior states.

See also: CONGO, DEMOCRATIC REPUBLIC OF THE (Vols. I, II, IV, V).

Further reading: Robert Harms, *River of Wealth, River of Sorrow: The Central Zaire Basin in the Era of the Slave and Ivory Trade, 1500–1891* (New Haven, Conn.:

Yale University Press, 1981); Jan Vansina, *Kingdoms of the Savanna* (Madison, Wisc.: University of Wisconsin Press, 1966).

Congo, Republic of the (Congo-Brazzaville)

Equatorial African country, approximately 131,900 square miles (341,600 sq km) in size and constituting the northern portion of the CONGO region. To its north lie CAMEROON and the CENTRAL AFRICAN REPUBLIC. The UBANGI RIVER and the CONGO RIVER, which are major river highways, constitute its western and southern border with the Democratic Republic of the CONGO except for the small CABINDA enclave along the Atlantic coast. The coastal Atlantic plain gives way to the southern or Niari River basin. This, in turn, rises to the sandy Central, or Téké, Plateau that eventually gives way to the Congo Basin, which covers nearly half of the country. Astride the equator, the country mostly consists of tropical forests.

The southern portion of the republic, where the great Tio, LOANGO, and KONGO kingdoms had emerged by the early 15th century, became increasingly caught up in the transatlantic SLAVE TRADE from the 16th into the 19th centuries. Further south in Angola, the trade into the interior was in Portuguese and Afro-Portuguese hands. North of the Congo River, Europeans were confined to the coast. In this area, though, the French and the British, rather than the Portuguese, dominated the trade. A political by-product of the trade was the emergence of a new African merchant elite that took over real power from the chiefs and kings. This was especially true of the Loango and Kongo.

By 1800 a vast trade network had developed throughout the northern Congo region. In addition, the steady increase in trade led to the rise of sizeable market towns. These emerged at key points along the banks of the Congo River and its principal tributaries.

See also: CONGO, REPUBLIC OF THE (Vol. I, II, IV, V).

Further reading: Phyllis Martin, *The External Trade of the Loango Coast, 1576–1870* (Oxford, U.K.: Clarendon Press, 1972); Jan Vansina, *Paths in the Rainforests* (Madison, Wisc.: University of Wisconsin Press, 1990).

corsairs

Mediterranean PIRATES who made a living by raiding and looting merchant vessels. During the late 15th and early 16th centuries, Portuguese and Spanish Christians vied with the Ottoman Turks for control of the western Mediterranean. The Christians captured the strategic North African ports of TANGIER, TRIPOLI, ALGIERS, and Tunis.

In retaliation, Ottoman corsairs recaptured these ports and used them as a base to attack Christian merchant vessels in the Mediterranean. While the Ottomans were unable to gain complete control of the Mediterranean shipping lanes, their control of these key ports ensured that the MAGHRIB would remain under Muslim rule.

The corsairs continued their attacks on Christian ships throughout the 17th and 18th centuries. The booty captured from these raids provided most of the revenue for these coastal ports.

See also: BARBARY COAST (Vol. III); OTTOMAN EMPIRE AND AFRICA (Vols. III, IV).

Further reading: Jacques Heers, *The Barbary Corsairs: Warfare in the Mediterranean, 1480–1580* (Greenhill, Penn.: Stackpole, 2003).

cotton

Throughout the world the fiber cultivated from the seed of the cotton plant has long been traded either in bulk or woven and then traded as cloth. Although cotton was an African trading commodity for centuries, the advent of European trade toward the end of the 15th century greatly increased the demand for African cotton and cotton textiles.

During the 16th century the Yoruba cotton growers in the kingdom of ALLADA, in present-day NIGERIA, attained great wealth from the trade of their cotton cloths. Their fame from their cottons was such that they were rumored to keep their wives dressed in finery that rivaled the outfits of women in the wealthiest trading states of the GOLD COAST. By the 17th century large Yoruba trade cities such as BENIN CITY had taken over the cotton trade by transporting it from surrounding towns such as Allada and WHYDAH and then trading it with the Europeans at their

Replica of Eli Whitney's cotton gin, invented in 1793. This machine for cleaning the seeds out of cotton helped make cotton the main crop of the American South and kept slavery as its dominant economic institution. © *Bettmann/Corbis*

own big markets. Hence the cloth bought from the two cotton towns was called *aso-Ado,* meaning "cloth for Benin." By the mid-17th century English and Dutch traders were accepting more than 10,000 pieces of these cotton cloths per year.

In the 17th century cotton began to replace other options, such as raffia and tree bark, as the preferred material for making cloth. The famed *kente* cloth of the Ashanti peoples of what is now GHANA was originally made out of raffia but changed to cotton. While the men were the weavers of the *kente* cloth, it was the women who were responsible for making the yarns out of raw cotton and dying them various colors.

While the late 17th century saw the beginning of cotton cultivation in other parts of Africa, such as the western Cape of southern Africa, cotton was already a staple crop of groups such as the DYULA of what is now GUINEA. In this region as in others, cotton cloth was used for currency, and so the Dyula traders became rich from the products of their fields. It was said that the Dyula used so many forced laborers that the cotton could be picked, spun and woven all in one day, thereby giving them the advantage over their local competitors in the cotton trade well into the 18th century.

Cotton and the textiles made from it remained a constant factor in both inland and overseas trade throughout the 18th and into the 19th centuries. However, the African cotton trade saw its heyday after 1861, when the start of the United States Civil War curtailed the production there.

See also: COTTON (Vols. II, IV); YORUBALAND (Vol. III).

Cross River   Waterway located mostly in southeastern NIGERIA and parts of western CAMEROON. The Cross River stretches approximately 300 miles (483 km) and joins the Calabar River before emptying into the Bight of Bonny (formerly the Bight of Biafra), on the Gulf of Guinea.

Two of the most important trading peoples located along the Cross River were the IBIBIO, especially active in the 16th century, and the EFIK, active in the 17th century. Both groups were located in and around the city of OLD CALABAR and used the Cross River to trade their goods

with both the Europeans on the coast and FULANI groups of the hinterland to the east. European explorations of the Cross River started early, as Portuguese sailors were familiar with the area in the 15th century.

The Cross River's banks were also used as a place for traditional ART, as evidenced by the 17th-century discovery of *akwanshi*—stone pillars carved into human-shaped figures by EKOI people—in the area.

Cugoano, Ottobah (John Stuart)   (1757–unknown) *African man who became a highly active and influential abolitionist in London in the late 1700s*

Cugoano was kidnapped into slavery in present-day GHANA and worked on plantations in Grenada before he was taken to England. In London he obtained his freedom, and in 1773 he was baptized into the Anglican Church, taking the name John Stuart. For the next 15 years he lived in the borough of Westminster in London, working as a servant in the home and studio of the artist Richard Cosway (1740–1821), a portraitist known for his miniatures. Cugoano was a friend of Olaudah EQUIANO (c. 1745–1797), another African abolitionist, then living nearby in London.

In 1787, while in Cosway's service, Cugoano wrote and published a book entitled *Thoughts and Sentiments on the Evil and Wicked Traffic of the Commerce of the Human Species,* an important antislavery tract and the first of its kind to be written in English by an African. That same year, 30 years in advance of its actual implementation, Cugoano suggested that Britain establish a naval squadron to patrol the African coast and suppress the trade of humans.

Little else is known about Cugoano's life after he published his book. He dropped from sight, and the time, place, and manner of his death are unknown.

See also: ENGLAND AND AFRICA (Vol. III); RECAPTIVES (Vol. IV); SLAVE TRADE, THE TRANSATLANTIC (Vol. III).

Further reading: Ottobah Cugoano, *Thoughts and Sentiments on the Evil of Slavery and Other Writings;* Vincent Caretta, ed. (New York: Penguin, 1999).

Dagomba (Dagamba) Ethnic group of present-day northern GHANA that was subjected to numerous invasions by their AKAN neighbors from the 16th through the 19th centuries. The Dagomba are one of the groups cthat make up the Mossi people, who also inhabited the states of MAMPRUSI, Fada-n-Gurma, Tenkodogo, Nanumba, and Yatenga. The Dagomba and Mamprusi speak Gur, a Niger-Congo language.

In the 15th and 16th centuries the Dagomba rapidly expanded their kingdom, known as Dagbon. In 1620, though, the neighboring kingdom of GONJA attacked the Dagomba, forcing them out of the western region of their homeland. They fled east, where they conquered the Konkomba, becoming their overlords, and established their new capital, Yendi (later YENDI DABARI). The Dagomba prospered during this period by taxing the profitable trade that traveled through their region.

Traders from the HAUSA STATES, to the east, brought GOLD, kola nuts, and human captives from the inland forest to the south. In return they procured cloth from other Hausa States and salt from the Sahara. The DYULA, West African traders, brought Islam to Dagbon, where it was later embraced by Ya Na Muhammad Zangina (r. c. 1700–1714), the 16th ruler of the Dagomba people.

The tensions between the Dagomba and the Gonja lasted a century, during which the Gonja served as their overlords. In 1720, under the leadership of Ya Na Andani Sigeli, the Dagomba were finally able to defeat the Gonja. However, their freedom was fleeting, as the Ashanti king, OPOKUWARE II (c. 1700–1750), began his subjugation of the Dagomba about 1744. The Dagomba were finally conquered in the early 1770s under the reign of Asantehene OSEI KWADWO (c. 1740–1777). Thereafter they became a major source of captives for the Ashanti, who amassed great wealth by trading them and others to Europeans for firearms and manufactured goods. Dagbon was forced to pay tribute to the ASHANTI EMPIRE until the middle of the 19th century, when the British conquered the Ashanti, and the Dagomba were able to return to independence.

See also: DAGOMBA (Vol. II); VOLTA BASIN (Vol. III).

Dahomey West African kingdom of the FON, a subgroup of the AJA people, located within present-day Republic of BENIN. The powerful Dahomey kingdom of the 18th century emerged from the unification of the kingdom of ABOMEY—whose principal city of the same name was to become the capital of Dahomey—with the neighboring Aja kingdoms of ALLADA and WHYDAH. Abomey started to gain influence during the 1600s under the leadership of the self-appointed king, WEGBAJA (c. 1645–1680). It was during his reign that some of the Fon people started referring to themselves as Dahomeans. In the years that followed, Dahomey became rich trading human captives with Europeans, and as its power grew the kingdom expanded. About 1724 Dahomey's King AGAJA (1673–1740) conquered Allada, and in 1727 he captured the nearby coastal trading kingdom of Whydah. The combined kingdoms of Allada, Why-

Women in the army of the king of Dahomey, with the king at their head. This engraving by Francis Chesham (1749–1806) was published in Archibald Daizel's 1793 *History of Dahomey*. As late as the reign of King Gezu (1818–1858), three regiments of 1,000 women were said to be serving in the Dahomey army. © *Historical Picture Archive/Corbis*

dah, and Abomey became the three provinces of the kingdom of Dahomey. With its expanded borders, Dahomey assumed control of coastal ports and gained further access to European trade, making it the dominant power in the region. The kingdom's expansion continued into the 18th century, at which time Dahomey was attacked by the OYO EMPIRE, to which it ultimately was forced to pay tribute.

Dahomey regained its power during the 1800s under the strong leadership of kings GEZU (r. 1818–1858) and Glélé (r. 1858–1889). Under Gezu, Dahomey continued to trade human captives, but a British blockade in 1852 forced him to agree to put an end to that practice.

See also: DAHOMEY (Vols. II, IV, V).

Further reading: Edna G. Bay, *Wives of the Leopard: Gender, Politics, and Culture in the Kingdom of Dahomey* (Charlottesville, Va.: University of Virginia Press, 1998).

Dakar Port city located in present-day SENEGAL on the Cap-Vert peninsula, the westernmost point in Africa.

> The term *Dakar* probably comes from the word *daxar,* the Wolof name for the tamarind tree that is common in the area. Others believe the name might be derived from Deuk Raw, or "land of refuge," a name that some exiles from the interior called the Cap-Vert.

The Lebu, a Muslim people, inhabited the fishing village of Ndaxaru (now Dakar) in the early 18th century. The French established a port there in 1750, and a century later a settlement was founded at Dakar to oversee the cultivation and trade of France's groundnut (peanut) crops. Throughout the 19th century many people relocated from GORÉE ISLAND to Dakar, and the city grew to become an important market for TRADE AND COMMERCE.

See also: DAKAR (Vols. IV, V); FRANCE AND AFRICA (Vols. III, IV, V); GROUNDNUTS (Vols. III, IV).

Damot Kingdom in ETHIOPIA located south of the Blue Nile River, between the Angur and Gibe rivers. The once-powerful kingdom of Damot was conquered in 1316–17 and was absorbed in the Ethiopian Christian state of Emperor Amda Siyon (r. c. 1314–1344). Damot went into decline over the next 200 years as Ethiopia became a battleground for the militant religious leaders of both Islam and Christianity. By the beginning of the 16th century the kingdom of Damot, which was largely populated by animists who were neither Muslim nor Christian, had lost most of its influence. Eventually, around 1590, great numbers of migrating OROMO people moved into the weakened kingdom, forcing many of its inhabitants to move to the Ethiopian kingdom of GOJJAM, to the northwest. By the 17th century Damot was completely absorbed and became a subdistrict of Gojjam.

See also: DAMOT (Vol. II).

Dangme (Dangbe) See GA-DANGME.

Dar es Salaam Capital of present-day TANZANIA, located on the Indian Ocean coast, separated from ZANZIBAR by the Zanzibar Channel. The site of DAR ES SALAAM was originally a small village named Mzizima, KISWAHILI for "healthy town." Later it became the site of plantations growing cassava, millet, and MAIZE. *Dar es Salaam*, an Arabic name meaning "haven of peace," was formally founded by the sultan of Zanzibar in 1866. It remained a small town until it was occupied by German colonial forces in 1887.

Darfur (Fur Sultanate) Islamic state founded in the mid-17th century by the FUR people; located in the western region of present-day Republic of the SUDAN, near the CHAD border.

Darfur means "house of the Fur people" in Arabic.

Little is known about the origin of Darfur, but oral history suggests that the state was preceded by the Daju and TUNJUR dynasties. The Daju prospered in the 13th and 14th centuries, owing mostly to thriving trade. By the 15th century, however, the Tunjur took control of the region's trade and seized power from the Daju. It is thought that Islam began to influence the region during the period of Tunjur rule. However, the religion took a firm hold in the region only with the founding of the Fur Sultanate in the 1600s.

SULIMAN SOLONG (r. c. 1640–1660) declared himself the first sultan of Darfur about 1640, beginning the rule of the KAYRA DYNASTY. The Kayra clan was influential even before Darfur became a Muslim enclave, tracing its ancestry back to a 15th-century Tunjur rebel leader

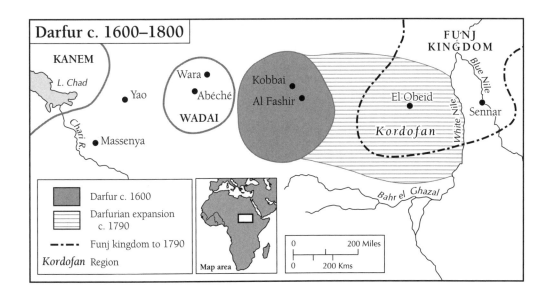

named Dali. The true Kayra dynasty, though, began with Suliman Solong.

From its beginnings Darfur was characterized by a political struggle between two rival factions of the Kayra dynasty. Nevertheless the sultanate prospered by selling captives for slave labor and by exploiting the North African IVORY TRADE. The wealth they amassed enabled their sultans to expand Darfur's territory by conquering smaller neighboring states.

In the middle of the 18th century Sultan Abd-al Rahman al-Rashed established his capital at the former caravan trading center of al-Fashir and centralized Kayra authority. From al-Fashir, Darfur's Muslim sultans expanded into FUNJ territory, in the KORDOFAN region, successfully converting the people they conquered to Islam.

See also: DARFUR (Vols. II, IV, V).

Further reading: P. M. Holt and M. W. Daly, *A History of the Sudan: From the Coming of Islam to the Present Day* (New York: Longman, 2000); R. S. O'Fahey, *State and Society in Dar Fur* (New York: St. Martin's Press, 1980).

date palm A type of palm tree that produces the date fruit. An important crop since long before the common era, dates were cultivated in groves throughout the Sudan and Sahara regions of North Africa. The versatile date palm is a hardy tree that had several uses in the generally treeless Saharan plains. Its leaves and bark could be used for building purposes, and the seeds from its fruit could be used as animal feed.

The Toubou people of Kawar, an oasis in present-day northeastern NIGER, cultivated date palm trees in the 17th and 18th centuries. The dates they produced were generally sent on southern caravan routes to be traded for goods and other foodstuffs. Dates were an easily stored source of nutrition during travel, so they were often stolen during raids conducted by bandits throughout the Saharan regions. Date palms bear spikes, making a fall from a date palm tree extremely perilous. However, the inhabitants of the Sudan region were noted for their agility in harvesting the fruit from the trees.

See also: FOOD (Vols. I, II, III, IV, V); SUDAN, THE (Vol. II); TOUBOU (Vol. II); TRANS-SAHARAN TRADE ROUTES (Vol. II).

Daud, Askia (Askia Dawud) (r. 1549–1582) *Muslim ruler of the Songhai Empire*

Daud was the sixth of the 10 members of the ASKIA DYNASTY who ruled the SONGHAI Empire from 1493 to 1591. First he was the governor of Kurmina, the western province of the Songhai Empire, but he assumed the Songhai throne when his brother, Askia Ishaq I, died in 1549. Daud ruled from the city of Gao, located on the NIGER RIVER.

Daud had a reputation as a devout Muslim, and he organized campaigns against the non-Muslim MOSSI STATES and BORGU to the south of Songhai. (Daud respected the power of traditional RELIGION, though, and was careful not to alienate Songhai's non-Muslim population.) He also successfully defended his territory from FULANI incursions and repelled numerous invasions from nearby TUAREGS. The captives seized during Daud's campaigns were turned into an agricultural LABOR force that served to help feed the growing Songhai Empire.

During Daud's reign TIMBUKTU reached the height of its influence as a center of Islamic culture. Daud was known to lavish the most devout Muslim scholars with gifts of land, slaves, and cattle.

Songhai enjoyed an extended period of prosperity under Daud, but it was during his reign that the seeds of the empire's destruction were sown. In 1578 the Moroccan sultan, ABD AL-MANSUR (r. 1579–1603), began collecting taxes on the salt exported from the Taghaza mines in northern Songhai territory. Instead of attacking his fellow Muslim, Askia Daud allowed al-Mansur to take control of the northern salt trade so that he might fund his campaigns against the Portuguese and Spanish Christians who were vying for control of Morocco's Mediterranean ports. Daud died in 1582 and his son Askia al-Hajj (r. 1582–1586) was chosen from among his many sons to succeed him. After Daud the Askia dynasty suffered from internal conflicts that weakened Songhai unity, and within four years MOROCCO had assumed authority in the northern Songhai territories. Five years later al-Mansur's well-armed ranks routed the Songhai army, and the empire quickly crumbled.

See also: MUHAMMAD TOURÉ, ASKIA (Vols. II, III); KURMINA (Vol. II); TAGHAZA (Vol. II).

degredados Individuals convicted of civil or political crimes and exiled from Portugal. By the 1500s many Portuguese *degredados* were being exiled to the islands that are now the Republic of CAPE VERDE; others were sent to ANGOLA or MOZAMBIQUE.

As a way to atone for their crimes, *degredados* were given the opportunity to perform hazardous duties on the continent in the name of the Portuguese crown. In the 16th century these duties included exploring the possibility of an overland route between Angola, on the Atlantic Ocean coast, and Mozambique, on the Indian Ocean coast. *Degredados* might also be asked to penetrate uncharted territories in the African interior. At the end of their sentences many *degredados* remained in Africa to live with their indigenous African wives and families or to continue trading GOLD or working in the lucrative IVORY TRADE.

One of the better known *degredados* was Antonio Fernandes, who was sent to Mozambique in southern East Africa. On three separate journeys between 1512 and 1516, his task was to reconnoiter the land and the indigenous peoples of the interior to see if there were prospects for trade. Fernandes's stories about the fabulous amounts of gold produced by the MWENE MUTAPA kingdom convinced some Portuguese that they had found the biblical land of Ophir, the legendary place where the queen of Sheba supposedly acquired her gold gifts for King Solomon.

Some of the offspring of Cape Verdean *degredados* and their indigenous wives formed a caste known as *lançados*, who were acculturated into both the European and African societies. *Lançados* acted as independent trade intermediaries, but those who took to illegal smuggling harmed the established Portuguese trade monopolies. Still other *degredados* joined the ranks of the *sertanejos* (backwoodsmen), Portuguese men who adapted well to the difficult conditions of the interior areas south of the ZAMBEZI RIVER. The *sertanejos* often became subjects of the local rulers in order to participate in their trade fairs.

See also: MAKEDA, QUEEN (QUEEN OF SHEBA) (Vol. I); PORTUGAL AND AFRICA (Vol. III).

Further reading: Malyn Newitt, ed., *The First Portuguese Colonial Empire* (Highlands, N.J.: Humanities Press, 1986).

Delagoa Bay Bay located on the southern Indian Ocean coast of present-day MOZAMBIQUE. Delagoa Bay was charted by the Portuguese during Vasco da Gama's expedition in 1502. In 1544, a Portuguese merchant named Lourenço Marques was the first European to explore the area . Originally Delagoa was a depot for Indian Ocean trading vessels. Later it became an ivory-trading market and a primary center for the trading of Africans abducted from ZIMBABWE, Mozambique, and the South African interior.

At the height of the local slave trade, in the first half of the 19th century, Delagoa was exporting several thousand captive Africans per year. The bay would later serve as a TRANSPORTATION and commercial gateway for the South African GOLD mines.

The word *Delagoa* derives from *Goa,* the name of a maritime trading port on the west coast of mainland India. In 1510 the Portuguese seized Goa, as part of their attempts to monopolize the sea routes to the lucrative Indian spice trade. To arrive at Goa, Portuguese ships had to make the long and treacherous journey around the southern tip of Africa, up the African east coast, and across the western reaches of the Indian Ocean. Once Goa had been established, it became important for the Portuguese to secure the coastal regions of southern East Africa as well. In the 16th century, then, the entire coastal region related to the Indian spice trade fell under the rule of the viceroy at Goa, and the stretch of African mainland was appropriately named Delagoa (Portuguese for "relating to Goa").

See also: DELAGOA BAY (Vol. IV); GAMA, VASCO DA (Vol. II); LOURENÇO MARQUES (Vol. IV); PORTUGAL AND AFRICA (Vol. III).

Further reading: Malyn Newitt, *A History of Mozambique* (Bloomington, Ind.: Indiana University Press, 1995).

Denianke dynasty (Denyanke) Dynasty of FULANI kings who ruled FOUTA TORO, a region in present-day northern SENEGAL, from the mid-16th century to the late 18th century. The founder of the Denianke dynasty was Koli TENGELLA (fl. c. 1530), who took charge of the army founded by his father, the Fulani chief Tengella (d. c. 1512). The elder Tengella was killed in battle against the forces of Amar, the brother of SONGHAI ruler Askia MUHAMMAD TOURÉ (r. 1493–1528). Koli Tengella then collected the remaining soldiers of his father's army and led them southwest, over the Senegal River, to a region known as Badiar. In this region he recruited a group of Mandinka warriors loyal to his cause and continued to travel until they reached the former Tuareg state of Tekrur in the northern parts of what is now Senegal. In 1559 the combined Fulani and Mandinka forces invaded Tekrur, overthrowing the ruling SONINKE.

Koli Tengella then established the state of Fouta Toro and began a ruling dynasty known thereafter as Denianke. The Denianke kings were called *silatigui*, meaning "commander." Throughout their successful two-century rule they never converted to Islam, despite the fact the religion was quickly spreading among the region's other Fulani groups.

By the early 18th century the dynasty was weakened by succession wars and attacks from the Muslim Brakna

Moors. An Islamic marabout, or mystical religious leader, named Suleyman Bal (fl. c. 1770s) took advantage of Denianke vulnerability to declare a jihad (holy war) in 1776. As a result of the successful jihad, Fouta Toro was declared an Islamic state.

See also: MUHAMMAD TOURÉ, ASKIA (Vol. II); MANDINKA (Vols. II, IV); TEKRUR (Vol. II); TUAREGS (Vols. II, III).

Denkyira (Denkyera) AKAN subgroup and the state they founded in the forest regions of present-day southwestern GHANA. In the late 16th century the Denkyira began to form a larger collective state out of several smaller Denkyira kingdoms. Over the next 100 years or so the Denkyira state expanded its territorial boundaries to encompass much of the southwestern region of Ghana and parts of what is now IVORY COAST. The state was ruled during this time by the kings of the Agona dynasty, who conquered the ADANSI people and seized the Ashanti capital of KUMASI by 1659. At its height the Denkyira kingdom also dominated the West African GOLD trade by controlling the trade routes in the western regions that connected the gold-producing territories with European coastal outposts, such as ELMINA Castle.

Denkyira was so rich in gold that the *denkyirahene* (Denkyira king) adorned most everything from shields to swords to ornaments with the precious metal. Denkyirahene Boa Amponsem (r. c. 1677–1692) commissioned the first Denkyira GOLDEN STOOL as a representation of the wealth and power of the kingdom and its people.

With its capital situated on the Ofin River at the city of Abankeseso, Denkyira thrived at its location near the heart of the gold-producing region. Since the smaller states it conquered were in the gold-MINING business as well, Denkyira became one of the wealthiest states in the region by the latter part of the 17th century. With its riches, Denkyira maintained a well-trained army that was successfully incorporated into the civilian government. The *denkyirahene* remained the highest authority over the army. Even with its powerful army, Denkyira tended to lack an overall cohesiveness, and some conquered territories were not completely integrated into the kingdom.

Despite its political problems Denkyira remained an important kingdom until the turn of the 18th century. Around that time the ASHANTI EMPIRE, also of the forest regions of present-day Ghana, was rapidly conquering the

gold-producing regions once held by Denkyira. By 1701 Denkyira itself had fallen to the forces of Asantehene (Ashanti king) OSEI TUTU (c. 1650–1717). A decade later the Denkyira attempted to overthrow the Ashanti but were once again soundly defeated, forcing many Denkyira to migrate to the east into territories ruled by the AKYEM peoples.

Further reading: Ivor Wilks, *Forests of Gold: Essays on the Akan and the Kingdom of Asante* (Athens, Ohio: Ohio University Press, 1993).

Denmark and Africa In the early part of the 17th century Denmark became interested in trading along the Guinea Coast in West Africa. In 1625 Jon de Willum established the Danish-Africa Company, a nationalized slave-trading company, to pursue this trade. In 1658 the Danish king, Frederik III (d. 1670), granted a monopoly to merchants hailing from Gluckstadt and Copenhagen on the condition that they maintain the formerly Swedish fort of Carolusborg situated along the GOLD COAST in present-day GHANA. These merchants later built the trading forts of Frederiksborg (1659) and Christiansborg (1661), where they traded for captives with the AKWAMU people, among others. In 1685, when Frederiksborg was acquired by the British ROYAL AFRICAN COMPANY after failure to repay a loan, Christiansborg became the primary departure point for African captives being shipped to LABOR on the sugar plantations in the Danish West Indies.

The Danish trade monopoly was lifted in 1735, granting all Danish subjects equal opportunities along the West African coast. The forts of Fredensborg and Augustaborg were built to further capitalize on the lucrative coastal slave trade. During the late 18th century a Danish governor named Kioge led an effort to seize Dutch possessions along the Guinea Coast and build the fortresses of Prinsensten and Kongensten. These last two forts gave the Danes a presence along the SLAVE COAST, east of the Volta River. But with the abolition of the slave trade in the early 19th century, Denmark's African possessions greatly decreased in value. Ultimately, the Danes sold their African assets to the British government in 1849.

See also: SLAVERY (Vols. I, III, IV); SLAVE TRADE, THE TRANSATLANTIC (Vol. III).

Dhlo-Dhlo (Dhlodhlo, Danagombe) Town located near Bulawayo, ZIMBABWE. In the late 17th century Dhlo-Dhlo became the successor to KHAMI as the capital city of the Torwa state that developed on the southern margins of the Zimbabwe plateau. Smaller than Khami, which had a population perhaps as large as 7,000, Dhlo-Dhlo had an architectural style that was similar to that of its predecessor.

Archaeological evidence indicates that Dhlo-Dhlo may have had trade contacts with Muslim merchants from the commercial towns of the SWAHILI COAST. It also might have traded through intermediaries with Portuguese merchants operating in the southeast African interior. The town's inhabitants probably traded GOLD, copper, and ivory in exchange for rare items like pottery, cloth, and glass beads that came to the East African coast via the Indian Ocean trade routes. By 1700 Dhlo-Dhlo and the entire Torwa state had probably come under the control of the ROZWI state.

Archaeologists have excavated what they believe is the town's main building. It is made up of two large, tiered platforms, the higher of which has a retaining wall nearly 20 feet (6 m) in height. The Dhlo-Dhlo ruins are notable for their intricately patterned walls covered in various herringbone, cord, and checkered patterns.

See also: ARCHAEOLOGY (Vols. I, II, III, IV, V); GREAT ZIMBABWE (Vol. II).

Diarra, Monson (r. 1790–1808) *Ruler of the Bambara state of Segu*

When the reigning *fama* (king), Ngolo DIARRA, died in 1790, his two sons, Nianankoro and Monson, began a struggle for the right to assume power in the kingdom of SEGU, located in present-day Republic of MALI. Monson fought for the throne from his camp at the city of Segu-Sikoro and eventually succeeded in imprisoning his brother and claiming the title of *fama*. Monson's main challenge thereafter came from the kingdom of KAARTA when King Dessé Koro (r. 1788–1799) attempted to gain control of Segu during the period of weakness caused by the succession struggle. Monson responded in 1794 by demolishing Kaarta, thereby establishing Segu as the more powerful of the BAMBARA kingdoms. Monson successfully ruled Segu until his death at the city of Sirakoro in 1808. Although several rulers in the Diarra dynasty followed, Monson was considered the last of the powerful rulers to extend the territory and control of the Segu kingdom.

Diarra, Ngolo (Ngolo Dyara, Ngolo Diara, Ngolo Jara) (r. 1766–1790) *Warrior under Mamari Kulibali who became the* fama, *or ruler, of the second Segu dynasty, in what is now Republic of Mali*

After the death of Mamari KULIBALI (r. 1712–1755), the SEGU government disintegrated and the kingdom was plagued with social unrest and civil war. For more than a decade the kingdom was ruled by a series of weak leaders whose reigns were both tumultuous and short-lived. From out of these circumstances emerged Ngolo Diarra, who seized the throne and consolidated the kingdom in 1766. He was a capable leader who was able to appease both his Muslim subjects and those who practiced Segu's traditional religion. Although he did not actually convert to Islam, he learned the Quran—the Muslim holy book—and often enlisted the help of Muslim clerics in settling internal disputes. He maintained good relations with the Muslim trading communities by not only protecting their interests but also allowing them a certain degree of autonomy.

During his reign Ngolo Diarra expanded the Segu territory by defeating both his FULANI and MACINA enemies. Ngolo Diarra's death in 1790 sparked another civil war as his sons vied for the throne. He was succeeded by his son Monson DIARRA.

See also: ISLAM, INFLUENCE OF (Vols. II, III, IV, V).

Dingiswayo (d. 1818) *Chief of the Mthethwa (Mtetwa) clan of the Nguni peoples; ruler of the region that would become Zululand*

Dingiswayo introduced to the Mthethwa the practice of maintaining a standing army, which he used to secure his supremacy over nearly 30 other NGUNI clans occupying the region between the Umfolozi and Tugela rivers, in present-day SOUTH AFRICA.

A rival Nguni chief named Zwide assassinated Dingiswayo in 1818. In turn, Dingiswayo's handpicked successor, SHAKA (1787–1828), defeated Zwide in the same year and continued Dingiswayo's system of nation-building. The result of Shaka's efforts was the birth of the ZULU nation.

Further reading: James O. Gump, *The Formation of the Zulu Kingdom in South Africa, 1750–1840* (San Francisco: EM Texts, 1990).

Dinka (Jieng, Moinjaang) Ethnic group in southeastern Republic of the SUDAN that is made up of more than 25 clans, including the Agar, Aliab, Bor, Rek, and Malual. The Dinka have long been seminomadic pastoralists. Throughout the 18th and 19th centuries the Dinka expanded their territory through the conquest of neighboring peoples. The result of this was that some of these peoples, including the NUER, were permanently displaced from their homelands.

In time, however, the Dinka were weakened by attacks from Muslim and Egyptian raiders, who brought Dinka captives to sell at interior markets in DARFUR and SENNAR, and to SUAKIN on the Red Sea coast. Despite their weakened state the Dinka vehemently resisted attempts by foreign powers to subjugate them. By the early part of the 19th century, however, Dinka territories were under Ottoman-Egyptian control.

See also: DINKA (Vol. II).

Further reading: Francis Mading Deng, *Dinka of the Sudan* (Long Grove, Ill.: Waveland Press, 1984).

disease in precolonial Africa

disease in precolonial Africa The presence of Europeans in western, eastern, and southern Africa had a profound effect on the diseases faced by African peoples. In addition to the diseases that Africans normally faced in their environment, new diseases and more virulent outbreaks of older diseases affected the population as a result of contact with Europeans.

The State of Medicine and Disease Control The state of European MEDICINE at the time of first contact with West Africa and continuing until the rise of modern scientific medicine in the 19th century was not sophisticated. Modern-day standards of sanitation and hygiene were rarely met in the major cities of Europe. Physicians had not yet isolated the factors that cause disease. For example, the root meaning of the word *malaria,* Italian for "bad air," indicates what early physicians thought brought about the typical chills and high fever of malaria. It was not until 1880 that the true cause was discovered: parasitic protozoans in the bloodstream spread by the bite of the *Anopheles* mosquito, especially *Anopheles gambiae* and *Anopheles funestus,* which feed and rest indoors.

Possibly aware of the contagious nature of malaria, the Mano people of what is now LIBERIA set aside a "sick bush" away from the village where malaria sufferers would be quarantined and nursed back to health by a single individual. Treatment with poultices would retard scratching and control infection. After the patient recovered, the area would be cleaned by fire.

In a centuries-old practice found throughout Africa, a thorn is used to scrape pus from a sore of an infected person into the skin of a healthy person as protection against smallpox.

Neither the indigenous populations nor colonists in the New World and in Africa were immune to major epidemics, although indigenous peoples suffered more and perished in greater numbers when they encountered a disease to which they had built up no natural immunity. In 1702, for instance, an outbreak of yellow fever, a disease African in origin, killed 10 percent of the inhabitants of New York City. Colonists in Boston faced major outbreaks of smallpox in 1666, 1677–78, 1702–03, and 1721–22.

Epidemics among African peoples, previously unexposed to smallpox, were more severe. Open conflict, first in 1659 and again in 1673–77, between the European residents of the CAPE COLONY and the local KHOIKHOI

population near the Cape of Good Hope, at the southern tip of SOUTH AFRICA, led to the imprisonment or death of many thousands of Khoikhoi. By 1677 there were only a few thousand Khoikhoi, and a smallpox epidemic in 1713 killed most of those who were left.

The aftereffects of disease sometimes transcended borders. When Spanish colonists tried to enslave the Taino (Arawak) peoples of Hispaniola (present-day Haiti and the Dominican Republic) in the West Indies to work on sugar plantations, a major epidemic of smallpox killed most of the indigenous population of the island by 1550. The Spanish then imported captives taken from Africa to provide the missing LABOR. Much dreaded, smallpox traveled in slave ships and along the trails into Central Africa and grew as the European trade of human captives expanded in the 17th and 18th centuries.

The experiments of the English physician Edward Jenner (1749–1823) to isolate a smallpox vaccine did not begin until 1796. Vaccination (injecting a small, weakened amount of a virulent material to generate immunity to its less benign form) was a major innovation. Jenner's work was so successful that by 1840 the British government banned alternate preventive treatments.

On the other hand, fear of contracting malaria, common inland and a disease to which Europeans had no immunity, kept Europeans from traveling into the interior of Africa except in more temperate regions, such as in South Africa. This curtailed the development of settlements any distance from the coast. Until World War II (1939–45), malaria was treatable (though not fully curable) only by quinine, which was made from cinchona bark, a tree native to the Andes Mountains of South America and brought to Europe for this purpose by Jesuits from Peru in about 1640. The extract was rare, however, because the tree had to be destroyed to obtain it. A more effective synthetic was finally created from coal tar in 1944. Until then access to the drug was limited by short supply and lack of information. It was not until late in the 19th century, for instance, that even the wealthiest and most informed traders in Central Africa were aware of the benefits of quinine.

The Europeans of earlier times who contracted malaria were likely to face a life of intermittent illness. Malaria is an acute, chronic disease characterized by recurring bouts of chills and fever, anemia, enlargement of the spleen, and often fatal complications. Many Africans, on the other hand, were resistant to the malignant and benign forms of this disease. The sickle-cell trait in the red blood cells of Africans limits the growth of *Plasmodium falciparum,* the parasite that causes malignant tertian malaria; and a genetic trait of these imune Africans, the absence of DARC (the Duffy antigen receptor for chemokines), limits the ability of *Plasmodium vivax,* the parasite that causes benign tertian malaria, to invade red blood cells.

Islamic culture added another element into the cultural mix of Africa, especially in its attention to hygiene. Inhabitants of the major Islamic cities and towns, for instance, including ones in North Africa and Muslim sub-Saharan Africa, enjoyed access to *hammam*, or public baths, because cleanliness was part of faith, whereas Europeans well into the 17th century considered frequently washing the body a dangerous custom.

Islamic medicine and Western medicine existed in parallel. African converts in CAPE TOWN, South Africa, in the 1700s and later were often drawn to Islam because they desired access to Muslim healers. Sufi sheiks, or local religious leaders, were often associated with healing, which combined herbal remedies and religious rituals.

Foreign and Domestic Causes of Disease

Diseases specific to Africa and other regions near the equator are known in Western medicine as *tropical diseases,* and the branch of medicine that treats them is called *tropical medicine.* Africa before the arrival of Portuguese explorers, traders, and MISSIONARIES was not a pristine continent untouched by outside influences. Although the indigenous peoples of Africa died in great numbers from diseases first encountered after contact with Europeans, they suffered less than the more isolated peoples of the New World after comparable exposure to new diseases. It is thought that partial exposure through long-term contact with Arab trans-Saharan traders from North Africa may have allowed local peoples in West Africa to develop some degree of immunity to diseases of the Mediterranean world. The Arab presence from about 1020 in the kingdoms along the Indian Ocean may have brought similar benefits to the peoples of East Africa, although Arab traders rarely ventured far inland from the SWAHILI COAST.

The interior, however, faced pressure from other sources. Between 1000 BCE and 1000 CE sub-Saharan Africa was the scene of the western and southern migrations of Bantu-speaking peoples, one of the largest in human history, from their original homelands near the present-day border between CAMEROON and NIGERIA to almost the entire southern portion of Africa. It is thought that by entering these lands, they inadvertently brought diseases to which the indigenous SAN and Khoikhoi lacked immunity and to which they succumbed in large numbers by the 16th century. Further, by clearing forest land for cultivation, the Bantu-speaking peoples increased the habitat of disease-bearing mosquitoes, causing further loss of life, including their own. As cities such as Gao, TIMBUKTU, and KANO grew more populous, inhabitants became more susceptible to feces-borne diseases such as dysentery and typhus and infectious diseases such as tuberculosis transmitted by close contact with carriers.

The interior of Africa was further affected by the development of the TRANSATLANTIC SLAVE TRADE in the early 1500s. Contact with Europeans introduced smallpox, measles, and nonnative forms of syphilis to sub-Saharan Africa, and Africans escaping slave raids were forced to move into less hospitable regions, where they faced greater exposure to mosquitoes and to tsetse flies, which cause sleeping sickness.

Measles It is unknown how many Africans succumbed to measles when Portuguese carriers introduced it to sub-Saharan Africa in the latter half of the 15th century. However, epidemics of measles, smallpox, and influenza decreased the population of Mexico from 25 million to 6.5 million before the arrival of the Spanish conquistador Hernán Cortés (1485–1547), in 1519. Measles is not usually a killer of adults; however, its splotchy eruptions were often found on the faces of children. Measles sometimes led to death from pneumonia and diarrhea, especially if the children were malnourished and living in overcrowded rural settings. A vaccine—unfortunately one that is not stable in tropical regions—was not developed until the 1960s. A replacement more suited to hot climates is under development.

River Blindness Onchocerciasis, or river blindness, is another native African disease that spread because of the TRANSPORTATION of African captives to Central and South America. The disease is caused by parasitical filarial, or thread-like, worms carried by a biting blackfly, the simulium, which breed in streams and rivers. The adult worms live under the skin and cause unsightly nodules; their larvae, however, travel to the eye, where they die, disintegrate, and often damage the cornea, causing blindness. The disease also produces changes in skin pigmentation, often causing an unsightly leopard-like mottling. People who live along rivers are most often affected. The land for several miles on either side of the VOLTA RIVER in West Africa, infested by tsetse flies and simulium flies, is largely uninhabited.

Schistosomiasis Schistosomiasis is a parasitical infection carried by small aquatic snails and transmitted to humans when they bathe in water contaminated by urine or feces that contains the parasite. The disease is widespread in sub-Saharan Africa and causes severe damage to the bladder and kidneys. Native to Africa, schistosomiasis spread to South America and the West Indies as a result of the trade of African captives.

Sleeping Sickness Trypanosomiasis, or sleeping sickness, is a parasitical infection of the blood and the brain that is caused by a protozoan flagellate called a *trypanosome,* which is a one-celled parasite with a sperm-like tail. The trypan-osome enters the bloodstream of humans or domestic animals, especially cattle, dogs, and horses, when they are bitten by a bloodsucking tsetse fly. Sleeping sickness exists in both human and animal forms (formally called trypanosomiasis in humans and nagana in animals), and because tsetse flies prefer African game animals as hosts, the range of this disease is limited to sub-Saharan Africa. Until the start of the 20th century the cause and the method of transmission of this disease were unknown.

The early stages of the disease may appear weeks, months, or even years after infection. The variant caused by *Tripanosoma brucei gambiense,* found in West and Central Africa, often takes years to reach an advanced stage, but the more malignant form, caused by *Tripanosoma brucei rhodesiense,* found in eastern and southern Africa, is fatal within weeks. The first symptoms include swollen lymph glands, followed by fever, general weakness and body ache, headache, and itching. In the disease's advanced stage the victim experiences delirium, convulsions, and sleep disturbances, followed by a state of extreme lethargy, coma, and death.

Sleeping sickness has had a profound effect on Africa. Cattle from North Africa could not survive below the Sahel because of the tsetse fly. Plowing by oxen can be done only in those drier areas of East and South Africa that are free from the tsetse fly; otherwise, hand hoes must be used, limiting productivity. In areas where tsetse flies are numerous, the land cannot be used for AGRICULTURE. The presence of the tsetse fly and the threat of sleeping sickness, however, kept European farming from expanding northward from southern settlements.

Syphilis and Related Diseases The sexually transmitted disease (STD) most closely associated with Africa at present is HIV (human immunodeficiency virus), but that disease and its related syndromes are of 20th-century origin. The most significant STDs in sub-Saharan Africa after the start of European contact were syphilis, yaws, and gonorrhea. Syphilis and gonorrhea may have come to Africa by direct contact with Europeans or through contact inland with infected individuals. According to early historians of southern Africa, syphilis was not present there among Africans when the Europeans first settled. The ZULU people called it "the disease of the town" or "the white man's disease."

Some medical researchers believe that yaws is a tropical, rural form of syphilis. Yaws are caused by a spiral-shaped bacterium, or spirochete, called *Treponema pertenue,* that closely resembles the *Treponema pallidium* spirochete that causes syphilis. There is speculation that both diseases may have a common ancestor in equatorial Africa. Yaws, however, which is endemic, or native, to large parts of Africa, is not transmitted by sexual contact but by close nonsexual contact aggravated by overcrowding and poor hygiene. Health complications from yaws later in life are significantly less common than they are from syphilis.

Early health workers in Africa often misdiagnosed this disease as syphilis because the lesions are similar. There is also a second form of syphilis in Africa, called *bejel* in Arabic, that is medically categorized as endemic syphilis. This form of the disease is caused by the same *Treponema pallidium* spirochete that causes venereal, or sexually transmitted, syphilis; but endemic syphilis is spread by nonsexual contact between children in unhygienic environments and, unlike venereal syphilis, rarely affects the central nervous system. Endemic syphilis was most common among the pastoralist peoples living in the areas of present-day CHAD, NIGER, Republic of MALI, and SENEGAL.

Traditional cures for STD symptoms were extremely limited until recent times. For centuries, medicine men and healers were called upon to eradicate diseases. The Bantu-speaking Swazi people of SWAZILAND, who thought that STDs were transmitted only through infidelity or by breaking a taboo, best illustrate traditional beliefs. Only a tribal healer could treat the disease because only he would understand the unique cause. Some peoples, such as the XHOSA people of South Africa, believed that STDs were evil curses caused by witchcraft. Treatment might include performing a special ceremony or ingesting herbal remedies, although these remedies usually met with limited success.

Yellow Fever Yellow fever is a viral disease native to Africa that was carried to the New World by African captives in the transatlantic SLAVE TRADE. It has since spread to other tropical regions. Yellow fever originated in African tree-dwelling monkeys and is generally transmitted from monkey to monkey by the *Aëdes africanus* mosquito and to humans by the *Aëdes aegypti* mosquito, which breeds in water containers and bites humans.

Yellow fever epidemics were rare in Africa before Europeans arrived in the late 1400s; the antibodies from other mosquito-transmitted viruses largely protected humans from infection and the disease was slow to spread. However, when Europeans began clearing forests to establish plantations and the habitats of other mosquitoes decreased, breeding sites of *Aëdes aegypti* increased, and epidemics of yellow fever became a serious problem. In the 19th century yellow-fever outbreaks among European explorers and colonists in West Africa were often misdiagnosed as malaria. The virus causing yellow fever was not isolated until 1927 when the virulent *Asibi* strain was identified in the blood of a man from GHANA. A highly effective vaccine was subsequently produced.

Symptoms of yellow fever appear several days after the victim is bitten. They include jaundice (a yellowing of the skin and eyes) and two or three days of severe headache, backache, rising fever, nausea, and vomiting, ending in recovery or a more severe attack characterized by high fever, the vomiting of blood, and death a few days.

See also: DISEASE IN ANCIENT AFRICA (Vol. I); DISEASE IN MEDIEVAL AFRICA (Vol. II); DISEASE IN COLONIAL AFRICA (Vol. IV); DISEASE IN INDEPENDENT AFRICA (Vol. V); TSETSE FLIES (Vol. II).

Further reading: Gerald W. Hartwig and K. David Patterson, eds., *Disease in African History: An Introductory Survey and Case Studies* (Durham, N.C.: Duke Univ. Press, 1978); Oliver Ransford, *Bid the Sickness Cease: Disease in the History of Black Africa* (London: J. Murray, 1983).

Djibouti, Republic of Small present-day East African country measuring about 9,000 square miles (23,300 sq km) and located on the Gulf of Aden. Djibouti shares its borders with ERITREA, ETHIOPIA, and SOMALIA. The city of Djibouti has served as the country's main port since about 1888 and as the capital city since 1892.

For centuries the two major ethnic groups that have inhabited the region in and around the Republic of Djibouti are the Afars and the Issas. Both groups are Islamic, have a nomadic history, and share many traditions and beliefs. The main difference between these tribes is in their social and political systems. The AFAR people subscribe to a hierarchical structure in which chiefdoms and sultanates hold the majority of the power while the social system of the Issas— among the males, at least—is egalitarian, meaning that all Issa men have an equal voice in matters of their own clan.

Having no NATURAL RESOURCES of their own to depend on, the people of Djibouti have relied on the importance of their region to Ethiopian coastal trade to support their ECONOMY. Afar and Issa leaders maintained their economies by charging tariffs on all caravans heading inland. Except for the Portuguese, who were involved in East African trade beginning early in the 16th century, it was primarily Muslims who controlled trade in the Horn of Africa. The three main ports in the region were Tadjoura, Obock, and ZEILA, which had long been used by Muslim Arab traders. In the 19th century the French became increasingly interested in Ethiopian trade and developed commercial and trading ties with both the Afar and Issa.

See also: ADEN, GULF OF (Vol. II); DJIBOUTI, REPUBLIC OF (Vols. I, II, IV, V); DJIBOUTI, CITY OF (Vols. I, V).

Dongola (Dunqulah, Dunkula) Nile River town in the northern part of the present-day country of Republic of the SUDAN. From the sixth to the 14th centuries Dongola served as the capital of MAQURRA, a Christian kingdom closely related to the kingdom of Nubia, to the north. After the collapse of Nubia in the 14th century, Dongola was taken by Muslim forces. Later, in the 16th century, the city became the headquarters of a Muslim state that extended north as far as the third cataract of the Nile. The state was controlled by the powerful FUNJ dynasty of SENNAR to the south.

In the 17th century several influential Islamic centers of learning were founded along the White Nile near Sennar. One of these schools, the Shayqiyah, pushed for independence, and Dongola subsequently came under the rule of local chieftains. Soon major trade routes were diverted around Dongola, and the town quickly declined.

When present-day Dongola, sometimes referred to as New Dongola, was established along the west bank of the Nile in the early 1800s, the old town to the southeast lay in ruins.

See also: DONGOLA BEND (Vol. I); NUBIA (Vol. I); NUBIA, CHRISTIAN (Vols. I, II).

Dutch East India Company (United East India Company) Trading organization established in the early 17th century to promote Dutch activities in the Indian Ocean. In 1602 a group of Dutch merchants banded together to protect their trade in the Indian Ocean. They were given a charter from the Dutch government, which granted the company a monopoly eastward from the Cape of Good Hope. The company was given the right to enter into treaties, build forts, maintain armies, and administer territories through officials loyal to the Dutch government.

At first the Dutch East India Company was not particularly interested in the African continent, focusing instead on the Indonesian spice trade. The company chose Batavia (present-day Jakarta) in Java as its headquarters. Their efforts proved fruitful, and the company prospered as a profitable arm of the Dutch trade empire. By the mid-17th century the company had successfully displaced British and Portuguese endeavors in the East Indies.

The Dutch East India Company needed a safe port about halfway between Europe and the East Indies, so the area around the southern tip of Africa was a logical place to establish a settlement. Originally they chose a location on St. Helena Bay, but they relocated farther south to CAPE TOWN, near the Cape of Good Hope, about 1652.

Late in the 17th century the company became less interested in Indian Ocean trade and focused its energies on its affairs in Java. By the beginning of the 18th century the Dutch East India Company had transformed from a trading power into an organization devoted to agricultural production on the Indonesian archipelago. At the Cape Town settlement, Dutch BOERS had begun extensive farming operations in the fertile surrounding region. To keep production costs reasonable, the Dutch began importing captives from West Africa and India to work their farms. Their agricultural products were used to supply Dutch ships heading to the East Indies and were also traded with local KHOIKHOI pastoralists. The early interaction between the Boers and the local populations was generally peaceful, but as the Dutch extended their farms farther into the interior, skirmishes became common, especially with the Khoikhoi. Riddled with debt and corruption, the company was dissolved by the Dutch government in 1799, and British representatives assumed responsibility for the company's CAPE COLONY.

See also: DUTCH WEST INDIA COMPANY (Vol. III); NETHERLANDS AND AFRICA (Vol. III).

Further reading: Nigel Worden, *Slavery in Dutch South Africa* (New York: Cambridge Univ. Press, 1985).

Dutch West India Company (West India Company)

Organization established in 1621 to capitalize on trade between Africa and the Americas. The company was founded primarily with the purpose of overtaking the Spanish and Portuguese trade monopoly in the West Indies and South America. During the 1630s the Dutch West India Company seized sizable areas of Brazil from the Portuguese. In order to support the Brazilian plantation ECONOMY the company initiated a campaign to conquer Portuguese trading bases in West Africa. This plan proved successful as the Dutch became the primary transporter of African captives across the Atlantic. They also briefly held ANGOLA but then lost it to the Portuguese.

By the late 1640s the Portuguese had begun to direct their energies toward protecting their colonies. They expelled the Dutch from many of their former territories and regained control of the trade of human captives south of the equator. The Dutch West India Company, however, did maintain its supremacy north of the equator. In the 1660s England and France sought to degrade the Dutch status as a major trading power by establishing their own trading companies. Suffering from depleted resources, the Dutch West India Company gradually succumbed to the competition. The company was eventually placed under government control and was permanently dissolved in 1794.

See also: DUTCH EAST INDIA COMPANY (Vol. III); NETHERLANDS AND AFRICA (Vol. III); ROYAL AFRICA COMPANY (Vol. III).

Further reading: C. R. Boxer, *The Dutch Seaborne Empire, 1600–1800* (New York: Knopf, 1965).

Dyakanke (Jahanka, Jahanque, Diakkanke)

Mande-speaking ethnic group in West Africa. The Muslim Dyakanke are believed to have originated in Dia, a trading town in the FULANI kingdom of MACINA, near the Niger Bend in present-day central Republic of MALI. Eventually they migrated to western Mali near the Bafing River, a tributary of the Senegal River, where they set up their own commercial center. Throughout the 17th century Dyakanke settlements were established on important trade routes in regions that today are in The GAMBIA and SENEGAL. Walled Dyakanke towns were heavily protected to prevent rivals from interfering with their trade.

Dyula (Douala, Jula, Diula, Wangara, Kangan)

Muslim traders who make up an ethnic minority in the present-day countries of BURKINA FASO, Republic of MALI, CAMEROON, The GAMBIA, IVORY COAST, GHANA, GUINEA-BISSAU, and SENEGAL. The Dyula are made up of Mande-speaking people thought to have originated in equatorial Africa. Little is known about their history prior to the 13th century, at which time they emerged as the primary merchant class of the Mali Empire. Eventually the term *dyula* came to mean "trader" or "merchant," with Malinke, BAMBARA, and SONINKE individuals all being called *dyula*.

The Dyula created a commercial network throughout West Africa, trading kola nuts, textiles, salt, and GOLD. According to many scholars, the Dyula are largely responsible for increasing textile manufacturing throughout West Africa during the 16th and 17th centuries. Another major contribution of the Dyula was their influence on the culture of the western Sahel. Through their trade networks, they helped to spread Islam as well as styles and techniques of Arabian and Sudanic ARCHITECTURE.

Because of their interest in trade, most Dyula settled in busy commercial centers throughout West Africa. Northern centers included the trans-Saharan trading cities of TIMBUKTU and JENNE, near the Niger Bend and BAMAKO, in Mali. To the west, Dyula traders could be found in Senegal and The Gambia, and as far east as the HAUSA STATES. Southern Dyula settlements extended as far south as the AKAN states of coastal Ghana, which were connected to the northern settlements by a chain of Dyula-occupied kingdoms and cities including BONO, BEGHO, GONJA, BANDA, KONG, and Bobo Dioulasso. The Dyula were spread out over a wide territory and lived among various ethnic groups, many of whom treated them as second-class citizens. Despite their intermingling with other peoples, however, the Dyula were able to retain their unique identity.

See also: DYULA (Vols. I, II, IV).

Further reading: Robert Launay, *Beyond the Stream: Islam and Society in a West African Town* (Berkeley, Calif.: Univ. of California Press, 1992); Robert Launay, *Traders Without Trade: Responses to Change in Two Dyula Communities* (New York: Cambridge Univ. Press, 1982).

E

ebony A hardwood tree producing heavy, dark wood that is prized for its color and durability. Used to make masks, figurines, and even swords, ebony wood has been a trade item in Africa since before the common era. Arabian, Persian, and Indian traders supplied ebony to artisans and craftspeople in their homelands as long-distance Indian Ocean trade developed in the first millennium, but the popularity of the wood increased tremendously with the arrival of Europeans in the 15th century. The clearing of ebony forests continued steadily through the next few centuries as European furniture-makers and craftspeople demanded more and more of the precious hardwood.

Ebony trees were found throughout Africa, but were especially concentrated in regions of what are now the countries of ANGOLA, The GAMBIA, GABON, SOUTH AFRICA, and TOGO. Thick stands of ebony trees grew also on the island now known as MAURITIUS, east of MADAGASCAR in the Indian Ocean. In the 17th century Dutch colonists on Mauritius reaped huge profits by harvesting virtually all of the ebony on the island and shipping the wood to be sold in Europe.

See also: EBONY (Vol. I); MASKS (Vol. I); NATURAL RESOURCES (Vols. III, IV, V).

economy In the centuries immediately after 1500, AGRICULTURE continued to be the base of the economy for most African societies, with most African peoples producing their own FOOD. However, Africa's economy was not based strictly on subsistence farming. Its population growth and social complexity increasingly led to corresponding growth in TRADE AND COMMERCE.

One reason for this increased trading activity was the need for iron tools and weapons. But not all societies had equal access to workable deposits of iron, a situation that helped promote trade among communities at the local level.

The markets that emerged to serve people at the local level also had ties to long-distance trade. Extensive trans-Saharan trade in GOLD, salt, and commodities such as CLOTH AND TEXTILES, books, and leather goods, continued to expand to serve local markets as well as more distant markets.

The arrival of Europeans via the sea about 1500 served to stimulate the economy of the coastal zones, particularly in West Africa. After that time the peoples of the coast and its hinterland had a more immediate means of making trading contacts with the external world. Previously they had to rely on the more remote interior routes across the Sahara.

In North Africa the growing strength of the Ottoman Empire also stimulated the economy, especially in terms of Mediterranean trade. Ultimately, however, clashes between Europe and the Ottoman Empire did more damage than good to the economies of the North African port cities.

More significantly the new trade contacts with Europe were ultimately to prove deleterious to sub-Saharan Africa. This was due to the dramatic rise of the transatlantic SLAVE TRADE, which began in the 17th century and continued for more than 200 years. The trade in human captives diverted a significant amount of African LABOR from productive uses within Africa to production in the Americas for the benefit of Europe and its American colonies. This was true for both manual and skilled workers. Moreover, within Africa the slave trade diverted the focus of much of the economy from the essential work of internal development to the task of gathering captives to serve as the human cargo of the slave ships. In this and many other ways the slave trade served to distort the natural development of an African economy. During this period the slave trade was just one of the several ways in which exploitation of the continent's resources for the benefit of the Western world was beginning to replace development of these resources for the benefit of Africans.

See also: ECONOMY (Vols. I, II, IV, V); OTTOMAN EMPIRE AND AFRICA (Vols. III, IV).

Further reading: Ralph A. Austen, *African Economic History* (Portsmouth, N.H.: Heinemann, 1987).

Efik People located mainly in the lower CROSS RIVER region of present-day southeast NIGERIA. The early 17th-century migrations of the Efik people down the Cross River led them to found the trading center of OLD CALABAR and the adjoining settlements of Creek Town, Old Town (or Obutong), Duke Town (or Atakpa), Henshaw Town, and Qua Town.

A subgroup of the IBIBIO people, the Efik speak a Kwa language known as Efik-Ibibio. They were traditionally a fishing and trading society. From the 17th through the mid-19th centuries the Efik successfully traded fish, PALM OIL, and bananas with both neighbors and Europeans. The European traders were forced to pay for the right to trade with the Efik with a system of duties called *comey*.

Efik society is based on patrilineal succession for the right to head a village or household within their settlement. These village leaders, or *etubom*, were responsible for dealing with the trade transactions of Europeans, including the collection of the *comey* as well as settling disputes and administering the finances of their respective villages.

Among the various household leaders, one was elected to become the *obung*, or chief, of the secret society of men called the EKPE SOCIETY. The Ekpe (meaning "leopard") functioned as a social structure by which the whole of the Efik population was organized, even though the society did not function as a true governing system. The Ekpe society determined social hierarchy, rendered decisions in judiciary matters, collected fines, and handed down punishments when needed. The power of the Ekpe was such that even the wealthiest men of the Efik households had to become members of the society in order to exercise any authority within their village.

Although many have been converted to Christianity, the Efik peoples mainly practice a traditional RELIGION based on the belief in a supreme God called Abasi, the existence of a soul, witchcraft and sorcery, and the honoring of ancestral spirits.

Egba Ethnic group located in present-day southwestern NIGERIA. A subgroup of the Yoruba peoples, the Egba traditionally have been an agrarian community that speaks a language of the Kwa family of languages. While they were led overall by their *alafin*, or king, Egba communities tended to be locally governed by a chief whose succession was determined by patrilineage. In addition, each community was known to honor its own ancestral spirits and abide by its own taboos.

The Egba were the main clan to occupy the southern portion of Old Oyo (also known as Katunga), the capital of the Yoruba empire. Weakened by political unrest throughout the latter half of the 18th century, the OYO EMPIRE was eventually conquered and destroyed by the FULANI JIHADS (holy wars) near the end of the first quarter of the 19th century. The Egba were able to survive the demise of the empire, however, and in the 19th century they established a new community on the rocky east side of the Ogun River. This community was named ABEOKUTA, meaning "refuge among rocks."

See also: *ALAFIN* (Vol. II); CLAN (Vol. I); OLD OYO (Vol. II); ODUDUWA (Vol. II); YORUBA (Vol. I, II, IV, V).

Egypt Present-day country located in northeast Africa and bordered by LIBYA and the Republic of the SUDAN. Egypt's long history continued to be somewhat turbulent in the 16th through the 19th centuries.

As early as the late 13th century parts of North Africa were ruled by the MAMLUKS, a warrior caste of Christian slaves converted to Islam. The Mamluks, trained from boyhood to be soldiers, rebelled and established their own state in Egypt. The Mamluk reign was marked by dissension and instability. By the second half of the 15th century the Mamluks' lack of political strength allowed the Ottoman Empire (fl. 1290–1922) to set its sights on Egypt. The Ottomans were already firmly established as a powerful empire in what is now the country of Turkey.

Egypt under Ottoman Rule Egypt at this time was in economic decline. The once-profitable Egyptian-European trade that relied on Mediterranean trade routes was compromised by the 15th-century Portuguese discovery of the sea passage to India around the southern tip of Africa. This route enabled Europeans to avoid the high taxes placed on the goods that passed through the Egyptian city of CAIRO. Despite their weakness, the Egyptians were initially able to fend off the Turkish invaders and remained independent for more than a decade into the 16th century.

The Ottoman Empire at that time was growing rapidly and poised for expansion. In 1514, after seizing more territory in the Middle East, the Turks turned to Egypt for their next conquest. Two years later the Ottoman ruler, Selim I (r. 1512–1520), led his elite soldiers, known as Janissaries, to victory over the Mamluks in the region of Mardj Dabik (a disputed area located north of the town of Aleppo in present-day Syria). The Janissaries' strength in war was heightened by their use of European firearms, which overpowered the Mamluks, who by tradition used only swords and shields. Although the Mamluk sultan Qansuh al-Ghauri (r. 1501–1516) was killed in battle at Mardj Dabik, Egypt was not officially under Ottoman rule until 1517, when the Turks routed the last vestiges of Mamluk power at the city of Raydaniyya. Khayr Bey (d. c. 1522), a former Mamluk who defected to the Ottoman side, was then placed in control as viceroy, or governor, of Cairo, ruling from there until 1522.

Although Egypt was a vassal territory of the Ottoman Empire, the political institution under Khayr Bey kept many of the Mamluk traditions alive. Mamluk administrative positions and functions remained intact, and the justice system led by four supreme judges was also kept. Khayr Bey himself also kept close ties with the Mamluk culture by keeping his former title of *malik al-umara* (king of commanders), and placing respected Mamluks in his administration as key personnel.

Khayr Bey's death in 1522 brought about the beginning of serious backlashes from those opposing Ottoman rule. A rebellion in 1524 led by Ahmad Pasha, the reigning vice-regent, forced the Ottomans, led by sultan Suleyman I (r. 1520–1566), to rethink how they governed Egypt. The outcome was an Ottoman mandate that attempted to control Egypt's politics, ECONOMY, and even the military. The mandate, known as the *qanun-name,* provided for additional sections of royal troops, or *odjaks,* which reinforced the respective factions of Mamluk and Janissary military units. The *qanun-name,* borrowed from the Ottoman style of rule, divided the Egyptian lands into 14 separate provinces and specified the rights and duties of those who governed Egypt. The provinces were to be administered by a *kashif* (district head), who collected taxes and maintained the irrigation systems. The sultan purposefully kept the *kashifs* at odds with each other so that no province became more powerful than the others.

Before Suleyman I, the *odjaks,* or imperial Ottoman troops of both Janissary and Mamluk origin, were broken into six distinct groups. A seventh, distinctively Mamluk army called the Circassians, from the region from which the soldiers were taken, was formed during Suleyman I's reign.

Due to the reforms set up by the Ottoman government known as the Sublime Porte, Egypt was relatively peaceful and economically successful for almost 60 years. The late 16th century saw a decline in the economy, how-

ever, and by the early 17th century, rebellions had once again strained ties between the Egyptians and the Turks. One of the results of these uprisings was the emergence of the Sandjak beys from one of the groups of Mamluk *odjaks.* The Sandjak beys, 24 in all, came from the elite ranks of emirs, or commanders, and while they held no formal position within the government, their political power was still significant. Their duties included governing the military groups that guarded the treasuries as well as the caravans making the pilgrimage to the Islamic holy city of Mecca (in present-day Saudi Arabia). The influence of the Mamluk rulers, each bearing the new title of *bey* (governor), thus increased within the Ottoman government throughout the 17th century. Even so, their political clout was compromised when they split into two rival political groups known as the Qasimiyya and the Faqariyya. It was the constant and intense conflicts between these two parties, which often pitted their *odjak* groups against each other in the process, that is blamed for crippling the Sublime Porte's authority in Egypt by the start of the 18th century.

The opposition between the two Mamluk factions finally came to a head in 1711 during the battle known as the "Great Insurrection." For more than two months the Faqariyya and the Qasimiyya fought against each other with the help of their respective Janissary collaborators. The war ended with the ousting of the Faqariyya and, ultimately, the beginning of the downfall of Ottoman rule. The Mamluk beys took the title of *sheikh al-balad,* or "chief of the city," from the reigning Turkish governor which, in effect, allowed them to control all of Egypt throughout the 18th century.

As the Ottoman Empire began to lose its grip on Egypt, the Mamluks once again looked to rule their lands independently of foreign influence. Then in 1760 a new *sheikh al-balad* named Ali Bey (1728–1773) was appointed by a political group led by the Janissary Abd al-Rahman. Ali Bey was noted for an aggressive and tireless nature that earned him the nickname *al-Djinn,* or "the devil." Immediately, Ali Bey persuaded the Sublime Porte to give him the chance to reverse the debt that the treasury had accumulated. Though successful in doing so, Ali Bey also made enemies by oppressing Egyptian landowners and was even forced to flee Egypt for a short time to escape those who opposed him. He returned within a year, however, and reinstated himself as *sheikh.* By 1768 Ali Bey had deposed the beys in the offices of vice-regent and deputy vice-regent and placed himself in command as both vice-regent and *sheikh al-balad.* A year later he officially overthrew the newly appointed Ottoman provincial governor and declared Egypt independent from the Turkish empire. With his new position of power over all of Egypt, Ali Bey quickly took advantage of many of the privileges reserved for sultans. He ordered the minting of official coins, established trade deals with Europeans, and even incorporated his name into the Islamic prayers that were routinely said on Fridays.

Despite Ali Bey's strong attempt to liberate his lands, his rule in Egypt remained threatened. Even with another victory over the Turks at the city of Damascus (in present-day Syria), Ali Bey's commanders were swayed by the still-powerful Ottoman Empire, eventually pledging their loyalty to the reigning sultan, Mustafa III (r. 1757–1773). Due to his turn of loyalty, one of Ali Bey's commanders, Muhammad Bey (r. 1772–1775), was forced to leave Cairo for the lands of Upper (southern) Egypt. There he recruited Arab renegades and was even able to turn some of Ali Bey's troops to his side along with another commander named Ismail Bey. This turn of events proved to be Ali Bey's undoing. By 1772 he had no other choice but to cede power to his former commander, Muhammad Bey. Despite two more failed attempts to recapture his former glory, Ali Bey died in exile in 1773.

With Muhammad Bey in power, the Ottomans once again had a loyal subject as governor of Egypt, though his reign lasted only until 1775. After his death there was a battle for succession that the Sublime Porte had little power in controlling.

In 1786 the Ottomams once again tried to restore the all-encompassing control of the *qanun-name* mandate, but to little avail. The Ottoman government made several more attempts to place loyal beys in power in Egypt, but the Mamluks continued to thwart the Turkish plans. More than a decade later the Mamluks were unseated following an invasion by Napoleon Bonaparte (1769–1821). As part of his plan to build a French empire, Bonaparte aimed to limit British influence in the region by blocking trade routes to India and by establishing Egypt as a French-speaking province of his empire. At the Battle of the Pyramids, in July of 1798, and exactly a year later at the conquest at the city of Aboukir, Napoleon I defeated both the Mamluks and the Turkish forces to conquer Egypt. During his reign Napoleon attempted to make much-needed repairs to the irrigation systems, roads, and bridges of Egyptian cities, but his efforts went largely unnoticed. French rule lasted only until 1801, at which time British forces arrived to support the Turks. The Turks subsequently took control of the cities of Cairo and Damietta, effectively forcing the French out of Egypt.

End of Ottoman Rule Napoleon's invasion, though unsuccessful, ended the power of the Mamluks. The Ottoman Empire was briefly able to regain control, but in 1803 Albanian troops under Ottoman rule rebelled and set up their own government. Leadership eventually fell to MUHAMMAD ALI (c. 1769–1849), who was named viceroy in 1805 by local authorities in revolt against the Ottoman sultan, Selim III. When the sultan's viceroy fled, Muhammad Ali was confirmed as the new viceroy by Selim III. The British captured Alexandria in 1807 but failed to es-

tablish a major foothold. Defeated by Muhammad Ali's troops, the British withdrew.

Muhammad Ali went on to become an important figure in 19th-century Egypt, largely independent of his Ottoman overlords. He worked with the Ottoman sultans to control revolts in Arabia. He destroyed the hegemony of the Mamluks and dominated Egypt. In 1820–21 he sent an expedition up the Nile River and captured much of the northern Sudan, putting Egypt in control of a major slave-trading route. A common soldier who rose to high power because of his military and political skills, he dominated Egypt for the first half of the century.

See also: EGYPT (Vols. I, II, IV, V); ENGLAND AND AFRICA (Vols. III, IV); FRANCE AND AFRICA (Vol. III); ISLAM, INFLUENCE OF (Vols. II, III); OTTOMAN EMPIRE AND AFRICA (Vols. III, IV); PORTUGAL AND AFRICA (Vol. III); RED SEA TRADE (Vol. II).

Further reading: Irene A. Bierman, ed., *Napoleon in Egypt* (Los Angeles: Gustave E. von Grunebaum Center for Near Eastern Studies, 2003); Afaf Lutfi Sayyid-Marsot, *Egypt in the Reign of Muhammad Ali* (New York: Cambridge University Press, 1984); Michael Winter, *Egyptian Society Under Ottoman Rule, 1517–1798* (New York: Routledge, 1992).

Ejagham People of present-day southeastern NIGERIA and southwestern CAMEROON. The Bantu-speaking Ejagham, who are closely related to the EKOI peoples of the CROSS RIVER region, migrated from the Niger Valley down to the Cross River area prior to the 16th century. During the era of European colonization, the agricultural Ejagham traded with other Cross River groups and were known to be fierce and strategic warriors. They also were admired for their skills as artists, especially in the making of realistic, skin-covered masks.

The household, or *nju*, and the FAMILY were important to the Ejagham, and each village (*etek*) was made up of several families. Villages were headed by a local chief called the *ntuifam etek* who was in turn governed by a council of elders from each of the village families.

Like other groups of the Cross River area, the Ejagham participated in the secret EKPE SOCIETY. The Ekpe (meaning "leopard") was a male society of differing levels of authority and influence that affected every part of the Ejagham society, from education of children to judicial matters. Beginning about the 18th century the Ejagham also practiced a secret form of Nilotic script called NSIBIDI WRITING, which consisted of hieroglyphic-like symbols representing words and phrases.

Ekoi Bantu-speaking people of present-day southeastern NIGERIA and parts of western CAMEROON. About the 16th century the Ekoi carved close to 300 low-relief human figures out of large stones. Called *akwanshi,* these stones are laid out in circles and are found near the middle CROSS RIVER banks.

In the 1600s the Ekoi became known for their mask- and pottery-making skills. The intricate Ekoi masks were often made of skin, but other materials, including metal and wood, were sometimes used to make teeth and hair.

Their masks, made to represent ancestor spirits, resembled human skull figures, with deeply imbedded eye cavities and gaunt faces. They were worn during secret EKPE SOCIETY rituals and burial ceremonies. Sometimes masks had two, three, or even four faces to represent the ability to see into the past and the future, as well as truth.

Though antelope hides were used later on, the skins for Ekoi masks initially came from the bodies of their slain enemies.

The Ekpe secret society of the Ekoi developed a secret script called NSIBIDI WRITING, which they used to mark important historical events or to record rulings made by the Ekpe elders.

Further reading: C. C. Ifemesia, *Southeastern Nigeria in the Nineteenth Century* (New York: NOK Publishers, 1978).

Ekpe society (Egbo, Ngbe)

Male secret society mainly associated with the ethnic groups of the CROSS RIVER in present-day NIGERIA. The Ekpe, or Leopard, society was probably developed during the early to mid-18th century by the EKOI people living along the Cross River and in parts of what is now CAMEROON. Thereafter it also became associated with other ethnic groups of Cameroon such as the Ododop and the Efut before becoming adopted by the EFIK and IBIBIO peoples of the Cross River by the late 18th century.

Ekpe, egbo, and *ngbe* all translate to "leopard" in the Efik, Ibibio, and Ekoi languages, respectively.

While the Ekpe was not a true government in the traditional sense, it was nevertheless a major ruling force of influential and wealthy men who used their power to affect all levels of society. The Ekpe had powers such as the ability to administer punishment, hand out fines, monitor trade, and pass down judgments. The society became so powerful that no man, however wealthy, could exercise power within his community without being a member of the Ekpe. It was also known to be such an important force in the Ekoi society that no new village could be established until a shrine and an *ekpa ntam,* or house without walls, was built to honor the Ekpe.

The Ekpe society was made up of varying levels or grades, each with its own level of power, secrets, and rituals. Initial entrance into the society was paid by a fee that went toward a feast for the current members, and each level attained thereafter was achieved by the payment of another fee. Each grade was then identifiable by particular symbols worn on the members' clothing, such as peacock feathers for the lower grades and ostrich feathers for the upper grades. In the Efik society of OLD CALABAR, the Ekpe had nine grades and the most important was that of the chief priest, or *obung* (also known as *eyamba*), who was elected to the position from among the leaders of various villages and was the spiritual head of the whole Efik community.

Ekpe society continued to be a strong presence in the Cross River area from the 18th to the mid-19th centuries. Their power in Old Calabar began to decline somewhat, however, when the harsh treatment of slaves was called into question by visiting MISSIONARIES.

Also associated with the Ekpe was a secret script called NSIBIDI WRITING. This written language began appearing in the 18th century and used symbols and characters similar to hieroglyphics that were used to form words and phrases. Associated mostly with the Efik and Ekoi peoples, Nsibidi writing was used to document Ekpe society meetings as well as to record local legends and stories.

See also: SECRET SOCIETIES (Vol. I).

Further reading: Elizabeth Isichei, *A History of Nigeria* (Essex, U.K.: Longman Group Limited, 1983).

Elmina

Trading town and castle established in the 1470s by the Portuguese in the Gulf of Guinea area of present-day southern GHANA. Elmina Castle holds the distinction of being the first fort built by Europeans in the tropical regions of West Africa. It remained a GOLD-trading post until 1637, when the Dutch took control of the town.

In 1471 the Portuguese landed off of the coast of what is now Ghana and were greeted by the local peoples bearing pieces of gold to exchange for clothes and other trinkets brought from Portugal. A town was then established by the Portuguese at Edina, which was soon referred to as *el mina,* meaning "the mine," in reference to the abundance of gold that was available through trade. Hence, the town became known as Elmina, and the Portuguese quickly became interested in building a more permanent fort. On January 19, 1482, the Portuguese

XXIV.

DELINEATIO CASTELLI ET

PROPVGNÁCVLI LVSITANORVM,

La Mina, &c.

A ſtellum La Mina, alias à S. Georgio etiam cognomi-
natum, à Luſitanis Anno 1482. de mandato Iohan-
nis II. Portugaliæ Regis extructum eſt, ut Aethiopi-
bus terrori eſſet, & peregrinos ſimul ab hoc littore
prohiberet. Cuius quidem delineationem tibi ob ocu-
los ponere viſum eſt. A. enim litera, Caſtellum vel propugnaculum

The Portuguese settlement of Elmina (The Mine) on the West African coast. This print by Theodor de Bry was created between 1561 and 1623. © *Corbis*

were granted permission by the reigning king, known as Caramansa or Kwamina Ansah (fl. 1480s), to build a castle at Elmina. Although Caramansa was opposed to the construction, the presence of an overwhelming force of Portuguese soldiers made his opposition meaningless. The castle was built under the direction of Diogo de Azambuja (fl. 1480s) and named São Jorge da Mina, which later became known by the same name as the town surrounding it.

For more than a century both the town and the castle were major trading points for the AKAN, DYULA, and Mande traders along the GOLD COAST (as Ghana was then known). At Elmina's markets gold was traded for African captives, cloth, and metal items. During the late 16th century, however, the gold trade began a slow decline, due partially to the increase in the trading of captives. Then, in 1637, Elmina was taken over by the Dutch, who had become increasingly active along the Gold Coast and forced the Portuguese to continue their trading practices from their ships docked off the coast. The Dutch then turned Elmina Castle into a compound where the captives would be held in cramped quarters until they were shipped overseas. By the late 17th century the profitable trade with Elmina Castle had become dominated by the

DENKYIRA kingdom. At that time, captives and gold were traded for the usual cloth and metal goods but also for the advanced European firearms that were coveted by some African groups.

In 1699 the ASHANTI EMPIRE, led by Asantehene (King) OSEI TUTU (r. c. 1650–1717), waged war against the Denkyira and decimated them. Along with the goods captured in the war, the Ashanti also gained control over a piece of paper called simply "the Note," which gave the holder rights to the trade with Elmina Castle and the Dutch. The Ashanti were then the controlling group in the slave and weapons trade along the Gold Coast, especially with the Dutch at Elmina. The Dutch continued to control Elmina town and castle until they were forced to withdraw from the Gold Coast by the British late in the 19th century.

See also: ARCHITECTURE (Vol. III); ENGLAND AND AFRICA (Vol. III); NETHERLANDS AND AFRICA (Vol. III); SLAVE TRADE, THE TRANSATLANTIC (Vol. III); SLAVERY (Vol. III); TRADING OUTPOSTS, EUROPEAN (Vol. III).

Further reading: Christopher R. Decorse, *An Archaeology of Elmina: Africans and Europeans on the Gold Coast, 1400–1900* (Washington, D.C.: Smithsonian Institution Press, 2001).

England and Africa As with most European countries, Britain's presence in Africa was limited primarily to the western and southern regions of the continent prior to 1800. England, the metaphorical heart of Britain, was a relative latecomer to the coastal trading endeavors initiated by Portugal in the late 15th century. About 1663 the British officially entered the African fray when Charles II formed the Company of Royal Adventurers. The company established its base at CAPE COAST, a town on the coast of present-day GHANA, and was given a monopoly on all English commerce on Africa's west coast between the Cape of Good Hope and Gibraltar, a British territory (from 1704) in southern Spain. The company's primary interest was to supply LABOR to the plantation colonies in the Americas.

Renamed the ROYAL AFRICA COMPANY in 1672, the trading giant attempted to maintain its monopoly against the endeavors of rogue slave merchants. However, by 1698 the British government had granted trade rights to all Britons who paid a fee. Between 1680 and 1686 the company transported an average of 5,000 African captives per year. The Company of Merchants Trading to Africa, which allowed all merchants to use its forts along the coast, replaced the Royal Africa Company in 1750.

About the same time, much of Europe was divided by the territorial conflicts of the Seven Years' War, which pitted Britain and its allies (Hanover and Prussia) against France and its allies (Austria, Saxony, Sweden, and Russia). In 1763 Britain and France ended the war by signing the Treaty of Paris. As a result of the peace agreement, Britain won India and territory in North America and emerged as the major European overseas trading power. Spurred by the need to supply slave labor to its American colonies, the British overtook Portuguese and Dutch strongholds along the western and southern African coasts.

By the end of the 18th century, though, the COTTON gin had been invented, drastically reducing the demand for African laborers on the cotton plantations in the United States. Simultaneously a strong abolitionist movement had taken hold in England. Ultimately the British Parliament officially outlawed the buying and selling of human beings in 1807, though the trade continued even without official sanction.

See also: CUGOANO, OTTOBAH (Vol. III) ENGLAND AND AFRICA (Vols. IV, V); EQUIANO, OLAUDAH (Vol. III); NEWTON, JOHN (Vol. III); SLAVE TRADE, THE TRANSATLANTIC (Vol. III).

Further reading: Trevor R. Getz, *Slavery and Reform in West Africa: Toward Emancipation in Nineteenth-Century Senegal and the Gold Coast* (Athens, Ohio: Ohio University Press, 2004); Raymond Howell, *The Royal Navy and the Slave Trade* (London: Croom Helm, 1987); Joseph E. Inikori, *Africans and the Industrial Revolution in England* (New York: Cambridge University Press, 2002).

Equatorial Guinea Country in tropical western Central Africa, some 10,800 square miles (28,000 sq km) in size, that is made up of the mainland coastal enclave of Río Muni and five volcanic islands located in the Atlantic Ocean. Río Muni, which is largely coastal plains and interior hills, shares borders with CAMEROON to the north and GABON to the east and south. The large island of FERNANDO PO (now called Bioko), which is about 780 square miles (2,030 sq km) in size, and the small islands of Corisco and Great and Little Elobey lie in the Gulf of Guinea, about 100 miles (160 km) northwest of the mainland portion of the country. The present-day capital city of Malabo is on Bioko. The fifth island, Annobón, also small, is 350 miles (565 km) southwest of mainland Equatorial Guinea.

Much of the country's history between 1500 and 1850 is intertwined with the transatlantic SLAVE TRADE. The Portuguese sugar plantations on Fernando Po and Annobón faded away once the larger, more productive, and more strategically located plantations in the Portuguese colony of Brazil emerged in the second half of the 16th century. Slave trading activities, however, continued to flourish along the mainland coast. In 1641, for example, the Dutch established trading posts on the coast. Despite the presence of European competitors the Portuguese continued to claim sovereignty over the area until 1778. Portugal then ceded control of the two major

islands and the coastal mainland to Spain in return for Spanish recognition of Portuguese claims to Brazil. Yellow fever was soon to drive Spain from Fernando Po, and the island lay unoccupied until 1827, when Spain leased the island and its port of Malabo (which at the time was called Port Clarence) to Britain as a base for its anti-slave-trade naval squadron. The British resettled some of the recaptives rescued from the seized slave ships on the island. The British navy continued to use the base until 1843, at which time it began to base its ships at FREETOWN, SIERRA LEONE. In 1844 Spain returned to the island to reestablish its colonial presence and also to start asserting its control to the mainland area of Río Muni.

See also: EQUATORIAL GUINEA (Vols. I, II, IV, V).

Further reading: Max Liniger-Goumaz, *Small is Not Always Beautiful: The Story of Equatorial Guinea* (Totowa, N.J.: Barnes & Noble Books, 1989); Ibrahim K. Sundiata, *From Slaving to Neoslavery: The Bight of Biafra and Fernando Po in the Era of Abolition, 1827–1930* (Madison, Wisc.: University of Wisconsin Press, 1996); Jan Vansina, *Paths in the Rainforests* (Madison, Wisc.: University of Wisconsin Press, 1990).

Equiano, Olaudah (Gustavus Vassa) (c. 1745–1797) *Former slave who became a highly active and influential abolitionist in London in the late 1700s*

Known also as Gustavus Vassa, Olaudah Equiano was kidnapped into bondage at age 12 from the IGBO village of Essaka in the West African kingdom of BENIN, and taken to the West Indies. He was later sold to a Virginia planter and then sold again, this time to a British naval officer named Captain Pascal, who bought Equiano as a present for his cousins in England. After working as a sailor for his English merchant master, he saved enough money (£40, or about $4,600 in today's money) to buy his way out of forced servitude. He remained in England, where, working with the British abolitionist and philanthropist Granville Sharpe (b. 1735), he became important in the antislavery movement and the leading figure of the small African community in London. Historians believe that he was acquainted with Ottobah CUGOANO (b. c. 1757), another African-born abolitionist in London. They are less sure whether he ever met Ignatius SANCHO (1729–1780), another prominent black Londoner of the day.

Equiano's involvement with the abolition movement led him in 1789 to write and publish his strongly abolitionist autobiography, *The Interesting Narrative of the Life of Olaudah Equiano, or Gustavus Vassa the African, Written by Himself.* In this book he describes the humiliations that enslaved humans endure. He also denigrates Africans who participated in the trade of human beings and speaks highly of his master and other English people who befriended him. His book is one of the first works in English describing SLAVERY that was written by a person formerly held in bondage. It became a best-seller and went through nine editions, including a German edition in 1790 and an American and a Dutch edition in 1791, before Equiano died in 1797. It rivaled in popularity the adventure novel *Robinson Crusoe*, by the English writer Daniel Defoe (c. 1660–1731). Three editions of Equiano's book also included poems by Phillis WHEATLY (1753–1784), who was kidnapped into slavery in SENEGAL and became the first black poet published in the United States.

At the end of his life he was appointed to an expedition that was intended to help settle London's poor blacks in the British colony of SIERRA LEONE in West Africa. He did not live to return to his native continent.

See also: ENGLAND AND AFRICA (Vols. III, IV, V); SLAVE TRADE, THE TRANSATLANTIC (Vol. III).

Further reading: Olaudah Equiano, *The Interesting Narrative of the Life of Olaudah Equiano, or Gustavus Vassa the African, Written by Himself,* Werner Sollors, ed. (New York: Norton, 2000); James Walvin, *An African's Life: The Life and Times of Olaudah Equiano, 1745–1797* (New York: Cassell, 1998).

Eritrea Present-day northeast African country located on the Red Sea. Eritrea, which covers approximately 46,830 square miles (121,200 sq km), shares borders with Republic of DJIBOUTI, ETHIOPIA, and the Republic of the SUDAN. Its present-day capital is ASMARA. Eritrea's and Ethiopia's histories are closely linked. Between the 14th and 15th centuries waves of Agaw and Tigre immigrants came north from Ethiopia, flooding Eritrea and dominating the Beja kingdoms. In the 15th and 16th centuries the Tigray, whose language is Tigrinya, arrived and conquered Eritrea's Tigre population (whose language is often spelled *Tigré,* with an accent). A social system soon developed in which the Tigrinya-speaking people formed the aristocracy and the Tigré speakers made up the lower caste.

The 16th century proved to be an eventful time in Eritrean history, as it was under constant threat by enemies from abroad. During his military campaign against Ethiopia, AHMAD GRAÑ (c. 1506–1543), the celebrated leader from ADAL, tore into Eritrea with his Muslim forces. Sensing the seriousness of the threat to Ethiopia, Christian Ethiopian emperor LEBNA DENGEL (r. c. 1508–1540) asked for the help of Christian Portuguese soldiers to repel the Muslim onslaught. Lebna Dengel died in 1540, but the Portuguese reinforcements landed in MASSAWA in 1541. The combined Christian forces defeated Ahmad's army in a battle in which Ahmad was killed, and the Muslims were forced to leave the territory. Eritrea's *bahr negash* (king), YISHAQ (r. c. 1540–1580), was rid of the Muslim threat, but another foreign invader was looming on the horizon.

By 1557 Turks of the Ottoman Empire had moved into the Eritrean highlands and held them for nearly two decades. During this time, King Yishaq was continually at odds with his Turkish overlords. These disputes ended when both the Turkish pasha (governor) and Yishaq were killed by the Ethiopian emperor, Sarsa Dengel (r. c. 1563–1597).

In 1589 Eritrean forces joined with the Turks in an attempt to defend themselves against the Ethiopians. Though they were run out of the highlands, the Turks managed to keep Ethiopia at bay over the following three centuries, during which they occupied Eritrea.

After the 16th century Eritrean society underwent massive changes. The old pastoral ways were pushed aside in favor of AGRICULTURE as the country's primary form of subsistence, and villages and districts replaced kinship groups as a way of social organization.

Early in the 18th century Eritrea and the Tigrinya-speaking Christians from the northern Ethiopian province of Tigray formed alliances against their southern Ethiopian adversaries, temporarily gaining control of the southern Eritrean region. Their control was challenged, however, and Eritrea remained a contested area until the era of European colonialism in the 19th century.

See also: AGAW (Vols. I, II); BEJA (Vol. II); ERITREA (Vols. I, II, IV, V); OTTOMAN EMPIRE AND AFRICA (Vols. III, IV); TIGRAY (Vol. I, IV, V); TIGRE (Vol. I).

Further reading: Richard Sherman, *Eritrea: The Unfinished Revolution* (New York: Praeger Publishers, 1980).

Ethiopia Country covering about 435,100 square miles (1,126,900 sq km) in northeast Africa. Today Ethiopia shares borders with ERITREA, Republic of DJIBOUTI, SOMALIA, KENYA, and the Republic of the SUDAN. Ethiopia's Christian kingdom endured tumultuous times between the 16th and 18th centuries. Ethiopia served as both the initiator and victim of a series of religious, trade, and territorial wars that left the kingdom nearly in ruins.

The Ethiopian Christian kingdom reached its zenith between the 14th and 16th centuries by launching intensive military campaigns for the purpose of controlling trade routes and subjugating the kingdom's Muslim population. This period of economic and military prosperity began under the kingship of Amda Siyon (r. 1313–1344) whose successful military actions not only halted Islamic penetration but eventually extended Ethiopia's borders. This paved the way for the spread of Christianity and earned him a reputation as one of the country's great warrior kings.

Under Amda Siyon's immediate successors, the kingdom suffered several setbacks. This was reversed by Zara Yakob (r. 1434–1468), an emperor whose rule was as feared as it was respected. He is credited with several victories over the Muslims, the most notable being his 1445 conquest of the sultanate of ADAL. Besides being a great warrior, Yakob was also politically astute. He revamped

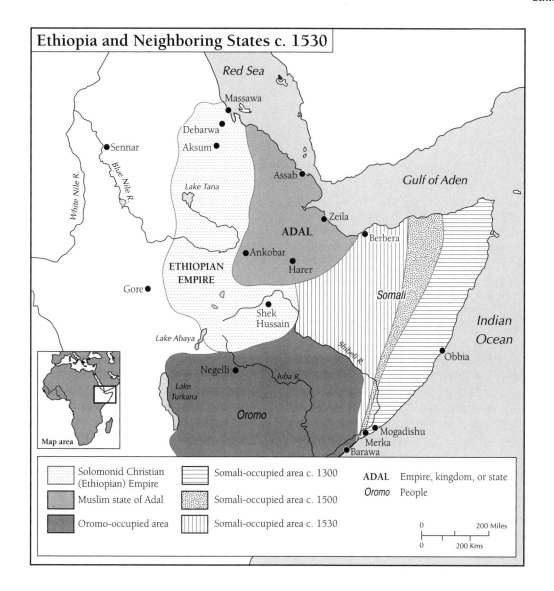

Ethiopia and Neighboring States c. 1530

Red Sea

Massawa

Debarwa

Sennar

Aksum

Lake Tana

Assab

Gulf of Aden

White Nile R.

Blue Nile R.

Zeila

ADAL

Berbera

Ankobar

Harer

ETHIOPIAN EMPIRE

Gore

Somali

Indian Ocean

Shek Hussain

Lake Abaya

Shibeli R.

Obbia

Map area

Negelli

Juba R.

Lake Turkana

Oromo

Mogadishu

Merka

Barawa

Solomonid Christian (Ethiopian) Empire	Somali-occupied area c. 1300	**ADAL** Empire, kingdom, or state
Muslim state of Adal	Somali-occupied area c. 1500	*Oromo* People
Oromo-occupied area	Somali-occupied area c. 1530	

0   200 Miles
0   200 Kms

the administration of his government, stripping away power from the once autonomous provinces in order to secure a tightly unified empire. In an attempt to consolidate the church and the state, he imposed Christianity on the entire kingdom through forced conversion and the suppression of all other faiths. After Yakob's death, however, his successors found it difficult to maintain control of the vast kingdom that he had built.

Despite the support of the Portuguese, the Ethiopian state was exhibiting signs of deterioration by the time of LEBNA DENGEL (r. 1508–1540). To a great extent this was because the kingdom was simply too large to control. Moreover, discontent was on the rise among many elements of the population, particularly among Muslims, who began to organize themselves under the leadership of Ahmad ibn Ibrahim al Ghazi (c. 1506–1543), known as AHMAD GRAÑ by his Christian adversaries.

After assembling a powerful army Ahmad Grañ waged a jihad against an unsuspecting Ethiopia. From

1525 to 1527 Ahmad's campaign was relentless, and the Christians suffered many losses. In 1527, after the Portuguese ambassador returned home, Ahmad Grañ took advantage of Ethiopia's vulnerability and forged ahead with an invasion. This cost Ethiopia most of its territory and forced Lebna Dengel to seek refuge in the Ethiopian Highlands. Lebna Dengel's requests for help from Europe were not answered until a year after his death, in 1541. However, his son Galawdewos (r. 1540–1559) was able to retrain the Ethiopian forces, and with the aid of 400 well-armed soldiers sent by the Portuguese, Galawdewos's forces were able to defeat and kill Grañ. After the death of their leader, the Muslim army was fragmented, and the territory he had won for them reverted to Ethiopian control.

The wars between the Muslims and Christians had substantially weakened both armies. This provided an opportunity for the mostly animist OROMO, who moved in quickly and forcefully to capture territory that neither the

Ethiopians floating wood in the Nile River to sell downstream in Cairo. This Richard Dalton print was created between 1735 and 1791.
© *Historical Picture Archive/Corbis*

Muslims nor the Christians were strong enough to hold. They came in masses, conquering and settling along Ethiopia's southeastern plateau, then infiltrating the regions in and around SHOA, AMHARA, and Lasta. They defeated the Muslim region of HARER, leaving that city's imam no choice but to move to Awssa. Still, with their territory significantly diminished and their military reduced in power, the Ethiopians ultimately were forced to live with the Oromo, who were firmly embedded in their country.

In the latter half of the 16th century the Roman Catholic Church became interested in bringing Ethiopia into its fold. It sent a series of MISSIONARIES to the country, but they had little luck in converting the monarchy. This continued until Pedro Páez, a Jesuit missionary from Spain, arrived in Ethiopia early in the 17th century. He earned the trust and respect of Emperor Susenyos (r. 1607–1632), leading to the emperor's acceptance of the faith and subsequent declaration of Roman Catholicism as Ethiopia's state religion.

Discontent among other members of the Ethiopian royalty and the public outcry from his subjects led Susenyos to abdicate the throne. He was succeeded by his son FASILIDAS (r. 1632–1667), who, upon taking power, removed the Jesuits and reinstated the country's Monophysite religion. The Jesuit mission, however, left in its wake a country theistically divided. Under constant threat from his Oromo and Muslim neighbors, Fasilidas

moved his capital from Manz to GONDAR, where he spent the rest of his rule in isolation. During his reign, he commissioned several castles and churches to be rebuilt, the most important being the cathedral at Aksum.

During the reigns of IYASU I (r. 1682–1706) and Iyasu II (r. 1730–1755) the Ethiopian monarchy tried to regain some of the territory lost in the previous century. To accomplish this they enlisted the support of some of the recently converted Oromo, adding them to the Ethiopian military. Oromo soldiers ultimately were even used in missions against their own people. Gradually some Oromo assimilated into Ethiopian society, and by the 19th century they were striving for political power.

Subsequent to this process the infamous *ras*, or regional ruler, Mikael Sehul acquired so much power during the kingship of Iyoas (r. 1755–1769) that on his command the emperor and his successor, Yohannis II, were assassinated. This gave rise to a dark period of anarchy, between 1768 and 1855, known in Ethiopian history as the ZEMENE MESAFINT, or Age of Princes.

See also: AMDA SIYON (Vol. II); CHRISTIANITY , INFLUENCE OF (Vol. III); ETHIOPIA (Vols. I, II, IV, V); ETHIOPIAN HIGHLANDS (Vol. I); ZARA YAKOB (Vol. II).

Further reading: Mordechai Abir, *Ethiopia: The Era of the Princes, 1769–1855* (London: Longmans, Green and Co., 1968); Donald Crummey, *Land and Society in the Christian Kingdom of Ethiopia: From the Thirteenth to the Twentieth Century* (Urbana, Ill.: University of Illinois Press,

2000); Harold G. Marcus, *A History of Ethiopia* (Berkeley, Calif.: University of California Press, 1995); Richard Pankhurst, *History of Ethiopian Towns from the Middle Ages to the Early Nineteenth Century* (Philadelphia: Coronet Books, 1985).

Ewe Ethnic group residing in present-day GHANA, TOGO, and the Republic of BENIN who are related to the AJA, ANLO, Mina, and Ouatchi people. Being a West African coastal group, the Ewe were involved early on in trade with the Portuguese, exchanging their agricultural products for European manufactured goods.

The name *Ewe* is pronounced "ay-vay" or "ay-way" in English.

According to tradition the Ewe emerged out of the Aja group that settled in the Yoruba province of KETU, in present-day Republic of Benin, after leaving Oyo in NIGERIA perhaps as early as the 13th century, but more likely during the 15th century. By 1600 they had migrated from Ketu to Notsie, in present-day Togo. In the 17th century a mass exodus of Ewe people fled from Notsie to escape the despotism of King Agokoli, dividing the Ewe into three distinct groups. The first group traveled north and occupied the region from Peki (Krepi) to Akpafu. The second group settled around the hills of Ho, to the east of the VOLTA BASIN. The third group moved south to the mouth of the Volta River, where they established the coastal town of KETA and eventually formed Anlo, a state that enjoyed relative peace until the mid-18th century.

See also: EWE (Vol. II).

exploration Prior to the era of European colonialism, which started in earnest in the 19th century, non-African explorers made numerous expeditions into the African interior to gather information about the geography and peoples of the continent. Although the entire coastline of Africa had been mapped by Europeans by 1514, little progress would be made exploring the interior of the continent before the 19th century. Uncharted African regions were often made inaccessible by deserts, including the Sahara in the north and the Namib and Kalahari in the south. The forbidding, almost impenetrable forests of Central and West Africa made exploration a difficult proposition. In many cases the task of accurately mapping Africa was made even harder because of the exaggerated descriptions of African cultures made by early explorers. All of the mystery surrounding Africa led some Europeans to refer to it as the "Dark Continent."

A Spanish-born Muslim named LEO AFRICANUS (c. 1485–1554) was one of the first explorers to venture into the African interior. Between 1507 and 1513 Leo traveled extensively throughout North and Central Africa, visiting TIMBUKTU, EGYPT, and KANEM-BORNU. In 1550 he published a geographical history of Africa.

Portuguese exploration of Africa, which was initiated in the 15th century, primarily focused on the coastal regions. However, several inland expeditions met with modest success. A *DEGREDADO* named Antonio Fernandes (d. c. 1522) visited the GOLD-bearing regions of present-day ZIMBABWE between 1511 and 1514. Gaspar Bocarro (fl. 1600s) reached TETE on the ZAMBEZI RIVER in 1616, and during the late 18th century the Portuguese established a settlement there. From Tete, Francisco Jose de Lacerda reached the southeastern border of present-day Democratic Republic of the CONGO in 1798. The Portuguese also gained valuable information about ETHIOPIA through the travels of the missionary Francisco ALVARES (fl. c. 1520).

Portuguese exploration sparked interest among other European powers, including the Dutch, who in 1652 established a shipping station at Table Bay, in present-day SOUTH AFRICA, near CAPE TOWN. By the early 18th century Dutch and British colonists had begun to investigate areas further north in the South African interior.

The British also made some inroads into the West African interior. On the Senegal River, merchants reached Barracuda Falls by 1651, and by 1659 Cornelius Hoges had reached Bambuk, in present-day eastern SENEGAL. The Scottish explorer Mungo PARK (1771–1806) reached the BAMBARA kingdom of SEGU, on the NIGER RIVER, in 1796.

During the 19th century waves of European explorers, many of them MISSIONARIES, would venture into the African interior. The knowledge they acquired on these expeditions would greatly facilitate the European colonizing of the continent.

See also: AGE OF DISCOVERY (Vol. II); NIGER EXPEDITION (Vol. III); PORTUGAL AND AFRICA (Vol. III).

Further reading: David Northrup, *Africa's Discovery of Europe: 1450 to 1850* (New York: Oxford Univ. Press, 2002); J. H. Parry, *The Age of Reconnaissance* (Berkeley, Calif.: Univ. of California Press, 1982); Robert I. Rotberg, ed., *Africa and Its Explorers: Motives, Methods, and Impact* (Cambridge, Mass.: Harvard Univ. Press, 1970).

F

factories, European See TRADING STATIONS, EUROPEAN.

family Family life in Africa from the 16th into the 19th centuries continued in many ways to flow along already well-established lines. Yet significant changes to family life on the continent accompanied the spread of SLAVERY that was brought about by the transatlantic SLAVE TRADE. A key feature of this trade was that European slave merchants and planters wanted a predominantly male LABOR force.

Indeed the ratio of male to female captives taken from Africa to the Americas was about 2 to 1. This in turn produced a shortage of marriageable males in much of the western regions of the continent and thus led to changes in marriage patterns. Most significantly the remaining males were in a position to have multiple wives. One can see the impact more clearly by looking at societies that were not affected by the slave trade. In those communities with a more balanced sex ratio, it was only the leading men who had the resources and social standing to support multiple wives. On the other hand, in the societies most affected by the slave trade, males of lesser social stature were also noted for having multiple wives.

See also: FAMILY (Vols. I, II, IV, V).

Further reading: Mario Azevedo, "The African Family," in Mario Azevedo, ed., *Africana Studies: A Survey of Africa and the African Diaspora* (Durham, N.C.: Carolina Academic Press, 2004).

Falasha See BETA ISRAEL.

Fante (Fanti) Kwa-speaking people of present-day GHANA. Little is certain about the origin of the Fante people other than that, according to oral history, they migrated to their present-day location from the Brong-Ahafo region of central Ghana. While it is unknown when the Fante settled along the coast, it is clear that they were established there by the time Europeans arrived in the late 1400s.

The Fante were organized into multiple independent states until the late 17th century, at which time they formed a confederation under the leadership of a high king, or *brafo*. While most Fante made their living through AGRICULTURE or fishing, many Fante became traders, acting as intermediaries in the GOLD trade between Europeans and the neighboring ASHANTI EMPIRE.

As members of a wealthy and powerful kingdom, the Fante expanded their territory throughout the 18th century and became brokers in the transatlantic SLAVE TRADE, supplying mostly British ships. In the latter half of the 18th century the growing Ashanti Empire to the east launched several attacks on Fante territory, hoping to monopolize the supply side of the European trade in gold and captives. Although they successfully defended their territory at first, the Fante eventually succumbed to the Ashanti in the early 1800s. During the 1820 and 1830s, however, the Fante's British allies helped them regain their independence.

See also: FANTE (Vol. II); FANTE CONFEDERATION (Vol. IV).

Further reading: Mary McCarthy, *Social Change and the Growth of British Power in the Gold Coast: The Fante States, 1807–1874* (Lanham, Md.: University Press of America, 1983).

Fasilidas (Fasilides, Fasiladas) (c. 1602–1667)
Emperor of Ethiopia who founded the city of Gondar as the capital of Christian Ethiopia

Fasilidas's reign as Christian emperor of Ethiopia was marked by conflict. His father, Emperor Susenyos (r. 1607–1632), had converted to the Roman Catholic Church from the Ethiopian Orthodox Church, bringing the country to the brink of civil war by pitting Ethiopia's Orthodox Christians against foreign Roman Ca-tholic MISSIONARIES and their converts. In 1632 Susenyos abdicated the throne in favor of Fasilidas in an attempt to end the bloodshed. Despite his father's conversion, Fasilidas remained a strong proponent of Ethi-opia's Orthodox Church. Prior to his becoming emperor, Roman Catholic missionaries had been pouring into Ethiopia for nearly 100 years, going back to the 1540s, when Portuguese Roman Catholics helped the Christian Ethiopian state repel attacks led by Muslim AHMAD GRAÑ (1506–1543). By the 1630s, however, Fasilidas felt that the Roman Catholic missionaries presented a threat to his Ortho-dox empire, so one of his first acts as emperor was to expel them from the country. He went so far as to enlist the help of Muslim Turks of the Ottoman Empire in barring European priests from entering the country at Massawa, a Red Sea port. His actions led to a period of Ethiopian isolation from Europe that lasted for several centuries.

Before becoming emperor Fasilidas had used the city of GONDAR, high in the hills above Lake Tana, as his military headquarters. When Fasilidas took the throne the city became the new capital of the Christian Ethiopian state. Under the direction of Fasilidas, Ethi-opian builders erected beautiful churches and fortified castles and towers that protected his capital against the threat of attack from bands of OROMO warriors, who were spreading throughout the Ethiopian countryside from the south.

Fasilidas maintained mostly peaceful political and commercial relations with the Muslims of Ethiopia. Gondar was an important trading center for the Muslim-controlled caravan routes that ran from the Ethiopian interior to Red Sea ports, and the city had a Muslim quarter. Fasilidas also made trade alliances with the Islamic OMANI SULTANATE, located across the Red Sea in present-day Saudi Arabia, but these ties were broken when the sultans presumed to send an Islamic holy man to Gondar in an attempt to convert the emperor. Fasilidas was succeeded by his son Yohannes (r. 1667–1682).

Further reading: Harold G. Marcus, *A History of Ethiopia* (Berkeley, Calif.: University of California Press, 1994).

Fernando Po (Bioko, Formosa) Small West African island located in the Gulf of Guinea off the coast of present-day southeastern NIGERIA. Fernão do Pó, a Portuguese explorer, discovered the volcanic island about 1472 and initially named it *Formosa,* Portuguese for "beautiful."

Although the Treaty of Tordesillas with Spain (1494) allowed Portugal to claim all parts of what is now EQUATORIAL GUINEA, the subsequent Treaty of Pardo (1778) forced the Portuguese to cede territory to Spain in exchange for land in the New World colony of Brazil. Included in this exchange was the island of Formosa, which was renamed Fernando Po in honor of the island's European discoverer.

In the 19th century Bubi and Fang people moved to the island from the mainland and began cultivating yams, cassava, rice, and manioc. Later, during the colonial era, they produced PALM OIL and coffee for European markets. Even though Spain officially owned the island and other parts of Equatorial Guinea, from 1827 to 1844 the British were granted use of Fernando Po's port for its naval vessels seeking to halt the transatlantic SLAVE TRADE.

See also: COFFEE (Vol. IV); FANG (Vol. II); PORTUGAL AND AFRICA (Vol. III).

Fez (Fes) Trade city and popular center of Islamic learning in north-central MOROCCO. The city reached its peak during the period between the mid-13th and mid-16th centuries, at which time Fez was under Marinid and Wattasid rule. These Islamic dynasties were led by BERBERS and controlled much of Morocco and the MAGHRIB.

In 1549 the Islamic SADIAN DYNASTY, came to power in MARRAKECH, to the southwest, and assumed control of Fez by 1554. Marrakech became the capital of the Sadian dynasty, and the political importance of Fez subsequently declined. Despite Fez's diminished political importance, the Sadian commander ABD AL-MANSUR (c. 1549–1603) built fortifications there, helping the city maintain its status as a cosmopolitan trading hub and a major center for Islamic scholarship.

In the 17th century Morocco was divided between the Sadian dynasty, which ruled from Marrakech, and the rival Alawite dynasty in Fez. By the late 17th century the Alawites managed to reunify the country under MAWLAY ISMAIL (r. 1771–1806), who forged close ties with European powers and ruled Morocco into the 18th century.

See also: FEZ (Vol. II).

Further reading: Titus Burckhardt, *Fez: City of Islam* (Cambridge, U.K.: Islamic Texts Society, 1992).

Fezzan (Fezan) Saharan region in present-day southwestern LIBYA. Known in ancient times to both the Greeks and Romans, the Fezzan was a center for trans-Saharan trade, with a popular route from Lake CHAD to the Mediterranean port of TRIPOLI running through it.

During the first half of the 16th century the region fell under the dominion of the KANEM-BORNU trading empire, located to the south, around Lake Chad. In the latter half of the century the Fezzan was ruled by independent states that fell under the nominal rule of the Ottoman Empire. Being an inland region, though, the Fezzan escaped the direct rule of the Ottoman Turks until the mid-19th century.

See also: FEZZAN (Vol. II); OTTOMAN EMPIRE AND AFRICA (Vols. III, IV).

Fipa Ethnic group that has long lived in what is now TANZANIA. The Fipa probably migrated to southwestern Tanzania well before the 18th century. Primarily an agricultural people, they traditionally have supplemented their crop cultivation by gathering fruit and by fishing.

During the late 18th century Fipa society was torn apart by two rivals who battled for the chieftainship. In the end the loser led his followers south to establish a new chiefdom. The conflict continued for many years, weakening the Fipa to the point that they were conquered, around 1840, by the NGONI.

Further reading: Roy Willis, *A State in the Making: Myth, History, and Social Transformation in Pre-Colonial Ufipa* (Bloomington, Ind.: Indiana University Press, 1981).

Fon See DAHOMEY.

food The Atlantic trade that the Portuguese initiated in the 15th century with their EXPLORATION of the South Atlantic Ocean led to the introduction of new food crops from the Western Hemisphere. The principal crops were cassava (manioc), GROUNDNUTS (peanuts), MAIZE (corn), and new kinds of beans. By the 16th century the Portuguese had introduced groundnuts from South America to the western Central African coastal area north and south of the mouth of the Congo River. The local Bantu-speaking people gave the crop a new name, *nguba*, a term that traveled back across the Atlantic Ocean and evolved into "goober pea," a common name for peanuts in the American South.

Unlike most grain crops, maize could grow in the rain forest as well as in more open areas, so it greatly enhanced the agriculture of the forest farmers. Maize became a major crop throughout much of the continent. Cassava, which is a tuber crop, could withstand drought and also could remain in the ground for a long time before harvesting it. While low in nutrition (though the leaves could be boiled for a garnish that provided vitamins), its hardiness gradually made it a popular crop. In the 17th century the Portuguese also introduced Asian strains of rice, which then spread widely in the Congo Basin.

See also: AGRICULTURE (Vols. I, II, III); CATTLE (Vol. I); FOOD (Vols. I, II, IV, V).

Fort Jesus Portuguese stronghold built to protect MOMBASA, an island off the Indian Ocean coast of present-day KENYA in East Africa. After almost a century of domination, Portuguese power on the east coast of Africa was on the decline during the late 16th century. By the 1850s the Portuguese were beset by Turkish raiders as well as by revolts by militant anti-Portuguese elements within the various city-states on the SWAHILI COAST. In response Portugal erected what it hoped to be an impregnable protection for its primary deep-water port, Mombasa.

For a number of years the fort provided a symbolically powerful reminder of the Portuguese presence. Then, in 1631, a discontented Arab sultan named Yusuf al-Hassan (1607–1638), a former Christian who actually was raised by the Portuguese in Goa, rose in rebellion against Portugal. Leading a force of 300 followers, he stormed Fort Jesus, taking the fort and stabbing the Portuguese governor. Yusuf held the fort until the arrival of Portuguese reinforcements and even then tried to dismantle and destroy the fortress.

After this the entire region entered a restive phase, and the Portuguese faced difficulties almost everywhere. In their attempt to drive out the Portuguese, local Africans turned to the leader of the Arab OMANI SULTANATE for support. By 1652 Omani PIRATES and raiders were at work throughout the region. This, combined with a general revolt among local people, threw Portuguese rule into turmoil. In 1661 the Omanis took Mombasa. Fort Jesus, however, held fast, and proved impossible to capture.

In 1696 an Omani fleet embarked on a major siege of the fort, which was garrisoned by a force of approximately 100 Portuguese and 1,500 Africans who had remained loyal to the Portuguese Crown. It took almost three years, but in the end the Omanis were successful, and when Portuguese reinforcements finally arrived in 1698, they found that the fort had fallen.

In the years immediately following the fall of Fort Jesus, KISWAHILI-speaking East Africans attempted to wrest control of the region from Oman. Although they were initially successful, maintaining their freedom was difficult. In the end, except for a brief return of the Portuguese in the 1720s, they were to remain under the influence of the Omanis for the next few centuries.

See also: ARCHITECTURE (Vol. III); PORTUGAL AND AFRICA (Vol. III).

Further reading: W. A. Nelson, *Fort Jesus of Mombasa* (Edinburgh, U.K.: Canongate Press, 1994).

Fouta Djallon (Futa Jalon) Highland region located in present-day GUINEA that was the site of the FU-

LANI JIHADS (holy wars) that successfully converted the region's inhabitants to the Islamic faith by 1750.

The Fouta Djallon region takes its name from the Yalunka peoples, sometimes called the *Djallonke,* who were the original settlers in the area. *Fouta Djallon* means "highlands of the Yalunka" in the Mande language.

During the 15th and 16th centuries a group of non-Muslim Fulani began southwesterly migrations from what is now the Republic of MALI to the Fouta Djallon highlands. There they encountered the agrarian Yalunka people, with whom they coexisted peacefully until the mid-18th century. At that time another migration of FU-LANI, this time Muslim Fulani, came to the Fouta Djallon and clashed with the non-Muslim Fulani, Yalunka, and neighboring SUSU peoples. In 1725 these tensions led to a Muslim jihad led by the TORODBE cleric Alfa Ba, who was quickly killed in battle. The jihad was then assumed by Alfa Ba's son, the religious leader Ibrahim Sambegu, who had taken the name KARAMOKO ALFA (r. c. 1725–1750). By 1727 the Yalunka and some Susu were pushed out of the Fouta Djallon region while the Fulani and the remaining Susu accepted the Islamic faith.

After the successful jihad, Karamoko Alfa was named the Fouta Djallon's first *almamy* (political and religious head). He divided Fouta Djallon into nine territories, called *diwe,* which were headed by local chiefs. The *diwe* were then sectioned into villages, or *misside,* with specific areas for both the free community and those in bondage. The area of town that housed the free people was called *fulaso* while those in bondage lived in *runde.*

Over the next century Fouta Djallon became an important center of Islamic education as well as a profitable regional trading outpost. After Karamoko Alfa's death about 1750, a Fulani warrior cleric named Ibrahim Sori (r. c. 1751–1784) continued the jihad. Despite wars of succession that ensued after Karamoko Alfa's death, the *almamy* of Fouta Djallon remained a powerful force in the region until the late 19th century, when France conquered and colonized the area.

See also: FRANCE AND AFRICA (Vol. III); FOUTA DJALLON (Vol. II); JIHAD (Vols. II, IV); YALUNKA (Vol. II).

Fouta Toro (Futa Toro) Highland region located between the lower Senegal River and the Gambia River in present-day SENEGAL. The Fouta Toro region was the original home of the FULANI people, who organized successful Islamic jihads (holy wars) in the 17th and 18th centuries.

The area was also the site of heavy slave trading in the same period.

Until the middle of the 16th century Fouta Toro was occupied by the TUKULOR people of the TEKRUR kingdom, which was part of the crumbling Mali Empire of the Mande. Around that time, the *silatigi,* or "commanders," of the ruling DENIANKE DYNASTY established an independent, non-Muslim kingdom. Though the kingdom flourished, Fulani Muslims took exception to the non-Muslim Denianke leadership. At the same time, European merchants began to arrive in West Africa in greater numbers, making Fouta Toro an increasingly influential trading kingdom.

Until the end of the 15th century, trade in the Fouta Toro region was relatively small-scale, as Muslim DYULA and Fulani traders exchanged salt, palm products, beeswax, and kola nuts with Mande merchants at local markets. After about 1480 Portuguese traders joined in the trade, exchanging their manufactured goods for local products with the people along the Senegal River. Some goods were sent north and east along trans-Saharan trade routes.

Before the slave trade was an important aspect of the economy of Fouta Toro, one of the most important trade items that was exported to Europe was gum arabic, a tree resin that was used in inks, dyes, and adhesives.

By the middle of the 17th century, however, the region had attracted other European powers, including the French, English, and Dutch, who came looking for exotic goods from the area, especially GOLD and ivory. There was also an increasing demand for human captives.

In 1673 a jihad was declared by Fouta Toro's *zawiya* clerics against the non-Muslim Denianke leadership, and some of the Denianke were replaced with Muslims. By about 1680 Islamic reformer Malik Si (d. c. 1699) had led his followers south from Fouta Toro to BONDU, where he established a new Muslim theocratic state. The reasons for these jihads were probably as much economic as they were religious, since the constant warfare in the region created a surplus of captives to be traded for European firearms.

During the 18th century the TORODBE, a wealthy class of Muslim clerics and scholars, rose to prominence in Fouta Toro. They gained influence by opposing the Denianke leadership and calling for extensive jihads against their Mande neighbors to the west and south. Around 1769, a Tukulor sheik named Sulayman Bal (d. c. 1776) declared a jihad in an effort to establish a Muslim state in Fouta Toro. By 1776 he managed to overthrow the last of the non-Muslim Denianke rulers, who had led Fouta Toro for more than 250 years.

After declaring a Muslim state Sulayman Bal seized Denianke land and redistributed it among the Torodbe who had supported him through the jihad. With the holy war won, Sulayman Bal stepped down from his position as leader and named the cleric Abd al-Qadir ibn Hammadi (d. c. 1806) the *almamy*, or *imam*, of the Muslim Fulani state of Fouta Toro. The jihads begun by the Fulani in the 17th century continued into the 19th century. One of the most successful of these FULANI JIHADS was waged throughout the 1850s and 1860s by a Muslim preacher from Fouta Toro named al-Hajj Umar Tal (1797–1864), who conquered the Bambara kingdoms of KAARTA and SEGU to the east of Fouta Toro.

See also: GAMBIA RIVER (Vol. II); ISLAM, INFLUENCE OF (Vols. II, III); IVORY TRADE (Vol. III); MANDE (Vol. III); SENEGAL RIVER (Vol. II); UMAR TAL (Vol. IV); WARFARE AND WEAPONS (Vol. III).

France and Africa Like most other European powers, France's precolonial activities in Africa centered on trade. First, in order to capitalize on the lucrative 17th-century spice trade, the French established trading centers on islands in the Indian Ocean, including MADAGASCAR and the MASCARENE ISLANDS. Later the French turned their attention to West Africa and the trade in human captives.

Trying to establish an Indian Ocean trading colony, the French founded Fort Dauphin on the southeastern coast of Madagascar around 1638. The soldiers at Dauphin suffered from deadly tropical fevers and were subject to attacks from the local peoples, so they abandoned their settlement for the less harsh environment of the Mascarene Islands (Réunion and MAURITIUS), to the east. By the 1670s the national French East India Company had begun trading from Ile Bourbon (later renamed RÉUNION ISLAND), and by 1715 the French also controlled Mauritius. On Ile Bourbon they established a rest and refueling station for ships sailing along the Indian spice trade routes and then quickly organized sugar, coffee, and vanilla bean plantations that used slave LABOR supplied by SAKALAVA traders from the island of Madagascar. The plantations were successful, but because of unrest back in France, the settlements on the Indian Ocean islands never developed into a comprehensive trading network.

The French had sought new territory in West Africa during the reign of Francis I (1515–1547), but it was not until 1659 that a permanent settlement was established on the island of St-Louis, at the mouth of the Senegal River. Initially the French explored the SENEGAMBIA region in search of a navigable route into the interior, but their attention quickly turned to the slave trade. St-Louis was one of several settlements from which the French exported captive Africans to their American sugar plantations in the West Indies. These settlements along the coast of what is now SENEGAL were run by the French West Indies Company until 1672, when that company was replaced by the Senegal Company. The French efforts in this trade met with limited success.

Around the turn of the 18th century France began to focus on the African interior. Under the leadership of André Brue (fl. 1798), the governor of St-Louis, French explorers moved nearly 500 miles (805 km) into the interior hoping to reach the famed GOLD-producing regions of the western Sudan. While the French were unsuccessful in their attempt to find gold, they ended up developing a lucrative trade in gum arabic, a tree resin that was prized in Europe to make dyes, inks, and adhesives. St-Louis prospered as a result, and by 1800 the settlement was one of the primary European trade centers in West Africa.

With the exception of a brief period from 1781 to 1784, when France controlled The Netherlands and therefore the southern Africa cape, France showed little interest in the rest of the African continent outside the West African coast until becoming a major colonial power in the 19th century.

See also: FRANCE AND AFRICA (Vols. IV, V); SLAVE TRADE, THE TRANSATLANTIC (Vol. III).

Further reading: William B. Cohen, *The French Encounter with Africans: White Response to Blacks, 1530–1880* (Bloomington, Ind.: Indiana University Press, 1980); Trevor R. Getz, *Slavery and Reform in West Africa: Toward Emancipation in Nineteenth-Century Senegal and the Gold Coast* (Athens, Ohio: Ohio University Press, 2004).

Freetown City located in present-day SIERRA LEONE that was a destination for emancipated slaves from Europe, Jamaica, and the Americas. Freetown succeeded the short-lived Granville Town, which was the first attempt by the British in Sierra Leone to establish a colony for former slave laborers.

In the early 1790s English abolitionist Granville Sharp (1735–1813) and like-minded businessmen and antislavery activists created the Sierra Leone Company, an organization designed to help repatriate former African slaves from Britain and British territories in North America. In 1792 a ship sailed from the Canadian province of Nova Scotia and returned more than 1,000 Africans to a new colony named Freetown. The area where Freetown was founded was sparsely populated and separated from the Mande trading network by thick forest, but a harbor and many waterways allowed for the easy transportation of people and goods.

Like Granville Town before it, the Freetown colony faltered at first, with the company's officials unsure how to proceed with the distribution of land and the collection of rent and taxes. In September 1794 French ships, disguised with British flags, docked off the coast of Freetown and attacked the colony with cannonballs before raiding and burning most of the town. Freetown survived the attack and slowly began to rebuild, but the colony continued to have financial troubles until it came under the protection of the British Crown, in 1808. Since SLAVERY had been officially abolished in 1807 by the British Parliament, Freetown soon became a regular port for the British navy to bring people rescued from ships bound for Europe and the Americas.

In 1787 Granville Sharp and fellow Englishman and abolitionist Thomas Clarkson (1760–1846) formed the Society for the Abolition of the Slave Trade, which supported the efforts of the Sierra Leone Company.

Some of the original settlers to Freetown came from Jamaica and elsewhere in the Caribbean and therefore possessed their own distinctive culture. Many were Christian and spoke English. These groups became known as Krio society, and they made a name for themselves by becoming active in the administrative and economic issues of the Freetown colony.

See also: ENGLAND AND AFRICA (Vol. III); KRIO (Vol. IV); NAIMBANA (Vol. III).

Further reading: Mary Louise Clifford, *From Slavery to Freetown; Black Loyalists After the American Revolution* (Jefferson, N.C.: McFarland & Company, 1999); Akintola Wyse, *The Krio of Sierra Leone* (London: Hurst, 1989).

Fulani (Fulbe, Peul, Pulo) Muslim people of the FOUTA DJALLON and FOUTA TORO regions of West Africa. Traditionally the Fulani were a pastoral people, although their culture changed as they conquered and absorbed neighboring peoples. The TUKULOR are a Fulani subgroup who occupy areas of present-day SENEGAL and Republic of MALI. At the height of their power in the 18th and 19th centuries the Fulani established several Muslim kingdoms that included much of the western Sudan.

By the 16th century Fulani pastoralists had settled throughout areas of present-day BURKINA FASO and NIGERIA. Beginning in the late 17th century Muslim Fulani clerics began declaring jihads against the non-Muslim MANDE peoples of Senegal, beginning in the kingdom of BONDU. Later, between 1750 and 1900, they engaged in a number of jihads led by, among others, USMAN DAN FODIO (1754–1817), a Fulani chief and religious scholar who considered the kings of the HAUSA STATES in northern

Nigeria to be heretical Muslims. In 1804 Usman declared a jihad against the sultan of GOBIR, the northernmost Hausa state, and by 1812 Usman's followers had conquered most of the other Hausa States. The Fulani also conquered ADAMAWA, NUPE, and YORUBALAND to the south, before finally being driven out of the Lake CHAD region by the forces of the KANEM-BORNU empire. Usman established the SOKOTO CALIPHATE from the states that he had conquered in northwestern Nigeria. He ultimately relinquished control of the eastern part of the empire to his brother, Abdullahi, and the western part to his son, MUHAMMAD BELLO (1781–1837), in order to devote himself to teaching and writing. After Usman's death, his son gained control of the entire empire. The Fulani ruled over the western Sudan until the early 20th century, at which time the British took power.

See also: FULANI (Vols. I, II, IV); FULFULDE (Vol. I).

Further reading: Paul Irwin, *Liptako Speaks: History from Oral Tradition in Africa* (Princeton, N.J.: Princeton University Press, 1981).

Fulani jihads Religious reform movements of the 17th through the 19th centuries led by the FULANI people in the FOUTA TORO and FOUTA DJALLON regions of SENEGAL and GUINEA as well as in the HAUSA STATES of present-day NIGERIA. These movements extended Muslim political and religious power and led to the establishment of two large West African states, the SOKOTO CALIPHATE, in 1808, and the vast TUKULOR empire, in 1854, as well as smaller ones, including BONDU, Fouta Djallon, Fouta Toro, and MACINA. Although some historians call this assemblage of states the Fulani empire, the individual states developed no central authority and had no common purpose except for the spread of Islam under the banner of its own charismatic jihad leaders.

Jihad, the Arabic word for "fight" or "battle," refers to the religious duty placed on believers to convert others to Islam (a name, from Arabic, that means "submission to the will of God") and the rule of Islamic law, either by peaceful means or by the sword. The jihads of the 17th century in West Africa were directed against unbelievers and had the added result of extending Muslim political power; the later jihads of the 18th and 19th centuries were true reformist movements aimed at restoring the full and pure practice of Maliki Sunni doctrine among West African Muslims whose practice of the faith had become syncretistic, or mingled with the "pagan" beliefs and rituals of traditional religion.

The Rise of Fulani Power Moving in search of better pasture land, by the 16th century the cattle-raising Fulani had extended their territory from Fouta Toro to the upper Niger Bend region and were moving eastward into Hausaland, where many eventually gave up pastoralism, became city dwellers in GOBIR and other Hausa

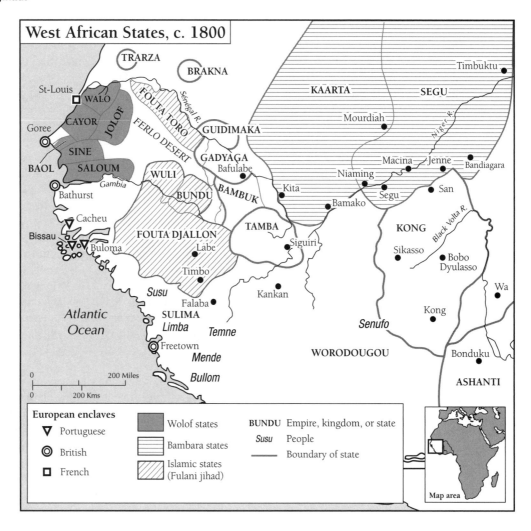

West African States, c. 1800

European enclaves
▽ Portuguese
◎ British
□ French

Wolof states
Bambara states
Islamic states (Fulani jihad)

BUNDU Empire, kingdom, or state
Susu People
— Boundary of state

Map area

states, and adopted Islam. By the 17th century the Fulani had spread across most of the West African savanna.

While they were still pastoralists the Fulani were generally content to tend their cattle and remain isolated from the peoples among whom they lived. However, they came under increasing pressure to pay taxes and tribute to the rulers and peoples on whose lands they grazed their animals. Restrictions placed on Fulani grazing rights and trading privileges intensified Fulani isolation from local sedentary populations, and the Fulani who settled in towns were no more than second-class citizens. Through contact with the Muslim traders in the towns and converted Tuareg pastoralists in the Sahel, many Fulani turned for protection to Islam. The religion offered the support of a broader community and the strength of *sharia,* or Muslim law, with which the Fulani could confront local rulers and demand greater rights. By the early 1700s a tradition of Islamic scholarship had arisen among the Fulani, and a reform movement led by literate, urban-based Fulani and Tuareg TORODBE, or cleric-scholars, pressed for greater rights for Muslims, to be granted by peaceful means if possible or by violence if necessary.

Bondu The first Fulani jihad took place in Bondu, a region near the Senegal valley. One of the Torodbe, Malik Si (d. c. 1699), organized the Fulani into political units called the *al-imam,* or "of the cleric," and led a successful revolt against local Mande rulers to establish a unified theocratic state based on the Quran.

Fouta Djallon Pressure built up in the early part of the 18th century in the nearby Fouta Djallon, a highland region of Guinea southwest of Bondu, below the Gambia River. Many Fulani from a variety of clans, but all members of the large QADIRIYYA Sufi brotherhood, had moved into the region. By 1700 the wealthier Fulani owned many cattle and held many people in bondage and resented paying tribute to local rulers. They sought relief from taxation and the confiscation of their property and the right to build schools and mosques. In 1720s the Fulani cleric Alfa Ba (d. 1725), acting as *amir al-muminim,* or "commander of the faithful," declared a jihad against the infidel SUSU and Mandinka inhabitants and against the non-Muslim Fulani dynasty in power. On Alfa Ba's death, his son, the cleric Karamoko Alfa (r. c. 1725–1750), and a war chief named Ibrahim

Sori (r. c. 1751–1784) continued the jihad, conquering and converting all but the most inaccessible parts of the Fouta Djallon. Sori became the *almamy*, the supreme head of the new regime. Sori attempted to consolidate Fulani rule and take control of the lucrative trade routes, through which GOLD, captives, and goods from Europe passed, but through the 1760s and 1770s he never fully succeeded in establishing a unified state. Although there was often dissension and rivalry among his successors, they always closed ranks when they were threatened by revolt or invasion. In this way the Fouta Djallon region managed to maintain its prosperity during the 19th century.

Fouta Toro The next Muslim Fulani state was established at Fouta Toro, northwest of Fouta Djallon. This area had been ruled in the 1600s and 1700s by the non-Muslim Fulani DENIANKE DYNASTY. About 1769 conflict arose between the ruling class and the Muslim clergy. Cleric Sulayman Bal (d. c. 1776) led the jihad against the Denianke; by 1776 a Muslim state headed by Abd el-Qadir ibn Hammadi supplanted them. Fouta Toro continued to expand in the Senegambia region after al-Qadir's death, eventually controlling some 40,000 square miles (104,000 sq km). Fouta Toro survived until French colonialists arrived early in the 19th century.

Macina The third Fulani kingdom was established in a BAMBARA kingdom, near TIMBUKTU, which had been the site of a large migration of Fulani in the 17th and 18th centuries. The Bambara kings ruled from SEGU. Muslim clerics led by Ahamadu ibn Hammadi (Amadu Sisi) (c. 1745–1844), a member of the fundamentalist Tijaniyya Sufi order, conducted a jihad against the Bambara to establish the state of Macina. In many respects a fanatic, Ahamadu ibn Hammadi believed in using any means necessary to establish a theocratic state, even to the point of destroying the mosques of those whose observance of Islam he judged lax. His jihadists captured the trading centers of Timbuktu and Jenne, and he established his capital of Hamdallahi (Praise Be to God) nearby. Ibn Hammadi's fervor established the Tijaniyya Sufi order as the dominant religious brotherhood in the western portions of West Africa, from which it began to spread eastward. Macina fell to French forces, in 1879.

Sokoto Caliphate One of the most influential of the Fulani jihads began in 1804 in what is now northern Nigeria and was proclaimed and led by a Fulani cleric named USMAN DAN FODIO (1754–1817), also known as "Shehu." The result of this sweeping jihad, which lasted over 30 years, was the formation of the Sokoto Caliphate, a Muslim kingdom that at its height included several of the Hausa States in Nigeria, as well as the nearby kingdoms of ILORIN and ADAMAWA.

The Fulani had been in the Hausa States since the 16th century. During the 18th century incessant warfare among the states, which historically were never more than a loose confederation, led to great instability in the region.

KATSINA and KANO fought over control of the trade routes; and GOBIR, a northern state with a large Fulani population, took advantage of the unrest to seize prime grazing land in the savanna, from ZAMFARA. Seeing themselves as protectors of Islamic orthodoxy, the Fulani had fomented many small revolts against Muslim Hausa rulers whose religious observance they deemed lax.

Born in Gobir, Usman dan Fodio was a Muslim cleric and member of the Qadiriyya Sufi brotherhood. Unable to win power by peaceful means and almost assassinated for his efforts, he proclaimed a jihad against Gobir with help from non-Muslim pastoralist Fulani, who had been repressed by the Hausa for years. Gobir fell in 1810, and within 10 years all of the Hausa States succumbed. To reach his goal, Usman dan Fodio allowed his followers to identify him with the Mahdi, a long awaited messiah-like figure, who believers thought would purify Islam. In the new Sokoto Caliphate that he founded, Usman held both religious authority as caliph and secular authority as sultan, under the title *amir al-muminin*. When Usman died in 1817 his son MUHAMMAD BELLO (1781–1837) took his place as *amir al-muminin*; his brother, Abdullahi, ruled the western emirates, including Gwandu, Ilorin, and Nupe. Under Muhammad Bello, who administered it under Muslim law, the Sokoto Caliphate reached the height of its power. The Sokoto Caliphate persisted until 1903, when Britain incorporated it into the colonial Protectorate of Northern Nigeria.

Other Local Jihads Usman dan Fodio's jihad in the Hausa States resulted in derivative jihads exploding in at least 15 surrounding states, including Bauchi, Adamawa, Nupe, and Ilorin. The neighboring Muslim state of KANEM-BORNU almost fell to jihad in 1811, but the jihad there met with firm resistance and was repulsed by the scholar-warrior-diplomat Sheikh Muhammad al-Amin al-Kanemi (r. 1814–1835), who claimed that the jihad was illegitimate because Kanem-Bornu was already a Muslim state. His defense revived Islam in Kanem-Bornu, and his descendants supplanted the former SEFUWA dynasty and ruled in their place.

The Fulani presence in Ilorin cut off the supply of horses to the OYO EMPIRE and forced the Yoruba people to move south to establish a new capital at the site of modern Oyo. The subsequent collapse of the empire shortly after 1800 led to a period of migration and unrest among the Yoruba that lasted until the end of the Yoruba civil wars, in 1886.

The Jihad of Umar Tal Umar Tal (c. 1797–1864) was a TUKULOR Muslim scholar, mystic, and reputed miracle worker who, in 1854, established the Muslim Tukulor empire between the upper Senegal and Niger rivers in land that is now part of upper Guinea, Senegal, and the Republic of Mali. Under Umar's son Ahmadu Séku (d. 1898), the empire persisted until 1897, when it was taken over by French colonial forces.

Son of a respected Tukulor scholar and teacher and, like Ahamadu ibn Hammadi of Macina, a member of the fundamentalist Tijaniyya Sufi Muslim brotherhood, Umar Tal set out on his hajj, or pilgrimage, to Mecca in 1823. He was well received in the Sokoto Caliphate, where its ruler, Muhammad Bello (d. 1837), gave Umar Tal his daughter Maryam in marriage. Umar Tal reached Mecca in 1827, stayed in CAIRO for a time, visited Jerusalem (where accounts say he miraculously cured the son of Ibrihim Pasha, the viceroy of Egypt), and then returned to Mecca. There he was named caliph, or religious leader, for West Africa by the head of the Tijaniyya brotherhood. Now entitled to the name al-Hajj, Umar Tal returned to Africa in 1833, where he lived in Sokoto under the tutelage of Muhammad Bello. He took as a second wife the daughter of Ahamadu ibn Hammadi, the jihad leader from Macina.

When Bello died in 1837 Umar Tal left for northeastern Guinea to preach Islam. By 1845 he went home to Tukulor for the same purpose. When preaching failed, he decided to use force. He preached a jihad in 1854 against pagans and non-practicing Muslims and spread terror throughout the region to force conversions. In 1855 the Bambara people of Mali accepted Islam under duress but revolted as soon as his armies left. He spent the years from 1850 to 1860 trying to contain his empire, quelling revolts and forcing further conversions, killing thousands and sending thousands more into slavery. Trying to keep the French neutral, in 1860 he signed a treaty with the French governor of Senegal accepting the Senegal River as a boundary for his empire.

In 1861, however, when he attacked the dispossessed Fulani people of Macina, who were adherents of the rival Qadiriyya Sufi Muslim brotherhood, Umar Tal was seen as a conqueror, not an agent of God with a divine mission. In 1863 he captured Timbuktu but soon lost the city to the Tuaregs; in a subsequent battle, his army was destroyed by combined force of Tuareg and Fulani soldiers. Umar Tal died when gunpowder blew up a cave in which he was hiding.

Assessment of Umar Tal's accomplishments is mixed. Some historians consider him the one leader able to have unified the Muslim Fulani states in West Africa, whose success was checked only by the arrival of the French and British colonial forces. Others consider him a spectacular failure. Some Muslims compare his life and glories with those of the prophet Muhammad (c. 570–632); others vilify him for shedding Muslim blood.

See also: AHMADU SÉKU (Vol. IV); ISLAM, INFLUENCE OF (Vols. II, III, IV, V); JENNE-JENO (Vols. I, II); JIHAD (Vols. II, IV); MAHDI (Vol. II); MALIKI SUNNI DOCTRINE (Vol. II); SUFISM (Vols. II, III); UMAR TAL (Vol. IV).

Further reading: R. A. Adeleye, *Power and Diplomacy in Northern Nigeria, 1804–1906: The Sokoto Caliphate and its Enemies* (London: Longman, 1971); John H. Han-son, *Migration, Jihad, and Muslim Authority in West Africa* (Bloomington, Ind.: Indiana University Press, 1996); David Robinson, *The Holy War of Umar Tal: The Western Sudan in the Mid-Nineteenth Century* (New York: Oxford University Press, 1984).

Funj (Fung) Nilotic African people of unknown origin who occupied the borderlands along the Blue Nile between the present-day countries of ETHIOPIA and the Republic of the SUDAN. The Funj sultanate was founded by Amara Dungas in 1504. About the beginning of the 16th century, the Funj, who were originally not Muslim, began a 100-year struggle for control of the Gezira region of the eastern Sudan. The Funj founded their capital at SENNAR, on the Blue Nile River, and began to wrest the surrounding territory from the SHILLUK and Abdullabi Arabs; by 1608 the Funj had established their dominance over the Abdullabi. In 1618 the Funj fought a war of expansion with neighboring Ethiopia. forcing Ethiopia's retreat into the mountains of ERITREA and Tigray.

The Funj dynasty reached its peak during the mid-17th century under Badi II Abu Daqn (r. c. 1644–1680). By that time most Funj had at least nominally converted to Islam, which was introduced by Arabic Sudanese missionaries. Led by Badi II, the Funj extended their rule westward into KORDOFAN and southward to Fazughli. Badi II formed an army made up of captives from his military conquests. This group became very loyal to the monarchy, and as a group they soon came to rival the ruling aristocracy for administrative power. Throughout the 17th century the Funj economy relied heavily on the trading of captives who were not fit for military duty. In addition, Funj merchants plied their trade on the caravan route that passed through Sennar along the southern edge of the Sahara on the way to Mecca, in Arabia.

The Funj monarchs were supported by a strong army. During the reign of Badu IV (1724–1762) this army turned against their king. Although the Funj dynasty continued for another 60 years, the monarchy was relegated to a mere puppet of the military leaders. In 1821 the Funj were conquered by the forces of MUHAMMAD ALI (1769–1849), the pasha and viceroy who ruled Egypt for the Ottoman Empire.

See also: OTTOMAN EMPIRE AND AFRICA (Vol. III).

Fur (Fota, Fordunga, Konjara) Central and East African agriculturalists. In the 16th century Arabic Muslim invaders forced the Fur to leave their kingdoms along the Nile. They traveled west, settling in Jebel Marra, a mountainous region of present-day Republic of the SUDAN. Terrace farming techniques enabled the Fur to cultivate cereals, onions, and pumpkins in an arid environment that is not ideal for AGRICULTURE.

During the 17th century the Arab Muslim leader SULI-MAN SOLONG (r. c. 1640–1660) arrived in Jebel Marra, ousted the TUNJUR ruler, and established the DARFUR state as a sultanate. The Nilotic word *Fur* was first used at this time to describe the people of Darfur. The Fur people would soon become active in the North African trade in captives, seizing members of neighboring communities and transporting them to the markets to the south. In the 19th century Darfur was captured by the Ottoman-Egyptian army, but it was turned over to colonial British forces shortly thereafter.

See also: SLAVERY (Vol. III).

Ga (Gan) See GA-DANGME.

Gabon Present-day country measuring approximately 103,300 square miles (267,500 sq km) and located on the western coast of Central Africa, at the equator. Today Gabon is bordered by EQUATORIAL GUINEA, CAMEROON, and the Republic of the CONGO.

Portuguese merchants landed off the coast in 1472, and by the 16th century they were actively trading with such groups as the Vili, the MPONGWE, and the ORUNGU. Trade with these groups at first involved mostly iron, cloth, ivory, and weapons. By the late 16th century other Europeans, including the Spanish, British, French, and Dutch, had joined the Portuguese. It was not long before all of the major European powers were using the coastal areas to barter their goods. Trading continued throughout the 17th century, with expansive networks of land and water routes forming in the Gabon region. While trade of human captives had initially been a small part of the lucrative business with the Europeans, it began to increase in Gabon during the mid-18th century.

One of the dominant forces in the slave trade were the Vili, who were located in the LOANGO kingdom in parts of what are now Gabon and Republic of the CONGO. The Orungu, another trading group, were located in what is now Cape Lopez, off the estuary of the Ogooué River. There the Orungu used the river to transport captives to the European trading outposts, from where they were later shipped to the Americas. The Fang, a seminomadic agriculturalist group, began entering the Gabon area from Cameroon in the late 18th century but did not engage in the widespread trade in captives.

The slave trade began to diminish in the early 19th century. However, bartering African goods for commodities from Europe remained a large part of Gabon's economy. This continued even after the region was colonized by France in the mid-19th century.

See also: GABON (Vols. I, II, IV, V); SLAVE TRADE, THE TRANSATLANTIC (Vol. III).

Further reading: Michael C. Reed and James F. Barnes, eds., *Culture, Ecology, and Politics in Gabon's Rainforest* (Lewiston, N.Y.: E. Mellen Press, 2003).

Gabu Autonomous West African kingdom, once part of the Mali Empire, that covered parts of modern-day SENEGAL, GUINEA-BISSAU, GUINEA, and The GAMBIA. Gabu became important in the salt and GOLD trades, as well as the transatlantic SLAVE TRADE, in the 17th and 18th centuries.

Gabu was founded in the mid-13th century by Tiramang Traore (fl. 1240s), as a tributary kingdom of the Mali Empire, in lands that FULANI people used for farming and grazing. Gabu's founders and leaders, however, were Mandinka by birth, as were the leaders of Mali. Mali's dominance in the region began to wane in the late 1400s and early 1500s, under continued pressure from the SONGHAI EMPIRE, and Gabu then became autonomous. The kingdom prospered and began a period of expansion that lasted until the middle of the 19th century.

Gabu grew rapidly after Mali's decline. The capital remained at Kansala, but the number of royal provinces grew from three to seven, encompassing 20 to 30 royal trading towns. In the land of present-day Senegal, Gabu established the states of Sine and Saloum, whose leaders were from the SERER people. By 1600, however, the Serer threw off Mandinka rule from Gabu and turned Sine and Saloum into independent kingdoms. In what is now Guinea-Bissau, the rulers of Gabu established two additional provinces at the headwaters of the Cacheu River, which flows to the Atlantic Ocean.

Gabu's wars in the region during the 1600s and 1700s provided many hostages for trade. According to one reliable estimate, up to half of the African peoples exported as war captives during this period were produced by Gabu's expansions. As time went on, relations between the ruling Mandinka people in Gabu and the subject Fulani people alternated between harmony and acrimony, and a long-term pattern of peace and open revolt emerged. At the end of the 18th century Gabu was attacked by Fulani raiders and the kingdom began to disintegrate.

See also: GABU (Vol. II); MALI EMPIRE (Vol. II); MANDINKA (Vol. II, IV).

Further reading: George E. Brooks, *Landlords and Strangers: Ecology, Society, and Trade in Western Africa, 1000–1630* (Boulder, Colo.: Westview Press, 1993).

Ga-Dangme (Ga, Ga-Adangme, Ga-Adangbe)

People of present-day GHANA and TOGO. According to tradition the Ga people claim that, during the 13th century, their ancestors migrated together with the Dangme people from what is now NIGERIA. They eventually settled throughout the Accra Plains, in southern Ghana. Although Dangme traditions vary slightly, today the two groups are considered the same people and are referred to as the Ga-Dangme. They reached their present coastal locations in the early 16th century, establishing the towns of AYAWASO, ACCRA, OSU, Labadi, Teshi, Nungua, and Tema as they migrated. Subgroups of the Ga-Dangme include the Ada, Gbugble, Kpone, KROBO, La, Ningo, Osudoku, Prampram, and the Shai. These groups inhabited the region spanning from the VOLTA BASIN to the coastal capital of Accra and from the Atlantic Ocean to the Akwapim Hills.

In the late 15th and early 16th centuries Ga-Dangme groups began trading with Portuguese merchants along the coast. In the 1570s, however, the Ga-Dangme expelled the Portuguese traders from region and burned their trading fort to the ground. Undeterred, Dutch, Danish, and British merchants continued to come to coastal Ga-Dangme villages to trade for GOLD and human captives. The region became known to the Europeans as the GOLD COAST.

In the 17th century the Ga-Dangme were pushed eastward by the rising AKAN state of AKWAMU. Despite the efforts of Okai Kwei (r. c. 1677), who is remembered as his people's greatest *mantse* (king), the Ga-Dangme had to flee their homelands. One group moved from Late to Aflao, and another group migrated east from Ladoku into the eastern hills of what is now Togo. This heavy migration into primarily EWE territory resulted in heated territorial disputes among the various ethnic groups, whose divisiveness allowed Akwamu to strengthen its control of the area.

By the 18th century the Ga-Dangme groups were banding together in order to move out from under Akwamu domination. Following the model set forth by the rival ASHANTI, another Akan subgroup, the Ga-Dangme *mantse* adopted a royal stool. This throne-like symbol of divine kingship served to unify the military might of the Ga-Dangme groups settled around Accra. Before long, however, the Ashanti state had supplanted Akwamu as the regional power, controlling the coastal trade with Europeans. The Ga-Dangme and other southern states eventually allied themselves with Britain to defeat the Ashanti. According to British first-hand accounts, Ga-Dangme warriors displayed special valor in helping deliver the decisive blows at the battle of Karamanso (1826). The Ga-Dangme were then free from Ashanti rule, but within half a century Britain had established its Gold Coast colony in territories formerly ruled by the Ga-Dangme. In fact, the British moved their colonial capital to the former Ga-Dangme capital of Accra.

See also: GA-DANGME (Vol. II); GOLD COAST COLONY (Vol. IV); VOLTA RIVER (Vols. I, II).

Further reading: C. O. C. Amate, *The Making of Ada* (Oxford, U.K.: African Books Collective, 1999); D. K. Henderson-Quartey, *The Ga of Ghana* (London: D. K. Henderson-Quartey, 2002); John Parker, *Making the Town: Ga State and Society in Early Colonial Accra* (Portsmouth, N.H.: Heinemann, 2000).

Gambia, The

Present-day West African country measuring approximately 4,360 square miles (11,290 sq km) and bordered by SENEGAL in all directions except along its western Atlantic Ocean coast. Before the arrival of Europeans in the 15th century, the inhabitants of the Gambia region included Wolof, Mandinka, and FULANI peoples.

Although the Portuguese were the first Europeans to settle and establish trade in the area, their interest waned by the 16th century, and they moved their enterprises to more profitable regions along the west coast. By the 17th century British and French traders took a renewed interest Gambia and forced out the remaining Portuguese. In 1651 a trading post was set up by the duke of Courtland on an island in the Gambia River. A decade later the British took control of the island, renaming it James Island after the duke of York and using it as their center for Gambian trade well into the 1700s. The British, however, were not without competition. In 1681 the French built a trading station nearby at Albreda.

Throughout the 18th century France and Britain battled continuously for dominance in the region. The British established the colonial province of SENEGAMBIA but handed it over to the French in 1783, following the Treaty of Versailles.

From the 16th to the 19th centuries nine independent Mandinka kingdoms, as well as the Serer and Wolof kingdoms, steadily developed. These kingdoms not only clashed with each other but also with the French who, unlike the British, remained very active in the region. Before the end of the 19th century the region was already a major exporter of GROUNDNUTS (peanuts), a trade item that would grow in importance during the colonial era.

See also: GAMBIA, THE (Vols. I, II, IV, V); SERER (Vol. II); WOLOF EMPIRE (Vol. III).

Further reading: Boubacar Barry, *Senegambia and the Atlantic Slave Trade* (New York: Cambridge University Press, 1998); Peter Mark, *"Portuguese" Style and Luso-African Identity: Precolonial Senegambia, Sixteenth-Nineteenth Centuries* (Bloomington, Ind.: Indiana University Press, 2002); Donald W. Wright, *The World and a Very Small Place in Africa: A History of Globalization in Niumi, the Gambia* (Armonk, N.Y.: M. E. Sharpe, 2004).

Ganda (Baganda, Luganda, Waganda)
Bantu-speaking people of the kingdom of BUGANDA, located in the GREAT LAKES REGION of East Africa, in what is now UGANDA. Buganda emerged as an independent kingdom by about 1500 and steadily increased its power over the next three centuries. The Ganda people were primarily agriculturalists, although there were some hunters and cattle herders among them. Antelope, wild pig, buffalo, and leopard were among the animals they hunted for FOOD and hides. Eventually elephants were hunted for the IVORY TRADE.

Musicians and their MUSIC were, and still are, highly regarded by the Ganda, who fashioned a wide variety of musical instruments, including flutes, trumpets, drums, xylophones, harps, fiddles, and lyres. Drums were especially important because they were associated with spirits and royalty. There were two types of Ganda drums, both made out of tree trunks. One was long and thin with a lizard skin stretched over one side; the other was larger and had cowhide skins on both sides. The Ganda king kept a large collection of royal drums (*mujaguzo*), possibly as many as 100, which were presided over by a special guardian, called *kawuka*.

The majority of Ganda cultivated bananas and the closely related plantain, their dietary staples. The Ganda distinguished between at least 100 different types of bananas, the main ones being cooking bananas (*bitoke*), beer bananas (*mbidde*), and roasting bananas (*ggonja*).

The people of Buganda, who are called Baganda, lived in agricultural villages, or *byalo*, made up of individual family households that were surrounded by plots of land, or *kibanja*. The *kibanja* generally included a banana grove, a parcel of land for raising chickens and goats, and another plot cultivated with such crops as TOBACCO, beans, millet, sweet potatoes, MAIZE, and, after about 1500, groundnuts (peanuts). The men cleared the *kibanja* and the women farmed it.

Because the Ganda were closely tied to their land, they developed stable and densely populated settlements. This pattern encouraged the construction of footpaths throughout the kingdom. The Ganda also traveled on Lake Victoria by canoe, which helped them to defend their territory against land-bound invaders and added another line of internal communication.

See also: GANDA (Vol. II).

Gatsi Rusere (d. 1624) *Ruler of the Mwene Mutapa kingdom during the 17th century*

Throughout the 16th century Portuguese traders along the ZAMBEZI RIVER paid tribute to the local ruler—an individual called the *mwene mutapa* , which was also the name of his kingdom—in exchange for the free passage through his territory. If this tribute were not paid, the ruler would seize the Portuguese assets within the kingdom. When this occurred in 1610, the *mwene mutapa* Gatsi Rusere declared a *mupeto,* or forcible confiscation, of Portuguese assets. The ensuing raid resulted in the deaths of many Portuguese merchants.

The Portuguese were unable to exert any control over the MWENE MUTAPA kingdom until the early 17th century. At that time internal conflict forced Gatsi Rusere to seek Portuguese military support in exchange for extensive MINING rights. This arrangement served little purpose because the Portuguese did not possess the capability to exploit these mines, and Gatsi Rusere ultimately was given no assistance in quelling his kingdom's civil wars. As a result, the internal conflicts continued until his death.

See also: PORTUGAL AND AFRICA (Vol. III).

Gezu (Guezo) (1797–1858) *King of Dahomey from 1818 to 1858*

Lacking the GOLD that enriched the neighboring ASHANTI EMPIRE, the kingdom of Dahomey, which flourished in present-day Republic of BENIN during the 18th and 19th centuries, grew prosperous as a result of the trading of captives. At the height of the transatlantic SLAVE TRADE at the end of the 1700s and the start of the 1800s, when Gezu's rule began, Dahomey exported roughly 20,000 humans per year in exchange for shipments of European muskets, as many as 150,000 annually. The kingdom used its military strength both to expand its territory and to take more captives, some of whom Dahomey sold to Europeans, primarily the British, on the slave market. Other captives were kept for LABOR on the royal plantations that provided food for the army and the royal court.

Under previous rulers, beginning with AGAJA (r. 1708–1732), Dahomey no longer served as an intermediary between Europeans along the coast and the inland peoples; it seized control of WHYDAH and ALLADA on the Gulf of Guinea and traded directly with the British. However, Dahomey remained a tributary state of the more powerful Yoruba OYO EMPIRE to the east. Oyo had gained superiority in the region by virtue of its cavalry, which gave it an advantage when it conducted raids in open country.

Gezu became king in 1818 when he seized the throne from Adandozan (r. 1797–1818). The new king took advantage of internal disputes within the Oyo empire and in 1818 declared that Dahomey would no longer pay tribute. To further expand his kingdom Gezu sent armies to seize ABEOKUTA, founded in 1830 by the EGBA people after the fall of Oyo. His attacks failed. About 1840, after Britain had drastically curtailed its overseas slave trade, Gezu successfully shifted the basis of Dahomey's ECONOMY from the trading of captives to PALM OIL, which was valued in Europe as a lubricant for machinery. Ultimately palm oil proved less lucrative than the slave trade, and Dahomey began to decline under Gezu's successor, Glele (r. 1859–1889).

Gezu enhanced the splendor of an already magnificent court and encouraged the arts. During Gezu's reign Dahomey became one of the most highly centralized states in West Africa. The king ruled with absolute power, and Dahomean society was sharply stratified, divided into royalty, commoners, and a servant class. Commoners, whose position could not threaten the king, staffed the central bureaucracy, and male officials in the field each had a female counterpart at court who reported on their activities to the king. Women also served with prominence in the armies of Dahomey. They functioned as royal bodyguards at court, took part in raids on neighboring people, and fought in battle in separate, all-female regiments. Gezu's court practiced human sacrifice, in accord with traditional Dahomean beliefs, to honor the king's ancestors and to bring benefits to the people; when Gezu's grandfather died, 1,300 servants were reportedly killed to accompany him into the afterlife. The polished skulls of Gezu's enemies were displayed on the supporting slats of his throne.

See also: WOMEN IN PRECOLONIAL AFRICA (Vol. III); WARFARE AND WEAPONS (Vol. III).

Further reading: Patrick Manning, *Slavery, Colonialism, and Economic Growth in Dahomey, 1640–1960* (New York: Cambridge University Press, 1982).

Ghana Present-day country located on the coast of West Africa and measuring approximately 92,100 square miles (238,500 sq km). Ghana is bounded by BURKINA FASO, TOGO, and IVORY COAST. Modern Ghana took its name from the ancient Ghana Empire, which flourished from about the ninth century through the mid-13th century in what is now the Republic of MALI. The region that is today's Ghana was also called the GOLD COAST by European explorers and traders due to the great amounts of the precious metal mined from the inland region.

By the 16th century Portuguese traders and settlers had sailed down West Africa's coast and were firmly established in the region at their castle-like fort called ELMINA, located on the Gulf of Guinea coast. Until the increase of the transatlantic SLAVE TRADE about the mid-17th century, Elmina was used as a Portuguese base. This allowed them to dominate the GOLD trade with local groups such as the AKAN, GA-DANGME, and Mande. During this time the area was also the site of the southern Mossi kingdoms of DAGOMBA and MAMPRUSI. In addition, the ASHANTI EMPIRE, in the central forest regions, and other states, including the coastal FANTE kingdoms, thrived in territories now in present-day Ghana.

Along with the gold, ivory, and cloth, human captives were another important trade item for the economies of the kingdoms in the Ghana region. During the first half of the 17th century the numbers of Africans entered into forced LABOR greatly increased—so much so that in 1637, the Dutch captured Elmina Castle from the Portuguese and used it to harbor captives until they could be transported overseas. European groups, including the Danes, Germans, and British (who coined the region's nickname of the Gold Coast), were also active slave traders and built more than 70 forts along the coast, some of which still stand today.

In the latter half of the 17th century the Ashanti kingdom moved toward building an empire under OSEI TUTU (r. c. 1650–1717). Tutu established the capital of his empire at the city of KUMASI and conquered smaller gold-producing towns, including TEKYIMAN, to position the Ashanti as the region's most powerful kingdom. His successor, OPOKUWARE II (r. 1720–1750), continued the territorial expansion of the Ashanti Empire by conquering more gold-producing cities and people, including BANDA, DAGOMBA, GONJA, and AKYEM. By the mid-18th century, the Ashanti were in control of a large portion of present-day Ghana and remained so until being conquered by Britain in the early 20th century.

As early as the 17th century the region had become so immersed in the European slave trade that the gold trade suffered. In the early 19th century Britain abolished slave trading, and the gold trade again became active, although it never regained the importance it once had during the late 15th and 16th centuries. By the 19th century Britain was extending its control over the area of present-day Ghana, and by 1874 the British had established the area as the crown colony of the Gold Coast.

See also: DENMARK AND AFRICA (Vol. III); ENGLAND AND AFRICA (Vol. III); GHANA (Vols. I, II, IV, V); IVORY TRADE (Vol. III); MANDE (Vol. II); NETHERLANDS AND AFRICA (Vol. III); PORTUGAL AND AFRICA (Vol. III); TRADING OUTPOSTS, EUROPEAN (Vol. III).

Further reading: Kofi Nyidevu Awoonor, *Ghana: A Political History from Pre-European to Modern Times* (Accra, Ghana: Sedco Pub.: Woeli Pub. Services, 1990).

Gimira One of many subgroups of the larger Cushitic language family. The two principal Cushitic languages are OROMO, spoken in ETHIOPIA and KENYA, and the language of Somali, spoken primarily in SOMALIA, Ethiopia, and DJIBOUTI. Among the many Cushitic language subgroups are the Saho-AFAR, Agaw, Beja, Burji, Geleba, Janjero, Konso, KAFFA, Maji, and SIDAMO.

Gimira-speaking people had established several small states in the southwest and western regions of Ethiopia by the 17th century. These states, formerly known as Shé, Benesho, and Mashengo, were incorporated into the neighboring Kaffa kingdom during the rule of the expansionist Tato Gali Ginocho (r. 1675–1710).

See also: AGAW (Vols. I, II); BEJA (Vols. I, II); KONSO (Vol. II); SOMALI (Vol. II).

Ginga (Nzinga) Central African people concentrated in present-day ANGOLA. The history of the Ginga can be traced back to the the early 16th century and the MATAMBA state, which served as an independent tributary of the KONGO KINGDOM. For more than 300 years the Matamba kingdom was in almost constant conflict with the Portuguese settlers who sought to colonize the region. In the late 16th century the Ginga formed an alliance with the neighboring NDONGO, IMBANGALA, and KONGO peoples, in an attempt to repel Portuguese infiltration of the region. This plan worked until the mid-18th century.

The Ndongo subjugated the Ginga in 1630 and used the Ginga kingdom as a base for attacks against Portuguese colonists. In 1684 a treaty was signed to end further Portuguese expansion. However, in 1744 the Portuguese overtook much of the Matamba territory, continuing their expansionist activities well into the 19th century.

Giriama Bantu-speaking ethnic group located south of the Galana River, near MALINDI on the SWAHILI COAST of KENYA. In the 18th century Giriama traders began to profit from the IVORY TRADE. Usually young, unmarried men, these traders used caravan routes to bring ivory from the Kenyan and Tanzanian interior to the ports of Malindi and MOMBASA. The journey was arduous, but the trade was so lucrative that a young Giriama man could buy land and cattle after only a couple of trips.

Later, in the first half of the 19th century, Giriama traders grew even wealthier when they joined with their KAMBA neighbors to monopolize the supply of Kenyan ivory going to ports along the Swahili Coast.

See also: GIRIAMA (Vol. II).

Further reading: Cynthia Brantley, *The Giriama and Colonial Resistance in Kenya, 1800–1920* (Berkeley, Calif.: University of California Press, 1981).

Gobir One of the seven original HAUSA STATES located in NIGERIA between Lake CHAD and the Niger River. While the state of Gobir was probably founded as far back as the 11th century, its actual rise to prominence took place several hundred years after that. According to traditions describing the inception of the seven Hausa States, sometime in the 10th or 11th century a prince from Baghdad named Bayajida married a Hausa queen. This, says the legend, led to the creation of Gobir and the other "true" Hausa states of KATSINA, Rano, Biram, Zazzau (later called ZARIA, after its capital), KANO, and Daura.

Because the individual Hausa states were not formally united, they constantly challenged each other for both political and trading rights—with Gobir beginning its preeminence during the early to mid-18th century. By the 1770s Gobir also had become known as the homeland of the Islamic scholar USMAN DAN FODIO (1754–1817), who later led the FULANI jihad of 1804. It was this holy war that, by 1808, led to Gobir's incorporation as an emirate of the SOKOTO CALIPHATE.

See also: BIRAM (Vol. II); DAURA (Vol. II); GOBIR (Vol. II); RANO (Vol. II).

Gojjam (Gojam) Kingdom located in the mountainous region south of Lake Tana and the Blue Nile River in ETHIOPIA. Gojjam was probably founded in the 13th century by the Agaw, most of whom had adopted Christianity by the 14th century.

During the latter part of the 16th century Gojjam was the the eventual settling place for waves of Christian refugees from DAMOT, to the south. These settlers were fleeing the OROMO who were moving into their territory in large numbers. Between about 1605 and 1617, under the leadership of Christian emperor Susenyos (r. 1607–1632), Gojjam itself resisted attacks by the Oromo. In 1627 the

Oromo tricked Gojjam's governor, Buko, by pretending to attack Enarya, a Christian region to the south of Damot. Feeling confident that the Oromo were busy elsewhere, the residents of Gojjam were unprepared when the Oromo attacked, ransacked the province, and escaped back across the Blue Nile before the people of Gojjam could retaliate. The Oromo carried out further expeditions against Gojjam over the next three decades, despite suffering a serious defeat at the hands of Emperor FASILIDAS (r. 1632–1667) in 1636.

The conversion of the Agaw in Gojjam took place as the result of a relentless campaign carried out by Ethiopian emperor Amda Siyon (c. 1314–1344). Gojjam's king, Zankimir (c. 1323–1324), resisted the new religion and became known to Ethiopian Christians as Sara-Qamis, meaning "enemy to God." Amda Siyon sent priests and monks to Gojjam, where they established monasteries and churches. This angered Zankimir, particularly when Amda Siyon sent the monk Yafqiranna-Igzi to Sana Qirqos, a small island near Gojjam that Zankimir once ruled. The efforts at Christianization took root, and by the middle of the 18th century the majority of Gojjam's inhabitants had converted.

See also: AGAW (Vols. I, II); AMDA SIYON (Vol. II); BLUE NILE (Vol I); CHRISTIANITY, INFLUENCE OF (Vol. III).

Further reading: Harold G. Marcus, *A History of Ethiopia* (Berkeley, Calif.: University of California Press, 1994); Richard Pankhurst, *The Ethiopians: A History* (Malden, Mass.: Blackwell Publishers, 2001).

gold The gold trade in Africa began as early as the seventh century, or perhaps even earlier, and the trade peaked around the late 16th century, when the slave trade gained momentum. While the trade of gold extended throughout most of Africa, the regions that produced gold were mainly concentrated in the southeast within areas of present-day ZAMBIA and ZIMBABWE, and in the west in parts of GHANA and GUINEA.

Gold Trade in West Africa From the 16th century on, the lucrative trade in gold had moved away from the trans-Saharan caravan routes that carried the gold to the northern regions of Africa from such important trading centers as GAO, JENNE and TIMBUKTU. Instead routes were established running away from the interior and toward the emerging trading outposts located on the coastlines of West Africa and southern East Africa. These areas had Portuguese, Dutch, and British mercantile ports, where local traders would bring their gold dust, nuggets, and bars to trade for other metals, weapons, and horses from Europe, as well as for cloth, salt and other items brought from other parts of Africa.

The Portuguese started trading on the GOLD COAST (present-day Ghana) about the 1470s. In 1482 they established São Jorge de Mina, the first fort within the tropics of West Africa. São Jorge later became known simply as ELMINA, as the gold-rich area had become known to the Portuguese as *el mina,* or "the mine." There the Portuguese conducted business mostly with the AKAN and Mande peoples, with whom they traded metal goods and cloth for gold and human captives, who were shipped back to Portugal for forced servitude. It is estimated that by the early 16th century the Portuguese had secured about one-quarter of their country's gold supply from their trade with West Africa.

Gold extracted from the regions of what is now Ghana represented about one-tenth of the entire world's supply of gold by the early 16th century.

In West African regions, such as the Gold Coast and present-day Guinea, the British became increasingly active in the gold trade beginning around the mid-16th century. The Dutch, Spanish, Danish, and French followed soon thereafter. While the gold trade reached its apogee by about the late 16th century, the Dutch and British in particular remained highly active and overcame the competing European nations for dominance of the trade by the mid-17th century. The Dutch, for example, were able to overtake the Elmina fort in 1637, forcing the Portuguese to trade mostly from their ships docked in the ports of the Gold Coast.

Around the beginning of the 18th century the gold trade began to wane in West Africa, due initially to the a combination of clashes between ethnic groups of the interior and the harshness of some of the European directors who governed trade relations. The Dutch attempted to revive the trade by offering gifts such as silk and velvet cloths, gilded mirrors, and large fringed umbrellas known as *quitasols* to the local chiefs. However, their offerings did little to increase the volume of gold exported back to Europe. Rather, the Akan peoples, who remained the main source of gold for the Europeans, began to use other methods to gain wealth in their kingdoms, including using cowrie shells in place of gold in their exchanges with North Africa. For their dealings with the Europeans, however, the gold-producing states became highly active in the trading of another commodity: human captives. By 1705 the Gold Coast was also known as the SLAVE COAST.

Gold Trade in East Africa The 16th century saw the Portuguese beginning to occupy parts of southern East Africa as well. By about 1510 they had conquered several of the Muslim city-states on the SWAHILI COAST, and beginning in the 1530s they had moved inland toward the gold-producing regions along the ZAMBEZI RIVER. The most popular gold-trading center at this time was SOFALA, on the coast, to the east of the MWENE MUTAPA kingdom in present-day Zimbabwe and MOZAMBIQUE. The Portuguese efforts at total domination of the gold trade failed, however, despite a treaty with the king of Mwene Mutapa. Their efforts were constantly thwarted by disease, hostilities with the local peoples, and resistance from Arab, Muslim, and Swahili merchants, who had been trading in the region for centuries. By 1529 the Portuguese also had to contend with increasing French presence in southeast Africa. The English and Dutch, too, had established trading rights in the region by 1580 and 1595, respectively. The gold trade in this region remained strong only until about 1650, when both the slave trade and the spice trade with India began to intensify. By 1698 the Portuguese were driven out of their headquarters at FORT JESUS, located in the city of MOMBASA in present-day KENYA. Although the African gold trade continued with the Europeans in the coming centuries, the powerful Swahili traders had shifted their profitable inland routes away from the coastline toward the southern regions of Africa.

The gold trade nevertheless continued, albeit at a reduced rate, throughout the 18th century, despite the fact that European manufactured items used to purchase captives became more and more valuable as the slave trade reached its height. After Britain outlawed the slave trade in 1807, the trade of gold once again increased, as Europeans and Africans alike began to look for ways to keep the successful, if not always equal, trade partnerships in place.

See also: NETHERLANDS AND AFRICA (Vol. III); ENGLAND AND AFRICA (Vol. III); GOLD (Vols. I, II, IV, V); PORTUGAL AND AFRICA (Vol. III); SPAIN AND AFRICA (Vol. III).

Further reading: Timothy F. Garrard, *Akan Weights and the Gold Trade* (London: Longmans, 1980).

Femme de la côte d'or.

Idealized image of a woman from the Gold Coast. Europeans got much of their knowledge about Africa from pictures like this 1796 book illustration by Grasset and Labrousse. © *Archivo Iconografico, S.A./Corbis*

Gold Coast Colonial name for the coastal region that extended from IVORY COAST to TOGO; in 1957 it became the present-day country of GHANA. GOLD mining was a common activity in the interior regions of Ghana as early as the eighth century. During the 15th century the Gold Coast was dominated by AKAN peoples, who were famous for their tremendous gold production and had grown rich by trading the precious metal with Muslim traders. In the latter half of the 15th century the Portuguese became the first Europeans to arrive on the coast. They quickly saw the opportunity to participate in the gold market that they found there, and they built their first trading outpost, ELMINA, by 1482.

In the centuries that followed the Portuguese were joined by other European countries, including France, Britain, the Netherlands, and Sweden. All told, by the end of the 18th century Europeans built nearly 40 forts and castles on land leased from local rulers along the Gold Coast. At these outposts West African gold was traded for European cloth, beads, iron and copper items, firearms, gunpowder, glass, and alcoholic spirits. From the beginning West African captives were also traded there. The African peoples who had developed commercial ties through the gold trade—including the Ashanti and the groups from the kingdoms of ABOMEY, AKWAMU, and WHYDAH—were poised to take advantage of the trading of captured Africans when the transatlantic SLAVE TRADE came to dominate the regional ECONOMY in the 17th and 18th centuries.

By the 19th century Britain had used trade alliances and military force to monopolize the commercial activity on the Gold Coast. Known for centuries by the Portuguese name *Costa d'Mina*, it became known as the Gold Coast after 1874, when it was renamed by the British.

See also: GOLD COAST COLONY (Vol. IV).

Golden Stool   Solid gold or gold-covered wooden stool symbolizing the divine rule of the kings of AKAN subgroups, including the Ashanti and the DENKYIRA. In West Africa stools were commonly used as thrones and were respected as having political importance. Most, however, were hand-carved from wood. The creation of the Golden Stool is attributed to *asantehene* (Ashanti king) OSEI TUTU (c. 1680–1720), who used the beauty and symbolic power of the stool to unite the people of his Ashanti state. About the same time, Boa Aponsem (r. c. 1677–1692), the *denkyirahene* (Denkyira king) commissioned the first Golden Stool for his people, as well. The Golden Stool was held in such high regard by the people that its power and authority were deemed greater than that of the king, and subjects remained loyal to the ideals represented by the stool even if a ruler died or was removed from office. In this way it allowed the unifying spirit of the kingdom to continue regardless of the fate of the ruler. According to popular legend, the Ashanti Golden Stool was sent down from heaven, landing in the lap of Osei Tutu to signify his divine rulership and the unification of his people.

See also: STOOL, ROYAL (Vol. II).

Further reading: Enid Schildkrout, ed., *The Golden Stool: Studies of the Asante Center and Periphery* (New York, N.Y.: American Museum of Natural History, 1987).

Gondar (Gonder)   City located north of Lake Tana in ETHIOPIA that served as the capital of the Ethiopian Christian empire from about 1632 to 1855. About the middle of the 17th century, Christian emperor FASILIDAS (1602–1667) established his capital in Gondar during his campaigns against the rising influence of Ethiopian Muslims. Located in an isolated region north of the Lasta Mountains, the city was an ideal location for the Christian capital, far from the threat of Muslim incursions. Because he was able to escape the constant pressure of military threats in Gondar, Fasilidas had the opportunity to focus on centralizing his powers using the state, church, and monarchy.

Under Fasilidas, Gondar became a center of Christian influence, independent from the Roman Catholic Church, which the Ethiopians found oppressive and threatening (even more so than Islam). He oversaw the construction of many beautiful churches and castles, most of which, unfortunately, do not survive today.

Fasilidas was succeeded by his son Yohannes (r. c. 1667–1682), who continued his father's practice of building churches and developing Gondar as the center of Christian influence in northeastern Africa. Yohannes was succeeded by his son, IYASU I (1682–1706), a Christian warrior-king who also ruled from Gondar, strengthening his empire by building military strongholds and through taxation. Iyasu I was deposed by his son, TEKLA HAYMONOT (r. 1706–1708), and died in 1706, marking the end of the glory of Gondar as the unrivaled center of Christian power in Ethiopia. The emperors who followed Iyasu I were weak and susceptible to court intrigue. From about 1769 to the middle of the 19th century the *negusa negast* (king of kings) at Gondar was a mere figurehead, unable to control either the rival OROMO chiefs or the Ethiopian kingdoms of AMHARA, GOJJAM, SHOA, and Tigray. This period, known as the ZEMENE MESAFINT (Age of Princes), marked a period of isolation and dissolution of the former Ethiopian Christian empire.

See also: TIGRAY (Vol. I, IV, V).

Further reading: Richard Pankhurst, *History of Ethiopian Towns from the Middle Ages to the Early Nineteenth Century* (Philadelphia: Coronet Books, 1985).

Gonja (Guan, Gongya, Ngbanya, Ntafo)   Kingdom in the north-central part of present-day GHANA that prospered in the 16th and 17th centuries by trading GOLD, captives, kola nuts, and other agricultural products with neighboring kingdoms. The most important trading centers in the kingdom were Yagbum, the capital, and Buipe. The people of Gonja spoke Gur and Guang, Niger-Congo languages related to Mande.

> As early as the 15th century, the forest region near Gonja was one of the major sources of kola nuts in West Africa. The nuts have a mildly stimulating effect that made them popular trade items among Muslim traders, whose religious beliefs prohibited the consumption of alcoholic beverages.

Gonja was founded between 1550 and 1575 by invading Mandinka cavalrymen from the SONGHAI EMPIRE. Under the direction of Askia DAUD (r. 1549–1582), the Songhai king, they took control of territory formerly held by the kingdoms of BONO and DAGOMBA and established a royal ruling class known as the *ngbanya*. By the mid-17th century Gonja began to expand under the leadership of Jakpa Lanta (c. 1622–1670), quickly developing a reputation as a strong trading nation. It accomplished this by dominating its tributary kingdoms, including Dagomba,

Stairways leading to the house that once held captives on Gorée Island, near Senegal. The photograph was taken between 1977 and 1998. © Wolfgang Kaehler/Corbis

and various smaller, stateless societies that traded in the region. Many of the captives resulting from these conquests were subsequently traded for gold.

Along with the AKAN states to the south and the MOSSI STATES to the north, Gonja remained a powerful empire until it was conquered and overthrown by the ASHANTI EMPIRE, an Akan state, during the 18th century. The Ashanti name for Gonja was Ntafo.

See also: KOLA NUTS (Vol. I); SLAVE TRADE, THE TRANSATLANTIC (Vol. III).

Further reading: J. A. Braimah, H. H. Tomlinson and Osafroadu Amankwatia, *History and Traditions of the Gonja* (Calgary, Canada: University of Calgary Press, 1997); Ivor Wilks, Nehemia Levtzion, and Bruce M. Haight, *Chronicles from Gonja: A Tradition of West African Muslim Historiography* (New York: Cambridge University Press, 1986).

Gorée Island Small island located off the coast of SENEGAL in West Africa. Gorée was the most heavily trafficked port during the transatlantic SLAVE TRADE. The Lebu people, the original occupants of the island, were pushed out upon the arrival of the Europeans in the 15th century.

The Portuguese were the first Europeans to establish settlements in the region. Calling the island Palma, they quickly set up a fort from which they conducted their commercial activities. Human captives and GOLD were their most valuable commodities, but they also traded gum, wax, hides, and ostrich feathers.

The Portuguese did not, however, enjoy exclusive rights to the trade. No sooner had the Portuguese landed than other European countries began to show interest. In 1588 Dutch traders assumed control of the island and changed the name to Goede Reede, from which the word *Gorée* is derived.

From the latter half of the 16th century to early in the 17th century, Portugal, France, the Netherlands, and England fought bitterly for control of the island and its valuable position in the slave trade. By the 17th century Gorée Island had become the nucleus for the European exportation of captives to the Americas. When Britain abolished slave trading in the early 19th century, Gorée

Island declined as a commercial center. It was under French dominance from 1817 until 1960, when Senegal achieved independence.

See also: FRANCE AND AFRICA (Vols. III, IV, V); NETHERLANDS AND AFRICA (Vol. III).

Further reading: James F. Searing, *West African Slavery and Atlantic Commerce: The Senegal River Valley, 1700–1860* (New York: Cambridge Univ. Press, 1993.

government, systems of By the end of the 15th century a wide variety of systems of government existed on the African continent. Islamic forms of government predominated throughout North Africa and also influenced some of the major states, including the empires of GHANA, MALI, and SONGHAI, in the western Sudan, south of the Sahara desert. In the same West African region, however, other forms of government also continued to exist, and not everybody lived under the rule of large states. The great diversity in the systems of African government can be seen in the region to the north of the great bend of the Congo River. The historian Jan Vansina has noted that there were eight major types of government in the region: kingdoms, principalities, village governments, segmentary lineages, urban governments with rotating leadership, chiefdoms based on matrilineal associations and territory, chiefdoms based on territory, and chiefdoms based on patrilineal associations and territory.

The continent saw several major shifts in the systems of government during the precolonial period. In North Africa the hold of the Ottoman Empire began to weaken over the course of the 18th century, so that by 1800 the states in the region were increasingly autonomous from the sultan in Istanbul. In the western Sudan it was the emergence of theocratic Muslim states from jihads led by individuals such as USMAN DAN FODIO (1754–1817) that introduced new systems of government based on Islamic precepts. A growing European presence was also making itself felt at key points on the coast. This led to coastal enclaves, such as Luanda in Portuguese-ruled ANGOLA, that were governed along European lines. The most important development in this regard was the establishment of the CAPE COLONY in southern Africa in 1652. It was to become the base for a spreading European dominance throughout the region. The early decades of the 19th century witnessed an increase in the European efforts to control larger areas of the continent, presaging the colonial governments to come.

See also: GOVERNMENT, SYSTEMS OF (Vols. I, II, IV, V); OTTOMAN EMPIRE AND AFRICA (Vols. III, IV).

Gqunukwebe South African ethnic group descended from the XHOSA and KHOIKHOI peoples. The Gqunukwebe inhabited the Eastern Cape just west of the Buffalo River.

The name *Gqunukwebe* derives from the Gkunukwa, a Khoikhoi group from the Zuurveld region.

According to tradition, in the middle of the 18th century a Xhosa chief named Tshiwo was to put a number of his subjects to death for practicing witchcraft. Rather than killing them, Tshiwo's executioner protected the accused by giving them sanctuary among a group of Khoikhoi residing along the Mzimvubu River. The two groups subsequently assimilated and formed the Gqunukwebe.

See also: WITCHCRAFT (Vol. I).

Further reading: J. B. Peires, *The House of Phalo: A History of the Xhosa People in the Days of Their Independence* (Berkeley, Calif: Univ. of California Press, 1982).

Grain Coast West African region that today makes up the coast of LIBERIA, also called the "Pepper Coast." The Grain Coast was so named because it was the part of the Gulf of Guinea coast that produced the MALAGUETTA PEPPER, also called "grains of paradise," a precious spice used for both culinary and medicinal purposes. In the 15th century an amount of Guinea pepper, as it was also known, was priced at par with gold. In the late 18th century the Grain Coast became home to freed slaves from the Americas.

Great Boer Trek Northern migration of about 6,000 BOERS, or Dutch-African farmers, that occurred between 1835 and the early 1840s. In 1795 the faltering DUTCH EAST INDIA COMPANY ceded control of the CAPE COLONY to Britain. Though the Dutch took the colony back in 1803, they lost it to the British again in 1806. By the mid-1830s, the first Boer migrants—called Voortrekkers—had begun an exodus from Cape Colony, believing that the British administration favored the indigenous African population and did not adequately address Boer concerns regarding LABOR laws and land rights. They left in a series of migrations, crossing the ORANGE RIVER into the Highveld to the north and the Natal coastlands to the northeast.

The Boers faced resistance everywhere they went. Nevertheless, they were able to forge ahead, largely because the territories into which they moved were occupied by groups that had only recently moved there themselves due to the MFECANE, forced migrations instigated by a ZULU territorial expansion that began around 1820. To the north some of the Boers settled in SOTHO and TSWANA lands, between THABA BOSIU and the Vaal River. Because of the unrest caused by the Zulu campaigns in the region, some Boers were able to make military alliances with the local groups, including the GRIQUA and Rolong, thereby facilitating their migration.

Other Boer groups migrated even further north, into Ndebele territory south of the Limpopo River, where they faced intense opposition. Those who migrated east into Natal, near the Indian Ocean coast, found their trek most dangerous, as fierce Zulu warriors controlled much of the pasture land that they sought. Eventually the Boers defeated many of the indigenous African groups by establishing fortified camps and using firearms and guerrilla tactics.

Although they persevered, the period of the Great Trek marked a difficult time for the Boers. As they moved into the southern-Africa interior in greater numbers, neighboring Bantu-speaking peoples put increasing military pressure on them. In the coastal regions the British, too, viewed the Boers as a threat, worrying that they could disrupt trade on the Indian Ocean. British policies in the 1840s resulted in further Boer migrations and the eventual establishment of the independent Boer republics of the Transvaal and the Orange Free State.

See also: AFRIKANER REPUBLICS (Vol. IV); AFRIKANERS (Vol. IV, V); ENGLAND AND AFRICA (Vol. III; NETHERLANDS AND AFRICA (Vol. III); SETTLERS, EUROPEAN (Vol. IV).

Further reading: Norman Etherington, *The Great Treks: The Transformation of Southern Africa, 1815–1854* (New York: Longman, 2001).

Great Lakes region Vast area in central East Africa that is dominated by Lake Victoria, Lake TANGANYIKA, Lake Malawi (Nyasa), and a number of smaller bodies of water. The Great Lakes region lies along the Great Rift Valley, a geological fault system that runs from western Asia through eastern Africa. In addition to the three large lakes mentioned, significant bodies of water in the Great Lakes region include Lakes Rudolf, Albert, Edward, and Kivu, to the north and east of Lake Victoria, Lakes Bangweulu, Rukwa, and Mweru, near the southern end of Lake Tanganyika, and Lake Chilwa, south of Lake Malawi.

The peoples who occupied the Great Lakes region during the period between the 16th and 19th centuries included the MAASAI, KAMBA, NYAMWEZI, NKOLE, GANDA, HEHE, MARAVI, and YAO. The area surrounding the Great Lakes region includes parts of the present-day countries of ETHIOPIA, KENYA, the Democratic Republic of the CONGO, ZAMBIA, UGANDA, RWANDA, BURUNDI, TANZANIA, MALAWI and MOZAMBIQUE.

See also: GEOGRAPHY (Vol. I); RIFT VALLEY (Vol. I); TANGANYIKA, LAKE (Vol. II); VICTORIA, LAKE (Vols. I, IV).

Further reading: Jean-Pierre Chrétien, *The Great Lakes of Africa: Two Thousand Years of History* (Cambridge, Mass.: MIT Press, 2003).

Griqua South African people of mixed KHOIKHOI and European descent. Dutch colonists began to establish permanent settlements in the southern African interior in the middle of the 17th century. These settlers—most of them young, single males—had sexual relations with the indigenous Khoikhoi women, and by the middle of the 18th century the Griqua had emerged. Most Griqua spoke Khoisan, though many also spoke Dutch.

The children of European men and Khoikhoi or San women in South Africa made up a mixed race that became known as *Coloureds* or, in Dutch, *Basters*. The Griqua are a Baster group.

In the late 18th century the Griqua sought relief from Dutch and then British oppression and migrated from the CAPE COLONY to the region north of the ORANGE RIVER. They quickly adapted to their new environment, becoming farmers, herders, and hunters. They regularly increased the size of their herds by raiding the cattle of neighboring groups.

Gronniosaw, Prince James Albert Ukawsaw (b. c. 1714) *Prince from Kanem-Bornu*

Prince Ukawsaw was the youngest of six children born to the daughter of the *mai* (king) of KANEM-BORNU, a kingdom surrounding Lake CHAD. Throughout the prince's childhood, as described in his autobiography, he possessed a "curious turn of mind." As a young man, too, he was restless, and he accepted an offer from an ivory merchant from the GOLD COAST to go on an expedition.

Upon reaching their destination Ukawsaw wrote that he heard "drums beat remarkably loud, and the trumpets blow." He later learned the drums and trumpets were in his honor, as he was a prince from the kingdom of Kanem-Bornu. Nevertheless his welcome did not last long, as the city's king thought that Ukawsaw might be a spy and sought to behead him. The king changed his mind when he witnessed the bravery at which Ukawsaw faced his execution and ordered him, not freed, but rather to be sold overseas as a forced laborer.

By the time he was sold for two yards of checked cloth and left the Gold Coast on a Dutch ship, Ukawsaw was about 15 years old. His first master was said to be kind and took him to Barbados, where, after some time, he was sold for $50 and brought to America, where he was a house servant for a family in New York. Later he was sold for £50 sterling to a Mr. Freelandhouse, a minister who taught him the Christian religion. Upon the death of Mr. Freelandhouse, Ukawsaw was released from bondage and given £10. He chose to stay on for six more years, serving the widow and her five sons.

When Ukawsaw did leave New York, he became a cook on a ship of the 28th Regiment, helping to attack and pillage ships in places such as Martinique and Cuba. Cheated out of his part of the spoils when the expedition was finished, he sailed to Spain with a shipload of prisoners and then, around 1762, traveled on to Portsmouth, England, with another group of prisoners.

Ukawsaw had long wanted to travel to England after learning about Christianity, as he thought it would be a land filled with holy people where he could live in peace. He instead found England to be inhospitable at first and was surprised at the profane language the British used. He was cheated out of his money and possessions and lived in poverty until he was helped by a preacher named Mr. Whitefield—a man whom Ukawsaw met after reading about him in his religious studies.

With the help of a Mr. Whitefield, Ukawsaw was able to stay in a boardinghouse, where he met Betty, a white woman who eventually became his wife. After making a seven-week trip to Holland to speak about his life to Calvinist ministers, Ukawsaw returned to England to marry Betty. Before he was married, he was officially baptized and took the Christian name of James Albert.

Ukawsaw and his wife had children and continued to live in poverty throughout most of their life together. He eventually moved his family to the town of Kidderminster, where, about 1774, Ukawsaw told his story and allowed it to be transcribed by the countess of Huntingdon, who lived in the town of Leominster. The countess at first chose to keep his autobiography for her personal collection but later decided to have it published with the intention of giving the proceeds to Ukawsaw and his family. The book was published in 1774 and titled *A Narrative of the Most Remarkable Particulars in the Life of James Albert Ukawsaw Gronniosaw, an African Prince, Written By Himself.*

By the time his autobiography was published, Ukawsaw was about 60 years old and frail. Nothing is known of his later life or whether he gained any wealth from his autobiography. His book later became known as one of the first publications by a free black man.

groundnuts (peanuts)

Legumes (*Arachis hypogaea*) originally from South America that ripen beneath the soil rather than above it. Groundnuts are highly nutritious in terms of protein, minerals, and vitamins, and they provide a high degree of food energy. In the United States, where they are called peanuts, groundnuts are usually consumed roasted or boiled. In Africa, however, they are usually pressed for oil for cooking and making stews.

The Portuguese encountered groundnuts in Brazil and introduced the crop to Africa by the 16th century. It became a major FOOD crop in the SENEGAMBIA region, the lower Congo River region, and MOZAMBIQUE, all of which were areas where the Portuguese were active commer-

cially. In the early decades of the 19th century, African farmers in the Senegambia region began to grow groundnuts commercially as a cash crop for export. The Gambia River, which is navigable from the sea for about 200 miles (322 km) inland, provided ready shipping access for this bulk crop.

> **The local Bantu-speaking people in the area of the mouth of the Congo River called groundnuts *nguba*. Many people from this area were taken captive and shipped to the American South in the transatlantic SLAVE TRADE. Groundnuts accompanied them as did the name, which eventually was transformed into the common term "goobers."**

The oil from groundnuts could be used as a lubricant for machinery in the era before petroleum products were available. It also was used to make foods such as margarine. France became the major importer of groundnuts from this region, and by the middle of the 19th century, the economy of the GAMBIA became almost entirely dependent on exporting groundnuts.

See also: CASH CROPS (Vol. IV); GROUNDNUTS (Vol. IV).

Gugsa, Ras (Gugsa Mersu Ras) (r. 1803–1825)

Regional ruler of Yejju Province in north-central Ethiopia

Ras Gugsa ruled YEJJU Province in north-central ETHIOPIA during the period called the ZEMENE MESAFINT (1769–1855), or the "Age of Princes." During this era the central monarchy was weak, and provincial ruling families wielded power behind the scenes.

Gugsa's father, Ras Ali Gwangwil (d. 1788), also known as Ali the Great, was the first of six rulers bearing the title *ras* (meaning "regional ruler" or "governor") to hold power in Ethiopia prior to ascension of Emperor Téwodros II (1820–1868), in 1855. Ras Ali's family conducted foreign policy and controlled royal appointments in the name of the emperor, Tekla Giyorgis I, who ruled, in evidence of the volatility of the times, from 1779 to 1784, from 1788 to 1789, and intermittently from 1794 to 1800. A member of the northern OROMO people who had converted to Islam, Ras Ali was the first of the rulers of Yejju Province to be baptized, although his embrace of Christianity was seen by many as insincere and merely a means to maintain control over the Christian emperor and the capital city of GONDAR.

Gugsa's succession did not come easily. When his father died in 1788, a period of anarchy ensued during which both the enemies and supporters of Ras Ali fought bitterly against one another, sacking Gondar and the trading province of Begemder and massacring and capturing the local peasants. Following his father's death Ras Gugsa struggled for 15 years to overcome his rivals, but finally won the throne in 1803. He married one of the daughters of Emperor Tekla Giyorgis and had eight children, although not all by his wife.

Gugsa was a ruthless ruler who tyrannized the nominal emperor, Egwala Siyon (1801–1817), and closely controlled every aspect of government, enabling him to enjoy, for the most part, a peaceful reign. He consolidated his relationship with the Christian lords—including Haile Mariam of SIMIEN, Maru of Dembya, and Welde Rafael and Wagshum Kenfu—by promising them his daughters in marriage.

The biggest threat to Gugsa's leadership was the campaign of Ras Wolde Selassie (d. 1817), of Tigray. He sought to destroy the ruling family of Yejju and reestablish the Ethiopian monarchy. A member of an old Christian family of Tigray Province who hated the Oromo from Yejju, Ras Wolde Selassie rallied the princes of Simien and Tigray provinces to join him in his war against Yejju. Gugsa's vigilance paid off between 1811 and 1812, when he cunningly played his enemies against one another until they eventually became disinterested in the cause and fragmented, leaving Wolde Selassie alone and defeated and bringing Sahle Selassie (r. 1813–1847) to the throne.

When Gugsa died in 1825, another great battle for the throne of Yejju Province ensued, resulting in the short and ineffective reigns of his sons Yeman (1825–1828), Marye (1828–1831), and Dori (1831, three months).

Guinea West African country situated in the Atlantic coast that is some 95,000 square miles (246,100 sq km) in size. It is bordered by GUINEA-BISSAU and SENEGAL to the north, Republic of MALI to the north and east, IVORY COAST to the east, and LIBERIA and SIERRA LEONE to the southwest.

Beginning in the late 15th century, *Guinea* was also the European term used to refer to the West African coast. Three independent nations in the region use the name today—the Republic of Guinea, Guinea-Bissau, and EQUATORIAL GUINEA, the southernmost of the three. The other present-day African countries whose coastlines made up the Guinea coast include, from north to south: WESTERN SAHARA, MAURITANIA, Senegal, The Gambia, Sierra Leone, Liberia, Ivory Coast, GHANA, TOGO, the Republic of BENIN, NIGERIA, and CAMEROON.

Guinea was renowned in Europe for its GOLD production, first attracting Portuguese traders in the 15th century. In later centuries traders from France, Britain, Spain, Sweden, and The Netherlands also participated in the gold trade.

Rising some 3,000 feet (914 m) above the coastal plains at the headwaters of the GAMBIA RIVER, the mountainous FOUTA DJALLON region of Guinea became prominent during the 15th and 16th centuries. Although the FULANI appear to have been present in this region from an early date, by the middle of the 15th century they were joined by additional Fulani migrants, many of whom were Islamic converts from Senegal. In the 18th century the Fulani developed a theocratic state steeped in Islamic RELIGION and culture.

See also: GUINEA (Vols. I, II, IV, V).

Further reading: George E. Brooks, *Landlords and Strangers: Ecology, Society, and Trade in Western Africa, 1000–1630* (Boulder, Colo.: Hestview Press, 1993); Walter Rodney, *A History of the Upper Guinea Coast, 1545–1800* (Oxford, U.K.: Clarendon Press, 1970).

Guinea-Bissau Small republic in West Africa measuring about 14,100 square miles (36,500 sq km) and bordered by GUINEA on the south and east and by The GAMBIA and SENEGAL to the north. Although the mainland portion of the country is small, Guinea-Bissau also includes 60 offshore islands—inhabited by the BIJAGO people—that are considered part of its overall land surface. The interior includes low-lying alluvial plains, massive mangrove swamps, and savanna woodlands. The country rises to a plateau on its eastern side, reaching a height of approximately 1,017 feet (308 m) in the southeast.

Guinea-Bissau has numerous rivers and tributaries, including the Geba, which have historically served as an essential means of transportation and trade. These rivers also provide a drainage network for the region. Although prone to flooding during heavy seasonal rains between May and October, the rivers may have sustained as many as 20 different ethnic groups beginning as early as 9000 BCE. Its original population consisted of hunter-gatherers who supplemented their subsistence diet with fishing.

A great influx of migratory groups occurred in the region between 900 and 1000 CE as a result of climatic changes, the need to secure reliable FOOD resources, and warfare in bordering regions. This secondary group included FULANI cattle herders and diverse groups of agriculturalists such as the Malinke, who grew COTTON and, later, GROUNDNUTS (peanuts). Other groups, such as the Balanta, one of the largest groups occupying the country's central and southern regions, practiced communal farming. The Balanta came to be paddy-rice growers with villages and small chiefdoms were organized according to paternal lineage. Other groups such as the Bijago and the

Manjaca and Pepel from the northern coast developed an economy based on the trade of sea salt, palm wine, and PALM OIL.

The region was the site of the powerful kingdom of GABU, founded in the 13th century. Between the 15th and 16th centuries the rise of the SONGHAI Empire, the demise of the Mali Empire, and the arrival of Portuguese traders ensured Gabu's continued power and independence. Wars between the Mandinka and surrounding Fulani people provided Gabu with captives, who were sold as forced laborers to further enrich the kingdom. Gabu remained a power in the region until the late 19th century.

See also: CACHEU (Vol. III); GUINEA-BISSAU (Vols. I, II, IV, V); MALINKE (Vol. II); MANDINKA (Vol. II); PORTUGAL AND AFRICA (Vols. III, IV, V).

Further reading: Laura Bigman, *History and Hunger in West Africa: Food Production and Entitlement in Guinea-Bissau and Cape Verde* (Westport, Conn.: Greenwood Press, 1993); George E. Brooks, *Landlords and Strangers: Ecology, Society, and Trade in Western Africa, 1000–1630* (Boulder, Colo.: Westview Press, 1993); Walter Hawthorne, *Planting Rice and Harvesting Slaves: Transformations Along the Guinea-Bissau Coast, 1400–1900* (Portsmouth, N.H.: Heinemann, 2003).

H

Hadya (Hadiya, Hadiyya, Gudela) Kingdom of the SIDAMO people established by the end of the 13th century southwest of SHOA, in ETHIOPIA. The people of Hadya speak an Eastern Cushitic language and refer to themselves as Gudela. They are called *Hadya (Hadiyya)* by their Ethiopian and OROMO neighbors. Although Hadya was a primarily Islamic sultanate, the people managed to preserve much of their non-Muslim traditional culture. The title bestowed upon their kings was originally *amano* but was later changed to *garad*. The Hadya have a tradition of cultivating barley, millet, and COTTON.

In his 14th-century observations, Muslim historian al-Umari includes Hadya as one of the six Muslim states in Ethiopia and describes it as an important and wealthy commercial center. Hadya had a long history of conflicts with Christian Ethiopia, dating back to the reign of Emperor Amda Siyon (r. c. 1314–1344), who took many of the Hadya people as slaves. Between the 15th and 17th centuries Hadya was raided several times by the Christian state for failing to make its tribute payments.

According to one account, the wars during the reign of Ethiopian Christian ruler LEBNA DENGEL (r. c. 1508–1540) were caused by his refusal to marry the daughter of the king of Hadya because she was buck-toothed.

In 1532, when the Islamic leader AHMAD GRAÑ (c. 1506–1543) was waging his jihad on Christian Ethiopia, Hadya's king once again sided with the Muslim leader, rather than the Christians. Hadya's interactions with the Christians were curtailed in the 17th century as a result of the disruptions caused by the influx of Oromo people, who migrated to the area in large numbers.

See also: AMDA SIYON (Vol. II).

Hamasien (Hamasen) Province located within the northern highlands of central ERITREA, in northeastern Africa. The inhabitants of Hamasien and the neighboring present-day provinces of Seraye and Akkele Guzay were mostly farmers who were physically similar, subscribed to the same religion, followed the same social structure, and participated in the same cultural traditions; there were, however, some regional differences in certain customs and laws.

During the colonial period Ras Alula (fl. 1870s), originally from Tigray, recognized the commercial importance of Asmara and moved his capital there. Asmara, still Eritrea's capital city, is located in Hamasien Province.

Hamasien's wealth was acquired through hundreds of years of commercial activity. A well-traveled trade route linking Hamasien and the nearby Red Sea port of Massawa with the Ethiopian provinces of Tigray, AMHARA, and SHOA was established in the 14th century.

Hamasien is home to the Mensa and Marya ethnic groups; both speak Tigrinya and adhere to Monophysite Christianity. Throughout the 17th and 18th centuries the province enjoyed political autonomy. Its rulers belonged to the House of Tsazzega from the 1700s until the 1830s and were among the wealthiest families in Eritrea. The founders of Tsazzega were the two youngest sons of Tesfazion Ate-Shum, who governed Hamasien in the 17th century. His elder sons belonged to the House of Hazzega, and for centuries the two houses were fierce enemies. Their rivalry eventually led to the downfall of both houses. Bahr Negash (King) Solomon (d. c. 1743) was Tsazzega's most notable leader, but after his death the position of *bahr negash* lost some of its authority because after him there were several claimants to the title, some of them Hamasien nobles.

See also: MASSAWA (Vol. II); MONOPHYSITE (Vol. I).

Hamdallahi Capital city of the second MACINA kingdom, located near the inland delta of the NIGER RIVER in present-day Republic of MALI. The first Macina kingdom dated to the 15th century. In the early 19th century Shehu Ahmadu Lobbo (1755–1845), a FULANI religious scholar, declared a jihad with the purpose of converting the remaining non-Muslim Fulani people to Islam. In 1810, after establishing his capital at Hamdallahi, Shehu Ahmadu ruled Macina as a theocratic state based on strict Islamic law. (*Hamdallahi* means "Glory to God" in Arabic.) After Shehu Ahmadu's death in 1845, the Macina kingdom fell into decline and later became a tributary state to the BAMBARA kingdom of SEGU.

See also: FULANI JIHADS (Vol. III); INLAND NIGER DELTA (Vols. I, II).

Harer (Harar) Ancient city in eastern ETHIOPIA known since the 14th century as an important center for trade and Islamic learning. Large numbers of captives and sizable amounts of agricultural products from the Ethiopian interior passed through Harer on the way to ports along the Red Sea and the Gulf of Aden, including BERBERA and ZEILA. As it grew in commercial importance, Harer also developed into a political and cultural capital.

> The original inhabitants of Harer were the Adere, a Hamitic people who spoke a southern Ethiopian Semitic language. The Adere were mostly agriculturalists who cultivated fruit, vegetables, grains, coffee, and saffron. They also raised a mildly narcotic plant called *qat.*

With a reputation as a Muslim holy city (it contained more than 90 mosques), Harer attracted pilgrims from all over the Islamic world during the 15th century. In 1520 AHMAD GRAÑ (c. 1506–1543), the devout Muslim leader of the Islamic state of ADAL, moved his capital from Deker to Harer. Over the next two decades he successfully penetrated Christian Ethiopia, conquering and pillaging much of the territory that had belonged to the once-mighty Christian empire. Ahmad Grañ's jihad (holy war) was ended in 1541 by Ethiopian emperor Galawdewos (r. 1540–1559) and his Portuguese allies.

About 1551 Ahmad Grañ's nephew Nur (d. 1567) became *imam,* or Muslim leader, in Harer. To defend the city against hostile invaders, Nur built a heavily fortified wall that still stands today. His army had to repel not only the Christian Ethiopians but also the OROMO, who were gradually moving into the Harer region. By the 1570s Harer's importance in the region had waned due to the Oromo migrations and the consequent diverting of Muslim trade away from the city.

In 1577 Imam Muhammad (b. Ibrahim Gassa), a relative of Ahmad Grañ, transferred his government from Harer to Awssa, in the desert to the north. The move proved to be a grave error, as Awssa could not maintain authority over Harer or the Somali clans living on the Harer plateau. Awssa also became vulnerable to AFAR attacks, which further hampered its power and prestige.

Harer's political instability continued on throughout the 17th and 18th centuries, as did Oromo occupation of the region. By the 18th century some Oromo clans embraced Islam and assimilated into Harer society so completely that they became farmers and even paid nominal tribute to the emir of Harer, although they maintained many of their tribal customs as well as their social and political systems. Most Oromo, however, did not assimilate. They stayed true to their pastoral roots and continued their fierce campaign on the Harare plateau.

Between 1647 and 1887, 18 different emirs ruled Harer, and by the end of the 18th century the city's importance as a trading center had declined. Arab, Somali, Afar, and Hareri merchants moved to Zeila, in Adal, which became the major trading post in the Harer region.

By the 19th century the trade route between SHOA and Harer was replaced by a new route that extended from Tajura to Shoa. Shoa also began to control the wealthy markets in Soddo and Gurage, and as a result many merchants left Harer for Aliyu Amba, Shoa's largest market. The governments of both Harer and Shoa worked together to see that the routes between these two centers remained open.

Despite losing its status as a great commercial center, Harer remained an important cultural and religious nucleus, facilitating the spread of Islam in southern Ethiopia.

See also: HARER (Vol. II); ISLAMIC CENTERS OF LEARNING (Vol. II); RED SEA (Vol. I); RED SEA TRADE (Vol. II).

Hausa States (Hausaland)

Group of 14 independent, self-governing states originally located between the NIGER RIVER and Lake CHAD. KANO, its major city, was one of the most important trading cities in Africa as early as the 15th century. At their peak in 1650, the Hausa States controlled territory that stretched from the Jos Plateau in central NIGERIA north to the Sahel, and from the Niger River to the border of Bornu, to the northeast. Hausa traders traveled extensively throughout West Africa. They continued dealing in captives from DAHOMEY (present-day Republic of BENIN) and the land of the Ashanti (in present-day GHANA) even after the European powers curtailed the slave trade in the early 1800s.

Situated between KANEM-BORNU and the Mali Empire in what is now Nigeria, the Hausa States began to emerge in the 13th century out of settlements that had been in existence as early as the fifth or sixth century. These states then became trading centers, with merchants from the rival areas of Mali and Bornu vying for the right to trade items such as GOLD, alum, salt, kola nuts, cloth, animal hides, and henna.

The Hausa States trace their founding to the legend of Bayajida, the mythical Middle Eastern ancestor of the Hausa, which says that there were seven original or "true" Hausa states, including Zazzau (later called ZARIA, after its capital), GOBIR, Daura, Biram, Rano, Kano, and KATSINA. These original states were referred to as Hausa Bakwai while the second set of states was referred to as the "bastard" states, or Banza Bakwai. Depending on the source, these outlying seven states included KEBBI, Gwari, KWARARAFA, ILORIN, Yauri, ZAMFARA, NUPE, and Yoruba.

By the 15th century most of the Hausa population had been converted to Islam, with a few remaining pagans, or MAGUZAWA, a legally protected religious minority, according to Islamic law. Thereafter the Hausa states continued to develop separately with only minor alliances between neighbors. By the end of the 17th century a succession of influential kings had helped their respective states to flourish, both economically and as centers of learning.

The 18th century was marked by phases of territorial growth in the Hausa States, but rivalry among the states kept them from uniting under one centralized authority. This lack of cohesiveness proved to be decisive in determining the success of the FULANI JIHADs waged by the Muslim fundamentalist USMAN DAN FODIO (1754–1818)

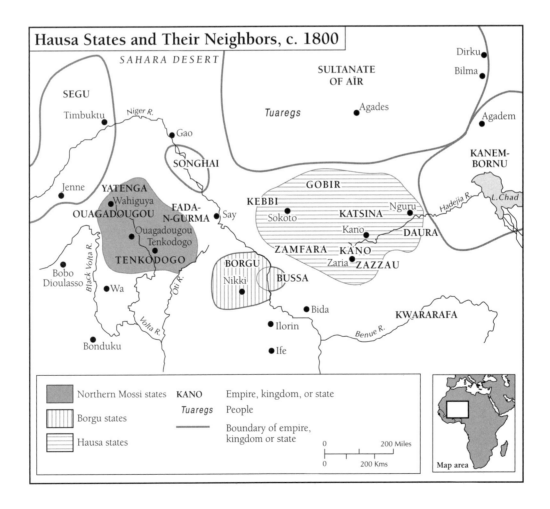

between 1804 and 1808. Ultimately Usman dan Fodio conquered the Hausa States and incorporated each of them into the SOKOTO CALIPHATE, an Islamic empire made up of individual emirates, or states, led by local Muslim rulers.

See also: HAUSA (Vols. I, IV, V); HAUSA STATES (Vol. II).

Hawkins, John (1532–1595) *Admiral and administrator in the English navy who later became the first slave trader in England's history*

Inspired by the exploits of his father, William Hawkins, who traded with Brazil in the 1530s, John Hawkins devised a plan to transport African captives to trading posts in the Caribbean. With the financial backing of English investors and a fleet of three ships, Hawkins set sail from England in October 1562. He landed in SIERRA LEONE, on what was then known as the Guinea Coast, where he acquired several hundred captives and merchandise that he then brought to the island of Hispaniola, in the West Indies, and traded for a wealth of goods. The Portuguese and the Spanish considered

Sir John Hawkins (1532–1595), the first English slave trader, in a print by H. Holland. Hawkins provoked conflict with Spain by transporting enslaved West Africans directly to the Spanish West Indies without the permission of Spain. *© Corbis*

Hawkins little more than a pirate and documented to the British government his capture of at least 16 vessels and their cargoes of African captives. The Spanish were also displeased with his unauthorized trading with their Caribbean colonies.

Because of the great profits from his first voyage, Hawkins's second trip was funded by another group of investors, which included Queen Elizabeth I (1558–1603) of England. On October 18, 1565, he set sail once again for Sierra Leone, where his group captured and then traded 400 Africans. In 1567 he made his third voyage to Africa, this time accompanied by the English explorer Francis Drake (c. 1540–1596). After selling their human cargo in the Caribbean, their fleet of ships was attacked in the harbor by Spanish vessels. Only the ships commanded by Hawkins and Drake sailed back home. This attack was the basis for the hostility between Spain and England that led to war in 1585.

In 1577 Hawkins became treasurer of the navy, and he was promoted to comptroller in 1589. On November 15, 1595, while on an expedition to the West Indies with Drake, Hawkins died at sea off the coast of Puerto Rico.

See also: SLAVE TRADE, THE TRANSATLANTIC (Vol. III).

Haya (Bahaya) Bantu-speaking people of present-day TANZANIA. Evidence suggests that ancestors of the Haya migrated into their homeland in about the 13th century. The Haya occupy some of the richest land in the entire region, and their traditional homes, which are beehive-shaped huts with thatched roofs, are well known.

From the earliest days the Haya have maintained a sophisticated social and political hierarchy. Eventually, they developed a system of kingship in which the monarch was both the ritual and the main administrative leader. Beneath this centralized authority, various princes administered the kingdom's smaller districts, and, although these districts were most often ruled by members of the royal family, it was not unknown for certain commoners to assume those tasks. Indeed, commoners generally held the most important positions at the royal court, giving them a substantial amount of power in the governance of the kingdom.

The Haya originally were divided into separate chiefdoms, with Karagwe in the west, Shangiro in the south, and Greater Kyamtwara in the east. A northern chiefdom, known as Kizibo, was ruled by LUO-speaking BITO people. This changed, however, when the Chwezi dynasty fell from power in the neighboring Kitara Complex about the beginning of the 15th century. Moving south, the HINDA aristocrats from Kitara spread their caste system to the Haya and other peoples with whom they came in contact.

See also: BUNYORO-KITARA (Vol. II); CHWEZI DYNASTY (Vol. II); KARAGWE (Vol. II); KITARA COMPLEX (Vol. II).

Further reading: Peter R. Schmidt, *Iron Technology in East Africa: Symbolism, Science, and Archaeology* (Bloomington, Ind.: Indiana University Press, 1997); C. M. Tibazarwa, *Economic Revolutions in Bahaya History* (Braunton, U.K.: Merlin Books, 1994).

Herero Seminomadic pastoralist ethnic group of southern ANGOLA, northwestern BOTSWANA, and northern NAMIBIA, where they are called *Himba*. This Herero group is not to be confused with the Himba of KAOKOLAND, in southern Namibia, who are a subgroup of the Herero, as are the Mbanderu, also of Namibia. The Bantu-speaking Herero migrated to southwestern Africa from Central Africa during the 16th century. The southern boundary of Herero territory abutted the northern territory of the Khoisan-speaking NAMA people, with whom the Herero traded and intermarried. Despite their close ties the two herding peoples frequently clashed over issues regarding land and water use.

Until the 19th century the Herero roamed the savannas, living off the products of their large herds of cattle, sheep, and goats. Herero women cultivated some crops, but the maintenance of the herds remained the most important feature of Herero culture. Herero life largely followed long-established traditional patterns until the arrival of European MISSIONARIES in the early 19th century. Eventually the Herero acquired German firearms and intensified their efforts to control disputed land that was claimed by them, the Nama, and the ORLAMS, another Khoisan-speaking group.

See also: HERERO (Vols. II, IV, V); HIMBA (Vol. II).

Hinda (Bahinda) Aristocratic ruling clan that rose to prominence during the 15th century, following the fall of the Chwezi dynasty in the Kitara Complex, a collection of chiefdoms in present-day UGANDA. Hinda clan members ruled in a number of East African kingdoms, including NKOLE, BURUNDI, and Karagwe. The Hinda in the Nkole and Burundi kingdoms, among others, were also known as TUTSI. Groups of Hinda aristocrats also moved to the southern shores of Lake Victoria, where they mixed with HAYA and Zinza groups to form states in what is now northern TANZANIA.

See also: CHWEZI DYNASTY (Vol. II); HINDA (Vol. II); KARAGWE (Vol. II); KITARA COMPLEX (Vol. II).

Horn of Africa See HORN OF AFRICA (Vol. I); SOMALIA (Vols. I, II, III, IV, V).

Hottentot Pejorative term coined by Dutch settlers in SOUTH AFRICA to describe the KHOIKHOI people. The word *Hottentot* apparently was derived from the Dutch phrase *hotteren-totteren,* meaning "to stammer." This probably was in reference to the fact that the Khoikhoi language utilizes numerous clicking sounds. The negative connotation of Hottentot developed during the 17th and 18th centuries, during which the Dutch were constantly warring with the Khoikhoi over grazing lands and trade.

See also: NETHERLANDS AND AFRICA (Vol. III).

Husseinid dynasty Succession of beys, or rulers, who governed what is now the country of TUNISIA from 1705 until the region became a republic in 1957. The founder of the dynasty was a military officer of the Ottoman Empire named al-Hussein ibn Ali (r. 1705–1735), who came into power in 1705 when the reigning Tunisian ruler was ousted by forces from present-day ALGERIA. Like the MURADID DYNASTY (r. 1631–1702) rulers before him, al-Hussein chose to assume the title of *bey* instead of the more commonly used Ottoman title of *dey*. Al-Hussein was also named *beylerbeyi,* or governor, of the region, and by 1710 he had secured a law stating his offices would be passed down through a line of hereditary succession.

From the beginning of al-Hussein's reign he was able to operate more or less independently of the Ottoman Empire. By 1728 he had made profitable trade alliances with such European powers as Britain, France, the Netherlands, Spain, and Austria, as well as with the Mediterranean privateers, or PIRATES, known as CORSAIRS. The reigns of the beys who immediately followed al-Hussein were marked by succession disputes as well as clashes with both Europeans and Algerians. For example, Ali Bey, who ruled Tunis from 1735 to 1756, was captured and beheaded by Algerians when they briefly took control of the city. Ali Bey's successor, Hammuda Bey (r. 1782–1814), was forced to discontinue relations with the Italians after they attacked two coastal towns in 1784 and 1785. Later Hammuda Bey fended off attacks from the Algerians in both 1807 and 1813, and he also managed to suppress uprisings by the professional Ottoman military corps known as Janissaries.

Despite these and other setbacks, the Husseinid beys continued to have successful reigns well into the latter half of the 19th century. However, after Tunisia was colonized by France in 1883, the beys became mere figureheads, a situation that lasted until the dynasty ended in 1957, when the former colony became the Republic of Tunisia.

See also: OTTOMAN EMPIRE AND AFRICA (Vols. III, IV).

Hutu (Bahutu, Wahutu) Bantu-speaking peoples of the GREAT LAKES REGION of Central Africa in what is now RWANDA and BURUNDI. The Hutu cultivated large fields of beans, peas, sorghum, sweet potatoes, cassava, and MAIZE.

They also tended smaller fruit and vegetable gardens, as well as groves of banana trees. Bananas were used for FOOD and to make beer.

Hutu farmers generally lived in small, valley communities ruled by local chiefs. When the pastoral TUTSI migrated to the area beginning in the 14th century, the Hutu also became cattle herders. The Tutsi were militarily superior, and occupied strategic positions in the hills.

A patron-client, or lord-vassal, system was slowly developed in central Rwanda. Within this system, which they called *buhake*, Hutu men tended Tutsi cattle and performed other services in return for patronage and protection. In the Hutu's Bantu language, the patron was called *shebuja*, and the client was called *guragu*. Similar patron-client systems were established in other parts of the region.

The *buhake* system has been called a caste system, but the social strata were not as strictly defined as in, for example, the Hindu caste system. Hutu were able to achieve higher social and political status, although they then ceased to be Hutu and were called Tutsi. As a group, Hutu were generally relegated to the client position and prevented from holding political power, a situation that led to increasing resentment of the Rwandan Tutsi in later centuries.

As *guragu,* the Hutu served as Tutsi messengers, travel companions, cattle herders, and field and household workers. *Guragu* were also required to give their patrons cow's milk and other gifts. In return the Tutsi *shebuja* provided the *guragu* with access to cattle, cattle products, and pasture lands for grazing. The *shebuja* helped cover dowry payments and other expenses if the *guragu* could not afford them, and provided for the client's immediate family after he died, if relatives could not support them. The patron also provided meat, tools, and other items to the *guragu* in times of shortage.

In Burundi the patron-client system was separate from the political system. The patron-client arrangement was more flexible so that many Hutu in Burundi were economically independent of the Tutsi. Hutu as well as Tutsi could become patrons, owning cattle and exercising political power.

See also: HUTU (Vols. I, II, IV, V).

I

Ibibio People of the CROSS RIVER area of southeastern NIGERIA. The Ibibio are agriculturalists who are known for their artwork, especially woodcarving, and share many cultural similarities with the neighboring IGBO. The traditional lifestyle of many of the Ibibio changed dramatically in the 16th century with the development of the transatlantic SLAVE TRADE. Ibibio groups living in the Niger Delta hinterland continued to cultivate cassava and yams and live in their traditional agricultural lifestyle, but the Ibibio people living near OLD CALABAR, an EFIK city, became heavily involved in the slave trade. These Calabar Ibibio fought often with their Igbo neighbors, with both groups capturing people who were then sold to both local buyers and to Portuguese traders.

In the early 18th century the Ibibio people were defeated by the Igbo, who established a confederation of Igbo-Ibibio towns led by prominent Igbo clan heads. The administrations in these towns came to rely on the proclamations of the AROCHUKWU ORACLE, the earthly representative of a mystical ancestral spirit that inhabited a shrine in Igboland originally built by the Ibibio. In the 1800s the oracle's proclamations often required that a debt be paid with captives, so the local trade in captives persisted even after the European governments began to officially abolish the practice in the early 19th century.

See also: IBIBIO (Vol. II); SLAVERY (Vols. III, IV).

Idah Nigerian town located east of the NIGER RIVER. Prior to the 16th century Idah was the capital of the Igala, a Muslim people. In the 1500s Idah was annexed by the kingdom of BENIN under Oba Esigie (d. c. 1504). Idah's prince Tsoede (fl. c. 1531) left and established himself as the head of the NUPE kingdom. It is believed that he acquainted the region with the art of bronze casting.

Over the years, Idah's political structure came to resemble that of the kingdom of Benin. It was controlled by a king known as an *obi* who had a group of title chiefs under him who were required to pay tribute. Throughout most of the 19th century Idah's economy flourished because of trade with both Europeans and the IGBO people.

See also: IGALA (Vol. II).

Idris Alawma (Idris Alooma, Idris Aluma) (r. c. 1570–1603) *Renowned king, or* mai, *of Kanem-Bornu, which during his reign was at its most powerful*

The reign of Idris Alawma brought great change to KANEM-BORNU. He was considered an innovative *mai*, or king, who helped the empire flourish economically and politically. Among his fellow SEFUWA, Idris Alawma was highly regarded for his military prowess, administrative reforms, and his strong belief in Islam. He was responsible for introducing new military tactics that helped in his battles with his main adversaries, including the Hausa, TUAREGS, Toubou, and the BULALA. He adopted the use of fixed military camps, armored horses and riders, and military camelry. His armies were able to sustain prolonged sieges. Alawma had a segment of his army trained in the use of firearms by Ottoman Turks, from whom he also bought arms. He established diplomatic relations with EGYPT and TRIPOLI, both of which were controlled by the Ottoman Empire. The Ottomans responded to his diplomatic efforts by sending a 200-member ambassadorial contingent across the desert to Idris' court at NGAZARGAMU, in Bornu.

Alawma's strong belief in Islam and Islamic law prompted him to introduce administrative and legal reforms in his empire. He supported the construction of several mosques and was inspired after a pilgrimage to Mecca to establish a hostel there to receive pilgrims traveling from his empire. He surrounded himself with loyal advisers and allies and created a council made up of the heads of the most influential Sefuwa clans. He also introduced economic reforms that helped the empire to prosper financially. Trade in goods and captives was very important to the empire's ECONOMY, and its location on one of the trans-Saharan routes brought the empire great wealth. Alawma was responsible for clearing roads, designing and improving boats for navigation on Lake CHAD, and introducing standard units of measure for grain. He also ensured the safety and security of travelers throughout his empire, thereby helping Kanem-Bornu to attain wealth. After Alawma's death, Kanem-Bornu gradually lost its dominance in the area.

See also: OTTOMAN EMPIRE AND AFRICA (Vols. III, IV).

Idris Katagarmabe (r. c. 1504–1524) *Mai (king) of Kanem-Bornu and a member of the Sefuwa dynasty*

Idris Katagarmabe succeeded his father, Mai Ali Gaji (r. c. 1472–1503), who consolidated power in KANEM-BORNU and built a new capital for the kingdom at NGAZARGAMU, west of Lake CHAD. Idris expanded his father's conquests in KANO, battling Kano kings Abdullahi (c. 1499–1509) and Muhammad Kisoki (c. 1509–1565). Early in his reign he recaptured the city of Njimi, the former SEFUWA capital, liberating it from the rival BULALA people. A few years later he launched an unsuccessful attack on KEBBI, one of the HAUSA STATES.

Idris developed diplomatic relations with North Africa, sending ambassadors to TRIPOLI in 1512 to renew commercial relations. He was succeeded by his son Mohammed, who reigned from about 1524 to 1545.

See also: NJIMI (Vol. II).

Ifa Yoruba divination system. Over the centuries, much of the Ifa system was integrated into Muslim practices, but the belief in Ifa still remained widespread in many areas. During the slave trade of the 16th through 19th centuries, Yoruba captives were shipped from YORUBA-LAND to British, French, Spanish, and Portuguese colonies in the Americas. Much of their culture, particularly such rituals as the Ifa divination system, was preserved in modified forms.

See also: IFA (Vol. I); YORUBA (Vols. I, II, IV, V).

Igbo (Ibo) Ethnic group of the southeastern regions of NIGERIA. The Igbo are a Kwa-speaking people who tradi-

tionally lived in small communities or villages based on a system of households, or *obi.* Beginning about the 15th century the Portuguese, and later the English and Dutch, began trading with the Igbo for, among other things, ivory and captives. Trade substantially increased after the development of the transatlantic SLAVE TRADE in the late 16th and 17th centuries. During the late 1700s the majority of the people being taken from the interior of Nigeria were Igbo, who were shipped to ports in the southern United States or the Caribbean.

The Igbo were in constant conflict with the IBIBIO, a neighboring delta group with whom they shared many cultural practices. In the early 18th century the Igbo defeated the Ibibio with the help of the Akpa, a Niger Delta group who had probably bought firearms from European traders. After their victory the Igbo developed a confederation made up of Igbo-Ibibio towns, led by Igbo head men, that used the authority of the AROCHUKWU ORACLE to dominate the delta slave trade.

The Aro, a subgroup of the Igbo, exploited the fearful respect that the Igbo, IJO, and Ibibio groups had for the proclamations of the Arochukwu oracle. Considered the earthly representative of powerful ancestral spirits, the oracle often demanded payment in captives, who could then be sold for profit.

Despite Britain's abolition of the slave trade in 1807, the Igbo continued to trade in captives with the Ijo and Ibibio people. Trade goods for the European merchants thereafter shifted to commodities such as spices, forest products, and PALM OIL.

See also: IGBO (Vol. I, II, IV, V).

Ijebu Subgroup of the Yoruba peoples of southwestern NIGERIA. During the 16th century the Ijebu people established a kingdom in present-day Ogun State of Nigeria. Its capital was located in the town of Ijebu-Ode. Along with serving as the residence for the reigning ruler, known as the *awujale,* the Ijebu-Ode was also a hub from which the Ijebu controlled trade from Lagos Lagoon to Ibadan until the 1820s. This control, however, was threatened by the Yoruba civil wars and was later lost completely to Ibadan.

See also: IJEBU (Vol. II); YORUBALAND (Vols. II, III).

Ijo (Ijaw) Southern Nigerian people of the Niger Delta region. Prior to the 16th century, groups of Ijo villages operated autonomously, relying heavily on fishing as a source of income. With the arrival of Europeans in the early 16th century, however, the Ijo began to develop more cohesive city-states. This ultimately transformed the villages of BONNY, OLD CALABAR, and Brass into more powerful entities.

As these states grew in size and power, they became major trading centers. They operated throughout the period during which the transatlantic SLAVE TRADE flourished, capturing people from the interior lands, often with the help of weapons garnered from Europeans. After Britain abolished the slave trade in 1807, the Ijo switched from trading in humans to trade in PALM OIL, fish, and salt.

See also: BRASS (Vol. II); IJO (Vol. II); NIGER DELTA (Vols. I, IV, V).

Ilesha Town located in present-day southwestern NIGERIA. The founder and original *owa* (king) of Ilesha was Owaluse, who was said to have descended from Oduduwa, the semi-mythical founder of the IFE kingdom of Nigeria. Owaluse established Ilesha during the early 16th century along a trade route between BENIN CITY and Old Oyo.

The main inhabitants of Ilesha, known as the Ijesha, are related to the Yoruba. They traditionally made their living from AGRICULTURE and, in later centuries, trading items such as cloth, PALM OIL, COTTON, kola nuts, and cocoa. The people were ruled by their *owa* who was elected and administered by a series of chiefs holding a variety of titles signifying their position as either a *iwole* (palace-chief) or a *t'ode* (town-chief). In the late 19th century Ilesha became the main military headquarters during the Yoruba civil wars (1877–92) against the neighboring town of Ibadan.

See also: ODUDUWA (Vol. II); YORUBALAND (Vol. III).

Ilorin City and emirate in western NIGERIA that was established by the Yoruba at the end of the 18th century. Ilorin had a significant impact on the downfall of the OYO EMPIRE, of which it was a vassal state. Kakanfo Afonja, the Oyo military leader stationed at Ilorin to protect the city from attack by the SOKOTO CALIPHATE, joined forces with Mallam Alimi, a FULANI Muslim from Sokoto, and together they led a revolt against the Oyo empire in 1817. Shortly after Afonja and Alimi won independence for Ilorin, the Oyo empire collapsed.

No sooner had Alimi arrived in Ilorin that the entire city was flooded with Alimi's soldiers. This became an increasing threat to Afonja's rule. He quickly discovered that siding with Alimi had been a grave mistake, and he was eventually overthrown by his one-time Fulani ally. Alimi's son Aba al-Salam became the emir of Ilorin in 1829. He waged a holy war on YORUBALAND

that lasted until the mid-19th century, when he was defeated by forces from Ibadan.

Imbangala (Jaga, Yaka) A Lunda-derived hunter-warrior society, descended from the MBUNDU, that settled in what is now ANGOLA, forming what later became the KASANJE kingdom. During the early 16th century a group of Lunda people left KATANGA and moved westward in search of territory. Their rulers, called by the titles *kinguri* and *makota,* led the Lunda across the Kasai River, where they encountered first the CHOKWE and then the SONGO. They continued westward until they met with resistance from the powerful LIBOLO kings, forcing them to stop and settle between the Kwango and Kwanza rivers, among the Songo, in what is now central Angola.

Here the leaders took on the name *Kasanje,* and the people began calling themselves the *Imbangala.* The rulers adopted a warrior-based political system, called *kilombo,* which gave the Imbangala the power to conquer weaker groups and move southward along the West African coast.

The *kilombo* was a radically different way of structuring society than the lineage-based systems of most Mbundu groups. There was no kinship in the warrior society. Men were chosen for leadership positions based on skill rather than kinship or lineage. Women were prohibited from giving birth inside the sacred walled encampments where the warriors trained and kept their weapons, and Imbangala infants inherited no standing in the *kilombo.* Only uncircumcised males, who were often the young captives of successful Imbangala conquests, could be initiated into the warrior society. During the 1680s some Mbundu began circumcising their boys at a very early age, between 5 and 9, making them ineligible for *kilombo* initiation and thereby making them unattractive as captives.

In the 16th century the Imbangala moved northward, conquering Mbundu and Kongo peoples along the coast and selling most of them to the Portuguese, with whom they had formed an alliance. In return the Portuguese aided the Imbangala in their conquests and provided them with European goods.

In the early 17th century an Imbangala ruler named Kulashingo led a band back north to the interior west of the Kwango River. During the 17th and 18th centuries the Imbangala became actively involved in the trade between the LUNDA EMPIRE, coastal Africans, and Europeans.

Ingombe Ilede Major trading center located in southeast Africa in the Zambezi Valley, near the junction of the Kafue and ZAMBEZI rivers. Ingombe Ilede was inhabited in the early 1400s by a small group of agriculturalists, hunters, merchants, and artisans. Archaeological evidence suggests that these inhabitants accumulated great wealth through trade. The town became an important trade center not only because of its strategic location in the ZAMBEZI RIVER valley but also because of the skill of the resident craftsmen. Ingombe Ilede was known for its textiles, ivory carving, and metalwork. Because of its connections with East African coastal merchants, Ingombe Ilede prospered. By the early 16th century, however, the settlement was inexplicably abandoned.

Inhambane Port town located on the coast of MOZAMBIQUE in southern East Africa that was an important trading settlement for Portuguese merchants in the 16th through the 18th centuries. Inhambane is also the name of the Bantu dialect that is spoken by the Tonga and Chopi peoples of southern Mozambique.

About 1534 Portuguese traders founded a fortified settlement in Inhambane and used it as a stopover for merchants working the Indian spice trade. By the end of the 16th century Inhambane was processing GOLD that was acquired at trading fairs in the African interior. In the 17th century Inhambane also began to process ivory for export to other Indian Ocean ports and India. By the mid-18th century the town—along with the other Mozambican coastal settlements of QUELIMANE and Mozambique Island—was used as an outpost in the trade of captives.

See also: INDIAN OCEAN TRADE (Vol. II); IVORY TRADE (Vol. III); PORTUGAL AND AFRICA (Vol. III); SLAVE TRADE ON THE SWAHILI COAST (Vol. III); TONGA (Vol. I).

Islam, influence of Islam and the traditional African religions were the dominant belief systems in Africa from the 15th through the 18th centuries. The influence had religious, commercial, and cultural aspects that strengthened Islam's presence in precolonial Africa.

By the 15th century Christianity existed in only small pockets of the continent, primarily in ETHIOPIA, in the Horn of Africa, where Christians practiced their religion freely, and in EGYPT, where the dwindling Coptic Church was often subject to bouts of restriction and persecution by the Muslim majority. Islam had totally replaced Christianity in North Africa by the 12th century and was making ever deeper inroads into West Africa. Trans-Saharan trade remained thoroughly dominated by Muslims, suffering only minor European interference in the 1400s when the Portuguese diverted a portion of the GOLD trade to the Atlantic coast.

The SWAHILI COAST, along the Indian Ocean, was the site of a thoroughly Arabized, and therefore Islamic, society that in the 16th through the 18th centuries came into conflict with Christianity. This conflict ended after 1698, when the Portuguese withdrew from the coast north of MOZAMBIQUE. Portuguese traders, however, gained control of much of the lucrative Indian Ocean trade that Muslim Arabs had dominated for more than 700 years.

Only southern Africa was untouched by Islam. Many of the original Muslims of the CAPE COLONY were political exiles from other Muslim lands. Islam took root among freed blacks and people in bondage. The latter were mainly from India, MADAGASCAR, the islands of RÉUNION and MAURITIUS in the Indian Ocean, and the east coast of Africa. Most were Muslim or had Muslim sympathies. Mainly white slave owners, afraid that they would have to free people who became Christian, tolerated the practice of Islam among captives on the grounds that a person should have some RELIGION. As southern Africa developed a wine industry, Muslims, forbidden by the Quran to drink alcohol, were prized as workers. By 1797 most Christian proselytization among enslaved populations had ended, but Islam did not become a major social force until the start of an Islamic revivalist movement in 1862. This movement was led by the Turkish scholar Abu Bakr Effendi (d. 1880), who worked among the Muslims of the Cape Colony.

The Appeal of Islam Belief in Islam simply required profession of faith in the One True God and the acceptance of God's will as revealed by the prophet Muhammad and recorded in the Quran. Islam lacked the complex theology and heresies of Christianity, was not concerned with elaborate rituals or liturgies, and was not governed by a hierarchical priesthood. As its primary observances, Islam called for regular private prayer, the practice of charity, a strict fast during the holy month of Ramadan, and, once in a believer's lifetime if the believer could afford it, a pilgrimage to the holy city of Mecca. Muslims tended to look upon other Muslims, even converts, as brothers in religion, as fellow believers, and superior to all infidels.

The Intellectual Influences on African Islam Islam in Africa is part of the Sunni branch of Islam, to which the majority of Muslims in the world belong; the smaller Shiite branch, with large communities particularly in present-day Iran and Iraq, accounts for roughly only 10 percent of Muslims worldwide. Different schools of Islamic law or jurisprudence govern the everyday behaviors and practices of Muslims. Because Islam reached Africa from two directions (both north and east), believers in Africa follow two different but compatible traditions: the Maliki school of law, which is dominant in North Africa and West Africa, and the Shafii school of law, which is dominant in East Africa and the neighboring Arabian Peninsula.

The Maliki school bases its practices on a code of law called al-Muwatta (The Beaten Path). Written by Malik ibn Anas (c. 713–c. 795), it covers the important areas of Muslim life ranging from prescribed prayer rituals and fasting to ethical conduct in business affairs. The Muwatta is supported by more than 2,000 traditions attributed to the prophet Muhammad. These reflect the legal principles dominant in the city of Medina, Saudi Arabia, the site of Muhammad's tomb and the city where much of the Quran was supposedly revealed to Muhammad.

The Shafii school of law is named for its founder, Muhammad ibn Idris al-Shafii (767–819), who was a pupil of Malik ibn Anas. In contrast to his teacher, al-Shafii began to believe in the overriding authority of the traditions from the prophet and identified them with the Sunna, the body of Islamic custom and practice based on Muhammad's life and sayings and the main source of Islamic law after the Quran. The Shafii school of law was dominant in Arabia until the Ottoman sultans of the 16th century supplanted it with the Hanafite school of law dominant in Constantinople. However, Shafii influence remained strong in East Africa.

Both East Africa and West Africa were further influenced by the Ibadi sect of Islam, which became important in the OMANI SULTANATE and other parts of eastern Arabia during the early centuries of the Islamic era. The Ibadi, unlike other Muslims, believed that the best qualified person should be elected imam, or religious leader, of the community, whereas the established tradition required him to be a descendant of the prophet Muhammad. Sunni tradition supported the choice of a single, central ruler with the title of imam or caliph; the Ibadi, in contrast, permitted regions to have their own imams.

Ibadi merchants from East Africa established trade routes across the Sahara and reached West Africa as early as the ninth century or even earlier. Their conversions among the Muslim faithful did not last; most reverted to Maliki practices by the 11th century. The Ibadi sect became dominant in ZANZIBAR when the Omani Sultanate captured the island in the 1700s. However, the Ibadi there did no missionary work among the African peoples; their influence extended only to the Arab population of the coast.

The Spiritual Influences on African Islam The story of Islam in Africa is closely tied to SUFISM, although there is disagreement as to whether the effect was radical, conservative, political, or religious. Central to Sufi practice is a *tariqa,* or a way by which a Muslim may achieve a personal religious experience. MUSIC, chanting, and dance is often used to create a mystical state among believers. The image of the dervish (from the Turkish word meaning "poor man," or "beggar"), pictured whirling in ecstatic dance, gives a reasonably accurate view of the externals of Sufi ritual. The word *tariqa* is also used to refer to groups of Sufis who share the same rituals, and the word is sometimes, therefore, translated as "order" or

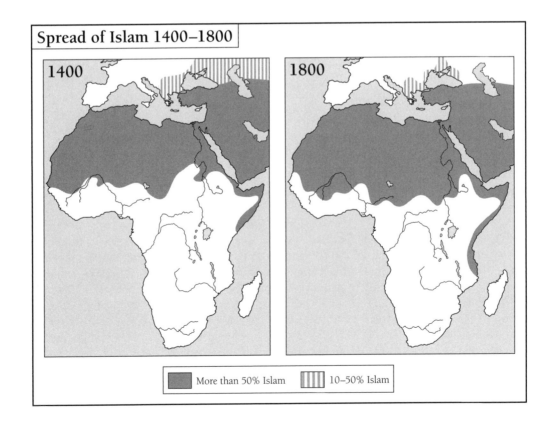

Spread of Islam 1400–1800

1400

1800

More than 50% Islam   10–50% Islam

"brotherhood." The beliefs and practices of the Sufi orders were shaped by the saints and holy men who founded them. The three most important Sufi brotherhoods in Africa were the QADIRIYYA, which is the oldest in Islam and active in North Africa and Arabia; the Khalwatiyya, who were active in the HAUSA STATES and the Sultanate of Aïr; and the Shadhiliyya, who were active in the Sahara and, after 1880, in East Africa. Each Sufi brotherhood traces its origins to the teachings of the mystic teacher who founded the order.

In 16th-century TIMBUKTU, the leading scholars were Sufi but belonged to no particular *tariqa*. The same was true in KANEM-BORNU. Sufism was especially strong in the MAGHRIB, in North Africa. Initially they were members of the Shadhiliyya brotherhood, which at the time lacked any kind of hierarchical organization. As early as 1500 the Qadiriyya brotherhood was active in the Somali city of HARER, in the Horn of Africa. Until the 1800s, however, holy men were associated with individual Somali clans rather than with a specific Sufi brotherhood. It was not until the 19th century that the *tariqa* became important in Somalia. The same is true for the Swahili Coast, especially PATE and the LAMU Archipelago, where Sufism appeared as early as the 16th century.

During the 18th century the Sufi brotherhoods underwent a shift from a decentralized and diffused method of organization to a more disciplined structure. This centralized organization, novel for the time, made them a growing social and political force. The important leader of the Qadiriyya in the second half of the 17th century was Sidi al-Mukhtar al-Kinti. His influence extended across the Sahara and the Sahel, and as far as FOUTA DJALLON. The Sufi brotherhoods represented an Islam of the people, rural rather than urban, pious and conservative rather than worldly. The impact of this more organized and energetic Sufism through 1800 was a growth in public observance of the rules of Islam and the encouragement to believers to live their faith more enthusiastically.

Islam in West Africa   Islam penetrated deep into the interior of West Africa in a steady process that began at the start of the millennium and continued well into the precolonial period. As early as the 11th century the Mande-speaking ancestors of the DYULA, a West African people with a long history as traders, set up commercial networks between the gold fields of West Africa and the trading towns from which caravans set off across the Sahara. Early converts to Islam, the Dyula shared a common bond of Muslim law, or *sharia,* with their fellow traders from the north. After a time, conversion to Islam became a necessity for anyone who wished to engage in trade. With these traders came Muslim clerics, who converted the local rulers. This process of conversion continued well into the 19th century, when some Ashanti people living in present-day GHANA, TOGO, and IVORY COAST were converted to Islam.

In many West African societies, Islam and traditional beliefs initially existed side by side. The primary point of contact between the common people and Islam was in the legal system and the courts of law. Important Islamic centers of learning were established in the major trading cities of Timbuktu, Gao, and JENNE. The Sankore mosque and university in Timbuktu, for example, where the leading scholars were Sufis, was a center of scientific learning and has been called by some historians the intellectual center of Africa in the 16th century.

In the precolonial period, as earlier, tensions existed between kings and clerics even if the king was a professed Muslim. The kings sometimes were warriors who drank alcohol and shed blood. In the major kingdoms of ancient, medieval, and precolonial Africa, including the Ghana , Mali, and SONGHAI empires, the ruler was also the titular head of the traditional religion; he risked alienating his followers and losing his authority if his practice of Islam was too strict. Even Mansa Musa I (r. 1312–c. 1337) of Mali and Askia MUHAMMAD TOURÉ (r. 1493–1538) of Songhai, both of whom were fervent believers, could not wrest their societies from their pre-Islamic traditions. The Fulani jihad of the late 1720s, led by the religious leader KARAMOKO ALFA (fl. 1720s) and the warrior Ibrahima Sori (fl. 1720s), led to the establishment of Fouta Djallon as a Muslim theocratic state; it dominated both central and coastal GUINEA until it was occupied by French troops in 1896.

In the 18th and early 19th centuries, the FULANI JIHADS led by the militant fundamentalist clerics USMAN DAN FODIO (1754–1817), his son MUHAMMAD BELLO (r. 1817–1837), and Umar Tal (1797–1864), were, in part, the result of attempts to return lax Muslims in the Hausa States to orthodox religious practices. Fodio's campaigns led to the foundation of the SOKOTO CALIPHATE, a fundamentalist theocratic Muslim state, in what is now northern NIGERIA. The power of these clerics was both religious and political. It is notable that Usman dan Fodio, who began his career as an itinerant preacher to rural Muslim communities, and other leaders of the jihads came from the countryside and not from the cities or the commercial community.

Usman dan Fodio's jihad caused a crucial change in Muslim thinking. He and his fellow reformers introduced the concept of *takfit,* according to which Muslims whose religious practices were considered tainted by paganism could be considered infidels even though they had not renounced Islam. Jihad against such unbelievers was both allowable and meritorious. Fodio used this principle to justify his campaigns against the Muslim Hausa.

The kingdom of Kanem (later part of KANEM-BORNU), with its capital of Njimi near Lake CHAD, was located on the trade routes that connected West Africa, the Nile Valley, and North Africa. Kanem was an exception to the standard that Islam was the religion of the rulers. Kanem became a Muslim state during the 11th century, when its ruler Mai Umme (r. c. 1085–1097) was converted by the scholar Muhammad ibn Mani, who first brought Islam to that land. Mai Umme adopted the name Ibn Abd al-Jalil. Later, during the reign of Dunama II (1221–1259), Kanem opened an embassy in TUNISIA in Muslim North Africa and a hostel and college in CAIRO, thus connecting the kingdom with the broader Islamic world. In the late 14th century, to replace Njimi, a new capital was established at NGAZARGAMU by the reigning *mai* (king), Ali Gaji (r. 1476–1503), also known as Ali Dunama.

The common language of prayer in Islam is Arabic. The Quran is read aloud in Arabic. Its verses are memorized in Arabic—phonetically if the learner does not understand the language but needs it for prayer. The expansion of Islam into the countryside was accompanied by a growth in the use of the vernacular languages and the development of a vernacular literature, which took the form of religious and didactic poetry. Some of the oldest written Fulani poems, dating from the second half of the 18th century, are religious verses meant to carry the message of Islam to rural peoples. Early Hausa written literature, also didactic and pious poetry, was also created for this purpose.

Ali Gaji led a revival of Islam in Kanem-Bornu. With the help of the leading cleric Imam Umar Masarambe and the power of his own good example, Ali Gaji convinced the nobles to limit their wives to four, the number permitted by the Quran. The process of Islamization continued in Kanem-Bornu under Mai IDRIS ALAWMA (r. c. 1570–1603), who went on hajj, or pilgrimage, to Mecca in the ninth year of his reign and built a hostel there for pilgrims from his homeland. Mai Idris revived traditional Islamic practices and imposed them on commoners and nobility alike. He instituted Islamic courts and replaced customary law with *sharia*, or Islamic law. He built a large number of brick mosques to replace the existing ones, which were built with reeds. As an indication of the depth to which Islam permeated the population, historians point to the existence of manuscripts of the Quran with interlinear translations and commentaries in the local language that date from as early as the 17th century. Kanem-Bornu remained a Muslim state until its demise in the early 1800s and incorporation into the Sokoto Caliphate. It remained, however, an important center of Muslim learning.

Many Hausa were Muslim as early as the 11th century. Islam did not reach neighboring YORUBALAND until

the 1800s as a result of the Fulani jihads. Yorubaland, however, never became a Muslim state, even though the practice of Islam was common among the people.

Islam in East Africa Islam first reached the Horn of Africa in the eighth century. By the ninth century there were Muslim settlements along the trade routes inland. However, ETHIOPIA, the dominant power in the Horn, was Christian. In the 14th century the Somali Muslim kingdom of ADAL arose in the Danakil-Somali region to challenge Ethiopia's control. Tensions and skirmishes marked the next two centuries. Conflict reached its height after 1516 when AHMAD GRAÑ (1506–1543) came into power in Adal. He assembled an army of nomadic Muslims and twice, in 1526 and again in 1531, he led Adal in a jihad against Christian Ethiopia. His attacks culminated in an invasion in 1535 that reached as far as the northern highlands, the heart of the Ethiopian state. The jihad of Ahmad Grañ weakened Ethiopia and led to the conversion of many of its people.

Mass migrations of the pastoral OROMO people late in the 16th century weakened Adal, and its leaders fled. By the 1700s the important families among the Oromo had accepted Islam; by the middle of the 19th century Islam had taken root among the common people as well. They guided their lives by Islamic law rather than customary law, circumcised their male children at an earlier age than had been traditional, tithed according to standard Muslim practice, and went on pilgrimage to Mecca.

Until the 19th century, Islam in East Africa was confined to the cities of the Swahili Coast. It did not penetrate into the interior either by missionary efforts or accompanying commercial activity. Even the YAO of what is today Mozambique and southern Tanzania, who were involved in the slave trade with the coast since the 17th century and who are today the most Islamized people of the interior, were not converted until Muslim scribes and traders finally went into the interior during the 1800s.

See also: MUHAMMAD TOURÉ, ASKIA (Vol. II); CHRISTIANITY, INFLUENCE OF (Vol. III); ISLAM (Vol. II); ISLAM, INFLUENCE OF (Vols. II, IV, V); ISLAMIC CENTERS OF LEARNING (Vol. II); MALIK IBN ANAS (Vol. II); MALIKI SUNNI DOCTRINE (Vol. II); MUSA I, MANSA (Vol. II); SHAFII SUNNI DOCTRINE (Vol. II); SHARIA (Vols. II, IV); UMME, MAI (Vol. II).

Further reading: Mervyn Hiskett, *The Course of Islam in Africa* (Edinburgh, U.K.: Edinburgh University Press, 1994); Nehemia Levtzion and Randall L. Pouwels, eds., *The History of Islam in Africa* (Athens, Ohio: Ohio University Press, 2000).

Iteso (Ateso, Teso) Nilotic ethnic group inhabiting the region between Mount Elgon, to the north, and Lake Nyanza, to the south, in present-day eastern UGANDA and KENYA. The Iteso speak an Eastern Sudanic language that belongs to the Chari-Nile branch of the Nilo-Saharan family of languages. Today the Iteso are the second-largest ethnic group in Uganda, after the Karamojong.

Little is known about Iteso origins, though it is believed that they are related to nearby groups such as the Langi, the Karamojong, the Jie, and the Kumam. Like those groups the Iteso probably migrated from the north and settled in Uganda by the early 18th century. The Iteso homeland is Teso, which extends south from Karamoja into the fertile region of Lake Kyoga. The Iteso were, and still are, farmers, growing millet as a staple crop.

Traditional Iteso villages were made up of homesteads scattered around a central stockade and granaries. Iteso social structure was organized by clans, each of which had a leader who was elected and advised by a council of elders. Iteso men were ranked by age sets, with higher status given to the older groups. With the help of priests, elders conducted religious rituals to honor ancestors. Although most Iteso eventually became Christian, they once believed in an omnipotent deity named Akuj and in a god of calamity named Edeke. After the Iteso were defeated by the GANDA near the end of the 19th century, many of their traditional beliefs and practices were lost.

Itsekiri People of the delta region of southern NIGERIA and the name of their kingdom, founded by emigrants from the kingdom of BENIN in the 15th century. The Itsekiri had extensive trade relations prior to the arrival of the Portuguese in the area in the late 15th century. Using canoes to travel through the delta, the Itsekiri traded salt, fish, and pottery to obtain agricultural products such as plantains, yams, and cassava from the neighboring people of the Niger Delta region, including the IJO to the southeast.

The Itsekiri quickly developed European trade, which also increased their dominance of local trade. They obtained firearms (often inferior or defective guns) from Portuguese traders and traded them with people from the Yoruba territories in the Nigerian hinterland, who used them on raids with the purpose of kidnapping Africans. The Itsekiri welcomed Portuguese traders but rejected the efforts of their MISSIONARIES to convert them to Christianity.

By the mid-16th century the Itsekiri kingdom of Warri, in the western delta, was a market for Portuguese manufactured goods. European merchants brought items such as wrought iron, glass, and cloth and traded them for ivory and captives. Traders from other delta kingdoms as well as from the interior brought their captives to Warri, and by the middle of the 17th century the kingdom was a major trading center. The Itsekiri maintained a strong trading ECONOMY into the late 19th century.

See also: ITSEKIRI (Vol. II); SLAVE TRADE, THE TRANS-ATLANTIC (Vol. III); WARRI (Vol. II).

Ivory Coast (Côte d'Ivoire) Present-day West African country that measures approximately 124,500 square miles (322,400 sq km) and is bounded by the present-day Republic of MALI, BURKINA FASO, GHANA, LIBERIA, and GUINEA. Prior to the period of European colonization, the region now known as Ivory Coast had already been a trading community for several centuries—possibly beginning as early as the eighth century.

Between the 17th and 18th centuries Mande peoples migrated to the area, establishing trading settlements that used the trans-Saharan trading routes to sell such items as kola nuts and GOLD northward to kingdoms in Mali. Even earlier, however, during the mid-15th century, the Portuguese began establishing trade relations with people of the Ivory Coast. The French also made a trip to the area, in 1483, but it was not until two centuries later, in 1687, that France attempted to permanently occupy Ivory Coast with the founding of a mission at Assini. Due to their precarious hold on Ivory Coast, the settlement at Assini was abandoned in 1704, and the French did not establish themselves firmly until the mid-19th century.

Ivory Coast received its name from the abundance of ivory that was available in the area. Ivory was so heavily traded throughout the 17th century that the elephant population was quickly depleted, putting an end to the IVORY TRADE by the early 18th century. Captives were also exported from the area from the 16th century onwards, but the country's lack of safe ports made the slave trade less profitable for both the local groups and the Europeans. To supplement the trade of captives, commodities such as pepper, gold, and ivory became main staples for trade throughout Ivory Coast. These wares were generally traded to the Europeans for cloth, weaponry, FOOD, and items made from iron.

Before Europeans controlled Ivory Coast, there were five main kingdoms that ruled the region. The earliest of these kingdoms, Jaman, was founded in the 17th century by members of the Abron ethnic group. The Abron had migrated west to escape the growing influence of the ASHANTI EMPIRE, in present-day Ghana. The Jaman kingdom became best known for its traditions of Islamic learning, which were spread mainly from its capital at Bondoukou.

During the early 18th century DYULA traders displaced the resident SENUFO group in the northern regions to found the kingdom of KONG. Before Kong was destroyed in 1895, it was an established agrarian community known for its trade and impressive works of ART.

The mid-18th century then saw the rise of three kingdoms founded by groups, like the Abron, attempting to distance themselves from the Ashanti. The first of these groups was the BAULE, who established their kingdom of Sakasso, while the other two kingdoms of Sanwi and Indenie were both created by members of the Agni people. These kingdoms were known for being fiercely independent and for having advanced political structures, which allowed them to better resist French rule.

See also: FRANCE AND AFRICA (Vol. III); IVORY COAST (Vols. I, II, IV, V); IVORY TRADE (Vol. III); PORTUGAL AND AFRICA (Vol. III).

Further reading: Robert E. Handloff, ed., *Côte d'Ivoire: A Country Study* (Washington D.C.: Library of Congress, 1991); Patricia Sheehan, *Cultures of the World: Côte d'Ivoire* (Malaysia: Times Media Private Limited, 2000).

ivory trade   Elephant tusks and other items made of ivory have been important trade commodities throughout much of African history. During the 16th to 19th cen-

Mask traditionally worn by members of the Poro Society of the Senufo people of Ivory Coast. Poro rituals are thought to guarantee a good relationship between the living and their ancestors. This mask was made in the 20th century. © *North Carolina Museum of Art/Corbis*

turies ivory was traded for valuable goods such as spices, cloth, GOLD, and salt. Ivory had been moving on Africa's trade routes since as early as 8000 BCE, when Egyptian artisans, who prized the material for its beauty and durability, began using it for carvings. It also was a profitable commodity traded in East Africa's ports from the foundation of the city-states of the SWAHILI COAST in the eighth century.

In the 15th century Europeans made contact with a number of ivory-collecting peoples of sub-Saharan Africa. As a result, demand increased for African and European goods alike. The trade of ivory, in particular, rose steadily and flourished from the late 16th century through the 20th centuries. In the 17th century Europeans named the West African region of IVORY COAST for the abundance of elephant tusks that were harvested there by such groups as the KRU people. Cities in what is now NIGERIA, including ASABA and BENIN CITY, were particularly active in the ivory trade.

The unfortunate result of the high demand for ivory was the large-scale slaughter of African elephants, which continued into the 20th century. By the 1980s the African elephant had been hunted nearly to extinction.

Prior to European colonization in the 19th century, the ivory trade in the eastern coastal regions of Africa was spurred by the Asian and Arabian demand for superior African ivory. Swahili traders of mixed African and Arabian descent exchanged Asian glass, beads, cloth, and metal goods for ivory supplied by groups such as the GIRIAMA and KAMBA of present-day KENYA as well as the NYAMWEZI of TANZANIA.

Farther down the east coast, YAO and Bisa traders acted as intermediaries between the ivory suppliers of the LUNDA EMPIRE, in the southern Central African interior, and the Muslim and Portuguese buyers at the coastal markets in MOZAMBIQUE. Skilled elephant hunters in their own right, the Bisa traded ivory at fairs held in Zambezi trading outposts, including TETE, SENA, and Zumbo. Zumbo was also a major outlet for the traders of BUTUA, who hunted ivory throughout the southern portions of Africa. Inhabiting present-day ZIMBABWE, the Butua traders obtained a majority of their tusks from the mountain region of Usanga near the SABI RIVER.

During the 19th century the ivory trade increased further, largely due to American demand. At that time present-day ZANZIBAR, located in the Indian Ocean nearly 30 miles (48 km) off the eastern coast of TANZANIA, took control of the eastern ivory markets.

See also: BISA TRADING NETWORK (Vol. III); ELE-PHANTS (Vol. I); IVORY (Vol. II); IVORY TRADE (Vol. IV).

Iyasu I (r. c. 1681–1706) *Solomonid ruler of Ethiopia*

In 1684 Iyasu I, known to his subjects as "the Great," launched a confrontational battle in order to bring the rebellious OROMO under his political and religious control. After sending out scouts to apprise him of Oromo lands and methods of resistance, Iyasu ordered a surprise attack on several Oromo groups, including the Wechales and the Wallos, which resulted in their lands being razed. Many Oromo were killed, their cattle seized, and their women taken captive. Although some Oromo groups apparently adapted themselves to imperial rule, others launched numerous, though largely unsuccessful counter-attacks for the remainder of the 17th century.

According to Ethiopian chronicles, by the early 18th century Iyasu had subdued the dissident Oromo groups and baptized captives. When he left the region, Iyasu stood at the Gibe River and ordered his men to fire their rifles as a celebration of military might and a victory for Christianity.

In spite of his popularity and success, however, Iyasu lost his throne. Returning from one of his military campaigns, he learned that his favorite concubine had died. Grief-stricken, he retreated to an isolated island on Lake Tana. During his absence, Iyasu's son, TEKLA HAYMONOT (r. c. 1706–1708), seized the throne. Iyasu returned to try to regain control, and, on the order of Tekla Haymonot, he was assassinated.

Further reading: Harold G. Marcus, *A History of Ethiopia* (Berkeley, Calif.: University of California Press, 1994); Richard Pankhurst, *The Ethiopian Borderlands: Essays in the Regional History from Ancient Times to the End of the 18th Century* (Lawrenceville, N.J.: The Red Sea Press, Inc., 1997).

J

Jaga See IMBANGALA.

Jenne (Djenné) Important center for the trade in GOLD, salt, and captives located in what is now the southern region of Republic of MALI. Ruled by the SONGHAI Empire in the late 15th century, Jenne and its sister trading city of TIMBUKTU were invaded in 1591 by an army from MOROCCO that conquered the Songhai and took control of both cities as well as their profitable caravan routes. Once the Moroccans established power in Jenne, a local chief, called the *Jenne-were*, was then appointed along with a representative of the Moroccan pasha (ruler) known as a *hakim*, or governor.

> Even though the BAMBARA kings who ruled Jenne in the 17th century were non-Muslims who practiced an animistic RELIGION, Jenne became a well-known center for Islamic learning, attracting Muslim scholars from all over the Sahara.

Although the *Jenne-were* initially accepted Moroccan command, tensions soon gave rise to clashes between the succeeding reigning chiefs of Jenne and the Moroccan pashas. About the mid-17th century, however, Moroccan power in the city began to wane, and by 1670 Jenne had been overtaken by the chiefs of the emerging Bamana-speaking Bambara kingdoms. Jenne remained part of the Bambara-led empire of SEGU until 1810, when the KUNTA, a local group of Arabic nomads, took the city. Kunta rule was short-lived as Jenne was again overtaken in 1818 by the forces of the Muslim leader Cheikou Amadou (1755–1845), also known as Shehu Ahmadu Lobbo. Amadou then incorporated the city into his Islamic kingdom of MACINA.

See also: JENNE (Vol. II).

Judar Pasha (c. 16th–17th c.) *Moroccan military commander*

Under the orders of ABD AL-MANSUR (r. 1578–1603), the reigning sultan of what became the present-day country of MOROCCO, a renegade soldier by the name of Judar was appointed pasha and given command of a 5,000-man military force. As commander or administrator, the pasha oversaw both the armed forces and the storehouse for the treasury monies, known as MAKHZAN. Judar's mission, however, was not to administer a region but to take his forces into what is now Republic of MALI and conquer the trading city of TIMBUKTU—ruled at that time by the SONGHAI Empire.

> The elite Moroccan army was made up of Muslim Spaniards, or Moors, as well as former Christians, known as *renegades,* who had converted to the Muslim faith. Judar was a member of the renegades who had successfully risen to a commanding position within the army.

By March of 1591 the difficulty of the trek across the western Sahara had cut the number of his Moroccan forces by about half. Nevertheless Judar's remaining troops were able to defeat the Songhai forces at the Battle of TONDIBI and gain control over Timbuktu. Acting on behalf of the sultan, Judar then negotiated a peace treaty with the Songhai ruler, Askia Ishaq II (r. 1588–1591). This agreement gave Morocco 100,000 GOLD pieces and 1,000 captives in exchange for a withdrawal from Timbuktu.

Al-Mansur quickly denounced Judar's deal with the Songhai ruler and removed Judar from his office as pasha. Although he was soon replaced by another pasha, Mahmud ibn Zargun (r. 1591–1618), Judar continued to have influence over the affairs of the Moroccan army in Timbuktu until his return to Morocco in the latter part of the 1590s.

See also: ASKIA DYNASTY (Vol. III); WARFARE AND WEAPONS (Vol. III).

K

Kaarta BAMBARA state located on the middle portion of the NIGER RIVER in present-day Republic of MALI; considered the sister state of SEGU. The Bambara states were known for succeeding the SONGHAI Empire as the most powerful West African kingdoms of the 17th through 19th centuries. Bambara king MASSA (r. 1650–1710) founded the original kingdom of Kaarta along the Niger River about 1650 and established his capital at the city of Sounsan. Massa ruled until 1710 and created the MASSASSI DYNASTY, which continued to be a prominent force in Kaarta until the kingdom's takeover by the TUKULOR empire, in 1854.

Kaarta was ruled by Massa's grandson, Foulakoro, until 1745, at which time the kingdom was demolished by Mamari KULIBALI (r. 1712–1755) from the neighboring Bambara kingdom of Segu. Kaarta was then reestablished in the same region near the city of Kumbi by a Bambara chieftain named Sey Bamana Kulibali (r. 1754–1758). During the first few years after Kaarta was recreated, the rulers increased their influence in the region by becoming seminomadic and overrunning weaker nations to acquire captives. However, Kaarta's emergence as a regional power did not begin until the 1761–81 reign of Sira Bo of the Massassi dynasty, who put an end to the nomadic way of life, established a capital at Guemou, and acquired cities such as Diawara and Khasso as tributary states.

Kaarta reached its height under the rule of Bodian Moriba (r. 1818–1832), who moved the capital from the city of Yélimané to the city of Nioro, where it remained until the Tukulor conquest of Kaarta in the 19th century. Moriba was also responsible for the formation of an alliance with the kingdom of Segu, effectively ending 30 years of war between the two Bambara states.

Kabre (Kabyé, Cabrais, Lamba) West African ethnic group in present-day northern and central TOGO, as well as parts of present-day Republic of BENIN. The largest Kabre subgroups include the Logba, Losso, and Lamba, whose languages are closely related and who have similar ethnic and cultural traditions.

> The Kabre call themselves *Lamba*—which is also the name of one of their subgroups—meaning "people of the forests" in their Bantu language.

Before 1600 the Kabre occupied a larger territory that included Djougou in present-day Benin. During the 17th and 18th centuries the Kabre were pushed by the MAMPRUSI, DAGOMBA, and Bariba kingdoms into the mountainous region around Kara and Sokodé, in central Togo, where many of them mixed with the indigenous Kotokoli. Despite their efforts to flee, many Kabre communities were raided for captives throughout the 18th and 19th centuries.

Traditionally the Kabre organized themselves through patrilineal descent and age-set societies. They practiced AGRICULTURE, with their primary crops being millet, GROUNDNUTS (peanuts), and yams. Kabre territory was later colonized, with Germany and France gaining control over the region in the late 19th century.

Further reading: Charles Piot, *Remotely Global: Village Modernity in West Africa* (Chicago: University of Chicago Press, 1999).

Kaffa (Kafa, Kefa) Ethiopian kingdom and the place where the coffee tree was discovered. The kingdom of Kaffa was established by the 14th century and was the largest of several western SIDAMO kingdoms to be founded at that time. Like many African rulers, the Kaffa's king, or *tato,* was seen as embodying both the spiritual and political worlds. Upon his death his spirit was believed to pass on to the next king. Kingship was based on heredity, and the king was given the utmost respect by his subjects. Below the king in rank were members of the nobility, whose position, like the king's, was based on lineage. The working class and the people in bondage consisted mostly of OROMO and AMHARA people. According to Francisco AL-VARES (fl. c. 1520), a Portuguese missionary who wrote in 1540 about his journey to ETHIOPIA, Emperor Sarsa Dengel (r. c. 1563–1597) converted Kaffa to Christianity late in the 16th century. Both Kaffa and the neighboring Sidamo kingdom of Janjero thrived until the latter part of the 19th century.

See also: COFFEE (Vol. II); KAFFA (Vol. II).

Further reading: Werner Lange, *Dialectics of Divine "Kingship" in the Kafa Highlands* (Los Angeles: University of California Press, 1976).

Kalenjin Inclusive name for a cluster of Nilotic-speaking peoples who occupy the highlands of the Rift Valley in present-day KENYA. Subgroups of the Kalenjin include the Pokot, Nandi, Kipsigis, Marakwet, and Sabaot, among others. Nandi and Kipsigis are also the most widely spoken Kalenjin dialects.

Kenyans, and the Kalenjin in particular, are recognized today as the finest long-distance runners in the world. In 2000, in the Boston Marathon, widely considered the most prestigious race among the world's elite runners, men from Kalenjin clans finished first and second, and took 12 of the top 18 spots.

Originally pastoralists, the Kalenjin groups migrated from the north, probably from the highlands of ETHIOPIA. They came during the first millennium of the common era, settling in western Kenya, near Mt. Elgon, on the present-day border with TANZANIA. Depending on where they settled, they also practiced limited AGRICULTURE, growing millet and MAIZE. Some Kalenjin converted to Christianity in the latter 19th century, but most have continued to practice an indigenous RELIGION that is based on ancestor veneration and sun worship—similar to the ancient Egyptians.

Kalenjin groups continued to roam the region during the period from the 16th through the 19th centuries. There is no uniform Kalenjin culture or tradition, as the different clans adopted some cultural practices of the people who occupied the lands they settled in. The Pokot, for instance, intermarried with and practiced the social customs of their Ugandan neighbors, the KARAMOJONG and the Turkana.

See also: ELGON, MOUNT (Vol. I); NILOTES (Vols. II, III).

kalonga (karonga) Honorific title given to the head of the MARAVI confederation, an alliance of chiefdoms spread throughout present-day MALAWI; when capitalized, also the name of the people led by that man. Though the history of the Kalonga people is not well preserved, Maravi oral tradition maintains that in the late 15th century, a member of the Phiri royal clan led a migration of his peoples out of Luba territory in Central Africa and headed southeast. By the beginning of the 16th century they had settled in the area south of Lake Malawi (Lake Nyasa). The leader of these peoples was named Kalonga Chidzonzi. His group, which became known as the Kalonga people, emerged as the founders of the Maravi confederation, a collection of kingdoms or chiefdoms with strong kinship organization that dominated Malawi during the 16th and 17th centuries.

From the town of Manthimba, at the southern end of Lake Malawi, Kalonga Chidzonzi governed with the assistance of Kalonga army commanders and advisers. Subordinate chiefdoms paid tribute to the *kalonga* in FOOD and valuable trade goods, such as ivor. He in turn protected them with his army and allowed them to use the land for grazing or AGRICULTURE. Kalonga Chidzonzi also wisely assigned important positions of authority to some of the headmen of the non-Kalonga groups that the confederation peacefully enveloped. As a result peoples such as the CHEWA, who pre-dated the Kalonga in the area, were represented in the Maravi confederation. This style of leadership contributed to the rapid expansion of Maravi dominion throughout the area. By the beginning of the 16th century the *kalonga* was recognized as the Maravi leader.

See also: LUBA (Vol. II).

Kamba (Akamba, Ukambani) Bantu-speaking ethnic group of present-day KENYA and northeastern TANZANIA. Closely related to the neighboring KIKUYU, the Kamba became major ivory traders in the 17th century. The Kamba were primarily agriculturalists, though during the 15th through the 17th centuries, many of their clans also lived a cattle-herding lifestyle in the region near the present-day Kenya-Tanzania border. The pastoralist Kamba moved often to avoid conflicts with the MAASAI, who also wandered the region in search of suitable land for their herds. By the latter half of the 17th century the Kamba had settled in the Mbooni Hills area that today is the Kamba heartland. The southern Kamba settled in the drier lowlands, cultivating drought-resistant grains and practicing some herding and hunting. Northern Kamba lived at higher elevations, where irrigation was possible, and practiced more extensive cultivation.

Mbooni, the name of the place where many Kamba settled in the 1600s, means "place of the buffalo."

During the 17th and 18th centuries the Kamba became active in the IVORY TRADE, bringing tusks from the Tanzanian interior to the trading port of MOMBASA on Kenya's SWAHILI COAST. Kamba ivory was traded for glass beads, cloth, copper, and salt. Later, in the 19th century, the Kamba became wealthy after arranging a monopoly on the ivory supply with the GIRIAMA people, a neighbor-ing Kenyan ethnic group that had traded ivory even more extensively than the Kamba.

See also: KAMBA (Vol. II).

Further reading: Joseph Muthiani, *Akamba from Within: Egalitarianism in Social Relations* (New York: Exposition Press, 1973); Sammy Nzioki, *Akamba* (London: Evans Brothers, 1982).

Kanem See KANEM-BORNU.

Kanem-Bornu   Two separate kingdoms, Kanem and Bornu, that evolved into a trading empire in the 16th century. In the early 1500s Bornu and Kanem came together under Mai (King) IDRIS ALAWMA (r. c. 1570–1603). Alawma extended the reach of the empire as far west as the eastern edge of the HAUSA STATES and as far east as the western border of the present-day Republic of the SUDAN. It's northern province stretched to the FEZZAN in present-day southern LIBYA. By the time the SONGHAI Empire fell in 1591, Kanem-Bornu was regarded as the most important state in the central Sudan. Alawma devised several

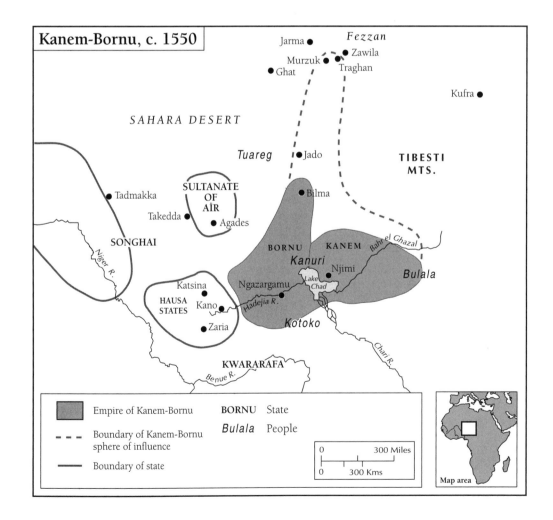

ways to increase his empire's wealth, including taxes on trade, the sale of captives for forced LABOR, and tributes paid to the king by inhabitants of areas controlled by Kanem-Bornu.

The Role of Idris Alawma The impetus behind Alawma's state building was largely religious. A devout Muslim, he sought to create an Islamic state that was larger than the one he had inherited. Ultimately, his military prowess and shrewd trade policies put Kanem-Bornu in the position to dominate the region for the next two centuries.

Alawma secured firearms from the Ottoman Turks of North Africa and initiated a style of waging war that was new to the region. Unlike previous military tacticians, Idris Alawma outfitted his soldiers with iron helmets and chain mail. Also, he ordered his armies to destroy everything in their paths and had them reside in highly organized military camps. Further, he was a wise ruler in that he negotiated well with other powerful leaders, and he heeded the sage advice of his counselors.

The success of Kanem-Bornu depended heavily on the revenue generated by taxing trade, so its commercial routes were among the best ways across the Sahara desert. Alawma made sure the routes were passable and worked to ensure the safety of those traveling them. Kanem-Bornu merchants carried slaves, COTTON, ivory, perfume, and hides north, while traders brought them salt, horses, glass, guns, and cloth.

The Decline of Kanem-Bornu Although Alawma died in 1603, the remarkable advances he made sustained the prosperity of the Kanem-Bornu empire for another 50 years. By the middle of the 17th century, though, the empire's influence was waning, and its borders began to contract. The 17th and 18th centuries marked a relatively peaceful time for Kanem-Bornu. By the middle of the 1700s the once-mighty empire was largely confined to the Lake Chad area, and the TUAREGS of the AÏR MASSIF assumed control of much of the trans-Saharan trade to the Fezzan.

About that time, the Islamic FULANI people from present-day eastern SENEGAL began waging jihads and conquering smaller kingdoms as they moved east. By about 1812 the Fulani cleric USMAN DAN FODIO (1754–1817) had taken control of most of the Hausa States and the kingdoms of YORUBALAND to the south, and even briefly seized NGAZARGAMU, the Kanem-Bornu capital. The Fulani jihad stalled in Kanem-Bornu, though, as the people of the kingdom were already devout Muslims and fiercely rejected the domination of a foreign sultan. Led by Muhammad al-Kanemi (d. 1837), Kanem-Bornu reasserted its independence and drove the Fulani from the Lake Chad region.

See also: BORNU (Vol. II); ISLAM, INFLUENCE OF (Vols. II, III, IV, V); KANEM (Vol. II); KANEM-BORNU (Vol. II); OTTOMAN EMPIRE AND AFRICA (Vols. II, III).

Further reading: Ronald Cohen, *The Kanuri of Bornu* (Prospect Heights, Ill.: Waveland Press, 1987); Agustin F. C. Holl, *The Diwan Revisited: Literacy, State Formation and the Rise of Kanuri Domination (AD 1200–1600)* (New York: Columbia University Press, 2000); Dierk Lange, *A Sudanic Chronicle: The Borno Expeditions of Idris Alauma (1564–1576)* (Stuttgart, Germany: F. Steiner, 1987).

Kankan Mande town in present-day GUINEA, located along the banks of the Milo River, a tributary of the NIGER RIVER. During the 17th century SONINKE and Islamic KUNTA and DYULA traders began to settle in Kankan, and by the 1720s they founded a trading center. As Islam penetrated Africa along Arab trade routes, Kankan became an important Islamic missionary post. It eventually emerged as a center for Islamic teaching.

See also: KANKAN (Vols. IV, V).

Kano One of the largest and most powerful of the ancient Hausa city-states. Kano is a commercial city known for its cloth manufacturing. Its chief industry is the weaving of cloth from locally grown COTTON and dyeing it with indigo at the Kofar Mata dye pits, the oldest in Africa. TUAREGS bought the indigo-dyed cloth and became known both as the "Men of the Blue Veil" as well as the "Blue Men of the Desert," because the blue dye often rubbed off on their skin.

Kano's prosperity sparked long-lasting rivalries with other HAUSA STATES, in particular KATSINA, which made it vulnerable to other competing African empires. As a result Kano became a tributary state of several rival powers, including Bornu in the 15th and 18th centuries and the SONGHAI Empire in the 16th century.

Subsequently a FULANI jihad that began in 1804 in the Hausa state of GOBIR significantly changed the history of the region. The holy war spread to Kano, and in 1807 the city was taken over by Fulani emirs. By 1815 Kano succeeded in overtaking Katsina as a commercial and political Hausa center. It retained that power until the 1880s, when changing trade practices and increasing domination by European colonialists began to limit its importance.

See also: KANO (Vols. II, IV, V).

Kanuri People living mostly in the northwestern parts of present-day NIGERIA and portions of present-day southeastern NIGER; also the language they speak. Traditionally an agricultural people who live in polygamous households and villages, the Kanuri have practiced Islam since as early as the 11th century. However, the Kanuri are most noted for their hand in the establishment of the Kanem kingdom, which evolved into the KANEM-BORNU trading empire. This empire, located around Lake CHAD, was situated along a busy trading route that passed through the Sahara desert on the way to LIBYA and the coast of the Mediterranean Sea. Kanem and Bornu had been linked for centuries, but their rise as a combined trading empire did not begin until about the 14th century, when the Kanuri, after facing clashes with the BULALA people, moved their capital to Ngazargamu, in Bornu.

The government of Kanem-Bornu was hierarchical, and the country was ruled by the *mai*, or king. From about 1570 to 1603 the kingdom was ruled by Mai IDRIS ALAWMA—a member of the SEFUWA dynasty that intermarried with the Kanuri and reigned throughout most of Kanem-Bornu's history. It was Idris Alawma who brought the empire to the peak of its power. The Kanuri had already gained significant wealth by trading agricultural goods, horses, and ivory along the trans-Saharan routes. During the reign of Idris Alawma the Kanuri moved successfully into the trade in human captives, thus expanding their influence and their boundaries as far west as the HAUSA STATES.

The Kanuri and Kanem-Bornu continued to flourish until the end of the 18th century, when less successful *mais* hindered the growth and power of the empire. During the early 19th century the FULANI JIHADS, led by the Muslim cleric USMAN DAN FODIO (1754–1817), attempted to overtake Kanem-Bornu. With the help of the Islamic scholar Muhammad al-Kanemi, the Kanuri were able to successfully resist the effort. This successful resistance, however, allowed al-Kanemi to take command of the kingdom, which in turn led to the end of the Sefuwa dynasty by 1846.

See also: KANURI (Vol. II); SAHARA DESERT (Vols. I, II).

Further reading: Ronald Cohen, *The Kanuri of Bornu* (Prospect Heights, Ill.: Waveland Press, 1987); Agustin, F. C. Holl, *The Diwan Revisited: Literacy, State formation and the Rise of Kanuri Domination (AD 1200–1600)* (New York: Columbia University Press, 2000).

Kaokoland (Kaokoveld)

Region in present-day northwestern NAMIBIA first settled by Bantu-speaking HERERO pastoralists, probably in the mid-16th century. Kaokoland is situated along the Atlantic coast, between the Kunene and Hoanib rivers. Despite its proximity to water, the region is extremely dry and, therefore, sparsely populated. At the heart of the region is the largely uninhabitable Namib Desert.

Kaokoland was first settled in the middle of the 16th century, when the Herero groups, including the Himba and Ovatjimba, migrated there from the central part of the continent. Dutch farmers called BOERS inhabited the region for a brief time in the late 1800s during their trek from the Transvaal, in present-day SOUTH AFRICA, to present-day ANGOLA, north of Namibia.

See also: HIMBA (Vol. II).

Further reading: Mary Rice and Craig Gibson, *Heat, Dust, and Dreams: An Exploration of People and Environment in Namibia's Kaokoland and Damaraland* (Cape Town, South Africa: Struik, 2001).

Karamanli dynasty

Line of rulers who, from 1711 to 1835, governed what is now LIBYA as an autonomous province of the Ottoman Empire. The Karamanli bore the title *bey* (from the Turkish, meaning "chief," or "gentleman"), a designation used by the Ottomans for a provincial governor. In 1835 the Ottoman Empire took advantage of local discord and disputes over succession to send officials from Istanbul to reestablish the empire's direct authority over the region.

The first bey, Ahmad Karamanli (r. 1711–1745), was a member of the elite Turkish military corps known as the Janissaries. Leader of the Ottoman cavalry, he killed his competitors in order to take office at the city of TRIPOLI. To put himself in good standing with the Ottoman sultan, Ahmed III (r. 1703–1730), in Istanbul, Ahmad Karamanli was said to have offered as tribute the properties of the rivals he had killed. By 1714 Ahmed III named the Karamanlis the rightful rulers of Tripoli.

A Janissary (from the Turkish word *yeniceri*, meaning "new soldier") was a member of an elite military corps within the standing army of the Ottoman Empire. The Janissaries existed from the late 14th century until 1826, when they were disbanded for revolting against the Ottoman sultan. The Janissaries were originally young enslaved Christians from the Balkans who were recruited into royal service and converted to Islam. Required to be celibate, Janissaries were famed for their military skills. By the late 16th century celibacy was no longer required, and their function became political rather than military.

Although the reign of Ahmad Karamanli's successor, Ali (r. 1754–1793), was long, it was beset by famine in 1767–68, by plague in 1785, and by the civil wars of 1791–93, the last of which nearly destroyed the Karamanli dynasty. Both rulers, however, became wealthy by selling human captives to the Europeans and by encouraging and protecting PIRATES along the BARBARY COAST, who brought their booty to trade at the Libyan port of Tripoli.

At the end of Ali's reign in 1793, Istanbul again attempted to gain control of Tripoli by ousting the Karamanlis from office. The effort failed, however, and in 1794 Yusuf Karamanli (r. 1794–1832) became the third Karamanli bey to rule at Tripoli. Yusuf's reign was characterized by his military successes, which expanded Libya's boundaries, and by the expulsion of marauding nomadic peoples from the region. He made alliances with both the SOKOTO CALIPHATE of present-day NIGERIA and with KANEM-BORNU in what is now Nigeria and NIGER, in order to reap benefit from their wars of expansion. These wars produced many slaves who were then shipped to the Americas as part of the transatlantic SLAVE TRADE. Ultimately the abolition of piracy along the Barbary Coast and the decline of the slave trade after 1807 greatly reduced the influence of the Karamanli dynasty. After Yusuf died in 1832, the Karamanli dynasty was economically and politically weak and had only as much power in the countryside as local nomadic peoples chose to grant to it. In light of this situation, the Ottomans easily regained control of Tripoli in 1835 and with it the province of Libya.

See also: OTTOMAN EMPIRE AND AFRICA (Vols. III, IV).

Karamoko Alfa (Ibrahim Sambegu) (r. c. 1725–1750) (d. c. 1751) *Muslim Fulani cleric and jihad leader in present-day Guinea*

Prior to the 18th century the pagan Yalunka peoples lived amicably in the FOUTA DJALLON with their FULANI neighbors, who also practiced a traditional African RELIGION. However in the mid-18th century a group of Muslim Fulani moved into the Fouta Djallon area and began spreading the Islamic faith. Among them was the religious leader Alfa Ba (d. c. 1751) and his son, Ibrahim Sambegu.

When, in 1725, the Yalunka kings began to regulate the preaching of the Muslim clerics, Alfa Ba called for the preparation of a jihad. Alfa Ba passed away before the jihad got under way and it was his son, Ibrahim Sambegu, who then became the leader of the jihadist forces. Taking the Muslim name *Karamoko* (meaning "scholar" or "teacher") and *Alfa* (possibly meaning "jurist"), he joined forces with a warrior named Ibrahim Sori (d. 1791), who garnered the nickname *Mawdo* (the Great). The two then launched a full-scale jihad against the Yalunka, the SUSU, and the Fulani of the Fouta Djallon region of present-day GUINEA. By 1750 the jihad had accomplished its mission, forcing the Yalunka and some of the Susu to flee the region and converting the remaining Susu and Fulani to the Islam.

Karamoko Alfa was then named the first *almamy* (religious or political head) of both the Fouta Djallon and its capital province of Timbo. He is also credited with designing the nine-region provincial system that defined the Fouta Djallon sultanate after the jihad. Karamoko Alfa

ruled as *almamy* until about 1750, when he reportedly began to go insane. He was replaced by his cousin Sory about 1751. After the death of Sory, a succession struggle began among the sons of both Karamoko Alfa and Sory. As a result, two political groups were formed in the region: the Alfayas, who gave allegiance to the successors of Karamoko Alfa, and the Soriyas, who backed the successors of Sory.

See also: FULANI JIHADS (Vol. III).

Kasanje
Kingdom of the 16th and 17th centuries located on the Kwango River in present-day ANGOLA, on Africa's Atlantic coast. The kingdom was founded by the 16th century by Lunda warriors who conquered the plains along the Kwango. Inhabitants of the area became known as the IMBANGALA, and the rulers adopted the title *kasanje*, thus the kingdom's name. The Kasanje kingdom quickly established commercial ties with the LUNDA EMPIRE and other interior states as well as with the Portuguese merchants of the Atlantic coast. By the late 17th century the Imbangala had a monopoly on the inland Portuguese-African trade in captives. This relationship lasted until the mid-19th century. Despite continuous attempts by the Portuguese to annex the kingdom, Kasanje remained independent until the early 1900s.

See also: PORTUGAL AND AFRICA (Vols. III, IV, V).

Kassala
Agricultural region in present-day east-central Republic of the SUDAN, near the nation's border with ERITREA. About 600 BCE Kassala was controlled by the Kushite dynasty of EGYPT. When the Kushites were later conquered by Aksum, the region was largely Christianized. Kassala remained under Christian rule until the Arab Abdullabi dynasty seized power in the early part of the 16th century.

By 1608 the Nilotic Muslim FUNJ dynasty dominated the Abdullabi and used the area as a military base during its war with ETHIOPIA. More than two centuries later, in 1821 Kassala was conquered by MUHAMMAD ALI (c. 1769–1849), an Egyptian vizier under nominal Ottoman rule who annexed the region as part of Egyptian Sudan.

See also: OTTOMAN EMPIRE AND AFRICA (Vols. III, IV).

Katagum
Town located along the Jamaare River of present-day northern NIGERIA. In 1809, during a Fulani jihad, the warrior Ibrahim Zakiyul Kalbi captured territory belonging to KANEM-BORNU on the northern side of the Jamaare River, making it the capital of his emirate. Upon his return to the capital in 1814, Kalbi, who was also called *Malam* (meaning "scholar" or "teacher"), officially established the city of Katagum. He commissioned a mosque and also ordered the construction of a pair of

city-encompassing walls with four gates, each with a 10-foot (3-m) base and a height of 20 feet (6 m). Katagum had become a trading center by 1824, when two Scottish explorers—Walter Oudney, who died and is buried in Katagum, and Hugh Clapperton—reached the town during their travels.

Although Katagum had been reclaimed by Kanem-Bornu and the KANURI people during the 1820s, the town was once again conquered by the combined forces of the reigning FULANI emir, Dan Kauwa, and the Bauchi king, Yakubu, in 1826. Katagum then resumed its position as an important emirate in the Fulani empire until clashes with the emir of Hadejia in the 1850s significantly weakened the town's authority.

Katanga (Shaba)

Province located in the southeastern region of present-day Democratic Republic of the CONGO known for its copper-mining industry. By the time Europeans arrived in the area in the late 15th century, Katanga was already being worked for its copper deposits by the Luba people. By the 16th century the LUBA EMPIRE had formed, with individual kingdoms situated around the Katanga region and its copper mines. The Luba were skilled in the working of copper, and by the 17th century the empire had become wealthy and powerful by trading both copper and iron ore for such commodities as foodstuffs and cloth. Even though a thriving trade in human captives greatly depleted the strength of many of the kingdoms of Central Africa, the Luba empire continued to have economic success throughout the 18th century because of the profitable copper industry of the Katanga region.

See also: COPPER (Vols. I, II); COPPERBELT (Vol. IV); KATANGA (Vol. V); SLAVERY (Vol. III).

Katsina

City and emirate in present-day north-central NIGERIA. It is thought that Islam was introduced to the area during the 15th century by Malian traders traveling along the camel caravan routes. By the 17th century Katsina was the largest of the seven "true" HAUSA STATES (also called Hausa Bakwai). Extensive and far-reaching trade brought wealth to Katsina, allowing it to grow larger than the neighboring Hausa states. The significant blossoming of Islamic culture further stimulated the city's development. Various forces fought for dominance of this important area.

In the early 16th century the city was conquered by the SONGHAI Empire of West Africa, which in turn collapsed in 1591. At that point Songhai's great rival in western Africa, Bornu, began exerting its influence, and Katsina became a tributary of Bornu. Although Katsina and several other Hausa states paid tributes to Bornu, they nonetheless continued to flourish and even fight among

themselves for political and economic leadership. Bornu's inability to control this infighting combined with a devastating drought in the middle of the 18th century to end its influence over Katsina.

In the early 1800s the FULANI Muslim leader USMAN DAN FODIO (1754–1817) started a revolutionary movement in the Hausa state of GOBIR. This led to a jihad that culminated in the fall of Katsina to the Fulani leader in 1806. About this same time, changing trade routes and the emergence of KANO as an economic center combined to end the period of Katsina's dominance.

Kayor (Cayor, Kajor)

Province of present-day SENEGAL that was a state of the WOLOF EMPIRE until the 16th century. Located on the Atlantic coast, Kayor shares its borders with Walo, Djoloff, and Baol. Its inhabitants are mostly of Wolof origin and speak a Western Atlantic language. Between the 16th and 19th centuries Kayor and Baol were at various times united under a single political administration.

Amari Ngoné Sobel (1549–1593) became the first *damel,* or ruler, of Kayor helped by helping the region, including Baol, achieve independence from Wolof in the mid-16th century. After Amari's reign, Kayor's and Baol's monarchies were split. As a result Amari's grandson became the *damel* of Baol and his son the *damel* of Kayor. Amari Ngoné Sobel and his descendants were able to build Kayor into a powerful and prosperous kingdom, its wealth resulting from Kayor's participation in the transatlantic SLAVE TRADE.

Although there were several attempts on the part of the succeeding *damels,* Kayor and Baol were not united again until the reign of Tegne Lat Soucabé (1697–1719), who, in addition to consolidating the two kingdoms, prevented them from being subjugated by the *burba,* or king, of Djoloff. Under Soucabé, the Fall Tié dynasty was established, lasting from 1697 to 1763. At that time it was replaced by the Fall Madior dynasty. Kayor and Baol were joined again under Tègne Macodou (r. 1766–1777), who founded the Fall Tié Ndella dynasty. Because of its strategic location, Kayor became a center of French colonial activities in the 19th century.

Kayra dynasty (Keira)

Ruling clan of DARFUR, an Islamic sultanate founded by SULIMAN SOLONG (c. 1596–1637) in the middle of the 17th century. Today Darfur lies in the western Republic of the SUDAN. The Kayra dynasty ruled from about 1640 until the late 19th century.

Under the leadership of Suliman Solong, the FUR people of the mountainous Darfur region broke free from the rule of the Bornu kingdom, located to the southwest of Lake CHAD, and drove the rival TUNJUR people out of Darfur and west, into WADAI.

Suliman Solong's successor, Ahmad Bakr ibn Musa (c. 1682–1722), expanded the role of Islam in the sultanate, building mosques and centers of Islamic learning. He also expanded the boundaries of the sultanate to the north and northwest, increasing the territory in which Darfur controlled trade. Five of Ahmad Bakr's sons eventually held the Fur throne, strengthening the dynasty's hold on power through marriage alliances and trading agreements. During this period it was not uncommon for the Kayra rulers to give local Muslim leaders and powerful allies gifts of slaves, firearms, and luxury items in order to strengthen their loyalty to the dynasty.

> Even though the sultans of the Kayra dynasty established Islam as the official RELIGION of the Fur state early on, many of its inhabitants continued to practice traditional African religions, especially on the isolated outlying plains northwest of KORDOFAN.

Until the late 1700s the Kayra clan was divided into two factions: one that wanted to expand the sultanate through military domination (the Darfur army was renowned for its expert horsemen) and the other that wanted to enrich and strengthen the dynasty itself. Despite the rift the Kayra clan ruled uninterrupted except for a brief period in the late 19th century.

In the 18th century Kayra sultans established al-Fashir as their capital. They consolidated their hold on Darfur by pushing east into the FUNJ sultanate and establishing trade relations with the Ottoman Empire in EGYPT. By the beginning of the 19th century Kayra sultans had grown rich by trading slaves to Egypt and continuing to heavily tax the trade caravans that passed through their territory on the way to Red Sea ports.

See also: OTTOMAN EMPIRE AND AFRICA (Vols. III, IV).

Kazembe (Cayembe)

Large Lunda kingdom of the 18th and 19th centuries located in present-day ZAMBIA and the Democratic Republic of the CONGO. The Kazembe kingdom was established in 1740 by dissenters from Central Africa's LUNDA EMPIRE, which had been founded before 1600. During the reign of its second king, Kazembe II (c. 1760–1805), the kingdom quickly expanded through the conquest of neighboring states. Kazembe IV, who ruled from 1805 to 1850, opened trade relations with Portuguese merchants in present-day ANGOLA. Kazembe controlled both the salt pans and the copper mines in what is now KATANGA Province in the Democratic Republic of the Congo.

> Kazembe was a title held by many of the chiefs who broke from the Lunda empire and established their own kingdoms in the 18th century.

The region became a major center for trade in salt and copper between the African interior and the Atlantic coast. Internal conflict led to the demise of Kazembe, which was overtaken by eastern groups around 1890.

See also: LUNDA KINGDOM (Vol. II).

Further reading: Giacomo Macola, *The Kingdom of Kazembe: History and Politics in North-Eastern Zambia and Katanga to 1950* (Münster, Germany: Lit. Verlag, 2002).

Kebbi

Founded around the beginning of the 16th century, one of the Banza Bakwai, or seven "illegitimate" HAUSA STATES in present-day northwestern NIGERIA and southwestern NIGER. The capital of Kebbi state, BIRNIN KEBBI, was an early settlement of the Kebbawa, a subgroup of the Hausa people.

Biram, Daura, GOBIR, KANO, KATSINA, Rano, and Zazzau (later renamed ZARIA, after its capital) were considered the *Hausa Bakwai,* or the seven "true" Hausa states. These states had seven outlying kingdoms, which were called the *Banza Bakwai,* or seven "illegitimate" states. The Banza Bakwai included ZAMFARA, Yauri, Gwari, NUPE, KWARARAFA (also called Jukun), Yoruba, and Kebbi. There was great rivalry among all of these states, and the fortunes of each rose and fell over the centuries. At times during the 16th and 17th centuries, Kebbi was the dominant Hausa state.

Kebbi was founded by Muhammadu Kanta (fl. 1516), a SONGHAI general who defected from the ranks of Askia MUHAMMAD TOURÉ (d. 1538). Muhammadu Kanta consolidated existing villages to build three new cities, Surname, Birnin Leka, and Birnin Kebbi, all of which repelled numerous attacks from neighboring peoples to become one of the great West African powers as a Hausa city-state. In 1674, however, Kebbi was defeated by forces from Agades, to the north, and the former glory of city rapidly declined.

The Sokoto River, also called the Kebbi River because of its proximity to the Hausa state, irrigates the surrounding savannah, allowing for year-round farming of GROUNDNUTS (peanuts), COTTON, tobacco, swamp rice, onions, sugarcane, and indigo. Much of the remaining land is used for grazing cattle, sheep, and goats. Today the FULANI, Hausa, Dakarki, and Kamberi peoples inhabit the region. They are primarily Muslims.

See also: MUHAMMAD TOURÉ, ASKIA (Vol. II).

Kenya East African country on the Indian Ocean coast measuring approximately 224,900 square miles (582,491 sq km). Kenya shares borders with ETHIOPIA, Republic of the SUDAN, UGANDA, TANZANIA, and SOMALIA.

Little is known of Kenyan history prior to the 19th century, especially regarding the interior regions. What has been recorded primarily concerns the Indian Ocean settlements that made up Kenya's stretch of the SWAHILI COAST. Kenya's interior was originally sparsely occupied by Bantu-speaking hunter-gatherers like the Okiek and Gumba. Later, Nilotic peoples of the KALENJIN group moved into Kenya, preceding groups of Bantu-speaking agriculturalists, including the KAMBA, KIKUYU, and GIRIAMA, who moved into the region to take advantage of the plentiful rainfall and fertile valleys. In the 16th and 17th centuries the pastoral MAASAI came from the north and wandered into southern Kenya with their herds of cattle.

The coast was dominated by Swahili city-states. The Swahili were commercially oriented Muslims who developed from generations of intermarriage between Arab traders and native coastal Africans. They established numerous Kenyan coastal chiefdoms, including MOMBASA, MALINDI, LAMU, and Pate, which thrived from the 12th through the 18th centuries. These cities were trading ports for the exchange of captives, cloth, ivory, glass beads, and GOLD. Swahili ports competed for control of the coastal trade, and by the end of the 15th century Mombasa had overtaken Malindi as the most powerful of the Swahili city-states. However, another shift in power was soon to occur.

Early in the 16th century, Portuguese forces led by explorer Vasco da Gama (1460–1524) arrived on the Kenyan coast seeking to control lucrative Indian Ocean trade routes. After aligning with the ruling dynasty of Malindi, the Portuguese attempted to capture Mombasa in 1505. However, the city resisted the Portuguese until 1529.

The Portuguese attempted to tax commerce in the Swahili city-states, leading to constant rebellion. Finally, in 1699 the Arabian OMANI SULTANATE, which had its African headquarters on the island of ZANZIBAR, drove the Portuguese from the Kenyan coast. Despite occupying Kenyan ports for nearly 200 years, the Portuguese had little influence on Swahili culture.

Although the Omani Arabs were interested in Indian Ocean trade, they did not immediately seize control of the Kenyan coast. Pate reigned as the most powerful city-state until the Lamu army defeated them in the early 1800s. It was not until 1820 that the Omanis, under sultan SAYYID SAID (1791–1856), came to dominate the Kenyan coastal region.

See also: GAMA, VASCO DA (Vol. II); INDIAN OCEAN TRADE (Vol. II); IVORY TRADE (Vol. III); KENYA (Vols. I, II, IV, V); SLAVE TRADE ON THE SWAHILI COAST (Vol. III).

Further reading: Robert M. Maxon and Thomas P. Ofcansky, *Historical Dictionary of Kenya* (Lanham, Md.: Scarecrow Press, 2000); Robert Pateman, *Kenya* (New York: Marshall Cavendish, 1998).

Keta Town in present-day southeastern GHANA located on the Gulf of Guinea, at the mouth of the Volta River. Prior to European settlement Keta was part of the ANLO kingdom. Europeans arrived at Keta in the 15th century and established a port to trade captives, ivory, spices, and GOLD. During the 1700s the Anlo kingdom was in constant conflict with the Ada people over fishing, MINING, and salt- and slave-trading rights. This made Keta a very important commercial center for the Anlo kingdom. A Danish settlement was constructed in the area in 1784. Ultimately, in 1850 Keta became part of a British colony.

See also: KETA (Vol. II).

Ketu Yoruba province and kingdom of the 16th through the 18th centuries located south of Sabe in central DAHOMEY (present-day Republic of BENIN). The capital of Ketu is the city of Ketu, and it was from here that the *alaketu* (a royal title meaning "owner of Ketu") set up his government. At its height in the 1700s, the Ketu kingdom extended east to Meko, west to the Weme (Oueme) River, north to Okpara, and south to the Ahori marshlands.

The date of the origin of the kingdom is obscure, but the existence of a kings list enumerating 38 kings who ruled before 1750 gives credence to the belief that Ketu was founded before Oyo in the early 16th century.

Until the 17th century the kingdom of Ketu enjoyed a relatively peaceful existence. But by the 18th century its territory was increasingly encroached upon by the OYO EMPIRE, to which it paid tribute. As time passed, however, Oyo began to lose its trade routes to the coast, and the stability of the kingdom was threatened from within by the resurgence of vassal states that had once paid tribute to Oyo.

The FON people of Dahomey posed the most serious threat. Since the mid-18th century the Fon had focused their attention on rebuilding and restructuring their kingdom. In 1789 Dahomey stormed Ketu, whose inhabitants were no match for the powerful Fon. However, Ketu tradition insists that Ketu was victorious in fending off Dahomey, maintaining that Dahomey plundered nearby Iwole instead.

See also: YORUBALAND (Vol. III).

Khami Capital of the Torwa state that emerged in the 16th century after the capital of Great Zimbabwe had been abandoned. Situated on the Khami River and with a population perhaps as large as 7,000, Khami had buildings with a distinctive architectural style. The key features were platforms on which houses were built and extensive low, intricately patterned walls covered in various herringbone, cord, and checkered patterns. The town's more important residents lived in a central group of buildings, with the hub being a hill topped with three platforms that formed a tiered structure. More ordinary residents lived in less substantial structures on the town's outskirts. Khami was a major center for trade, as indicated by the presence of goods such as pottery and glass beads originating from the Indian Ocean basin and even Europe. In exchange Torwa supplied GOLD, copper, and ivory, among other goods. Trade contacts were with Muslim merchants from the commercial towns of the SWAHILI COAST or through intermediaries with Portuguese merchants operating in the southeast African interior. In the late 17th century DHLO-DHLO succeeded Khami as Torwa's capital city. In 1986 the Khami ruins were declared highly culturally significant and were named a UNESCO World Heritage Site.

See also: ARCHAEOLOGY (Vols. I, II, III, IV, V).

Further reading: Graham Connah, *African Civilizations: An Archaeological Perspective* (2nd ed.; New York: Cambridge University Press, 2001); Martin Hall, *Farmers, Kings, and Traders: The People of Southern Africa, 200–1860* (Chicago: University of Chicago Press, 1990).

Khartoum Capital city of present-day Republic of the SUDAN, located at the convergence of the Blue Nile and White Nile rivers. Prior to the early 19th century Khartoum served as little more than a small agricultural community. However, in 1821 an Egyptian army led by Uthman Bey (fl. 1820s) was sent to claim the area for the Ottoman Empire and established an army camp there. Due to Khartoum's strategic location, a fort was built, and the city served as a military outpost for the Ottoman Empire until 1865. Khartoum developed into a primary marketplace for the trade in ivory and captives. The captured peoples were often traditional DINKA and NUER pastoralists from the Nile basin, to the south of the city.

See also: KHARTOUM (Vols. I, IV, V); OTTOMAN EMPIRE AND AFRICA (Vols. III, IV).

Khoikhoi (Khoe Khoe, Namaqua, Khoi, Hottentot) Pastoralist people who inhabited areas of present-day BOTSWANA and SOUTH AFRICA for thousands of years prior to the era of European colonization. The Khoikhoi aggressively repelled Portuguese incursions into their territory in the late 15th century, and their anti-European sentiments continued into the 16th century. By the mid-17th century Dutch and British colonists were fighting often with the Khoikhoi over land and water rights in the CAPE COLONY. Eventually, the superior European firepower took its toll, and the Khoikhoi were

forced from their homeland into present-day NAMIBIA. At the same time, an outbreak of smallpox decimated the Khoikhoi population. The remaining Khoikhoi divided into two subgroups, the NAMA and the ORLAMS. Some of these Khoikhoi peoples intermarried with BOERS, or Dutch South Africans, creating a new ethnic group called the Basters, of which the GRIQUA are a subgroup.

See also: KHOIKHOI (Vol. II).

Further reading: Emile Boonzaier, et. al., *The Cape Herders: A History of the Khoikhoi of Southern Africa* (Athens, Ohio: Ohio University Press, 1996); Elizabeth Elbourne, *Blood Ground: Colonialism, Missions, and the Contest for Christianity in the Cape Colony and Britain, 1799–1853* (Montreal: McGill-Queen's University Press, 2002); Susan Newton-King, *Masters and Servants on the Cape Eastern Frontier, 1760–1803* (New York: Cambridge University Press, 1999).

Kikuyu Bantu-speaking ethnic group residing in the foothills and ridges of the central highlands between Nairobi and Mt. Kenya in present-day KENYA. Today the Kikuyu make up almost one-quarter of Kenya's population. They probably migrated to their homeland from the north by the middle of the 17th century, slowly spreading throughout the region over the next three centuries. They practiced both herding and farming, which allowed them to trade with the earlier inhabitants of the region, including the MAASAI and Okiek.

In Kikuyu culture, both men and women were able to conduct trade. Kikuyu women often exchanged their goods with Maasai women, even if the men of their respective clans were warring. Kikuyu men secured trade alliances with Maasai and GIRIAMA men by becoming "blood brothers." Each man would taste the other's blood and declare oaths vowing to protect the other.

The Kikuyu secured peace alliances with their neighbors by intermarrying with them and by establishing strong trade relations. Once they were settled in the region, they held regular markets that further solidified social and economic ties with the other groups. With the Maasai, the Kikuyu settlers exchanged their agricultural products for animal skins, pots, gourds, and goods from the Kenyan plains. Nomadic Maasai pastoralists, for their part, often sought refuge among their Kikuyu relatives during times of drought or famine. With the Okiek the Kikuyu traded their livestock for large amounts of land and forest products, including honey.

Early in the 19th century the Kikuyu joined the Giriama and the KAMBA in monopolizing the Kenyan ivory supply. Their fortunes quickly turned for the worse, however, with the arrival of British colonial interests. First, MISSIONARIES converted many Kikuyu people to Christianity, weakening the Kikuyu's shared cultural traditions. Then, later in the 19th century, valuable Kikuyu lands were claimed by Britain, leaving many Kikuyu men with no option but to work as wage laborers for British railroad builders to earn income.

See also: IVORY TRADE (Vol. III); KIKUYU (Vols. II, IV); TRADIE AND COMMERCE (Vol. III).

Further reading: Jomo Kenyatta, *Facing Mount Kenya; The Tribal Life of the Gikuyu* (New York: Vintage Books, 1962); Godfrey Muriuki, *People round Mount Kenya: Kikuyu* (London: Evans Bros., 1985); David P. Sandgren, *Christianity and the Kikuyu: Religious Divisions and Social Conflict* (New York: P. Lang, 1989).

Kilwa (Kilwa Kisiwani or "Kilwa on the Island")
Island port on the Tanzanian coast of East Africa, south of MOMBASA and Mafia Island and north of the Kerimba Archipelago and COMOROS. East Africa's SWAHILI COAST possesses two natural harbors, both of which could handle ships of substantial size, and Kilwa became a major trading port as early as the 12th century. For the next 500 years it handled an extensive commerce in GOLD, ivory, and human captives. When Vasco da Gama (1460–1524) visited Kilwa in 1502, he found a large, prosperous city of narrow streets and tall, three- and four-story houses running right down to the harbor itself.

Within three years of da Gama's arrival, Kilwa fell under Portuguese domination when its king, Ibrahim (fl. 1505), defaulted on tribute payments that he had promised to make. Denied their money, the Portuguese launched a punitive raid that damaged the city and led to the carting off of numerous prisoners. To solidify their control, the Portuguese erected a fort, through which they hoped to regulate the SOFALA gold trade.

Although Kilwa figured prominently in Portuguese activities, the city's commerce was effectively weakened by Portuguese domination. It revived at the beginning of the 18th century, however, with the withdrawal of the Portuguese from Africa's Swahili Coast. By the end of the century it had once again become a major port, this time concentrating on the trade in humans. Its independence proved difficult to maintain, and it ultimately fell under the control of the rising Arab-led OMANI SULTANATE, with the sultan of Kilwa serving as a puppet under an Omani governor.

See also: GAMA, VASCO DA (Vol. II); KILWA (Vol. II); MAFIA ISLAND (Vols. I, II); PORTUGAL AND AFRICA (Vol. III); SLAVE TRADE ON THE SWAHILI COAST (Vol. III); TRADE AND COMMERCE (Vol. III).

Kimbu Bantu-speaking ethnic group of present-day west-central TANZANIA. The area inhabited by the Kimbu, which is known as *Ukimbu*, occupies about 20,000 square miles (51,799 sq km) of densely forested woodlands and river-fed grasslands. Most of the territory is infested with tsetse flies, making herding difficult, if not impossible because of the threat of sleeping sickne ((called *nagana* in animals).

Little is known of the original Kimbu inhabitants of this region, but it is believed that, perhaps during the 18th century, one or more waves of immigration brought numerous peoples from the south and east coast into the territory. This is borne out by various Kimbu social and governmental institutions, many of which seem to have been specifically aimed at successfully assimilating newcomers into the overall society.

Traditionally the Kimbu supported themselves by hunting and gathering, practicing only a limited amount of simple AGRICULTURE. Because of this they frequently moved their villages from place to place in search of new and better foraging areas. Kimbu villages required a fairly substantial population level in order to be both economically and socially viable. They contained 300 to 350 inhabitants and were located about 30 to 40 miles (48 to 64 km) apart.

Traditional Kimbu religion was similar to that of the NYAMWEZI, and the two groups even used the same or similar names for many of their deities, spirits, and ritual offerings. In Kimbu theology the Sun was the symbol of the primary deity, who was known as Ilyuva and who was seen as both a supreme being and a life-giving force. Like the Sun, Ilyuva was associated with the east, and the Kimbu looked to the east as the source of life and health. In contrast the west, particularly the area around Lakes Tanganyika and Rukwa, was seen as the home of the evil spirits responsible for the negative factors in life, such as disease and death. The Kimbu also believed in various lesser spirits, many of whom were linked with specific family lineages. These were, for example, associated with village clearings and abandoned village sites.

Puberty rites long figured prominently among Kimbu religious rituals. However, the traditional circumcision of boys at puberty, which once was a central part of Kimbu life and religion, apparently began to disappear as early as the 1860s.

Although Kimbu society was relatively small and rather heterogeneous, it was highly structured, with a complex system of kingship. The Kimbu chief was associated with the life-giving deity Ilyuva. As a result the chief's family enjoyed a share in the dominions belonging to Ilyuva, which included forests, villages, and virtually everything else within a carefully established territory that had clearly defined landmarks. Water as well as firewood, building materials, and agricultural products were seen as public property that could be used by anyone. However, all other NATURAL RESOURCES, such as honey, game, and even iron ore, were the property of the chief, and anyone who collected these resources owed a share to the chief.

Each individual chief had the responsibility of being a well-meaning and successful father to his people. During his reign the chief was responsible for ensuring both peace and prosperity by properly carrying out various ritual offerings to the chieftain's ancestors. These rituals, carried out at the ancestors' graves in the forests, were crucial to Kimbu society, for the ancestors were seen as the true source of authority and power. A chief was seen as the representative of the ancestors, and could be deposed if he was believed to have lost favor with his ancestors.

It was not only his ancestors who limited the power of a Kimbu chieftain, however. They also shared power with a council of elders, called *ivanyaampala*. This council was made up of older men of great respect in the community, and they generally used the name associated with the royal family. Membership in the council apparently was based on the notion of respect and achievement, since there seems to have been neither a set number of members for the council nor an established system by which members were elected or appointed.

The council traditionally held great power within Kimbu society, and even strong chiefs feared the elders. The council controlled who would be nominated for the chieftainship and had the power to depose a chief.

Subordinate to the main Kimbu chieftain were various lesser chiefs, who were grouped into associations, usually on the basis of specific pieces of regalia. Each of these associations had its own myths to explain its political origins and the systems by which it divided land among its people.

Among the main responsibilities of the Kimbu chiefs was the administration of justice, which they did in conjunction with their councilors. Within this system cases were brought to the council by parties who believed that they had suffered some kind of wrong. If possible these cases were settled by the council alone. If, however, the council believed that an individual case was particularly important or if it could not reach a decision, then the elders brought their findings to the chief.

If the chief disagreed with the council's decision, he would demand that the council's discussions continue until a unanimous decision was reached. Those judgments generally involved some form of compensation for victims and aggrieved parties; debtors were made to render LABOR or service to their creditors, thieves and rapists were forced to give compensation. Other violent crimes were punished with death.

See also: ANCESTOR WORSHIP (Vol. I); LAW AND JUSTICE (Vol. III).

Kimpa Vita See BEATRIX, DOÑA.

kingdoms and empires of eastern Africa and the interior

A major distinction exists between the peoples and kingdoms of the interior and the peoples and kingdoms of the coast. Little documentary evidence exists about the peoples of the East African interior, although for the period following the 15th century, the oral traditions of the present-day peoples of the region, carefully used, can supply a reasonably reliable understanding of the history of the region. On the other hand, the SWAHILI COAST, bordering the Indian Ocean, had been a major center of commerce and trade since at least the second century. Its Arab Muslim culture was urban and cosmopolitan, with links by trade to the Islamic world outside Africa.

The East African Interior The 15th and 16th centuries are characterized by a growing migration of Nilo-Saharan-speaking pastoralists from southern present-day Republic of the SUDAN and southwestern ETHIOPIA into the grasslands of the East African interior. Generally called Nilotes from their language, they intermarried with their Bantu-speaking predecessors and established new local cultures. They are generally divided into three separate groups: the southern Nilotes, the eastern Nilotes, and the western Nilotes.

The southern Nilotes migrated southward from Sudan near Lake Turkana and moved into the highlands east of Lake Victoria. The eastern Nilotes also migrated from the grasslands near Lake Turkana. They held on to their language and culture, forming the Karamojong people of present-day northeastern UGANDA and the MAASAI of present-day central KENYA and TANZANIA.

The Nilotic LUO-speaking peoples from the southern Sudan had reached the northern border of Uganda by the middle of the 15th century. From there they moved throughout the the interlacustrine, or inter-lake, region (the land between Lakes Victoria, Albert, Edward, and Tanganyika) and also northeast of Lake Victoria. From there the BITO clan of the Luo overthrew the Chwezi rulers of Kitara to the east of Lake Albert and founded the kingdom of BUNYORO, which flourished from the 16th to the 19th centuries. In this new kingdom the cattle-raising Luo became a privileged caste that ruled over the Bantu-speaking agriculturalists. As time passed the western Nilotic Luo generally blended with the local people and adopted the Bantu language. For the most part Bunyoro remained a loose confederation of settlements governed by local rulers under the overall authority of a central king. These settlements supplied the king with soldiers for raids against neighboring peoples. In the 16th and 17th centuries these raids, which were a source of cattle and tribute, extended as far south as BUGANDA and present-day RWANDA.

Some historians believe that protection from raids by Bunyoro was a significant reason why Buganda developed the strong central government that distinguished it from

Bunyoro. So successful were its administration and productive ECONOMY that by 1800 Buganda had surpassed Bunyoro in influence. The king of Buganda bore the title *kabaka;* territorial sub-rulers, or chiefs, held the land directly from the king, not by heredity, and owed him loyalty and obedience. The major crops of Buganda were bananas and plantains, and because the cultivation of these plantation-grown crops required only seasonal LABOR, the population was free to develop public works projects, especially the extensive network of roads that stretched from the capital in the town of Buganda throughout the region.

In Rwanda, to the south of Bunyoro and Buganda, a dominant clan of TUTSI pastoralists held power over a much larger population of Bantu-speaking HUTU agriculturalists. The ancestors of the Tutsi may have been Luo. The Tutsi generally did not intermarry with local populations, and they eventually assumed the role of a warrior caste, receiving herding services and other tribute from the farming peoples in return for protection from rival Tutsi clans. By the 18th century the Tutsi had formed the kingdom of Rwanda and the less powerful kingdom of BURUNDI. Both kingdoms developed very late in the precolonial period, however. Rwanda was not united into a single kingdom with defined borders until after the middle of the 19th century when Kilgeri Rwabugiri (r. 1860–1895), who is considered Rwanda's greatest king, assumed the throne.

As the Maasai moved with their herds of cattle through Kenya into the plains of Tanzania, they found the grasslands already occupied by local peoples such as the KALENJIN of central Kenya. With the Kalenjin, as with peoples they subsequently encountered, the Maasai acted on their traditional belief that all cattle belong to the Maasai and seized the pasture lands by force. The clan-based Maasai, ruled by councils of elders, never developed a central government or a central kingdom. In this regard, the Maasai were much like their clan-based, Bantu-speaking neighbors with whom they developed peaceful trading relations. Near Mount Kilimanjaro some large states developed among the clan-based CHAGGA, PARE, and SHAMBAA people. In addition the NYAMWEZI, who lived south of Lake Victoria, were establishing themselves as traders in ivory and, later, captives, using their advantageous location along the trade routes to the East African coast. No centrally governed kingdoms, however, developed from among these peoples.

By the middle of the 19th century the Lunda kingdom of KAZEMBE had become the central pivot of a long-distance trading network that stretched across eastern and Central Africa from the Atlantic Ocean to the Indian Ocean. At its height around the beginning of the 19th century, Kazembe controlled what is now KATANGA Province in the present-day Democratic Republic of the CONGO and northern ZAMBIA. Its major exports were cop-

per as well as ivory, salt, and captives. Imports included firearms, cloth from Europe and India, cowrie shells, beads, and manufactured goods.

The greatest Kazembe king, who amassed most of the territory of the kingdom, was Kazemba II (r. 1740–1760), also known as Kaniembo. The Kazembe Lunda kingdom was the largest and the most highly organized of the Luba-Lunda states of Central Africa and was an offshoot of the LUNDA EMPIRE ruled by the Mwata Yamvo dynasty. By the 1750s Kazembe was all but independent of the Lunda Empire and paid only nominal tribute.

Kazembe's trade routes to the west lay through the neighboring Lunda Empire. Professional Bisa traders who lived to the east of the Lunda Empire transported Kazembe's goods to the Portuguese traders in the Zambezi valley. The BEMBA kingdom, located in the northern reaches of present-day Zambia, dominated the land through which Bisa caravans passed and gained most of its revenue by raiding these caravans from the safety of their fortified towns. The Bantu-speaking YAO people, who lived south and east of Lake Malawi and traded in ivory and captives, were the main links to the port of KILWA on the Swahili Coast. The Yao were never united and established no central kingdom; they lived in settlements of 75 to 100 persons under a traditional headman.

The original Lunda kingdom itself, which developed into a centralized empire during the 15th century, became rich from MAIZE and cassava, two crops that the Portuguese introduced into Africa from the Americas. Trading these crops along with ivory and slaves, the Lunda Empire was able to obtain firearms and European-made cloth. The use of guns enabled the Mwata Yamvo rulers to extend their dominion within Central Africa. The Kazembe Lunda kingdom was the result of this expansionist move.

The Interior of Southern Africa Three important kingdoms with trading ties to the Indian Ocean coast arose in the interior of southern Africa after the abrupt disappearance of Great Zimbabwe in the second half of the 1400s. The first was the Bantu-speaking MWENE MUTAPA kingdom that stretched from ZIMBABWE to present-day northern SOUTH AFRICA. Over time, rebellious vassals broke away to establish their own kingdoms, including the important ROZWI kingdom of the Shona people, ruled by the CHANGAMIRE DYNASTY. Situated inland west of SOFALA, the Rozwi kingdom arose in the 1670s and dominated the Zimbabwe plateau well into the 18th century.

The second important kingdom, located in present-day MALAWI was the kingdom of the Bantu-speaking MARAVI people that lasted until the late 1700s. The Maravi, who entered the region in the 1400s, were important manufacturers and exporters of iron, and their kingdom controlled most of the Zambezi Basin when Portuguese explorer Vasco da Gama (1460–1524) landed at MOZAMBIQUE ISLAND in 1498. The most powerful Maravi ruler was Masula (r. c. 1600–1650), a KALONGA, or king, whose realm stretched from north of the ZAMBEZI RIVER, in the west, to Mozambique Island, in the east. He failed to set up a central government that could outlast him, however, and his empire disintegrated after his death.

Starting in the early 1500s the Portuguese had made many inroads along the coast and slightly into the interior, with trading stations at Sofala and QUELIMANE along the coast. By the 1530s the Portuguese had established trading stations inland at SENA and TETE along the Zambezi River and a string of large estates called PRAZOS, defended by slave armies, in the Zambezi valley. Although European trade was at first welcomed, from 1693 to 1695 the Changamire Rozwi kingdom expelled the Portuguese from the interior. They kept the MINING and trading of GOLD under strict royal control, restricted the Portuguese mainly to their *prazos,* and allowed only the African agents hired by the Portuguese to trade within the borders of the kingdom. The kingdom was destroyed by the rise of the NGONI and Ndebele peoples during the period called the MFECANE (the crushing) that resulted from ZULU expansion in South Africa during the 1820s and 1830s.

The Swahili Coast   Arab traders favored the Swahili Coast region rather than the closer Somali coast because they could use the monsoon winds to carry them back and forth. The culture of the coast was tied to the sea and linked with the rest of the Arab world. The ruling aristocracy was Muslim of mixed Arab and African descent, almost all of whom were involved in trade. The Muslim population had little or no direct contact, commercial or religious, with the peoples of the interior.

Between 1500 and 1700 the Portuguese were able to wrest control of the highly lucrative Indian Ocean trade from Arab hands. By force of arms they eventually controlled all the prosperous seaports along the coast, including MOMBASA in what is now Kenya, Kilwa in what is now Tanzania, and Sofala in present-day MOZAMBIQUE. They controlled the important islands of ZANZIBAR, LAMU, Pemba, and Mozambique. Their tactic was to sail their cannon-armed ships into a harbor and demand that the ruler become a Portuguese subject and pay annual tribute. If the Africans resisted the Portuguese would bombard and pillage the town and kill any Muslims they found.

The first to fall was MALINDI, north of Mombasa, which submitted quickly to avoid destruction. In a move typical of the rivalries that kept these cities from presenting the Portuguese with a united front, the sultan of Mombasa was so enraged that he declared war on the sultan of Malindi for being a turncoat. Zanzibar, in 1503, was the first coastal city to come under major Portuguese attack. By 1509 the Portuguese were firmly established on the southern end of the Swahili coast, with fortresses built in Kilwa and Sofala, and on Mozambique Island. Because the sultan of Mombasa, further north along the coast, continued to resist, Mombasa was sacked in 1528.

It was attacked again in 1589, this time by a fleet sent from the Portuguese colony of Goa, in India. Because the sultan of Mombasa died without an heir, the Portuguese were able to install the sultan of Malindi, their vassal, on the throne. To maintain dominance over Mombasa, the other northern cities, and the trade routes to India, Portugal built the massive FORT JESUS in Mombasa, completing it in 1599.

The Portuguese also controlled part of the Arabian coast. Their conquests included the island of Hormuz in the channel linking the Persian Gulf with the Gulf of Oman, and the city of Muscat, the capital of the OMANI SULTANATE, on the Gulf of Oman. The Portuguese captured Muscat in 1508 and held it until they were driven out in 1650. They captured Hormuz in 1514 and lost it in 1622 to a combined force from Britain and the shah of Persia (present-day Iran). Portugal's interests in this region were commercial rather than territorial, and it made no attempt to establish permanent colonies.

The resurgence of Oman ultimately led to Portugal's loss of the Swahili Coast. In 1652 Omani forces occupied the islands of Zanzibar and Pate, near Kenya. Pate became the center of resistance to Portugal. In 1696 Sayf ibn Sultan (r. c. 1690s), the ruler of Oman, as an ally of Pate, sailed to Mombasa with a large fleet. Fort Jesus finally fell to his forces in 1698, following a two-year siege. Zanzibar fell shortly thereafter. Portuguese control over Mombasa was briefly restored in 1728–29 in order to oust the Omanis, but Portugal was soon driven out again, and Kilwa, Zanzibar, Lamu, and Pate remained independent of both Portugal and Oman.

The Omani MASRUI dynasty came into power in the 1740s and reestablished Omani rule in Pate, Mombasa, and Zanzibar. This dynasty was to maintain firm control over much of the Swahili Coast during the 1800s.

See also: BISA TRADING NETWORKS (Vol. III); CHANGAMIRE (Vol. III); HIMA (Vol. II); INDIAN OCEAN TRADE (Vol. II); KARAMOJONG (Vol. II); KINGDOMS AND EMPIRES OF EASTERN AFRICA AND THE INTERIOR (Vol. II); PORTUGAL AND AFRICA (Vol. III); RWABUGIRI, KILGERI (Vol. IV).

Further reading: David M. Anderson, *Maasai: People of Cattle* (San Francisco: Chronicle Books, 1995); Jean-Pierre Chrétien, *The Great Lakes of Africa: Two Thousand Years of History,* Scott Straus, trans., (Cambridge, Mass.: MIT Press, 2003); John Middleton, *African Merchants of the Indian Ocean: Swahili of the East African Coast* (Long Grove, Ill.: Waveland Press, 2004).

kingdoms and empires of the Horn of Africa

The present-day countries located on the Horn of Africa are ETHIOPIA, ERITREA, Republic of DJIBOUTI, and SOMALIA. Ethiopia is the oldest kingdom in the region, tracing its roots to ancient Aksum, which flourished in the fourth through sixth centuries. The history of Ethiopia and neighboring Eritrea have long been intertwined because the present-day state of Ethiopia is landlocked, and the principal ports of ancient Aksum were in Eritrea, which borders the Red Sea. Despite this, until the 16th century Eritrea retained much of its independence, even from Ethiopia. After about 1557, however, Eritrea increasingly came under the domination of the Ottoman Empire.

During the fourth century the kings of Aksum became Christian. However, because of the its proximity to the Arabian Peninsula, the Horn of Africa was among the earliest regions of Africa to be visited by Islamic MISSIONARIES. The AFAR people of Djibouti, which adjoins Somalia, received Islam in 825. Further to the east, Muslim trading posts had been founded as early as the seventh century along Somalia's Indian Ocean coast and the Gulf of Aden. By 900 the nomadic Somali peoples had been converted. By the end of the 10th century Islam was firmly established in the trading cities of MOGADISHU, Marka, BRAVA, ZEILA, and BERBERA. The Muslim state of Ifat flourished in the eastern Shoa Plateau of central Ethiopia from 1285 to 1415. Ifat dominated the various small Muslim sultanates in the region, including Fatajar, Dawaro, Bali, and ADAL, incorporating them into an emerging and powerful Ifat state.

To contain Ifat, Ethiopian emperor Amda Siyon (r. 1314–1344), who is sometimes considered the founder of the Ethiopian state, marched southward in 1328. He established garrisons, distributed fiefs to his followers, and made Ifat into a tributary state, placing heavy taxes on the shipments of GOLD, ivory, and slaves that were sent from Ifat to Arabia through its port at Zeila on the Gulf of Aden. The rulers and people of Ifat remained in an almost continuous state of revolt against Ethiopian authority, but Amda Siyon and his successors brutally quelled those revolts and extended Ethiopia's dominance as far as Zeila on the Gulf of Aden. Ifat's independence ended in 1415 when emperor Yeshak I (r. 1414–1429) made Ifat a province of Ethiopia. Finally, in 1445, fearing Muslim encirclement, the emperor Zara Yakob (r. 1434–1468) utterly destroyed Ifat, overrunning the land as far south as present-day SIDAMO.

Ifat's place was taken by an emerging sultanate of Adal, once a tributary state of Ifat, in the Shoa region near HARER. About 1520 a Muslim religious reformer named Ahmad ibn Ibrahim al-Ghazi (c. 1506–1543) came to power in Adal. Known also as AHMAD GRAÑ (Ahmad the Left-Handed), he established his brother as puppet king and declared a jihad against Christian Ethiopia. Ahmad Grañ created a military force from the swelling population of nomadic Somali and Afar Muslims who responded to both his teachings and the hope of plunder. He received firearms from the Muslim Ottoman Empire and the assistance of a small force of Ottoman troops. He trained his own troops in Ottoman tactics. To provoke Ethiopia, he stopped paying tribute and held back the taxes that Ethiopia imposed on Adal's trading profits.

In 1526–27 Ahmad Grañ's forces attacked and defeated an Ethiopian army led by emperor LEBNA DENGEL (r. c. 1508–1540) at the Battle of Shimbra Kure. In 1528 his highly mobile Afar and Somali cavalry forces overran the SHOA region, and in 1531 he began his invasion of Ethiopia. By 1535 Adal troops had successfully overrun the central highlands and began to penetrate the staunchly Christian northern highlands, along the way burning monasteries and churches and forcibly converting a substantial portion of the population to Islam.

The newly crowned Ethiopian emperor, Galawdewos (r. 1540–1559), sought help from the Portuguese. For their part, the Portuguese were willing to offer military assistance because Muslim successes in Ethiopia were jeopardizing Portuguese trade in the Red Sea. The Portuguese sent 400 riflemen to Ethiopia and trained Galawdewos's army in European tactics and weaponry. They used hit-and-run tactics and the difficult mountainous terrain of the highlands to their advantage. In 1543 Ethiopian forces defeated Ahmad Grañ's army at Weyna Dega near Lake Tana; Ahmad Grañ lost his life in that battle, and the Adal threat to Ethiopia came to an end.

The cost to Ethiopia of the war with Adal was great. Its land was laid to waste. A substantial portion of its population had to be reconverted from Islam. Hundreds of thousands had been killed, and the treasury was exhausted. Ethiopia in the 1550s retreated into the feudalism that had characterized the Solomonid era at its inception centuries earlier. Discontent filled the border provinces, and the Christian population there felt exploited by the central government. The garrisons that earlier emperors Amda Siyon and Zara Yakob had established at the edges of Ethiopia were destroyed in the war with Adal and were thus no longer able to keep out the OROMO, a Cushitic-speaking pastoralist people from the south. The Oromo began moving into the Shoa region, establishing farming communities as far north as the Blue Nile valley. Waves of Oromo migrations in the 1500s brought the newcomers into southern Ethiopia, the central and western provinces, and into Tigray near the Eritrean border. In response to these Oromo invasions, Christian Ethiopia under Emperor Sarsa Dengel (r. 1563–1597) retreated into its mountain strongholds, in what was called Abyssinia. This territory, with its new capital at GONDAR, included Eritrea, the northern regions of Tigray and Gondar, and parts of GOJJAM, Shoa, and Welo.

The early 1600s were marked by religious struggles, as Roman Catholic missionaries tried to bring the Ethiopian Orthodox Church into community with Rome. Emperor Susenyos (r. 1607–1632) became a convert, as did many of the aristocracy, but the masses were repulsed by the emperor's rejection of tradition. He was forced to abdicate, and his son FASILIDAS (r. 1632–1667) assumed the throne. The later 1600s saw the rise of an assimilated Oromo aristocracy that slowly eroded the influence of the traditional monarchy. By early the next century and the brief reign of Emperor TEKLA HAYMONOT (r. 1706–08), the central government was little more than a façade. The ZEMENE MESAFINT, or "Age of the Princes," had begun.

Historians describe the next 150 years, until 1850, as a time of feudal anarchy. Alliances constantly shifted. The armies of local warlords fought each other, conscripted farmers into military service, and plundered the land. The self-sufficient rural ECONOMY of the north broke down, lawlessness prevailed, and the common people lived without hope.

See also: ABYSINNIA (Vol. I); AKSUM (Vols. I, II); CHRISTIANITY, INFLUENCE OF (Vols. II, III, IV, V); COPTIC CHRISTIANITY (Vol. II); ISLAM, INFLUENCE OF (Vols. II, III, IV, V); WARFARE AND WEAPONS (Vol. III); ZARA YAKOB (Vol. II).

Further reading: P. T. W. Baxter, Jan Hultin, and Alessandro Triulzi, eds., *Being and Becoming Oromo: Historical and Anthropological Enquiries* (Lawrenceville, N.J.: Red Sea Press, 1996); Tom Killion, *Historical Dictionary of Eritrea* (Lanham, Md.: Scarecrow Press, 1998); Virginia Luling, *Somali Sultanate: The Geledi City-state over 150 years* (Piscataway, N.J.: Transaction Publishers, 2002); Harold G. Marcus, *A History of Ethiopia* (Berkeley, Calif.: University of California Press, 2002).

kingdoms and empires of the Lower Guinea and Atlantic coast From the middle of the 15th century through the 19th century the growing European involvement in African political and economic affairs—and the explosive growth of the slave trade—dominated the history of the Lower Guinea coast. The region was untouched, however, by the Muslim-dominated FULANI JIHADS that embroiled the rest of West Africa during the 18th and 19th centuries.

The Yoruba States: Ile-Ife, Benin, and Oyo The Yoruba states, located in what is now western NIGERIA, began to develop in the 11th and 12th centuries; their strength was in AGRICULTURE. The Yoruba became well known for the excellence of the artifacts that their artists and craftsmen produced, and these became important trade goods. Ile-Ife was the original Yoruba state and the one with the strongest artistic tradition. It remained the chief religious center for the Yoruba, even though the kingdoms of BENIN and Oyo became more important politically in the region. Its religious position protected it

from its more powerful neighbors. When the *alafin* (ruler) of Oyo received the *ida oranyan* (sacred sword of state) at his coronation, he had to promise to safeguard Ife in return for receiving the spiritual authority of the sword. In the 1700s Oyo had become a major exporter of human captives. In 1793 the attempt of Alafin Awole (r. 1790s) to raid Ife to obtain captives led to internal uprisings and civil war that brought about the eventual fall of Oyo after 1817.

Benin, located in the forest region to the south and west, was founded by the Edo people in the 11th century, at about the same time as Ife. Both the *oba* (ruler) of Ife and the *oba* of Benin claim to hold their authority from Oduduwa, the legendary founder of the Yoruba. By the 1400s Benin was a large, walled city several miles across. By 1500 Benin was the head of an extensive empire. Oba Ewuare the Great (r. c. 1440–1480), who created a stable succession to the throne by making the monarchy hereditary, built up a powerful standing army and vastly expanded the boundaries of his domain so that it stretched from the Niger Delta in the east to the Lagos Lagoon in the west.

Benin was still in a period of expansion when the Portuguese landed there in the late 1400s, and, following a common practice, Benin sold to the Portuguese the captives it took during its wars with its neighbors. The Portuguese, in turn, exchanged them with AKAN groups for GOLD. Early in the 1500s Benin's wars and its participation in the slave trade ceased until the 18th century. During the 1600s and 1700s Benin grew wealthy by selling gold, pepper, ivory, acacia gum, and COTTON cloth to Portuguese and Dutch traders, becoming their principal link to the peoples of the interior.

During the 18th and early 19th centuries Benin fell into decline. Dynastic disputes led to a period of civil war, during which each side sold its captives into SLAVERY in exchange for firearms. A growing aristocracy became a drain on the kingdom's resources. The kingdom retreated into empty rituals of kingship to support the claims of the weaker *obas*. Ultimately Benin was taken over by the British in 1897.

At the height of its power, between 1650 and 1750, the Yoruba state of Oyo in present-day southwestern Nigeria, dominated most of the kingdoms between the Volta River in the west and the NIGER RIVER in the east. Oyo had a beneficial position on the trade routes between the other Yoruba kingdoms and the HAUSA STATES. The land was fertile, and because it was beyond the range of the tsetse fly, the country was suited for horses—a fact the rulers of Oyo took advantage of. The formidable Oyo cavalry helped extend the OYO EMPIRE to the southwest, where the terrain was suitable for cavalry maneuvers. In the late 1600s Oyo's reach extended as far as the coastal kingdom of ALLADA, which it forced to pay tribute. Through Allada Oyo had contact with European traders.

Oyo's sub-Saharan trade and wars of expansion produced more captives than were needed to work on the *alafin's* royal farms. Accordingly, many captives were sold to European traders in exchange for firearms, metal goods, cloth, and other trade items. These items were often shipped to North Africa for more horses and more slaves. Thus in the 1780s Oyo became a major conduit for human captives from north to south. This trade enriched the kingdom greatly until the market withered in the 1790s, largely as a result of the Napoleonic Wars in Europe. To maintain revenue levels and to support a growing though nonproductive aristocracy, the *alafin* overtaxed the people, a decision that led to social unrest and rebellion.

The Oyo cavalry, largely composed of Muslim conscripts from north of Oyo and the main source of the *alafin's* power, was headquartered at ILORIN, an Oyo vassal state. In 1817 an attempted revolt by the head of the cavalry failed when the cavalry itself rebelled and switched its loyalty to the new Muslim SOKOTO CALIPHATE during the FULANI JIHADS. The government of Oyo collapsed, and by 1830 the rest of YORUBALAND was caught up in civil war.

Dahomey One of the major states involved in the slave trade in the 18th century, DAHOMEY was situated in what is now the Republic of BENIN. In 1650 its first king, WEGBAJA (c. 1645–1680), transformed it from a decentralized group of villages inhabited by the FON people into a centralized state dominated by the AJA people, who migrated there from the kingdom of Allada along the coast. Under Wegbaja and his successors Dahomey developed an absolute monarchy without parallel in Africa. The king was at the pinnacle of society and governed through a strong, centralized bureaucracy. Human sacrifice in honor of the royal ancestors became an annual practice.

Allada was a major embarkation point for captives in the transatlantic SLAVE TRADE. The main tasks of Dahomey's army were to expand the territorial boundaries of the kingdom and to procure captives, who were sold for firearms or kept to work on the royal plantations. In the 1720s Dahomey captured both Allada and the neighboring kingdom of WHYDAH along the coast, where European forts had already been established. Dahomey thus gained even better access to European traders.

Dahomey's major rival in the trade of captives was Oyo, which invaded Dahomey four times in the 1720s. In 1730 Dahomey became a vassal state of Oyo when AGAJA (1716–1740), the reigning king of Dahomey, realized that he could not withstand the attacks of the powerful Oyo cavalry and agreed to pay tribute to Oyo.

Throughout the 1730s to nearly 1800 Dahomey continued to add provinces and prospered on the proceeds of the sale of captives. The royal plantations produced enough crops to feed the army and the royal court. Dahomey reached the height of its power under king GEZU (1818–1858). He freed Dahomey from subservience

to Oyo, and to make up for the loss of revenue that occurred when Britain curtailed the slave trade in the 1840s, he helped Dahomey make a smooth transition to a post-slavery ECONOMY. The royal plantations, as producers of PALM OIL, became a major source of the kingdom's revenue in the 19th century.

Ashanti and the Akan States The AKAN were farming peoples who lived in the area of West Africa between the Volta and the Komoé rivers, in the forests and the coastal lands of what is now TOGO, GHANA, and IVORY COAST. Muslim DYULA traders penetrated as far south as the region of the upper Volta River during the 1400s in search of new merchandise. They bought gold and kola nuts from the Akan people and paid them, in part, in human captives. The presence of such captives and hostages made it possible for the Akan to clear the forest for planting and to mine gold on more than a small-scale, seasonal basis. Early settlements combined AGRICULTURE and MINING, and these became the foundations for a more organized Akan society.

The kingdom of BONO, established in c. 1450, was the earliest of the northern Akan states. Of the southern Akan states the most important were DENKYIRA, AKWAMU, FANTE, and Ashanti. In the late 1400s the Akan found in the Portuguese a new market for their gold, and the Portuguese erected trading posts on the Akan coast at which they traded captives and hostages from Benin and European cloth and metal goods for Akan gold. They also introduced MAIZE and other crops from the New World.

The ASHANTI EMPIRE was founded in the 1670s. Its first king was OSEI TUTU (d. c. 1712), who believed that the only way for the smaller Akan states to free themselves from the domination of Denkyira to the south was to unite into a single kingdom. Ashanti began as a loose confederation, but gradually Osei Tutu assumed leadership and won the religious leaders to his side. It was during his reign that the GOLDEN STOOL became the all-important symbol of Ashanti royalty.

By the beginning of the 18th century Ashanti under Osei Tutu became an empire that had conquered Denkyira and most of the other Akan states and controlled most of the Akan goldfields. Its area had tripled, but even more important it had contact with the coast, where it sold captives to the Portuguese and the Dutch in exchange for firearms and other goods.

Osei Tutu's successor, OPOKUWARE II (r. 1720–1750), expanded the boundaries of the Ashanti Empire until it covered most of present-day Ghana. A period of chaos preceded Opokuware's reign, but during his tenure the Ashanti Empire reached its fullest territorial extent, reaching far into the interior. Later kings, especially OSEI KWADWO (r. c. 1764–1777), Osei Kwame (1777–1801), and Osei Bonsu (c. 1801–1824), developed a strong, stable, centralized government. Friction with Britain over the

Fante region led to armed conflict, known as the ANGLO-ASHANTI WARS, beginning in the 1820s. The Ashanti defeated the British in 1824 and made peace with Britain in 1831, a peace that continued for the next 30 years until the Ashanti once again rose to challenge the British.

Atlantic Coast Kingdoms During this same period the KONGO KINGDOM, which had been formed from the scattered villages south of the Congo River, became a power in the region. Drawing on agricultural resources as well as access to both trade goods and routes, the Kongo kingdom became the nexus of a trading effort stretching across much of the central part of Africa. The kingdom's power initially increased with the arrival of the Portuguese in the late 15th century. Welcoming the newcomers and hoping to gain both knowledge and superior tools and weapons, many of the Kongo people became actively involved in trade with the Portuguese. By the end of the 15th century the Kongo kingdom had become the main supplier of slave and forced labor for the Portuguese sugar plantations on SÃO TOMÉ AND PRÍNCIPE.

At the same time, the kingdom's rulers, beginning with AFONSO I (r. 1506–1543), attempted to spread Christianity—at times by force. It was not long, however, before it became clear that being a supplier of captives and forced laborers would only weaken the kingdom. By the mid 16th century, the Kongo kingdom fell to the IMBANGALA, who overran the country from the east. Although the Kongo king Alvaro I (r. 1567–1576) eventually regained power with the help of the Portuguese, the kingdom never regained its prominence. The central authority gradually collapsed, and by the end of the 17th century it had disintegrated into independent regions.

One of the kingdoms that arose out of the collapse of the Kongo kingdom was LOANGO. Located on the coast, north of the Congo River, this one-time province of the Kongo kingdom gained its independence early in the 16th century. Its inhabitants, the Vili, established an economy based on hunting and fishing as well as on agriculture and crafts. In time, however, the thriving trade in everything from cloth and metalwork to ivory and copper had given way to the commerce in human captives, which proved to be of much more interest to European traders. Beginning in the early 17th century this trade increased steadily, peaking during the latter part of the 18th century, when at least 10,000 people were shipped from the Loango coast each year.

See also: EDO (Vols. I, II); KINGDOMS AND EMPIRES (Vol. II); KINGDOMS AND EMPIRES OF THE LOWER GUINEA COAST (Vol. II); KINGDOMS AND EMPIRES OF SENEGAMBIA (Vol. II); KINGDOMS AND EMPIRES OF THE WEST AFRICAN SAVANNAH (Vol. II); OYO KINGDOM (Vol. II); SALT TRADE (Vol. II); WARFARE AND WEAPONS (Vol. III).

Further reading: Dominique Malaquais, *The Kingdom of Benin* (New York: F. Watts, 1998); Patrick Manning, *Slavery, Colonialism, and Economic Growth in Da-*

homey, 1640–1960 (New York: Cambridge University Press, 1982).

kingdoms and empires of the Maghrib See ALGERIA (Vol. III); BARBARY COAST (Vol. III); CORSAIRS (Vol. III); KINGDOMS AND EMPIRES OF THE MAGHRIB (Vol. II); LIBYA (Vol. III); MOROCCO (Vol. III); OTTOMAN EMPIRE AND AFRICA (Vol. III); TUNISIA (Vol. III).

kingdoms and empires of West Africa Changes in the patterns of trade, especially as a result of the presence of Europeans, the growth of the slave trade, the continued spread of Islam, and the militancy of Muslim states, deeply affected precolonial West Africa.

The West African savanna prior to 1450 was the location of the largest and most prosperous kingdoms of sub-Saharan Africa up to that time. The ancient Ghana Empire, located in present-day Republic of MALI, emerged as a state around 300 CE and grew wealthy in the trade of GOLD and salt. Ruled by the Mande-speaking SONINKE people, it dominated two of the most important trans-Saharan trade routes: the route north to present-day MOROCCO and the North African coast and the route to the Nile Valley by way of KANEM-BORNU. At its peak the Ghana Empire had a population of several million, an army of 200,000, and a territory that encompassed 250,000 square miles (647,500 sq km). It was also the first Muslim state in West Africa, having accepted Islam during the 11th century.

The Mali Empire Conditions in the Ghana Empire became unsettled after it was attacked by Berber Almoravids from Morocco in the late 11th century, and the empire disintegrated. The Mali Empire arose in the wake of the decline of the Ghana Empire, as the legendary Sundiata (r. 1235–1255) united Malinke speaking peoples into a new state. After defeating Sumanguru (d. c. 1235), the leader of the Susu, Sundiata quickly established a major empire. Mali regained control of the trans-Saharan trade routes, controlled the MINING of West African gold, and developed itself into a major agricultural state. At the Mali Empire's height, its population the territory it controlled was double that of ancient Ghana. Its land extended north into present-day MAURITANIA and south into the HAUSA STATES. In the 1300s Mali also became an important center of Muslim culture, as the major trading cities of Gao, TIMBUKTU, and JENNE became the sites of important Muslim mosques and schools. SANKORE UNIVERSITY in Timbuktu still thrives today.

The Rise of Songhai The Mali Empire began to decline around 1400, and the SONGHAI Empire emerged from Mali's vassal state of Gao. In 1468 Sunni ALI (r. 1464–1492), the founder of the great trading empire of Songhai, captured Timbuktu and began to dominate the lands bordering the NIGER RIVER, controlling them with his war fleet. After his death in 1492, the throne was seized by Askia MUHAMMAD TOURÉ (r. 1493–1528), who was a more devout Muslim than Sunni Ali. He restored Islam and built Songhai into the largest empire in the history of West Africa. The commercially significant salt mines at Taghaza in the Sahara were brought under control of the empire. On his return from his hajj, or pilgrimage, to Mecca in 1496, Askia Muhammad was named caliph of West Africa by the last Abassid caliph of EGYPT, al-Mutawakil II (1479–1497). The title gave Askia Muhammad a new Islamic legitimacy.

Songhai went into decline, however, when the aging Askia Muhammad went blind and was deposed by his son. Songhai's trans-Saharan trade then began to decline, in part because of competition from Portuguese gold traders whose dealings along the Atlantic coast undercut the trans-Saharan gold trade and because of increased commercial competition from the Hausa States, Kanem-Bornu, and the Tuareg sultanate of Aïr. A series of succession disputes, droughts, outbreaks of disease, and rebellions and civil war in the 1580s diminished the empire's strength. Because it still felt safe from its powerful Ottoman and Moroccan neighbors across the broad Sahara, Songhai had made no attempt to modernize its army by adopting the firearms, primitive and unreliable as they were, that were beginning to become available from Europe. Consequently Songhai's formidable cavalry was surprised and decisively defeated by the guns of Morocco's elite musketeers at the Battle of TONDIBI in 1591. Driving Morocco's venture was its plan to revive and control the trans-Saharan trade in gold.

Morocco, however, was unable to hold onto the territory it conquered. Resistance in the countryside forced Morocco to keep a large and costly army in the field, and insufficient gold was being acquired in trade to pay for its upkeep. After 1603 Songhai broke into several small states under the rule of local Moroccan governors who were independent of central Moroccan control. By 1660 all aspects of central rule had disappeared. In 1737 the TUAREGS of Aïr seized Timbuktu and imposed their control over the region of the Niger bend.

The Bambara Kingdoms SEGU became one of the more important states to rise in the land of the former Songhai. Segu was one of the two BAMBARA kingdoms in the region; the other was KAARTA in present-day Republic of Mali. In the 1680s a Bambara empire extended as far as Timbuktu, but it disintegrated after the death of its founder, Kaladian Kulibali (r. 1652–1682). Segu finally came into its own during the reign of Mamari KULIBALI (r. 1712–1755), who extended the empire as far as Jenne and Timbuktu and established a professional army and navy that gave it the might to dominate its local rivals. After a period of instability following Kulibali's death, Ngolo DIARRA (r. 1766–1797) seized the throne, eventu-

ally ruling for almost 30 years. Under Diarra and his sons, the empire continued to expand southward toward the Black Volta River. In 1818, however, Segu fell to the kingdom of MACINA during the FULANI jihad led by Muslim reformer Shehu Ahmadu Lobbo (1775–1844).

Kanem-Bornu Kanem-Bornu was made up of two kingdoms whose history is so conjoined that they are often treated as a single entity. Kanem was converted to Islam as early as the 11th century and had grown to become the major power in the region northeast of Lake CHAD. Kanem reached the height of its power during the first half of the 13th century when the powerful, far-ranging cavalry of Mai (King) Dunama Dibbalemi (r. 1210–1248) extended Kanem's control over trans-Saharan trade as far north as the FEZZAN, in present-day LIBYA. Kanem's attempts to maintain such an expansive realm overextended its resources, and Kanem began to fall into decline during the 14th century. Bornu, its tributary state southwest of Lake Chad, became the site of a revived Kanem when around 1400 the SEFUWA dynasty of Kanem moved its capital from Njimi, in Kanem, to NGAZARGAMU, in the fertile grasslands of Bornu. Kanem then became the tributary state of Bornu. The move to Bornu improved the Sefuwa dynasty's access to trade routes heading to the West African coast. During the 15th century Bornu established commercial links with the Hausa States and traded salt and horses for AKAN gold.

During the first half of the 16th century Bornu underwent a number of peasant revolts that were brutally quelled by jihads led by its rulers. In the second half of the century, Mai IDRIS ALAWMA (r. c. 1750–1603) armed his soldiers with muskets purchased from North Africa. He established ties with the Ottoman governor of TRIPOLI and had Ottoman soldiers brought in to train Bornu's troops. KANO and other Hausa states paid tribute to Bornu, and trade began to shift away from Songhai.

Little is known about Bornu in the 17th and 18th centuries. It became a center of Islamic culture and learning, and the trade in captives provided a substantial part of its income. The Hausa States continued to pay tribute until the end of the 1700s. The Tuareg sultanate of Aïr, however, was successfully vying with Bornu for control of trade in the region, and the Fulani were challenging them for dominance of the Hausa States. Bornu began to decline in 1808 when the reigning Sefuwa *mai* was forced to flee from Ngazargamu. Although the Sefuwa dynasty was able to return to power for a time and defend its interests, the dynasty died out in 1846.

The Hausa States Situated in present-day northern NIGERIA, between Songhai and Kanem-Bornu, the Hausa States first began to develop between 1000 and 1200 as fortified towns. These towns grew into walled cities, which later became the capitals of individual city-states. GOBIR, the northernmost state, originally developed near the Tuareg sultanate of Aïr. In the 15th century pressure from the Tuaregs forced Gobir to relocate southward at the edge of the Mali Empire. This advantageous choice of location helped Gobir develop into an important trading center, rivaling KATSINA, which was founded much earlier, before 1300. Kano became a manufacturing center and later a center of the cloth and dyeing trades. The important Hausa states of ZAMFARA, KEBBI, and Zazzau (later renamed ZARIA, after its capital) also developed in and before the 1500s. The Hausa States were a loose confederation, sometimes warring, sometimes cooperating, but never developing a central authority. They never united into an empire or set forth on wars of conquest. Each had a specialty. Zazzau became the purveyor of captives and hostages, both for internal use in the agricultural state of Kebbi, where they labored in the fields, and for export to Kanem-Bornu, to which the Hausa States paid tribute. The Hausa States also exported captives to North Africa, where they were exchanged for horses and guns.

During the 1300s Muslim MISSIONARIES from Mali introduced Islam into the Hausa States, and following the familiar pattern of conversion in West Africa, the upper classes became Muslim, perhaps to benefit their trading relationships. The common people maintained their indigenous beliefs into the 18th century. In the 17th century the rulers of the Hausa States needed money to continue the local wars that were devastating the countryside. Because the common people were overtaxed, the rulers resorted to increasing the supply of slaves, which they did by enslaving Muslim peasants—a clear violation of a core principle of *sharia,* or Muslim law—and selling them in North African markets. These acts, considered corrupt and abusive by pious Muslims, alienated the Hausa rulers from the peasants, many of whom were newly converted to Islam. The disaffection of the peasants had long-term consequences: During the jihads conducted by fundamentalist religious reformers among the neighboring Fulani in the early 19th century, many Hausa peasants joined the Fulani against their rulers.

The West Africa Jihads The Fulani were a pastoralist people who by the 1600s had spread across much of the West African savanna. They were a stateless people, on the move, rarely settling down, strangers among the people with whom they dwelled. They were often resented as intruders by the settled agriculturalist peoples, and their grazing and trading rights were often restricted. Many were converted to Islam either by passing Muslim traders or by contact with Muslim TUAREGS from the AÏR MASSIF. Islam gave the Fulani a sense of cultural identity, and Muslim law gave them a standard against which to measure the behavior of the local rulers who demanded onerous taxes and tribute from them. The Fulani converts were strong in their faith, and some became important Islamic scholars. The Fulani became the driving force behind a Muslim reform movement that affected many of the major kingdoms of the region. One of their motives was to fight for Fulani rights; another motive was righteous indignation at the activities of infidels whom, as fervent Muslims, the Fulani were obligated to convert by preaching or by the sword.

The Fulani jihads, as this reform movement is often called, began in BONDU, near the Islamized Senegal valley. In the second half of the 17th century Fulani clerics wrested control from the local Mande rulers to establish a Muslim state. The movement spread to the highlands of FOUTA DJALLON in what is now GUINEA, where the Fulani had been pasturing their cattle since the 1500s. In 1725, in alliance with local Muslim Mande traders, Fulani and Mandinka Muslims condemned the paganism of their non-Muslim Fulani and Mandinka rulers and rose up in rebellion. By 1750 their conquest was complete. Fouta Djallon was organized as a Muslim theocracy, and trade links were established with the Upper Guinea coast. The 25 years of struggle produced thousands of captives who were sold on the coast to European traders.

Islamic law forbade Muslims from enslaving fellow Muslims who were prisoners of war, but no similar restrictions were placed on non-Muslim prisoners, who were considered pagans or infidels. Later, during the rise of the SOKOTO CALIPHATE, leaders sometimes stretched the law and treated nonobservant Muslims as if they were little more than infidels and thus subject to enslavement.

The movement spread northward to FOUTA TORO, below the Senegal River, where the kingdom of Tekrur once stood. The region has a long history of involvement with both Islam and SLAVERY. Tekrur was one of the earliest African kingdoms to convert to Islam. The Zanaga BERBERS converted the TUKULOR people of Tekrur in the middle of the 11th century and founded, on the banks of the Senegal River, a monastery to which the ascetic Almoravid sect traces its roots. Later the Almoravids spread northward to dominate Morocco and bring Islam as far as Spain and southern France. Dominated in subsequent years by Mali, however, Tekrur's fortunes fell, and the Wolof and the Serer states, initially resistant to Islam, emerged in their place. Until the end of the 1500s the SENEGAMBIA region in which these states flourished was the largest provider of captives for the transatlantic SLAVE TRADE. The competition to supply captives led to continuous fighting among the kingdoms of the former WOLOF EMPIRE, as well as GABU to the southeast and Fouta Toro to the northeast. During the late 1670s Muslim clerics tried to topple the governments of the states in Senegambia that supported the slave trade, but firearms sold by the French helped rulers quell the revolts. However, many peasants were influenced to accept Islam and became fervent Muslims as a result of this unrest. RELIGION became a source of solace, protection, and power. Between 1769 and 1776 the Tukulor people rebelled against their lax, though nominally Muslim, rulers and turned Fouta Toro into a theocracy on the model of Fouta Djallon.

In the early 1800s a Muslim-dominated Tukulor empire, with roots in Fouta Toro, was to arise under the leadership of the Tukulor cleric Al-hajj Umar Tal (c. 1795–1864), a member of the austere Tijaniyya Sufi brotherhood. Controlling a territory that extended from the Atlantic Ocean to Timbuktu in what is now Mali, the Tukulor Empire was almost as large as the vast SOKOTO CALIPHATE, the theocratic successor to the Songhai Empire.

Early in the 19th century the jihads of Fouta Djallon and Fouta Toro inspired similar jihads in the Hausa States in the northern parts of present-day Nigeria. The leader of the most successful of these jihads was USMAN DAN FODIO (1754–1817), a Fulani cleric from the Hausa state of Gobir whose dual aim was to convert those Hausa who had not yet accepted Islam and to bring back to religious discipline the lax Muslim rulers of the state. His movement had the support of the Fulani pastoralists, Muslim and non-Muslim alike, who were highly taxed by these rulers. Rumors circulated that Usman dan Fodio was the long-awaited Mahdi, or redeemer, the precursor of the prophet Muhammad's return. The jihad began in 1804 after an unsuccessful assassination attempt on Fodio by the king of Gobir.

The Hausa jihad was a series of simultaneous uprisings. By 1804 Zamfara, Kebbi, Katsina, ZARIA, Kano, and Gobir had fallen to the jihadists. Without the support of the peasants and because of their traditional inability to cooperate, the Hausa States fell. By 1817 the capital had been moved to the city of Sokoto, in Kebbi, and the empire began to expand into neighboring lands. The Sokoto Caliphate, as the empire became known, emerged as the largest single West African state of the early 19th century, with a population of 10 million and a large and well-equipped army. It unified its rival constituent states, which continued to exist as emirates that owed fealty to the caliph. Bondage of various kinds remained an important feature of Sokoto, as vast numbers of field workers were needed to feed the people in the prosperous towns. Pockets of non-Muslim resistance provided an ongoing supply of captives to enslave in the service of the growing ECONOMY.

See also: ALI, SUNNI (Vol. II); ALMORAVIDS (Vol. II); ISLAM, INFLUENCE OF (Vols. II, III, IV); KANGABA (Vol. II); KINGDOMS AND EMPIRES (Vol. II); KINGDOMS AND EMPIRES OF THE LOWER GUINEA COAST (Vol. II); KINGDOMS AND EMPIRES OF THE SENEGAMBIA (Vol. II); KINGDOMS AND EMPIRES OF THE WEST AFRICAN SAVANNA (Vol. II); MAHDI (Vol. II); SALT TRADE (Vol. II); SERER (Vol. II); SUFISM (Vol. III); WEAPONS AND WARFARE (Vol. III).

Further reading: Harold Courlander and Ousmane Sako, compilers, *The Heart of the Ngoni: Heroes of the African Kingdom of Segu* (New York: Crown, 1982); Sundiata A. Djata, *The Bamana Empire by the Niger: Kingdom, Jihad, and Colonization, 1712–1920* (Princeton, N.J.: Markus Wiener, 1997); Paul Staudinger, *In the Heart of the Hausa States,* Johanna Moody, trans. (Athens, Ohio: Ohio University Center for International Studies, 1990).

Kinshasa Capital of present-day Democratic Republic of the CONGO. Although it is not known exactly when the area was first settled, by the 14th century Kinshasa was a major slave-trade center of the KONGO KINGDOM. Located along the Congo River, the city emerged from two villages, Nshasa and Ntamo, that were inhabited by people of the Humbu ethnic group. Europeans established a major trading post in Kinshasa in 1881. The city, which was renamed Leopoldville, later became the capital of the Belgian Congo.

See also: BELGIAN CONGO (Vol. IV); KINSHASA (Vols. II, V); LEOPOLDVILLE (Vol. IV).

Kisama Town located 30 miles (48 km) inland from the Atlantic coast near the Kwanza River in present-day ANGOLA. Kisama's ECONOMY was long based on the production and trade of salt. By the mid-16th century the Kisama salt mines were controlled by the MBUNDU rulers of the nearby LUNDA EMPIRE. Salt was exported in 24-inch (60-cm) blocks to be used as both a foodstuff and as a form of currency to purchase other trading commodities, including slaves.

The Portuguese tried to take over the salt mines at Kisama from the late 16th century onwards, but they were largely unsuccessful. By the 18th century, because the land was inhospitable, the Kisama region had become a haven for people who had escaped bondage in coastal LUANDA, a Portuguese colonial town. The salt trade continued to attract new traders, with the Portuguese ultimately controlling the salt trade only in the 20th century.

See also: PORTUGAL AND AFRICA (Vol. III); SALT MINING (Vol. II); SALT TRADE (Vol. II).

Kissi (Kisi) West African people located in the forest region that links present-day LIBERIA, SIERRA LEONE, and

GUINEA. The Kissi, who speak a Niger-Congo language known as Mel, were settled in this forest region by at least the 16th century. They were an agricultural people who grew rice in the savanna marshes and practiced a cult-like religion based on both AGRICULTURE and the honoring of ancestor spirits. The Kissi nearly faced extinction as an ethnic group, however, when they were the subjects of numerous slave raids in the late 18th century.

See also: ANCESTOR WORSHIP (Vol. I); SLAVE TRADE, THE TRANSATLANTIC (Vol. III).

Kiswahili National language of present-day TANZANIA, KENYA, and UGANDA. As Arab-Swahili trade expanded beginning in the 19th century, Kiswahili spread through eastern Africa. According to some estimates, Kiswahili is now spoken by between 50 million and 100 million people. This would make it, after Arabic, the most widely understood language in Africa. Used mainly in eastern and Central Africa, Kiswahili also is spoken, though somewhat less frequently, in present-day Democratic Republic of the CONGO and southern Republic of the SUDAN, as well as in the COMOROS, the northern part of MADAGASCAR, and some Persian Gulf states.

Kiswahili is considered a Bantu language of the Sabaki subgroup of the Northeastern Coast Bantu languages. These languages are spoken as a first language in sub-Saharan Africa by nearly a third of Africa's population, and many second language speakers of Kiswahili are native speakers of another Bantu language. The main characteristic of Bantu languages is their class system of nouns in which linguistic changes come in the form of prefixes attached to nouns, with nouns divided into classes referred to as grammatical genders. While most European languages divide the genders into masculine, feminine, and neuter classifications, Kiswahili uses a system of semantic classification, with classes for humans, animals, plants, artifacts, countries, abstract places, and so on. Verbs are equally complex, using a system of affixes to mark grammatical relations.

A thousand years of contact with peoples around the Indian Ocean resulted in the incorporation into Kiswahili of a large number of borrowed words from Persian and various Indian languages. Beyond this, thousands of Arabic words also were absorbed into the Bantu system of noun classes and verb categories, leading to a completely new linguistic structure. Moreover, during the 16th and 17th centuries many Portuguese words were added to the vocabulary, and since then Kiswahili has borrowed extensively from English. Despite the large number of foreign words in usage, Kiswahili remains a distinctly African language due in large part to its typical Bantu structure.

There are a large number of dialects among Kiswahili speakers, differing from each other primarily in phonological and lexical features. Unlike other Bantu languages, Kiswahili is not characterized as a tone language. Stress is usually on the penultimate syllables of words. The language also contains somewhat unique sounds, called implosives, that are made by drawing air *into* the lungs rather than by expelling it. Since the mid-19th century, a Roman-based alphabet has been used for writing Kiswahili. Prior to this an Arabic-based orthography was in use, and some older-generation speakers of Kiswahili continue to write in this style.

Kiswahili is one of the few African languages with a precolonial written tradition, and its literature is rich in songs, poetry, proverbs, and stories. The oldest surviving Kiswahili documents, written in Arabic script and reflecting the influence of Islamic culture, date from the early 1700s. Most of these early documents are transcriptions of Kiswahili epic poetry intended for chanting or singing. During this time, prose was generally restricted to practical purposes, such as the discussion of theological and historic subjects.

See also: KISWAHILI (Vols. II, IV); SWAHILI COAST (Vols. II, III, IV).

Komenda Trading city located in what is now the central region of present-day GHANA. Komenda was a major town in the state of Eguafo, which came into prominence in the early 17th century. Prior to this Komenda paid tribute to the larger and more powerful state of Assin. It was known, however, to have a strong social structure of its own, consisting of complex social grades that included a ruling elite known as the *caboceers*.

The town's trading community soon attracted British merchants, who set up a trading outpost in 1663. Later, the Dutch established a presence in the area, building a fort called Vredenburg. The French also became active traders in the area, dealing mostly with the famous African trader named John Kabes (d. 1734).

Kabes was one of a handful of Africans who became wealthy and influential along the GOLD COAST by becoming brokers with the European traders in their areas. From 1680 to 1716 Kabes controlled the trade out of Komenda by diversifying his business from to include salt, agricultural products, and even canoe-building. With the protection of a personal army made up mostly of captives and hostages, Kabes was able to barter successfully with the Europeans as well as the surrounding states, which enabled him to move up the chain of political command to become one of the most powerful independent coastal traders of his day. Kabes's ability to work the coastal trade was such that he was able to remain successful despite the tensions between Komenda and the Dutch, tensions that led to initial clashes in 1688 and eventually to a five-year war that began in 1694. The fort was abandoned in 1816.

See also: ENGLAND AND AFRICA (Vol. III); FRANCE AND AFRICA (Vol. III); NETHERLANDS AND AFRICA (Vol. III); SALT TRADE (Vol. II).

Kong Islamic city in the north-central region of present-day IVORY COAST. Early in the 18th century Mande-speaking DYULA immigrants from the north established Kong in a region populated by the SENUFO people. Kong became an Islamic center of learning at the same time that its rulers prospered through the salt and kola-nut trades in the southern Sudan, at the edge of the forest. Ethnic diversity and religious discord caused the kingdom to decline. By middle of the 18th century the Kong were at war with their northern neighbors, the BAMBARA, as well as with the Ashanti, in the south. In 1895 Samori Touré (c. 1830–1900) conquered Kong, making it part of his Mandinka empire.

See also: MANDE (Vols. I, II); SAMORI TOURÉ (Vol. IV).

Kongo (Bakongo) Bantu-speaking people of present-day ANGOLA, the Republic of the CONGO, and the Democratic Republic of the CONGO.

Kongo Social Structure The Kongo people, commonly called the Bakongo, were traditionally an agrarian people, and by the 16th and 17th centuries individual Kongo villages (*libata*) were organized into townships (*mbanza*). Most *mbanza* were organized as large farming communities. Each community was led by a chief, or *kitome*, a priestly figure whose function was to help the Kongo people find harmony with the natural world. The people believed the *kitome* controlled rainfall, so he was given the honorable task of blessing the planting seeds and tasting the first fruits of the harvest. When a *kitome* felt he was nearing death, he gathered the Kongo people in a public forum and demanded that his successor, a member of the priestly lineage, strangle him to death. To ensure the Kongo people would never be without a *kitome*, a successor was chosen as soon as a new *kitome* took power. The Kongo believed the soil would become infertile unless a *kitome* was constantly in office.

Kongo Spiritual Life In addition to the *kitome*, Kongo social and political structure relied heavily on matrilineal lineage groups called *kanda*. The *kanda* functioned as the spiritual link between the villagers and their ancestors. Ancestor worship was the primary religious practice among the Kongo people. They believed that otherworldly powers were the root of all earthly good and evil. Spirits were divided into three main groups, the category of the dead (*mbmba*), the water and earth spirits, and the sky spirits. The category of the dead was the most influential on their daily life. The Kongo people believed that the soul (called *moyo*) withdrew to the water when a person died. The soul remained the same, but its physical manifestation changed by taking on a new body and name.

The Kongo people performed elaborate rituals to guide the *moyo* properly into the afterlife. An unsuccessful ceremony could result in the soul haunting its living relatives. A mourning period of eight days followed the ceremony, during which time the relatives of the deceased wore only white, which they viewed as "the color of the dead." The women smeared their faces with black charcoal as an antidote to death. When buried, the body was completely covered with cloth, for the Kongo people believed it was so important for a body to be covered that wealthy villagers gave cloth to the poor.

If the burial rituals were not performed properly, the Kongo people believed that the dead would infect the body of a living person. An evil spirit (*nkwija*) would make the person sick, possibly resulting in death. To solve the problem, a Kongo priest specializing in resurrections would have the corpse dug up. He would call a public gathering and make the body appear to walk and speak. The body was then reburied properly so the evil spirits could be put to rest.

Europeans and the Kongo In 1483 Portuguese explorers arrived on the coast of the KONGO KINGDOM. Their relationship with Kongo was originally amicable, but the Portuguese quickly lost interest due to the lack of riches in the area. In spite of this, however, the rulers of the Kongo kingdom maintained cordial relations with the Portuguese, even exchanging ambassadors with the European power. During this period, Christianity spread in the area, and, under Nzinga Mbembe (later known as King AFONSO I), who came to the throne in 1506, Catholicism became the state religion.

In 1512 King Manuel of Portugal renewed his interest in the Kongo as a possible trade center. As a result, Kongo rulers, or *manikongos*, armed with Portuguese firearms, began raiding neighboring villages and abducting their inhabitants for the trade. The Portuguese exchanged gifts and new crop seeds, as well as the services of stonemasons, carpenters and priests. During this time, many Kongo people converted from their traditional religion to Christianity. The Portuguese also established schools for Kongo children, so for the first time many of the villagers became literate.

Eventually the trade in humans isolated Kongo from its neighbors and led to its downfall. By 1570 the kingdom had lost much of its power and became increasingly vulnerable to the attacks of neighboring peoples. In 1641 the Dutch began a short period of occupation in Kongo territory, but by 1648 the Portuguese were able to expel them. After gaining control of the territory, the Portuguese were able to break up what was left of the Kongo central government, after which the Kongo kingdom quickly declined. Still, the Kongo people longed for restoration of the Kongo kingdom, and this sense of loss

King of the Kongo kingdom of western Central Africa receiving ambassadors from Europe. Note the mixing of African and European décor and dress in this 18th-century print, perhaps intended to create an exotic air. The identity of the king is not known. © Corbis

underlay the remarkable career of Dona BEATRIX (1684–1706) at the turn of the century.

See also: AFTERLIFE (Vol. I); ANCESTOR WORSHIP (Vol. I); CHRISTIANITY, INFLUENCE OF (Vol. III); KONGO (Vols. II, IV); NETHERLANDS AND AFRICA (Vol. III); PORTUGAL AND AFRICA (Vol. III).

Further reading: Anne Hilton, *The Kingdom of Kongo* (New York: Oxford University Press, 1985); John Thornton, *The Kingdom of Kongo: Civil War and Transition, 1641–1718* (Madison, Wisc.: University of Wisconsin Press, 1983).

Kongo kingdom During the 14th century the scattered villages of the region south of Zaïre River began uniting, and by 1400 they had formed a loosely organized kingdom whose capital was at Mbanza Kongo. The ruler of the kingdom was known as the *manikongo*, and he ruled a land that had both extensive agricultural resources and an extensive trade network. By the beginning of the 16th century metalwork, cloth, and pottery from Kongo were being traded for salt and seashells from as far away as the Atlantic coast.

Portuguese explorers first made contact with the kingdom in the late 15th century and, in the years that followed, developed strong diplomatic and trade relations with the Kongo. In 1506 a pro-Portuguese Christian convert came to power, and, as AFONSO I (r. 1506–1543), he not only fostered the spread of Christianity but also began supplying captives for use as laborers on the Portuguese-held islands of SÃO TOMÉ AND PRÍNCIPE.

The Kongo kingdom soon developed into a major center for the trade in captives, raiding neighboring peoples to keep up with the Portuguese demand. These actions, however, eventually led to the kingdom's downfall, when Kongo's program of conquest resulted in its isolation by other peoples of the region. In the 16th century an invasion by the IMBANGALA drove Alvaro I (d. 1587), the Kongo king, from his throne. It was five years before Alvaro I was able to return to power, and only with the aid of the Portuguese. The kingdom began to decline in the 17th century, and with the development of new slave routes, even that trade lessened. The kingdom split into several rival states; by the late 19th century the Kongo kingdom had been effectively dismantled.

See also: KONGO (Vols. II, IV); KONGO KINGDOM (Vol. II); POMBEIRO (Vol. III).

Further reading: J. S. Cummins, ed., *Christianity and Missions, 1450–1800* (Brookfield, Vt.: Ashgate, 1997); John K. Thornton, *The Kingdom of Kongo: Civil War and Transition, 1641–1718* (Madison, Wisc.: University of Wisconsin Press, 1983).

Kordofan (Kurdufan) Central region of present-day Republic of the SUDAN, located between DARFUR and the White Nile River. The early history of the Kordofan is largely unknown. It is believed that the Christian TUNJUR dynasty ruled the region from the 10th to 13th centuries. After this, Kordofan was incorporated into KANEM-BORNU. By the early 1300s Arab nomads from EGYPT infiltrated the area and began mixing with the Nubian-speaking indigenous peoples.

From the the 17th to 18th centuries both the FUNJ and Darfur sultanates ruled the region. However, neither of these sultanates garnered any permanent influence within Kordofan. Egypt gained control of the Kordofan in the early 1820s. This rule was unchallenged until 1882, when the Muslim leader Muhammad Ahmad al-Mahdi raised a rebellion. Al-Mahdi and his successor ruled until 1899, at which time Kordofan became a province of the Anglo-Egyptian Sudan.

See also: ANGLO-EGYPTIAN CONDOMINIUM (Vol. IV); MUHAMMAD AHMAD AL-MAHDI (Vol. IV); WHITE NILE (Vol. I).

Koyam Ethnic group located in parts of the Lake CHAD region in northeast NIGERIA. The nomadic Koyam were one of the main groups within KANEM-BORNU, a trading empire that flourished around Lake Chad between the 14th and 18th centuries. The Koyam, who were devout Muslims, arrived in the Kanem-Bornu region around the mid-17th century and established the city of Belbelec, which then became a center for Islamic scholarship. The Koyam did not remain in Kanem-Bornu for long, however. By the end of the 17th century, famine and raids by

TUAREGS pushed them out of the area and further west into areas of the HAUSA STATES. Led by sheik Umar ibn Abdullah, the Koyam returned to Kanem-Bornu during the early decades of the 18th century and established another religious center in the town of Gaskeru. Supported by the *mai* (king) of Kanem-Bornu, who sent military defenses to protect the city, Gaskeru flourished until Tuareg invasions once again decimated the city. The Koyam were dispersed further by attacks from the pastoral FULANI people. Despite their history of relocation and dispersal, the Koyam were one of the most successful groups at bringing Islam and its teachings to the people around the Lake Chad region.

See also: ISLAM, INFLUENCE OF (Vols. II, III).

Kpengla (Kpengla Adahoonzou)   (r. 1774–1789)
King of Dahomey

In 1774 Kpengla succeeded his father, TEGBESU (1732–1774), as king of DAHOMEY. Upon taking the throne Kpengla was warned by Abiodun (r. 1770–1789), the *alafin* (ruler) of Oyo, that Dahomey would remain autonomous as long as the kingdom paid Oyo the yearly tribute of cowries, coral, and other goods. In 1775 Kpengla vowed that he would free Dahomey from Oyo repression, though he continued to pay his annual tribute.

Conflict arose between Oyo and Dahomey when Kpengla tried, by military action, to stop the diversion of trade from his own port at WHYDAH to PORTO NOVO. To the annoyance of Kpengla, Abiodun of Oyo supported both Porto Novo and Badagry, a town and lagoon port in present-day southwestern NIGERIA. Kpengla was helpless to do anything about his lost trade.

In 1781, when Porto Novo and Badagry were at war, Abiodun convinced Kpengla to join him in backing Porto Novo. Kpengla agreed on the condition that trade would be redirected back to his port at Whydah. In 1784, after Kpengla successfully sacked Badagry, Alafin Abiodun reduced Dahomey's tribute by half. Pleased with Kpengla's victory over Badagry, Abiodun requested that Dahomey punish Weme, a village in what is today northern Republic of BENIN, whose people had assaulted Oyo traders. Kpengla carried out his mission and was once again victorious.

Relations between Dahomey and Oyo began to break down when trade from Porto Novo was not redirected to Whydah. When Kpengla sought Abiodun's permission to invade Porto Novo, he was given a stern warning that if he attempted to move into Porto Novo, Abiodun would have no choice but to attack Dahomey. Kpengla ignored the threat and attacked Porto Novo. Despite his warnings, Abiodun did not retaliate. After his death in 1789, Kpengla was succeeded by Agonglo (r. 1789–1797), who continued Dahomey's expansion.

See also: OYO EMPIRE (Vol. III).

Krobo (Krobou, Klobi)   Ethnic group of West Africa located mostly in present-day IVORY COAST and GHANA. Prior to the 18th century the Kwa-speaking Krobo peoples were considered a minor branch of the GA-DANGME peoples. About the 1730s, though, they were able to establish greater autonomy by becoming independent from the AKAN state of AKWAMU, which extended along the coast from Ghana to present-day TOGO and the Republic of BENIN. The Krobo then began to expand their territories, moving into agricultural lands vacated by Akwamu and enlarging their domain over the next century to more than 200 square miles (518 sq km).

As the Krobo were not involved in the slave trade, they participated mainly in agrarian trade. During the 18th century, with the ASHANTI EMPIRE threatening the Krobo and other Ga-Dangme subgroups, the Krobo defended themselves by forming trading alliances with neighboring communities. By the late 18th century, these alliances had the effect of weakening the Ashanti Empire by shutting them out of the important trade routes.

In 1826 the Ashanti were finally defeated by the Ga-Dangme and other indigenous groups, with the help of the British and the Danes. Although the Krobo forces were small, their valiant efforts to dispel the Ashanti were noted by the European commanders of the war. However, even as the Krobo were able to gain importance and reap the economic benefits that began after the Ashanti defeat, their culture did not begin to flourish until the latter part of the 19th century.

See also: DENMARK AND AFRICA (Vol. III); ENGLAND AND AFRICA (Vol. III).

Further reading: Louis E. Wilson, *The Krobo People of Ghana to 1892: A Political and Social History* (Athens, Ohio: Ohio University Center for International Studies, 1991).

Kru (Krou)   Ethnic group located in the southwestern portions of present-day IVORY COAST and the southern portions of LIBERIA. Between the 15th and 17th centuries the Kru people migrated to the area from the northeast. There were several culturally different subgroups within the Kru, but they were all peoples who lived in fishing and agricultural communities. Their society was traditionally structured around clans that offered succession only through the paternal side of the FAMILY, and marriage was sought outside their local clans (a practice called *exogamy*). Government among the Kru peoples was mainly decentralized with the family chiefs forming a council to advise the local ruler.

While the transatlantic SLAVE TRADE developed during the 18th century, the Kru peoples were known to be adamantly against the trading of captives and hostages and offered to trade with the Europeans only in items such as ivory. As the Kru traded a large portion of their ivory for weapons to protect their state, the Europeans' attempts to attack and quell the Kru's resistance were mostly unsuccessful.

See also: CLAN (Vol. I); IVORY TRADE (Vol. III); WARFARE AND WEAPONS (Vol. III).

Kuba (Bakuba)

Bantu-speaking people in present-day Democratic Republic of the CONGO, in Central Africa. Little is known of Kuba origins. It is believed, however, that at some time during the latter half of the 16th century, wars with the IMBANGALA forced the Kuba people, commonly called the Bakuba, to migrate to their current lands from their original home south of the mouth of the Congo River. By the end of the 16th century the Kuba were organized into a loose confederation of about 18 clans. Then, under the direction of the capable BUSHONGO clan chief Shyaam, or SHAMBA BOLON-GONGO (r. c. 1600–1620), the Kuba people established a unified kingdom, also called Kuba. An army was raised, a capital was established, agricultural production was encouraged, and craftspeople—including weavers and wood carvers—were held in high esteem.

The Kuba kingdom was known for producing high-quality raffia cloth with symbolic geometrical designs. For their funeral ceremonies, the Kuba people dressed the bodies of the deceased in their finest cloth. They did this because of the belief that their ancestors in the land of the dead might not recognize them otherwise.

The Kuba agricultural ECONOMY promoted wealth, trade, and, subsequently, population growth. Because of this, Kuba was able to maintain its hold on the area despite the influx of new peoples who came to enjoy the kingdom's prosperity. During the 19th century, however, internal conflict among the Kuba clans greatly weakened the kingdom, and by the end of that century outsiders were able to successfully invade. Ultimately, however, it fell victim not to neighboring peoples but to Belgium's King Leopold II (1835–1909) and his Congo Free State.

See also: BANTU LANGUAGES (Vol. I); CONGO RIVER (Vol. I).

Further reading: Jan Vansina, *The Children of Woot: A History of the Kuba Peoples* (Madison, Wisc.: University of Wisconsin Press, 1978).

Kulango (Koulango, Kulago, Kulano)

Ethnic group located in the eastern portions of present-day IVORY COAST, portions of GHANA, and BURKINA FASO. The Kulango speak a Kwa dialect of the Niger-Congo group of languages. Despite the efforts of DYULA traders in the 17th and 18th centuries, very few Kulango converted to Islam.

Related to the LOBI, with whom they often fought, the Kulango migrated to the Ivory Coast region prior to the period of European colonization. They were later subjugated by the Abron peoples from the 17th century until French colonization in the 19th century.

Kulibali, Mamari

(r. c. 1712–1755) *Eighteenth century ruler of the Bambara state of Segu located in present-day Mali*

Although the foundation legend of the SEGU state declares that both Segu and the state of KAARTA were established by two brothers in the mid-17th century, the ruler credited with the true founding of Segu was Mamari Kulibali. Under Kulibali the Segu state expanded its borders to encompass both TIMBUKTU and JENNE to the northeast and BAMAKO to the southwest. Known to his people as "The Commander," Kulibali was also credited with the formation of a navy and army that helped to fend off threats to his vast territories.

See also: BAMBARA (Vols. II, III).

Kumasi

Capital of the ASHANTI EMPIRE located in the tropical forests of present-day central GHANA. According to oral tradition, the city was founded in 1680 and was named Kumasi by its founder, OSEI TUTU (r. c. 1680–1720), because he sat under a Kum tree during territorial negotiations. Rich in GOLD and kola nuts, it also was a junction for converging trade routes. As a result Kumasi quickly became an important trading town.

As the center of Ashanti culture, Kumasi was home to the influential *asantehene* (Ashanti king). The sacred GOLDEN STOOL, a symbol of royal authority, was housed in Kumasi, making it a truly royal city.

See also: KUMASI (Vols. IV, V).

Further reading: *The City of Kumasi Handbook: Past, Present and Future* (Cambridge, U.K.: Cambridge Faxbooks, 1992).

Kunta

Ethnic group of nomadic Arabs who inhabit present-day southern ALGERIA and the northern banks of the NIGER RIVER, having migrated there along caravan routes. The Kunta peoples were known for bringing the rigorous teachings of the Islamic Sufi QADIRIYYA brotherhood to West Africa in the late 15th to mid-16th centuries. This branch of SUFISM insisted on strict adherence to the basic principles and beliefs of Islam and disapproved of laxity in religious practices. The beliefs of the Qadiriyya brotherhood took deep root among the FULANI people of West

Africa, who used political conquest to further their religious aims during the FULANI JIHADS of the 17th through the 19th centuries.

Kwararafa (Kororofa, Jukun)

One of the seven Banza Bakwai, or "illegitimate" states of Hausaland located near the Benue River in present-day NIGERIA. Like the other HAUSA STATES, Kwararafa has its origins in the legend of Prince Bayajida. According to the traditional tale, this prince, who originally came from Baghdad, in present-day Iraq, married a Hausa queen and founded the seven "true" Hausa states, or Hausa Bakwai. In addition he established seven outlying states that were considered "illegitimate" and were therefore called Banza Bakwai.

While it is possible the area of Kwararafa was occupied as early as the 11th century, the state did not truly begin to form until the mid-14th to early 15th centuries. The state became a trading center and benefited from its position between the southern parts of Nigeria and the northern Hausa States, which led to its becoming the go-between for many trading activities.

Because of this, Kwararafa came into direct contention with the Hausa state of ZARIA (formerly called Zazzau but renamed after its capital city); wars for regional trading rights often broke out between the two states. Ultimately Zaria successfully held sway until after the 17th century. At that time Kwararafa gained enough power to conquer Zaria and other northern states such as KANO. Peace accords between the states were successful, but when the FULANI JIHADS broke out in 1804, Kwararafa was conquered by the forces of USMAN DAN FODIO (1754–1817). This brought Kwararafa under the rule of the SOKOTO CALIPHATE.

L

Lagos Town and port island located in present-day NIGERIA. Originally named Oko, the port was founded by Yoruba fishermen during the late 15th century. In 1472 the Portuguese arrived at Lagos, calling the island *Onim,* and later *Lagos.* The town soon became a trading center. By the 16th century the Portuguese had established such a profitable relationship with the Yoruba *obas* (kings), that they were granted full rights to the slave trade in Lagos. By the latter part of the 16th century, however, Lagos was taken over by the kingdom of BENIN and was renamed Eko. Under Benin rule the area prospered, primarily by means of the transatlantic SLAVE TRADE. This continued until the mid-19th century when the British navy besieged the island in an effort to put down the slave trade, which had continued to flourish despite its abolition by the British Parliament in 1807.

See also: LAGOS (Vols. IV, V); PORTUGAL AND AFRICA (Vol. III); YORUBA (Vols. II, IV).

Lamu Port, island, and archipelago in present-day KENYA; known as a distribution center for the gold, ivory, spice, and slave trades. Although it was initially settled almost two thousand years ago, Lamu was established at its current site some time at the beginning of the 14th century. In 1505, when a Portuguese warship came to the island, Lamu agreed to pay tribute in exchange for a pledge not to destroy the town. This initiated a period of Portuguese domination that lasted more than 150 years.

By the end of the 17th century, however, the Portuguese were ousted by the Arab forces of the OMANI SULTANATE, and Lamu entered into a period of great success. Loosely linked to Oman, Lamu became a wealthy Indian Ocean trading port, as well as a cultural center for Arab and Swahili poetry, the arts, and politics.

This golden age lasted until 1812. At that time, fearing reprisals from the MASRUI rulers of MOMBASA for Lamu's victory at the Battle of Shela, the city's council of elders petitioned for increased protection from the Omani Sultanate. Oman's conquest of the Masruis led to a tightening of the sultanate's grip on the entire SWAHILI COAST. As a result Lamu went into decline, and leadership of the coastal cities fell to Mombasa and ZANZIBAR.

See also: LAMU (Vol. II).

Further reading: Patricia Romero, *Lamu: History, Society, and Family in an East African Port City* (Princeton, N.J.: Marcus Wiener, 1997).

Lebna Dengel (r. c. 1508–1540) *Ethiopian emperor*
Because Lebna Dengel was named the emperor of ETHIOPIA at the age of 12, his grandmother, Empress Eleni (c. 1468–c. 1522), acted as regent until Lebna Dengel was old enough to assume the responsibility of running the empire himself. During this time Eleni initiated a diplomatic relationship with Portugal whereby the Europeans would join Ethiopia as an ally against their common Muslim enemies. Between 1520 and 1526 Portuguese diplomats visited Ethiopia in an attempt to consolidate this union.

In 1526, after a series of disputes, Lebna Dengel secured a truce with the Muslims by agreeing to have the Portuguese ambassador return home. Despite this truce ADAL obtained weapons and training from the Ottoman Empire and enlisted newly converted Somali pastoralists into their military. This put Ethiopia in a vulnerable position when Adal, under Ahmad ibn Ibrahim al Ghazi (1506–1543), declared a holy war against Ethiopia a year later. In 1528 Ahmad, known to the Portuguese as AHMAD GRAÑ, was victorious over the Christian army at the Battle of Shimba Kure, and his army subsequently occupied AMHARA, Dawaro, Lasta, and SHOA.

During the next six years the Muslims plundered their way through southern Ethiopia, forcing Lebna Dengel to take refuge in the Ethiopian Highlands. By 1535 little remained of Lebna Dengel's once powerful Christian kingdom. In desperation he begged the Portuguese for help, which finally came, six years later, in the form of 400 reinforcements armed with muskets. The Ethiopian army regrouped, and in 1543, under Lebna Dengel's successor, Galawdewos (c. 1540–1559), they killed Ahmad Grañ and drove his army out of the region.

See also: PORTUGAL AND AFRICA (Vol. III); SOMALI (Vol. II).

Further reading: Harold G. Marcus, *A History of Ethiopia* (Berkeley, Calif.: University of California Press, 1994); Richard Pankhurst, *History of Ethiopian Towns from the Middle Ages to the Early Nineteenth Century* (Philadelphia: Coronet Books, 1985).

Leo Africanus (Giovanni Leone, Al-Hasan Ibn Muhammad Al-Wazzan Az-Zayyati, Al-Fasi) (c. 1485–1554) *Arab traveler and geographer*

Born in the city of Granada, in Muslim Spain, Leo Africanus was raised in present-day MOROCCO after he and his family were forced to flee Spain when the monarchs Ferdinand and Isabella expelled the Muslims in 1492. He studied in the city of FEZ and as a teenager accompanied his uncle on various diplomatic and commercial expeditions. In 1512 they traveled throughout North Africa and, in 1513, to the city of TIMBUKTU, at the time a major trading city of the SONGHAI Empire in sub-Saharan Africa. Between 1517 and 1520 Leo made three trips to EGYPT, ultimately reaching Aswan. His supposed travels in Persia, Arabia, and Armenia are unsubstantiated.

In 1520, while returning home, he was captured by Christian PIRATES in the Mediterranean. He was presented as a slave to Pope Leo X, who later befriended, freed, and baptized him Giovanni Leone de Medici. Leo flourished in Rome, learning Italian and Latin and teaching Arabic. He was commissioned by the pope to write a detailed survey of Africa in Italian, the first of its kind. His *Descrittione dell'Africa* was finished in 1526 and published in 1550. An English version was later published in 1600. According to popular belief he ultimately returned to Tunis in North Africa and reconverted to Islam. He died there in 1554.

Further reading: Amin Maalouf, *Leo Africanus*, Peter Sluglett, trans. (New York: W. W. Norton & Company, 1989).

Lesotho Small, mountainous country, 11,700 square miles (30,300 sq km) in area, that is wholly surrounded by present-day SOUTH AFRICA; more than 80 percent of the country lies 5,905 feet (1,800 m) above sea level. The origins of present-day Lesotho (pronounced la-SOO-too and meaning "the country of the SOTHO people") lie with the founding of the Sotho kingdom. The Sotho kingdoms spread out in the 1820s, when the ZULU initiated the MFECANE, or "crushing." As they expanded their empire in the east, the Zulu drove the people of other kingdoms north, south, and over the Drakensburg Mountains. At this time King MSHWESHWE (1786–1870) founded the Sotho kingdom of Basutoland at Butha-Buthe and later on the mountain of THABA BOSIU.

About this time the BOERS, or Voortrekkers, moving inland from CAPE COLONY, challenged the Sotho for their land. This simultaneous expansion of growing Sotho and Boer populations brought the two into conflict over a limited resource—land. By 1840 the Sotho people numbered about 40,000. Worried by the aggressive tactics of his Boer neighbors, in 1833 Mshweshwe invited French MISSIONARIES to bring Christianity and knowledge of the outside world to his people, reasoning that if European missionaries were there, it would stop Boer encroachment.

See also: BASUTOLAND (Vol. IV); LESOTHO (Vols. I, II, IV, V).

Further reading: Scott Rosenberg, Richard F. Weisfelder, and Michelle Frisbie-Fulton, *Historical Dictionary of Lesotho* (Lanham, Md.: Scarecrow Press, 2004).

Liberia Independent republic on the Atlantic Ocean coast of West Africa measuring about 38,300 square miles (99,200 sq km) and bordered by the present-day countries of SIERRA LEONE, IVORY COAST, and GUINEA. Although Liberia was the only black state in Africa to avoid European colonial rule, from an African perspective, the creation of Liberia was very much a case of colonial conquest.

In 1807 Britain banned the transatlantic SLAVE TRADE, and opposition to SLAVERY in general became more vocal. Sierra Leone became a home to free blacks who had been living in London and Canada as well as recaptives freed by Britain from slave ships on the high seas. In the United States, abolitionists saw the coastal region south of Sierra Leone as a prime location to establish a settlement for both America's free blacks and emancipated slaves.

Founded in 1816 by wealthy, white Americans, the American Colonization Society (ACS) sought to establish a private colony on the African coast. Americans such as James Madison (1751–1836), Bushrod Washington (1762–1829), and Henry Clay (1777–1852) had a dual purpose for establishing the colony: first, free African-Americans were competing with immigrant LABOR for wages, undercutting white labor, and second, to remove emancipated Africans or African-Americans away from white settlement. The ACS received funding from philanthropists and from James Monroe (1758–1831), the sitting president, and sold memberships to free blacks in the United States to promote the Christianizing of the indigenous inhabitants.

Many free African-Americans refused to go, but others, planning a new life in missionary work or commerce with the United States, chose to go. Two-thirds of those who went "Back to Africa" were free African-Americans who had property and money, and one-third were emancipated slaves who had little more than the shirts on their backs.

A wide social gulf existed between the Americo-Liberians, as the free black settlers were called, and the indigenous peoples of Liberia. Laws prohibited "tribal" people from most jobs in civil service and schools, and attempts were made to impose Christian practices by law. It was difficult, though not impossible, for indigenous Liberians to enter colonizer society, although the colonizers accounted for less than 3 percent of society. Often, however, servants, adopted children, and children born of intermarriage and informal polygamous unions were allowed to pass into the ruling class. Most power in Liberia remained concentrated in the hands of the Americo-Liberian elite until 1980, when riots after a long period of civil unrest toppled the government and a new constitution was imposed by the army, led by a 31-year-old sergeant named Samuel Doe (1951–1990).

The first attempt to return to Africa failed due to the first arrivals lacking immunity to tropical diseases. The second attempt began with the 1821 negotiations with indigenous people at the coast and the selling of the land at what was called Providence Island at Cape Mesurado. Settlers arrived in 1822. Not only did this settlement provide a home for African-Americans but it also provided a place where U.S. war ships could deposit captives rescued from those still plying the slave trade. In 1822 a white American Episcopal clergyman, Reverend Jehudi Ashmun (1794–1828), became the ACS's first colonial agent of the colony. During his stay, which ended in 1828, he became the official founder of the country that the people named *Liberia* (from the word *liberty*). Ashmun also named the capital *Monrovia,* after American president and ACS member James Monroe, who had helped to fund the trip. Ashmun also instituted

the country's first government, which was based on the Constitution of the United States. Liberia then adopted the motto, "The love of liberty brought us here."

The ACS administered the colony until 1841, when the settlement received its own constitution and Joseph Jenkins Roberts (1809–1876) became the settlement's first black governor. In 1847 Liberia became fully independent, with Roberts as the first president. At this time the African-Americans became Americo-Liberians, the owners of the new country. However, they were not alone on the land, with 16 indigenous groups surrounding their fledgling country. President Roberts expanded Liberia's boundaries through diplomatic means and established the University of Liberia, in Monrovia. Although most European powers recognized Liberia by 1856, the United States did not grant Liberia formal diplomatic recognition until 1862, during the U.S. Civil War (1860–65).

See also: CUGOANO, OTTOBAH (Vol. III); DOE, SAMUEL (Vol. V); EQUIANO, OLAUDAH (Vol. III); LIBERIA (Vols. I, II, IV, V); ROBERTS, JOSEPH J. (Vol. IV).

Further reading: G. E. Saigbe Boley, *Liberia: Rise and Fall of the First Republic* (New York: McMillan, 1983); D. Elwood Dunn and Svend E. Holsoe, *Historical Dictionary of Liberia* (Metuchen, N.J.: Scarecrow Press, 1985); Jane J. Martin, *Krumen "down the coast": Migrants on the West Virginian Coast in the Nineteenth Century* (Boston: African Studies Center, Boston University, 1982); Tom W. Schick, *Behold the Promised Land: A History of Afro-American Settler Society in Nineteenth-Century Liberia* (Baltimore: Johns Hopkins University Press, 1980).

Libolo Ethnic group and kingdom of the MBUNDU people of what is now ANGOLA, in western Central Africa. The Libolo kingdom had emerged by the early 16th century. A ruling dynasty, which probably came from the southern state of Kalembe, moved north and established a new kingdom just south of the Kwanza River. The new Libolo kings, who held the title *hango,* ruled from the Ngango River valley and extended their territory into the Mbundu communities living to the north and northeast, including the Mbondo and the SONGO.

The Libolo kings were successful at expanding their kingdom largely because they appointed governors, called *mavunga,* to rule outlying provinces that the king could not control directly. Unlike in the northern Mbundu kingdoms, in which ruling positions were inherited, the *mavunga* title did not belong to any particular lineage. Because the Libolo kings appointed rulers who depended on them entirely for their offices, they were able to command greater loyalty and encourage greater stability than the Mbundu kings.

During the second half of the 16th century the Mbundu kingdoms to the north were strengthened by newly developed trade routes from the interior to the port of LUANDA on the Atlantic coast of Angola. They began to expand their influence, pushing the Libolo back south of the Kwanza. The advance of the Mbundu kingdoms cut off Libolo from its northern province of Mbondo, which soon formed its own independent kingdom. Songo came increasingly under the influence of the LUNDA EMPIRE.

During the 1600s the Libolo people suffered increasing retaliation from the Portuguese for their attacks on trade caravans traveling through their territory to Luanda. Wars and slave raids by the Portuguese and the IMBANGALA contributed to the kingdom's decline during the 17th century.

See also: PORTUGAL AND AFRICA (Vol. III); SLAVE TRADE, TRANSATLANTIC (Vol. III).

Libya North African country situated on the Mediterranean coast and bordered by present-day EGYPT, Republic of the SUDAN, CHAD, NIGER, ALGERIA, and TUNISIA. As Christians and Muslims vied for control over Mediterranean trade in the 15th and 16th centuries, cities along the North African coast became strategic locations from which CORSAIRS and naval vessels could tax and seize passing merchant ships. Libya was no stranger to the fray in the Mediterranean. The coastal town of TRIPOLI was stormed and occupied by the Spanish in 1510. In 1551 Tripoli was conquered by the Turkish Ottoman Empire, which wrested it from the control of the Knights of St. John of Malta as part of their attempt to extend the empire across North Africa. The Ottomans hoped to profit not only from coastal trade but also from the inland trade passing through the FEZZAN in the upper Sahara. However, other than exacting annual payments of tribute from the interior regions, Turkish power remained in the coastlands. Much of the interior of present-day Libya fell under the authority of Muslim religious states and Berber confederations.

Much of the Ottoman power was concentrated in Tripoli. The city was home to a large population of Janissaries, members of an elite corps of soldiers in the Ottoman army. As the region slowly gained autonomy from the distant Ottoman government, the power of the Janissaries increased. In 1611 the Janissary commander, Dey Suleiman Safar (fl. 1610s), staged a coup and took control of the government.

By the end of the 17th century Tripoli had become a wealthy city due to the efforts of the corsairs. Despite the region's prosperity, there was a constant struggle for control of the government. A wave of military coups followed. In 1711 the KARAMANLI DYNASTY wrangled power from the existing government. While the Karamanlis succeeded in strengthening Tripoli's power over the Libyan interior, they did little to quell the region's political turmoil.

In 1793 a Turkish military officer, Ali Benghul, took advantage of this civil unrest and seized control of the government. In 1799, however, he made a grave mistake that would lead to his downfall. He agreed to aid the French general Napoleon Bonaparte (1769–1821) in his quest to conquer Egypt. This agreement greatly angered the British, who already felt estranged from Benghul's government because of corsair activity in the region against their merchant fleet.

In 1801 Britain, with the help of the United States, bombarded Tripoli in an attempt to end corsair activity against passing merchant ships. No longer able to tax and seize merchant ships, the government was forced to borrow heavily from French and British merchants. The population resisted the heavy taxation imposed by the government to pay the debt. Due to lack of repayment, the French and British blockaded Tripoli, and the entire region became embroiled in a civil war. Taking advantage of this situation, the Ottoman Empire stepped in to restore direct control in 1835.

Enslaved African family from the kingdom of Loango. The innocence of this picture contrasts greatly with the reality of the trade in humans. The engraving from which this print by John Gabriel Steadman was made (c. 1792) is by the famed English Romantic poet and engraver William Blake (1757–1827). © *Historical Picture Archive/Corbis*

See also: LIBYA (Vols. I, II, IV, V); OTTOMAN EMPIRE AND AFRICA (Vols. III, IV).

Further reading: Ronald Bruce St. John, *Historical Dictionary of Libya* (Lanham, Md.: Scarecrow Press, 1998).

Loango Kingdom and port city of the Bantu-speaking Vili people located along the African Atlantic coast north of the Congo River and the land of SOYO, in what is now ANGOLA. Loango was an important trading zone from the 1500s. Formerly a province of the KONGO KINGDOM, Loango became an independent city in the early 16th century under the divine rule of the *maloango*. The king and his court lived in the capital city of Buali, which had a population of 15,000 by the middle of the 18th century. Most Vili resided in villages ruled by the local nobility, or *mfumu*, who paid tribute to the king.

A holy fire, called *ntufia,* was lit during the coronation of the *maloango.* During the ceremony, men kindled fires from the *ntufia* and carried them throughout Loango to each of the local chiefs, who kept the holy fires burning in recognition of the *maloango's* political and spiritual authority. In turn, Vili commoners kindled their fires from the fires of the local rulers. The *ntufia* burned until the *maloango's* death and was a symbol of his divine rule.

The Vili people were fishermen, hunters, weavers, blacksmiths, farmers, and salt processors. They raised cattle and poultry and cultivated millet, sorghum, MAIZE, and cassava. They also made wine, oil, cloth, and fishing nets from the palm trees that grew throughout their territory. The Vili traded their wares at local markets, which were an important part of Loango life. By the 17th century Vili palm cloth was used as currency, indicating a highly developed ECONOMY.

In northern Loango major exports included wildlife, lumber, animal skins, and ivory. The kingdom's interior was rich in copper, which was also an important commodity for trade.

By the late 1500s Loango was trading regularly with the southern port of LUANDA in the MBUNDU kingdom. By the early 1600s both the Dutch and the Portuguese were heavily participating in the coastal trade. Because the Dutch lacked tropical colonies until the 1630s and were accordingly more interested in ivory and other commodities rather than human captives, their slave trade was later in starting than elsewhere along the coast. However, by the 1630s the Europeans, including the Dutch, had established a slave trade at Loango, which increased steadily over the next four decades and continued through the 18th century. The trade peaked in the late 1700s, when at least 10,000 humans were shipped from the Loango coast each year. For Europeans Loango became one of the most significant areas of the transatlantic SLAVE TRADE along the entire Atlantic coast of Africa.

See also: NETHERLANDS AND AFRICA (Vol. III); PORTUGAL AND AFRICA (Vol. III).

Lobi Ethnic group located in present-day GHANA, IVORY COAST, and BURKINA FASO. By the 16th century the Lobi people were mining GOLD from fields that lay along the Black Volta River. During the first half of the 18th century the Lobi gold mines were attacked and taken over by the army of the ASHANTI EMPIRE from present-day central Ghana. Possibly due in part to the Ashanti expansion, the latter half of the 18th century saw Lobi migrations from Ghana into regions of present-day Burkina Faso and Ivory Coast.

The Lobi people were a traditionally agrarian community and were also skilled hunters and fishermen. While their political system tended to be unorganized and made up of autonomous villages governed by a religious head, or *thil,* the Lobi banded together and fiercely opposed French colonial rule in the 19th century.

See also: FRANCE AND AFRICA (Vols. III, IV).

Lozi (Aluyi, Barotse, Barutsi, Barozi, Luyi, Malozi, Marotse, Rotse, Rozi, Rutse, Silozi, Tozui) Bantu-speaking agriculturalists of present-day ZAMBIA. Because of similarities to the Lunda people, the Lozi are thought to have originated in the Congo basin. The Lozi probably migrated to their present location on the ZAMBEZI RIVER floodplains during the 17th century.

The Lozi people established their kingdom by conquering neighboring peoples. Their expansionist state grew to include nearly 25 ethnic groups. A hierarchical social system developed with an elite nobility ruling over the commoners and serfs. At the head of this nobility was a paramount chief, who ruled with the aid of clan chieftains. Despite a highly organized society, the Luyi lacked a clear policy of monarchal succession, a situation that led to internal disputes that greatly weakened the kingdom.

Because of the seasonal flooding of the Zambezi River, the Lozi spent part of each year living on mounds they built. As Lozi territory expanded during the 18th century, the Lozi were confronted with a Kololo invasion that left them in a subjugated status for several decades. It was not until the 1860s that the Lozi successfully revolted and regained control of their territory.

See also: LOZI (Vol. IV).

Luanda Major port city on the west coast of Central Africa, south of the Bengo River, in what is now ANGOLA. Founded as the capital of the Portuguese colony in 1575, the city was the principal port in the transatlantic SLAVE TRADE until about 1800.

The natural port of Luanda had previously belonged to the MBUNDU kingdom of NDONGO, which was a tributary of the KONGO KINGDOM. Competition between the two kingdoms to control trade with the Europeans caused a major war in 1556. The forces of the Ndongo leader, the *ngola a kiluanje,* beat the forces of the Kongo king, or *manikongo,* and as a result Ndongo became independent and traded directly with the Portuguese at Luanda.

Across from the port city was the island of Luanda. *Nzimbu* shells, which were used throughout Angola as currency, came from the waters around the island. Women would collect the shells by diving down to the ocean floor and bringing up handfuls of sand. They separated the sand from the shiny, black *nzimbu,* which they collected in small bags hung around their necks. During the 1600s the Portuguese destroyed the *nzimbu* currency system through their practice of importing foreign shells, which caused major inflation.

By the 1570s the Portuguese were attempting to colonize the area, leading to a series of wars with the armies of Ndongo, MATAMBA, and Kongo, among others. In 1575 the Portuguese began building fortifications at Luanda, as the wars continued well into the 1600s. In 1641 the Dutch seized control of the port, which they held until 1648. That year the Portuguese sent more than 1,000 troops to Angola and recaptured Luanda.

By the end of the 1700s Luanda was still a small commercial town in arid and uncultivable land. FOOD had to be imported from Portuguese plantations farther north, from overseas, and from Kongo, which also supplied the town with wood for ships, shelter, and fuel. The majority of Luanda's 2,000 inhabitants were in bondage, and the rest were primarily traders and troops. Portuguese officials also resided in Luanda, which was the seat of the colony's government. Luanda was ruled by a town council, or *camara,* which had to be consulted in important matters by the Portuguese governor of Angola. The *camara* often urged him on to war, because captured peoples could be sold for profit.

Slave trading was the most lucrative commercial activity for Portuguese merchants, although there was also a small ivory-exporting industry. Captives were procured largely from the Kongo and Ndongo kingdoms by OVIM-BUNDU and Matamba armies, and by the IMBANGALA warriors of the KASANJE kingdom. Most of the captives were sent to Brazil to work in the mines of that new Portuguese colony. The majority of the ships and their crews were Brazilian, as were the imported goods, including food, textiles, and alcohol. Humans were traded to the Portuguese in exchange for cloth from Europe and Asia and for alcohol, especially the highly prized Brazilian spirit, *geribita.* The Portuguese also purchased captives with African products obtained from the coastal kingdoms, including salt, elephant tails, animal skins, and palm cloth. As many as 30 slave ships passed through Luanda each year, carrying away about 10,000 people annually. During the 1700s alone, Luanda exported about 1 million captives.

During the 18th century the commercial supremacy of Luanda was increasingly challenged by the northern ports of LOANGO and Mpinda, as well as by the southern port of BENGUELA. Total Portuguese domination on the African coast was gradually undermined by competition from the Dutch, French, and British.

See also: LUANDA (Vols. IV, V); PORTUGAL AND AFRICA (Vol. III).

Luba empire Wealthy Bantu empire of Central Africa that emerged during the 16th century in what is now southern Democratic Republic of the CONGO. Closely associated with the LUNDA EMPIRE, the Luba people lived primarily in agricultural and fishing villages in the Central African savannas and fertile valleys west of the Congo River. This was the Luba heartland, from which the empire was born. Luba villages were organized into chiefdoms, which were ruled by local leaders, or *kilolo,* who inherited their positions based on patrilineal descent. The *kilolo* paid tribute to the spirit-hero king, or *vidye,* who ruled by divine right and was believed to have supernatural powers.

The Luba king ruled from his capital, or *kitenta,* along with appointed titleholders who were usually members of his FAMILY. The Luba court oversaw the empire's regional trade network, as well as the collection and redistribution of wealth through the tribute system. The royal court was a major cultural center, and inspired great artwork in the form of sculpture, masks, poetry, and MUSIC. Metalwork, especially in copper, was particularly noteworthy and was built upon a tradition that dated as far back as the fourth century.

The Luba heartland was rich in salt and iron deposits, which attracted long-distance traders from throughout the Luba empire and neighboring territories. Trade strengthened the tribute system and enriched the royal court. Fish, salt blocks, iron tools, palm cloth, animal hides, and copper crosses, which were used as currency, were among the most valuable trade goods in the region.

Until the 14th century the Luba lived primarily within a number of chiefdoms. Economically they relied on a combination of trading and farming. With only a limited amount of land available for farming, however, there was intense competition between the various chiefdoms for resources. In time chiefdoms began to merge together, pooling their resources in order to strengthen their societies.

By the beginning of the 15th century a number of Luba chiefdoms located east of the Lualaba River had united, forming a single kingdom. However, this kingdom's ruling dynasty, known as the Nkongolo, was replaced later in the century. According to tradition, the new ruler, Ilunga Kalala, was a noted hunter and warrior with heroic, even magical powers and qualities. The new Ilunga dynasty expanded westward, taking possession of territory west of Lake Kisale. It also established a relatively centralized state, with the king ruling in conjunction with governors who collected tribute in the provinces of the empire. In spite of widespread faith in the king's almost mystical authority, disorder often broke out as rivals within the royal family and clans vied for the kingship. In the mid-15th century this dissension led to the formation of the LUNDA kingdom, as rivals for power moved westward and established their own, new kingdom.

During the 17th and 18th centuries the Luba kings extended the tribute system by creating client states of neighboring peoples around the heartland's periphery. At its height the Luba empire stretched east to Lake Tanganyika and south to the Congo copperbelt, near the Lunda kingdom of KAZEMBE.

The Luba developed a secret society called *bambudye* into which all kings, chiefs, and other political leaders were initiated. The Luba believed that in the past the *bambudye* and the spirits were the same, and that members of the secret society continued to possess spiritual powers. The *bambudye* society legitimized Luba rulers, united village leaders with each other and the royal court, and transcended the local kinship ties that often led to inter-lineage disputes. The society thus strengthened political cohesion and promoted stability within the empire.

The central Luba kingdom within the Luba empire influenced the LUNDA EMPIRE, which was established along the Luba model. The Luba, however, were less successful than the Lunda at integrating conquered peoples into their society because of their strict patrilineage-based system of rule, which could not as easily incorporate local lineages and was prone to internal power struggles.

See also: LUBA (Vol. II).

Lulua (Luluwa) Bantu-speaking peoples who migrated from the west in the 18th century and settled in the Kasai Basin in what is now southern Democratic Republic of the CONGO. Related to the Luba of the Kasai region, the Lulua were primarily farmers who cultivated cassava, MAIZE, GROUNDNUTS (peanuts), tobacco, and hemp. They were skilled potters, weavers, and ironworkers and today, Lulua wooden masks and sculptures are prized for their fine design. Eventually the Lulua also participated in the trade of ivory and rubber.

The Lulua lived in small villages presided over by chiefs who received their tribute. They were influenced by both the Lunda and Luba, although they did not recognize the supremacy of the Lunda *mwata yamvo*, or king.

See also: LUBA EMPIRE (Vol. III); LUNDA EMPIRE (Vol. III).

Lunda empire Expansive collection of Bantu-speaking kingdoms that stretched across what is now the southern region of Democratic Republic of the CONGO, northern ANGOLA, and northern ZAMBIA. By the 18th century there were as many as one million people living in this vast empire.

Until the mid-15th century the Lunda lived primarily within small chieftainships with no centralized authority. Around this time, however, Luba aristocrats, often individuals who had been disappointed in their attempts to gain power in their own Luba kingdom, began moving into the region. Marrying into the families of Lunda chieftains, the newcomers carried with them the more centralized traditions of the Luba as well as the Luba's advanced ironworking and agricultural techniques. Rather than altering the basic fabric of Lunda society, the newcomers left both religious and political institutions relatively intact and simply forced the Lunda to pay tribute to their new Luba-Lunda kings. By the 16th century the new rulers had begun centralizing their power until, adopting the title *mwata yamvo*, meaning "lord of vipers," there was a single king for all of the Lunda territory.

By the latter part of the 17th century the Lunda empire had expanded considerably and included a number of important offshoots. Part of this growth stemmed from the great wealth of the Lunda, much of which came from their adoption of crops brought to Africa from America by the Portuguese. Both MAIZE and cassava proved to be valuable crops in the African interior, and they constituted a central element in Lunda wealth.

There was more to the Lunda economy than farming, however, as much of the power of the *mwato yamvo* came from the tribute that was collected from his subjects. Tribute collectors were assigned to each chieftainship, and these officials were highly successful in bringing a wealth of goods—food, salt, iron, copper, and even baskets and pottery—back to the royal court of the *mwato yamvo*.

Some of this tribute was handed out as gifts to the ruler's favorites. But much of it was used as the foundation of a long-distance trading network that formed a fundamental part of the Lunda economy. Ivory, metals, and even captives were exchanged for cloth, guns, and other goods in a complex system that stretched across the continent from the Atlantic to the Indian oceans. As time went on a number of Lunda tribute collectors went on to form their own chieftainships and kingdoms, as did various disappointed rivals to the Lunda throne.

The most important offshoot of the Lunda empire, however, was formed when, in the early 18th century, the *mwata yamvo* sent Lunda warriors to the upper part of the Lualaba River to seize control of the salt flats. Taking the title *kazembe,* their leader eventually established his own kingdom, also called KAZEMBE. Eventually extending as far as the great Copperbelt, the kingdom of Kazembe grew until, by the second half the 18th century, under Kazembe III, it had become an empire in its own right, rich in both natural resources and long-distance trade. By 1800 Kazembe had become the nexus of a trading network that stretched virtually across the entire continent. Iron and copper, salt, ivory, and slaves all were sent out to be exchanged for European and Indian cloth, guns, beads, and other luxury items destined for the royal court.

The Lunda kingdom was very successful at expanding into an empire largely because of the institutions of perpetual succession and positional kinship. According to perpetual succession, the holder of a particular office assumed the title and identity of the original office holder. The complementary practice of positional kinship held that a new office-holder also assumed the kinship ties of the original holder of that position. Thus the lineages of local chiefs were easily incorporated into the political power structure.

See also: BEMBA (Vol. III); BISA TRADING NETWORK (Vol. III); IMBANGALA (Vol. II); KASANJE (Vol. II); KINGDOMS AND EMPIRES OF EASTERN AFRICA AND THE INTERIOR (Vol. III); LUBA EMPIRE (Vols. II, III); LUNDA KINGDOM (Vol. II).

Luo (Lwo, Lwoo, Dholuo, Kavirondo) Niloticspeaking ethnic group who, beginning about the 15th century, migrated south from present-day Republic of the SUDAN to what are now KENYA and UGANDA. Groups of Luo gradually moved south along the Nile River into the GREAT LAKES REGION near Lake Victoria. They were mostly seminomadic cattle herders who settled among native Bantu-speaking agriculturalists and recently arrived Hamitic pastoralists. The Luo migration had an enormous impact on the area, contributing to the end of Chwezi rule in Kitara. In its place the Luo-speaking BITO clan founded the kingdom of BUNYORO-KITARA. Other Luo settled to the east in BUGANDA and BUSOGA. The Luo migrations into the region probably pushed Bantu-speaking TUTSI pastoralists further south, where they founded the kingdoms of NKOLE, RWANDA, and BURUNDI.

The Luo migrations occurred in three waves. In the first, which occurred near the beginning of the 15th century, Luo groups left the Sudan, probably due to environmental changes that caused a lack of suitable pasture. Along the way to new lands, the Luo relied on barter for their livelihood, trading iron weaponry and wooden tools for FOOD. The Luo first established their rule in Bunyoro, and then moved north into Alur, Palwo, Lango, and ACHOLI and east into Buganda and Busoga. They continued to raise cattle, but along the shores of Lake Victoria the Luo also fished and cultivated crops of bananas and millet.

The second wave of Luo migration, during the 17th century, saw the settlement of the region knownn as Padhola. This area was a previously unoccupied forestland north of Lake Victoria and east of Lake Kyoga and was better suited to farming than cattle rearing. To the Luo, Padhola was their "promised land," which they believed had been preserved for them by God and which they later vigorously defended. In Padhola the Luo embarked on the especially LABOR-intensive process of clearing the forest for cultivation. Through this process the Luo claimed rights to the land, and the Luo clans developed a tie to it that they had not previously felt as nomadic cattle herders. The ownership of land began to influence their political and spiritual life. For example, Luo clans began to construct shrines (*kuni*) for worship, something that they did not do before establishing permanent settlements.

The third stage of Luo migration, from the 16th to the 19th centuries, was the movement into what is now western Kenya, in the savanna country of NYANZA. Here the Luo again encountered Bantu groups with which they mingled. The Luo intermarried with local peoples, absorbed aspects of the cultures they encountered, and made their own contributions to other cultures. Some Luo groups started speaking Bantu, and others gave the Nilotic language to Bantu speakers. Here as elsewhere, land settlement, population expansion and absorption, and dispersed lineages encouraged the evolution from a society based solely on kinship relations to one based on territorial chieftainships. Southern Luo migrations continued during the 19th century, and related ethnic groups are among the most populous in the region.

See also: LUO (Vols. II, IV, V).

Luvale (Lubale, Lovale, Lwena, Luena) Bantu-speaking people of present-day ZAMBIA and ANGOLA. The Luvale were part of what became the LUNDA EMPIRE, in the 15th century. In time, however, they split off from the Lunda and established their own kingdom in the southern CONGO. During the late 1700s the Luvale raided neighboring peoples in order to procure captives for MBUNDU slave traders. While trade proved to be an important economic activity for the Luvale, they were best known for their skill as hunters and fishermen.

M

The Eunoto ceremony of the Maasai people of western Kenya. This week-long ceremony, here photographed c. 1984, marks the coming of age of the young Maasai warriors from the *moran*, or novice stage, to the level of junior warrior, at which point they may marry and start families. © *Yan Arthus-Bertrand/Corbis*

Maasai (Masai) Nilotic pastoralist ethnic group that migrated to the highlands of present-day central KENYA during the 16th, 17th, and 18th centuries. The Maasai were skilled in defending their own land and stock—typically cattle and sheep—and were known for their fierce raids on other groups and their territories. Their reputation as warriors was so widespread that trading caravans traveled miles out of their way to avoid Maasai territories entirely. Despite their reputation, the Maasai did maintain some peaceful relations with neighboring peoples, including the KIKUYU, with whom they traded skins and other animal products for iron tools and foodstuffs.

Early in the 19th century the southward migration of the Maasai was thwarted by the Hehe people, and the Kikuyu, a much larger group than the Maasai, expanded their territory from the north, confining the Maasai to Kenya's central highlands. At this time several Maasai clans, finding the available pasture land shrinking, turned to AGRICULTURE as a way of life. During the 19th century the Maasai remained relatively unaffected by the turmoil that was generated by European attempts to colonize East Africa.

See also: MAASAI (Vols. I, II, IV, V); PASTORALISM (Vols. I, IV).

Further reading: Elizabeth L. Gilbert, *Broken Spears: A Massai Journey* (New York: Atlantic Monthly Press, 2003); Lisa McQuail, *The Masai of Africa* (Minneapolis, Minn.: Lerner Publications, 2002).

Macina (Masina) FULANI kingdom, lasting from the 15th to 19th centuries, located on the floodplain region of the inland Niger Delta, in present-day Republic of MALI. Although it was a kingdom of considerable power, throughout much of its existence Macina remained a tributary state to various other kingdoms.

During the early 15th century Maga Diallo (c. 1400), a Fulani vassal from the Mali Empire, broke away and founded the kingdom of Macina. He became the founder of the Diallo dynasty, which remained the ruling family until Macina was destroyed in 1810. Macina remained under the control of the Mali Empire for most of the 15th century, fending off attacks from both the SONGHAI ruler, Sunni Ali (r. 1464–1492), and the Mossi peoples. In 1494 the Songhai Empire finally conquered the kingdom and made it a tributary state for the greater part of the 16th century.

Macina's name was taken from the name of a lake located within the original capital city of Kéké.

From 1539 to 1559 the throne of Macina was disputed among the successors to the Diallo dynasty. This period of unrest finally ended with the successful reign of Boubou-Mariama (r. 1559–1589). During the latter part of his rule, Boubou-Mariama attempted to overthrow Songhai rule in Macina, but he was captured and eventually died while being forced to help the Songhai *askia* (king) fend off the Moroccan invasion of 1591. The soldiers from present-day MOROCCO, however, quickly defeated their counterparts since they fought with European armor and firearms that easily outmatched the less sophisticated ones used by the Songhai and Fulani.

Beginning in 1598 the ruler Hamadou-Amina (r. 1583–1603) waged an extensive war against the Moroccans in which he was initially unsuccessful, forcing him to abandon his kingdom in favor of the city of Diara. Moustapha el Turki (d. 1598), a Moroccan army leader, then named the Moroccan royal Hamadi-Aissata the *ardo* (ruler) of Macina. Upon Moustapha's death Hamadou-Amina returned to Macina, where he defeated Hamadi-Aissata and regained his throne. Nevertheless the Moroccans remained powerful in the kingdom until Hamadou-Amina, at the end of his reign, finally defeated their forces during a battle at the city of Tie along the Bani River. The Moroccans then retreated, but later clashes kept them powerful enough to force Macina to pay tribute to their pashas throughout most of the 17th century.

In 1670 the increasingly powerful kingdom of SEGU took Macina from the Moroccans and brought it under the dominion of the non-Muslim BAMBARA kingdom. Even as Macina lacked true political independence, the kingdom continued to thrive under the kings of the Diallo dynasty throughout the 18th and early 19th centuries. In 1810 the Fulani Muslim Shehu Ahmadu Lobbo (1755–1845) waged a jihad (holy war) and succeeded in destroying the kingdom—which was considered a pagan kingdom since the Fulani of Macina practiced a traditional African religion. Lobbo then founded a new capital in HAMDALLAHI, establishing Macina as a theocratic Muslim state.

See also: FULANI JIHADS (Vol. III); INLAND NIGER DELTA (Vol. II); MALI EMPIRE (Vol. II); MOSSI STATES (Vols. II, III); SUNNI ALI (Vol. II).

Madagascar Indian Ocean island country of 226,700 square miles (587,200 sq km), the fourth-largest island in the world, located 242 miles (390 km) off the coast of present-day MOZAMBIQUE, on the southern coast of East Africa. During the 16th through the 19th centuries several powerful states developed on Madagascar, the most important of which were those formed by the SAKALAVA and the MERINA peoples. Smaller kingdoms included those of the ANTANKARANA, in the north, the BETSILEO and BARA, in the south, and the BETSIMISERAKA, on the east coast. Also during that time Madagascar was visited by Portuguese, Dutch, English, and French colonists, none of whom managed to establish a significant presence on the island until later in the 19th century.

Madagascar's population was, and still is, a complex mix of these various colonists, traders, and settlers. Although it is believed by some historians that an initial group of immigrants, probably from Indonesia, might have arrived as early as the fifth to 10th centuries, the bulk of Madagascar's early population apparently came to the island starting in the 11th century. Included in these groups are the original Malayo-Polynesian colonists from Indonesia, Bantu-speaking groups, most of whom probably came from the African mainland in bondage, and Arabic-speaking Muslim traders, who had settled along Madagascar's northern coastal stretches as early as the 12th century. The language spoken by most people on the island was, and still is, Malagasy, a unique tongue that incorporates words from several languages, reflecting the many influences of Madagascar's diverse population.

The modern Republic of Madagascar is made up of Madagascar Island—the fourth largest island in the world—and many smaller islands, including Nosy-Bé, in the northwest, and Île Sainte-Marie in the northeast.

By the time the Europeans discovered the island in 1500, the northern coastal regions had been settled by Muslim and Swahili traders. For centuries, ports in northern Madagascar had been stops along the Indian Ocean trade routes, where merchants could exchange human captives and manufactured goods for fruit, dried fish, beeswax, and, most important, rice. Thinking that the island might become an important trading stop on the Indian spice route, Christian Portuguese settlers established trading forts in ANTEMORO territory, in the southeastern region, in an effort to suppress the rise of Muslim settlements there.

Local oral traditions from the early 16th century, supported by Portuguese accounts from the time, describe many small, independent fishing villages along both east and west coasts, but without any dominant ruling kingdom or centralized power. Similar small pastoral and farming villages had developed inland. These small villages frequently clashed, but only rarely was any one group able to expand into a greater political entity. About the mid-16th century, however, monarchical rule was established among three of the islands larger groups, the Sakalava, Antemoro, and Merina.

In 1613, two Portuguese Christian Jesuit priests, Antonio d'Azevedo and Luis Mariano, arrived from Goa, in India, to convert the Madagascar population. Their records provide invaluable information on the island at that time.

Their reports describe a thriving trade in human beings in the northern coastal areas of the island. Muslim traders from both Arabia and the city-states of the SWAHILI COAST—LAMU, PEMBA, PATE, MOMBASA, MALINDI, and ZANZIBAR—arrived on the Boina coast, in the northwest, and traded African and Arabian goods for non-Muslim Malagasy captives.

During the 17th century the Sakalava empire emerged, moving up the coast from the south, and founding the kingdoms of MENABE and Boina. Sakalava rulers maintained a great army of fierce, capable warriors who easily conquered the farming and fishing villages that they encountered. By the end of the 17th century the Sakalava empire controlled nearly half of the island of Madagascar.

European efforts to colonize Madagascar generally met with failure. Early on, the Portuguese found that the indigenous Malagasy groups did not mine GOLD and that they were difficult trading partners. French colonists had arrived in southeastern Madagascar as early as 1638, establishing Fort Dauphin on the southeastern coast. They, too, were unsuccessful in their attempts to establish a colony and abandoned Dauphin for the island of Réunion, in 1674. Both the Portuguese and French colonists were further discouraged by the tropical fevers that decimated their numbers.

Madagascar was famous for being a haven for PIRATES and privateers, both Arab and European, who used the island as a base to prey on Indian Ocean trading ships. Toward the end of the 17th century it is widely believed that an organization of English, French, and American pirates even established their own democratic republic in the northeast, calling it Libertalia. In the 18th century one of these English pirates is supposed to have taken a Malagasy princess and produced a son who founded the Betsimisaraka state. During the 18th century this eastern kingdom conquered smaller coastal kingdoms and controlled much of the eastern Madagascar coast until the rise of the Merina empire in the 19th century.

See also: INDIAN OCEAN TRADE (Vol. II); INDONESIAN COLONISTS (Vol. II); MADAGASCAR (Vol. I, II, IV, V), MALAGASY (Vol. II).

Further reading: Mervyn Brown, *A History of Madagascar* (Princeton, N.J.: Markus Wiener Publishers, 2000); Philip Kottak Conrad, *Madagascar: Society and History* (Durham, N.C.: Carolina Academic Press, 1986); Pier Martin Larson, *History and Memory in the Age of Enslavement: Becoming Merina in Highland Madagascar 1770–1822* (Portsmouth, N.H.: Heinemann, 2000); Deryck Scarr, *Slaving and Slavery in the Indian Ocean* (New York: St. Martin's Press, 1998).

Maghrib (Maghreb) Muslim region of Northwest Africa along the Mediterranean Sea that extends from the Atlas Mountains to the coasts of present-day MOROCCO, ALGERIA, TUNISIA, and LIBYA. Originally inhabited by BERBERS, this mountainous region was conquered by Muslim Arabs in about the eighth century. Although the Maghrib faced subsequent invasion by the French, the Arabs remained dominant. Today the majority of the Maghrib's inhabitants is Muslim.

See also: MAGHRIB (Vols. I, II, IV, V).

Further reading: Jamil M. Abun-Nasr, *A History of the Maghrib in the Islamic Period* (New York: Cambridge University Press, 1987).

Maguzawa (Bunjawa) Subgroup of the Hausa peoples located in present-day NIGERIA. They retained their indigenous religion and became a protected religious group within the Muslim-dominated SOKOTO CALIPHATE (1808–1903).

Although most of the HAUSA STATES were converted to Islam by the late 14th century to early 15th century, a group of Hausa peoples called the Maguzawa resisted conversion and remained true to their traditional religious practices. Muslims called this religion "pagan" because it was not based on Muslim principles, but instead focused on the worship of nature deities known as *bori* or *iskoki*.

In 1804 USMAN DAN FODIO (1754–1817), a FULANI cleric, began a sweeping jihad (holy war), eventually capturing the states of Hausaland and making them emirates within his caliphate of Sokoto. One of the main motives behind the jihad was to convert those who practiced a syncretistic Islam mixed with pagan rituals to a purer form of Islam based on *sharia,* or Islamic law. However, despite the fact that the Maguzawa were non-Muslims, Usman dan Fodio did not force them to convert. Rather, the Maguzawa were allowed to continue their traditional religious practices and were given protection under Islamic law as a minority group. Although it is not clear why the Maguzawa were not forcibly converted to Islam by Usman dan Fodio, they were reportedly treated both kindly and fairly by both Usman and his son and successor, MUHAMMAD BELLO (1781–1837).

See also: FULANI JIHADS (Vol. III); ISLAM, INFLUENCE OF (Vols. II, III); *SHARIA* (Vol. II).

Mahajanga (Majunga)

Mahajanga (Majunga) Port town located in northern MADAGASCAR, on the north side of the alluvial delta of the Betsiboka River. Originally called Majunga, the port became the capital of the Boina kingdom, which was established in the late 17th century as part of the SAKALAVA empire.

Besides being an important port for Madagascar's seafaring peoples, Mahajanga was also the terminus of overland routes that were used to bring fruit, rice, beeswax, and other products from the island's interior to the coast for export to Arabia and East Africa.

See also: INDIAN OCEAN TRADE (Vol. II).

Further reading: Michael Lambek, *The Weight of the Past: Living with History in Mahajanga, Madagascar* (Basingstoke, U.K.: Palgrave Mcmillan, 2003).

maize Crop also known as corn. Indigenous to the Americas and transported across the Atlantic Ocean by Europeans, maize had long been a staple in the diets of native peoples throughout the Americas. Maize, cassava, and GROUNDNUTS (peanuts) were brought to Africa via the transatlantic trade conducted by European merchants.

See also: AGRICULTURE (Vols. I, II, III, IV, V).

makhzan The governing body active in the MAGHRIB region of Northwest Africa. Literally translating to "storehouse," the *makhzan* was initially the location where tax monies were housed prior to the 17th century. Later the word became synonymous with the treasury that was both collected and reserved for governmental purposes. During the reign of the SADIAN DYNASTY (r. c. 1553–1669) of present-day MOROCCO, however, the term *makhzan* came to mean "government" or "central authority." By the time the Moroccan Alawite dynasty ruler MAWLAY ISMAIL (c. 1645–1727) came to power, the word *makhzan* was used to designate one of the two types of regional lands. The *bilad al-siba* was the "land of dissidence," and the *bilad al-makhzan* was the "land subject to governmental authority." While the *bilad al-siba* were regions that lay outside of the government's bounds and did not pay taxes to the *makhzan*, the *bilad al-makhzan* were lands that were subject to taxation as well as governmental control.

The English word *magazine,* the original meaning of which is "storehouse," especially for munitions, comes from *makhzin,* the plural form of *makhzan.*

Makonde Ethnic group that has long lived in present-day southeastern TANZANIA as well as MOZAMBIQUE, inhabiting those areas since well before the 18th century. Primarily an agricultural people, the Makonde practice slash-and-burn farming, growing sorghum and, after their introduction from South America by the Portuguese, MAIZE and cassava. Makonde villages tend to operate fairly independently, without strong centralized authority outside themselves.

During the 18th and 19th centuries the Makonde were central to Arab caravans of the East African trade in captives. Despite these and other contacts with Islam, the Makonde managed to retain both their indigenous religion, which was focused on the veneration of elders, and their indigenous customs, including the creation of detailed tattoos on their faces, chests, and backs. Over time, the Makonde became famous for their carvings, notably their wooden masks and human figures.

See also: AGRICULTURE (Vol. III); SLAVE TRADE ON THE SWAHILI COAST (Vol. III).

Makua (Macua) Ethnic group, located on Africa's east coast near MOZAMBIQUE ISLAND in present-day MOZAMBIQUE. The Makua, who are related to the Lolo and the Lomwe of the same region, were a hunting and farming society that was organized along clan lines. Although their oral traditions do not recount exactly when they arrived in the region, they were almost certainly established in the area between the southern end of Lake Malawi and the coast when the MARAVI groups began immigrating there in the 15th century.

In the 16th century the Makua often made alliances with neighboring peoples in an effort to repel the encroaching Maravi groups, with mixed success. To that end they also joined in trade alliances with the Portuguese, who had arrived in the area about 1500. Makua territory included the coastal town of QUELIMANE, which became a Portuguese trading station in 1544, allowing the Portuguese greater authority in their dealings with the caravans of traders who brought goods, including grains, salt, captives, GOLD, and ivory.

Makua peoples also lived in the coastal towns of Mossuril and Angoche, and populated the area between Mozambique Island (which was taken by the Portuguese early in the 16th century) and the Shire River, to the west. In the 1580s the Makua faced an invasion from the west by an army of Lundu and ZIMBA warriors of the Maravi federation. These fierce, marauding bands hoped to contain Portuguese expansion and take control of the lucrative IVORY TRADE by occupying the coastal towns between Mozambique Island and MOMBASA, some of which were Makua settlements. At the time, the Makua were a stateless, segmentary society, so they were unable to mount a serious defense against the invaders. The history of the Makua after this period is more complete than before, as the Portuguese records describe in detail the region of Bororo, which was the name they gave to the Lundu-dominated Makua territory. By the end of the 16th century the Makua had organized into a couple of powerful chiefdoms and were able to reclaim some of their lost lands.

There was a sizeable community of Makua people on the island of MADAGASCAR, about 250 miles off the coast of present-day Mozambique. It is theorized that these Makua were brought there by Arab traders, who acquired them from the MAKONDE, a group that lived to the north of the Makua on the continent.

In the 17th century Makua territory became important to the ivory trade. There was a trade route that ran through the middle of Makua territory, from the southern end of Lake Malawi, where hunters from the interior brought their tusks, to the coastal port of Mossuril, which was used by Maravi, Arab, and Portuguese merchants and sea traders.

Portuguese records show that in the 17th century the Makua were considered friendly trading partners and good neighbors, unlike the Maravi states to the west.

Unknown to the Portuguese at the time, the Makua resented their dictatorial trading practices and the stern policies of the Portuguese landowners, or *prazeros,* who often showed little respect to the original inhabitants of the land that comprised their PRAZOS.

Later in the 17th century Makua warriors joined Lundu and Zimba warriors to carry out raids against the Portuguese, who periodically attempted to make inroads from their coastal settlements toward the interior.

From the middle of the 18th century to the beginning of the 19th century the Makua developed a state mentality, based on a clan hierarchy, which evolved into a type of Makua nationalism. At first they directed their efforts against the Portuguese, using firearms purchased from French traders to confront their enemies more forcefully than they ever had before. Two Makua chiefs, Mauruka and Murimuno, were especially adept at unifying their people against the Portuguese. When the Makua were not fending off Portuguese incursions, they were directing their hostilities toward the Maravi groups who had invaded their territories in the 16th and 17th centuries, or toward the YAO, who, from their territories to the north of the Makua, regularly made raids for captives.

See also: PORTUGAL AND AFRICA (Vol. III); SLAVE TRADE ON THE SWAHILI COAST (Vol. III); WARFARE AND WEAPONS (Vol. III).

Malaguetta pepper (Malagueta, Melegueta)

West African spice that became a prized trade item during the 15th century; also known as "grains of paradise." The spice became such a popular trade item that the coast of present-day LIBERIA became known to European traders as both the Grain Coast and the Pepper Coast.

Like black pepper, the reddish brown Malaguetta pepper grains grow in large pods. Compared to black pepper, though, Malaguetta pepper tastes spicier but has a subtler aroma.

Prior to the 15th century African peoples in regions of present-day GHANA, IVORY COAST, TOGO, and SIERRA LEONE traded Malaguetta pepper for kola nuts and other forest products. It was also brought north by trans-Saharan caravans, eventually becoming a common spice in Moroccan and Tunisian dishes. Later, when Portuguese merchants began trading on the West African coast in the 15th century, it became one of the first spices that they brought back to Europe, where demand for the spice made it an even more valuable trade item.

See also: KOLA NUTS (Vol. I).

Malawi Present-day southeastern African country measuring about 45,700 square miles (118,400 sq km) and bordered by the present-day countries of TANZANIA, MOZAMBIQUE, and ZAMBIA. Between the 16th and 19th centuries the region was controlled by the MARAVI peoples, who migrated there from Luba territory to the west in the 15th century, and for whom the region is named.

Malawi's original inhabitants were Bantu-speaking groups, who migrated there largely between 300 and 1200. By 1400, though, several nomadic pastoralist and agriculturalist peoples had moved into the area. Among these early settlers in Malawi were the Phiri, CHEWA, TUMBUKA, and NGONDE peoples, among others. By the end of the 15th century the Maravi peoples had emerged under a centralized power led by a KALONGA, who was always a high-ranking member of the Phiri clan. The seat of Maravi authority was the trading center of Manthimba, located at the southern end of Lake Malawi.

By the 1600s the Maravi peoples completely dominated the Malawi region, controlling trade and wielding political and religious influence. The most lucrative trade item in the 17th century was ivory, and since the expanses of thinly populated savanna and grasslands to the west of Lake Malawi made ideal habitats for elephants, the Malawi region had a plentiful supply. The Tumbuka, a Maravi subgroup that occupied the western shores of Lake Malawi, were visited by eastern traders from across the lake, who came with Arabic beads, shells, cloth, guns, and gunpowder to trade for ivory. The Chikulamayembe state, founded by the Tumbuka, thrived by taxing the IVORY TRADE. Besides the Tumbuka, the other most powerful Maravi subgroups during this period were the Kalonga, Lundu, and Undi, each of which profited from ivory trading.

Ivory hunting and trading was a relatively peaceful pursuit, but the nature of the commerce in the region changed greatly in the 18th century with the development of the trade in human beings. This trade was not new to the region, as Arab and Swahili merchants had been trading manufactured goods for people from the interior with groups, such as the MWENE MUTAPA, since the ninth century. But the trade in humans took on a more violent and urgent aspect when the Portuguese began to look to East Africa for the captives that would be shipped to their colonies in the Americas, especially Brazil.

By the beginning of the 19th century the demand for captives in the region was so great that the Portuguese and Swahili traders were joined by fierce NGONI traders, who invaded from the south and possessed a highly disciplined and regimented army, and the YAO, who lived to the east of Lake Malawi and became the major traders in the area.

See also: LUBA EMPIRE (Vol. III); MALAWI (Vols. I, II, IV, V); PORTUGAL AND AFRICA (Vol. III); RIFT VALLEY (Vol. I); SLAVE TRADE ON THE SWAHILI COAST (Vol. III).

Further reading: Owen J. M. Kalinga and Cynthia A. Crosby, *Historical Dictionary of Malawi* (Lanham, Md.: Scarecrow Press, 2001); J. M. Schoffeleers, *River of Blood: The Genesis of a Martyr Cult in Southern Malawi c. AD 1600* (Madison, Wisc.: University of Wisconsin Press, 1992).

Mali, Republic of Present-day land-locked central West African nation 478,800 square miles (1,240,100 sq km) in size stretching north into the Sahara desert, where it shares borders with ALGERIA and MAURITANIA. Other countries bordering Mali include (east to west) NIGER, BURKINA FASO, IVORY COAST, GUINEA, and SENEGAL. Mali is known for its history of encompassing several powerful empires, including the 11th-century SONINKE empire of Ghana, the Muslim Almoravid empire (c. 1060–1147), and the Mandinka empire (13th to 15th centuries) of Mali—after which the country is named—and the SONGHAI Empire (c. 1375–1600). The region was colonized by France in the late 19th century.

With their capital at the city of Gao, the Songhai people had already been established as a trading community in areas of what is now western NIGER and eastern Mali by the 11th century or earlier. Under their most influential leader, Sunni Ali (r. 1464–1492), the Songhai assumed control of trans-Saharan trade routes, and the towns of JENNE and TIMBUKTU. Their state subsequently grew to become the largest and most important empire of the Sudan region as well as a major center of Islamic scholarship. The Songhai Empire continued to flourish under Askia MUHAMMAD TOURÉ (r. 1493–1528) and his successors but then collapsed after a Moroccan army, aided by the use of guns, conquered the Songhai in 1591. One of the consequences of the Moroccan invasion was the redirecting of the trade routes toward the European outposts of West Africa's coastline instead of across the Sahara desert.

The Moroccan occupation of present-day Mali was concentrated in the region around the NIGER RIVER at such former Songhai strongholds as Gao and Timbuktu. The Moroccans were routed by TUAREGS in 1737, but they remained active in areas to the west of the Niger until they were effectively crushed by the kingdom of MACINA, in 1833.

Inhabited by the FULANI, Macina had become a tributary kingdom of the declining Mali Empire until 1494, when it was conquered by the Songhai. The kingdom then remained under Songhai rule until the Moroccans began to control the area in the late 16th century. It was the Fulani ruler Hamadou-Amina (r. 1583–1603) who eventually overthrew the Moroccans and forced them to retreat from the kingdom. The Moroccans retained some power over Macina, however, until it became a tributary of the SEGU state in 1670. More than a century later, the kingdom of Macina was again conquered during the jihad (holy war) led by an Islamic Fulani scholar named Shehu Ahmadu Lobbo (1755–1845). He later established a new Macina kingdom in 1810 and founded his capital at the city of HAMDALLAHI.

Between the 16th and 19th centuries the two other major kingdoms that were situated within the borders of modern-day Mali were the Bamana-speaking BAMBARA states of Segu and KAARTA. Prior to 1650 Segu had been established between the Niger and Senegal rivers by the Bambara chief, Kaladian Kulibali (r. c. 1652–1682). Although a powerful state, Segu did not become an official kingdom until 1712 when Kaladian's great-grandson, Mamari KULIBALI (r. 1712–1755), was named the first king. He was thereafter also considered the true founder of Segu.

Although located on a savanna that was becoming increasingly Islamic, the Bamana-speaking Bambara states resisted the influence of Islam. The other Bambara kingdom of Kaarta was originally established in 1650 by Bambara ruler MASSA (r. 1650–1710). The forces of Mamari Kulibali later destroyed the kingdom in the mid-18th century and a second Kaarta kingdom was then established, in 1754, by Bambara chief Sey Bamana Kulibali (r. 1754–1758). It was located along the middle Niger River.

The name *Mali* is from the Bamana language and translates to "mighty hippo."

Both Segu and Kaarta continued to gain importance until the mid-19th century when a TUKULOR cleric from Senegal known as al-Hajj Umar Tal (1794–1864) waged a series of jihads in the region in an effort to convert the inhabitants to Islam. Umar Tal succeeded in conquering Kaarta, in 1854, and Segu, in 1862, bringing both kingdoms, as well as other Malian kingdoms such as Macina, under the reign of the Tukulor empire.

See also: ALMORAVIDS (Vol. II); GHANA EMPIRE (Vol. II); FRANCE AND AFRICA (Vol. III); MALI (Vols. I, II, IV, V); MALI EMPIRE (Vol. II); MUHAMMAD TOURÉ, ASKIA (Vol. II); MUSA I, MANSA (Vol. II); UMAR TAL (Vol. IV).

Further reading: John H. Hanson, *Migration, Jihad, and Muslim Authority in West Africa: The Futanke Colonies in Karta* (Bloomington, Ind.: Indiana University Press, 1996); Pascal James Imperato, *Historical Dictionary of Mali* (Lanham, Md.: Scarecrow Press, 1996).

Malindi Reportedly founded as far back as the 10th century by Arab traders, Malindi became, by the 13th

century, one of the most important city-states and trading centers on the SWAHILI COAST. Its links with the outside world were so widespread that, by 1414, its king apparently established diplomatic and trade relations between Malindi and China.

In 1498 Vasco da Gama (c. 1460–1524) landed at Malindi, building a monument in the form of a cross. Unlike many other coast TOWNS AND CITIES, Malindi welcomed the Portuguese, who, in return, made Malindi their headquarters on the East Africa coast. In 1593, however, the Portuguese transferred their headquarters to MOMBASA. The city continued to play a part in the commercial and political affairs of the East African coast for centuries, although, beginning in the 16th century, its power began to wane.

See also: GAMA, VASCO DA (Vol. II); MALINDI (Vol. II).

Mallamai Professional Muslim scholars who are revered for their perceived ability to interpret the supernatural. The elite Mallamai are experts in Arabic and the teachings of the Quran, and they maintain that knowledge brings Muslims closer to Allah, or God. As the most learned Muslims, the Mallamai are thought to possess supernatural powers that could alleviate earthly ailments. Mallamai write horoscopes, interpret dreams, and cast healing spells. Their elevated status enables them to become government officers and judges.

With their daily prayers and healing rituals, the Mallamai played a central role in unifying the Hausa people. Hausa trading communities (*zongos*) relied on the confidence instilled by the Mallamai for their economic success. Under Mallamai leadership, merchants gained enough trust to extend credit and other financial services to one another.

Mallamai influence in Africa is closely tied to the 19th-century victory of the FULANI over the HAUSA STATES. A radical Mallamai, USMAN DAN FODIO (1754–1817), rallied the local Fulani and conquered the Hausa States in 1808. In 1809 the Fulani founded a new state, the SOKOTO CALIPHATE, which recognized the power of the Muslim sultan.

Because the Fulani intermarried with the Hausa and shared customs and religious practices, the Mallamai became a significant part of Hausa life. By 1850 the new Sokoto empire stretched almost 930 miles (1,500 km) and was the largest kingdom in Africa. The Mallamai used their newfound popularity to spread the word of Allah and became important teachers of Islam. The popularity of the Mallamai was pivotal in converting many local African populations to Islam in the 20th century.

See also: HAUSA (Vols. I, II); ISLAM (Vol. II); QURAN (Vol. II).

Mamluks Caucasian and Turkish soldiers, once held in servitude, who formed a dynasty that ruled EGYPT from the mid-13th until the early 16th century. The Mamluk dynasty was an intimidating military dictatorship, with new soldiers continuously being brought in from Turkey, the Balkans, and Russia. This kept the military perpetually renewed and gave the dynasty the strength to extend its control into Palestine and Syria.

The Mamluk army was known for a skillful cavalry, expert in its use of the sword and the bow and arrow. For centuries, Mamluk domination relied on these skills. By the 16th century, however, failure to utilize modern firearms and artillery led to the Mamluks' demise. In 1517, the Ottoman Turks conquered Egypt and the Mamluks.

See also: MAMLUKS (Vol. II); OTTOMAN EMPIRE AND AFRICA (Vol. III); WARFARE AND WEAPONS (Vol. III).

Further reading: Amirea El Azhary Sonbol, *The New Mamluks: Egyptian Society and Modern Feudalism* (Syracuse, N.Y.: Syracuse University Press, 2000); Phillip Thomas and Ulrich Haarmaan, *The Mamluks in Egyptian Politics and Society* (New York: Cambridge University Press, 1998).

Mamprusi (Mampruli, Manprussi) One of the seven main MOSSI STATES, named for the Mamprusi people, who settled in present-day northeastern GHANA and BURKINA FASO in the 14th century. The Mamprusi language is More-Gurma and is classified as a branch of the Niger-Congo language group.

Under Mossi rule, the Mamprusi kingdom flourished from the 14th to 18th centuries. During the Ashanti conquests of the mid-18th century, Mamprusi, along with DAGOMBA and GONJA, fell to Ashanti leader Asantehene Opokuware I (r. 1720–1750). In 1894 Mamprusi came under British control. Despite converting to Islam in the 18th century, the Mamprusi have maintained many of their traditional religious customs and practices.

See also: ASHANTI (Vol. II); ASHANTI EMPIRE (Vol. III); MAMPRUSI (Vol. II).

Mandara (Wandala) Kingdom of the Wandala people located to the south of the Lake CHAD region in what is now northern CAMEROON and NIGERIA. Also known as the Wandala state, Mandara was in its formative stages during the 15th century. It reached its height in the mid- to late 18th century.

By the 16th century the Mandara kingdom was dominated by four main groups—the Wandala, Gamergu, Velle, and Kerawa. It was the Wandala, however, who, because of their expertise in iron working and trading, controlled the kingdom. The Gamergu, on the other hand, were an agricultural and hunting people, while the Velle and Kerawa, although skilled in iron work, remained a weak group because of internal clashes.

The Mandara kingdom's location to the south of the Lake Chad area enabled it to participate in the trade of iron, agricultural products, and even human captives. In fact, Mandara became so powerful as a trading kingdom that, by the late 16th century, it had become a threat to KANEM-BORNU. As a result it was repeatedly attacked during the reign of Mai IDRIS ALAWMA (r. c. 1571–1603).

The Wandala and the KANURI of Kanem-Bornu apparently had been in contact with each other since the 13th century. Indeed, the name *Mandara* is the Kanuri-altered version of the word *Wandala*.

While it is known that the Wandala and other groups had inhabited the Mandara region for centuries, the kingdom's establishment is steeped in a 15th-century legend about a famous hunter named Gaya. Along with his two older brothers, Dunama and Rika, Gaya and his brothers were said to have traveled from Yemen (a present-day country in the Arabian Peninsula) to various towns before stopping to hunt near the capital town of Ishga-Kewe in the Mandara region. There they encountered the reigning queen, Sukda, and while Dunama and Rika gave the proper respect to the queen, Gaya is said to have walked past her to seat himself at her royal throne. Instead of punishing him, Queen Sukda was intrigued by Gaya's confidence. Showing him deference, she ignored his two brothers. The legend goes on to tell how Gaya and Sukda were married—Sukda then taking the title *nahungi*, or queen consort—and all but one subsequent ruler of the Mandara kingdom can be traced to their union. The capital was also moved from Ishga-Kewe to the town of Kerawa, and the villages later established by Rika and Dunama known as Kamburwa and Gawa, respectively, became provinces of Kerawa.

During the 17th century the Mandara kingdom faced conflicts with Hausa forces from KWARARAFA and ZAMFARA. Still it managed to grow, due in part to the decline of Kanem-Bornu after the death of Idris Alawma. Also contributing to this growth was the move of the kingdom's capital from Kerawa to the coastal trading town of Douala, which allowed for trade with Portugal, France, Britain, and Germany.

A successful army was also established at this time, led primarily by a cavalry force that became famous for horses bred in the Mandara region. Iron, usually in the form of bars and balls, also was traded, and the iron trade continued to grow as the kingdom gained more territory in the north and west. The 17th century also saw an influx of peoples such as the pastoral FULANI, Tubu traders, and nomadic Shuwa Arabs.

By the beginning of the 18th century continued Fulani migrations had begun to bring Islam to the Mandara kingdom. It was during the reign of Tlikse (King) Bukar Aji (r. c. 1715–1737) that Islam, despite the fact that it had been first resisted, became a powerful force within the region. Ultimately, Islam was accepted and became the predominant religion.

Of the Muslim kings who reigned after Bukar Aji, the two most prominent were Tlikse Bladi-a-Wandala (r. c. 1755–1773) and his son, Tlikse Bukar-a-Jama (or Bukar Guiama) (r. c. 1773–1828). Bladi was known to have been an active ruler who built mosques and fought battles to expand his kingdom. He is also credited with ending the Wandala tradition of killing the mother of each successive *tlikse*, even staying at the capital for an unusual length of time to be near his mother when she was ill. His successor, Bukar-a-Jama, was also known to be a strong ruler. Among his accomplishments was a great wall with six gates that encompassed the capital city of Douala. It was also during his reign that Mandara reached its apogee after successfully defeating the kingdom of Kanem-Bornu.

The Mandara kingdom continued to be an important power well into the 19th century. It was then that a series of clashes with the Fulani of the Fumbina (Fombina) states led to the kingdom's decline. Fulani dominance was short-lived, however, as Mandara was incorporated into German colonial territory in 1902.

See also: IRON (Vol. II); ISLAM, INFLUENCE OF (Vols. II, III, IV); TRADE AND COMMERCE (Vol. III); SLAVE TRADE, THE TRANSATLANTIC (Vol. III).

Mane Mande-speaking peoples largely located in present-day SIERRA LEONE, IVORY COAST, and LIBERIA. It is thought the Mane migrated toward the western Atlantic coast from the upper NIGER RIVER region by the early to mid-16th century. Their westward migrations were marked by intermittent stops where they conquered small communities and left behind a group to establish a new ruling state. The Mane were reputed to be outstanding soldiers who wore war shirts covered with feathers and amulets and carried shields fashioned from tight bundles of reeds.

In roughly 1540 a powerful Mane leader named Farma Tami (fl. c. 1540) invaded what is now Sierra Leone, conquered the local peoples, and from them founded the Temne people. The more powerful Mane, it was said, taught the Temne the art of war. With their talents at war, the Mane also brought improved methods of weaving and iron manufacture and more advanced systems of GOVERNMENT. Farma Tami moved the capital of his kingdom to the town of Robaga, near what is now the city of FREETOWN in present-day Sierra Leone.

By 1545 other groups of Mane people had turned back inland somewhat to reach the FOUTA DJALLON region in present-day GUINEA. Despite their reputation for being fierce warriors, the Mane were halted there in battles with the SUSU people and were forced to retreat toward the Atlantic coastline. Once established along the coast, the Mane began to trade commodities including cloth and salt with the DYULA and other merchant peoples for kola nuts, captives, and GOLD.

See also: KOLA NUTS (Vol. I); SALT (Vol. I); SALT TRADE (Vol. II); SLAVERY (Vol. III); TRADE AND COMMERCE (Vol. III).

Manyika (Manica) Shona-speaking people of present-day eastern ZIMBABWE and MOZAMBIQUE. The Manyika have historically been organized into small, independent communities. However, two large Manyika kingdoms, Mutasa and Makoni, emerged by the early 17th century. The Manyika organized into a more cohesive society in response to the presence of European colonists. Although primarily agriculturalists, the Manyika became prosperous traders after the discovery of GOLD in the region. From the 17th century, gold from Manicaland was traded along the Mozambique coast with Arab, Indian, and Portuguese merchants.

See also: SENA (Vol. III).

Maputo Port city and capital of present-day MOZAMBIQUE. Maputo was established as a trading post by Portuguese merchants who explored the area in 1544. It was not until 1787, however, that the Portuguese built a fortress around which a large settlement grew. Due to its deep harbor and proximity to present-day northern SOUTH AFRICA, the town thrived as a commercial center. In 1907 it became the capital of Portuguese East Africa.

See also: MAPUTO (Vol. V); PORTUGAL AND AFRICA (Vol. III).

Further reading: Mario J. Azevedo, *Historical Dictionary of Mozambique* (Lanham, Md.: Scarecrow Press, 2003).

Marabout War Religious movement led by Nasir al-Din (fl. 17th century), a cleric in present-day southern MAURITANIA, to curb European influence and establish orthodox Muslim rule in SENEGAMBIA. A marabout is a charismatic Islamic religious personality who inhabits a *ribat,* a fortified convent similar to a *zawiya.*

In 1659, hoping to capitalize on regional trade, France established a settlement on the island of Saint-Louis, at the mouth of the Senegal River. However, the settlement also had the effect of drawing trade away from the local BERBERS, who were led by the marabout, thus creating a grave economic crisis in the Senegal valley. The economic downturn fueled tensions between the marabout and the ruling Hassan warriors.

In response to the situation, Nasir al-Din started a religious movement, based on orthodox Islam, to save Berber society from economic collapse. The movement sought to create a Muslim theocratic state, thereby ending what it saw to be the arbitrary rule of the Hassan warriors. The movement also sought to reclaim some of the lucrative trade of the Senegal valley that the Berbers had lost to the French.

Quickly gaining popular support, the movement took on the aspects of a jihad, or holy war, and was able to overtake the ruling aristocracies of Walo, FOUTA TORO, KAYOR, and Jolof. But Nasir al-Din died in 1674, and the movement soon deteriorated. The French, fearing the emergence of a centralized marabout state, threw their support behind the former Hassan regimes in Walo, Fouta Toro, Kayor, and Jolof. By 1677 al-Din's movement faded, and, although the marabout retained religious authority, the old Hassan regime regained military and political control of the region.

See also: FRANCE AND AFRICA (Vol. III); ISLAM, INFLUENCE OF (Vol. III); JIHAD (Vols. II, IV).

Maravi Ethnic group that controlled the regions to the west and south of Lake Malawi in southern East Africa during the 16th and 17th centuries. The Maravi migrated eastward from the Luba regions of Central Africa. They settled over a vast geographical area that includes regions of three present-day countries: MALAWI (named after the Maravi), ZAMBIA, and MOZAMBIQUE.

About 1400 the Phiri clan assumed precedence among the peoples just south of Lake Malawi. By around 1480, a Maravi confederacy was established by the head of the Phiri clan. This confederacy acted as a centralized government for the various Bantu-speaking groups in the area. The chief of this confederacy, known as the KALONGA, was a member of the Phiri clan.

The name *kalonga* probably comes from the clan name of the original Luba peoples who migrated east and became known as the Maravi.

Much of the history of the various Maravi groups, and the region in general, is reconstructed from the oral traditions as well as the European accounts of the area, which begin shortly after 1500, when Portuguese merchants first arrived there. According to this history, the TUMBUKA, one of the oldest Maravi groups, settled along the western shore of Lake Malawi. They were a simple agriculturalist and pastoralist people who stayed in the northern Lake Malawi region as the Maravi moved further south. Another Maravi group, the Ngonde, led by a dynastic succession of chiefs called Kyungu, established dominion over the Karonga plain, in the northern region of present-day Malawi.

In the late 16th century the Lundu, a people of Maravi descent, instituted a reign of terror in reaction to the Portuguese attempts to control the IVORY TRADE in the region. Lundu warriors, known as ZIMBA, attacked settlements in regions of Zambezia, including the trading centers of SENA and TETE. The Zimba pushed east into the territory of the stateless MAKUA peoples of present-day Mozambique, routing the Portuguese from the area in 1592 and continuing up the coast to present-day KENYA, where they were finally repelled by a Swahili-Arab confederation. The reputation of the Maravi peoples as fierce warriors, largely derived from the actions of the Zimba, served to contain the Portuguese, who were reluctant to move inland from their coastal settlements, including MOZAMBIQUE ISLAND.

By 1624 the Maravi had established their dominion over the CHEWA inhabitants near Manthimba, a populous trading center at the southern end of Lake Malawi. They centralized their power and began a period of territorial expansion that spilled into regions of present-day Mozambique, to the south and east, and Zambia, to the west. Maravi chiefs increased their control by wisely integrating the head men of other non-Maravi groups—including the BANDA and Chewa—into their ruling hierarchy.

The most powerful Maravi ruler was Kalonga Masula (r. c. 1600–1650), whose kingdom stretched from Zambezia, in the west, to Mozambique Island, in the east. However, because Kalonga Masula failed to name a successor or establish centralized power, his Maravi empire gradually disintegrated after his death. Internecine rivalries between the Lundu and Kalonga slowed eastward expansion, but the Maravi enjoyed great success and influence in the 17th century as traders and regional power brokers.

The most influential activity of the Maravi in the 17th and 18th centuries was the ivory trade. Elephants were plentiful in the region to the west of Lake Malawi, so Maravian trading networks brought the tusks from the interior to the Shire River, the outlet of Lake Malawi, for TRANSPORTATION to the ZAMBEZI RIVER, and then on to the Arab and Swahili merchants who worked the markets on the Indian Ocean coast. The Portuguese, recognizing how lucrative the ivory trade was, tried to ally themselves with the Maravi as trading partners. Portuguese merchants and landowners called *prazeros* even recruited soldiers from among the Maravi in their attempts to expand their trading ties into Shona and Karanga territories, south of the Zambezi River.

By the middle of the 18th century several groups, including the Kalonga, Lundu, and Undi, had clearly become independent of central Maravi control. Undi (r. c. 1750), a chief of the Kalonga peoples, established a tributary kingdom by conquering the Nsenga peoples, southwest of Lake Malawi, and then establishing commercial ties with the Portuguese and the MWENE MUTAPA kingdom. Other peoples who began to identify less with the Maravi empire included the Sena, to the south, the Manganja, who were Lundu subjects, the Chewa, and the Zimba. Although these peoples distanced themselves from Maravi authority, they continued to participate in trade with them, producing iron goods and cloth and MINING salt.

One of the more conspicuous factors that contributed to the dissolution of the Maravi confederation was the loss of a powerful, centralized religious authority in the region. As they migrated, the Maravi peoples generally followed similar naturalistic religious practices that relied heavily on rain and fire rituals. The Manganja, for example, maintained the MBONA religious practices. These institutions began to disintegrate with the weakening of the central authority at Msinja in Lilongwe, who performed rituals that ensured the well-being of the semidivine rulers of the Maravi and, therefore, the well-being of the entire state. The sense of a Maravi spiritual community dissipated as the various groups developed their own ritual authorities over time.

During the 18th century the absence of a strong, centralized power left the Maravi unable to defend their territories against an influx of new waves of immigrants, who arrived from all directions. The influx of peoples, many of whom were looking to capitalize on the burgeoning trade in human beings, included settlers and traders from such diverse groups as the YAO, the BEMBA, the Bisa, and the NGONI, as well as Arabs and the Portuguese. By the beginning of the 19th century the former Maravi territory was overrun by these groups.

The Maravi name means "people of the fire," referring to the fact that the peoples who make up their group practiced a RELIGION that centered around fire rituals.

See also: INDIAN OCEAN TRADE (Vol. II); LUBA (Vol. II); LUBA EMPIRE (Vol. III); PORTUGAL AND AFRICA (Vol. III); SLAVE TRADE ON THE SWAHILI COAST (Vol. III).

Maroserana Dynastic ruling family of MADAGASCAR that produced the chiefs of several Malagasy-speaking ethnic groups, most important among them the SAKALAVA. Maroserana oral tradition tells of a semimythical ancestor called Andriandahifotsy, or "White King," who was not Malagasy but instead came with his family from India, having gotten caught in a storm and shipwrecked off Madagascar's southern coast around 1300.

The Maroserana dynasty was also known as the Volamena, or "Kingdom of the Gold." Since GOLD is not an especially prized metal among the Malagasy of Madagascar, the name Volamena indicates a possible connection to the gold-trading kingdom of the MWENE MUTAPA of southern Africa.

Maroserana rulers led the Lahefouty clan in Mahafaly, a southern Madagascar kingdom, around 1550. By around 1625, the dynasty emerged as the leaders of a confederacy of Malagasy peoples that included the Sakalava, a group of warriors who occupied land to the north of Mahafaly. Andriandahifotsy (r. c. 1660–c. 1685), a supposed descendant of the original White King, is generally considered the first Sakalava king. He led his warriors north along the west coast, conquering smaller kingdoms as they moved into new territories. Eventually, they controlled western Madagascar from the southern tip of the island to the northern parts of MENABE, on the central stretch of the west coast.

Upon Andriandahifotsy's death around 1685, his sons fought for succession. The victor, Tsimanongarivo (c. 1668–1718), remained in Menabe, to rule the Sakalava. Tsimanongarivo's brother, Tsimanatona, continued north to conquer the Muslim Boina peoples, adding their kingdom to the growing Sakalava empire.

European accounts of Tsimanongarivo written during his reign described him as a tyrant, bedecked in gold and silver, and living in a state of grandeur that was unknown in other kingdoms of Madagascar at the time. Tsimanatona, too, lived in high style, wearing a great silver chain and holding court on an EBONY throne decorated with ivory. By the end of the 18th century kings related to the Maroserana dynasty had ruled over nearly half of the island of Madagascar, including the kingdoms of the BARA, Antandroy, Antesaka, as well as the Sakalava, Mahafaly, and Boina.

The elaborate 16th-century tombs of the Sadian dynasty in Marrakech, Morocco. One of the two main mausoleums houses the tomb of the most important Sadi ruler, Abd al-Mansur (1578–1603). He conquered Songhai in 1591 and kept Morocco out of the hands of the Ottoman Empire. © *Karen Hunt/H. Mason/Corbis*

Marrakech (Marrakesh)   City located in present-day west-central MOROCCO. Founded in 1062, the city saw frequent changes in power and domination over the centuries. By the time the SADIAN DYNASTY seized control of the city in 1522, however, it was a poor place, largely in ruins. The Sadian caliphs revitalized Marrakech, making it the new capital of southern Morocco. Under Caliph ABD AL-MANSUR (1578–1603), the royal palaces of Marrakech were rebuilt, and the city recaptured the glory that it last enjoyed under the rule of the Almohads in the 12th and 13th centuries. By the end of the 16th century Marrakech was, culturally and economically, the leading city of Morocco, boasting about 60,000 inhabitants. The succeeding Alawite rulers, though, lived at FEZ or Meknès, using Marrakech primarily as a military post.

See also: MARRAKECH (Vols. II, IV, V).

Mascarene Islands   Group of islands in the western Indian Ocean, to the east of the large island of MADAGASCAR. The individual islands of MAURITIUS, RÉUNION, and Rodrigues are collectively known as the Mascarene Islands. They are named after the Portuguese sailor and eventual "vice-king" of Goa, Pedro Mascarenhas (1484–1555), who first visited the islands in 1512 while on his way to Portuguese India.

Masrui   Family dynasty associated with MOMBASA and East Africa, which, beginning in the mid-18th century, helped transform Mombasa into a major economic and political power. After their arrival, beginning with Vasco da Gama (c. 1460–1524) in 1498, the Portuguese dominated not only Mombasa but much of the East Africa coast. They continued this domination through both the 16th and 17th centuries. By the 18th century, however, Portuguese power had begun to wane, and the region came under the influence of the OMANI SULTANATE.

Although Omani power was considerable in the region, Oman was never able to take complete control. In part this was due to the fact that the various populations of the East African coast did not acquiesce to Omani rule any more than they did to that of the Portuguese. Instead, those populations sought help from anyone—even the Portuguese, who tried to return to Mombasa in 1748—willing to assist them in freeing themselves from a particular foreign invader.

Another factor in Oman's inability to assume firm control were the frequent conflicts and periods of unrest that marked its political life. These resulted in frequent civil and dynastic wars, one of which, beginning in 1741, led to rise of the Masrui family to power in Mombasa.

Oman launched its effort in East Africa by dispatching ships to Pate and ZANZIBAR in 1652. Although this expedition resulted in an Omani victory, Portugal continued to resist, and battles between the two powers went on for almost a half-century. It was not until the Omani victory at and capture of the Portuguese citadel of FORT JESUS, in 1698, that they finally were able to wrest control from their European adversaries.

In 1741 a member of the BUSAIDI family, Ahmad ibn Said, became involved in one of these dynastic wars and eventually seized control of Oman. In response the Omani governor of Mombasa, a member of the Masrui family, declared Mombasa's independence, only to be murdered by Busaidis. Eventually, however, the governor's brother was able to take power in Mombasa, establishing the Masrui dynasty that would play a major role in the region's political life for many years to come.

In contrast to the Busaidis, the Masruis identified themselves with Africa and African interests rather than with Arab ones, a fact that helped them solidify their position as Mombasa's main political family. In addition, they worked to mediate long-standing conflicts between the community's major civil federations. This led to a period of peace, cooperation, and prosperity at home.

Building upon this, the Masruis extended Mombasa's trade networks, particularly to the NYIKA people, who became important suppliers of goods and soldiers for Mombasa. Growing more ambitious, the Masruis sought to carry Mombasa's influence still further. Focusing, at first, on Pate, by the early 1800s they managed to assume control of that island as well.

Ultimately, however, the Masruis stretched Mombasa's power too far and too thin. In fact their victory over Pate, in 1807, proved to be their highwater mark. A few years later, they attempted to conquer LAMU, but met with a crushing defeat. More than this, their efforts resulted in direct involvement on the part of Oman's new ruler, SAYYID SAID (1791–1856). Shrewdly maneuvering his alliances with such European powers as Britain and France, Said managed to quickly consolidate and expand his own power. He was so successful that, by 1823, he managed to put Masrui power in check, limiting their sphere of influence to Mombasa itself.

A period of British and then Omani dominance ensued in Mombasa, followed by the return of the Masruis, in 1828. The dynasty's renaissance, however, proved to be short-lived. By 1837 the dynastic quarrels they had carefully avoided until then weakened them and gave Sayyid Said the opportunity he needed to take complete control of Mombasa.

Massa (r. 1650–1710) *Founder and first ruler of the Bambara kingdom of Kaarta*

King Massa was known for expanding the territory and influence of his kingdom during his 60-year reign in KAARTA, in present-day Republic of MALI. Massa descended from the Kulibali line of BAMBARA rulers, as did the early kings of Kaarta's sister state of SEGU, and founded his kingdom around the middle portion of the NIGER RIVER about the same time that Kaladian Kulibali (r. c. 1652–1682) established Segu in an area between the Niger and Senegal rivers. The ruling dynasty that Massa established in Kaarta, however, assumed his name and was known as the MASSASSI DYNASTY.

Massassi dynasty Succession of rulers who reigned in the BAMBARA state of KAARTA, located in present-day

MALI. The Massassi dynasty was comprised of descendants of MASSA (r. 1650–1710), the first king and founder of Kaarta. After the death of King Massa in 1710, his son Benefali (r. 1710–1745) assumed the throne and defended Kaarta in clashes against the forces of Mamari KULIBALI (r. 1712–1755) from the Bambara state of SEGU. In 1754 Mamari Kulibali was finally successful in conquering and destroying the original kingdom of Kaarta, ceasing the reign of Benefali's son and successor, Foulakoro (r. 1745–1754).

Kaarta was rebuilt in 1754 by the next Massassi successor, Sey Bamana Kulibali (r. 1754–1758). He was followed by his brother, Doni Babo (r. 1758–1761), who was known for leading the Bambara peoples into a more nomadic existence, as they gained wealth through raiding and ransacking smaller kingdoms. The ruler most often credited with Kaarta's rise as an important kingdom, however, was Sira Bo (r. 1761–1780). Sira Bo reestablished the Bambara as a sedentary people and, in 1777, extended the boundaries of Kaarta with the acquisition of tributary cities, including Bélédougou and Khasso. He also established a capital at the town of Guemou and forced several local groups, including the SONINKE and Diawara, to pay tribute to the Kaarta rulers.

Sira Bo's reign was followed by that of Dessé Koro (r. 1788–1799), who was defeated in battle in 1794 by the Segu king, Monson DIARRA (r. 1790–1808). Kaarta was demolished during this battle, and the next three Massassi rulers reigned over a weakened Kaarta kingdom. Beginning in 1818, with the rule of Bodian Moriba (r. 1818–1832), Kaarta was able to slowly recapture much of its former glory. Bodian Moriba became known as a powerful and influential ruler. Under his rule the capital was moved to Nioro, and much of Kaarta's former territory was regained. He was perhaps most famous, though, for finally ending the tensions between the kingdoms of Kaarta and Segu by making peace with the reigning Segu ruler, Da Monson (r. 1808–1827).

Bodian Moriba's successful tenure was followed by the reign of Garan, who ruled from 1832 to 1844. The Massassi dynasty came to an end shortly thereafter when the last Massassi ruler, Mamady Kandian (r. 1844–1854), was killed in 1854 during the jihad of TUKULOR cleric al-Hajj Umar Tal (1794–1864), who overthrew the kingdom of Kaarta and made it a part of his Muslim caliphate.

See also: FULANI JIHADS (Vol. III); UMAR TAL (Vol. IV).

Matamba MBUNDU kingdom of western Central Africa in what is now ANGOLA. Matamba reached the height of its influence during the 17th century under Queen NZINGA (1581–1663). In the early 16th century Matamba was a tributary state of the KONGO KINGDOM. The female chief, *muhongo Matamba,* offered payment to the king, or *manikongo,* in exchange for European goods traded in his kingdom. By the end of the 16th century, however, the *muhongo Matamba* had switched allegiance to the *ngola a kiluanje* ruler of the Mbundu kingdom of NDONGO. The *ngola a kiluanje* controlled new southern trade routes from the interior to the Portuguese-controlled port of LUANDA. In the 1570s Matamba fought along with Ndongo and Kongo armies against Portuguese efforts at colonization in Angola.

About 1630 the chiefdom of Matamba turned into a full-fledged kingdom. Queen NZINGA, the sister of the reigning *ngola a kiluanje,* seized power upon the death of the *muhongo Matamba.* Under Nzinga's rule Matamba became a formidable presence in the region, developing a strong military inspired by the IMBANGALA, and extending its territory to the Kwango River in the east and beyond the Lukala River in the west.

Matamba continued to resist Portuguese domination and played a large role in confining their rule to Angola. During the short-lived Dutch occupation of Luanda in the 1640s, which Nzinga had helped enable, Matamba warriors almost succeeded in destroying the last Portuguese bulwark in the colony. However, the Portuguese regained control of the region in 1648, and Matamba began to negotiate peace. In 1656 Matamba signed a treaty with the Portuguese that relinquished the kingdom's lands west of the Lukala River but retained its independence from the Europeans.

Hostilities between the two did not end, however, and another war broke out between Matamba and the Portuguese, in 1680. Matamba had irritated the Portuguese by bypassing Luanda for trade with the northern port and kingdom of LOANGO. Matamba armies defeated the Portuguese forces, and another peace treaty was signed in 1683. That treaty lasted until 1744, when a five-year war ensued after Matamba sacked a Portuguese market in the interior.

Matamba was a key player in the trade in human beings during this period. Trade fairs were set up in the capital, where Portuguese-sponsored traders, or *POMBEIROS,* purchased captives and ivory. The captives were often acquired through raids on the Kongo and Ndongo kingdoms by Matamba armies. By the middle of the 17th century Matamba and the KASANJE kingdom were the principal suppliers of captives to the Portuguese at Luanda. Traders from the northern Loango coast also traveled to Matamba to sell their goods, including firearms, which were especially valuable commodities in the southern kingdoms because they had been banned by the Portuguese authorities for sale to Africans. The Matamba rulers continued to control much of the interior trade during the 18th century, when routes began to penetrate further east into the LUNDA EMPIRE. The Lunda launched an attack on Matamba during the 1760s in an attempt to end Matamba's domination of the trade routes, but they were unsuccessful.

See also: IVORY TRADE (Vol. III); PORTUGAL AND AFRICA (Vol. III); SLAVE TRADE, THE TRANSATLANTIC (Vol. III); WARFARE AND WEAPONS (Vol. III).

Mauritania Present-day country of northwestern Africa, some 398,000 square miles (1,030,800 sq km) in size and bordered by ALGERIA, Republic of MALI, SENEGAL, and WESTERN SAHARA. During the 19th century the region of present-day Mauritania fell prey to the French campaign of colonial conquest in West Africa.

The BERBERS of Mauritania have been Muslims since the rise of the Almoravids in the 11th century. In the process, the Almoravids gained control of key Berber trading towns, which they dominated until the mid-13th century. Tensions between the Berber and Arab populations in Mauritania worsened over the next several hundred years. In 1673 Nasir al-Din, a Berber cleric, initiated a holy war against Arab warriors (Hassan). The Berbers were defeated, and the Hassan established a strict social order. Occupying the top rank were the Hassan Arabs, followed by Berber religious scholars (*zawiya*), Berber farmers and herders (*znaga*), former captives (*haratine*), and persons still in bondage (*abid*). The Hassan Arabs were primarily traders and soon developed a lucrative trade empire by selling captives and gum arabic to European traders. Dutch, French, Spanish, and Portuguese merchants all vied for Hassan Arab favor, paying them handsome sums for trade rights.

In 1814 France acquired Mauritania in the Treaty of Paris. The European power was primarily interested in controlling the coastal port towns and the fertile Senegal River region and therefore left the northern interior largely untouched. France ruled Mauritania until 1960.

See also: FRANCE AND AFRICA (Vol. III); MAURITANIA (Vols. I, II. IV, V).

Further reading: Anthony G. Pazzanita, *Historical Dictionary of Mauritania* (Lanham, Md.: Scarecrow Press, 1996).

Mauritius Small island nation in the Indian Ocean, situated approximately 500 miles (805 km) east of MADAGASCAR. Measuring approximately 720 square miles (1,870 sq km), Mauritius includes the inhabited island of Rodrigues and other scattered coral atolls, such as Cargados Carajos and Agalega. Mauritius was formed more than 10 million years ago by an active volcano. The main island is almost completely surrounded by coral reefs, and contains a wide range of terrain, including low-lying plains, mountains, rivers, forests, and a central plateau. This terrain, coupled with the tropical climate, has provided the island with hundreds of square miles of arable land. Mauritius's ECONOMY has historically relied on one crop, sugarcane.

Although visited for centuries by Arab, Malay, and Portuguese sailors, Mauritius remained unsettled until the late 16th century. The Dutch occupied the island in 1598 and remained there until the early 1700s. The French took possession in 1715, but the British captured the island during the Napoleonic Wars (1801–15). Mauritius was formally relinquished to Great Britain in 1814, and Britain ruled the country for the next 150 years.

The history of the island has resulted in a diverse population, much of which is of French or Creole (mixed African and European) descent. There are also small groups of Europeans and Chinese in the country. Nearly two-thirds of the population is descended from people from India who, with the end of the slave trade, were brought to Mauritius as indentured LABOR by British and other plantation owners.

See also: MASCARENE ISLANDS (Vol. III); MAURITIUS (Vols. I, II, IV, V).

Further reading: Anthony J. Baker, *Slavery and Antislavery in Mauritius, 1810–1833: The Conflict between Economic Expansion and Humanitarianism* (New York: St. Martin's Press, 1996); Marina Carter, *Servants, Sirdars, and Settlers: Indians In Mauritius 1834–1874* (New York: Oxford University Press, 1995); Perry J. More, *A Concise History of Dutch Mauritius, 1598–1710* (New York: Kegan Paul, 1998); Auguste Toussaint, *History of Mauritius* (London: Macmillan, 1977).

Mawlay Ismail (Mulay Isma'il) (c. 1645–1727)
Second sultan of the Alawite dynasty of Morocco

Malawi Ismail's half-brother, Mawlay al-Rashid (d. 1672), founded the Alawite dynasty of present-day MOROCCO in 1666 and by force brought order to a region that had suffered from 50 years of religious and political warfare between local sheiks and the holy men, known as marabouts, who led Sufi religious brotherhoods. To reach his goals Mawlay al-Rashid mobilized the Arab peoples who had moved into the region during the Almohad period (c. 1147–1271) and pitted them against the BERBERS, who dominated the Atlas Mountains and parts of northern Morocco since the 1640s. He died an accidental death before he could consolidate his rule, and the Berbers remained a threat. Furthermore, England, Spain, and Portugal were in control of Morocco's coastal cities and the trade revenues they generated. The Alawite dynasty has ruled in Morocco until the present day.

Not much is known about the early life of Mawlay Ismail, whose full name is Ismail ibn Sharif, until he became the provincial viceroy of the city of FEZ during the rule of Mawlay al-Rashid. After al-Rashid died in early 1672, Ismail seized control of the treasury storehouse, known as the MAKHZAN, and had himself declared sultan in April of the same year.

Sharif and *mawlay* are titles, not names. *Sharif*, meaning "noble" or "high born" in Arabic, is a title of nobility that, in the early days of Islam, was used to designate members of the prophet Muhammad's Hashim clan. The Alawite dynasty claims descent from the Prophet through Muhammad's daughter Fatima and her husband, Ali, the fourth caliph. Females in the Sharifian line bear the title *Lella*.

Mawlay, from an Arabic word meaning "lord," is the same word that comes into English spelled *mullah*. In the Middle East, *mullah* designates a religious leader. In Morocco and other parts of North Africa, *mullah* is an honorific used with the name of a king, a sultan, or other noble.

Until 1677, Ismail's rule was disputed by his brother, his nephew Ahmad ibn Muhriz (d. 1686), and a northern Moroccan leader named al-Khidr Ghilan (d. 1673). These rivals had the support of the Ottoman Turks' regent in neighboring ALGERIA, who desired to weaken Alawite control and dominate Morocco. By 1673, however, Ghilan had been defeated by the sultan's forces and, in the years that followed, both Ismail's brother and nephew were brought into the administration as regional governors. Nevertheless, the peace between Ismail and his nephew, Muhriz, did not last. It ended only when Muhriz was finally killed by Ismail, in 1686, after Muhriz successfully enticed the people of Fez into rebellion against Mawlay Ismail's rule. With the defeat of his rivals, Mawlay Ismail was finally able to bring Morocco under unified leadership.

Like the reign of his brother Rashid before him, the major part of Mawlay Ismail's rule was spent at odds with the Ottoman Empire. The Ottomans were seeking to displace the Alawite rulers and regain control of Morocco from their base located to the west in the city of ALGIERS, located in present-day Algeria. To counteract this threat, Mawlay Ismail created an elite professional military force of captives known as the *Abids*. The Abids were made up of descendants of prisoners of war who had been brought back to Morocco after Morocco's defeat of the SONGHAI Empire (present-day Republic of MALI), in the 1590s. The Abids, who numbered over 150,000 soldiers at full strength, were given intense, specialized training and armed with European firearms. This army allowed Mawlay Ismail to effectively defeat the Ottoman forces in 1679, 1682, and 1695–96, thereafter securing Moroccan independence from Ottoman rule.

Mawlay Ismail also mounted campaigns to control Morocco's coastal cities. He recaptured TANGIER from the British (1684), Arzila from the Portuguese (1691), and both al-Mahdiyya (1681) and Larache (1689) from the Spanish. Despite these campaigns against the Europeans, Mawlay Ismail understood that Morocco's ECONOMY was, to a large extent, based on trade with countries in Europe. He chose to forge a strong relationship with France because of that country's political rivalry with Spain. This alliance provided Mawlay Ismail a military edge in his fight to regain the cities that the Spanish occupied.

Ruling for 54 years, Mawlay Ismail is credited with having one of the longest and most successful reigns in the history of Islamic states, second only to the 58-year reign of the 11th-century Egyptian ruler al-Mustansir (r. 1036–1094).

In addition, Mawlay Ismail greatly admired the French king, Louis XIV (r. 1643–1715), and attempted to emulate him by his manner of ruling and by designing his capital at Meknès in the architectural style of the French court at Versailles. With this French-Moroccan alliance came greater military strength for Ismail's armies and an increase in economic benefits for both France and Morocco.

On a personal level, Ismail himself was an extremely devout Muslim who was known to have adhered to the strict rules of Islamic law and who consistently sought to convert others to the Muslim religion. His rule was also marked by allegations of cruelty and brutal force. Mawlay Ismail had four wives and possibly as many as 700 children and 500 concubines. After his death in March of 1727, his most successful son, Mawlay Ahmad, was proclaimed sultan.

See also: ALMOHADS (Vol. II); ENGLAND AND AFRICA (Vol. III); FRANCE AND AFRICA (Vol. III); ISLAM, INFLUENCE OF (Vols. II., III); MARABOUT WAR (Vol. III); PORTUGAL AND AFRICA (Vol. III); TRADE AND COMMERCE (Vol. III); SPAIN AND AFRICA (Vol. III); SUFISM (Vols. II, III, IV); WARFARE AND WEAPONS (Vol. III).

Further reading: Rahma Bourqia and Susan Gilson Miller, *In the Shadow of the Sultan: Culture, Power, and Politics in Morocco* (Cambridge, Mass.: Harvard University Press, 1999).

Mazagan (el-Jadida) Port city in north-central MOROCCO settled by the Portuguese in 1502. Mazagan was fortified as the last stronghold in the Portuguese struggle against the Filali sultanate. The Portuguese lost control of the city in 1769. Deemed an infidel city and unsuitable for Muslim habitation, Mazagan was not resettled until Moroccan Jews occupied the town in 1821.

See also: PORTUGAL AND AFRICA (Vol. III).

Mbona Legendary priest who is worshiped as a rain god by the Manganja people of the southern Shire River valley in present-day MALAWI. The rituals related to Mbona worship functioned as an expression of shared values and as a way of retaining a symbolic history of past events. From the 1580s to the 1620s Mbona worship practices were especially influential in determining the way land was distributed among the MARAVI peoples.

According to Manganja oral tradition, Mbona was a rain priest who was decapitated by his enemies. Even after dying, his blood continued to pour from his headless body, eventually forming a river. The Ndione Pool, located not far from the Mbona shrine in Nsanje, Malawi, is celebrated as the place where Mbona was martyred.

Worship practices like the Mbona rites, sometimes called "Earth cults" or "fertility cults," serve functions both spiritual and political. In many traditional African cultures, the spirits of the ancestors are thought to exercise extraordinary influence over local natural phenomena. Venerating and placating the ancestors, then, is a way of warding off floods or droughts and guaranteeing a plentiful harvest. When other Maravi peoples moved into their region in the late 16th century, the Manganja were able to use the Mbona myth as a charter, or original claim, to the surrounding land. If outsiders could not simply force their own beliefs on the Manganja, they had two options: either accept and perpetuate the Mbona myth and settle alongside the Manganja, or move on to unoccupied territory.

It was thought that the consumption of millet beer helped the priests and headmen to commune better with the spirits during the Mbona rites. On the other hand, celebrants were instructed to abstain from sex during the ritual cycle, for fear that the "heat" of sexual thoughts might work against the desired effect of bringing cool rain.

The Mbona shrine, located on the Shire just north of SENA on the ZAMBEZI RIVER, was a simple circular hut with a clay floor and a roof made of sticks. Mbona celebrants annually gathered at the shrine at the end of the dry season to pray to their ancestors and to beseech Mbona for plentiful rain in the upcoming wet season. When an older shrine fell into disrepair, it was disassembled and a new one was constructed following a prescribed ritual.

The Mbona shrine was traditionally maintained by an older woman selected by the priests to be Mbona's "spirit wife." The spirit wife, named Salima after Mbona's original wife, supposedly received Mbona's messages in her dreams. The Salima also oversaw female initiation rites at Nsanje.

See also: ANCESTOR WORSHIP (Vol. I); RELIGION (Vols. I, II, III, IV, V).

Further reading: J. Matthew Schoffeleers, *River of Blood: The Genesis of a Martyr Cult in Southern Malawi, c. A.D. 1600* (Madison, Wisc.: University of Wisconsin Press, 1992).

Mbundu Large Kimbundu-speaking ethnic group of western Central Africa whose homeland is located in what is now the country of ANGOLA. The Mbundu kingdoms were greatly affected by the transatlantic SLAVE TRADE and Portuguese colonization during the 1600s. By the 16th century Mbundu ethno-linguistic subgroups included the LIBOLO, SONGO, Mbondo, Lenge, NDONGO, PENDE, and Hungu, among others. They occupied primarily the highlands of modern-day Angola, from the Longa River in the south to the Bengo and Dande rivers in the north, and past the Kwango River to the east. Steep escarpments separated them from the African coast. The Mbundu were bordered in the south by the OVIMBUNDU and in the north by the KONGO KINGDOM, which by that time was more similar in language and culture to the Mbundu than were the Ovimbundu.

The Mbundu were mostly farmers who cultivated millet and sorghum as staple crops, which they supplemented with fruits and vegetables. During the 17th century they began to cultivate cassava, which had been introduced from the Americas. The Mbundu also fished, hunted game, and kept small animals, including chickens and goats. They herded some cattle, but only at the highest elevations, where the deadly tsetse fly could not reach. Salt and iron were important commodities for trade with groups in the interior, who supplied the Mbundu with copper, palm cloth, ivory, and other items.

During the 16th century local symbols of political authority, the *ngola,* gave way to the formation of the more centralized *ngola a kiluanje* and *kinguri* kingships, which were adopted by most Mbundu states in Angola. Formerly autonomous chiefdoms were consolidated into kingdoms, including Ndongo and MATAMBA. These kingdoms developed lucrative trade routes from the African interior to the ports of LUANDA and LOANGO. They successfully competed with the Kongo for European trade and challenged their status as the most powerful kingdom in western Central Africa during the precolonial period.

During the 1600s the Portuguese began to aggressively colonize Angola and sought to subjugate the Mbundu. Despite frequent wars, the eastern Mbundu state of Matamba was able to resist Portuguese domination and maintain profitable trade relations, largely because they remained outside the immediate sphere of Portuguese influence in western Angola, and because of their participation in supplying captives for the slave trade. Other western kingdoms, including Ndongo, were unable to maintain their independence. Their kings became puppets of the Portuguese colonial administration, and their kingdoms were frequent targets of predatory raids. By the 17th century, European MISSIONARIES in Angola reported that the previously heavily populated Mbundu country had become a wasteland.

See also: MBUNDU (Vol. II).

medicine While medical practices differed from region to region, most African groups engaged in one or more traditional healing techniques that included such concepts as magic potions, amulets, incantations, and divination. These remedies were often performed by healers, diviners, or village priests, who were revered for their abilities and sometimes considered divine or quasi-divine because of their talents. Through documented reports written by European travelers who traversed the continent in the 16th through the 18th centuries, it has become evident that Africans maintained a highly complex knowledge of medicine and surgical techniques. Medicine in Africa was often deeply rooted in lore not typically associated with the Western scientific tradition of medicine (i.e., so-called ancestor worship and the supernatural). Still, African medicine often reflected knowledge of biology, physiology, and psychology that was decades, if not centuries, ahead of European or Asian knowledge of the same period.

One of the areas in which African medicine excelled was the derivation of healing potions, both ingested and topical, through the use of herbs, roots, fruit extracts, and other naturally occurring substances such as honey. While the application of these concoctions was often the realm of the healers, it was known that village women were often instrumental in the collection, preparation, and proper use of the medicine on an ailing member of the community. Many women also acted as midwives and greatly facilitated the birthing process of the pregnant women they attended through the use of massage. This hands-on method was widely used by such groups as the MAASAI of present-day KENYA and helped to relax certain muscles, stimulate the production of contraction-producing hormones, and even enabled the midwife to help rotate a breached child so that it was properly positioned in the birth canal. When the birthing process became protracted, however, African healers such as those in the villages of the BUNYORO in present-day UGANDA were known to have performed a Caesarean section as a last resort.

In fact, detailed accounts by European witnesses state that African healers were extremely skilled in performing the Caesarean operation as well as other centuries-old procedures, such as amputations. Especially noted in these accounts was that the African surgeons were knowledgeable in certain herbs and alcohols that aided in both the sedation of the patient as well as the sterilization of both the instruments used for surgery and the body parts involved. They were extremely clean in their practices did not overuse the tools at their disposal. For example, red hot irons were sometimes used to quickly cut off and seal bleeding points, but were known to cause great harm if used too often or for too long a time. Therefore the irons were used sparingly and, hence, to their greatest effect. Whether it was potions, ointments, or surgical tools, the use of these items was usually well thought out and to the maximum benefit to the patient and his or her healing time.

The use of sun exposure to aid in the health and growth of a sick or premature baby was a common treatment used by some African midwives. These women would take the child out into the sun for variable lengths of time to give the newborn child strength. This practice was a precursor to today's method of incubation, whereby a newborn child is placed in a warm enclosure to facilitate its healthy development.

Another aspect of African medicine that had been intact long before European colonization was the idea of community health procedures, such as the prevention of disease spread through quarantine. When European traders brought the smallpox disease to areas of sub-Saharan Africa that were previously unexposed, certain groups, such as the Mano people of what is now LIBERIA, already had in place a quarantine procedure to deal with the spread and treatment of the disease. When a member of their community became infected, that person would be taken away from the village to an area known as the "sick bush." There, the patient would be treated with topical ointments that helped treat the itching and would be fed a special diet to speed up the healing time. The treatment was carried out by a solitary attendant in order to reduce the likelihood of the disease spreading throughout the village. Once the patient had recovered, the "sick bush" was burned, thereby killing any lingering germs and further decreasing the chances of the smallpox affecting others within the community.

It is also thought that the Africans were the first peoples to effectively introduce inoculation as a method of fighting off a disease epidemic such as smallpox. Possibly centuries before the renowned British doctor Edward Jenner (1749–1823) gave the first smallpox vaccine in England in 1796, African traditional doctors were using thorns laced with the infected fluid from a smallpox lesion to scratch an uninfected person. This process induced the uninfected patient's body to produce an immune response to the smallpox contagion, generally without developing the disease itself. If the illness progressed, however, it was more often than not a weak, non-life-threatening form of smallpox, which still successfully triggered the immune response and protected the patient from any further outbreaks of the disease.

Before European medicine made its way to the African coast, indigenous African doctors were also known to be capable in treating a host of ailments. Examples include the setting of and use of traction on broken bones, the surgical extraction of foreign objects—such as arrowheads and bullets—from the body, the draining of abscesses, the reduction of tumors, and the removal of cataracts from the eyes. These early traditional healers mostly learned by being highly observant and cognizant of the reactions—good and bad—that their methods produced. This knowledge would then be passed down to future generations, with the recipients acquiring the accumulated knowledge and skills of thousands of years of treatment and observation.

See also: DIVINATION (Vol. I); DISEASE IN ANCIENT AFRICA (Vol. I); DISEASE IN COLONIAL AFRICA (Vol. IV); DISEASE IN MEDIEVAL AFRICA (Vol. II); DISEASE IN MODERN AFRICA (Vol. V); DISEASE IN PRECOLONIAL AFRICA (Vol. III); HEALERS AND DIVINERS (Vols IV, V); MEDICINE (Vols. I, II, IV, V); SCIENCE (Vols. I, II, III, IV, V).

Further reading: Ivan Van Sertima, ed. *Blacks in Science: Ancient and Modern* (London: Transaction Books, 1983).

Menabe Kingdom and ethnic group of the western coastal region of the island of MADAGASCAR. Menabe was founded by the SAKALAVA people in the late 17th century. Along with Boina, Menabe was one of the most powerful kingdoms of the Sakalava empire.

Several Sakalava traditions say that the name *Menabe,* meaning "The Great Red," comes from a red bull that was employed by the Sakalava to defeat the Antanandro during their campaigns of territorial expansion in the latter half of the 17th century. Thereafter, according to the legend, the Sakalava were forbidden from killing red bulls.

Before the founding of Menabe, the territory was known as Ansakuabe, a sparsely populated region of small villages. After many years of warfare and conflict, the MAROSERANA king, Andriandahifotsy (r. c. 1660–1685), led his Sakalava warriors to victory over the local peoples, including the Vazimba, Vezo, and Antanandro. Eventually, the Menabe kingdom controlled the stretch of coast from the Onilahy River in the south to Boina Bay in the north and even exacted tribute from inland kingdoms.

Upon the death of Andriandahifotsy, the "White King" of the Sakalava, his two sons, Tsimanongarivo (c. 1668–1718) and Tsimanatona, fought for succession. The victor, Tsimanongarivo, established his capital in Menabe, while his brother moved north to conquer more territory for the Sakalava empire.

Mende West African peoples who migrated to their locations in present-day SIERRA LEONE, GUINEA, and LIBERIA by the 16th century or earlier. During the 16th century, however, some Mende who lived in the FOUTA DJALLON region of present-day Guinea fled the area and moved to what is now Sierra Leone. This migration was forced by the pressures the Muslim FULANI peoples were exerting as they swept through the area in an attempt to convert those practicing traditional religions to Islam. The mid-16th century also saw a group of Mende travel from present-day Liberia to Sierra Leone and establish regional states that eventually became the Koor, in the east, and the Kpa and Wajama, in the south.

The Mende speak a Mande language, possibly indicating a cultural origin in the western Sudan. Historically, they are an agrarian people who cultivate yams, PALM OIL, cassava, and rice. They are also known for their secret societies, which get encompassed into their daily lives as ways to help in legal, educational, and social protocol decisions. The men's society is called *poro* and is important to any Mende man wishing to have authority within his community. The women also take part in their own version of the secret society, called *sande*, and, like the men, their ceremonies utilize masks that represent important spirits. It is believed that the Mende are the only African ethnic group practicing a secret society in which both the women and the men wear ceremonial masks.

See also: SECRET SOCIETIES (Vol. I).

Further reading: Arthur Abraham, *An Introduction to the Precolonial History of the Mende of Sierra Leone* (Lewiston, N.Y.: Edwin Mellen Press, 2003); Melissa Leach, *Rainforest Relations: Gender and Resource Use among the Mende of Gola, Sierra Leone* (Washington, D.C.: Smithsonian Institution Press, 1994).

Merina Ethnic group inhabiting the city of TANANARIVE and the surrounding central highlands of the island of MADAGASCAR. In the 18th century the Merina began a period of territorial expansion that eventually brought nearly the entire island under their rule. Today, the Merina are the most populous of the Malagasy-speaking people of Madagascar.

The name *Merina* means "people from the place where one can see far," in Malagasy, the language of Madagascar. This appellation refers to the fact that they are from the mountainous central region of the island.

The Merina emerged from the conflicts between the Vazimba people and Indonesian invaders called the Hova. The Vazimba were probably of African or Afro-Indonesian origin and settled in the central region of Madagascar, perhaps as early as the 13th century. Around the middle of the 16th century, Hova groups began penetrating Vazimba territory from the southeast, beginning a conflict that lasted nearly 100 years. An early Hova king was Andriamanelo (r. c. 1540–1575), who introduced the use of iron-tipped spears, giving his warriors an advantage over the Vazimba, who fought with only clay-tipped spears.

According to Merina oral tradition, the wars between the Vazimba and the Hova were eventually settled through the intervention of a group of Antonosy sages, known as Marinh, which is probably the source of the name Merina. When the territorial dispute was settled, the combined Vazimba and Hova peoples rapidly consolidated their power, and early Merina society reflected influence from both groups. For example, the traditional practice of so-called ancestor worship came from the Vazimba. The Hova brought to Merina culture the practice of endogamy, or marriage within the group.

By the middle of the 17th century the Merina were expanding in all directions, cultivating vast areas of rice paddies and acquiring good cattle and grazing lands. The Merina kingdom, Imerina, was protected by disciplined clan militias, who were supported by the state.

Much of what is known of Merina history comes from the *Tantara ny Andriana* (History of Kings). The Tantara was assembled from the accounts of numerous Merina oral historians by a French Jesuit priest named Father François Callet, who arrived in Tananarive in 1864.

During the 17th century, while the SAKALAVA were building their western coastal empire in Madagascar, the Merina thrived in their isolated highland kingdom and remained relatively unknown. By the middle of the 18th century they were in good position to challenge the Sakalava for control of the greater part of the island. Merina king ANDRIANAMPOINIMERINA (r. c. 1782–1810), a dynamic ruler and statesman, established his capital at Tananarive (today's Antananarivo). From there he began to centralize his authority over the vast Merina territories. It was early in his reign, around 1785, that the first European visited Imerina. Under Andrianampoinimerina's capable leadership, the Merina grew rich and powerful by trading Malagasy captives for French firearms. By 1830 the Merina had overwhelmed the Sakalava and controlled practically the whole island except for the kingdoms of the BARA and a few other southern groups.

Further reading: Pier Martin Larson, *History and Memory in the Age of Enslavement: Becoming Merina in Highland Madagascar 1770–1822* (Portsmouth, N.H.: Heinemann, 2000).

Mfecane (Difaqane) Period of ZULU warfare and migration lasting from 1817 to the 1840s. The Mfecane, (meaning "The Crushing," led to the breakdown of the traditional clan system within the Zulu kingdom and caused the formation and reorganization of several kingdoms. It also accounted for the deaths of more than 2 million people.

The perilous middle passage, the slave ship's journey from Africa to the Americas. The terminally ill and the mutinous were often thrown overboard, as this undated woodcut shows. Some 14 to 20 percent of the enslaved humans aboard ship generally perished during this part of the journey. © *Corbis*

The Mfecane began in 1817, when Zulu king SHAKA (1787–1828) embarked on a program of conquest. In order to expand his kingdom, which was located in the present-day province of KwaZulu-Natal, SOUTH AFRICA, Shaka set out to conquer or subjugate a number of neighboring peoples, including the Ndwandwe and Qwabe. Shaka's efforts at conquest expanded further by 1820, leading to large-scale migrations throughout the region, as people fled the Zulu forces. Some peoples fled to places as far away as present-day TANZANIA, MALAWI, and ZAMBIA.

The Mfecane resulted in the formation of several kingdoms. MSHWESHWE (1786–1870), for example, united his followers in present-day LESOTHO, which led to the formation of the SOTHO nation. Elsewhere, Mzilikazi (1790–1868) established the Ndebele kingdom in present-day ZIMBABWE, while the Gaza empire was founded by Soshangane (d. 1858) in MOZAMBIQUE, and the NGONI settled in present-day Tanzania.

See also: NDEBELE (Vol. IV); WARFARE AND WEAPONS (Vol. III).

Mfengu (Fingo) Ethnic group inhabiting the Eastern Cape province of present-day SOUTH AFRICA who were forced from their homelands in Natal during the MFECANE, a migration forced by ZULU military campaigns in the early 19th century. The Mfengu are primarily descendants of Hlubi, Bhele, and Zizi peoples, and they made their way to the eastern Cape, where they helped the British fight the XHOSA during the CAPE FRONTIER WARS. In return for their service the victorious British government gave the Mfengu former Xhosa lands in the Transkei and Ciskei regions. The Mfengu occupation of those lands served to buffer any further Xhosa attacks on the British colony. These new Mfengu lands were annexed into CAPE COLONY in 1879.

See also: SHAKA (Vol. III).

middle passage Name given to the The 21- to 90-day voyage of captive Africans' across the Atlantic Ocean from Africa to the Caribbean. The transatlantic SLAVE TRADE is often visualized as a triangular trade. On the first leg of the triangle, goods from Europe were loaded aboard ships and brought to Africa. On the second leg, the so-called middle passage, the ships were loaded with Africans, who were transported amid conditions of great squalor and danger to destinations in the Caribbean. On the third leg of the triangle, agricultural products and other commodities, sometimes bought from the proceeds of the sale of Africans to local purchasers, were shipped to Europe. Although the visualization is inexact when North American trade and ports of call are added to the trade, the term *middle passage* has maintained its traditional meaning.

Sailing ships were generally not built to specifically carry captives. Instead, a ship's standard hold inside the hull was modified to accept human cargo. Manifests list from 150 to 600 Africans depending on the size of the vessel. They were chained to platforms that were stacked in tiers in the hold, given limited headroom, and allowed a space not much more than 16 inches (40 cm) wide in which to lay their bodies.

Africans sold into captivity came into the barracoons, or slave pens, at WHYDAH, GORÉE ISLAND, and other slave ports in West Africa a few at a time as they were brought from the interior to the coast. A slave ship might wait in port for a month or even the better part of a year before collecting enough slaves to continue the journey. The slaves were generally housed and fed ashore during that time, while the ship was being refitted to carry a human cargo. When the Africans were loaded aboard ship, a barrier was generally erected to block their last views of their homeland.

The crowded conditions aboard slave ships was so severe, the ventilation so poor, and the rations of rice, yams, or millet so limited that ship owners expected that 14 percent to 20 percent of their human cargo would die during the crossing. An estimated 10 to 12 million captive Africans reached the Americas after surviving the middle passage.

The causes of death were many. Despondent about being forced from their homes or fearful of the unknowns they might encounter at the end of the voyage, a number of the individuals committed suicide. In good weather the captives were allowed to sit on deck to get fresh air and exercise, during which time their quarters were cleaned and aired out. In bad weather, however, they were forced to remain below deck for days, seasick, amid excrement and vomit, in conditions that often led to death from dysentery and fever. Males were generally kept shackled to the deck or to one another to prevent mutiny, which was the fear of every captain whose vessel carried a human cargo. Attempted mutinies were viciously and quickly quelled, and the bodies of the mutineers thrown overboard.

The number of deaths in the middle passage often went unrecorded. They could be as few as four of the 207 captives from the Congo River region who were taken to Havana, Cuba, in 1835 aboard the Spanish ship *Amalia* or as many as 360 of the 560 human captives from MADAGASCAR destined for Cuba aboard the *Aguila Vengadora* in 1837 or the 702 Africans drowned while chained below deck aboard the *Leusden* near Surinam, in 1738.

Most of the Africans on board were destined for Portuguese Brazil or the hot, humid sugar plantations in the Caribbean. In the 18th century, for example, Spanish Cuba and Barbados, St. Christopher, the Bermudas, and Jamaica in the British-owned West Indies all required constant replenishment of their LABOR force. As many as 40 percent of the Africans brought directly into British North America were landed at Charleston, in South Carolina. They were held in quarantine on Sullivan Island in the harbor until they were sold in Charleston's slave market.

See also: SLAVERY (Vols. I, III, IV).

Mijikenda (Wanyika) People inhabiting the East African coast of present-day KENYA not considered to be Swahili in language, culture, or economic activity. The name *Mijikenda,* meaning "Nine Towns," refers to the nine fortified centers, called *kayas,* occupied by these peoples, who include the Chonyi, Digo, Duruma, GIRIAMA, Jibana, Kauma, Kambe, Ribe, and Rabai.

Although oral traditions of both the Swahili and the Mijikenda maintain that the Mijikenda, like the POKOMO, originated in the town of SHUNGWAYA and migrated to their eventual homeland during the 16th century, the true origins of these peoples remains unknown. What is known is that, for centuries, they inhabited the hinterlands immediately beyond the narrow coastal band occupied by the Swahili.

Resisting conversion to Islam, the Mijikenda developed a culture that was at once independent and closely linked to that found on the SWAHILI COAST. Over the centuries, the Mijikenda enjoyed a client-group relationship with the Swahili. The Mijikenda provided the Swahili with protection from attacks by the MAASAI and OROMO. They also engaged in trade with various inland peoples, acting as intermediaries between those inland groups and the Swahili traders of the coast. In exchange for all this, they received a share of the profits enjoyed by the Swahili, whose extensive trade network carried inland goods to ports as far away as Arabia and India. The Mijikenda also received Swahili protection from attacks from the sea.

The arrival of the Portuguese in the 16th century disrupted this relationship between the Mijikenda and Swahili. As more and more people fled the coast, moving inland to escape the Portuguese, the Mijikenda increased and grew more powerful. Building fortified areas, from which they could attack the coast, they soon began to assume a far more dominant role than they had in the past. By 1592, in some areas, they were even collecting tribute from the Portuguese.

In the years that followed, the Mijikenda grew even stronger. The Portuguese, however, consistently carried out a policy that included ambushes, looting, and raids to take captives. These weakened the Mijikenda considerably, eventually forcing them to move further into the hill country beyond the coast.

See also: INDIAN OCEAN TRADE (Vol. II); PORTUGAL AND AFRICA (Vol. III).

Mindouli Town located in what is now western Republic of the CONGO known for its large deposits of copper. Mindouli was part of the LOANGO kingdom, which was founded prior to the 16th century but reached the height of its influence from the late 16th century to the late 17th century during the reign of kings from the Vili ruling clan. The MINING of copper in Mindouli was extremely profitable to the Loango, and the metal became a powerful symbol of wealth throughout the groups of the outlying savanna regions. Copper mined at Mindouli was formed into necklaces, bracelets, and other adornments, and then traded along with other items, such as raffia cloth and ivory, by the Vili merchants. In the 17th century the MINING operations at Mindouli were controlled by the neighboring TEKE people, but the export and trade of the copper that was mined was successfully retained by the Vili. Also at this time, the Loango kingdom had begun trading copper on a fairly large scale with the Dutch, which further expanded the wealth of the kingdom. The mining of copper was then increased, and by about 1660 a tradition had been established by which groups of coppersmiths and novice miners from the Niari valley would come to the Mindouli region and beyond to work the copper mines from September until the onset of the next year's dry season.

See also: COPPER (Vol. II); IVORY TRADE (Vol. III); NETHERLANDS AND AFRICA (Vol. III).

mining Minerals and metals such as salt, GOLD, copper, and iron have long been extracted from the earth. While mining for various materials had been commonplace in Africa for centuries, the advent of the Europeans helped boost mining, and the trade which resulted from it, by the 16th century and beyond.

One of the largest gold-producing regions was present-day GHANA. The abundance of gold mines in the region led the Europeans to dub the region the GOLD COAST. Prior to the 18th century the group most responsible for mining in the Gold Coast were the AKAN peoples of the forest regions who worked gold in such towns as BEGHO, as well as the states of BONO and BANDA. These areas became wealthy from the deposits they extracted and often used intermediaries from the Mande groups to trade the gold both with inland kingdoms as well as with the Europeans along the coast. In the early 18th century, however, the ASHANTI EMPIRE began to overtake these regions from the Akan and thereafter gained control of the

lucrative gold-mining industry until the area was colonized by the Europeans.

Elsewhere, between the 16th and 19th centuries gold mining was concentrated southwest of the ZAMBEZI RIVER, in MWENE MUTAPA territory. When trading their gold the people of Mwene Mutapa dealt mainly with Indian Ocean Muslim traders and, later, the Portuguese, primarily at SOFALA.

The mining of salt was another profitable economic venture for various regions, such as parts of present-day Republic of MALI, SOUTH AFRICA, ANGOLA, and ZIMBABWE. During the 16th century and earlier, salt was known to have been quarried into large slabs in such towns as Taghaza in what is now Republic of MALI and then shipped to TIMBUKTU and other trading centers where it was bartered for FOOD and cloth. Another group that engaged in the mining of salt in exchange for cereals and grain was the peoples of the SHONA KINGDOMS in present-day Zimbabwe. From the 16th to the 19th centuries the Shona, who lived in areas of low rainfall, used salt mining to gain the needed foodstuffs for sustainable living. This period also saw the salt mines at KISAMA become the major source of income for the SOTHO peoples located near the coastal region of present-day Angola who shaped their salt into blocks to trade both with the Portuguese and into the lands of the interior.

Metals such as copper and iron also made up a large segment of Africa's mining industry. As copper was often a symbol of wealth among many ethnic groups as well as currency for trade, the regions that could boast copper mines became wealthy and powerful. Two of the best examples were the MINDOULI and PHALABORWA MINES located in present-day Republic of the CONGO and South Africa, respectively. Governed by the Vili peoples of the LOANGO kingdom and then later controlled by the TEKE, Mindouli was an important source of both copper and iron for a 100 years beginning in the late 16th century. The copper mining industry at Mindouli benefited from a partnership between the Loango kingdom and Dutch traders, who sought to control the copper trade. The mines at Phalaborwa produced copper and iron since about the eighth century but became important from the 16th to the 19th centuries, when the Sotho dominated the metals industry in the Transvaal province of South Africa.

See also: COPPER (Vols. I, II); COPPER MINES (Vol. II); COPPERBELT (Vol. IV); DIAMOND MINING (Vol. IV); IRON AGE (Vol. I); MINERALS AND METALS (Vol. V); MINING (Vols. II, III, IV, V); SALT (Vol. I); SALT MINING (Vol. II); SALT TRADE (Vol. II).

missionaries Individuals who spread religious doctrine in hopes of gaining converts.

Spreading Islam Muslim traders helped to spread Islam through West Africa along the trade routes, a process that began in the early days of Islam in the seventh century and continued through the following centuries. With the traders often came scholars, called *malams*, who in 14th-century GHANA, for example, exerted influence on the local rulers by means of fortune-telling and the preparation of charms and amulets to promote healing and to bring success in battle. Islam was propagated in West Africa along the trade routes as late as the 18th when Islam reached the Ashanti people along IVORY COAST and began to win converts from among the traditional believers.

The concept of jihad can refer to a process of personal spiritual purification or to actual physical combat with unbelievers, apostates, and enemies of Islam in a war of conversion. The FULANI JIHADS of the 18th and 19th centuries led to the conversion of many traditional religionists and the return to fervor of many backsliding Muslims. Charismatic figures such as USMAN DAN FODIO (1754–1815), who founded the SOKOTO CALIPHATE on the ruins of the SONGHAI Empire in present-day Mali, and the fundamentalist reformer Umar Tal (c. 1797–1864), who founded the TUKULOR empire in SENEGAMBIA, often led these bloody jihads.

The brotherhoods of the mystical Sufi movement within Islam gained many adherents in North Africa. It was largely through the preaching of wandering Sufi missionaries that Islam spread in sub-Saharan Africa. In the 14th century, when Sufi beliefs and practices began to permeate religious life in North Africa, these preachers were called marabouts. They espoused the teachings of Abu Madyan (1115–1198), from FEZ in MOROCCO, the most influential Sufi teacher in the formative period of Sufism in the MAGHRIB. His writings strongly influenced the practices of the QADIRIYYA and Shadhiliyya Sufi orders, or brotherhoods.

Spreading Christianity Christian missionary activity was dormant in North Africa after the rise of Islam in the seventh century. The exploration of the West African coast in the late 1400s led to a resurgence in missionary activity. Religious, commercial, and political interests, however, were frequently intertwined. After explorer Diogo Cão (fl. 1480s) sailed into the mouth of the Congo River in 1482, missionaries followed in 1491 with the purpose of converting the king. They built a church in the KONGO KINGDOM and baptized the *manikongo* (king) NZINGA NKUWU (r. c. 1490), who abandoned his new religion soon after converting. On Nzinga Nkuwu's death in 1506, the Portuguese installed his son, Nzinga Mbemba, baptized as AFONSO I (d. c. 1550), as *manikongo*. Afonso made Christianity the state religion and encouraged the Portuguese to convert his people. He also traded captives and ivory with the Portuguese to increase his wealth and prestige. However, as the Portuguese involvement in the trade in humans increased, relations between the two states faltered. Relations be-

tween the Kongo and neighboring peoples also soured because of Portuguese-sponsored raids against them.

Portuguese missionaries entered the kingdom of BENIN in the early 1500s in an attempt to convert the *oba*, or king. However, except for the adoption of the cross as a design in Benin sculpture, little further developed. Missionaries generally met with limited success in Africa. Many peoples felt alienated by the missionaries' denunciation of their religious and social customs. Others were angered at Europeans' role in the buying and selling of human beings. In the 1560s Portuguese missionaries first reached the MWENE MUTAPA kingdom in what is now ZIMBABWE and MOZAMBIQUE. There the people proved somewhat receptive to Christian doctrine. Most efforts were simply hindered by a lack of clergy.

Groups elsewhere in Africa proved more receptive to the work of the missionaries. Ethiopians, for example, welcomed a large contingent of Jesuit missionaries that remained in the country for centuries. These Ethiopians were already Christians but saw the Jesuit presence as a way to build alliances with the European powers. However, they resisted the Jesuits' attempts to convert them to standard forms of Roman Catholicism, preferring instead to maintain their own rites and liturgical practices.

The Roman Catholic Church undertook most mission work until about 1650. The Protestants showed little interest in Africa until the late 1700s, when groups in the United States, Great Britain, and northern Europe saw mission work as necessary to "civilize" the African peoples.

See also: CHRISTIANITY, INFLUENCE OF (Vols. II, III, IV, V); ISLAM, INFLUENCE OF (Vol II, III); JIHAD (Vol. II); MISSIONARIES (Vols. IV, V); SUFISM (Vols. II, III, IV).

Mogadishu Commercial port town and capital of the present-day country of SOMALIA, located on the BENADIR COAST, in northeast Africa. Mogadishu flourished as a center along the Indian Ocean trade routes into the 16th century. Between the 16th and 19th centuries the town was controlled by various Arabian, Somali, and Turkish forces until the era of European colonization in the 19th century.

Mogadishu was founded and populated by Arab, Persian, and Indian sea merchants. In addition to its maritime commercial activities, the town produced fine glass beads and COTTON weaving. In the 16th century Mogadishu was visited by several Portuguese explorers, including Vasco da Gama (c. 1460–1524). The mostly Muslim town was heavily populated and well protected, so the Portuguese did not try to mount an invasion, as they had done at other port cities on their way up Africa's east coast. In fact Mogadishu was the only town on the SWAHILI COAST that successfully avoided Portuguese occupation, even at the height of Portuguese influence in the 16th and 17th centuries. During that time, Mogadishu was controlled by Islamic sultans, first under the Muzaffar dynasty and then, around 1581, under the Ottoman Turks. The Turks assumed control of the town by threatening ruin and destruction to those who would oppose them. At the time, Turkish naval might was widely respected, and in Mogadishu they faced little resistance.

During the early 1600s the population of the Mogadishu region swelled as Somali Hawaya clans began migrating there from northern regions, drawn by the town's peace and prosperity. By the middle of the century, though, waves of OROMO immigrants from ETHIOPIA had begun to displace the Hawaya nomads, many of whom migrated south in search of suitable pasture lands. Outlying coastal areas around Mogadishu were occupied by the Amarani, people of Arabian and Persian descent who settled in small fishing communities.

In the late 17th and early 18th centuries captives in bondage were brought to Mogadishu in great numbers, eventually comprising about one-third of the population. These captives were transported along caravan routes that ran from the African interior to the coastal towns of BRAVA and Marka, as well as Mogadishu. Many were Bantu-speaking farmers who worked the land that was owned by the wealthy trading families. By the 18th century their agricultural activity had expanded far into the Mogadishu hinterlands, or interior regions.

Like other settlements along East Africa's Swahili coast, Mogadishu was characterized by distinctly Arabic buildings and ARCHITECTURE. It had multi-story stone houses, lighthouse towers, and mosques with minarets that could be seen from afar. It also had a harbor fortified with walls of piled rocks and coral, a type of structure unfamiliar in other parts of Africa.

During the 1700s Mogadishu became the most important city on the Horn of Africa, not only for its continuing Indian Ocean trade but also as a center of Islamic influence. Islam had been a unifying force in the town for hundreds of years, but in the 18th and 19th centuries there was a renewed interest in the religion. Clerics who subscribed to the ascetic Islamic movement called SUFISM penetrated the Mogadishu hinterland, finding converts among the Oromo and Somali peoples who still practiced a traditional religion. The spread of Islam throughout the countryside made it easier for the OMANI SULTANATE of Muscat, in Arabia, to take control of Mogadishu in the 19th century.

See also: ISLAM, INFLUENCE OF (Vol. III); MOGADISHU (Vols. II, IV, V); OTTOMAN EMPIRE (Vol. III).

Mombasa Major trading city, located in present-day KENYA on the East African coast, situated mostly on Mombasa Island. After the fourth century, Mombasa saw a period of Arab settlement, during which the intermingling of Arabs with local inhabitants led to Swahili culture and language. From the eighth to the 16th centuries it was a thriving center for the Arab Indian Ocean trade in ivory and humans.

Vasco da Gama (c. 1460–1524) stopped at Mombasa in 1498 on his way to India, and the city quickly came under Portuguese sway. On three different occasions they burned Mombasa, and in 1593 the Portuguese erected FORT JESUS as the headquarters for their East African operations. Portugal retained control of Mombasa until 1698, when the city was seized by the OMANI SULTANATE. The Portuguese regained control in 1729, holding it for a brief time until Mombasa came under the sway of the MASRUI rulers of ZANZIBAR, under whom the city remained until the mid-19th century.

See also: GAMA, VASCO DA (Vol. II); MOGADISHU (Vols. IV, V); MOMBASA (Vol. II); SLAVE TRADE ON THE SWAHILI COAST (Vol. III); SWAHILI COAST (Vols. II, III); ZANZIBAR (Vol. III).

Further reading: W. A. Nelson, *Fort Jesus of Mombasa* (Edinburgh, U.K.: Canongate Press, 1994).

money and currency In precolonial Africa objects used as money varied depending on the region and the traders involved in the markets. The period was characterized by the emergence of market-oriented trade, which, unlike barter or subsistence-based trade, necessitated the use of money.

For thousands of years most trade in Africa was conducted using the barter system, whereby one desired trade commodity was exchanged for an equal value of another desired commodity. The trading parties discussed the value of their goods until both sides were pleased with the exchange. By the 16th century, though, trade routes had become more extensive than ever before, and relations between distant trading partners required currency that might be used as a medium of exchange among traders in disparate markets across great geographical expanses.

Ideally the units of money they used had several characteristics: they were relatively uniform in size, they were dividable into smaller units for low-value purchases and to make change, and they were easily transported. For these reasons the most common currencies used in Africa included metals (especially GOLD, but also silver, copper, bronze, and iron), salt, cloth, and cowrie shells. In general the value of an object used as currency increased the further one got from its source. A few objects, like gold, cloth, and salt, were valuable throughout the continent at all times, but the use of different objects as money created "currency zones." The zones did overlap and inter-penetrate, but what was valuable in one zone was often either worthless or too expensive to transport to another, limiting its usefulness. A notable exception was the western Sudan (at the western edge of what is now Republic of MALI), where three distinct zones converged: the metal zone of North Africa, the cowrie zone in sub-Saharan Africa to the west and south, and a mixed commodity zone (glassware, cloth, iron, and other items) along the Atlantic coast. Traders there had to be able to determine the value of currency in one zone and relate it to the value of the currencies of the other two zones.

The most stable and efficient currency zones used a "bar" system to determine the relative value of other currencies. After the 17th century, for instance, the abstract value of a healthy male was used as the bar within the West African zone, and the value of other currencies, such as cowries and gold, was expressed in relation to that bar. Bars varied depending on the region.

Muslim North Africa Unlike the currency zones of sub-Saharan Africa, the currency zone of North Africa used metal coins as money. (Gold dust and nuggets were commonly used all over Africa, but the use of minted coins was particular to the North African currency zone.) Mediterranean people in Europe and Asia used gold and silver coins from ancient times, and since North African Muslims and Arabs maintained close ties with these people, it was natural that those metals were used as money in regions north of the Sahara as well.

Whereas some religions disparage the use of money, it was commonly believed among Muslims that to trade was to emulate the prophet Muhammad. Writings in the Muslim holy book, the Quran, provide a set of rules for the use of money and for righteous behavior in trading and at markets. Coinage that was used in Islamic markets included the gold dinar and the silver *dirham*. The dinar was equal in value to the *mithqal*, a measured amount of gold dust that was used in the Sahel and parts of Islamic West Africa as well. Other items that were used as currency included salt from northern deposits along the coasts and grains from Sahelian farms. However, grains were not honored throughout all of North Africa, as they were perishable. The use of metal coins slowly penetrated sub-Saharan markets worked by Muslim traders, but even as late as the 19th century, the use of coins was largely restricted to North Africa.

In the late 17th century French traders were unsuccessful at introducing silver coins to the markets in Saint-Louis, at the mouth of the Senegal River. Although some African traders accepted the French coins as a commodity to be melted down and made into jewelry, the coins were generally not accepted as currency. The more widely accepted currency along the Senegal River at that time was the *guinee*, a standardized piece of Indian-made cloth introduced by Portuguese traders. A little further south, in the Gambia region, British silver coins were sometimes accepted by Gambian groundnut exporters, who began to realize their value among other Europeans and in outlying Moorish markets to the north.

West Africa Another currency zone was the region stretching from the savanna to the coastal kingdoms in West Africa. Commonly accepted currencies in this region included salt, gold, glass beads, iron implements, and copper, but as of the 16th century, the most widely accepted currency for low-value transactions in this zone was cowries, the shells of a mollusk found in the Indian and Pacific oceans. It is not known if cowries were first brought to the area via land or sea routes. They may have been introduced by Islamic merchants in the Sudan, whose trading network stretched as far as the Indian Ocean coast. Or, they may have been introduced by European traders moving up the Atlantic coast of West Africa on their return trip along the Indian Ocean spice trade route. Either way, it seems that they were being circulated as money no later than the 15th century and perhaps as early as the eighth century. The Portuguese reported the heavy use of cowries in the kingdom of BENIN when they traded there early in the 16th century.

Cowrie shells were not a convenient form of currency for high-value transactions, such as bride-wealth payments. An anonymous Islamic historian described a transaction in which the receiver of a large payment of cowries ultimately lost money in the deal because it cost him more than the value of the payment to hire porters to carry such a great number of shells back to his village.

In YORUBALAND and the West African coastal kingdoms of DAHOMEY (and ALLADA and WHYDAH before it), cowries were the preferred currency beginning in the 16th century. Dahomey tradition does not mention any sort of currency in use before cowries in the 16th century, when Europeans began trading there. When European traders needed food for their trading stations, they were not able to barter for it, but instead had to sell their goods for cowries and then purchase provisions with them. Muslim traders came to the kingdom of Dahomey late, probably around the beginning of the 18th century, and quickly began using captives to purchase cowries from Europeans.

The arrival of greater numbers of Europeans in West Africa in the 16th century had a profound effect on the economic relations of the region. They brought with them the idea of extending credit—rarely done in most African economies prior to their arrival—as a regular practice. It is thought that Dutch traders in the middle of the 17th century were the first to extend credit to African traders in Dahomey. By the end of the century the king of Dahomey made it his policy not to pay cash to Europeans, preferring credit represented by written "notes." Once the practice became common, the Dahomean kings saw the advantage of storing a small piece of paper over storing a mountain of shells. Paper notes also allowed the king to be more secretive about his true wealth if it served his purposes. In Allada the local traders did not use writing to record transactions but instead used knotted cords of different colors.

Dutch traders reported that African merchants in Dahomey who were unfamiliar with paper and writing were highly suspicious of the European promissory notes, checking them frequently to make sure that the writing hadn't disappeared, leaving them a worthless scrap of paper. Similarly, European traders were at first wary of trading their manufactured goods for shells until they saw that cowries were widely accepted as money throughout the region.

Although there was no "banking system," West African kings often had special rooms in their royal compounds that were reserved for the storage and counting of the cowrie shells that they accumulated through taxation and tribute. In these rooms, larger amounts of shells were often strung to facilitate counting and transport.

Before the 19th century the relative value of cowries to gold remained steady at about 3,000 cowries to the *mithqal*. That ratio changed drastically, though, when Europeans began flooding the West African markets with thousands of pounds of cowrie shells early in the 18th century. The Dutch and Portuguese imported great amounts of cowries from the coastal regions of the Indian Ocean where the shells were simply harvested and sold cheap, using the shells to buy captive humans for export to the Americas. By the beginning of the 20th century the ratio was about 12,000 cowries to the *mithqal*, effectively ending the use of shells as currency.

Northern East Africa In the 16th century blocks of salt called *amolehs* were the most common form of currency on the plains of what is now ETHIOPIA and KENYA, in northern East Africa. Salt was important for cattle rearing and was also used to pay soldiers in the OROMO standing army. Pastoralist nomads in the eastern highlands of Ethiopia, as well as in the western Sahel, sometimes accepted cattle as currency to pay off debts and to buy captives or salt.

Swahili Coast Much of the trade on East Africa's SWAHILI COAST during the period was simple exchange of goods. Because of the Muslim and Arabian influence on the coast, however, metal coins were used at markets from the BENADIR COAST in SOMALIA to SOFALA in MOZAMBIQUE, perhaps as early as the 700s. Merchants in the Swahili city-states regularly conducted transactions with Arab, Persian, and Indian traders, all of whom used metal coins. Gold dust was also a widely accepted currency at Swahili markets.

The extreme southeastern region of the African continent around DELAGOA BAY was not a well-defined currency zone. Gold, ivory, and salt were highly valued trade items, but even after the arrival of Portuguese traders in the 16th century, and the Dutch and English in the 17th century, the trading system remained one of an exchange of goods rather than a money system.

The African Interior Similar to the southeastern region, the markets of the interior zone from present-day Democratic Republic of the CONGO to ZAMBIA were primarily exchange markets, though some of the trade goods, such as gold, copper, salt, beads, and cloth, were accepted as currency on the outer fringes where the region converged with other currency zones. Ivory, which was produced in massive quantities in the African interior, was mostly an exchange item.

Up until the 19th century salt and iron were the bases of regional trade in central and western TANZANIA. While iron was traded in an area ranging from Lake Tanganyika to Usagara, salt was even more widely exchanged. The best salt in the region came from the Uvinza pans, where salt-working had apparently been carried out for more than 1,500 years. The salt from Uvinza was traded within an area extending from the southern end of Lake Malawi to the southern end of Lake Tanganyika and from the eastern CONGO to the Ruaha valley. Ugogo, in central Tanzania, was another source of salt, but its products were inferior to those of Uvinza.

The works that produced the iron for regional trade in Tanzania were located in the northwest, where the smelting process was firmly in the hands of just a few clans. The most common tool made from the iron was the hoe, which helped transform AGRICULTURE in the area. Hoes were traded so extensively that they actually became a widely accepted form of currency.

Western Central Africa When the Portuguese arrived in present-day ANGOLA in the 16th century, the item they found most readily accepted as currency was salt.

The KISAMA salt mines, located to the south of LUANDA near the Kwanza River produced high-quality slabs that could be used to purchase other goods. A letter written by a Portuguese missionary from 1563 described how one block could purchase six chickens, three blocks could buy a goat, and about 15 blocks purchased a cow. By the beginning of the 19th century the salt slabs were being further processed down to foot-long bars about an inch in diameter, making for easier transportation into the Angolan hinterland, where the salt was also accepted as currency. Portuguese traders introduced tobacco from the Americas to the western Central African region in the late 16th or early 17th century, and bundles of cured tobacco leaves eventually became an accepted currency in the KONGO KINGDOM.

Paper money was widely used in Europe beginning in the 17th century, but the lack of centralized banking systems in sub-Saharan African kingdoms made paper money useless. Therefore, paper notes as currency were not circulated in Africa until the 19th century when the French, and later the Portuguese, Germans, and Italians, imposed their colonial banking systems on the indigenous markets.

See also: COPPER (Vols. I, II); COWRIE SHELLS (Vol. I); IVORY (Vol. II); MONEY AND CURRENCY (Vols. I, II, IV, V); SALT TRADE (Vol. II); TRADE AND COMMERCE (Vol. III).

Morocco North African country located in the MAGHRIB ("West" in Arabic), bordering the Mediterranean Sea. Morocco also borders ALGERIA and WESTERN SAHARA. Its population includes both the BERBERS, who were the original inhabitants of the region, and Arabs, who moved into the region during the seventh and eighth centuries. The Maghrib was converted to Islam by these Arab newcomers, and the region fell into the orbit of the Muslim world, where it has remained to the present. Located at the northern end of many trans-Saharan trade routes, the Maghrib has benefited commercially as the intermediary in trade, including the trade in humans, between Africa south of the Sahara and the states of Europe and the wider Muslim world. Most of the Maghrib fell to Ottoman expansion in the early 1500s, but Morocco maintained its independence.

The Islamic mystical movement called SUFISM was strong in North Africa among both the urban people of the coastal cities and the rural peoples of the interior. In Morocco, the Almohad empire of the 13th century, which supplanted the Almoravid empire of earlier centuries, was based on the religious reformist-fundamentalist teachings of Ibn Tumart (d. 1130), who proclaimed himself the long awaited Mahdi, or Muslim redeemer. At the apex of its power in the 15th century, the Almohad empire controlled not only Morocco but Muslim Spain as well. The Christian reconquest of Spain, culminating in

their victory at Grenada in 1492, resulted in the influx of many exiled Spanish Muslims and Jews into Morocco and the addition of Iberian elements into Moroccan life and culture.

With the fall of Muslim Spain came a shift in the balance of power, as Spain and Portugal became active in Moroccan affairs. Between 1471 and 1505, Portugal occupied the port cites of TANGIER and Agadir. Agadir remained in Portuguese hands until 1541, when it was won back by the Sadian king of Sus in southern Morocco. Tangier remained under Spanish and Portuguese control until 1662. It then fell into English hands—transferred there as part of the dowry of a Portuguese princess who married Charles II (1630–1685) of England—until it reverted to Moroccan control in 1684.

European activity was not restricted to Morocco but extended further along the Mediterranean coast as well. In 1509 the Spanish established a garrison at ORAN in Algeria, a city to which many Spanish Muslims had fled while escaping forced conversion to Christianity. The city remained under the domination of the European powers until it fell to the Ottoman Empire in 1708. TRIPOLI in LIBYA was in Spanish hands from 1510 to 1551, when it became the capital of the new Ottoman province of Libya.

The incursions of the Spanish and the Portuguese prompted a strong reaction among the Arab peoples of Morocco, and they rose in jihad (holy war) against them to found a new state in Morocco that lasted from 1511 to 1603. The leaders of this revolt, the Sadi family, claimed to be sharifs—direct descendants of the prophet Muhammad through Muhammad's son Ali. This ancient form of Islamic legitimacy and the acceptance and promotion of it by Sufi holy men preaching among the people gave the Sadi family the start it needed to attain power.

Europeans called Morocco, Algeria, TUNISIA, and Libya the "Barbary states," and the part of the Mediterranean Sea they border was called the BARBARY COAST. The name *Barbary* is derived from the word *Berber*, the name of the original inhabitants.

The SADIAN DYNASTY reached the height of its power under ABD AL-MANSUR (1578–1603), who with Turkish and

Spanish help established Morocco's first standing army and equipped them with firearms from Europe. He led this army against the Muslim SONGHAI Empire in 1591 because an expansionist Songhai, in what is now Republic of MALI, was competing too strongly with Morocco for control of the trans-Saharan trade routes. Moroccan firearms frightened the Songhai cavalry, which fled the field, leaving Morocco free to capture TIMBUKTU, Gao, JENNE, and other key centers of Songhai strength. Morocco ruled Songhai as a vassal state for 40 years.

Conflict after the death of al-Mansur led to the division of Morocco into a number of feuding principalities. They were united in 1668 by the Alawite dynasty—another sharif family—from the town of SIJILMASA. With the help of strong Arab support, the affirmation of the Sufi holy men, and the legitimacy that sharifian descent provided, the Alawites under their founder Mawlay al-Rashid (d. 1672), began their rise to power in 1664. They seized FEZ from the powerful Dila Sufi brotherhood and ruled as absolute monarchs. Al-Rashid died in an accident before he could solidify his holdings; his half-brother, MAWLAY ISMAIL (r. 1672–1727), assumed the throne and completed the reunification of Morocco with the help of an expensive-to-maintain army of black Africans. These soldiers were said to be descendants of the prisoners of war that were brought to Morocco after its victory over Songhai.

Ismail's army, which was equipped with European firearms and artillery, was called the Abid al-Bukhari. At its height it numbered 150,000 men, of whom about 70,000 were kept as a strategic reserve. Although he hated the Europeans as infidels, he needed their armaments and other products for his soldiers. To challenge Spain over its settlements in Morocco, he cultivated the friendship of Spain's enemy, French king Louis XIV (1638–1715). As a result of this friendship, French officers trained his artillery, and France received commercial benefits. Ismail's palace at Meknès, the political and military capital of Morocco from 1675 to 1728, was designed to resemble Versailles, the royal palace of the monarchs of France.

Dynastic struggles after Mawlay Ismail's death led to 50 years of political instability and economic decline. The country regained stability and began a period of economic recovery during the reign of Muhammad ibn Abd Allah (1757–1790) and his successor as sultan, Mawlay Sulayman (1792–1822). The French occupation of present-day Algeria in 1830 and European political and economic pressure on Morocco after 1800 led to a diminishing of Moroccan power.

See also: ALMOHADS (Vol. II); ALMORAVIDS (Vol. II); ISLAM, INFLUENCE OF (Vols. II, III, IV); MAHDI (Vol. II); MOROCCO (Vols. I, II, IV, V).

Further reading: Rahma Bourgia and Susan Gilson Miller, *In the Shadow of the Sultan: Culture, Power, and Politics in Morocco* (Cambridge, Mass.: Harvard University Press, 1999); Thomas Kerlin Park, *Historical Dictionary of Morocco* (Lanham, Md.: Scarecrow Press, 1996).

Mossi States (Moshe, Moose, Mohe, Mosi)

Confederation of states, including YATENGA, FADA-N-GURMA, Nanumba, OUAGADOUGOU, MAMPRUSI, Tenkodogo, and DAGOMBA located in present-day GHANA and BURKINA FASO. Between 1500 and 1800 the Mossi States controlled territories in the region south of the Niger bend.

Twentieth-century wood sculpture of a Mossi ancestor figure. The Mossi States, which flourished from the middle of the 16th century through 1895, centered around the headwaters of the Volta River. © *Bowers Museum of Cultural Art/Corbis*

According to Mossi tradition, their ancestors were cavalrymen who invaded the Volta River basin from the south, conquering the indigenous Dogon, Lela, Kurumba, and Nuna peoples. Though each of the states that make up the Mossi confederation was established prior to 1500, the foundation of formal political alliances between them dates to later in the 16th century.

By 1450 Ouagadougou, in present-day central Burkina Faso, had become the center of Mossi political authority. Mossi social organization was a strict hierarchy of nobles, commoners, and retainers in slave status. The sacred kings, or *nakomse*, of the Mossi States had to be the direct descendants of the original invaders. In exchange for tribute and gifts, the *nakomse* offered protection from hostile invaders. Nakomse were aided by a trusted group of chief advisers, or *naba*. The *nyonyose*, or peasant class, were descendants of the conquered farmers, who were allowed to continue to farm the land and practice their traditional religion, but they were forced to pay taxes, serve in the military, and learn Moré, the Mossi language.

The *mogho naba* (great king), of the Mossi confederation ruled from Ougadougou. From the founding of the Mossi confederation, *mogho nabas* allowed Muslim traders to pass through their lands, but they were especially careful to maintain the unity of their kingdoms by preserving indigenous religion and culture. Their efforts allowed the Mossi States to successfully resist a series of invasions by the Songhai and FULANI in the 16th, 17th, and 18th centuries.

The Mossi are well known for their ART, which incorporates both political and spiritual themes. The creation of wooden figures by the *nakomse* are used to validate their political power, while the *nyonyose* fashion wood masks to honor the spirits of nature.

During the 17th century the number of minor Mossi kingdoms increased as the confederation enjoyed remarkable stability, and trade in the region became more impor-

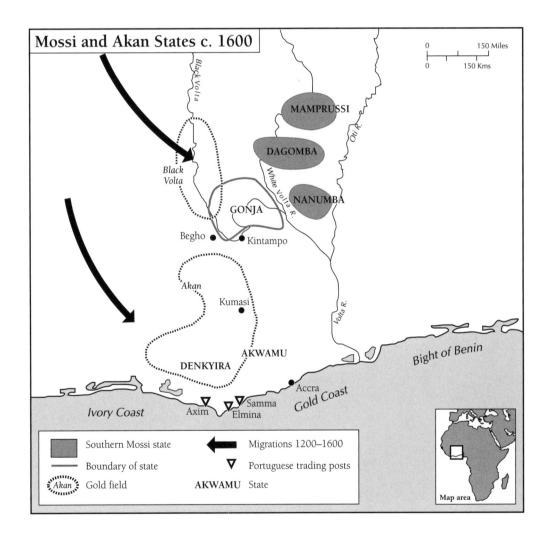

Mossi and Akan States c. 1600

Southern Mossi state — Migrations 1200–1600
Boundary of state — ▽ Portuguese trading posts
Akan Gold field — AKWAMU State

tant. Mossi trading outposts lay along trans-Saharan routes, and merchants traded their captives, iron tools, livestock, and agricultural goods for kola nuts, salt, and dried fish.

By the end of the 18th century the Mossi States were no longer as tightly unified as they had been, and their power began to wane. Trade had allowed outside influences to infiltrate the kingdom, and years of instability had pushed many of the former Mossi tributaries to declare independence from the central rule of Ouagadougou. Islam became the religion of the people sometime around 1800, when Mogho Naba Dulugu (r. c. 1796–1825) converted. The period of European (especially French) colonization that began in earnest toward the middle of the 19th century marked the end of the Mossi confederation as a regional power.

See also: FULANI JIHADS (Vol. III); MOSSI STATES (Vols. II, IV); TRANS-SAHARAN TRADE ROUTES (Vol. II); VOLTA RIVER (Vol. II).

Mozambique Present-day country on Africa's southern Indian Ocean coast. Mozambique measures approximately 297,800 square miles (771,300 sq km) and is bordered by SOUTH AFRICA and SWAZILAND to the southwest, ZIMBABWE and ZAMBIA to the west, MALAWI to the northwest, and TANZANIA to the north.

Prior to the arrival of Europeans in the late 15th century, the ZAMBEZI RIVER was already a well-developed commercial waterway for the transport of ivory and GOLD from the interior to the SWAHILI COAST ports of INHAMBANE, MOZAMBIQUE ISLAND, and SOFALA. The region was inhabited by Bantu-speaking groups such as the Tonga, MAKUA, and YAO. These peoples were typically agrarian and stateless, but their societies became more organized as they increasingly turned away from AGRICULTURE to become more active as hunters as the coastal demand for ivory and animal hides increased.

In the 16th century the arrival of Portuguese seafaring merchants radically altered the nature of trade in the area. When they realized the profits to be made from the great amounts of gold and ivory that were being traded locally, the Europeans began violently forcing the coastal Arab merchants to leave the ports. They also attempted to force African gold suppliers on the interior, including the MWENE MUTAPA traders, to deal exclusively with them, with mixed success.

Although they created much resentment among the local peoples, by the end of the 17th century the Portuguese traders had established trading forts up and down the Swahili Coast and as far south as MAPUTO. Because of the fierce resistance they met in the northern interior, especially from the ZIMBA people, the Portuguese settled mostly along the coast. However, Portuguese traders also settled throughout the Zambezi River valley, especially

near the trading centers of SENA and TETE. These settlers often began families with African wives. They also used African workers to grow their crops, transport their trade goods to the fairs, and protect their landholdings, called PRAZOS. In the course of their activities, the *prazeros* started what would become known as the mestizo, or "mixed," culture of Mozambique. Some of the *prazeros* grew rich and powerful trading gold and ivory.

However, as the gold and ivory trades dwindled because of the disruption caused by the Portuguese incursions, many of the *prazeros* turned to the trade in human captives to make a living. The captives, most of whom were shipped to the Portuguese colonies in the Americas were largely supplied by Yao slave traders, who used firearms purchased from Arab arms dealers in slave raids on peoples from the interior. The extensive presence of Portuguese settlers in Mozambique led Portugal to declare the region a colony in the middle of the 18th century.

In the middle of the 19th century waves of NGONI peoples fleeing ZULU expansion came north from the Natal region of present-day South Africa to settle in the interior. The Ngoni clashed often with the Portuguese colonists, but their resistance was not enough to dissuade Portugal from further establishing its colonial presence.

See also: MOZAMBIQUE (Vols. I, II, IV, V); PORTUGAL AND AFRICA (Vols. III, IV, V); QUELIMANE (Vol. III); SABI RIVER (Vol. III); SLAVE TRADE ON THE SWAHILI COAST (Vol. III).

Further reading: Mario Joaquim Azevedo, *Historical Dictionary of Mozambique* (Lanham, Md.: Scarecrow Press, 2003).

Mozambique Island Coral island located off of the mainland coast of East Africa, across the Mozambique Channel from the island of MADAGASCAR. Beginning in the 16th century Mozambique Island served as a Portuguese trading outpost and commercial center and was the capital of Portuguese East Africa until the 19th century. The present-day country of MOZAMBIQUE was named after this island.

From the 10th through the 15th centuries Mozambique Island was used as a port by Zanj and Swahili traders along the SWAHILI COAST. Then, in 1498, Portuguese explorer Vasco da Gama landed on Mozambique Island while mapping the southern route to India. Recognizing the need for a safe port between the trading centers of KILWA, to the north, and SOFALA, to the south, the Portuguese established Mozambique Island as a trade settlement around 1505. Under the direction of Francisco de Almeida, the island became a stopover for the Portuguese merchants on the Indian spice route as well as a trading center for those Portuguese traders who were active in the established ivory and GOLD trade and the trade in human beings.

Portuguese activity in the area disrupted the established Muslim-controlled coastal trade, leading to several confrontations. With their powder, arms, and larger vessels, the Portuguese rather easily established superiority in the area. Because of its strategic location, Mozambique Island was becoming a busy Indian Ocean port, handling more merchandise than even Sofala, and by 1522 the Portuguese had begun building St. Sebastian's Fort in order to protect their interests.

Between 1600 and 1608 the Portuguese moved to monopolize the increasingly lucrative trade fairs in the area. First they forged agreements with the MWENE MUTAPA kingdom, which controlled inland trade routes in the area. Then they secured MOMBASA, another Indian Ocean port to the north. This action effectively cut off Arab merchants from the protection of their northern allies, thereby strengthening Portuguese control of the coastal routes.

Despite their military and naval might, the Portuguese at this time were reluctant to penetrate areas beyond Mozambique Island, to the north of the ZAMBEZI RIVER, which were occupied by the powerful MARAVI peoples. Instead they acquired land from the Mwene Mutapa kingdom, in Zambezia, and instituted the PRAZOS system, a semifeudal arrangement that allowed Portuguese settlers to run their leased estates as they saw fit. The prazos system resulted in the dissolution of the Mwene Mutapa kingdom by the end of the 17th century.

During the 17th and 18th centuries Portuguese interest in the area intensified, but the hard living conditions, the long distance from the Portuguese homeland, and the difficulty of realizing a quick profit from their trading activities made it an increasingly unattractive place for settlement. Most Portuguese trading activity during this period was limited to fairs conducted with peoples from the interior along the lower Zambezi River. After about 1750, the Portuguese began to intensify gold MINING and trading in the area, trying to participate in the BISA TRADING NETWORK, which also moved large amounts of ivory to the coast for export.

By the beginning of the 19th century the Portuguese were using Mozambique Island as a port for sending large numbers of Africans to their colonies in the Americas, especially Brazil.

See also: GAMA, VASCO DA (Vol. II); INDIAN OCEAN TRADE (Vol. II); IVORY TRADE (Vol. III); PORTUGAL AND AFRICA (Vol. III); SLAVE TRADE ON THE SWAHILI COAST (Vol. III).

Mpondo (Pondo) NGUNI people who have inhabited the area between the Mtata and Mtamvuna rivers in present-day SOUTH AFRICA for nearly two centuries. The Mpondo were forced to flee their homelands during the MFECANE, a series of ZULU military campaigns begun in the 1820s. Chief Faku reorganized the Mpondo and established an agricultural state west of the Mzinvubu River between present-day Durban and Port Edward.

Good trade relations with the Europeans coupled with increased agricultural productivity created a seemingly stable Mpondo nation. However, internal conflict among rival clans made the Mpondo vulnerable to European conquest. Mpondo territories, coveted for their agricultural richness as well as for grazing lands, were overtaken by the British and incorporated into CAPE COLONY in 1894.

See also: ENGLAND AND AFRICA (Vol. III); SHAKA (Vol. III).

Further reading: Timothy Joseph Stapleton, *Faku: Rulership and Colonialism in the Mpondo Kingdom c. 1760* (Waterloo, Ontario: Wilfrid Laurier University Press, 2001).

Mpongwe West African people inhabiting the coastal regions of the present-day countries of GABON, CAMEROON, and EQUATORIAL GUINEA. Although the exact timeframe is unknown, the Mpongwe migrated to their present-day location throughout the first millennium. During these migrations the Mpongwe split into multiple clans, each headed by an *oga*, or chief. These early Mpongwe were farmers, fishers, hunters, and skilled artisans who traded among themselves.

With the increase of European coastal trade in the 16th century, the Mpongwe assumed a new role as mediators in the transatlantic SLAVE TRADE. This relationship with European merchants allowed the Mpongwe to prosper. Despite a smallpox epidemic that cut the Mpongwe population in half during the early 19th century, the Mpongwe continued to be a powerful force in coastal West Africa.

See also: DISEASE IN PRECOLONIAL AFRICA (Vol. III).

Mshweshwe (Moshesh, Moshoeshoe) (1786–1870) *Founder and king of the Sotho nation*

Mshweshwe united SOTHO refugees fleeing the Zulu-led MFECANE (the crushing). During the early 19th century he relocated his people to an impenetrable mountain plateau at THABA BOSIU, in present-day SOUTH AFRICA. He then engaged in wars against both Britain and the BOERS, who were attempting to colonize southern Africa.

Ultimately the Sotho were not powerful enough to prevent encroachment upon their lands. In order to prevent the Boers and other Europeans from settling Sotho lands, Mshweshwe sought British protection in 1868. The region officially became a British protectorate and was renamed Basutoland.

See also: BASUTOLAND (Vol. IV); ENGLAND AND AFRICA (Vols. III, IV, V).

Mswati I (Mswazi) (1820–1868) *Chief of the Ngwane; one of the founding fathers of the Swaziland state*

In 1750 the Ngwane people left the area around MAPUTO in present-day MOZAMBIQUE and moved southward settling in the northern part of the ZULU empire. However, they were unable to compete with the Zulu militarily, so in the 1800s they moved just north of the land claimed by the Zulu establishing what is today SWAZILAND. In the 1840s Mswati I assumed leadership of the Ngwane, who came to be known as the SWAZI, taking their name from a variation on Mswati's name.

Muhammad Ali (Muhammad Ali Pasha; Mehmet Ali) (1769–1849) *Founder of the modern Egyptian state*

Originally from Albania, Muhammad Ali arrived in EGYPT in 1798, assisting the Ottoman Empire in driving French emperor Napoleon Bonaparte (1769–1821) out of its Egyptian province. Following a protracted political struggle in CAIRO, in 1806 the Cairenes invited Muhammad Ali to become Egypt's viceroy, or governor, for the Ottoman Empire.

Under Muhammad Ali, Egypt began transforming itself into a modern nation able to compete with European powers in TRADE AND COMMERCE. He built a canal between Alexandria and the Nile to expedite the movement of goods. To improve the ECONOMY he forced a systematization of imports and exports. In AGRICULTURE he introduced the cultivation of hemp and COTTON and then built textile mills to process it. He built steel mills to support his industrial complex.

Regarding education, he invited European instructors to teach the best students who would then go to European countries for higher education. He introduced an educational system of schools and colleges, and promoted literacy by supporting publishing houses.

In government, Muhammad Ali formulated a new constitution, implemented a new system of taxation, and introduced health legislation. He constructed a new military complex to strengthen Egypt's armed forces. The new army was a civilian army, raised by conscript, that trained Egyptian peasants.

Besides being a crafty statesman, Muhammad Ali also displayed formidable talent as a military technician. He put down the Greek rebellion against the Ottomans in 1821 and then led Egypt to military victories that earned him greater autonomy within the Ottoman Empire. His successes did not go unnoticed, however, as the European powers—Britain, France, and Russia, in particular—moved to check Egyptian expansion. Muhammad Ali's Egypt continued as a vassal state of the Ottoman Empire, although the pasha enjoyed much autonomy and even managed to make the leadership of Egypt a hereditary right to be passed on to his son, Ibrahim Pasha.

See also: ISMAIL, KHEDIVE (Vol. IV); OTTOMAN EMPIRE AND AFRICA (Vols. III, IV).

Muhammad Bano, Askia (Muhammad IV Bani) (r. 1586–1588) *Grandson of Muhammad Touré and eighth askia of the Songhai Empire*

Upon the death of Askia DAUD, in 1582, al-Hajj Muhammad II (r. 1582–1586) was chosen by his brothers to succeed their father as the seventh *askia*, in spite of the fact that Askia Daud had wanted his eldest son, Muhammad Benkan, to take the throne. Like many *askias* before him, however, al-Hajj felt threatened by his other brothers and treated them harshly. His fears were not unfounded. In 1586 he was dethroned in favor of another brother, Muhammad Bano.

Though Bano's brothers elected him as their eighth *askia*, they disliked his leadership and set into motion a plan to overthrow him. Askia Bano quickly uncovered the conspiracy and disciplined all those who had betrayed him.

In 1588 another plot against Askia Bano was developed. This time it came from the western SONGHAI provinces, and it was led by al-Sadduk, the *balama* from TIMBUKTU. Askia Bano perished unexpectedly on the same day he sent the Songhai troops to deal with the dissidents.

Bano's brother Ishaq II (r. 1588–1591) was chosen as successor, becoming the ninth *askia* of the Songhai Empire. He immediately began to deal with al-Sadduk, who had been designated by his army as the next *askia*. After killing al-Sadduk, Ishaq took a firm stand with the western provinces, but the civil war upset the stability and power that the Songhai Empire had previously enjoyed. As a result, Songhai became vulnerable to the Moroccans, who invaded in 1591.

See also: ASKIA DYNASTY (Vol. III); MUHAMMAD TOURÉ, ASKIA (Vol. II).

Muhammad Bello (c. 1781–1837) *Sultan of the Sokoto Caliphate and son of Fulani religious leader Usman dan Fodio*

Led by FULANI cleric USMAN DAN FODIO (1754–1817), and commanded by both Muhammad Bello and his uncle, Abdullahi dan Fodio (c. 1756–1828), the FULANI JIHADS (holy wars) began in 1804. They became widely successful attempts to convert the regional peoples from a variation of the Muslim RELIGION mixed with more traditional rituals and practices to the *sharia,* a more pure form of Islamic law. The main result of the jihad was the formation of the SOKOTO CALIPHATE, a vast empire formed from such conquered kingdoms as the HAUSA STATES.

Initially the caliphate was ruled by Usman dan Fodio (also known as the *Shehu,* or "Chief"). At his retirement from the jihad movement in 1812, Muhammad Bello was given the northern and eastern emirates to govern, while Abdullahi dan Fodio was given the emirates to the south and west. Upon the Shehu's death in 1817, Muhammad Bello was granted his father's title as *amir al-muminin* (commander of the faithful) of Sokoto.

A religious scholar who published works on law, SCIENCE, history, and the Muslim faith, Muhammad Bello adamantly continued the work of the jihad. His major accomplishments in this included converting further territories to Islam and enlarging the borders of the caliphate. Bello's success as the leader of Sokoto allowed both trade and learning to flourish. This was especially true in the area of education for women, which he believed to be important for any learned Muslim society.

See also: ISLAM, INFLUENCE OF (Vols. II, III).

Muhammad Touré, Askia (r. 1493–1528) *Ruler of the Songhai Empire in West Africa*

Askia Muhammad Touré assumed the throne of the SONGHAI Empire in 1493 after the death of Sunni Ali (1464–1492), the leader of the Sunni dynasty. He established Islam as the official state RELIGION, and he consolidated the region of west-central Sudan into one political unit.

Muhammad controlled a vast area, with lands, according to some sources, extending to the Atlantic Ocean to the west, the salt mines of Taghaza to the northwest, to Bendugu in the southwest, and to Busa in the southeast. He also gained control of trade routes that stretched to Tripoli and EGYPT. In time Muhammad subdued the Mossi state of Yatenga, and his army established a colony in the Tuareg sultanate on the Aïr Massif, giving him access to the caravan markets to the north.

Oral tradition has it that Muhammad was able to communicate with the *jinni,* spirits that have supernatural powers, such as the ability to change shapes. Some sources claim that the *jinni* were responsible for the appointment of Muhammad to caliphate. Oral traditions from a later period assert that Muhammad even became a *jinni* himself.

Muhammad spent much of his time in Gao, the capital, organizing his state. He created a complex system of tithes and taxes, initiated regulations for AGRICULTURE, and arranged for the selection and training of regional governors. He also established Islam as the official religion of the Songhai nobility. Among his other acts was to create for his brother Umar (fl c. 1518) a powerful position and

title—*kurmina fari*—allowing Umar to govern the western provinces and to act for Muhammad in the ruler's absence.

Muhammad's reign ended in 1528 when his son Musa (r. 1528–1531) took power by means of a series of successful plots. Ultimately Muhammad was banished to an island, remaining there until 1537, when his son Askia Ismail (r. 1537–1539) came to power and recalled his father to the capital.

Further reading: David Conrad, *The Songhay Empire* (New York: F. Watts, 1998); Thomas A. Hale, ed.; recounted by Nouhou Malio with the assistance of Mounkaila Maiga [et al.], *The Epic of Askia Mohammed* (Bloomington, Ind.: Indiana University Press, 1996).

Muradid dynasty (Muradite) From 1631 to 1702, ruling family of the nominally independent Ottoman province of TUNISIA in North Africa. Instead of using the traditional Ottoman civil title *dey* to denote their status as ruler, the Muradids adopted the military title *bey* in respect of their origin as local military commanders. In principle, they ruled in the name of the Ottoman sultan; in practice, Istanbul had little control over ALGIERS, Tunisia, and TRIPOLI.

The dynasty was established by the descendants of a soldier named Murad Corso (r. 1628–1631) who came from the island of Corsica (then under the control of Genoa), in the Mediterranean Sea, northwest of Tunisia. Corso was known to have formed a powerful army that defeated the unruly ethnic groups to the south. These campaigns put him in favor with Murad IV (1612–1640), the reigning Ottoman sultan. The sultan honored Corso in 1631 by granting him the nonhereditary title of pasha and giving him the right to confer the title of bey on his heirs. This made the House of Murad relatively independent of the power of the local deys, or leaders of the CORSAIRS in ALGERIA, who, in years to come and in years past, kept trying to intervene in Tunisian affairs.

The Muradids gained approval by identifying with the people by seeing themselves as Tunisian. (This was something that the Ottoman deys never did.) They brought both the urban merchants and the rural peoples into their government and, despite periods of local unrest, countered Algerian ambitions in the region.

European economic interests dominated Tunisia during Mudadid era. With the curtailment of corsair activity along the BARBARY COAST and because of poor harvests inland, the Muradid beys were forced to depend on European trade. They signed commercial agreements with France in 1662, 1672, and 1685 giving France substantial privileges. The beys had some success controlling the Tunisian side of this trade by creating government monopolies, but European traders dominated the economy. The Muradid dynasty ended in 1702, giving way to the HUSSEINID DYNASTY, which came to power in 1705.

See also: FRANCE AND AFRICA (Vol. III); OTTOMAN EMPIRE AND AFRICA (Vol. III); TRADE AND COMMERCE (Vol. III).

music The traditional sources that historians have relied on to understand the various influences as well as the social, political, and religious role that music has had on African societies include ARCHAEOLOGY, illustrations, oral history, writings, and, more recently, musical notations and sound recording.

Archaeological sources include bronze plaques and iron findings such as lamellophones, or bells. Archaeologists have been able to place the introduction of the *dundun* pressure drum to the western savanna around the 15th century thanks to the illustrations on plaques discovered in the present-day BENIN CITY, in NIGERIA. Excavations have also dated the use of three kinds of bells (the double iron clapperless bell, the pellet bell, and the tubular bell with clappers) to the 15th century. These bells have been found in the KATANGA region of the Democratic Republic of the CONGO, as well as in parts of ZIMBABWE.

The artistic depictions of musical instruments such as horns, bells, drums, and bow lutes on bronze plaques have been an important source for historians in documenting African music traditions, particularly in terms of their ceremonial or religious significance. Also available to historians, from the 15th century onwards, are the illustrations of travelers and explorers such as Dutchman Jan Huvghen van Linschoten (1563–1611), whose work is the first documented proof of the existence of mouth-bows along the coast of MOZAMBIQUE, in southeast Africa, in the 16th century. Giovanni Antonio Cavazzi (unknown–1692) produced several watercolors in the 17th century during his visits to the Central African Atlantic coast kingdoms of KONGO, NDONGO, and MATAMBA. From the work of travelers like Van Linschoten and Cavazzi, much can be learned about the culture, playing methods, and tuning layout of African musical instruments and the periods in which they recorded their observations.

European musical notations made in the 18th and 19th centuries are not entirely reliable as historical sources. While they offer the musicologist an approximate idea of what the sound was like, the music cannot be directly produced from notations, as the Western system fails to address or encompass the full nature of African music. In addition the musical interpretation from one listener to another is so subjective that it is impossible to give an accurate account of African music based solely on these notations.

Like many aspects of African life, African music has always been affected by both external and internal influences, such as migration patterns, trade, politics, economics, war, religious and cultural shifts, clashes or assimilation, climate fluctuations, NATURAL RESOURCES, population growth or decline, and ecological factors.

African migrations took place for a variety of reasons. People traveled great distances in search of new land or prosperity. Many were forced out of their own regions by invasions and war as well as from changes in the climate. For instance, ethnic groups migrated southward when the Sahara dried up, circa 3000 BCE, and when they moved, they brought with them and were introduced to new forms and styles of music, instruments, and dance. When the MAASAI migrated many centuries later, their vocal songs had a profound effect on the vocals of the Gogo of central TANZANIA, as is demonstrated in their *nindo* and *msunyunho* chants. Likewise, migrations that took place in the 17th century were responsible for bringing lamellophones with iron keys from the ZAMBEZI RIVER valley to locations as far north as the Lunda kingdom of KAZEMBE and the Luba province of KATANGA, and as far west as ANGOLA. The limitations of traveling affected the style and design of these instruments and they eventually were made smaller so they were easier to transport.

Historians are also able to use, albeit in a limited and indirect way, information about African music from locations outside of Africa, most significantly in Latin America. Between the 18th and 19th centuries Europeans did not have access to areas such as inland Angola and Mozambique but were able to study the music and instruments that Africans brought with them to the New World. For instance, there is a link between 18th and 19th century *orisha* worship of the Yoruba of present-day Nigeria and the music of the Candomble religious cult in Brazil in South America.

African music not only influenced music on other continents but itself was influenced by people arriving from other parts of the world. *Goombay*, a drum dance from the Maroons of Jamaica, was brought to SIERRA LEONE in 1800 when the British settled Maroon rebels there. Eventually *goombay* infiltrated into areas of present-day GHANA, Nigeria, BURKINA FASO, Republic of MALI, IVORY COAST, and CAMEROON. Colonialism brought marching bands to West Africa in the 19th century.

Islamic musical influences resulted from the trans-Saharan trade in West Africa and from Indian Ocean trade in East Africa. The Muslim people of northern ETHIOPIA can trace their musical heritage from their interaction with Muslims on the Red Sea coast. Further south, Arabian music and instruments, such as the guitar-like *oud,* were commonplace on the SWAHILI COAST. In central southern Africa, the NGUNI and SOTHO musical traditions incorporated Khoisan bows, songs, and dances.

Powerful kingdoms and states had a great impact on the cultural traditions of music. For example, the Turks of the Ottoman Empire standardized the use of oboes, long trumpets, and barrel drums in court ensembles. Musicians, and particularly bards and the griots of West

Africa, have long held prestigious roles within African society. Through oral and musical traditions they would pass on to the next generation the histories of their ancestors. They also provided advice or counsel to the king. It was often the "talking drummer" who relayed messages to the monarchy about the state of the empire, such as plans for the abdication of the king.

See also: DRUMS (Vol. I); GRIOT (Vol. II); MUSIC (Vols. I, II, IV, V).

musumba Word used to describe the royal center of the LUNDA EMPIRE, which began in the 16th century and was located east of the lower Kasai River in what is now southern Democratic Republic of the CONGO. *Musumba* derives from the Bantu word for a center of royal activity.

Each Lunda ruler, or *mwata yamvo,* assembled his court in the *musumba,* a region that was surrounded by a moat and earthen wall. Within the *musumba* were neatly laid out roads, public squares, and several courtyards enclosed by stakes. These areas served both political and ritual functions, including royal burials.

The king and his council, or *citentam,* ruled from the *musumba.* The council was made up of ritual titleholders, military officials, representatives of the Lunda colonies, and other administrators. Here the *mwata yamvo* received tribute from his territories, coordinated Lunda trade, and directed the empire's expansion.

The *musumba* was situated on the route along which the Lunda transported captives abducted on raids against neighboring peoples. The *mwata yamvo* conducted raids to the north and northeast, including the Luba. Beginning in the 17th century, captives were either brought to the capital to work the Lunda fields or sold into the transatlantic SLAVE TRADE on the coast.

mwami Head of the TUTSI political structure; believed to be of divine lineage. According to Tutsi mythology, three children were born in heaven and placed on earth by accident. One of these children, Kigwa, was the founder of the most powerful Tutsi family and the being to whom the Tutsi *mwamis* have traditionally traced their beginnings. As early as the 1300s the Tutsi, who were always a pastoralist, or cattle-raising, people, began to settle throughout present-day RWANDA and BURUNDI, an area that had been occupied by the HUTU people for centuries. Because they possessed cattle and had superior skills in warfare, the Tutsi slowly gained political control over the Hutu. By the 1800s the Hutu were completely under Tutsi rule.

The *mwami* was at the top of the Tutsi political, economic, and social pyramid, presiding as king in the Tutsi's monarchical society. The *mwami* controlled all affairs of the state and eventually took possession of all

Hutu land. Therefore, a contractual relationship, called the *ubuhake,* was formed between the Hutu and Tutsi. Under this system the Hutu became indentured servants in exchange for the use of Tutsi land and cattle. This feudal system was so strong that it remained intact through the period of German and Belgian colonial rule that lasted from the late 19th century well into the 20th.

See also: BELGIUM AND AFRICA (Vol. IV); RUANDA-URUNDI (Vol. IV).

Mwari The high god of the Shona people of present-day ZIMBABWE, considered a fertility god and rain-giver. Elaborate Mwari worship practices were an expression of the shared values and beliefs of the Shona people and also served to centralize their religious authority in the oracle at the main Mwari shrine, which was located near present-day Fort Victoria. Mwari worship practices continue to this day.

According to the tradition of the ROZWI people, a Shona subgroup that came to rule Zimbabwe about the beginning of the 18th century, the Mbire clan, from whose ranks the Mwari priests came, migrated south from the Lake Tanganyika region in the 14th century. (There is still a religious tradition surrounding a rain god named "Muali" in the Tanganyika region.) The cult gained strength after that as Shona monarchs attempted to unify the diverse tribes in the area south of the ZAMBEZI RIVER. Later, in the late 17th century, Rozwi kings conquered the MWENE MUTAPA kingdom of Zimbabwe, located to the south of the Zambezi River, and instituted the Mwari worship practices.

> Neither male nor female, Mwari is considered a fertility god and rain-giver. Mwari's multiple functions are indicated by the various praise-names that are used to invoke the god during worship ceremonies. *Dzivaguru,* the most common praise-name, means "great pool" and refers directly to Mwari's ability to send rain to the people; *Mbuya* means "grandmother"; *Zendere* is Mwari's emanation as a young girl; *Sororezhou* means "head of the elephant" and probably refers to Mwari's manifestation as a clap of thunder; *Nyadenga* means "possessor of the sky"; *Wokumusoro* means "the one above"; and *Musikavanhu* means "creator of humankind."

At Zimbabwe the Rozwi's Mwari worship tradition was combined with the preexisting ancestor-worshiping rituals of the people of Mwene Mutapa. That tradition centered on a figure named Chaminuka, who evolved into the "Son of Mwari," although the two religious systems retained their individual identities and traditions. Mwari was certainly important, but the spirits of ancestors were considered even more powerful than Mwari in traditional Shona religious practices.

Although the date and reason for moving the shrine are not certain, the Rozwi kings relocated the main Mwari shrine from its original place north of Zimbabwe, at present-day Fort Victoria, to a cave at Matonjeni in the Matopo Hills, near modern Bulawayo, about 125 miles (200 km) to the west. Despite the shrine's new location the Mwari tradition remained strong among the Shona, and a number of other shrines appeared in the Matopa Hills. The tradition's influence could be seen in the way Shona chiefs demonstrated their loyalty to the Rozwi kings by their affiliation with Mwari and the shrines.

In the 1830s Mwari's authority gained even more influence. At that time the Ndebele, an NGUNI subgroup, fled north into Zimbabwe to escape the military expansion of the ZULU. Ndebele priests, rather than trying to change the Mwari tradition, respected its power and incorporated it into their own religious rituals. Later in the 19th century the Mwari worship practices would prove influential again when the warring Shona and Ndebele people were united by their shared tradition against a common enemy in the form of European colonists.

See also: RELIGION (Vol. III); SHONA (Vols. II, IV); SHONA KINGDOMS (Vol. III).

Further reading: Gwinyai H. Muzorewa, *Mwari: the Great Being God: God is God* (Lanham Md.: University Press of America, 2001).

Mwene Mutapa (Mwene Matapa, Mwene Mutabe, Monomotapa, Mwenenutapa, Mbire) Title of the monarchs who ruled the ZIMBABWE plateau between the ZAMBEZI and Limpopo rivers from the 15th century through the 17th centuries; also the name of the kingdom over which these monarchs ruled. By the late 15th century the Mwene Mutapa state was an active trading kingdom, with a virtual monopoly on the ivory, GOLD, and salt trades in the region and the trade in human beings. Gold was collected from gold fields and panned from the Mazoe River in the interior parts of the kingdom and then brought by caravan to the Indian Ocean ports of SOFALA and QUELIMANE, where it was traded for valuable Arab and Indian goods such as glass, ceramics, spices, and cloth. The height of Mwene Mutapa trading power coincided with the rise of the great East African Swahili and Arab ruling dynasties that built their kingdoms on profits from the gold trade.

By the beginning of the 16th century Swahili, MARAVI, Arab, and even Portuguese traders from around the region all participated in the fairs that were conducted in Mwene Mutapa territory near the Zambezi Valley.

After the 1530s, however, the Portuguese presented a serious threat to Mwene Mutapa as they moved inland from their coastal trading posts. By 1571 the Portuguese had begun hostile invasions for the purpose of seizing Mwene Mutapa's gold mines. In order to keep peace, and probably because the its hold on power may have been slipping, around 1575 the kingdom forged a trade agreement with Portugal that prohibited Arab and Muslim merchants from trading in Mwene Mutapa territory. Around 1623 the kingdom was invaded by warriors from the Maravi federation of states, located to the north of the Zambezi, leaving Mwene Mutapa vulnerable to incursions from the east. The Portuguese took advantage of the situation and had seized vast expanses of Mwene Mutapa territory by 1629. The territory was subsequently divided into estates called *PRAZOS*, which were leased to Portuguese settlers by the Portuguese king.

By the middle of the 17th century the influx of Portuguese merchants and *prazeros,* as the Portuguese lessees were called, had done irreparable damage to the Mwene Mutapa kingdom, which previously had vehemently opposed the spread of foreign influences in their territory. By the late 1600s the weakened kingdom was rather easily conquered by the emerging ROZWI kingdom. By the end of the century the militaristic Rozwi had expelled both the Portuguese and Mwene Mutapa traders from the Zambezi River valley. These conditions enabled the Rozwi to dominate the region and reduce the Mwene Mutapa to a minor state.

See also: IVORY TRADE (Vol. III); LIMPOPO RIVER (Vol. II); MWENE MUTAPA (Vol. II); PORTUGAL AND AFRICA (Vol. III); SALT MINING (Vol. II); SENA (Vol. III); SLAVE TRADE ON THE SWAHILI COAST (Vol. III); TETE (Vol. III).

Mzilikazi (Umsiligasi, Mozelekatse) (1790–1868) *Founder of the Ndebele kingdom in what is now Zimbabwe*

During the period of war and migration known as the MFECANE, the ZULU leader, SHAKA (1787–1828), succeeded in defeating several neighboring peoples, including the Ndwandwe. This brought the Khumalo clan, led by Mzilikazi, under Zulu control. Mzilikazi refused to submit to Zulu authority and, following an unsuccessful rebellion, began leading his followers to the highveld of the Transvaal. From there, beginning circa 1822, the clan raided areas occupied by the SOTHO peoples.

Using variations of the military techniques and organizational system of the Zulu, Mzilikazi was able to subjugate neighboring peoples and organize the strong, centralized nation of Ndebele. However, he continued to suffer attacks from both the Zulu and the BOERS. By 1837 Mzilikazi was forced to move his people once again, this time leading them north of the Limpopo River into what is now ZIMBABWE. There Mzilikazi overcame the Shona people led by the ROZWI rulers of the CHANGAMIRE DY-

NASTY. He then built his kingdom anew. The Ndebele remained strong enough to repel repeated attacks by the Boers, who eventually made peace with Mzilikazi in 1852. Gold was discovered in the region in 1867, bringing increased numbers of European settlers, and unable to control the influx of outsiders, the Ndebele nation ultimately disintegrated.

See also: LIMPOPO RIVER (Vols. I, II); PORTUGAL AND AFRICA (Vols. III, IV); SHONA (Vols. II, IV); SHONA KINGDOMS (Vol. III).

Further reading: R. Kent Rasmussen, *Migrant Kingdom: Mzilikazi's Ndebele in South Africa* (London: Collings, 1978).

Nabahani dynasty Swahili rulers of PATE ISLAND originally from the OMANI SULTANATE; they were at the height of their power in the 1600s and 1700s. The Nabahani family of Oman settled in Pate in the 1200s but did not attain power until the 1600s. During the second half of the 17th century the Nabahanis rebelled, on numerous occasions, against Portuguese influence, contributing to the decline of Portuguese power in the region. (The Portuguese first visited Pate around 1510.) The Nabahanis also struggled against other rulers, including the MASRUI dynasty, for dominance on the East African coast. The Nabahanis retained control of Pate well into the 1800s and at times extended their rule to PEMBA ISLAND and KILWA. In Songo Mnara, just south of Kilwa, an impressive Nabahani mosque still stands today.

The Nabahani commissioned court records, which are referred to as the *Chronicle of Pate*. Some of the earliest Swahili poetry that can be definitively dated was included in the chronicle, probably composed during the 14th century. The poems' formal style was derived from Arabic verse, but its subjects and spirit reflected Swahili culture. One of the poems included in the records, *al-Inkishafi* (The Soul's Awakening), chronicled the economic decline of Pate in terms of man's neglect of God. *Al-Inkishafi* eloquently describes the sinful acquisitiveness of island merchants, who it says consorted with women on beds inlaid with ivory and silver.

Nafata (r. c. 1795–1802) *Sultan of the Hausa state of Gobir*

When Sultan Nafata became *sarkin* (ruler) of GOBIR about 1795, he faced the growing threat of a jihad from the forces led by USMAN DAN FODIO (1754–1817), a FULANI cleric also from Gobir. Fodio's rigorous teachings were accepted and welcomed early in his career, but by the mid-1780s he had become a threat to the authorities of the HAUSA STATES for his ability to attract a large group of followers demanding political and religious change. Usman dan Fodio was also considered dangerous for his attempts to "purify" Islam by outlawing the practice of traditional religion, calling it "pagan" because it was not based on true Islamic law, or *sharia*.

Usman dan Fodio's teachings were initially so well received he was brought to the royal court of Gobir to tutor young rulers, including Nafata's son, Yunfa, in the Islamic faith.

Earlier, in 1789, the reigning *sarkin* of Gobir, Sultan Bawa (r. c. 1781–1790), met with Usman dan Fodio (also known as the *Shehu*, meaning "chief") initially to assassinate the religious leader. When the strength of the Usman dan Fodio's following became apparent, however, Bawa negotiated terms of economic and religious change instead, including the freeing of religious prisoners, the right to preach Islam, the prohibition of taxation, and the right of Muslims to identify themselves by wearing veils or turbans. These reforms brought the state of Gobir to the verge of becoming an independent theocratic state, and this shift in power worried the traditionalist sultanate.

After Bawa's death he was succeeded briefly by a son who was killed in war. A few years later Nafata gained control as sultan of Gobir. Reacting partly to pressure from the nobility as well as from a desire to preserve the sultanate, Nafata soon rescinded the rights granted to Muslims by Sultan Bawa. Nafata also persecuted believers and made attempts to force resident Muslims to practice traditional religion. These actions by Sultan Nafata caused Usman dan Fodio to encourage his followers to arm and defend themselves, a step toward jihad because Muslim reform was generally sought first through peaceful processes.

Before his death in 1802, Nafata clashed strongly with Usman, only increasing tensions between the religious leader and the sultanate of Gobir. However, it was not until the reign of Nafata's son and successor, Yunfa (r. c. 1802–1808), that Usman dan Fodio felt compelled to go on the hajj (or pilgrimage to Mecca), which prefaced the start of the jihad in 1804.

See also: FULANI JIHADS (Vol. III); ISLAM, INFLUENCE OF (Vols. II, III); MECCA (Vol. II); *SHARIA* (Vol. II).

Naimbana (r. 1720–1793) *King of the Temne peoples of present-day Sierra Leone*

By 1786 the British government agreed to help the London-based Committee for the Relief of the Black Poor by sending a group of free blacks to West Africa to form a colony. On April 9, 1787, the *Nautilus* sailed with 344 blacks and 115 whites and landed on May 9, 1787, off the coast of what is now SIERRA LEONE. Once on land the British sought to purchase land from the Temne peoples and their ruler, King Naimbana.

Without Naimbana's knowledge, an agreement was soon made with one of his local chiefs named Tombo, called "King Tom" by the English. King Tom, who could not understand nor read the agreement, signed an initial treaty on June 11, 1787, permanently giving the British claim to the piece of land that was thereafter known as the Province of Freedom. The town that was then built for the former slaves was called Granville Town after the expedition's promoter, Granville Sharp.

After the death of King Tom, Naimbana realized the implications of the land agreement with the British and immediately called for a new treaty to be made. The British complied and the treaty was again confirmed, with Naimbana's signature, in 1788.

Naimbana was said to have been a kind ruler who expressed a desire to learn Christianity and had an interest in European-style education. In 1791 his son, known as Prince John Frederic Naimbana, was sent to England to attend school but later died on his trip back to Sierra Leone. Naimbana's capital was the city of Robana, situated up the Rokel River, where he ruled with absolute power but was known always to consult with his kingdom's chiefs in matters of importance.

See also: ENGLAND AND AFRICA (Vol. III).

Further reading: Mary Louise Clifford, *From Slavery to Freetown; Black Loyalists After the American Revolution* (Jefferson, N.C.: McFarland & Company Inc., 1999).

Nama Subgroup of the nomadic KHOIKHOI inhabiting the southern region of present-day NAMIBIA. Little is known of Nama history prior to 1800, but it is thought that they moved into the Namibia region early in the 17th century. They were originally part of a larger migration of Khoisan-speaking people who came up from the south in search of grazing lands and reliable water sources. The Nama Khoikhoi established their territory, NAMALAND, in areas directly north and south of the ORANGE RIVER, which they called the Gariep (Great) River. The ORLAMS, another Khoikhoi subgroup, migrated to regions to the south of the Nama.

The Nama were herders, and the patterns of their life revolved around the challenges of raising fat-tailed sheep and cattle in an arid environment. They were often plagued by droughts and FOOD shortages, so they celebrated with ancient traditional religious rituals when the seasonal rains finally came. On the occasions when the nomadic Nama could not produce food from their cattle, they would resort to bartering with SAN hunter-gatherers or even hunt and gather themselves.

By the middle of the 17th century the Nama were firmly established as the dominant ethnic group of southern Namibia. They carried out trade with the Ovambo kingdoms to the north, exchanging animal hides and milk for metal goods and other handicrafts. Around the middle of the century Dutch settlers and copper prospectors began to come across the Olifants River, just north of CAPE TOWN on the southern edge of Namaland. Starting around 1660 there were regular clashes between the Nama and the recent Dutch arrivals, with the Nama eventually accepting nominal Dutch sovereignty by the end of the century.

By the end of the 18th century five of the seven major Nama clans had united as the "Red Nation," so called because of the reddish tint to their dark skin. The Dama, a fellow Khoikhoi subgroup that lived to the north of the Nama, were referred to as the "Black Nation." Dama were often hired as servants of the Nama, tending to their herds and sometimes cultivating a small plot of their land.

The northern boundary of Nama territory abutted land ruled by the HERERO, another pastoralist group. The relationship between Nama and Herero was complex, as they had frequent battles over grazing lands and water

The Bantu-speaking Ovambo people of Namibia traditionally constructed enclosures like this kraal. The kraal, shown in a 1983 photograph, is a traditional enclosed set of individual family compounds grouped around a central meeting place. © Nicole Duplaix/Corbis

rights, but they also traded with each other and even intermarried. When European firearms were introduced in the late 18th century, their battles became more deadly.

Present-day Namibia remained an uncharted region of southern Africa until the beginning of the 19th century, when European powers began sending more mineral prospectors and MISSIONARIES hoping to convert the Nama to Christianity. The Europeans were not always welcome, however, as Britain and Germany both sent missionaries who were killed by plundering bands of Nama. Due in large part to these violent reactions, the Nama Khoikhoi, called *Hottentots* by the Dutch, developed a reputation in Europe as one of the fiercest groups in Africa.

See also: HOTTENOT (Vol. III); NAMA (Vol. IV); NETHERLANDS AND AFRICA (Vol. III); OVAMBO (Vols. II, IV); WARFARE AND WEAPONS (Vol. III).

Namaland (Namaqualand)

Region historically inhabited by the NAMA people of southern NAMIBIA and the northern Cape Province of SOUTH AFRICA. The ORANGE RIVER divides Namaland into Great Namaland to the north and Little Namaland to the south. Today the northern limit of Namaland is the city of Windhoek, its eastern border is the Kalahari Desert, and it borders the rugged

Atlantic coast to the west. The history of this region of Africa before 1800 is unreliable, but it is known that the indigenous Nama people herded their cattle in the area and occasionally clashed with local HERERO and SAN groups over land disputes and accusations of stolen cattle.

As early as the 17th century Namaland was also the site of violent disputes between the Nama and Dutch and British settlers. The Europeans came up from the southern Cape region of present-day South Africa, prospecting for copper and looking for suitable farming and grazing lands to support further settlement. In the late 19th century many Europeans came to Namaland to try to mine and trade diamonds, which were found in great concentrations along the floodplains and other alluvial areas of Namibia.

See also: COPPER (Vol. II); HOTTENTOT (Vol. III); KALAHARI DESERT (Vols. I, II); NETHERLANDS AND AFRICA (Vol. III).

Further reading: Brigitte Lau, *Southern and Central Namibia in Jonker Afrikaner's Time* (Windhoek, Namibia: National Archives, Dept. of Nat. Education, 1987).

Namibia

Present-day country measuring approximately 313,300 square miles (824,400 sq km) and located along the coast of southwest Africa. Namibia is bordered by ANGOLA, BOTSWANA, and SOUTH AFRICA. Bantu-speaking peoples migrated to the region between the ninth and 14th centuries and settled the area of present-day Namibia. These peoples established mixed agricultural and pastoral communities that generally lacked any centralized authority. However, several groups, including the Ovambo, Okavango, and HERERO, founded centralized confederations. These peoples dominated the northern and central regions of Namibia, monopolizing NATURAL RESOURCES and the trade routes throughout southwest Africa. The southern regions of Namibia were the exclusive territory of the Khoisan-speaking NAMA people, who probably arrived in the region early in the 17th century.

Namibia's climate is harsh. Strong, blinding winds blow across the Namib Desert, which runs along most of the Namibian coast, making it dangerous territory. One stretch of coast was so littered by bleached animal bones that European explorers referred to it as the SKELETON COAST. Due to its climate and isolated geographical location, little is known about Namibia prior to the 19th century. Several Portuguese sailors touched down on the Namibian coast in the late 1400s, but few foreigners explored the interior until the DUTCH EAST INDIA COMPANY sponsored a brief expedition in the 1650s. The rocky coastline made it virtually impossible to land there. While American, Dutch, French, and British whaling vessels operated along the coast during the 1700s, it wasn't until the 1790s that Europeans, especially the Dutch, began settling the region.

See also: NAMIBIA (Vols. I, II, IV, V); NETHERLANDS AND AFRICA (Vol. III); OVAMBO (Vols. II, IV).

Further reading: M. Hinz, *Without Chiefs There Would Be No Game* (Windhoek, Namibia: Clarkes, 2003).

natural resources Africa's natural resources, including its lush forests and significant mineral resources such as coal, copper, diamonds, GOLD, iron, natural gas, and petroleum make Africa one of the world's richest continents. Except for some metals, however, the mineral resources were not commercially exploited in any widespread way before the colonial period, many not until the 20th century.

Copper, gold, and iron were first exploited by Africans thousands of years ago. The use of copper to make castings dates as far back as 6000 BCE. About 3500 BCE copper was first alloyed with tin to make bronze, a more durable material for making both weapons and adornments. Iron was mined and worked in the ancient kingdom of Aksum before 750 BCE, and recent archaeological evidence points to the development of ironworking technology in East Africa as early as 1400 BCE. Gold was both an important trading commodity and source of adorn-

ment since 5000 BCE in ancient EGYPT and early in the common era in West Africa.

Africa's vast resources first gained worldwide attention in the 15th century. The Portuguese explored the coastal regions of the continent in order to establish trade routes to India. They also sought to tap into the gold and ivory trades and the trade in human beings along Africa's eastern and western coasts. This natural wealth spurred European imperialism. Much of the continent's natural and human resources were exploited for the benefit of the ruling nations. It is difficult to ascertain the exact effect this exploitation had on the course of history.

Much of Africa's natural wealth is contained in its mineral deposits. Africa has major portions of the world's reserves of bauxite, cobalt, tantalum, and germanium. The continent is a major producer of coal and contains one of the largest uranium-producing regions in the world. The sedimentary Precambrian rocks of western Africa make the continent one of the world's greatest producers of iron ore. Southern Africa contains one-half of the world's gold reserve and nearly all of the world's supply of chromium.

Africa also contains vast nonmetallic minerals. Some of the largest kaolin, bentonite, and fuller's earth deposits are found on the continent. There are also large sodium deposits, and present-day MADAGASCAR is the world's foremost producer of flake graphite. Many of the world's building materials come from Africa, as there are huge quantities of basalt, pumice, granite, marble, and limestone.

Africa is best known for its immense deposits of precious stones. Today more than 40 percent of the world's industrial diamonds come from African mines. Africa also has large deposits of gem diamonds, garnets, opals, amethyst, emeralds, and topaz.

Immense botanical resources are also prevalent in Africa. Lush forestation provides valuable timber, and vast expanses of grassland allow for diverse populations of mammals. The tremendous numbers of animals, such as water buffalo, oxen, horses, mules, camels, sheep, pigs, and antelope, are used in land cultivation, TRANSPORTATION, FOOD, tourism, skins, and even game hunting.

See also: COPPER (Vols. I, II); COPPERBELT (Vol. V); COPPER MINES (Vol. II); EBONY (Vols. I, III); ELEPHANTS (Vol. I); IVORY (Vol. II); IVORY TRADE (Vols. III); MINING (Vols. I, II, III, IV, V); NATURAL RESOURCES (Vols. IV, V).

Ndlambe (Ndlamba) South African ethnic group residing in the Eastern Cape province and related to the XHOSA. They are one of the nine groups, including the ZULU and the Thembu, who make up the NGUNI people. They speak a language unique among the Bantu because it combines Bantu elements with imploding clicking sounds that were absorbed into their language through intermarriage with the region's earlier Khoisan-speaking peoples.

Ndlambe (c. 1740–1828) is also the name of a Ndlambe regent who acted on behalf of his nephew, NGQIKA (1775–1829). Throughout his regency, Ndlambe continually looked for opportunities to raise his status. When Ngqika came of age, he accepted his position as sovereign of all the Xhosas, much to the dismay of Ndlambe. Thereafter, the two became rivals.

In the late 18th and early 19th centuries the Ndlambe people joined forces with the GQUNUKWEBE to resist the incursion of Dutch farmers known as BOERS. Much of this contention arose from land and cattle disputes.

As a result of a steady increase in the European settler population and mismanagement of property, there was a huge land shortage on the eastern frontier in the early 19th century. About 1811–12 the British embarked on a massive campaign to push the Gqunukwebe, Zuurveld, and Ndlambe peoples across the Fish River. At the same time, the British worked to their advantage the hostilities that arose as a result of this mass exodus. Conflict between Ngqika's followers and those of his enemy Ndlambe became more intense. As Ngqika's people had always inhabited the region beyond the Fish River, Ngqika was not affected directly by the efforts of the Europeans. In the 1818 Battle of Amalinde, the Ndlambe people conquered Ngqika's forces.

The Ndlambe and Ngqika were in the process of consolidating under Chief Makanna (d. 1820), a subject of Ndlambe's, when the British, with the help of Ngqika, tried to intervene. Under Makanna the Ndlambe retaliated by invading Grahamstown. No sooner did it appear that the Ndlambe would be victorious than the British reinforcements came through. Makanna surrendered and was quickly banished to isolated Robben Island, in Table Bay, 5 miles (8 km) west of the mainland. He died a year later trying to escape. The British designated Ngqika leader of all Xhosa in the Fish River territory.

See also: ENGLAND AND AFRICA (Vol. III).

Ndongo Early 16th-century kingdom of the MBUNDU, a Bantu-speaking peoples from a region of what is now northern ANGOLA. The Mbundu who founded this kingdom are often called the Ndongo after the kingdom's name. The Ndongo recognized the authority of the KONGO KINGDOM in the early 16th century. By the 1540s, however, they attempted to free themselves of these feudal bonds.

The modern country of Angola gets its name from *ngola,* the title of Ndongo's ruler.

As part of their efforts the Ndongo began to establish commercial ties with Portuguese merchants in order to curb the Kongo trade monopoly. Despite KONGO efforts to maintain this monopoly, the Ndongo defeated the Kongo in 1556 and achieved their independence.

The Ndongo soon became embroiled in constant conflict with the Portuguese. The Portuguese Crown authorized the conquest and Christianization of Ndongo in 1571. The Ndongo held off Portugal's colonial efforts for nearly a century, in part by banding together with the Kongo and IMBANGALA peoples. Portuguese forces, however, ultimately prevailed, and the Ndongo were incorporated into Portuguese Angola in 1671.

See also: PORTUGAL AND AFRICA (Vol. III).

Netherlands and Africa The Netherlands' interest in Africa was the result of economic and political necessity. In the 16th century the Dutch were the leading northern European distributors of African goods brought to Europe through Spanish and Portuguese commerce. The provinces of the Netherlands, ruled by Philip II of Spain (1527–1598) as part of his inheritance, rebelled against the Spanish Crown, finally gaining independence in 1609. As a result of this conflict, however, the Dutch sea merchants of the united Netherlands' provinces were cut off from Asian and African goods arriving through Lisbon in Portugal, which was a Spanish holding at the time. Therefore they quickly sought a direct means of obtaining these goods, which led to increased military and commercial competition with Portugal and Spain.

Even before independence the Dutch were able to supplant the Portuguese as the most powerful European force involved in the Indian Ocean spice trade. They developed a commercial empire under the leadership of the national DUTCH EAST INDIA COMPANY, which was established in 1602 near the Cape of Good Hope. This development was matched on the Atlantic coast, as the Dutch looked to monopolize the transatlantic SLAVE TRADE to the Americas. Led by officers from the DUTCH WEST INDIA COMPANY, the Dutch attacked Portuguese and Spanish strongholds in West Africa, eventually seizing fortified trading outposts on GORÉE ISLAND, Arguin Island, and at São Jorge da Mina (ELMINA). For a few years in the mid-17th century the Netherlands had a virtual monopoly on the supply of captives coming from West Africa.

In 1652 the East India Company was charged with founding a station along the South African coast to resupply its ships traveling between Europe and the Indian Ocean. The station was not intended to be permanent, but by 1657 the company had to grant farming rights to its employees in order to increase FOOD production for the Dutch who worked there. To maintain the necessary LABOR force, the Dutch began acquiring captive labor from East Africa—and from India and Indonesia, where they maintained strong trading ties—and the once-small shipping depot became converted into a permanent colony centered around CAPE TOWN. The company began to augment the inconsistent KHOIKHOI cattle supply with its own herds, and disputes over grazing land led to armed conflict with the Khoikhoi people. Dutch soldiers fought using superior European weapons and easily defeated the Khoikhoi. Smallpox, brought to the Cape by Dutch traders, further decimated the Khoikhoi people, who had no immunity to the disease.

Dutch is a Germanic language spoken by people from the "Low Countries" (modern Netherlands, Luxembourg, and Belgium, where it is called Flemish). The English used the term *Dutch* to refer to people from the Republic of the United Netherlands, which was established in 1588 and lasted until 1795.

During the 18th century Dutch and other European colonists immigrated to the cape in waves. Vast stretches of arable land were settled beyond the coast, and a group of farmers known as BOERS, or Trekboers, moved into the northern reaches of the colony, encroaching upon the lands of the XHOSA people. This resulted in an explosive relationship between the colonists and the Xhosa. Forts were erected to protect colonists from attacks, and in 1780 a colonial border was established at the Great Fish River to separate settlers from the Xhosa. Those Xhosa residing west of the river were forcibly removed from their homelands, resulting in nearly a century of war.

By the turn of the 18th century the Dutch had lost their trading superiority to the French and British, who captured many of their coastal strongholds. By 1806 the CAPE COLONY was a British protectorate.

See also: CAPE FRONTIER WARS (Vol. III); ENGLAND AND AFRICA (Vol. III); PROTECTORATE (Vol. IV); SLAVERY IN SOUTH AFRICA (Vol. III).

Newton, John (1725–1807) *English seaman, trader, minister, and author*

Newton's book *An Authentic Narrative* is a valuable first-hand account of the transatlantic SLAVE TRADE during the 18th century. In 1788 Newton also wrote an antislavery pamphlet, *Thoughts upon the African Slave Trade,* that was influential in convincing the British House of Commons to consider abolishing the trade in human beings.

John Newton was born to a London maritime merchant and a deeply religious mother. He became a sailor while still in his teens, working on a Mediterranean commercial vessel and later sailed as a midshipman with the British Royal Navy. Eventually Newton was transferred out of the navy and got hired on as a mate on an Africa-bound trading ship. Once in Africa he ended up working for a European named Clow, a farmer and slave trader in SIERRA LEONE. After a disagreement with the white trader's black African "wife," Newton was forced to work on the plantation as a manual laborer. After about one year of this work Newton was happy to see his fortunes change when another slave trader arrived and hired him to work on his ship. Newton wrote later that it was at this time, about 1748, that he had a powerful religious experience during an especially rough transatlantic voyage.

Eventually, about 1750, Newton came to be the first in command on his own ship, which carried cargoes of enslaved Africans. His journal entries from this time, which he used to compose *An Authentic Narrative,* describe brutal conditions in the holds of these ships and the cruel treatment of the typically poor and uneducated sailors who worked the ships. In 1756 Newton retired from his captaincy because of illness and returned to England, where he eventually became an ordained Anglican minister, hymn writer, and author.

In *An Authentic Narrative,* written around 1764, he expresses remorse for his past actions and emphasizes that his livelihood as a trader in human beings was always in conflict with his professed Christian religion, though he did not realize it at the time. By the time he wrote *Thoughts upon the African Slave Trade,* he describes the buying and selling of human beings as a "business at which my heart now shudders." Newton died in England in 1807.

When he returned to England, Newton became a minister in the small town of Olney, in Buckinghamshire. He became a close friend of the English poet William Cowper (1731–1800), and the two collaborated on a collection of church hymns, or songs of praise. One of the most popular of these Olney Hymns was adapted to an African-American spiritual melody to become the well-known "Amazing Grace."

Ngazargamu Capital of KANEM-BORNU, from its establishment by Mai Ali Gaji (fl. 1470s), about 1472, until 1808. Ngazargamu remained the capital of Kanem-Bornu even after the trading empire managed to defeat the BULALA people and recapture Njimi, Kanem-Bornu's

original capital, in the early 1500s. Despite Njimi's historical significance to Kanem-Bornu, the rulers elected to remain in Ngazargamu, which offered richer lands for farming and livestock. Ngazargamu was also known for its cloth production.

In the early 19th century the FULANI living in what is now NIGERIA fell under the influence of the Islamic religious scholar USMAN DAN FODIO (1754–1817). Considering the people of Kanem-Bornu to be irreligious, the Fulani launched a holy war that ended in 1808 with the destruction of the Kanem-Bornu capital.

See also: BORNU (Vol. II); FULANI JIHADS (Vol. III); NGAZARGAMU (Vol. II).

Ngbandi (Gbandi, Mogwandi)
Ethnic group that, between the 15th and 16th centuries, migrated west from southern regions of the present-day Republic of the SUDAN. Ngbandi groups settled in the northwest region of the CONGO and also on the left bank of the Ubangi River, in what is today the CENTRAL AFRICAN REPUBLIC.

The Ngbandi speak an ADAMAWA-Ubangi language that belongs to the Niger-Congo language family. Their language is similar to that of the BANDA and Baya. They are also related to the Ngbaka people.

One group of Ngbandi established the Nzakara kingdom in the 16th century while others set up feudal systems. In the 18th century Ngbandi from the Bandia clan conquered territory belonging to another Sudanic group, the AZANDE, eventually combining with them, adopting the Azande's language and customs.

Traditionally the Ngbandi were a hunting and gathering society but they gradually moved into AGRICULTURE, producing primarily grains and nuts as well as fruits and vegetables. Their society is organized by patrilineal descent. They have long been skilled artisans known for their knives, harps, statues, wood carvings, and masks. Some of these items were traded with neighboring peoples.

Ngonde
Ethnic group of present-day TANZANIA. For centuries, the Ngonde lived in villages that were organized by age-sets, meaning that the inhabitants were all of approximately the same age. Eventually, however, the Ngonde were centralized under a king, known as the *kyungu*. Although exactly when this took place is unknown, according to Ngonde traditions, the first *kyungu* held his position for approximately 10 generations before the arrival of Arab traders in their area toward the end of the 18th century.

See also: AGE SETS (Vol. I); ARABS (Vol. II); SWAHILI COAST (Vol. III).

Further reading: Owen J. M. Kalinga, *A History of the Ngonde Kingdom of Malawi* (New York: Mouton, 1985).

Ngoni (Angoni, Abangoni, Mangoni, Wangoni)
Ethnic grouping of 12 NGUNI peoples originally inhabiting modern-day Natal in SOUTH AFRICA. The Ngoni were forced to flee their homelands during the MFECANE (the crushing), a period of migrations caused by the ZULU military campaigns of the early 19th century. They migrated to areas in present-day MOZAMBIQUE, MALAWI, TANZANIA, and ZAMBIA, settling into small patrilineal states. The Ngoni factions were able to increase their territory by conquering neighboring peoples, utilizing the same military techniques used by the Zulu who had displaced them.

Each Ngoni group attained regional dominance for nearly 50 years. However, by the end of the 19th century, Portugal, Britain, and Germany had placed the Ngoni under colonial rule.

Ngoyo (Ngoy)
Kingdom that lasted from the 16th to the 19th centuries on the west coast of Central Africa, just north of the mouth of the Congo River. The kingdom of Ngoyo probably started during the late 15th century in the lush equatorial rain forest north of the Congo River. Like the neighboring kingdom of LOANGO, Ngoyo was originally a tributary state of the KONGO KINGDOM. Loango broke from Kongo during the 16th century, and Ngoyo followed in the 17th century. Although there was tension among the three kingdoms, they continued to maintain close ties through trade and the shared language of Kikongo. Ngoyo continued to pay tribute to the Loango king, or *maniloango,* who was often married to an Ngoyo princess. By the 18th century, however, Ngoyo's wealth from trade at its port of CABINDA and its formidable military enabled the state to become an independent power, equal in status to the larger kingdoms of the region.

During the 18th century Ngoyo and SOYO, another breakaway state from the Kongo kingdom, vied for control of the burgeoning northern trade with the Portuguese, French, Dutch, and British. The Ngoyo port of Cabinda began to divert trade from the southern Portuguese port of LUANDA and from the nearby port of Mpinda at the mouth of the Congo River, which belonged to Soyo. As the local trade became increasingly lucrative, the two kingdoms frequently warred with each another.

The northern trade in captives increased substantially during this period, reaching its peak during the late 1700s. It heightened tensions with Ngoyo's neighbors, especially the KONGO, whose territory was often plundered for captives. These captives were increasingly traded at Cabinda rather than at the more remote port of Luanda, prompting Portuguese intervention in Ngoyo. In 1783, anxious to establish a foothold in the north coast of ANGOLA and subdue their rivals, the Portuguese built a fort at Cabinda. But Ngoyo quickly ousted them with the help of the French and the Kongo people, and the Portuguese were forced to concede a free-trade zone north of the Congo River. The agreement helped stabilize commerce at Cabinda, which had previously suffered from a rivalry between European merchants that often resulted in armed conflicts that frequently interrupted trade.

The trade at Cabinda—and the power it conferred on those who controlled it—also caused internal disputes between the king of Ngoyo, whose capital lay in the interior, and the port's governor and minister of trade. By the end of the 18th century Cabinda's officials refused to pay royal tribute and began to act independently. Despite this the Ngoyo kingdom remained intact into the 1800s and managed to resist Portuguese colonization until the end of the 19th century.

See also: PORTUGAL AND AFRICA (Vols. III, IV); SLAVE TRADE, THE TRANSATLANTIC (Vol. III).

Further reading: Zdenka Volavkova, *Crown and Ritual: The Royal Insignia of Ngoyo* (Toronto: University of Toronto Press, 1998).

Ngqika (Gaika) (1775–1829) *Chief of the Amararabe branch of the Xhosa people*

Ngqika's father, Umlao, died before Ngqika was old enough to accept his rightful position as chief of the Amararabe (later called the Ngqika) branch of the XHOSA living in what is now SOUTH AFRICA. Umlao's brother, NDLAMBE, who would have ascended to the throne if not for his nephew, acted as regent until Ngqika came of age. During his tenure Ndlambe grew to become very powerful and gained the support of a group of loyal followers. When Ngqika was ready to assume the throne, Ndlambe was not willing to step down. The Amararabe people immediately sided with Ngqika and designated him king of all the Xhosas. Ndlambe retreated and took his large following with him.

In 1796 the forces of Ngqika and Ndlambe were engaged in a bitter war from which Ngqika emerged victorious. He then imprisoned his uncle for two years. While Ndlambe was imprisoned Ngqika reportedly stole one of his uncle's wives, offending many of Ngqika's own supporters and creating a great rift within Xhosa society. Many of Ngqika's people migrated to the western side of the Fish River with Ndlambe's supporters. It was from this split that the Ngqika and Ndlambe groups were formed.

After Ndlambe's escape, the series of wars that ensued were precipitated by British interference. In 1818, at the Battle of Amalinde, the Ngqika people were defeated by their Ndlambe enemies. A year later Ngqika returned with the help of his European allies, and together they conquered Ndlambe and his people. Thereafter the British acknowledged Ngqika as the supreme Xhosa chief. His title came with a price, however, which was the

British acquisition of all the Ngqika land between the Kei and Keiskamma rivers. Ngqika quickly lost the support of his people. He died in 1829.

See also: ENGLAND AND AFRICA (Vol. III); KEI RIVER (Vol. I).

Nguni Group of related Bantu-speaking peoples who occupied areas of southeast Africa from CAPE COLONY, in present-day SOUTH AFRICA, to southern MOZAMBIQUE. By the end of the 18th century the Nguni had organized into three main kingdoms, the Nganwe, the Ndwandwe, and the Mthethwa. The broad geographic dispersion of the Nguni peoples is largely the result of the MFECANE, a series of forced migrations caused by the ZULU military campaigns beginning in the 1820s. The Zulu were originally a chiefdom in the Mthethwa kingdom, so some Nguni were easily assimilated into the conquering Zulu society. Most Nguni, however, fled to other regions.

Many refugee groups adopted Zulu warfare methods, allowing them to easily conquer other African peoples. In this manner, many great Africa states, such as the Ndebele, the SWAZI, and the Gaza, were established in central and southern Africa. In the 19th century the NGONI, an eastern branch of the Nguni, conquered territories around Lake Malawi, to the north of the ZAMBEZI RIVER.

Europeans gradually overtook many Nguni groups during the CAPE FRONTIER WARS. With the discovery of GOLD and diamonds on Nguni lands in the late 1800s, European conquest was further accelerated. By the turn of the 20th century traditional Nguni societies were virtually nonexistent in South Africa.

Ngwaketse (Bangwaketse) Southern African ethnic group that migrated to present-day BOTSWANA between the 17th and 18th centuries. The Ngwaketse were originally descended from the TSWANA dynasty. According to oral tradition, Kwena, Ngwato, and Ngwaketse were the great grandsons of Tswana chief Masilo. After a bitter dispute over succession, the three brothers separated with their followers and founded their own kingdoms. Ngwaketse and his people moved into the Kanye region in southeastern Botswana. By the mid-18th century the Ngwaketse kingdom was firmly established as a strong military force. They subjugated the Kgalagadi communities and controlled all of the commercial activities, including hunting, cattle raiding, and copper MINING, in the Kalahari Desert region. The Ngwaketse also fought with the neighboring Tlhaping and Hurutshe peoples over CAPE COLONY and MOZAMBIQUE trade routes.

In the early 19th century Ngwaketse power began to decline as Cape Colony raiders in search of ivory, cattle, and captives initiated a series of invasions into Ngwaketse territory.

See also: IVORY TRADE (Vol. III); KALAHARI DESERT (Vol. I, II); SLAVERY IN SOUTH AFRICA (Vol. III).

Nkole (Ankole, Banyankole Nkore, Nyankole)

Bantu-speaking people living in what is now UGANDA; also the name of the kingdom they established at the beginning of the 15th century. The Nkole are made up of the cattle-raising TUTSI and the agricultural HUTU. Nkole's Tutsi members descended from Nilotic pastoralists who, between the 14th and the beginning of the 15th centuries, migrated into the region from the northeast. Upon their arrival in the region, they peacefully began to establish dominion over the agricultural Hutu.

By the early 16th century Nkole was led by kings from the HINDA ruling clan. The Hinda belonged to the Hima, a cattle-owning social caste made up mostly of Tutsis. About 1520 the Hinda rulers were able to achieve independence from the neighboring kingdom of BUNYORO with the aid of a natural phenomenon: in the midst of the Battle of Biharwe, the area underwent a solar eclipse, which Bunyoro's BITO rulers took as a sign to leave Nkole. During the first half of the 18th century Nkole again warred with Bunyoro. This time, the *mugabe,* or king, of Nkore expelled Bunyoro's Bito rulers permanently.

Although they were an ethnic minority, the Tutsi instituted a hierarchical political system with Tutsi court officials and regional chiefs serving as the highest authorities. The majority Hutu, descendants of the region's original Bantu-speaking inhabitants, made up the Nkole underclass. They were forced to pay tribute to the Tutsi and were obliged to feed the Tutsi lords and care for their herds; in return, Tutsi warriors protected the kingdom. The Tutsi and Hutu traditionally were forbidden to intermarry. In Nkole society the Hutu were considered legally inferior and were not allowed to possess their own cattle, which were considered a symbol of status. To prevent Hutu rebellion, only Tutsi men were allowed to serve in the army.

See also: NKOLE (Vol. II).

Niger

Large, landlocked West African country measuring approximately 458,100 square miles (1,186,500 sq km) and bordered by LIBYA, CHAD, NIGERIA, Republic of BENIN, BURKINA FASO, Republic of MALI, and ALGERIA. The present-day borders of Niger were created during 20th-century French colonial occupation. Prior to the period of European colonization, several important kingdoms occupied parts of the country.

From the 14th century on, the region around the AÏR MASSIF, which is a group of mountains in central Niger rising 6,628 feet (2,020 m) at its highest peak, changed hands several times. It was important as a center of trans-Saharan trade with the regions to the south and west. The region also was important because of the copper mines at Takedda, a small kingdom ruled by TUAREGS that later developed into a sultanate centered around AGADES, the chief city of the region. The Tuareg Aïr sultanate was captured by SONGHAI in 1515, and it later fell to KANEM-BORNU in the 17th century.

The main power to the west was the SONGHAI Empire, which ruled successfully in portions of Niger and Mali until the late 16th century. To the southeast, around the Lake CHAD area, were the KANURI peoples of the Kanem-Bornu empire, who flourished until the early 1800s. This empire ultimately began losing territory to the emerging SOKOTO CALIPHATE.

Between the NIGER RIVER in the extreme southwest and Lake Chad in the southeast lay the powerful HAUSA STATES. These walled city-states reached their pinnacle in the 17th and 18th centuries before succumbing to the early 19th-century FULANI JIHADS led by Islamic cleric USMAN DAN FODIO (1754–1817). The jihad launched in 1804 succeeded in incorporating the Hausa States—and later Kanem-Bornu—into the vast SOKOTO CALIPHATE, which stretched throughout the northern regions of Nigeria and the southern regions of Niger.

See also: NIGER (Vols. I, II, IV, V); TAKEDDA (Vol. II).

Niger expeditions

European interest in exploring the regions of West Africa and charting the course of the NIGER RIVER began late in the 18th century with the founding, in 1788, of the British Africa Association (known formally as the Association for the Discovery of the Interior Parts of Africa). The first expedition down the Niger did not begin, however, until Scotland's Mungo PARK (1771–1806) traveled the waterways for the Africa Association during two separate journeys that began, respectively, in 1795 and 1805. Although, with these journeys, Park succeeded in mapping a major portion of the river from SEGU to Bussa, he drowned in 1806 during an assault by a Bussa-area people.

Between 1823 and 1825 British explorer Hugh Clapperton (1788–1827) also made attempts to explore the Niger and its waterways, focusing his efforts in the northern region of present-day NIGERIA. After his death near the SOKOTO CALIPHATE, his former servant, Richard Lander, continued Clapperton's efforts at charting the Niger. Lander eventually made his way from the Hausa state of KANO to the YORUBALAND coastline of present-day Nigeria. After his journey he returned to England, publishing both Clapperton's and his own memoirs. Clapperton's journals, published in 1830, are entitled *Records of Captain Clapperton's Last Expedition to Africa* and *Subsequent Adventures of the Author.* Lander's memoirs, *The Journal of Richard Lander from Kano to the Sea Coast,* were published in 1829.

At the request of the British government, Lander again explored the Niger River, this time accompanied by his brother John. The Landers began their expedition on March 22, 1830, and were successful at drafting a map of the river that picked up where Park's expeditions left off at Bussa and extended to the river's eventual outflow into the Atlantic Ocean. Lander died while on a journey back up the Niger, but his exploits were posthumously published in 1832 with the title *Journal of an Expedition to Explore the Course and Termination of the Niger.*

See also: EXPLORATION (Vol. III).

Nigeria West African country located on the Atlantic coast and bounded by the present-day nations of CHAD, CAMEROON, NIGER, and Republic of Benin. Nigeria covers approximately 356,700 square miles (923,900 sq km) of southeastern West Africa. By the 16th century, when the Portuguese had firmly established trade contacts with parts of West Africa, the numerous states and kingdoms in the region were governed by two different systems. The first was a centralized system controlled generally by a monarch, who usually held both religious and secular authority. This monarch exercised sole control over the kingdom's lands and resided in the kingdom's capital, which also served as the kingdom's main trading center. KANEM-BORNU, the OYO EMPIRE, and the kingdom of BENIN all flourished under this centralized system; ruling dynasties grew increasingly wealthy from tribute collected from the outlying, generally agrarian, provinces.

Other precolonial states in this area had decentralized governments. In these cases, smaller groups of villages were governed by councils of elders and the heads of the families within each village. The concepts of house and FAMILY were essential to these decentralized states, and most villages tended toward self-government. Examples of these states include those of the EFIK and the IGBO peoples, which, along with councils of elders, also included the use of secret societies, such as the EKPE SOCIETY of the Efik people, whose function was to collect tribute, educate the younger generations, and enforce laws or punishments when required.

The vast territory of empires and states in Nigeria from the 16th century onward were highly active in the trading of captives, FOOD, PALM OIL, and metals with both the interior and the Europeans. Kingdoms such as Oyo, Benin, ITSEKIRI, and the HAUSA STATES owed their economic success to their contact with Europeans, especially the Portuguese and, later, the British, with their demand for humans captives, which reached its peak in the 17th and 18th centuries.

While the trade in captives dominated Nigeria in the 17th century, other factors were gaining in importance. The kingdom of Oyo had become a major transfer point for internal and external trade. Oyo also built up a powerful army, led by a large cavalry, that brought the empire both economic and military success. The dominance of Oyo lasted until the 18th century when political unrest began to undermine the kingdom and set the stage for the FULANI JIHADS, or holy wars, that destroyed Oyo in the early 19th century. Thereafter Oyo became known as Old Oyo. About 1830 a new city, also named Oyo, was built 62 miles (100 km) to the south.

The Hausa States of Nigeria were also experiencing a period of economic prosperity during the late 17th century because of the efforts of a series of rulers who increased the educational and political strength of their respective states. Hausaland continued to gain strength and territory into the next century but, like Oyo, was unable to withstand the might of the FULANI JIHADS. Between 1804 and 1808, the Muslim FULANI leader, USMAN DAN FODIO (1754–1817), successfully captured the Hausa States and incorporated them into the SOKOTO CALIPHATE.

The year 1807 brought the abolition of the slave trade by the British Parliament. Even though the trade in human beings continued over the next few decades and the demand for palm oil increased, the once-powerful kingdoms and states of Nigeria began to decline. The modern boundaries of Nigeria were set in 1861, when the former capital of LAGOS was officially annexed by Britain, a move that presaged the coming colonial era.

See also: NIGERIA (Vols. I, II, IV, V).

Further reading: Toyin Falola and Steven J. Salm, *Nigerian Cities* (Trenton, N.J.: Africa World Press, 2004).

Niger River Major West African river, the fourth-longest in the world. Although the complete course of the river was not mapped until after 1830, the river's geography and length had long been under speculation by African and European mapmakers.

The waterways of the Niger were an important means of TRANSPORTATION and commerce in West Africa even before Europeans began to use it extensively in the 18th century. The most important precolonial kingdoms and states of West Africa, including the empires of ancient Ghana, Mali, and SONGHAI, relied on the Niger for trade and territorial conquest. Further, during the 15th through the 19th centuries newer kingdoms, including BENIN, BONNY, Oyo, Ife, and BORGU, were established around the valley areas of the Niger and utilized the river for commerce.

The fact that the Niger flows from east to west was first mentioned in 1550 in the writings of the Arab traveler LEO AFRICANUS (1485–1554). The Arab geographer al-Idrisi (c. 1100–1165), whose major work, the *Kitab nuzhat al-mushtaq fi ikhtiraq al-afaq (The pleasure excursion of one who is eager to traverse the regions of the world)*, was finally published in Rome in 1592, also wrote of the east-west flow of the river and speculated that the Niger emptied into the Atlantic Ocean at SENE-GAL. In 1796 a Scot named Mungo PARK (1771–1806) mapped the course of the river from SEGU as far as Bussa, but it was not until the 1830 expedition of John and Richard Lander (the latter the servant of Captain Hugh Clapperton (1788–1827), who had made expeditions to chart the Niger from 1823 to 1825) that the rest of the Niger's course, from Bussa to its outflowing from the delta at the Bight of BENIN into the Atlantic Ocean, was finally defined.

See also: NIGER DELTA (Vol. I); NIGER EXPEDITIONS (Vol. III); NIGER RIVER (Vol. I).

Nilotes A pastoralist people of the southern Sudan, the Nilotes traced their ancestry to the Late Stone Age. Between 200 BCE and 1000 CE, the Southern Nilotes, known as the Paranilotes, migrated into the highlands east of Lake VICTORIA. Then, around 1500, the western Nilotes of the southern Sudan moved in clan groups to the area northeast of Lake Victoria. One of these LUO-speaking clans, the BITO, deposed the Chwezi, took control of the Kitara Complex, and began the new dynasty of BUNYORO-KITARA. The Bito established several other kingdoms, including Buganda, Koki, Kiziba, and Toro. The Bito adopted some of the traditions of the Chwezi and also adopted the Bantu language. Thus the Bito ruled without much opposition from their Bantu-speaking subjects, and the merger of the two cultures formed a new one that had elements of each of the parent cultures.

In other cases the Bito imposed their political systems and language on the people they conquered. In the highlands the Luo sent out minor chiefs from already established chieftainships to rule over non-Luo-speaking groups. The impact of the Nilote migrations went beyond the assimilation and integration of other cultures, however. Some peoples responded to the invaders by withdrawing into other areas. For example, the pastoral HINDA withdrew to NKOLE, Karagwe, and RWANDA—where they were known as TUTSI—and established new kingdoms there. The later migrations of the eastern Nilotes were responsible for the formation of the Karamojong of northeast Uganda and the MAASAI of central KENYA.

See also: CHWEZI DYNASTY (Vol. II); KITARA COMPLEX (Vol. II); NILOTES (Vols. I, II); KARAMOJONG (Vol. II).

Further reading: Audrey Butt, *The Nilotes of the Sudan and Uganda* (London: International African Institute, 1964).

Nkole (Ankole, Banyankole, Nkore, Nyankole) Bantu-speaking people living in what is now UGANDA; also the name of their kingdom established at the beginning of the 15th century. The Nkole are made up of the cattle-raising TUTSI and the agricultural HUTU. The Nkole occupied a kingdom in what is now the Mbarara district of Uganda. Nkole's Tutsi members descended from Nilotic pastoralists who migrated into the region from the northeast from the end of the 14th to the beginning of the 15th centuries. Upon their arrival in the region, they peacefully began to establish dominion over the Hutu.

By the early 16th century the Nkole kingdom was led by the HINDA ruling dynasty of the Hima caste, made up mostly of Tutsi. The Hinda rulers were able to achieve independence from the neighboring kingdom of BUNYORO in 1520 with the aid of a natural phenomenon: in the midst of the Battle of Biharwe, a solar eclipse occurred, which the Bunyoro rulers took as a sign to leave Nkole. During the first half of the 18th century Nkole again warred with Bunyoro. This time the *mugabe,* or king, of Nkore expelled Bunyoro's BITO rulers permanently.

Although they were an ethnic minority, the Tutsi instituted a hierarchical political system with Tutsi court officials and regional chiefs serving as the highest authorities. The majority Hutu, descendants of the region's original Bantu-speaking inhabitants, made up the Nkole underclass. They were forced to pay tribute to the Tutsi and were obliged to feed the Tutsi lords and care for their herds; in return, Tutsi warriors protected the kingdom. The Tutsi and Hutu traditionally were forbidden to intermarry. In Nkole society the Hutu were considered legally inferior and were not allowed to possess their own cattle, which were considered a symbol of status. To prevent Hutu rebellion, only Tutsi men were allowed to serve in the army.

See also: NKOLE (Vol. II).

Nsibidi writing System of writing found in CAMEROON and NIGERIA. Probably invented as early as the 18th century, the Nsibidi form of script was made up of symbols and characters that represented words and ideas. It was used generally by the EKOI and EFIK peoples as a form of communication within the Ekpe (leopard) secret society. Nsibidi writings were used to record court proceedings, anecdotes, and traditional adages, as well as for tattoos, wall inscriptions, mask decorations, carvings, and drawings.

See also: EKPE SOCIETY (Vol. III).

Ntinde XHOSA subgroup from the Eastern Cape Province of SOUTH AFRICA. According to oral history the Ntinde group descended from a man of the same name whose father, Togu, was the Xhosa chief and whose mother was the daughter of Chief Ngosini of the neighboring Lawo people. In the 17th century Ntinde and his brother Ketshe migrated with their followers to the region between the Chalumna and Buffalo rivers. The Ntinde royal and administrative center was located just east of the Keiskama River. By the late 18th century many Ntinde people had settled in the Zuurveld region.

Between the 18th and 19th centuries the Ntinde, as well as the neighboring Xhosa groups, including the Gcaleka, Ngqika, NDLAMBE, GQUNUKWEBE, Dushane, and Qayi, fought against Dutch farmers, known as BOERS, in a series of conflicts known as the CAPE FRONTIER WARS. The Boers were eventually victorious and the CAPE COLONY took control of the Xhosa territory.

Nuba Ethnic group residing in the Nuba Hills located in the predominantly Arab KORDOFAN province in the central part of the present-day Republic of the SUDAN. During the 16th century the Nuba migrated to their present location in the mountains, probably to escape raids by Baggara and Kababish Arabs in the Sudan.

There are several Nuba groups, each of which has its own distinct traditions and customs. The central and northern groups are organized by patrilineal descent while the southern groups follow matrilineal descent. They are all tied linguistically, however, speaking Kordofanian languages that belong to the Nilo-Saharan language family. The exact origin of the Nuba is unknown; it is thought that they are one of several people who migrated to ancient Meroë after its decline in the fourth century.

Traditionally the Nuba have farmed and kept livestock. Although some Nuba have converted to Islam, many have held onto their traditional religious beliefs and customs, which are based on animal sacrifice and the honoring of ancestors. In Nuba society rain priests and headmen hold prominent positions of authority. It is important to note that the people of the Nuba Hills are often confused with Nubians, due to the similar spelling of their names. However, these two groups are unrelated.

See also: ANCESTOR WORSHIP (Vol. I); MEROË (Vol. I); NUBA (Vol. I).

Nuer Seminomadic pastoralists of the southern region of the present-day Republic of the SUDAN. Like the neighboring DINKA, the Nuer are a Nilotic group that has inhabited the arid savanna on either side of the Nile River for thousands of years. Little is known of the history of the Nuer people before the 19th century, when Turkish and Egyptian forces arrived in the Sudan to establish trade monopolies. However, oral tradition and anthropological studies have been used to reconstruct some of their activity.

Between the 16th and 19th centuries the Nuer continued their traditional lifestyle of moving seasonally and living off of the products of their cattle. They also continued their practice of raiding the cattle of neighboring groups, including the LUO, SHILLUK, and especially the Dinka. Infighting among the Nuer was common, as they lacked a centralized authority, but during times of conflict against outsiders the Nuer would put their differences aside and unite against the foreign enemy.

In the 1820s the Nuer and other southern Sudanic peoples were subjected to predatory raids by the Turkish forces of the Ottoman Empire, which occupied northern Sudan. Later in the 19th century Nuer territories were claimed by France, Belgium, and Britain, although the Nuer themselves did not feel the effects of colonial rule until the 20th century.

See also: NUER (Vol. I).

Nupe Inhabitants of a region in present-day west-central NIGERIA centered on the confluence of the NIGER RIVER and the Kaduna river; also the state they founded. In the 16th century the Nupe state was continuously at war with its Hausa State neighbor, KEBBI, as well as with smaller local states. By the late 19th century Nupe was one of the most powerful states in central Nigeria. Bida, the chief Nupe city, established trade relations with the British Royal Niger Company in 1871. Subsequent trade disputes led to the British occupation of Bida, beginning in 1901. In 1908 the Nupe state was incorporated into the new British protectorate of Nigeria.

Traditionally the Nupe were known for their glass beads, brass trays, fine cloth, and leatherwork. Farming played a major role in the Nupe ECONOMY, with rice, GROUNDNUTS (peanuts), COTTON, and shea nuts all being cultivated for commercial trade. The area also had a large fishing industry. Primarily Muslims, the Nupe also maintained traditional rituals.

See also: IDAH (Vol. III); ROYAL NIGER COMPANY (Vol. IV).

Nyakyusa Bantu-speaking ethnic group that has long resided in the region of present-day TANZANIA. Unlike many other Bantu-speaking peoples, the Nyakyusa maintained a long-standing tradition of organizing their villages according to age sets rather than kin. There also was a rapid proliferation of independent chiefdoms that were divided in each generation.

Among the Nyakyusa, inheritances were passed down to a person from neither the father nor the mother. Instead, inheritance was from brother to brother.

Skilled agriculturalists, the Nyakyusa raised bananas, finger millet, cassava, sweet potatoes, and, after its introduction from South America, MAIZE (corn). Cultivation generally was carried out by men and boys. Cattle were raised as well. The dialect they speak is one of the few Bantu languages that does not make use of tones.

See also: AGE SETS (Vol. I); BANTU LANGUAGES (Vol. II).

Nyamwezi Second-largest ethnic group of present-day TANZANIA. Their name translates as "the people of the moon," which probably originates from their location in the west. The Bantu-speaking Nyamwezi moved into their homeland about 1350. They have long been noted for the wooden statues—semi-abstract depictions of various ancestors—that are used in their religious rituals. Ethnologists have observed close similarities between Nyamwezi religious beliefs and practices and those of the KIMBU, another Bantu-speaking people living further to the south.

Originally farmers and herders and living in a decentralized group of chiefdoms in a dry but fertile land, the Nyamwezi became important traders between 1700 and 1800. During this time entire families and clans would gather their cattle and take them as far west as the CONGO forest. There the Nyamwezi would exchange the cattle for captives, wax, ivory, and copper. The copper they sold to the kingdoms surrounding Lake Tanganyika, where it was used to make ceremonial items and personal adornments. Other trade goods were carried to the east coast and traded for cowries, metal tools, and cloth.

The lands of the Nyamwezi were well situated to give them a commercial advantage. A major caravan route extended eastward from the principal town of Unyanyembe to Bagamoyo on the mainland directly opposite the island of ZANZIBAR on the coast, covering a total of some 500 miles (805 km). Additional caravan routes extended to Lake Victoria and Lake Tanganyika. The Nyamwezi developed a high level of skill—and pride in their skill—as porters on the great caravans to the coast. Caravan pack animals, usually mules, were lightly loaded, and most of the merchandise on these trips was carried by human porters. The Nyamwezi held a virtual monopoly on the carrying trade.

The Nyamwezi were less skillful as traders, lacking the effective bargaining skills and understanding of commercial credit that would give them an advantage in Zanzibar. Thus as the 19th century went on, the Nyamwezi formed a number of commercial alliances with coastal Arabs. These agreements allowed the Nyamwezi to share in the profits of the Arab trading expeditions that made their way through Nyamwezi territory.

See also: NYAMWEZI (Vol. IV); SWAHILI COAST (Vol. III).

Further reading: Laura S. Kurtz, *Historical Dictionary of Tanzania* (Metuchen, N.J. and London: Scarecrow Press, 1978); Aylward Shorter, *Chiefship in Western Tanzania* (Oxford, U.K.: Clarendon Press, 1972).

Nyanza Province in present-day southwestern KENYA that was primarily inhabited by LUO and Gusii peoples in the 16th through the 18th centuries. Nyanza's Nilotic-speaking Luo inhabitants originally came from the Bahr el-Ghazal area in present-day southern Republic of the SUDAN, beginning in the 16th century. Because of overpopulation and changing environmental conditions, the Luo migrated in search of new land for nearly two centuries. They first headed north into DINKA and NUER territory, and then they headed south into present-day UGANDA, where it is believed that the group split up into subgroups. The Alur Luo settled near Lake Albert, a second Luo group occupied ACHOLI, and a third ended up in the Lake Kyoga region. Lake Kyoga was only a temporary home for latter group of Luo migrants, as they were quickly forced south by a new wave of Luo invaders, eventually landing on the eastern shore of Lake Victoria in the present-day city of Nyanza.

Many of the Bantu communities in Uganda assimilated with the Luo migrants while others resisted Luo domination and were gradually pushed into southern Nyanza during the 17th and 18th centuries. The right to live and work on the land was contingent on whether one belonged to a prominent clan, so both Luo and Bantu societies began to organize themselves in geographically based clans. At the same time, small chiefdoms were beginning to develop in the region around the lower Nzoia and Yala rivers. The largest Bantu chiefdom in the region was Wanga, and the largest Luo chiefdom was Alego. After periodic wars and rivalry the two groups eventually came together and formed one chiefdom.

Toward the end of the 18th century Wanga expanded with the help of the pastoralist MAASAI warriors. Chief Netia of the Wanga agreed to allow the Maasai to settle in the region on the condition that their warriors were at the disposal of the Wanga. Although Wanga gained territory through this tactic, the chiefdom never grew to rival the large Nilotic-speaking states to the west of Lake Victoria.

See also: VICTORIA, LAKE (Vol. I).

Nyika (Nyiha) Ethnic group of present-day TANZANIA, thought to have originated in Mbizi. Traditionally the Nyika were hunters, but they eventually became agriculturalists and cattle herders. In the mid-19th century, during the rule of Omani Sultan SAYYID SAID (1791–1856), the Nyika became traders in MOMBASA and other towns in East Africa, exchanging captives and other goods between the KAMBA, Arab, Swahili, and Indian coast merchants.

See also: OMANI SULTANATE (Vol. III); SLAVE TRADE ON THE SWAHILI COAST (Vol. III).

Nzima (Nzema, Apollonia) Ethnic group and kingdom located on the coast of present-day GHANA that, in the 18th century, flourished in the region around the Tano and Ankobra rivers. Europeans often called the territory Apollonia, and in 1768 the British constructed Fort Apollonia at Beyin in the Nzima kingdom.

In 1707, a young Nzima boy was taken to Europe by the Dutch and presented to the Duke of Wolfenbüttel. The boy was given the name William Amo and went on to attend the University of Halle in 1727 to study law and philosophy before earning his doctorate at the University of Wittenberg in 1734. Despite distinguishing himself as a scholar, Amo was eventually forced to leave Europe in 1747 due to increasing racial tensions.

The Nzima are a subgroup of the AKAN peoples who migrated to the Guinea coast from the regions around the Ashanti-controlled city of KUMASI beginning in the late 17th century. The Nzima kingdom itself was founded by three brothers, Amihere II (fl. 1760s), Annor Blay Ackah, and Bua Kpanyili, who ruled the trading states of Ankobra, Jomoro, and Abripiquem, respectively. In the early 18th century the brothers decided to combine their states to form one large kingdom and continued to prosper by trading salt, fish, and GOLD with European merchants. The Nzima kingdom rose to the height of its power in the 1760s under Amihere II (fl. 1760s), who expanded the boundaries of his kingdom. Nzima grew as it absorbed other groups who migrated into the territory and continued to be a strong force on the coast of Ghana throughout the 18th century.

See also: ASHANTI EMPIRE (Vol. III); GOLD COAST (Vol. III).

Nzinga, Queen (Jinga, Nzingha) (c. 1582–1663) *Queen of the Mbundu people in present-day Angola*

Nzinga was the daughter of King Kiluanji of the NDONGO and MATAMBA kingdoms of the MBUNDU people. These kingdoms were located in the Malanje highlands region of present-day Angola. A dictatorial ruler, King Kiluanji was dethroned by his people, after which his illegitimate son Mbandi (fl. 1610s) rose to power and forced Nzinga to flee the kingdom in order to keep her from claiming the throne.

About 1617, however, the Portuguese invaded the Malanje highlands, and Nzinga was called upon by her brother to help secure the independence of Ndongo. In 1622 she went to LUANDA and brokered an arrangement that, in addition to freeing a number of Portuguese captives in exchange for Portuguese recognition of the Ndongo kingdom, guaranteed the kingdom's assistance in the trading network. It was reported that during this meeting, Nzinga found an ingenious way to demonstrate her equality to the Portuguese governor by using one of her female attendants as a human throne when no seat was offered to her by the governor.

Also around this time, Nzinga converted to Christianity and accepted the name Dona Anna de Sousa (or Souza). Apparently, this was done primarily for political reasons and to ingratiate herself to the Portuguese. This view is supported by the fact that, when her pact with Portugal subsequently fell apart, she is reported to have abandoned Christianity. Ironically she is reputed to have reconverted for sincere religious reasons during the last years of her life.

When Nzinga's brother proved himself to be unable to resist impending colonization, Nzinga formed her own army using warriors of the IMBANGALA people. Claiming both trading rights and the throne of Matamba, she used Matamba as her home base for numerous attacks on the Portuguese and their figurehead rulers in Ndongo. She even formed a strategic alliance with the Dutch in order to fight the Portuguese. The alliance failed to produce results, and after the combined forces were defeated Nzinga regrouped her own army and continued to mount attacks on the opposition. When her forces were finally worn down, Nzinga eventually agreed to negotiate peacefully with the Portuguese, yielding to them on trade issues. She died on December 17, 1663.

Nzinga was famous for her bravery and for the inclusion of women in both her armies and her royal entourage. She was also known for always taking personal command and being at the forefront of every battle, even those that took place late in her life.

See also: PORTUGAL AND AFRICA (Vol. III); WOMEN IN PRECOLONIAL AFRICA (Vol. III).

Nzinga Nkuwu (r. c. 1490) *King of Kongo*

The KONGO KINGDOM, inhabited by Bantu-speaking peoples, was established at the mouth of the Congo River in the 14th century. Nzinga Nkuwu was the fifth *manikongo*, or king. Although the king was referred to as *nzambi mpunga*, or "superior person," the king's person was not considered sacred, only his power.

A Portuguese sailor named Diego Cão sailed into the mouth of the Congo River in 1483 and found Kongo villages there. He returned in 1485 and again in 1491. On this third visit he brought missionary priests, soldiers, and trade goods. The MISSIONARIES baptized Nzinga Nkuwu and built a church. The king converted in the hope that it would help him develop trade relations with the Portuguese. He later abandoned Catholicism, but his son and successor, Nzinga Mbemba I (r. 1506–1543), became a devoted Catholic, taking the name AFONSO I and making Catholicism the state religion of Kongo.

See also: CHRISTIANITY, INFLUENCE OF (Vol. III).

Obiri Yeboa (Nana Obiri Yeboa, Obiri Yeboa Manu) (r. c. 1660–1680) *Chief of Kwaman and uncle of the first* asantehene, *Osei Tutu*

Obiri Yeboa succeeded his brother, Oti Akenten (r. c. 1630–1660), as chief of the Kwaman, near the Ashanti town of KUMASI. After inheriting his brother's title he assumed his brother's ongoing conflict with the Domaa, against whom he declared war. Obiri Yeboa was known for his ambitious plans regarding the future of the ASHANTI EMPIRE. It was his goal to unite the states under one chief, thus making them powerful enough to be freed from their overlords, the DENKYIRA, who controlled trade in the region and to whom the Kwaman were paying tribute. Ultimately he convinced other Ashanti chiefs to establish a confederation, thereby strengthening the political unity of the various clan states, which led to the founding of the Ashanti Empire. Obiri was unable to see his plans of Ashanti unification come to fruition, as he was killed in battle with the Domaa.

See also: OSEI TUTU (Vol. III); OYOKO (Vol. III).

Ogaden Plain Dry and desolate lowland region in southeastern ETHIOPIA, north of the Shebelle River near the eastern limit of the Horn of Africa. Ogaden was primarily occupied by Somali people who, by 1500, had pushed out OROMO pastoralists to establish themselves in the region. The Somali of Ogaden conducted trade with the HARER caravans that moved along the southern Ethiopian provinces on their way to the port cities of the BENADIR COAST, on the Indian Ocean in today's SOMALIA.

Ogaden became a source of contention between Ethiopia and Somalia with the military conquests of AHMAD GRAÑ (c. 1506–1543), the 16th-century ruler of the Islamic state of ADAL. In the 17th century the Somali of Ogaden faced a new threat as the Oromo infiltrated back into Ogaden and overran many parts of Ethiopia. This left the Christian monarchy in a state of disarray and ushering in a period of anarchy known as the ZEMENE MESAFINT, or "The Age of Princes."

See also: SOMALI (Vol. II).

Old Calabar City along the CROSS RIVER in present-day southwestern NIGERIA, near the Niger Delta. Founded by the EFIK peoples and made into a trading center in the early 17th century, Old Calabar was highly successful in trading with both the Europeans and the peoples of the hinterland well into the 19th century. The Efik traded fish, PALM OIL, and bananas with peoples of the hinterlands. To the Europeans, however, they exported mostly ivory and human captives, for which they obtained pewter items, beads, iron, cloth, and copper. In the 17th century, for instance, a male captive could be bought for 38 copper bars, while a female was obtained for either 36 or 37 bars. When the trade of human beings was abolished by the British in the early 19th century, palm oil and kernels became the main export commodity of Old Calabar.

The Efik founded several communities in and near Old Calabar, including Atakpa (Duke Town), Obutong (Old Town), Creek Town, Qua Town, and Henshaw Town. These towns initially operated separately and were generally equal on a political level. Eventually, they were united under Old Calabar by the members of the EKPE SOCIETY, a secret society made up of influential Efik males.

See also: ENGLAND AND AFRICA (Vol. III); IVORY TRADE (Vol. III); NIGER DELTA (Vol. I); SLAVE TRADE, THE TRANSATLANTIC (Vol. III).

Further reading: A. J. H. Latham, *Old Calabar, 1600–1891: The Impact of the International Economy upon a Traditional Society* (Oxford, U.K..: Clarendon Press, 1973).

Omani Sultanate Succession of rulers of Oman, located on the coast of the Arabian Peninsula, between the present-day countries of Yemen and the United Arab Emirates. An Islamic country from the seventh century, Oman was occupied by the Portuguese at the beginning of the 16th century. After slightly more than a century of Portuguese occupation, during which time Oman served as port of call for Portuguese ships going back and forth to India, the Omanis revolted. Driven from their headquarters at Hormuz, the Portuguese fell back on Muscat, which they managed to hold until 1650. The Omanis then succeeded in ridding themselves entirely of the Portuguese, establishing their own independent state.

Beginning in the mid-17th century Oman created an extensive trading empire that, by the end of the next century, extended throughout the Persian Gulf and Indian Ocean and stretched as far as the East African coast. In 1749 the BUSAIDI dynasty assumed control in Oman, and the Busaidi sultans—who have ruled Oman right up to the 21st century—extended Omani power and wealth even further.

The Omani Sultanate reached its peak in the early years of the 19th century under SAYYID SAID (1791–1856). Shrewdly manipulating the European powers, Said also pushed East Africa into new industries and trading systems. These transformed ZANZIBAR into a thriving center for the clove trade and led to the establishment of trade networks that brought ivory and slaves to the sultanate for export to Arabia, Europe, and the United States. All this helped turn Oman into the dominant regional power.

See also: MOMBASA (Vol. III).

Further reading: C. S. Nicholls, *The Swahili Coast: Politics, Diplomacy and trade on the East African Littoral, 1798–1856* (New York: Africana Pub. Corp., 1971).

Omdurman Second-largest city in the Republic of the SUDAN, located north of KHARTOUM on the Nile River.

Al-Khandaq Fort in Oman in southeast Arabia. This castle-like fort was built in the early 1600s in what is now the town of Buraimi. The power of the Omani sultans was felt up and down the Swahili coast throughout the 18th and 19th centuries. © Arthur Thévenart/Corbis

Omdurman is an ancient Islamic center and is the site of Sudan's College for Arabic and Islamic Studies. The tomb of al-Mahdi is located in Omdurman. Born Muhammad Ahmad (1844–1885), al-Mahdi was one of the most respected and influential religious leaders in the history of present-day Sudan.

See also: MAHDI, MUHAMMAD AHMAD AL- (Vol. IV); OMDURMAN, BATTLE OF (Vol. IV).

Onitsha Trading town in what is now southern NIGERIA, east of the NIGER RIVER in the state of Anambra; it became the capital of the small IGBO kingdom of the same name. In the 16th century, during the reign of Oba Esigie (c. 1517–c. 1550) a group of Igbo people from Ado na Idu, west of the kingdom of BENIN, immigrated to the Onitsha region. This led to the establishment of a number of communities, including Aboh, along the Niger. These ultimately were referred to as *Umuchima*, after Chima (fl. early 1500s), the leader of the area's inhabitants. Unlike other Igbo communities, these tended to follow the monarchic systems of Benin.

At the town of Illah, Chima's group divided into several factions, with some people going to Agbor and others to Aboh, while a third group founded Onitsha. Before these people reached Onitsha, however, Chima died, and his son Oraeze deceitfully beat out his rivals for the vacant leadership position of and proclaimed himself king.

Opokuware II (c. 1700–1750) *Great Ashanti warrior and king and creator of the Great Oath of the Ashanti*

Opokuware was related to the great OSEI TUTU (r. c. 1680–1717), the first *asantehene,* or ruler, of the unified Ashanti nation, which eventually became the predominant power of West Africa's GOLD COAST. Chosen by Osei Tutu to be his successor, Opokuware eventually assumed the title of *asantehene* following Osei Tutu's death in 1717.

As a means of further unifying his people, Opokuware created what became known as the Great Oath of the Ashanti. The oath was based on the words *Koromante ne memeneda,* which referred to "Saturday," and "Kormante," the day and place of Osei Tutu's death. The oath made binding—and unrecantable—any pledge with which it was uttered. As a result it played an important role in pledges of allegiance between chiefs and the *asantehene,* because the oath bound the chiefs and their ruler together forever.

Opokuware's initial concern as a ruler was restoring stability to his kingdom. Once that was achieved, however, his chief interest became expanding and consolidating Ashanti power and prestige. He soon moved against the Sehwi state, which, in 1717, had attacked KUMASI, the Ashanti capital, during the war with AKYEM. Opokuware quickly defeated Sehwi, incorporating vast amounts of territory into the ASHANTI EMPIRE. He then attacked the states of TEKYIMAN and Gyaman, conquering these lands that lay to the northwest. By 1726 he had also subjugated AKWAMU, to the northeast, and had begun what would become a long-term war with WASSAW, which lay to the southwest. Soon Opokuware's domain encompassed virtually all of present-day GHANA.

By the 1730s, however, Opokuware was confronted with a threat in the form of the rising power of Akyem. In 1742 Opokuware and his army attacked and defeated Akyem, spreading Ashanti political and economic dominance to the coast. After subsequent attacks on DAGOMBA, which took place in 1744–45, the Ashanti became the Gold Coast's largest supplier of captives, ivory, and GOLD.

After this Opokuware worked to centralize and improve the administration of his kingdom. One of his primary moves was to decrease the power of the various provincial chiefs, or governors, by increasing the number of subordinates who would be directly reporting to the *asantehene.* The provincial chieftains rebelled, and their initial uprisings forced Opokuware to flee from Kumasi. Stirred on by this, such subjugated peoples as the Akyem and Wassaw revolted, attempting to free themselves of Ashanti domination.

Ultimately Opokuware overcame this opposition. By the time he died, in 1750, he had forced the governors to accept his reorganization of the government and prevented the newly expanded Ashanti nation from falling apart. The seeds of disaffection, however, had been sown, and in subsequent years discontent and rebellion continued to afflict the kingdom.

See also: OYOKO (Vol. III).

Oran (Wahran, Ouahran) Port and city located on the Mediterranean coast of northwest ALGERIA. During the 10th century merchants from Andalusia, Spain, founded the port of Oran, giving themselves much-desired access to the inland trading routes of North Africa. The short-lived TLEMCEN kingdom, established about 1437, maintained Oran as its main port, which helped the city secure its importance as a trading center until the early 16th century.

Oran became a port for PIRATES, known as CORSAIRS, during the first decade of the 16th century. Initially the port harbored Muslim Spaniards, in 1492 and 1502, who sought to escape pressure to convert to the Catholic faith. Between 1509 and the early 18th century, several Mediterranean countries wanting trading privileges fought over the port. Ultimately, this battle narrowed to the Ottoman Turks and Spain, with the Turks gaining control by the latter part of the 18th century. By 1831, however, France had taken control of Oran, using the port as a military base until the Algerian religious leader Abd al-Qadir (1807–1883) seized power in 1832.

See also: OTTOMON EMPIRE AND AFRICA (Vol. III).

Orange River Located in southern Africa, this 1,200-mile (1,931-km) river stretches from LESOTHO across the Republic of SOUTH AFRICA, through both the Kalahari and Namib deserts to the Atlantic Ocean. The Orange River was known to the KHOIKHOI people as the Gariep, or "Great," River. In 1779 a Scottish merchant who worked for the DUTCH EAST INDIA COMPANY renamed the river in honor of the royal Dutch House of Orange.

The first inhabitants along the Orange River were the Khoikhoi people, who most likely settled there some time after the 14th century. During the 18th century it was settled by TSWANA people. Around the same time, Europeans made their way across the river. The BASOTHO and GRIQUA came to the region a century later, as did MISSIONARIES and Dutch Trekboers (BOERS) fleeing the British.

The Orange River and the surrounding territory were at the center of many of the disputes that took place between the various groups that settled in the area. In 1848, the British under Sir Harry Smith claimed the land extending from the Orange River to the Vaal River, designating it the Orange River Sovereignty. After six years of strife over the territory, the British handed it over to Boer farmers in 1854, at which time the Boers established the Orange Free State.

See also: ENGLAND AND AFRICA (Vol. III); KALAHARI DESERT (Vols. I, II); NETHERLANDS AND AFRICA (Vol. III); ORANGE FREE STATE (Vol. IV); ORANGE RIVER (Vol. I).

Orlams (Oorlams) A subgroup of the KHOIKHOI people, related to the Amraal, Berseba, Bethanie, and Witbooi. They lived mainly in western southern Africa, where they still reside today. During the 18th century the Orlams, like the Kora and GRIQUA, migrated northward to avoid the expansion of the BOERS. As a result they were able, for a time, to preserve some degree of independence.

Oromo (Galla) Ethno-linguistic group that migrated in the 16th century from southeast ETHIOPIA to their present locations in the northern, central, and western parts of the country. They also settled as far south as the Tana River region in KENYA. The Oromo are also known as the *Galla,* primarily by the AMHARA; however, it is a word that has been phased out for its derogatory implications.

The Oromo were originally pastoralists who organized in small bands and initiated attacks not only on their Christian and Muslim neighbors but among their own groups as well. The Oromo expansion was due in part to a population explosion that forced the Oromo to search for new land for themselves and pastures for their cattle. Because the Oromo had no centralized political system, each group tended to adopt the culture and RELIGION of the people among whom they settled. For instance, as the Oromo in the eastern and northern provinces mixed with the SIDAMO and Amhara people, they gradually changed their way of life from pastoralism to AGRICULTURE. And depending on where they lived, most Oromo converted either to Islam or Christianity. Even so, many maintained their language and sense of Oromo ethnicity, and some even held on to their traditional religion, especially in the south.

Prior to the Oromo invasions, the greatest threat to the Ethiopian Christian kingdom had come from the Muslim state of ADAL. By the 17th century, however, the Oromo dominated most of the northeastern and western territory, including Arsi, GOJJAM, SHOA, Welega, Harerge, and Welo. During this time the Ethiopian Christian state fell into a period of political anarchy and decentralization known as ZEMENE MESAFINT (The Age of Princes). In the 18th century the YEJJU, a Muslim Oromo group, nominally converted to Christianity and dominated GONDAR for almost 100 years.

The Ethiopian kingdom had been so devastated by the Oromo that it took more than a century to rebuild the fragmented monarchy. During this time the Oromo became acculturated to either the Muslim or Christian segments of Ethiopian society, where they have remained, making up almost half the population of Ethiopia at the beginning of the 21st century.

See also: OROMO (Vols. I, II, IV, V).

Further reading: Mohammed Hassen, *The Oromo of Ethiopia: A History, 1570–1860* (New York: Cambridge University Press, 1990).

Orungu Kingdom and peoples located around the mouth of the Ogooué River along the coast of present-day GABON. The Orungu kingdom developed in the early 17th century after the Orungu peoples (formerly known as the Ombéké) migrated down the Ogooué to establish themselves at places near the Ogooué estuary. It was there that the Orungu traded wood and ivory with a subgroup of the MPONGWE called the Adyumba, who then taught the Orungu how to work iron and build boats.

During the latter parts of the 17th century the Orungu migrated further toward the Cape Lopez area, as well as into portions of what is now the northern coast of Gabon. With this move came clashes with the Adyumba for control of the trade with Europeans.

The Orungu eventually prevailed and became dominant in the region and began trading in ivory, EBONY, beeswax, and honey with merchants from Portugal, France, Spain, and Britain. When the slave trade began to gain momentum in the area during the mid-18th century, the Orungu used their positions along the Ogooué River to transport captives down the river's waterways to sell to European slave traders. This allowed the Orungu to flourish until the mid to late 19th century, when French occupation and the forced end of the slave trade—which had continued well beyond the 1807 decree by the British to abolish the slave trade—reduced their power in the region.

See also: ENGLAND AND AFRICA (Vol. III); FRANCE AND AFRICA (Vol. III); IVORY TRADE (Vol. III); PORTUGAL AND AFRICA (Vol. III); SLAVE TRADE, THE TRANSATLANTIC (Vol. III); SPAIN AND AFRICA (Vol. III).

Osei Kwadwo (Osei Kojo) (c. 1740–1777) *Ashanti king*

In 1764 Osei Kwadwo became the *asantehene,* or king, of the ASHANTI EMPIRE when Kusi Obodum (r. c. 1750–1764) was deposed. He acquired the title during a time of strife. The rebellion of their neighbors to the south, the Twifo, WASSAW to the southwest, and AKYEM to the southeast denied Ashanti traders access to the coast, leaving the Ashanti unable to purchase weapons and goods from the Europeans. Kwadwo's first act as king was to suppress the rebellion. He enlisted the aid of the FANTE, who were also blocked from accessing the trade routes. In 1765 the Ashanti and the Fante attacked, causing the Twifo and Wassaw to retreat. In subsequent battles, the allied forces of the Ashanti and Fante also defeated Akyem. The alliance between the Ashanti and the Fante unraveled, however, when the Ashanti established a camp within Fante territory. A battle ensued, which the Ashanti lost.

Osei Kwadwo had to face a new threat with the re-emergence of the Akyem and its new king, Obirikoran, who had become an ally of two of the region's smaller chiefdoms, the KROBO and the Akwapim. Fearing that the Akyem would also form an alliance with the Fante, Osei Kwadwo quickly moved against them. Although the Akyem were defeated and their king deposed, the Ashanti were beaten by the Krobo.

In the early 1770s Osei Kwadwo headed north to conquer the DAGOMBA in a campaign that provided the Ashanti with a large number of captives, who were sent to the coast and sold to the Europeans.

One important administrative change that Osei Kwadwo made during his reign was the appointment and installation of Ashanti nobles as regional commissioners. These administrators were responsible for overseeing the provinces in the name of the kingdom. He also dis-patched representatives to other towns on the coast in order to guarantee that European traders paid rent for their forts and castles, an action that enabled the Ashanti to exercise control over the coast more effectively.

See also: TWIFO (Vol. II).

Osei Tutu (c. 1680–c. 1717) *Warrior king of the Ashanti Empire; credited as the creator of the Golden Stool*

Osei Tutu became the fourth ruler of the ASHANTI EMPIRE—and the first to hold the title *asantehene*—upon the death of his uncle, OBIRI YEBOA (r. c. 1660–1680). Osei Tutu's greatest accomplishment was the unification of local clan groups into the powerful ASHANTI EMPIRE.

From the mid-16th century to the late 17th century a number of clan groups that had migrated into the region of KUMASI, in what is now GHANA, formed several AKAN states, including Ashanti and DENKYIRA. Being the most powerful of these Akan states at the time, Denkyira reaped most of the benefits generated by the trade of GOLD and kola nuts in the region. However, the oppressive Denkyira rule created dissent among the other Akan groups. Osei Tutu used this deep hatred of Denkyira to merge the smaller states into one union.

The first step toward unification was the creation of the GOLDEN STOOL, a symbol that was used to solidify the creation of the new kingdom. Osei Tutu named KUMASI his capital and established an annual unifying event, the Odwira Festival, for all the states to attend. He designed a new constitution, appointing himself the divine king and forming a council of the heads of the states.

The last step in creating the Ashanti Empire was to remove the Denkyira from power. Between 1699 and 1701 Osei Tutu led a newly formed army into war and defeated Denkyira. One of the primary effects of this was to allow the Ashanti access to trade with Europe. Under Osei Tutu's rule, the Ashanti Empire tripled in size and became a strong warring nation. His rule continued until 1717, when he was killed during a war against AKYEM, another Akan state.

See also: OYOKO (Vol. III).

Oshogbo Town in the southwestern part of present-day NIGERIA located on the Oshun River in the state of Osun. Founded in the 17th century by ILESHA settlers from Ibokun, Oshogbo was, until the 19th century, tributary to the kingdom of Ilesha. The Ilesha strategically picked the Oshogbo site so they could observe the activities of the Oyo, who had expanded their kingdom and trade route to the nearby town of Ede. The Ilesha also wanted to monitor the *timi,* the Ede ruler designated by the Oyo.

According to oral tradition, Oshogbo was founded by the goddess Oshun, after whom the Oshun River is named.

Legend states that Oshun placed the town beside the deepest levels of the river so that the people of Oshogbo would have an abundance of fish. The king of Oshogbo was called *ataoja* (*atewogbeja*), which means "the one who accepts the fish." Tradition maintained that the first *ataoja* was Laro, who, it was said, fed the fish of the river Oshun and for his good deed was given a potion that ensured fertility among the Oshogbo women. The two most notable shrines dedicated to the goddess Oshun are the Ile Oshun and the Ojubo Oshun.

Although primarily an agricultural society, the Oshogbo people have long been famous for their weaving and for a dying procedure called *adire*. In earlier times the process was used for renewing old cloth. In more recent times, however, it has become an important industry. In it, starch is painted or stencilled onto cloth using techniques similar to tie-dying. Although *adire* cloth now is seen in many different colors, it was originally produced only in an indigo blue.

Osu (Christiansborg)
Coastal GA-DANGME village, in present-day GHANA, that ultimately became one of the nuclei of ACCRA, Ghana's modern capital and its largest city. During the 17th century traders from many European countries were looking for accessible ports along what they called the GOLD COAST of West Africa. Beginning in the 1650s, they established trading forts at Fort James, Fort Crèvecoeur, and Christiansborg Castle. These grew into, respectively, James Town, Dutch Accra, and Osu, the three towns around which the city of Accra eventually developed. Like the other independent Ga-Dangme towns, Osu had its own royal stool, or symbol of leadership.

In 1661 the town passed from Swedish to Danish hands, at which time the Danes built Christiansborg Castle, naming it after King Christian IV of Denmark. Then, between 1679 and 1683, the castle was a Portuguese possession. It was acquired by the British in 1850, at which time it began serving as their colonial headquarters in the region.

See also: DENMARK AND AFRICA (Vol. III); ENGLAND AND AFRICA (Vols. III, IV); PORTUGAL AND AFRICA (Vol. III); TRADING STATIONS, EUROPEAN (Vol. III).

Ottoman Empire and Africa
Vast and powerful Islamic empire that lasted from 1290 to 1922. It was ruled from the province of Anatolia, located in the western region of what is now the country of Turkey.

By the mid-16th century the Ottoman Empire stretched over portions of southeast Europe and most of the Middle East. It controlled most of North Africa, including present-day ALGERIA, TUNISIA, LIBYA, and EGYPT. MOROCCO, too, came under the Ottoman influence, but

The "conqueror," Muhammad II (r. 1451–1481), ruler of the Ottoman Empire. Here he is depicted in the turban of a sultan. His capture of the city of Constantinople, in 1453, brought about the fall of the Byzantine Empire. © *Bettmann/Corbis*

its strong sultans managed to escape the political domination endured by the the rest of North Africa.

> Located in what is now the Turkish city of Istanbul, the government of the Ottoman Empire became known as Bâbiâli (in Turkish), or Sublime Porte (from the French), both meaning "High Gate" or "Gate of the Eminent," in reference to the gate that guarded the city's government buildings.

Established by the Turkish chief Osman (r. c. 1290–1324) in the early 14th century, the Ottoman Empire completed numerous conquests over the next two centuries to rule areas in the present-day Balkan Peninsula, as well as in several other modern European countries, including Austria and Hungary.

Beginning around the early 16th century, however, the focus of Ottoman expansion shifted to the continent of Africa with the reign of the ninth Ottoman ruler, Selim

Ottoman Empire in Africa 1683–1699

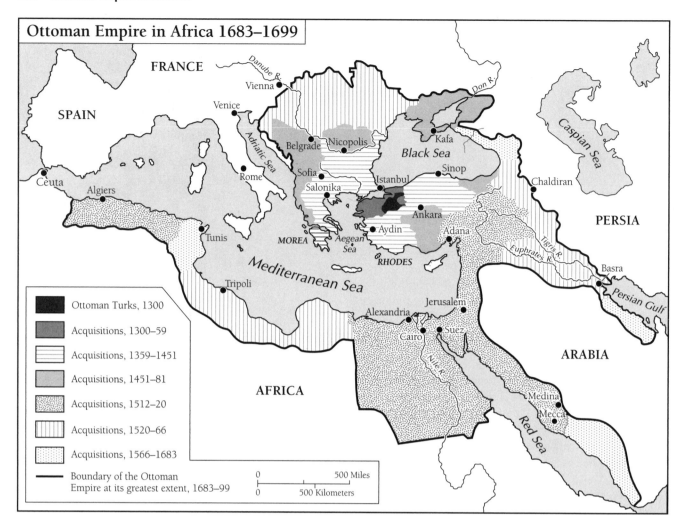

FRANCE

SPAIN

Danube R.

Vienna

Venice

Venice

Adriatic Sea

Rome

Ceuta

Algiers

Tunis

MOREA

Aegean Sea

RHODES

Tripoli

Mediterranean Sea

Belgrade   Nicopolis

Sofia

Salonika

Istanbul

Kafa

Black Sea

Sinop

Ankara

Aydin

Adana

Chaldiran

Euphrates R.

Tigris R.

Caspian Sea

PERSIA

Basra

Persian Gulf

Alexandria

Jerusalem

Cairo   Suez

Nile R.

AFRICA

ARABIA

Medina

Mecca

Red Sea

Don R.

■ (black)	Ottoman Turks, 1300
■ (dark gray)	Acquisitions, 1300–59
▤	Acquisitions, 1359–1451
▥ (gray)	Acquisitions, 1451–81
▦	Acquisitions, 1512–20
▥	Acquisitions, 1520–66
▨	Acquisitions, 1566–1683
——	Boundary of the Ottoman Empire at its greatest extent, 1683–99

0   500 Miles

0   500 Kilometers

I (r. 1512–1520). The reign of Selim I, who was known as "the Grim," was characterized by a militant territorial expansion that nearly doubled the size of the empire. In 1516–17 Selim led the effort to establish a new sultanate in what is now Egypt. The war pitted his artillery-laden army corps, known as Janissaries, against the sword-carrying Egyptian MAMLUKS. Emerging victorious, Selim became the spiritual and secular ruler of the new Ottoman territory of Egypt by assuming the Islamic title of *caliph*. During the same time, he also sent the Turkish pirate Khayr ad-Din Barbarossa (c. 1466–1546) to the west, where he succeeded in taking the city of AL-GIERS, in present-day Algeria, in the name of Selim I and Ottoman rule.

After Selim I died, in 1520, the sultanate passed to his son, Suleyman I (r. 1520–1566), who eventually came to be called "the Magnificent" for bringing the Ottoman Empire to the height of its power. Under Suleyman's reign, larger areas of what is now Algeria were taken, and Barbarossa was put in command of the Ottoman naval forces. By 1551 the city of TRIPOLI in present-day Libya was overtaken by Suleyman's forces, and, as the annexa-

tion of regions of North Africa became more widespread, the influence of the empire was felt further to the west in what is now Morocco. Fearing the threat of a possible invasion, the Moroccan sultan, Muhammad II (r. 1540–1557), led an invasion to capture Algiers from the Ottomans in 1554. Although Muhammad's forces were successful in capturing the Algerian city of TLEMCEN, they were unable to either depose the Turks from Algeria or loosen the empire's hold over the rest of northern Africa.

The final Ottoman conquest of the North African territories came in 1574, under the reign of Selim II (r. 1566–1574), when the city of Tunis, in what is now Tunisia, was captured from Spain. While the empire continued to grow with the taking of Tunis and other European territories, the reign of Selim II, who became known as "the Drunkard," was characterized by other political setbacks, which would mark the beginning of the empire's slow decline.

Over the next two centuries the relationship of the Ottoman Empire to North Africa was one of tension and political change. Whereas in the 16th century the North African territories were controlled by Turkish rulers, by the 17th century local military leaders had regained control of their governments. These provinces then began to operate as tributary states, rather than true Ottoman territories, and gained wealth and power by engaging in the pirating of European ships. Although piracy was effectively outlawed in 1699, the practice continued in the waters off of North Africa well into the 18th century.

Although northern Africans resented Ottoman rule, the majority of them were allied with the Turks through their common Islamic beliefs. So, despite the resentment, the Ottomans were often looked to for diplomatic and military aid against non-Muslim powers. In 1574, for instance, Mai IDRIS ALAWMA (r. 1571–1603) of the KANEM-BORNU empire in the central Sudan region needed Ottoman aid. He sent an envoy to Istanbul to ask the reigning Ottoman sultan, Murad III (r. 1574–1595), for protection for his people in Turkish territories and for help in containing threats from the TUAREGS. Three years later, in 1577, Murad III sent a letter of agreement to help the empire. Later diplomatic efforts between the Ottomans and Kanem-Bornu brought about political ties and beneficial trading agreements.

The country of Morocco also forged a relationship with the empire in the late 18th century, the purpose of which was mostly to obtain firearms for Moroccan soldiers, as well as to establish the Turks as a political ally against the threat of French invasion.

Even though the Ottomans never ruled beyond North Africa, their influence was also felt in the present-day African countries of ERITREA, DJIBOUTI, Republic of the SUDAN, TANZANIA, and in ZANZIBAR.

During the course of the 18th century the Ottoman Empire's decline began in earnest as a succession of wars broke out in Europe and internal dissension within the Turkish military ranks increased. In Egypt the warrior Mamluks were also regaining their strength, and in 1757 an influential Mamluk bey, or governor, named Ali Bey al-Ghazzawi (1728–1773), came to power. Known as al-Djinn (the Devil), Ali Bey led a revolt against the Ottoman Empire in 1769 after which he proclaimed himself sultan of Egypt and asserted his country's independence from the Ottomans. His reign lasted until he was defeated by Turkish forces in 1773 and was forced to give up the title of bey to his rival. Though the Ottomans once again had control over Egypt, their rule lasted only another quarter of a century. At that time France was becoming increasingly powerful under Napoleon Bonaparte (1769–1821). Napoleon advanced from Europe, setting his sights on

taking Egypt from the Ottomans. In July of 1798, he succeeded in defeating the Mamluks at what became known as the Battle of the Pyramids. Later, in July of 1799, he defeated the Ottoman armies under the leadership of Sultan Selim III (r. 1789–1807) at the city of Aboukir to take control of Egypt.

The Ottoman Empire was ruled by the Osmanli dynasty. The word *Ottoman* comes from the anglicized version of *Osmanli*, which translates as "sons of Osman."

Egypt remained under French rule until 1801, when the Ottomans once again regained control of their former territory. Their rule was short-lived, however, and by 1805 the Egyptians were able to regain much of their independence under the pasha, or military commander, known as MUHAMMAD ALI (r. 1805–1848). Despite this setback the Ottoman Empire still held sway over what is now Algeria, Libya, and Tunisia until the latter part of the 19th century, when Algeria and Tunisia were lost to the French. Tripoli, in Libya, was the only Ottoman territory to remain under the empire's dominion until it, too, was taken by the Italians, in the early 20th century.

See also: CORSAIRS (Vol. III); FRANCE AND AFRICA (Vol. III); ISLAM, INFLUENCE OF (Vols. III, IV); OTTOMAN EMPIRE AND AFRICA (Vol. IV).

Further reading: Justin McCarthy, *The Ottoman Turks: An Introductory History to 1923* (New York: Longman, 1997); Donald Quataert, *The Ottoman Empire, 1700–1922* (Cambridge, U.K.: Cambridge University Press, 2000).

Ouagadougou (Wagadugu) Capital city of the Mossi state of the same name, located in present-day central BURKINA FASO. Ouagadougou, the city, was founded in the mid-11th century; the Ouagadougou kingdom was founded in the 15th century, and the city then became the seat of the Mossi *mogho naba*, or ruler. The MOSSI STATES, or kingdoms, included YATENGA, DAGOMBA, FADA-N-GURMA, Nanumba, and MAMPRUSI.

Although the Mossi States never unified to become a true empire, they maintained a strong military presence and occupied a vast stretch of land in the area of present-day northern GHANA and Burkina Faso. The Ouagadougou ECONOMY was based mostly on the trading of local agricultural products, but Ouagadougou did achieve some regional economic importance because it lay between the GOLD-producing AKAN states of the forests and the trans-Saharan trade centers of TIMBUKTU, JENNE, and Gao. Traders carried gold north to be brought across the desert and came back with salt and dried fish, which were sold at Ouagadougou's central market.

The Mossi exported some COTTON, iron tools, and slave laborers, and they imported kola nuts from the forest regions to the south. The Yarse, Muslim merchants who lived in Ouagadougou, conducted trade with DYULA merchants, whose commercial ties stretched eastward to the HAUSA STATES in present-day NIGERIA, and westward to present-day SENEGAL. In the 19th century Ouagadougou also traded with the FULANI traders of the SOKOTO CALIPHATE.

Ouagadougou began its rise to prominence among the Mossi States in the 15th century under Niandfo (c. 1441–1511). The *mogho naba* became powerful collecting agricultural products from the outlying villages and levying heavy taxes on the sale of captives in the kingdom. The city reached its height during the rule of Mogho Naba Waraga (c. 1666–1681), who organized the royal court and laid out the city so that his residence was near those of his senior officials and earth priests.

See also: OUAGADOUGOU (Vol. II, V).

Ovimbundu Large Umbundu-speaking ethnic group of what is now ANGOLA in western Central Africa; major intermediaries in the transatlantic SLAVE TRADE after the end of the 1700s. The Ovimbundu lived in the highlands of the BENGUELA plateau below the Kwanza River and the NDONGO kingdom of the MBUNDU. They were primarily agriculturalists who cultivated MAIZE, beans, and other vegetables, as well as fruits. The Ovimbundu also engaged in hunting, fishing, ironworking, cattle herding, and salt MINING.

During the 17th and 18th centuries IMBANGALA emigrants from the LUNDA EMPIRE founded states among the Ovimbundu. In the 1700s there were more than 20 Ovimbundu kingdoms, the smaller of which were generally tributaries of the larger ones, which included Bailundu, Bié (Bihe), and Wambu. The Ovimbundu kingdoms were ruled by the king, his queen, and his royal council and court. The council consisted of members of the royal dynasty, as well as free men and slaves, and had the power to both elect and depose the king. The Ovimbundu king was an important religious leader but held less political power than his equivalent in the Lunda states or the KONGO KINGDOM. His principal authority lay in representing the kingdom to foreign powers, waging war, and dispensing justice.

The Ovimbundu kingdoms were divided into districts and sometimes subdistricts, each containing a number of villages (*ovaimbo*) that were presided over by a local patriarch (*sekulu*). Some districts resembled independent tributary kingdoms, which were governed by princes who established ruling dynasties in their territory. Other districts were administered by officials appointed by the king, and still others were governed by local chiefs whose positions were inherited.

The center of Ovimbundu village life was the dance floor. Each village (*imbo*) was divided into four units (*ovitawila*), and the dance floor was placed in the largest unit. The dance floor, where festivals and ceremonies were held, was the social and religious heart of the village. Dancing was vital to the Ovimbundu, who danced from the afternoon through the night, and often for several days in a row. They had a saying: "When you see a drum, dance: A drum may not be seen twice."

Besides the dance floor, the men's clubhouse was an important village institution. Men and boys gathered in the clubhouse every evening for meals of corn porridge and relish, beans, meat, mushrooms, or greens. Here the men discussed work, settled disputes, gossiped, and educated their youth.

During the 17th century the Portuguese began trying to penetrate the interior of Angola. But steep mountains isolated them from the Benguela highlands, and they did not succeed in infiltrating the region until the next century. In 1769 the Portuguese built their first *presidio*, or fort, in the highlands, causing clashes with the Ovimbundu that led to major wars from 1774 to 1776. At the end of the conflict, during which two Ovimbundu kings were captured, the Ovimbundu began trading reluctantly with the Portuguese. By the end of the century the Ovimbundu were major players in the slave trade, raiding neighboring groups to the east and southeast, whom they referred to as *ovingangela*, or "less than human." By 1800 the Ovimbundu were important intermediaries in the regional trade networks between the ports of LUANDA and LOANGO and the interior, where they exchanged cloth, guns, alcohol, corn, and PALM OIL for wax, ivory, and slaves.

See also: DANCE (Vol. I); OVIMBUNDU (Vols. II, IV); PORTUGAL AND AFRICA (Vols. III, IV).

Oyo empire Located in southwestern NIGERIA, this Yoruba state flourished from the mid-17th to mid-18th centuries. At the height of its power, from 1650 to 1750, the Oyo empire controlled the region between the Volta and Niger rivers, including the kingdoms of BENIN, and NUPE, as well as the areas occupied by the EGBA. Historians generally consider Oyo the most important of the early Yoruba states.

The ruler of Oyo was called the *alafin*. He initially ruled from Igboho and, after the late 18th century, from Old Oyo. Oyo was a relatively minor state at the beginning of the 16th century and was even conquered, in 1550, by its northern neighbors, BORGU and Nupe. Under the leadership of Alafin Orompoto (fl. 1560–1570), however, Oyo began to strengthen and expand. Orompoto, who had acquired a great deal of wealth in commercial trading, could afford to finance a trained army and a force of cavalry. As its military forces became more powerful, so did the kingdom.

By the 18th century Oyo territory had grown substantially, as did its ECONOMY, which flourished as a result of increased trade with the Europeans. In 1738, at the peak of Oyo's military power, it subjugated the kingdom of DAHOMEY (in today's Republic of BENIN). Although a series of struggles between Oyo and Dahomey to its west ensued, the Oyo empire dominated Dahomey until 1748, when Dahomey once again rebelled.

The Oyo empire dominated a vast region, but each state was governed by its own administration. The states, however, were required to pay yearly tribute, and in return for their homage and loyalty to the *alafin*, they were protected by the empire's military forces.

During the rule of Alafin Abiodun (r. 1770–1789), the empire continued to prosper economically, but with a lack of interest in the army, the kingdom became vulnerable to its enemies both at home and abroad. By the time Alafin Awole (fl. 1793) succeeded the throne, the empire was in steady decline. Disgruntled tributary states, internal strife within the government, and the loss of trade routes all contributed to the downfall of the Oyo empire. It was finally conquered by the FULANI early in the 19th century.

See also: OYO KINGDOM (Vol. II); OYO MESSI (Vol. II); TEGBESU (Vol. III); VOLTA BASIN (Vol. III); YORUBA (Vol. II); YORUBALAND (Vol. III).

Further reading: Robin Law, *The Oyo Empire c. 1600–c. 1836: A West African Imperialism in the Era of the Atlantic Slave Trade* (Oxford, U.K.: Clarendon Press, 1977).

Oyoko AKAN royal clan that ruled the ASHANTI EMPIRE for nearly 200 years. Under the first Oyoko ruler, OBIRI YEBOA (d. c. 1680), the Ashanti embarked on a series of campaigns against the rival DENKYIRA state. They succeeded in conquering the Denkyira, under the second Oyoko king, OSEI TUTU (d. 1712), and established themselves as the dominant military and commercial power along the GOLD COAST of present-day GHANA.

Considered the founder of the Ashanti nation, Osei Tutu continued the Ashanti conquests and established the GOLDEN STOOL as the kingdom's sacred symbol. By the time the third Oyoko king, OPOKUWARE II, died in 1750, the Ashanti ruled supreme along the Gold Coast. The Ashanti, led by the Oyoko clan, maintained their power until the mid-1800s.

Ozolua (Ozolua the Conqueror, Prince Okpame) (r. 1481–1504) *Warrior king of the kingdom of Benin*

Prince Okpame, as Ozolua was then known, had been exiled from the kingdom of BENIN since the death of his father, Ewuare, in 1473. While in exile he remained active, conducting military campaigns against the Uzea, Uromi, Akoko, NUPE, Igallas, and Igbirras.

After a series of unsuccessful rulers the people of Benin asked Prince Okpame to return. In 1481 he was designated Oba (King) Ozolua at Usama and later assumed the title *ogie-akpolo-kpolo,* meaning "emperor." Ozolua led Benin to victory in as many as 200 battles and was celebrated for his military prowess. Many of his campaigns were against the Iye-korhimowo people who occupied the region east of the Orhiomwo River. Much of Ozolua's success can be attributed to his relationship with the Portuguese, who supplied him with firearms and weaponry. At the height of Ozolua's rule Benin's borders stretched across present-day southwestern NIGERIA from the NIGER RIVER to LAGOS, on the coast.

Eventually Ozolua's troops grew tired of his appetite for war and turned against him. After an attack on Uromi, near the Niger River, Ozolua's general, Laisolobi, betrayed him and assisted in his assassination. Ozolua was succeeded by his son Esigie (r. c. 1504–1550).

See also: EWUARE (Vol. II); PORTUGAL AND AFRICA (Vol. III); WARFARE AND WEAPONS (Vol. III).

P

palm oil Liquid extracted from the fermented fruit of the oil palm, a tree found throughout regions of West Africa. Groups including the IGBO, EFIK, IJO, Yoruba, ITSEKIRI, and Ijesha, all located in present-day NIGERIA, were successful traders of palm oil. The extent to which palm oil was traded slowly increased after the 16th century, when the Europeans began to acquire more of the product to ship overseas. Thereafter, palm oil was brought from the Nigerian interior to the coast and bartered for other African goods, such as ivory, GOLD, yams, salt, and kola nuts, while European traders offered such items as metals and weapons for the oil.

During the 17th and 18th centuries when the West African trading ECONOMY was dominated by the slave trade, palm oil was a minor trade item. The most popular palm oil at that time was red palm oil, which was a staple product on the slave ships crossing the Atlantic. By the late 18th century, however, palm oil was being exported in larger amounts to both France and England, where it was used not only for foodstuffs but also for making candle wax, and as a lubricant for machinery. After the British abolished their slave trade, in 1807, the demand for palm oil jumped significantly. For instance, in the year 1790, only 130 tons (132 metric tons) were sent overseas, generally in large casks, or barrels. By 1810 the amount was up to 1,287 tons (1,308 metric tons), and it had reached 10,673 tons (10,844 metric tons) by 1830.

See also: CASH CROPS (Vol. IV); ILESHA (Vol. III); PALM OIL (Vol. IV); TRADE AND COMMERCE (Vol. III); WARFARE AND WEAPONS (Vol. III).

Palm oil being pressed at Whydah, along the Gold Coast of West Africa. The oil palm (*Elaeis guineensis*), the fruit of which is pressed to produce the oil, is native to Africa and was exported to Malaysia, Indonesia, and other areas around the globe. *© Corbis*

Pare Bantu-speaking group that has long resided in the Pare Mountains, an area named after them in present-day northeastern TANZANIA, south of Mt. Kilimanjaro. Although little is known about the early history of the various peoples inhabiting the area, it is believed that, about 1500, the ruling clan of blacksmiths, the Washana, was overthrown by a clan known as the Wasuya. At about the same time, another group, the Wagwamba, moved into the southern part of the region and were joined by various groups originating in the Taita Hills as well as nearby mountains and grassland regions. Between these two zones a middle area was populated by peoples from North and South Pare. This area eventually became home to people migrating from areas outside Pare as well.

Between then and the 19th century various trade routes and caravan routes passed through the region, and it became known as an area in which ivory and human captives were traded. Until the mid-1800s the Pare remained quite separate from the neighboring Gweno people. Gradually, however, the two groups grew closer together, and in time they came to be seen as similar; today they are indistinguishable.

The Pare were in frequent contact with the neighboring MAASAI, and the two peoples found many ways in which to interact. For their tools, for example, the Maasai needed iron, a material manufactured by the Pare. In turn, the Pare needed the livestock that was fairly abundant among the Maasai. As a result the two peoples developed the custom of leaving offerings for each other at Pare religious shrines.

See also: IVORY TRADE (Vol. III); KILIMANJARO, MOUNT (Vol. I); SLAVE TRADE ON THE SWAHILI COAST (Vol. III).

Park, Mungo (1771–1806) Scottish explorer known for his travels on the Niger River

In 1795 Park, a surgeon, led an expedition funded by the British African Association to study the course of the NIGER RIVER. From the mouth of the Gambia River, Park journeyed nearly 200 miles (322 km) upstream to the British trading post of Pisania. In 1796 he reached the BAMBARA state of SEGU, in today's Republic of MALI. His account of this journey, *Travels in the Interior Districts of Africa*, was published in 1797.

Mungo Park's reports from his first Niger Expedition contained information about shea butter, a greasy substance extracted from the nut of the shea tree and used both in cooking and as a skin moisturizer. Because of Park's report, the scientific name for shea butter is *Butyrospermum parkii*.

The British government asked Park to lead another expedition up the Niger in 1805. His team made it to BAMAKO and then continued through the interior delta. They made it as far as Bussa, in present-day NIGERIA, before being attacked by unknown indigenous inhabitants. Park drowned in the attack.

See also: EXPLORATION (Vol. III); GAMBIA RIVER (Vol. II); NIGER RIVER (Vol. I); SHEA BUTTER (Vol. I).

Further reading: Mungo Park (Kate Ferguson Marsters, ed.), *Travels in the Interior Districts of Africa* (Durham, N.C.: Duke University Press, 2000).

pashalik of Timbuktu Reign of pashas, or military commanders, sent to govern the city of TIMBUKTU from 1591 until 1617; the pashas were sent to this city, in present-day Republic of MALI, by the sultan of what is now MOROCCO. These pashas were elected by the army and were generally Timbuktu-born descendants of the original Moroccan military officers.

The first such pasha to govern the merchant city of Timbuktu was JUDAR PASHA (fl. 16th–17th c.). A military officer, Judar led the formidable Moroccan force that, in 1591, overcame the SONGHAI armies controlling the city. He was, however, quickly relieved of his office by the Moroccan sultan, Mawlay ABD AL-MANSUR (r. 1578–1603), when Judar attempted to return the army to Morocco in exchange for a monetary deal with the Songhai ruler, Askia Ishaq II (r. 1588–1591). Judar Pasha's replacement, a military officer named Mahmud bin Zarkun (d. 1594), drove the Songhai from Timbuktu and began the process of exiling Muslim scholars from the city's famed SANKORE UNIVERSITY. After Zarkun was killed by the Songhai, Judar briefly came back into service before the role of pasha was once again passed to another.

By 1617 the office had been filled eight times. In the years that followed, the pashalik began to lose touch with the Moroccan sultanate, and most of the subsequent pashas were born in Timbuktu. Without the financial and military aid of Morocco, the pashalik slowly began to become less stable, and the reigns of the pashas grew shorter. By 1660, for example, 19 pashas had taken office; by 1750 another 86 had attempted to govern the affairs of Timbuktu—with most being forcibly ousted from their elected post. By the late 18th century the office was handed down a hereditary line of succession, but the era of the pashalik did not last much longer. The last pasha, known as Uthman, ruled Timbuktu just before the TUAREGS permanently routed the Moroccans from the city in 1833.

The reigning pasha was generally in charge of both the military as well as the MAKHZAN, or local treasury house, that was used for the collection of taxes. Beyond requiring approval for any newly elected chief, the pashas rarely intervened in the political affairs of the remaining

Songhai peoples. At the beginning of a new term in office, each new pasha demanded that the local brokers of Timbuktu pay him tribute, which he in turn shared with the men under his command. When a particular pasha became greedy about his wealth, his army was known to immediately remove him from power.

See also: ISLAMIC CENTERS OF LEARNING (Vol. II).

Pate Island   Small mangrove-lined island in the LAMU archipelago off the coast of KENYA. Pate was an important trading post and, from the 15th to the 18th centuries, was one of the great city-states of the SWAHILI COAST. The island was ruled by the NABAHANI DYNASTY, which originated in Oman, Arabia, starting in the 17th century.

Pate's KISWAHILI-speaking inhabitants lived in towns protected by sturdy coral walls. They built ships, wove cloth, and cultivated crops. The people of Pate maintained a close relationship with Kenya's other coastal port cities, including MALINDI and MOMBASA, from which they obtained ivory, iron, and other items that they could not get on the island.

During the 16th and 17th centuries Pate developed a sophisticated cloth industry. Weavers there produced high-quality silk and embroidered COTTON, which they traded with Arabs, the Portuguese, and the African peoples of the Swahili coast. Fine cloth was a symbol of wealth and status in Swahili society, and it was worn primarily by kings and cultured aristocrats.

Beginning in the 16th century Pate came under constant siege from warring Swahili and Arab dynasties, as well as from the Portuguese, who established settlements there in the 1500s. The Portuguese built Christian missions as well as a factory and a customhouse to administer taxes on trade. The Muslim inhabitants soon grew restless under Portuguese influence and appealed for assistance to the imam of the OMANI SULTANATE, under whose protection the island fell. During the second half of the 17th century Omani Arabs sacked the Portuguese forts at Pate. The older Swahili families did not resign themselves to Omani rule, however. As a result, in 1727, they formed an alliance with the Portuguese to oust the Omanis, but turned against them soon after.

When the BUSAIDI dynasty gained power in Oman, in 1741, the rival MASRUI dynasty, which ruled in the nearby coastal city of Mombasa, took the opportunity to declare itself independent from Oman and extend its influence to other settlements in the area. The two families continued to fight among themselves as well as with the Nabahani for control of Pate well into the 19th century.

See also: PATE (Vol. II).

Pemba Island   Island off the northeastern coast of present-day TANZANIA. A lush, green island, it was one of the leading city-states of the SWAHILI COAST. Its population, which included the descendants of Persian Gulf traders who immigrated to the island well before the 10th century, was long engaged in both trade and AGRICULTURE. Over the centuries Pemba became the landing place for many of the immigrants arriving on the East Africa coast from Arabia and Asia. The island was taken by the Portuguese during the 16th century, but at the end of the 17th century it fell under the influence of the OMANI SULTANATE. Several periods of unrest marked the island's history between the Portuguese pullback and the 19th century, when the Omanis, under SAYYID SAID (1791–1856), solidified their control.

See also: PEMBA ISLAND (Vol. II); PORTUGAL AND AFRICA (Vol. III).

Pende   Large ethno-linguistic subgroup of the MBUNDU that emigrated from ANGOLA in the 1600s. Before the 17th century the Pende lived to the northeast of the LIBOLO, SONGO, and the kingdom of NDONGO, and the KONGO KINGDOM lay to the northwest. The Pende controlled valuable salt mines, whose wealth encouraged the emergence of several Pende kingdoms. Pende kings derived their power from the *lunga*, a sacred emblem of lineage that was believed to have originated in the waters, along with the ancestors of the Pende. The *lunga* usually took the form of a human figure sculpted in wood, and the guardian of the *lunga* controlled the waterways, rainfall, and fields of his territory. During the 1500s the power of the Pende *lunga* kings declined due to the expansion of the neighboring kingdom of MATAMBA and the rise of a different system of Pende kingship, the *ngola a kiluanje*. During the same period, some Pende groups were absorbed by the Libolo to create a new ethno-linguistic subgroup called *Mbondo*.

In the late 16th century the Portuguese founded the colony of Angola and began expanding the slave trade. In response to these developments the Pende migrated further into the interior, east of the Kasai River and the Kongo kingdom. From their new home outside of the immediate sphere of Portuguese influence, the Pende established relations with the other peoples of Angola in order to continue their salt-trading activities.

About the turn of the 18th century the Pende came under the influence of the LUNDA EMPIRE, though they managed to retain most of their own cultural traditions. The Lunda introduced new ruling titles to the Pende, who were required to pay tribute to the Lunda *mwata yamvo*, or king.

See also: SCULPTURE (Vol. I); SALT MINING (Vol. II); SALT TRADE (Vol. II).

Phalaborwa mines Important copper and iron mines located in the present-day eastern Transvaal province of SOUTH AFRICA. Beginning about the 16th century Phalaborwa was ruled by the SOTHO people. Known as a copper-rich area since before the eighth century, the Phalaborwa region began to gain prominence during the 16th and 17th centuries. (It was at that time that the Sotho moved northward into Phalaborwa from parts of what is now SWAZILAND.) Even though the number of Sotho who lived in Phalaborwa was small, the emerging line of chiefs built upon the already profitable MINING industry. In part this was achieved by trading iron and copper bars and, in part, by making agricultural utensils. The latter were traded with their agrarian neighbors for FOOD and cattle.

By the mid-18th century the success of the Phalaborwa mines allowed the Sotho to assert control over the neighboring Lovedu peoples, which led to an even greater stake in the iron and copper trade. Nevertheless, the Sotho's domination of the area was short-lived, primarily because the lack of good soil left them unable to establish an agricultural community. (The Phalaborwa region also harbored the cattle-killing tsetse fly, which further limited the Sotho's efforts at establishing themselves in the region.) The mining industry, however, continued to thrive, despite the lack of a large, powerful state. The mines, in fact, remained consistently profitable throughout the 19th century.

See also: COPPER (Vols. I, II); IRON (Vol. II); TRADE AND COMMERCE (Vol. III).

pirates Maritime mercenaries who travel from port to port attacking and plundering commercial vessels for profit. Although piracy had been practiced in various parts of the world since before the common era, pirates were not too common around Africa until the beginning of the 16th century, with the beginnings of truly international sea trade.

The most successful pirates working the Mediterranean coast of North Africa were known as CORSAIRS. The Ottoman Empire employed groups of corsairs, some of them Greek, to help them control the movement of European trading ships along the Mediterranean coast. In the early 16th century the Ottoman government even formed an alliance with the Turkish brothers and corsairs, Khayr al-Din (d. 1546) and Aruj (d. 1518) Barbarossa. The Barbarossas helped the Ottomans challenge Spain for control of what is now the Mediterranean coast

of ALGERIA. Although Aruj was killed during the ensuing battles, Khayr al-Din was eventually successful in bringing the city of ALGIERS under Ottoman rule by 1518. Al-Din was later made an admiral of the Ottoman navy by Sultan Suleyman I (r. 1520–1566). Barbarossa also helped the Turks establish a presence at the port of Tunis, in TUNISIA, which along with Algiers would eventually become two of the main ports for the empire.

Piracy, in fact, contributed to the economies of many coastal cities in northern Africa. Until the early 19th century, coastal towns in present-day MOROCCO and Ottoman territories of Algeria, Tunisia, LIBYA, and EGYPT (an area known collectively as the BARBARY COAST), derived much of their income by trading pirated goods. Until the late 18th century the main targets of Barbary pirates were European ships from France, Britain, the Netherlands, and Italian city-states. After the end of the American Revolution in 1783, North African pirating ships took to plundering American ships on the Atlantic, too.

The Europeans and Americans were heavily involved in piracy themselves and often competed against one another for control over the best sea routes and their ports. In East Africa the European pirates worked the Indian Ocean trade routes, intercepting ships laden with goods either destined for or coming from ports on the SWAHILI COAST. Pirates were especially active around the island of ZANZIBAR, located about 22 miles (35 km) off the coast of TANZANIA. Portuguese pirates were well aware of the value of the ivory, metals, and cereals that made up the cargo of the Indian Ocean trading ships. Their raids were frequent beginning around 1503.

Another island that was a favorite haunt of pirates was MADAGASCAR, located about 250 miles (400 km) off the coast of what is now MOZAMBIQUE, in southeastern Africa. Madagascar became a pirate haven toward the end of the 17th century, and there was even rumored to be a utopian-style republic, Libertalia, founded by a band of like-minded American, French, and British pirates. Although the existence of Libertalia has not been confirmed, it is certain that the island of Madagascar was home to hundreds of European, Arab, Persian, and Indian sailors seeking individual wealth through piracy. Many of these pirates were active in the trade of human captives and used islands as their bases for raids on the coastal kingdoms of Africa and Madagascar.

A form of legalized European piracy called privateering began in the latter part of the 16th century. Similar to the Turkish corsairs of the Mediterranean, privateers were commissioned by their governments to attack and loot enemy ships as a means of protecting their nation's interests. The written commission that legalized the raids of privateers was called a "letter of marque." If a privateer carried a letter of marque, he was spared the harsh punishment of imprisonment, hanging, or beheading that was normal punishment for such actions.

Other bounty sailors who preyed on seagoing commercial ships were the buccaneers, who were mainly of French, British, and Dutch origin. Buccaneers operated much the same way as pirates but they were active in the Caribbean Sea, plundering ships around such places as Jamaica, Haiti, southern Mexico, and Brazil. The ships on which they preyed were often bound for Europe and filled with proceeds from the transatlantic African slave trade.

The word *buccaneer* comes from the Taino/Arawak word for the grill, or *boucan,* on which beef was smoked to preserve it for sale or later use. The Spanish call this method of cooking *barbacoa,* from which the English word *barbecue* is derived. Originally, the buccaneers were the illegal cattle hunters in western Hispaniola (modern Haiti) who used this kind of grill. The term later became applied to pirates operating in the region.

Piracy in northern Africa began to decline around the turn of the 17th century. After their 1697 defeat by the combined forces of Austria, Poland, and the Italian city-state of Venice, the Ottoman Turks were forced to sign what became known as the Treaty of Karlowitz. Among other things, this pact between the Turks and the three European powers required the Turkish government to defend European merchant ships from North African pirates. Nevertheless, raids on the European vessels continued for almost two more decades, until the Ottoman sultan Ahmet (Ahmed) III (r. 1703–1730) pressured his corsairs into stopping attacks on the foreign trading ships. Despite European efforts to put an end to the corsairs, piracy remained a profitable activity along the Barbary Coast well into the 18th century.

The end of the American Revolution brought about major changes in the status of the sea adventurers of the Barbary Coast. In 1786, three years after the end of the Revolutionary War, the U.S. government and North African leaders from Morocco and the Ottoman Empire began signing treaties that called for the respectful and fair treatment of crews and cargo on ships from all signatory countries. The first of these agreements, known as the Barbary Treaties, was signed by the Moroccan sultan Sidi Muhammad Ben Abdullah (r. 1757–1790), and American diplomatic ministers Thomas Jefferson (1743–1826) and John Adams, who helped to draft the treaty in conjunction with fellow diplomat Benjamin Franklin (1706–1790). In the 19th century the United States continued forging diplomatic relations by signing eight more treaties with North African states. Included in these treaties were three agreements with Algeria (1795, 1815,

and 1816), three with TRIPOLI in present-day Libya (1796, 1797, and 1805), one with Tunis (1797) and one more with Morocco (1836). Although pirating continued into the 19th century, these treaties contributed to reducing the violent and often merciless activities of pirates, corsairs, and privateers.

See also: OTTOMAN EMPIRE AND AFRICA (Vol. III); SLAVERY (Vol. II, III); SLAVE TRADE, THE TRANSATLANTIC (Vol. III); TRADE AND COMMERCE (Vol. II, III).

Pokomo Bantu-speaking ethnic group located along the banks of the Tana River in southeastern KENYA. The Pokomo are related to the MIJIKENDA and trace their origins to the Kashur people, who, in the 16th century, were dispersed by the movement of OROMO pastoralists from southern ETHIOPIA. Ancestral Pokomo first lived in SHUNGWAYA, near the border between Kenya and present-day southern SOMALIA, and eventually spread to the islands of LAMU, Manda, and Pate. Pokomo traders began using caravan routes to bring grains north to the SWAHILI COAST port of BRAVA, where they traded for cloth, glass beads, and metal goods, including Arabian and Persian flintlocks.

In the middle of the 17th century the Pokomo settled along the fertile floodplains of the Tana River, between the KAMBA and Orma peoples of southern Kenya. Along the Tana they cultivated a wide array of crops, including rice, MAIZE, bananas (plantains), mangoes, squash, pumpkins, and coconut palms. They also fished and raised small domestic animals like chickens and dogs. It is thought that the Pokomo also tried to raise cattle, but Oromo and MAASAI pastoralists raided their herds and put an end to that practice.

Both the Oromo and Somali call the Pokomo *Munyo,* which means "sedentary farmer."

The Pokomo are divided into four major subgroups: the Upper Pokomo, who are mostly Muslims; the Lower Pokomo, who are mostly Christians; the Welwan, or Elwana; and the Korokoro, also known as the Munyo Yaya. Each Pokomo group is organized into patrilineal clans that are further divided into age sets.

See also: POKOMO (Vol. II).

pombeiros Professional slave traders of Central Africa. During the late 1560s the IMBANGALA people overtook the KONGO KINGDOM and exiled its ruler, King Alvaro I (r. 1567–1576). With the aid of the Portuguese, Alvaro I was restored to the throne in 1574. However, his power over the kingdom had become diminished, and in order to maintain Portuguese military aid, it became crucial for Alvaro to meet their demand for captives.

To accomplish this, Alvaro had to combat growing competition from the Dutch. Therefore, professional African and European slave traders created an alternative route that, it was hoped, would circumvent the Dutch slave trade. These traders working this new route became known by the Portuguese term *pombeiros*. Over time *pombeiro* came to be used to refer to all professional traders of human captives in the region.

See also: NETHERLANDS AND AFRICA (Vol. III); PORTUGAL AND AFRICA (Vol. III); SLAVE TRADE, THE TRANSATLANTIC (Vol. III).

Popo (Mina, Peda, Xwla)

Popo (Mina, Peda, Xwla)   West African ethnic group inhabiting two small coastal kingdoms located west of WHYDAH on the Gulf of Guinea. The ports of Little Popo and Great Popo were situated in Aného and Agbanakan, near the border between present-day GHANA and TOGO. Known as Mina and the GOLD COAST in the 17th century, the stretch of coast that marked the Popo kingdoms was an important center during the transatlantic SLAVE TRADE. One of the most important of the Portuguese trading posts and slave depots, ELMINA, was built near there. It also served as a place where kings from the coastal kingdom of Whydah sought asylum during raids from DAHOMEY (present-day Republic of BENIN) to the north. The EWE-speaking Popo, who inhabit the Popo coast, are descended from GA-DANGME and FANTE peoples who migrated into the region during the 17th century. Because of their linguistic affinities, the Popo are sometimes categorized as an Ewe subgroup.

According to oral tradition, the Popo kingdoms were founded by descendants of Oduduwa, the legendary founder of Ile-Ife, the principal city of the Oyo people. Historians now believe that the Popo ties to Ile-Ife did not arise until the 18th century, when the OYO EMPIRE subjugated their kingdoms and revised Popo traditions in order to justify demanding tribute from them.

See also: ILE-IFE (Vol. II); ODUDUWA (Vol. II); POPO (Vol. II).

Porto Novo   City located on the Porto Novo lagoon, an inlet on the Gulf of Guinea on the coast of West Africa. Originally the town of Ajase, in the 18th century Porto Novo became a part of the DAHOMEY kingdom, then a trading center for the OYO EMPIRE, and ultimately a Portuguese slave-trading center. Today it is the capital of Republic of BENIN. About 1625 a prince named Te-Agdalin from the ruling family of ALLADA founded the town of Ajase. In the 1720s, King AGAJA (c. 1673–1740)

of ABOMEY—a kingdom later known as DAHOMEY—conquered neighboring kingdoms, including Allada and WHYDAH; led by Allada royalty, Porto Novo remained independent. Throughout the 18th century the slave trade dominated the region's ECONOMY, and Ajase and the Dahomey coastal towns became busy slave-trading ports. By the 1750s the OYO EMPIRE, which traded heavily with the Portuguese, dominated the area, and Dahomey became an Oyo tributary kingdom.

About the same time, Portuguese traders renamed Asaje, calling it *Porto Novo* (New Port). Porto Novo began to lose its importance later in the 18th century, with the fall of the Oyo empire, and was further weakened by conflicts with LAGOS, Dahomey, and the EGBA peoples of NIGERIA.

See also: PORTUGAL AND AFRICA (Vol. III).

Portugal and Africa   Portuguese sailors sparked European interest in Africa as they explored further and further down the West African Atlantic Ocean coast during the latter half of the 15th century. After 1500, when Portuguese explorer Vasco da Gama (c. 1460–1524) rounded the Cape of Good Hope at the southern tip of the continent, the entire African coastline was opened for European EXPLORATION. Nevertheless Portugal was unique among European countries in that it was heavily involved in ventures along both West and East African coasts. Portuguese merchants maintained a virtual monopoly on European trade with sub-Saharan Africa for nearly 100 years.

By the late 15th century Portugal's empire stretched from Brazil to China. Therefore, Portugal did not have the resources to devote to permanent settlement or conquest on the African continent. Portugal's interest in Africa was strictly trade-related, as it looked to exchange manufactured European goods for African cloth, beads, peppers, and slaves. The Portuguese established a series of trading forts along West Africa's GOLD COAST, in present-day GHANA, in hopes of drawing some of the GOLD trade away from the trans-Saharan routes. Although the Portuguese held many of these coastal fortresses until the Dutch conquests of the 17th century, they made little impact further inland.

One exception was the Portuguese interaction with the KONGO KINGDOM, in present day Democratic Republic of the CONGO and ANGOLA. Since Diogo Cão (fl. 1480) discovered the mouth of the Congo River in 1483, the Portuguese had exchanged ambassadors with the people of the Kongo kingdom. The Kongo people welcomed MISSIONARIES and sought technical aid from the Portuguese, but the Europeans were more interested in supplying slave LABOR to their nearby island possession of São Tomé. Portugal's insatiable demand for slave labor and its imperious attitude regarding the people of the Kongo led to the eventual disintegration of the kingdom. By the 18th century the Kongo state was all but defunct.

The Portuguese sought a similar relationship with the powerful kingdom of BENIN, further north up the West African coast. They occupied a trading outpost at UGHOTON as early as 1487 but lacked the resources to dominate Benin and soon lost interest in the region. About the same time, Angola became appealing to Portuguese slave traders. A small missionary settlement was established in 1575 and was soon placed under direct control of the Portuguese monarch. Military force was used to ensure the continuous supply of slave labor to work the plantations in Portugal's New World colonies, especially Brazil.

On the east coast of Africa the Portuguese relied on naval superiority to occupy many of the coastal Swahili city-states, including KILWA, ZANZIBAR, and MOMBASA, where they built FORT JESUS. After defeating an outgunned Muslim navy in 1509, Portugal remained the dominant Indian Ocean power until the end of the 17th century, when it was ousted from the region by Arabs of the OMANI SULTANATE. The Portuguese established strongholds up and down the eastern coast, from present-day SOMALIA to SOFALA in MOZAMBIQUE, in order to gain access to the lucrative, interior gold trade run by the MWENE MUTAPA kingdom. To access this trade, the Portuguese Crown awarded PRAZOS, or large estates, to hardy traders and backwoodsmen who were willing to settle in interior regions of southeastern Africa. The most successful Portuguese trading centers, or fairs, were located on the ZAMBEZI RIVER at SENA and TETE. Portuguese *prazeros* often took local women for their wives, and by the beginning of the 17th century, there was a new class of *mestizos,* or mixed-blood individuals, in the region. Despite years spent among the native population trying to develop trading ties in this region, the profits from these endeavors were small and slow in coming.

With the exception of Kongo and Angola, the Portuguese presence in Africa prior to 1800 had little impact. As a result of Portugal's absorption by Spain in the late 16th century, the Dutch had overtaken Portugal's control of the West African coast by the mid-1600s. Some small settlements and trading companies remained in operation, but most Portuguese activity was limited to the exportation of slave labor from Angola.

See also: AFONSO I (Vol. III); AGE OF DISCOVERY (Vol. II); ALVARES, FRANCISCO (Vol. III); CHICO REI (Vol. III); CHRISTIANITY, INFLUENCE OF (Vol. III); DELAGOA BAY (Vol. III); ELMINA (Vol. III); IMBANGALA (Vol. III); MOZAMBIQUE ISLAND (Vol. III); NZINGA NKUWU (Vol. III); NZINGA, QUEEN (Vol. III); PORTUGAL AND AFRICA (Vols. IV, V); SLAVE TRADE, THE TRANSATLANTIC (Vol. III); TRADING OUTPOSTS, EUROPEAN (Vol. III).

Further reading: David Birmingham, *Portugal and Africa* (New York: St. Martin's Press, 1999).

prazos Land grants allocated by the Portuguese government to colonial settlers beginning in the 16th century. The assigning of *prazos* was a system of land tenure through which the Portuguese Crown received income by leasing land in Africa to Portuguese settlers, traders, and backwoodsmen called *sertanejos.* The leaseholders, or *prazeros,* were given rights by local rulers to acquire captives and to cultivate the land, though their safety was not guaranteed. For that reason, many *prazeros* hired Africans to help them protect their *prazos* and ran them like medieval feudal kingdoms in Europe.

Prazos were especially prevalent in the eastern region of the MWENE MUTAPA kingdom, near the ZAMBEZI RIVER valley in MOZAMBIQUE. Through the *prazo* system, the Portuguese were able to become involved in local politics and extend their colonial influence.

See also: PORTUGAL AND AFRICA (Vol. III); ROZWI (Vol. III).

Further reading: Allen F. Isaacman, *Mozambique: The Africanization of a European Institution; The Zambesi Prazos, 1750–1902* (Madison, Wisc.: University of Wisconsin Press, 1972).

Q

Qadiriyya Islamic Sufi brotherhood popular in western Africa and the Nile River valley. In 1166 Abd al-Qadir al-Jilani, a Sufi scholar and mystic, died in Baghdad, in what is now Iraq. By the end of the 12th century his followers, called the Qadiriyya, had spread his teachings to the Sudan, in northeast Africa. By the 19th century Qadiriyya SUFISM had spread throughout western Africa, as well, brought there by Muslim traders along trans-Saharan trade routes. Like other Sufi brotherhoods, the Qadiriyya order stressed faith and submission through personal interaction with God. Followers strived to reach a state of divine meditation that allowed them to connect with God and perform magic and miracles.

Sufism emerged in the seventh century in the Middle East. It spread to Africa by the 12th century and became widespread in the 19th century, in both North Africa and in sub-Saharan Africa.

See also: ISLAM, INFLUENCE OF (Vols. II, III, IV, V); KUNTA (Vol. III); SUFISM (Vol. II, IV).

Quelimane Indian Ocean port town in east-central MOZAMBIQUE. Established in 1544 as a Portuguese trading station, Quelimane maintained an active market for the trading of human captives throughout the 18th and 19th centuries. By 1761 it was important enough to be recognized as a colonial town; it was recognized as a township in 1763.

See also: PORTUGAL AND AFRICA (Vol. III); SLAVE TRADE ON THE SWAHILI COAST (Vol. III).

R

religion As in earlier centuries, African religious practices continued along well-worn paths in many parts of the continent, especially south of the Sahara. In more traditional societies elders and ritual specialists—including priests, oracles, medicine men, and prophets—continued to engage in time-honored religious rituals as they sought to understand and engage with the supernatural world. Even in this context, however, religious practices were not static, and they often evolved to keep pace with other changes affecting African culture. However, more dramatic changes took place outside the realm of traditional religion.

During period just prior to colonial European conquest, the monotheistic religion of Islam became an even greater religious force across the belt of savanna grasslands south of the Sahara desert, in the Horn of Africa, and along the SWAHILI COAST. Of particular importance in the West African interior were a series of jihads in the 18th and early 19th centuries led largely by FULANI religious leaders deeply immersed in SUFISM. The most important of these jihads was that of USMAN DAN FODIO (1754–1817), which led to the founding of the SOKOTO CALIPHATE, in what is today northern NIGERIA.

Christianity also became a greater influence after 1500. The Orthodox Church in ETHIOPIA faced severe challenges in the war between Ethiopia and the Muslim forces led by AHMAD GRAÑ (c. 1506–1543). The church gradually recovered, however, and by 1850 it was again a major force in the recovering Ethiopian state. In other parts of the continent Christian MISSIONARIES from Europe began to arrive in Africa alongside European traders. One of the earliest areas where missionaries succeeded was in western Central Africa, beginning early in the 16th century with the conversion of the kings of KONGO to Christianity. By and large, however, missionaries were not active in most of the continent until the late 18th and early 19th centuries. In FREETOWN, SIERRA LEONE, for example, British missionaries led the efforts to care for captives freed by British naval vessels as part of the effort to suppress the Atlantic SLAVE TRADE. They also laid the basis for an African church leadership in the second half of the 19th century. Similarly, other British missionaries in southern Africa, particularly in the eastern CAPE COLONY, built the foundation for a vibrant African church through their work in evangelization and EDUCATION. Up to 1850, one of the principal differences between Christianity and other religions in Africa was that the leadership rested primarily in the hands of European missionaries. It was not until after 1850 that a genuinely African church came into widespread existence.

See also: ANCESTOR WORSHIP (Vol. I); ANIMISM (Vol. I); AROCHUKWU ORACLE (Vol. III); CHRISTIANITY (Vols. I, II); CHRISTIANITY, INFLUENCE OF(Vols. II, III, IV, V); COPTIC CHRISTIANITY (Vol. II); CRUSADES, THE (Vol. II); DIVINATION (Vol. I); DIVINE RULE (Vols. I, II); IFA (Vol. III); ISLAM, INFLUENCE OF (Vols. II, III, IV, V); MARABOUT WAR (Vol. III); MBONA (Vol. III); MWARI (Vol. III); QADIRIYYA (Vol. III); RELIGION (Vols. I, II, IV, V); RELIGION, TRADITIONAL (Vol. I); SHRINE (Vol. I); ZAWAYA (Vol. III).

Réunion Island Volcanic island, uninhabited before the era of European EXPLORATION, located 420 miles (680 km) east of MADAGASCAR and 110 miles (180 km) southwest of MAURITIUS. Until the Suez Canal opened in 1869, Réunion was a port of call on voyages to India and Asia.

Cartographer Pedro Reinel, who charted the west coast of Africa about 1485, was the first mapmaker to draw the now standard 32-point compass rose as a legend on a chart to show compass directions. On his chart of West Africa, he used a fleur-de-lis to point to north and a cross (for the Holy Land) to point to east. Reinel's son Jorge (fl. c. 1510–1540) was also a renowned mapmaker.

By most accounts the 16th-century Portuguese explorer Pedro de Mascarenhas landed at Réunion Island during his expedition to India in the early 1500s. Others, however, suggest that in 1507 Tristão da Cunha (c. 1460–c. 1514), another Portuguese explorer, was the first European to land at Réunion. Some sources, however, claim Phoenicians, Indians, and Arabs knew of the island much earlier. Regardless, the island was first charted by the Portuguese mapmaker Pedro Reinel (fl. c. 1485–1522) in 1518, under the name Santa Apolonia Island.

In 1642 the French visited the island for the first time. When mutineers exiled there from Madagascar were found in perfect health, though they were expected to be dead, the French took possession of the island, made attractive because of its prime location along the Indian Ocean trade routes. The newly renamed Île Bourbon was not formally settled until 1665 when the French East India Company established a rest station for ships en route to India. A plantation ECONOMY quickly developed, incorporating forced LABOR for coffee and sugar production. In 1764 the East India Company went bankrupt, and the island became the property of the king of France. In 1792, during the French Revolution (1789–99) in Europe, the island was renamed Île de la Réunion (Réunion Island) by the French National Convention in memory of the union of troops from Marseilles who burned Tuileries, a royal palace in Paris, in 1781. In 1806 the island was renamed Île Bonaparte, after Emperor Napoleon I (1769–1821). In 1810 Britain took possession of the island, calling it Île Bourbon once again, but in 1815, they returned it to France, under whose control it has remained.

Royal African Company

Organization chartered by the British government in 1663 as the Company of Royal Adventurers to combat the Dutch monopoly on West African trade. Beginning in the early 17th century the Dutch started the practice of chartering companies—such as the DUTCH EAST INDIA COMPANY and DUTCH WEST INDIA COMPANY—to trade with Africa and transport captives to America. These types of companies were granted exclusive trade rights by their respective governments and provided with military protection under which they pursued their commercial and expansionist endeavors. In return they were expected to build and maintain forts to protect the European trading posts along the coast.

It was not until the 1660s that other European powers attempted to thwart the Dutch monopoly in West Africa. The Company of Royal Adventurers, later the Royal African Company, held a monopoly on the English slave trade until 1698, when the industry was opened to all English traders.

See also: ENGLAND AND AFRICA (Vol. III); NETHERLANDS AND AFRICA (Vol. III); SLAVERY (Vol. III).

Rozwi (Rozvi)

Name given to the Shona people who were ruled by the leaders of the CHANGAMIRE DYNASTY, in present-day ZIMBABWE. The Changamire-Rozwi empire dominated southeastern Africa in the 18th century. Changamire, a title first assumed by a wealthy herdsman named Dombo (d. 1696), rose to prominence in the area south of the ZAMBEZI RIVER in the 1680s. Changamire Dombo organized a formidable army by recruiting young, single males from the surrounding SHONA KINGDOMS related to the disintegrating MWENE MUTAPA kingdom. He then used these soldiers to extract tribute payments of cattle and FOOD from the very kingdoms that had supplied the them.

Rozwi, meaning "the destroyers," was originally the name given to the Shona warriors of the Changamire's army. Over time, the name came to refer to all of the people of the empire.

Before the end of the 18th century Changamire Dombo and his well-trained army drove Portuguese settlers from their interior settlements, or PRAZOS, thereby assuming control of the lucrative southeast-African GOLD trade. The Changamire-Rozwi simultaneously came to control the burgeoning southeastern IVORY TRADE, and cemented their commercial dominance by not even allowing the Portuguese to travel through Rozwi territory.

By the early 18th century the powerful Changamire-Rozwi state had grown into an empire that covered most of the territory south of the Zambezi River, from Tonga territory in the west to the SABI RIVER in the east.

Succession disputes weakened the Changamire dynasty, and the empire was subsequently destroyed in the 1830s during the MFECANE, a period of forced migrations caused by ZULU invasions from the south.

Rwanda Country in the southern GREAT LAKES REGION of eastern Central Africa measuring 9,600 square miles (24,900 sq km). Today Rwanda borders on the Democratic Republic of the CONGO, TANZANIA, BURUNDI and UGANDA. Located just south of the equator, Rwanda was also the name of a kingdom occupied by HUTU, TUTSI, and pygmoid Twa during the precolonial period. The country's capital and largest city is Kigali.

During the 14th and 15th centuries Tutsi cattle herders began settling among the agriculturalist Bantu-speaking Hutu already occupying the area. As the 15th century progressed Rwanda assumed the aspect of a stratified, feudal society. Due to their cattle ownership and military prowess, the Tutsi emerged as the ruling class. The Hutu, on the other hand, were peasant farmers, supplying the Tutsi with FOOD in exchange for protection from outside threats. The Twa, for their part, remained hunter-gatherers. Eventually, Rwanda emerged under a Tutsi king, or MWAMI, named Ruganzu Bwimba (r. c. 1532–1559). The precolonial government of Rwanda was highly centralized and revolved around the divine rule of the *mwami*. The *mwami* occupied the highest position in a strict hierarchy of power, and all authority descended from him.

As in BUGANDA, the kings of Rwanda consolidated their power by appointing chiefs rather than allowing accession based on heredity. The *mwami* divided the kingdom and ruled with the help of a council of great chiefs, known as *Batware Bintebe*. A group of lesser chiefs governed districts, with each district divided into hills. The hill chiefs presented the *mwami* with tributes of food, labor, and milk that they gathered from the common people who lived in the villages.

Both Hutu and Tutsi practiced polygamy, but the Tutsi to a far lesser extent, due to economic circumstances. The Hutu were farmers, and their wives and children were the primary source of LABOR. More wives (and thus more children) meant that more land could be cultivated. On the other hand, Tutsi cows were tended by men because the cattle had to be defended against raiders. Therefore, Tutsi men had less incentive to take more wives.

In the 1600s Mwami Ruganza Ndori, a Tutsi, ruled the kingdom, and later Mwami Kigeri Rwabugiri unified many of the outlying Rwandan states. The kingdom reached the height of its power during the rule of Mutara II, in the early 19th century, and under Kigeri IV, who ruled from 1853 to 1895. Kigeri IV established a Rwandan army, led by powerful chiefs, whom he equipped with guns purchased from traders from the East African coast.

See also: BELGIUM AND AFRICA (Vol. IV); GERMANY AND AFRICA (Vol. IV); RUANDA-URUNDI (Vol. IV); RWANDA (Vol. I, II, IV, V).

S

Sabi River (Save) River in southern East Africa that was the main waterway for the transport of GOLD from the interior to the Indian Ocean port town of SOFALA, in MOZAMBIQUE. The Sabi River rises in ZIMBABWE and runs in a southerly direction before joining the Lundi River near the Mozambique border. From its confluence with the Lundi to its mouth on the Mozambique Channel, the river is also known as the Save.

At the height of its influence in the 16th century, the MWENE MUTAPA kingdom was supplying Swahili and Muslim Arab coastal traders with great amounts of gold from its goldfields between the Zambezi and Sabi rivers. Since the most important gold-trading center, Sofala, lay only about 50 miles (80 km) north of the mouth of the river, the Sabi was the preferred means of transport to the coast. Other trade goods transported by canoe on the Sabi included ivory, iron tools, tortoiseshell, cloth, salt, and handcrafts.

By about 1525 armed Portuguese settlers had taken Sofala from the previous Muslim inhabitants, disrupting the dynamics of the gold trade in the region. During the rest of the 16th century, as Sofala declined as a major gold-trading port, the ZAMBEZI RIVER to the north became the primary means of transporting the Mwene Mutapa gold to the coast.

See also: IVORY TRADE (Vol. III); PORTUGAL AND AFRICA (Vol. III); TSONGA (Vol. III).

Sadi Abd al-Rahman (c. 1569–1655) *Islamic scholar and historian*

Sadi Abd al-Rahman was born about 1569 in the prosperous trading city of TIMBUKTU, in what is now the Republic of MALI. He was educated at the city's well-known Islamic institution, SANKORE UNIVERSITY. In 1591 al-Rahman was a witness to the devastation caused when elite military forces from MOROCCO invaded the city and deposed the previously established rule of SONGHAI.

One result of the Moroccan occupation of Timbuktu was that many Muslim scholars were driven out, with followers of the religion suffering many casualties. It was because of the events and outcomes he lived through that al-Rahman decided to write the text known as the *TA'RIKH AL-SUDAN*, (History, or Chronicle, of the Sudan). This book became widely known as one of the best sources for the history of the western Sudan. It also was a chronicle of the powerful Songhai Empire and its rulers, detailing events from the latter half of the 15th century through most of the 17th century.

See also: ISLAMIC CENTERS OF LEARNING (Vol. II); SUDAN, THE (Vol. II); *TA'RIKH AL-FATTASH* (Vol. III).

Sadian dynasty

Islamic dynasty that ruled MOROCCO during the 16th century. The Sadians were a sharifian dynasty, which meant that they traced their lineage back to the prophet Muhammad. This greatly legitimized their authority within Morocco. In the mid-16th century the Sadians sought to oust Morocco's ruling dynasty, the Wattasids, and their Portuguese allies in Agadir.

In 1525 the Sadians took control of MARRAKECH, and they soon controlled all of southern Morocco. In 1541 they were able to expel Portuguese settlers and traders from Agadir. By 1550 the Sadians had driven the Portuguese from the Moroccan coast and captured the Wattasid capital of FEZ.

The Sadian dynasty reached its peak during the reign of Ahmad al-Mansur (1578–1603), under whom Moroccans were able to repel Ottoman expansion from ALGIERS. This gave the country a unique identity from the rest of the MAGHRIB. Al-Mansur also built the country's first professional army, and in 1591 they succeeded in conquering the SONGHAI. After al-Mansur's death, in 1603, Morocco split into several principalities until the Alawite dynasty reunited the country in the 1640s.

See also: ISLAM, INFLUENCE OF (Vol. III); OTTOMAN EMPIRE AND AFRICA (Vols. III, IV).

Sakalava Ethnic group and empire that emerged in the 17th century, unifying several kingdoms in western MADAGASCAR. The origins of the Sakalava are not clear, but their larger historical significance began around 1650. By the end of the 18th century the Sakalava empire ruled most of the western half of Madagascar, united by a common dialect and shared religious beliefs.

Around 1660 the MAROSERANA ruling dynasty of the southern region of Mahafaly began a campaign of territorial expansion under Andrianahifotsy (c. 1660–1685). That leader, whose name means "White King," led his Sakalava warriors north, conquering smaller Malagasy kingdoms as they went. Eventually, in the 1670s, they established the kingdom of MENABE.

Upon his death Andrianahifotsy was succeeded by his son Tsimanongarivo (fl. 1696), who migrated northward, conquered the Muslim Iboina, and founded the kingdom of Boina. By that time the kingdom ruled by the Maroserana leaders had taken on the aspects of an empire.

Conflicting Sakalava oral traditions suggest that the Sakalava name comes either from the Sakalava River, where they first settled, or from a previous group called the *Suculambe*.

Sakalava society under the Maroserana kings was divided into a "white" (perhaps Indian) ruling class and an underclass of Malagasy and Malagasy-Bantu people. The upper class was made up of cattle herders and warriors who were supported by the fishers and sedentary farmers who made up the lower class. Despite these differences,the Sakalava kings and subjects alike conformed to customs defined by their oral history and a strong tradition of honoring their ancestors.

By the beginning of the 18th century the Sakalava were active seafaring merchants. At the height of their power, the towns of Tulear, in the south, and MAHAJANGA (Majunga), in the north, were the most important trading ports of the Sakalava. Along with rice and beeswax, the Sakalava also began to trade in humans. They exchanged Malagasy captives for European firearms and manufactured goods, and, later in the 18th century, they traded their excellent cattle for MAKUA people from the African mainland. With the guns acquired from trade, the Sakalava empire built up an imposing army of skilled warriors. As the Sakalava came to understand the power of guns, their trading activity increased. By late in the 18th century it was a common practice for Sakalava traders to conduct raids by sea on the people of the COMOROS, to the north of Madagascar. Because of the difficulty of travel over the terrain in western Madagascar, the Sakalava usually relied on sea routes for travel. They were expert oarsmen and built large outriggers that could hold up to 50 people.

Sakalava religious practices involved the *dady,* or "ancestor cult." The relics—including teeth, bones, nails, and hair—of deceased kings were carefully preserved and became a source of power for those who possessed them. Warriors often kept these relics in decorated boxes that they attached to their belts, carrying them into battle for the protection that they thought they provided.

Though their power was unchallenged in western Madagascar, by about 1710 the Sakalava had been greatly diluted by intermarriage with the peoples they conquered. Internal power struggles weakened the ruling hierarchy, and the growing influence of Islam on the traditional RELIGION negatively affected the homogeneous cultural identity that previously unified their empire. Still they controlled nearly one-third of the island until the early 19th century, when the kingdom of MERINA began invading Sakalava territories from the east.

San (Sarwa) Khoisan-speaking nomadic hunter-gatherers of southern Africa. The San of today primarily inhabit semiarid areas in BOTSWANA, NAMIBIA, and ANGOLA. It was to these regions that the San fled, as early as the third century, when faced with waves of migrating Bantu-speaking agriculturalists. The arrival of European settlers in the 17th century forced them even further from their original hunting grounds.

The Dutch who settled on the Cape of Good Hope in 1652 established CAPE TOWN, first as a supply station for ships to Asia and then as a permanent settlement. At that time the San lived on the fringes of the CAPE COLONY, beyond the lands surrounding the colony that the KHOIKHOI inhabited. Although they lived by highly prescribed rituals, the San were nomadic and lived in autonomous bands, lacking central leadership. For this reason the Dutch settlers considered the San to be wild *Bosjiemen* (Bushmen), and viewed them as nothing more than mischievous bandits who plagued them with their cattle raids. During the 17th and 18th centuries these harsh judgments were used by the Dutch governors of the colony to justify ordering the murder of San people. The sporadic Dutch-San Wars, which lasted from 1676 to 1861, marked two centuries of ruthless conflict as Europeans dispatched punitive expeditions, called *commandos,* in retaliation for San cattle raids. Records for the years 1785–95 indicate that 2,500 San were killed and an additional 700 taken captive and held in bondage. Those who lived in the inhospitable Kalahari Desert generally survived; those who lived beyond its fringes did not.

See also: NETHERLANDS AND AFRICA (Vol. III); SAN (Vol. I); SLAVERY IN SOUTH AFRICA (Vol. III).

Sancho, Ignatius (1729–1780) *Former slave who later became the first African writer published in England*

Before Britain emancipated persons held in slavery, in 1834, Ignatius Sancho was one of a handful of blacks who reached success as butlers or valets, the highest levels in British domestic service. Born on a ship from the Guinea Coast bound for the Spanish West Indies, Ignatius was orphaned early in life. His mother died in transit, and his father committed suicide. At the age of two, his master took him to Greenwich, England, where the boy worked in servitude for three sisters. They nicknamed him Sancho after a perceived resemblance to Sancho Panza, the servant in the novel *Don Quixote,* by Miguel de Cervantes (1547–1616).

The wealthy and powerful duke of Montague befriended Ignatius and took an active interest in educating him. His friendship with the duke gave him a small taste of freedom not usually afforded to Africans, and he ran away. Sancho passed through a number of jobs until he became the butler to the duke's widow. Upon her death he was left a small sum of money and an annuity for life that Sancho used in 1773 to open a small grocery store with his wife on a fashionable street in London. In his spare time he composed MUSIC and indulged in a love for letter writing. His letters to the popular writer Laurence Sterne (1713–1768), the author of *Tristram Shandy,* were collected and published in 1782, two years after Sancho's death. In those letters he asks Sterne to use his influence on people's minds and speak out to oppose SLAVERY.

Further reading: Reyahn King, et al., eds. *Ignatius Sancho: An African Man of Letters* (Wappingers Falls, N.Y.: Antique Collectors Club, 1997); Ignatius Sancho, Vincent Caretta, ed. *Letters of the Late Ignatius Sancho, an African* (New York: Penguin, 1998).

Sankore University Historic institution of Islamic education located in the city of TIMBUKTU in present-day Republic of MALI. Sankore University was established during the reign of Mansa Musa I (r. c. 1312–1332) of the Mali Empire. It was formed around the great Sankore mosque built during Mansa Musa's lifetime by an architect from Granada named Abu Ishaq al-Sahili. (See photo next page.) Under the rule of the SONGHAI leader Askia MUHAMMAD TOURÉ (r. 1493–1528), Sankore University began to flourish as a center of Islamic learning. Throughout the 16th century the university was known to have held more than 20,000 Muslim students and had up to 180 *madrasas,* or Quranic schools. Islamic scholars throughout the western Sudan, as well as the entire Muslim community, traveled to Timbuktu in order to attend the renowned university and be educated in such subjects as RELIGION, Islamic law, and Arabic literature.

Throughout their education, students at Sankore lived with and were taught by other renowned scholars. After their education was completed, the students were given documentation of their *isnad*—the chain of scholars in their line of study from which each previous scholar was taught—and formed a sort of line of succession to the teacher who originated that particular field of study.

The university at Sankore also became known for educating three of the most important Islamic scholars of the 16th and early 17th centuries: Mahmud Kati (b. 1468), Abd al-Rahman SADI (b. 1516) and Ahmad Baba (b. 1556). Kati, who was a part of the royal cabinet of Askia Muhammad I, was famous for writing the TA'RIKH AL-FATTASH (History of the seeker of knowledge). Along with another historical compilation written by as-Sadi called TA'RIKH AL-SUDAN, these books were known to be two documents from which later historians gained most of their knowledge about the western Sudan. The works of Ahmad Baba were also crucial, as he wrote many books about Islamic law as well as a series of biogra-phies on famous Islamic teachers. Some of Baba's works became so widely read that they are still in use by Muslim scholars today.

In 1591 a Moroccan army sacked the city of Timbuktu, killing or dispersing most of the Muslims who resided there. Sankore University, however, remained standing and eventually reclaimed its status as an important Islamic academic institution in the western Sudan.

See also: ISLAMIC CENTERS OF LEARNING (Vol. II); MALI EMPIRE (Vol. II); MUHAMMAD TOURÉ, ASKIA (Vol. II); MUSA I, MANSA (Vol. II); SAHILI, AL- (Vol. II).

The Sankore mosque in Timbuktu, around which Sankore University arose. By the 16th century Sankore was an important center of Islamic learning. The photograph shows the Sankore mosque as it looked in the mid- to late 20th century. © *Sandro Vannini/Corbis*

São Salvador Capital of the KONGO KINGDOM located in the central hills south of the Congo River, in what is now ANGOLA. At its height, in 1650, São Salvador was a densely populated stone city inhabited by more than 60,000 people. Formerly called *Mbanza Kongo,* São Salvador was occupied largely by the ruling classes, which enjoyed a high standard of living. The king, the royal council and other noblemen, judges, and a supporting bureaucracy of secretaries, military officials, tax collectors, and personal servants all lived there. Beginning in the 16th century São Salvador was also the seat of the Catholic Church in Kongo, and was home to many clergymen, MISSIONARIES, and cathedrals.

The king's palace was so huge that it was said to form a second city within São Salvador. The noblemen also lived in large complexes in the town and owned plantations in the fertile plains just outside it, where peasants cultivated millet, sorghum, and cassava. The ruling classes levied taxes on the surrounding rural villages, or *lubata,* which were paid in the form of LABOR, metal goods, cloth, and animal products.

During the second half of the 17th century succession disputes brought war to the capital. Challengers from SOYO and elsewhere sacked the city, looting property and burning buildings. By the end of the 1670s most of the inhabitants had fled and the crops in the surrounding fields were left untended. According to a Capuchin monk named Michele da Torre di Camerino, who reported about his visit to the area, São Salvador was so deserted at this time that the elephants had taken it over, tramping through the ruins and feasting on banana trees.

The city was repopulated in the early 1700s by the followers of DOÑA BEATRIX (c. 1684–1706), and the Portuguese king, Pedro IV, rebuilt São Salvador a few decades later. However, the city never regained the splendor that it had achieved as capital of the Kongo kingdom.

See also: MBANZA KONGO (Vol. II).

Further reading: John K. Thornton, *The Kingdom of Kongo: Civil War and Transition 1641–1718* (Madison, Wisc.: University of Wisconsin Press, 1983).

São Tomé and Príncipe Country measuring about 390 square miles (1,010 sq km) made up of the volcanic islands of São Tomé (600 square miles) and Príncipe (40 square miles), as well as a number of smaller islets. The smallest country in Africa, São Tomé and Príncipe is located off the coast of GABON, in western Central Africa. São Tomé is the major city and capital. The country's population descended from six ethnic groups, which moved to the islands after 1400. A large portion of the original population descended from Africans formerly held in bondage.

The Portuguese sent to the islands African captives, exiles, criminals, and Jewish orphans, all of whom assimilated to form a Creole population called *Forros*. Throughout the 16th century the two islands prospered from sugar production. The Portuguese brought Africans in large numbers to work on their plantations (*roças*). Toward the end of the century, however, sugar production steadily decreased. In part this was due to the fact that São Tomé's LABOR force revolted against the conditions they endured at the hands of their Portuguese overlords. In addition, the crops from these islands could not compete, in either quality or quantity, with what Brazil was producing.

In the 17th century the Portuguese turned their attention to the slave trade in order to rebuild the failing ECONOMY. The islands not only served as a stopover for slave ships on the way to the Americas but they also became an important trading center for the slave market. In 1753 the capital was moved from São Tomé to Santo Antonio, on Príncipe Island.

When the slave trade was abolished, in the 19th century, São Tomé once again became the capital, with coffee and then cocoa being the colony's economic staples. Although enslaving humans was no longer legal, a form of SLAVERY existed in the practice of forced labor.

Working conditions were particularly deplorable in the islands' cocoa plantations. When, in the early 20th century, this was made known to the European public, both Britain and Germany led public boycotts against chocolate made from the islands' cocoa.

See also: COCOA (Vol. IV); PORTUGAL AND AFRICA (Vol. III); SÃO TOMÉ AND PRÍNCIPE (Vols. I, II, IV, V); SLAVE TRADE, THE TRANSATLANTIC (Vol. III).

Sayyid Said (Sa'id Imam, Sa'id ibn Sultan) (1791–1856) *Ruler of Oman, Muscat, and Zanzibar*

Said came to the throne of the OMANI SULTANATE in 1804, supposedly to share power with his brother Salim. However, his cousin Badr seized power, and it was not until two years later that Said was able to engineer the murder of Badr and take power. Reserving for himself the title *sayyid*, which was one of respect, he allowed his brother to retain nominal control of Oman until Salim's death in 1824.

Said assumed power in a time of turbulence in the region, with Britain and France fighting for control of the Indian Ocean, PIRATES raiding local shipping, and internal battles in Oman and other Arabian states causing still further conflict. Said, however, gradually solidified his power and expanded Oman's sphere of interest.

During his early years he shrewdly played the European powers against each another, using the security he gained from this to defeat the Masruis of ZANZIBAR, who were his main rivals for power in East Africa. By 1837 he was virtually in complete control of Zanzibar and the East African coast. He transferred his capital from Muscat to Zanzibar during this period and, realizing the potential of a new industry, transformed Zanzibar into a thriving clove-growing commercial center. He also revolutionized the traditional trading system of the region, and soon Zanzibar caravans were bringing ivory, captives, and other products of the African interior to the coast. Said's wide-ranging trade network carried these products to Arabia, India, Europe, and even the United States. He died at sea, in 1856.

See also: ARAB COASTAL TRADE (Vol. II); BUSAIDI (Vol. III); PORTUGAL AND AFRICA (Vol. III).

science Historically, Africans have made contributions to scientific inquiry in the fields of mathematics, engineering, astrology, metallurgy, and MEDICINE. Between the 16th and 19th centuries these fields continued to develop. The study of mathematics, which had a great tradition in North Africa, spread throughout parts of sub-Saharan Africa, and botany, or the science of plants and their uses, became more sophisticated, extensive, and complex.

During the 17th century the *ulama*, or scholars, of the kingdom of KANEM-BORNU, located in the Lake CHAD region in the central Sudan, had become skilled astrologists and mathematicians. Of special concern was *ilm al-awfaq*, or the science of magic squares, a mathematical principle whereby a group of numbers, each only occurring once, are placed into a matrix so that the sums of the numbers in each column, row or diagonal are always equal. These scholars also studied a science called *ilm al-huruf* (the science of letter magic), or cryptology. This and other secret sciences, known as occult sciences, became so avidly and widely studied by Islamic scholars that they were eventually denounced by the *ulama* as being damaging to the more conservative and practical studies of Quranic interpretation and Islamic law.

European science benefited from significant advancements made by Europeans working in Africa in the field of botany, since Africa was host to numerous species of flora that were unknown in Europe at the time. In the 17th and 18th centuries numerous European expeditions came to the continent to conduct research on, identify, and catalog the new species of plants. The area around the Cape of Good Hope, on the coast of present-day SOUTH AFRICA, was rich in different species of plant life. One of this area's most thoroughgoing explorers was Carl Peter Thunberg (1743–1828), a Swedish doctor and botanist. Thunberg studied the plants of southern Africa during three expeditions between 1772 and 1775, eventually earning the nickname, "The Father of South African Botany."

In the Hausaland area of present-day NIGERIA, the indigenous African knowledge of botany was combined with the knowledge of biology to produce organic chemicals that were effective as early weapons of biological warfare. Traditional African scientists inherited the knowledge gained through thousands of years of observations made of the reactions that were produced by various secretions and toxins from plants and animals. Their scientific knowledge was employed to dominate their opposition during wartime. Hausa soldiers made poison for arrowheads using a toxin referred to as the *dafin zabgai mai kare dangi* (poison that can destroy a whole generation). It caused asphyxia and eventually killed its victim if he or she went untreated. The poison was made either from a concoction of several kinds of plants and barks, or from the venom extracted from the heads of snakes and millipedes.

African warriors and medicine men alike realized that, even as some biological potions increased their abilities and heightened their perceptive powers, others served only to decrease their effectiveness in war. For this reason, alcohol and TOBACCO were forbidden to warriors before a battle, since they impaired the senses, coordination, and alertness.

Biological chemicals derived from plants and animals also had other uses in battle, sometimes being applied to make a warrior fearless and strong or to make an enemy fearful and weak. Also in Nigeria, a potion was used to make an enemy soldier extremely nearsighted, rendering him nearly blind and unable to fight. Warriors also were known to attempt to gain an extra source of power simply by displaying a plant that was known to have powerful chemical properties. These charms might be used to decorate the bodies of the warrior and his horse.

Across much of West Africa the study of sciences accelerated during the 18th and 19th centuries by virtue of various Islamic jihads, or wars fought for religious reasons. Muslim leaders generally held scholarship and the sciences in high regard and promoted scientific study in the regions they conquered.

See also: SCIENCE (Vols. I, II, IV, V).

Further reading: Ivan Van Sertima, ed. *Blacks in Science: Ancient and Modern* (London.: Transaction Books, 1983); Gloria Thomas-Emeagwali, ed., *Science and Technology in African History with Case Studies from Nigeria, Sierra Leone, Zimbabwe, and Zambia* (Lewiston, N.Y.: The Edwin Mellen Press, 1992).

Sefuwa African dynasty of *mais*, or kings, who, from about 1075 through the 19th century, ruled KANEM-BORNU in the region surrounding Lake CHAD. The most notable of the Sefuwa kings was Mai IDRIS ALAWMA (r. 1571–1603). It was during his reign that the dynasty saw the height of its military power and economic prosperity. Eventually FULANI warriors captured the Sefuwa capital of NGAZARGAMU, in Bornu, leading to the fall of the Sefuwa dynasty, in 1846.

See also: BORNU (Vol. II); KANEM (Vol. II); KINGDOMS AND EMPIRES OF THE WEST AFRICAN SAVANNA (Vol. II); KINGDOMS AND EMPIRES OF WEST AFRICA (Vol. III).

Further reading: Augustin F. C. Holl, *The Diwan Revisited: Literacy, State Formation and the Rise of Kanuri Domination (AD 1200–1600)* (New York: Columbia University Press, 2000).

Sefwi (Sahwi, Segwi) Subgroup of the West African AKAN peoples that spent most of its history dominated by neighboring powers. The Sefwi lived in the western region of present-day GHANA. Much of their early history is unrecorded, but it is known that, by the end of the 17th century, the Sefwi were under the dominion of DENKYIRA. By 1717 the Sefwi were strong enough to invade the neighboring Ashanti, sacking their capital, KUMASI, and pillaging the royal mausoleums. Several members of the Ashanti royal family were murdered during the conflict, including the mother of the Ashanti ruler, OPOKUWARE II (c. 1700–1750). The Ashanti counterattacked, eventually conquering the Sefwi and annexing them to the ASHANTI EMPIRE until the late 1800s.

Segu (Segou) BAMBARA kingdom located between the Senegal and Niger rivers in what is now the Republic of MALI. Segu and KAARTA, its sister kingdom, are known for succeeding SONGHAI in regional dominance from the 17th century until their defeat by the TUKULOR, in the mid-19th century.

Although the state of Segu was established about 1650 by Kaladian Kulibali (r. c. 1652–1682), a Bambara chief, Segu also has a foundation legend built on the story of two brothers named Nia Ngolo and Barama Ngolo. These brothers were known for pillaging other towns and were said to have come to live and establish their kingdom at the trading city of Segu prior to 1650. Regardless, it is neither the Ngolo brothers nor Kaladian Kulibali whom the people of Segu regard as their founder. Rather it was Mamari KULIBALI (r. 1712–1755), the great-grandson of Kaladian Kulibali, who was credited with founding the kingdom of Segu as well as becoming its first *fama*, or king.

Known as "The Commander," Mamari Kulibali led an aggressive military expansion that came to include territories such as the southwestern market village of BAMAKO along the NIGER RIVER, as well as the former Songhai-controlled trading centers of JENNE and TIMBUKTU, to the northeast. He also formed special armies such as the *ton djon*—a group that guarded the king and was made up of soldiers captured or conscripted from rival peoples—as well as a navy that utilized canoes for TRANSPORTATION up and down the Niger River.

After Mamari Kulibali's death, in 1766, there was a power struggle for the throne amongst his successors and some powerful members of the *ton djon*. In 1766 Ngolo DIARRA (r. 1766–1790), a member of the the the *ton djon,* was able to become *fama* and establish a dynasty that survived throughout the remainder of Segu's history. Diarra became known as the most powerful king of Segu as he increased the size and influence of his state, defeating such other states as MACINA and gaining a more firm hold of Timbuktu and Jenne. In 1790 Diarra was killed in a battle against the MOSSI STATES, leading to another succession struggle. Diarra's son, Monson, became king in 1790, reigning successfully until 1808 after further expanding Segu's territory.

The kingdom of Segu began its decline in the years after King Monson's death. In 1862 the weakened Segu state was conquered during the jihad of al-Hajj Umar Tal (1794–1864) and became part of the Islamic Tukulor empire.

See also: FULANI JIHADS (Vol. III); TUKULOR EMPIRE (Vol. IV).

Further reading: B. O. Oloruntimehin, *The Segu Tukulor Empire* (London: Longman, 1972).

Sena Trading town located on the banks of the ZAMBEZI RIVER, in present-day MOZAMBIQUE. Sena was established early in the 16th century by Portuguese traders who wished to take advantage of its position on the best water route between the GOLD fields of the MWENE MUTAPA kingdom and the Swahili trading network on the Indian Ocean coast. It also lay near the confluence with the Shire River, the major waterway of the MARAVI traders of the Lake Nyasa region, to the north.

Sena was located in Tonga territory in the Zambezi valley, surrounded by cultivated fields that easily supported its relatively small population. Toward the end of the 16th century the declining Mwene Mutapa kingdom to the southwest made pacts that allowed Portuguese traders to occupy land in the Zambezi valley, including the towns of Sena and TETE, farther up the river. Although the Portuguese were subsequently attacked by Lunda warriors from the KAZEMBE kingdom (which the Portuguese had helped to establish), by the beginning of the 1600s the Portuguese had a strong presence in central Mozambique. *Prazeros*, as Portuguese landowners were called, had secured large fortified holdings around the Sena settlement and had bought or captured many native inhabitants to work their land and protect their interests. Around 1630 the most powerful *prazero* in Sena was Sisnando Dias Bayao (d. c. 1645). With the help of his African laborers, Bayao managed to take territory on the opposite side of the Zambezi from the chiefs of the Maravi federation. Controlling land on both sides of the river allowed Bayao to offer safe crossing to favored traders, while at the same time letting him deny passage to the unwelcome African, Muslim, and Arab merchants who also settled and traded in the region.

From his stronghold at Sena, Bayao and his followers expanded southward and exerted their influence in political skirmishes in the BUTUA region until being driven out by the CHANGAMIRE DYNASTY. After Bayao's death, around 1645, the Changamire came to control the areas surrounding Sena and made trade agreements that excluded the Portuguese from participating in the gold-trading fairs along the Zambezi. By the end of the 17th century Portuguese trading activity in the region had practically come to a standstill.

Toward the middle of the 18th century the few remaining Portuguese traders in Sena revived their gold-trading activities with the MANYIKA chiefs to the south. Under a new agreement, though, the Portuguese were forced out of all MINING activities and had to offer large annual tributes to the Manyika in order to occupy the lucrative gold-trading fairs. As the Sena trading fairs proved to be less and less profitable, both Portuguese and Muslim merchants gradually moved away from the gold and ivory trades and into the burgeoning trade in humans. By the end of the 18th century Sena, like other outposts in the region, had become a stop on the routes that brought captives from inland regions to the Indian Ocean coast for export to French colonies in the MASCARENE ISLANDS or to the Americas.

See also: IVORY TRADE (Vol. III); LUNDA EMPIRE (Vol. III); PORTUGAL AND AFRICA (Vol. III); PRAZOS (Vol. III); SLAVE TRADE ON THE SWAHILI COAST (Vol. III).

Senegal Country located in West Africa measuring about 76,000 square miles (196,800 sq km). It is bordered by the Atlantic Ocean to the west, MAURITANIA to the north, the Republic of MALI to the east, and GUINEA and GUINEA-BISSAU to the south. DAKAR, Senegal's capital and largest city, is located near Africa's westernmost point.

Beginning in the eighth century, most of present-day Senegal was part of the ancient Ghana Empire. From the 11th to the 14th centuries, however, the powerful Tekrur kingdom of the TUKULOR dominated the eastern regions, using conversion to Islam to unify the people they conquered. By the 14th century non-islamic Wolof kingdoms were also gaining strength and supplanting the Tekrur kingdom between the Senegal River and the coast. The Wolof kingdoms included Walo, KAYOR, Baol, and the Serer kingdoms of Sine and Saloum.

It was the Portuguese explorations of the 15th century and their subsequent commercial activities that turned the West African coast into a major trading outpost by the 16th century. At that time, England, France, and the Netherlands began moving in on Portugal's commercial monopoly. Dutch merchants set up trading posts along the coast, the most notable on GORÉE ISLAND in 1588, and by the mid-17th century they controlled almost all trade in the region. But by the end of the century it was the British and French who were vying for commercial dominance. The British operated from the Gambia River and the French from the Senegal River, where they set up a trading post on Saint-Louis Island. The French moved in on Dutch territory and, in 1677, took Gorée Island away from them. The European influence had a devastating impact on the WOLOF EMPIRE in particular. The empire eventually fragmented, with its various states breaking away and establishing independence.

Meanwhile, Muslim clerics facilitated the spread of Islam during the 17th century. Their opposition to slave trading enlisted them in a series of expeditions between 1673 and 1677 in which they attempted to hinder European trading activities on the coast. The clerics were no match for the French, whose superior weaponry put an end to the rebellions, but the Muslim influence nonetheless converted many of the West African peoples whose villages were often raided for their inhabitants.

The antagonism between Britain and France continued on into the 18th century and culminated with the outbreak of the Seven Years' War, a worldwide conflict fought in Europe, North America, and India between 1756 and 1763. From 1756 to 1815 control over French posts went back and forth between the two rival nations until the British eventually handed everything back at the Congress of Vienna, in 1815.

The trade in humans began to decline early in the 19th century as a result of the industrialization of Europe and the decreased demand for forced LABOR in the Americas. France compensated first by extending its commerce to the Casamance region, south of The GAMBIA, along the Gambia River, and then, by the mid-century, developing the trade in GROUNDNUTS (peanuts).

See also: ENGLAND AND AFRICA (Vols. III, IV); FRANCE AND AFRICA (Vols. III, IV); PORTUGAL AND AFRICA (Vol. III); SENEGAL (Vols. I, II, IV, V); SERER (Vol. II); SLAVE TRADE, THE TRANSATLANTIC (Vol. III); TUKULOR EMPIRE (Vol. IV).

Further reading: Basil Davidson, *A History of West Africa 1000–1800* (London: Longman, 1977).

Senegambia Region in West Africa that includes the present-day countries of SENEGAL and The GAMBIA. It was a British Crown colony from 1765 to 1779, passed briefly to French control, until 1783, and then reverted to British control. In 1763 Britain and France ended their Seven Years' War, and the British returned GORÉE ISLAND to the French as a peace offering. Over the next two years the British found that the French trading operations were a threat to their own commercial interests. So, in 1765, they reevaluated their deal with France and established the Province of Senegambia, which was made up of the three small islands of Saint-Louis, Gorée, and James island.

The colony of Senegambia was run by a governor, who chose his own council. Colonel Charles O'Hara was the first governor and headed the colony from 1765 to 1775; his three companies of troops were called "O'Hara's Corps," but the name was later changed to the Royal African Corps. O'Hara held his office for almost 11 years, during which time he was continually at odds with the French over trading territory.

Matthias MacNamara was the second governor of Senegambia, but his leadership was short-lived, lasting only from November 1775 to April 1777, as internal conflicts with his lieutenant resulted in his dismissal. After the death of John Clark, the province's third governor, in 1778, the colony was substantially weakened.

In 1779 the French destroyed the fort at James Island, leaving it in such a state of disrepair that the British did not occupy it again. In the 1783 Treaty of Versailles, the British handed the Province of Senegambia over to the French but retained control of the Gambia River and James Island.

See also: ENGLAND AND AFRICA (Vol. III); FRANCE AND AFRICA (Vol. III); SENEGAMBIA CONFEDERATION (Vol. V); SENEGAMBIA REGION (Vol. IV).

Sennar (Senaar, Sennaar) City located in central Republic of the SUDAN that served as the capital city of the FUNJ sultanate from the 16th to the 18th centuries. The people of Sennar lived in small farming communities and paid taxes to their local overlords, as well as to the sultan, in exchange for the use of the land. Society was organized by matrilineal descent. Although Islam was the state RELI-GION and Arabic the state language, many of Sennar's farmers maintained traditional African beliefs and spoke African languages.

In 1504 the Funj sultanate was founded at Sennar by Amara Dunqas, who established the Funj dynasty, the family that ruled in the Nilotic Sudan from the 16th to the 19th centuries. For the Funj the 16th century was a turbulent time, as they were engaged in numerous terri-torial conflicts with Arabs from the surrounding regions around the Blue and White Nile rivers. By the 17th cen-tury Sennar under Funj leadership reached its political, economic, and territorial zenith.

Sennar's most notable warrior-king was Badi II Abu Dagn (r. 1644–1680). During his reign he extended the kingdom's territory and established a powerful military caste comprised primarily of warriors he had captured during his many campaigns. Eventually these captives began to compete with the Funj aristocracy for control of important state offices. They united and rebelled against the nobility and their traditional power. Under the Funj king Badi IV Abu Shulukh (r. 1724–1762), the power of the aristocracy was broken and the king became an abso-lute ruler, with the support of his army. By 1762 the army, too, was out of control, and they revolted against the monarchy, driving Badi IV Abu Shulukh out. The power of the succeeding Funj kings rapidly dwindled. In 1821 Sennar was conquered by the Egyptians under MUHAM-MAD ALI (1769–1849), whose dynasty ruled EGYPT until the middle of the 20th century.

Senufo (Senuofo)

West African people who inhab-ited areas of northern IVORY COAST and southeastern parts of present-day Republic of MALI. After the deterioration of the Mali Empire in the 16th century, the Senufo moved southwards and began to inhabit land in central Ivory Coast, in a region that would become the short-lived kingdom of Sakasso, in the mid-18th century. During the 17th century, however, the Senufo were forced to flee the Sakasso region in an attempt to escape subjugation by the Mandinka peoples.

The early 18th century again forced the migrations of the Senufo, who had resisted conversion to Islam when they were under Malian control, when the Muslim Juula peoples established themselves in the region and began the foundation of the KONG kingdom. The Senufo were still unable to establish themselves in a region until the 18th century, when they finally settled near the kingdom of Korhogo. They remained a fairly independent and di-verse group throughout most of the 19th century until another faction of Senufo, the Muslim Senufo who had remained in the original region of Sakassa, began to at-tack and overthrow the non-Muslim Senufo settlements to the south.

The Senufo were traditionally an agrarian group who spoke more than four different dialects of the Gur branch of the Niger-Congo language family. Their FAMILY units were based along matrilineal lines, and marriages were often arranged. The Senufo were also widely recognized as skilled carvers of wooden masks and sculptures.

See also: MALI EMPIRE (Vol. II).

Seychelles

Island country covering approximately 180 square miles (470 sq km) located off mainland Africa, north of MADAGASCAR, in the Indian Ocean. Victoria is the capital and largest city. The country is made up of 115 is-lands, of which Mahe is the largest. Approximately 85 per-cent of the population lives on Mahe island. Other major islands are Praslin and La Digue. During the 18th century the islands served as an important Indian Ocean trading base. According to legend, the Seychelles were visited by Arab and Phoenician traders before the beginning of the common era. The first recorded sighting of the islands, however, was by Vasco da Gama (1460–1524), in 1502, when he discovered part of this uninhabited island group and named it the Amirantes Islands.

In 1609 the British made the first documented land-ing, when members of the British East India Company spent several days restocking their ships there with sup-plies and produce, especially tortoises, which they boiled for meat. After several visits by the French in 1742 and 1744, France formally claimed the Seychelles, on Novem-ber 9, 1756, and renamed them after the French minister of finance, Jean Moreau de Sechelles.

Colonization began in 1778, when French planters and their captive African laborers settled the area to grow crops used to supply passing French trading vessels. The islands were also utilized to smuggle captive Africans into nearby MAURITIUS. The French lost control of the Sey-chelles in 1814, when the islands were signed over to Britain in the Treaty of Paris. The British, however, ac-quired the islands only as a means of halting French trade and saw little use for them. After 1834, the year in which Britain, having outlawed the slave trade in 1807, formally emancipated all slaves, more than 6,000 Africans were freed, causing many of the settlers to flee the islands with their enslaved workers.

See also: FRANCE AND AFRICA (Vols. III, IV); INDIAN OCEAN TRADE (Vol. II); SEYCHELLES (Vols. I, II, IV, V); GAMA, VASCO DA (Vol. II).

Shaka (Chaka, Tshaka)

(1787–1828) *Great Zulu warrior chief and empire builder*

Shaka was born the son of a ZULU chief but spent his childhood living in exile and disgrace with his mother, whom his father had repudiated. The Zulu of the time were only one of many Bantu-speaking NGUNI clans in what is now SOUTH AFRICA. At the age of 23 Shaka was commissioned by DINGISWAYO (d. 1817), the head of the clan that had taken in the young Shaka, to serve as a warrior for the Mtetwa (Mthethwa) clan of the North (Natal) division of the Nguni people, where he served with honor for six years.

Shaka's childhood was a troubled one. His father, Senzangakona, was a chieftain of the Zulu clan, but his flirtation with Nandi, a princess from the neighboring Elangeni clan, who bore Shaka out of wedlock, defied Zulu laws and customs. The union of Senzangakona and Nandi brought conflict, shame, and humiliation to the young Shaka, whose name is derived from *iShaka,* the Zulu name for an intestinal beetle that was blamed for menstrual irregularities. By the age of six he was taken by his mother to live with the Elangeni clan. In 1802 the Elangeni drove them out, and Shaka and his mother eventually found refuge with the Dietsheni, a subgroup of the powerful Mtetwa clan. Shaka harbored a deep hatred for his persecutors for the rest of his life.

After the death of his father, in 1816, Shaka was discharged from military service, and Dingiswayo dispatched him to rule the Zulu clan. The first task he set for himself was the reorganization of the Zulu military. He introduced a short thrusting spear, called an *assegai,* and trained his soldiers in the tactics of hand-to-hand combat. More important, he also developed innovative military strategies. To this end he divided each of his available regiments, collectively called the *impi,* into four fighting units, each with its own battle plan. One group would attack the enemy head on, while two groups moved around the flanks and encircled the enemy. During these maneuvers the fourth group remained in reserve, ready to aid wherever it was needed. Shaka also was a proponent of total warfare. His strategy was to destroy his enemies as completely as possible, incorporating any survivors into the Zulu. Within a year he had quadrupled the number of people who owed him allegiance.

After the death of Dingiswayo, in 1817, Shaka decided to further increase the power of the Zulu, beginning by taking over the only nearby clans who could threaten him, the Ndwandwe and Qwabe. Then, over the next 10 years, he launched a series of annual campaigns against the clans to the south, which set off mass migrations of people seeking to escape the Zulu aggression. By 1820 these attacks, known as the MFECANE (The Crushing), eventually broke down the clan system and left an estimated 2 million people dead.

Throughout his life Shaka was obsessively fearful of being replaced by an heir. Thus, although he had at the height of his power more than 1,200 wives, he called them his "sisters" and practiced a form of external sexual intercourse, called *ukuHlobonga,* allowed to the unmarried, that led to no offspring.

The death of his mother, in 1827, had a profound effect on Shaka. His grief was so extreme—some authorities call it deranged—that he ordered the executions of several men. The chaos that followed quickly led to the almost immediate deaths of 7,000 Zulu. In reverence for his mother, he ordered his clan to starve itself. Shaka's erratic behavior ultimately led to his death, in 1828, at the hands of a group of his military leaders and his half-brothers, DINGANE and Mhlangana.

See also: WARFARE AND WEAPONS (Vol. III).

Further reading: John Laband, *The Rise & Fall of the Zulu Nation* (New York: Sterling Publishing, 1997).

Shambaa Agricultural people who have long lived in the Usambara Mountains, in the northeastern portion of present-day TANZANIA. The region they inhabit is called *Shambaai.* Their language, also known as Shambaa, is a Bantu language. The pantheon of their traditional RELIGION is divided into two kinds of deities: those associated with ancestors and those associated with nature. Observances involve rituals owed to the ancestors of each FAMILY.

The Shambaa have lived in their homeland since at least the 18th century. They primarily inhabit the mountainous part of the region but are close enough to the lowlands to have ready access to the nearby plains. This allows them to use the mountainsides for growing crops and the plains for hunting game and tending herds. Given the prevalence of famine in Africa, this economic flexibility meant that the Shambaa had a far greater chance for survival than some other groups.

Although hunting and the IVORY TRADE were important supplements, AGRICULTURE was the mainstay of the Shambaa ECONOMY. However, before the beginning of the 19th century revenue from the ivory trade apparently was the property of Shambaa kings and chiefs and was not shared with the population in general.

During the early part of their history, tribute also formed an important part of the Shambaa economy and society. The tribute system grew as new groups were added to the Shambaa kingdom. New arrivals showed their allegiance and submission to the larger group by paying tribute in the form of services, livestock, and other products. In return the Shambaa king supplied his new subjects with meat.

This tribute system that developed over time was relatively informal and based on the king's needs. When he desired particular goods or services, he simply sent out courtiers to collect what was wanted. Collectors could also go out in quest of tribute on their own accord; they simply had to supply the king with his proper share.

A large population was to the king's advantage, as it increased his royal wealth in the form of tribute and LABOR on his farms and allowed him to increase his military force. This led to attempts to further Shambaa size, either by conquest or assimilation.

Among the Shambaa, the amount of tribute that a subject owed to the king did not depend upon how much that individual owned or produced but rather on services requested of the king. Thus, the more frequently a subject came to the king to settle a dispute or request other assistance, the more he or she owed in tribute.

In the early 19th century political control of Shambaai passed to the king of the Kalindi, Mbegha (fl. c 1800), who, according to tradition, was awarded the kingship of Shambaai because he managed to kill the bush pigs that had been destroying Shambaa land. The Kalindi rulers further centralized Shambaa government, establishing a system of lesser kingdoms and chiefdoms, ruled primarily by the royal sons.

See also: ANCESTOR WORSHIP (Vol. I); BANTU LANGUAGES (Vols. I, II).

Further reading: Steven Feierman, *The Shambaa Kingdom: A History* (Madison, Wisc.: University of Wisconsin Press, 1974).

Shamba Bolongongo (r. 1600–1620) *Greatest of the Shongo kings of the Kuba kingdom*

Shamba Bolongongo, the ninety-third KUBA *nyim*, or king, introduced to the kingdom the cultivation of MAIZE, TOBACCO, beans, and cassava, and expanded trade both east and west. He also strengthened the central government and expanded the territory of the Kuba kingdom. His reign inspired a golden age in Kuba culture.

Shamba was widely admired as a peacemaker among his people. He encouraged the pursuit of arts and crafts and relegated warfare to a standing army. He forbade the use of a traditional BUSHONGO weapon, the *shongo*, or throwing knife. Shamba's philosophy of peace was represented by his famous decree: "Kill neither man, woman nor child. Are they not the children of Chembe (God), and have they not the right to live?"

Weaving, sculpture, pottery, and other arts flourished under the king's rule. The practice of honoring Bushongo royalty by portraying them in sculpture, called *ndop,* began with Shamba Bolongongo.

Shamba was often represented in Kuba sculpture. One example is an elegant carved wooden figure that depicts Shamba Bolongongo sitting with legs crossed on a low throne, with his left hand holding a ceremonial sword and his other hand resting on his right knee. He wears a crown and dons bracelets around his wrists and ankles. Geometric patterns crisscross his stomach and extend around to his back.

Shankella
Name given by rival AMHARA and Tigray peoples to the Hamitic-Nilotic groups that inhabited the region along what is now the border between the Republic of the SUDAN and ETHIOPIA. According to Arabic records, the Shankella originally came from KHARTOUM, the capital of present-day Republic of the Sudan, and eventually settled in the villages of Alguma, Amoda, Afillo, Bisaka, Debatara, Debintana, Henditaga, Karakada, Saderda, Tabara, Tagada, and Tamada. They were an agricultural people made up of several sub-groups, each with its own culture and language. The most notable groups include the Kunama, Barya, and Bani Shangul.

Between the 15th and 18th centuries the Shankella endured a series of attacks and invasions by soldiers from the Ethiopian Christian empire. They were often the targets of raiders from both sides of the Ethiopia-Sudan border. The Shankella were less desired as captives than the OROMO or SIDAMO, who were favored for their lighter skin and what was believed to be a milder temperament. On the hierarchy of captives the Shankella were at the lowest level, and they paid for their low status by being given the least desirable work, such as hard domestic LABOR or fieldwork.

Shilluk (Collo)
Nilotic people inhabiting the area along the White Nile and Sobat rivers in present-day Republic of the SUDAN. The Shilluk settled in their present location during the early 16th century. In the early 17th century, they began to expand their territory, overtaking the frontier areas surrounding the Nile River. By the second half of the 17th century a centralized state was established under the rule of the *reth,* or divine king, who was elected from the sons of former kings. The *reth* was the representative and the reincarnation of the mythical hero Nyiking, the legendary founder of the Shilluk,

and his health was thought to be closely related to the spiritual and material health of the people.

The Shilluk, who led a lifestyle that was both pastoral and agricultural, remained in control of the region until the early 19th century, when MUHAMMAD ALI (1769–1849), the pasha of EGYPT, established Turco-Egyptian rule in the area.

See also: DIVINE RULE (Vols. I, II); NILE RIVER (Vol. I).

Shirazi dynasty Powerful Swahili families who were instrumental in developing Indian Ocean trade; the Shirazi controlled many of the city-states that supported a flourishing urban culture along the East African coast. Beginning in the 1600s the Shirazi dynasty declined at MOMBASA, ZANZIBAR, and other coastal cities, due in part to the increasing influence of the Portuguese and Omanis, who sought to control the ocean trade. Some Shirazi, however, made deals with the OMANI SULTANATE, which allowed the Shirazi to retain their local authority. The Shirazi remained in power in some coastal towns well into the 19th century.

Previously, it was thought that the Shirazi came from the Persian city of Shiraz. In both African and Arab societies, however, genealogy communicated social status. People adopted a more desirable genealogy to reflect a new social identity. Often, the name of a prestigious foreign place was taken as a *nisba,* or family name. Currently, scholars think that Swahili people on the African coast adopted Shirazi as their *nisba* to indicate their elite status as merchants, since some of the Arab traders they dealt with had come from Shiraz. The term *Shirazi* has also been used generally to distinguish older Swahili families from people who arrived more recently, during the 19th and 20th centuries.

See also: AFRO-SHIRAZI PARTY (Vol. V); SHIRAZI ARABS (Vol. II); SWAHILI COAST (Vols. II, III, IV).

Shoa (Shewa, Showa) Province of ETHIOPIA located between the Blue Nile and the Awash rivers. Throughout Ethiopia's long and turbulent history, Shoa has been an important political region. Indeed, between the 10th and 14th centuries many of Shoa's towns, including Tegulet and Dabra Berhan, were royal centers and residences for local rulers.

In 1528, during the Battle of Shimbra Kure, a Muslim army from neighboring ADAL, headed by Ahmad ibn-Ibrahim al-Ghazi (1506–1543), also known as AHMAD GRAÑ, overthrew the Ethiopian emperor LEBNA DENGEL (r. c. 1508–1540) and took Shoa as well as the neighboring regions of Dawara, AMHARA, and Lasta. Before Lebna Dengel's death, in 1540, he appealed to the Portuguese for aid. A year later Portugal supplied the Ethiopians with 400 musketeers.

Subsequently the governor of Tigray revamped his military forces, training them to fight in the style of the Europeans. These forces went on to defeat Ahmad Grañ's army. Their success did not last for long, however, because Ahmad Grañ sought the help of the Ottomans and, in 1542, conquered substantial portions of the Christian empire of Ethiopia.

As a result Ethiopian emperor Galawdewos (r. 1540–1559) implemented a new military strategy, switching to a strike-and-run war against the Muslims. This left Ahmad Grañ's men unsure when Galawdewos would strike next. In 1543, after a long and vicious battle, Grañ was killed in action. His army fled, and Ethiopia once again belonged to the Christian empire.

During the 17th century OROMO pastoralists moved to the area and dominated Shoa as they did in other Ethiopian territories, including Arsi, Welega, GOJJAM, Harege, and Welo. Many Oromo settled in these regions and, over the years, took up AGRICULTURE and adopted the culture and RELIGION (either Muslim or Christian) of the societies in which they lived.

Resentment against the Oromo was strong, however, especially in Shoa. There the Amhara had been pushed out and were forced to live in Manz, a plateau high in the mountains northeast of Shoa. But Shoa was resilient, and the kingdom's rulers, including Negassi Kristos Warada Qal (r. c. 1703), Sebastiye (r. 1705–1720), Abiye (r. 1720–1745), and Amha Iyasu (r. 1745–1775), spent much of the 18th century regaining the territory lost to the Oromo. As a result, Shoa had grown considerably by the end of the 19th century.

See also: AKSUM (Vols. I, II); OTTOMAN EMPIRE AND AFRICA (Vol. III); SHOA (Vol. IV); TIGRAY (Vols. I, IV, V).

Shona kingdoms Kingdoms established by the Shona peoples in present-day ZIMBABWE, ZAMBIA, and MOZAMBIQUE. During the first millennium Shona peoples began to move into the region south of the ZAMBEZI RIVER that had once been inhabited by the SAN. The Shona intermarried with other Bantu-speaking peoples already there, either absorbing them or pushing them south, and began to mine the deposits of GOLD, establishing thousands of small mines. The Shona began to form centralized states in the 11th century, foremost among them Great Zimbabwe, which flourished in the 12th through the 15th centuries and grew prosperous on the gold and ivory trades. By the middle of the 15th century the Shona had extended their territory from the Indian Ocean to the Kalahari Desert.

Great Zimbabwe was succeeded by two offshoots of the Shona kingdoms: the gold-trading Torwa empire to the west and the MWENE MUTAPA kingdom to the northeast. The ROZWI kingdom of the Shona, ruled by the CHANGAMIRE DYNASTY, dominated the region until the mid-19th century. At that time the Shona kingdom went into a state of decline as migrating NGUNI groups conquered the region.

See also: PORTUGAL AND AFRICA (Vol. III); SHONA (Vols. II, IV); TOGWA (Vol. III).

Shungwaya Supposedly the ancestral homeland of the MIJIKENDA and POKOMO people of the KENYA coast of East Africa. According to the oral traditions of both the Mijikenda and Swahili peoples, the Mijikenda left the town of Shungwaya during the 16th century, migrating to the coastal hinterlands fairly rapidly. This, however, seems to be refuted by the bulk of the historical and archaeological evidence available, since the various Mijikenda peoples seem to have been in place near the coast substantially before the 16th century. Nor do the governmental traditions of the Mijikenda seem related to either the system of kingship or the Islamic religion associated with Shungwaya.

Sidamo (Sidama) Culturally diverse people groups who, until the 16th century, populated much of southwestern ETHIOPIA. The major Sidamo groups include Bako, Amar, Gibe, GIMIRA, Janjero, Kaffa, Maji, and WOLAMO. The Sidamo, who speak dialects of the Cushitic language family, founded several kingdoms that were firmly established by 1400, among which KAFFA and Janjero were the largest. The religious and political structures of all the Sidamo kingdoms were similar in that they worshiped a pagan god, whom their king was believed to represent. Especially among the Kaffa, Janjero, and Gibe, caste distinction between the royalty, nobility, and commoners was strictly observed. Upon the king's death there were elaborate ceremonies (some involving animal sacrifice), during which his successor was chosen from among his sons.

The Sidamo were primarily agricultural and cattle-rearing people who also participated in the trade of salt, cloth, cattle, and, more significantly, GOLD. They used iron bars for their currency.

By the 16th century the OROMO moved into the region, conquered the Sidamo people, and dismantled their monarchies. During this time, many Sidamo converted to Islam, although there were also Christian converts and groups that managed to preserve their traditional religions.

See also: AHMAD GRAÑ (Vol. III); SIDAMO (Vol. II).

Sierra Leone Country measuring about 27,700 square miles (71,700 sq km) located in West Africa. It is bordered by GUINEA to the north and east, LIBERIA to the south, and the Atlantic Ocean to the west. The capital and largest city is FREETOWN, located on the coast.

Sierra Leone was known for becoming a refuge for freed Africans from abroad. From the 15th century to well into the 18th century, Sierra Leone took active part in the transatlantic SLAVE TRADE, although it was a minor source of captives. The Temne people lived along the coast when the Portuguese arrived. By 1425 the Portuguese had built a fort on the site of what is today Freetown, and from then on European merchant ships visited the coast in search of ivory and humans. In the mid-1500s the Mande migrated there from what is now Liberia. The British built trading posts on Bund and York islands during the 1600s, but the land was under the control of no European state. In the early 1700s FULANI and Mande Muslims from FOUTA DJALLON converted many Temne to Islam.

In 1787 a group of emancipated Africans from England attempted to form a colony for other Africans. This original colony was unsuccessful until 1791, when an English antislavery group formed the Sierra Leone Company and took up the cause, establishing the settlement of Freetown as a safe harbor for Africans once held in servitude in Europe, Jamaica, and the United States.

In 1807 the slave trade was officially abolished by the British Parliament, and in 1808 a naval base was established at Sierra Leone by the British to accept ex-slaves into the country and help incorporate them into a new life of freedom. By the time the last ship stopped in Sierra Leone, in 1864, more than 50,000 Africans from abroad had been brought to the country by the British navy.

As these people, commonly called Krios (Creoles), came from various homelands, they generally lacked a common RELIGION, language, and cultural background, and the government then combined forces with Protestant MISSIONARIES and other Freetown pastors to adopt a policy that would Christianize the Krios and create a uniform community. This unification met with great success and saw the establishment in 1827 of Fourah Bay College, a part of the Anglican Church Missionary Society, which educated and trained many Africans and their children to work as missionaries or in such fields as teaching and business.

See also: FOURAH BAY COLLEGE (Vol. IV); KRIO (Vol. IV); SIERRA LEONE (Vol. I, II, IV, V); SLAVERY (Vol. III).

Further reading: Joe A. D. Alie, *A New History of Sierra Leone* (New York: St. Martin's Press, 1990).

Sijilmasa Trans-Saharan trading center located in what is now MOROCCO. Once a flourishing city, Sijilmasa was described by the Arab traveler and historian LEO AFRICANUS (c. 1485–c. 1554) as a mere shadow of its former grand self, with the gated walls that formerly surrounded the city lying in ruins. Although technically ruled by the SADIAN DYNASTY of the Moroccan city of MARRAKECH, Sijilmasa during the early 1600s was practically independent, with people living in more than 350 *ksours,* or villages. By the late 17th century, however, Morocco had come under the rule of the powerful Alawite dynasty, and during the reign of MAWLAY ISMAIL (c. 1645–1727) Sijilmasa was once again occupied by Moroccan forces. During Mawlay Ismail's reign the city was outfitted with an extensive irrigation system that made agricultural activities much more viable.

Thought to have fathered as many as 700 children, Mawlay Ismail faced succession conflicts when his numerous sons came of age. After attempting first to give each of them some form of commanding office, Ismail later deposed all but one of his sons and sent them to live in Sijilmasa. There they were given houses, land, and a number of bondservants to help cultivate the land.

See also: SIJILMASA (Vol. II).

Further reading: Julian Clancy-Smith, ed., *North Africa, Islam, and the Mediterranean World: From the Almoravids to the Algerian War* (Portland, Oreg.: Frank Cass, 2001).

Simien (Semyen) Ethiopian province located south of Tigray, near Lake Tana. The BETA ISRAEL have inhabited the region in and around Simien since the 14th century. As a Hamitic group who practice a form of Judaism, the Beta Israel have been in conflict with their Muslim and Christian neighbors for centuries, and as a result have been the target of many attacks and invasions.

The first order of business of Emperor Minas (r. 1560–1564), after succeeding his brother Galawdewos (r. 1540–1559) as emperor of ETHIOPIA, was to attack the Beta Israel who were living in the Simien Mountains. Although the campaign was not a success, it gave Minas the opportunity to replace the governor of Tigray with one of his own men. In the latter half of the 16th century Emperor Sarsa Dengel (r. 1564–1597) turned his attention to Simien, Wagera, and Dembya. He led several missions against the Beta Israel, ultimately occupying their areas. Susenyos (r. 1607–1632) continued Sarsa Dengel's war against the Beta Israel, his campaign even more ruthless. Under Susenyos any Beta Israel who refused to convert to Christianity were killed or sold into captivity. As a result of these and other activities the Beta Israel were eventually driven out of the region altogether.

See also: TIGRAY (Vols. I, II, IV, V).

Skeleton Coast Stretch of arid shoreline in northeast NAMIBIA that is bordered by the Namib Desert. Throughout the ages, many animals—and people—who could not survive the desert's harsh, waterless environment eventually perished in its sands. The area got its name from early European sea explorers who were impressed by the great number of sun-bleached human and animal bones that had been exposed by the blasting wind. The nomadic KHOIKHOI were the only group to inhabit this arid environment.

Slave Coast Coastal stretch on the Gulf of Guinea in West Africa that is made up of the coastlines of the three present-day countries of TOGO, Republic of BENIN, and NIGERIA. By the mid-16th century Europeans had named the lower coastal area of West Africa according to the trade commodities found in each specific region. The westernmost of these areas was known for the abundance of elephants—and therefore ivory tusks—and became known as the IVORY COAST. The stretch to the east of the Ivory Coast became known for its abundance of GOLD mines and was quickly named the GOLD COAST (now GHANA). When human beings became an important trade commodity around the 17th century, the West African coastal regions below the Gold Coast became known as a plentiful source of captives. The Slave Coast was loosely defined as the region between the mouths of two rivers—the NIGER RIVER in the east and the Volta River in the west.

The same stretch of coastline referred to as the Slave Coast is also called the Bight of BENIN.

Although such European powers as Portugal, Spain, France, Denmark, and Sweden all attempted to control the commerce in the area, the Slave Coast was dominated especially by the Dutch and British, who worked with indigenous traders well into the 19th century.

See also: DENMARK AND AFRICA (Vol. III); NETHERLANDS AND AFRICA (Vol. III); ENGLAND AND AFRICA (Vol. III); FRANCE AND AFRICA (Vol. III); PORTUGAL AND AFRICA (Vol. III); SLAVERY (Vol. III); SLAVE TRADE, THE TRANSATLANTIC (Vol. III); TRADE AND COMMERCE (Vol. III).

slave rebellions Historical records show that many Africans never accepted SLAVERY and rebelled against, ran away from, and resisted enslavement at every opportunity, some even killing themselves rather than submitting to bondage.

In North America Letters and diaries from the American South in the 1800s indicate that slaveholders lived in constant fear of rebellion. In 1791 the ferocity of the initial slave revolt in Haiti, on the island of Hispaniola in the Caribbean, made it clear to Europeans that unrest easily led to violence. In this revolt 280 sugar plantations were destroyed and 2,000 European planters and their families killed. In some instances their children's bodies impaled on stakes and used as standards to lead the rebels. The French responded by committing equally gruesome atrocities against the rebelling Africans.

To repress and control slave rebellion, especially in those places, such as South Carolina and the Caribbean islands, where persons in slavery outnumbered the free sometimes ten to one, Africans were forbidden to meet in groups or to learn to read, and they lived under the constant scrutiny of their overseers. Families were often separated, further increasing their isolation from one another and from white society.

In 1800 an African named Gabriel Prosser (c. 1775–1800) led the first large-scale revolt of enslaved Africans in the United States. His plan was to create an independent black state in Virginia, with himself as its head. His plan to march on Richmond, Virginia, at the head of an army of 1,000 followers failed because heavy rains washed out the bridges and flooded the roads that led to the arsenal and powderhouse. The state militia captured Prosser and 34 of his followers before they could regroup their forces. All were hanged.

In 1811 nearly 500 Africans on a plantation near New Orleans, Louisiana, took up weapons with the intent of marching on New Orleans and freeing all the Africans there. They killed an unrecorded number of people and burned a number of plantations along the way until they were stopped by government troops 10 miles (16 km) from the city.

In 1821 a freedman named Denmark Vesey (c. 1767–1822) began to organize the most extensive slave revolt ever planned in the United States, which was to take place among the African laborers in the plantations surrounding Charleston, South Carolina. By 1822 he and his fellow leaders had gained widespread support in the region. However, the rebels were betrayed from within by a traitor who knew all their plans, and Vesey and his lieutenants were hanged. In 1831 Nat Turner (c. 1800–1831) led 75 followers in what was to become the only rebellion by Africans in United States history that did not quickly die out. It took place near Jerusalem, Virginia; 60 whites were killed, including Turner's "master" and his family. (The only local family spared was one that held no one in bondage.) Hundreds of whites fled, and many left the state for good. Turner was captured and hanged, but whites became keenly aware of the anger and resentment among Africans unwillingly held in bondage.

Unrest among Africans was not restricted to the Southern states. An insurrection in New York City in 1712 led to the murder of nine whites and the execution of 17 blacks. In 1741, again in New York City, where one in five inhabitants was an African in bondage, a number of conspiracy trials were held as a result of a series of incidents of arson and burglary that led many to believe that an African revolt was immanent. The supposed revolt's "leader," Ceasar, and five other Africans were hanged. Some historians have compared these trials to the Salem witchcraft trials of 1692.

In Haiti In the 1780s, 20,000 whites, 30,000 free persons of color, and an unknown but large number of fugitive Africans called *maroons* lived in the French colony of Saint-Domingue, as Haiti was then known. An estimated 500,000 Africans worked on the sugar, coffee, indigo, and other plantations in the colony. The slave system in Haiti had the reputation of being the cruelest in the Western Hemisphere. Recalcitrant Africans in other colonies were threatened with being sent there. Despite a willingness to admit the human status of slaves, at least on religious grounds, the French plantation owners in Haiti were known to work their African laborers to death, preferring to replace them rather than to improve their living and working conditions—a common practice in Brazil and in many parts of the Caribbean and North America. In 1791 a religious leader named Boukman Dutty (d. 1791) led a revolt that in its ferocity expressed the African population's desire for vengeance as well as liberty. France at the time was embroiled in the French Revolution (1789–99), its own revolt against the monarchy that made France a republic.

Leadership of the revolt in Haiti was soon assumed by the charismatic 50-year-old general named François Dominique Toussaint Louverture (1743–1803), who had once been held in bondage. Toussaint's ability to play the three contenders for the island, the French, British, and Spanish, against each other won him the allegiance of the French, who made Toussaint governor-general of the island and Haiti a French protectorate. Toussaint's rule came to an end when, in 1802, Napoleon sent an army of 20,000 soldiers to invade Haiti and restore slavery. A guerrilla war led by Toussaint ensued. Although Toussaint made peace with the French and retired from office, in 1802, he was tricked into a meeting, arrested, and sent to France, where he died in prison, in April 1803. In 1804 Haiti won its independence from France and became the first black republic in the Western Hemisphere.

Elsewhere in the Caribbean Most slave revolts in the Caribbean, as elsewhere, involved a limited number of Africans and were quickly quelled. The more prominent of them occurred in Brazil (1630), in St. Kitts–Nevis (1639), in Jamaica, (1720, the so-called First Maroon War), in Surinam (1733), in Monserrat (1768), and in Belize (1773). In most cases the rebellions were crushed.

At Sea Two famous revolts occurred at sea after the 19th century began: the revolt aboard the *Amistad* on a voyage from West Africa to Cuba in 1839 and the revolt on board the American brig *Creole* on a voyage from Richmond and Hampton Roads in Virginia to New Orleans in 1841. Those held responsible for the revolt aboard the *Amistad* were defended in court by former president John Quincy Adams (1767–1848). In a judgment that surprised many people of the time, the U.S. Supreme Court ruled that the 53 Africans aboard the *Amistad,* who overwhelmed the crew and brought their vessel into American waters for protection, were justified in their actions. With the help of missionary and abolitionist groups, the mutineers returned home to SIERRA LEONE, in 1842.

No such clemency was shown to the mutineers aboard the *Creole*. Because their legal status as slaves made them, according to the law of the day, the property of American citizens, the courts demanded their return by the British, who had declared them free when they landed at Nassau in the Bahamas. The British later agreed to compensate the Americans for their loss.

In the Arab World The largest revolt of African bondsmen in Islamic times occurred in what is now Iraq in the ninth century among laborers in the salt marshes. Known to historians as the Revolt of the Zanj (from the Arabic word for "black"), the longest of the rebellions lasted from 868 to 883. The ranks of the enslaved blacks were augmented by black soldiers who defected from the army of the Abassid caliph in large numbers. The revolt spread to within 70 miles (113 km) of Baghdad until it was quelled by the army with the offer of amnesty and rewards to rebels who chose to surrender.

No other revolts of any magnitude are recorded. It may be speculated that differences in the status of slaves in Islam, the greater ability of slaves in Islam to win their freedom and join the general populace, the number of females in the urban slave population, and the relatively infrequent concentration of many fieldworkers in a single place contributed to the lack of organized resistance and unrest. Further, groups originally made up of slaves, such as the MAMLUKS of EGYPT and the Janissaries of the Ottoman Empire, could attain their freedom and reach positions of high authority and influence in their societies.

See also: OTTOMAN EMPIRE AND AFRICA (Vol. III); SLAVERY, CULTURAL AND HISTORICAL ATTITUDES TOWARD (Vol. III); SLAVE TRADE, THE TRANSATLANTIC (Vol. III); ZANJ (Vol. II).

slavery Slavery is a condition in which human beings are kept in a state of forced servitude. Many non-African historians use the term as a shorthand to encompass all forms of slavery, giving the misleading impression that all systems of servitude and bondage are alike. They are not. The brutal and dehumanizing system of chattel slavery that arose in the Americas and into which millions of Africans were abducted against their wills, sold, and held as the property of their purchasers was a Western, non-African development. Numerous so-called SLAVE REBELLIONS attest to the unwillingness of Africans to accept this attack on their humanity and limitation on their freedom.

Scholars of African culture note that the system of domestic bondage or slavery that existed in West Africa before Portuguese explorers arrived in 1441 bore little resemblance to chattel slavery, a system unique to the Americas, by which human beings were legally defined as property. In African society, prisoners of war, people who violated a traditional custom or prohibition or committed a crime, and people who were unable or unwilling to settle a just debt could be held in a condition of servitude. This condition was not perpetual. These slaves were not considered property, and they enjoyed certain rights. Families were typically not separated, and children of the enslaved were not automatically slaves. People held in a state of slavery often married into the kinship group of their masters and became members of their masters' extended families.

Islam took root in Africa starting in the seventh century, first in North Africa and along the SWAHILI COAST and later in West Africa. Muslim law provided protections for persons in slave status, but these protections resulted in reinforcing the institution of slavery in Muslim lands. Most slaves performed domestic tasks, but some did field LABOR or comparable jobs. In the parts of North Africa occupied by the Ottoman Empire, slaves entered military or government service, sometimes achieving high rank. Even though books often call people held in this kind of servitude slaves, the distinction between chattel slavery and what might be called "traditional slavery" or servitude should be noted.

Slavery after 1441 became the story of chattel slavery in the Americas and its impact on African life. It is possible that some Africans transported into slavery in the Americas already lived in a traditional form of slavery in their own states or villages. It is probable, however, that the majority were abducted in raids against their people and transported as captives in chains to work in the mines and, later, the fields of the New World.

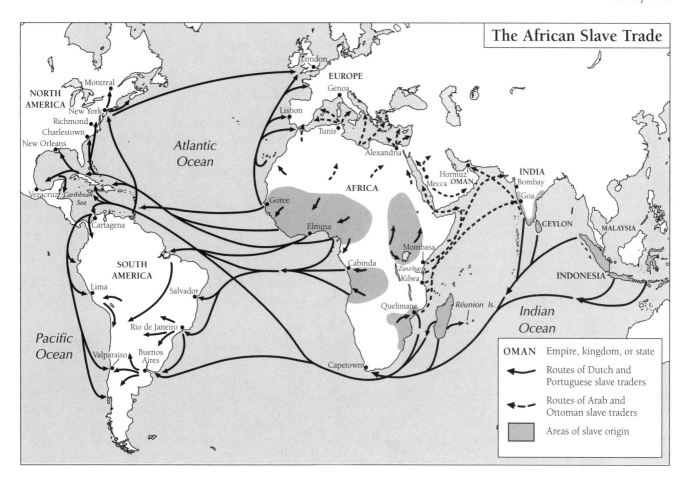

The African Slave Trade

OMAN Empire, kingdom, or state

Routes of Dutch and Portuguese slave traders

Routes of Arab and Ottoman slave traders

Areas of slave origin

Background and Overview During the Age of Discovery that began in the 1430s, Europe, led by Portugal, began to expand beyond its borders, exploring first the coast of Africa and later the Americas. The prevalent cultural and religious attitudes of the day among Europeans legitimized slavery in their minds. When the exploitation of commercial resources in the Western Hemisphere required a large labor force, they did not hesitate to enslave the native American populations of the lands they colonized. When this source of labor dwindled, they increasingly imported African laborers and held them in a state of chattel slavery.

In 1415 the Muslim city of CEUTA, a center of the North African slave trade, became Portugal's first permanent conquest in Africa. Ceuta is located directly across from the Iberian Peninsula on the Moroccan side of the Strait of Gibraltar, a channel that is at its narrowest point just 8 miles (13 km) wide. Ceuta was the gateway to the Atlantic and the starting point for the explorations of the West African coast and the Atlantic islands that Prince Henry the Navigator (1394–1460) of Portugal sponsored in the years following 1420. In 1441 the first African captives from West Africa were brought to Portugal.

At first the Portuguese trade in human captives took place directly between West Africa and Europe, cir-cumventing the Arab traders in Ceuta and in other North African ports, and provided servants and farm laborers for Spain, Portugal, and other parts of Europe. Europeans did not enter into the African (domestic) slave trade. Very soon, however, a much more extensive transatlantic trade in humans began to emerge in response to the need to supplement or replace native workers on plantations in the Americas. With the influence of superior European weaponry, a system of raiding villages and abducting people was begun, without regard to any concept of slavery as previously practiced in Africa, and it was totally foreign to those who were suddenly caught up in its practices.

The first voyages of slave ships from Africa to the Western Hemisphere began in the 1520s. Their human cargo sailed on Portuguese vessels destined for the Spanish colonies on the Caribbean island of Hispaniola (now Haiti and the Dominican Republic).

As the need for laborers grew or their commercial interest in Africa expanded, other European kingdoms joined the Portuguese in the trade in Africans. These include the Spanish (after 1479), the English (1562), the Dutch (1625), the French (1640), the Swedes (1649), the Danes and Norwegians (1651), and the German states (1685). After declaring its independence from Britain, in

1776, the United States continued North American involvement in the slave trade, which began as early as 1619, in the Jamestown colony in Virginia. The largest traders overall, however, were Portugal, France, and especially Britain. By the middle of the 18th century Britain was the most active exporter; British ships carried more than half of all the enslaved Africans being transported across the Atlantic.

The transatlantic SLAVE TRADE from ports in ANGOLA, SENEGAMBIA, in West Africa, and MOZAMBIQUE, in East Africa, was of long duration and did not end even when formal declarations to abolish slavery were promulgated by the major slave-trading countries in the 19th century. These declarations served only to make slaving operations covert; British and American naval vessels on antislavery patrols on the African coast were generally evaded and their cargoes of human beings were carried off to the plantations of the New World.

The process of abolition and emancipation took most of the 19th century to accomplish worldwide. Wide-ranging abolition movements arose after the start of the Industrial Revolution, which began in Britain about 1760 and spread to Europe and then to the United States in the 19th century. Some historians argue that the shift from an ECONOMY based on AGRICULTURE to an economy based on industry and manufacturing enabled abolition to occur because it made the system of chattel slavery less economically advantageous. As evidence of this, they cite the fact that abolition occurred earlier in industrialized areas such as Britain and the New England states, where manufacturing dominated the economy, and it spread more slowly in the agrarian economies of the American South and the Caribbean region, where extensive field labor was still required.

Abolition Formal abolition of chattel slavery did not necessarily entail the emancipation, or freeing, of

Arab dhow trying to elude a British warship on an antislavery patrol. Lateen-rigged dhows like this one transported slaves up the Swahili Coast and on to Arabia. © *Corbis*

peoples already enslaved, which often occurred at a later date. France temporarily outlawed the slave trade in the aftermath of the French Revolution, during the early 1790s, but soon lifted the ban and did not reimpose it until 1817. In 1805 the Danish government forbade its citizens from taking part in the slave trade. Sweden banned the slave trade in 1813, and Netherlands followed in 1814. The United Kingdom officially outlawed the slave trade in 1807, and in 1834 Africans living in British lands were emancipated.

In the United States the path to abolition was complicated by the slave-based economies of the southern states. In order to win the ratification votes of the southern states, a clause prohibiting the federal government from interfering with the slave trade until 1808 was included in the U.S. Constitution (1787). When the clause expired, the slave trade was outlawed, but the United States did not emancipate captive Africans until 1863, at the height of the Civil War (1860–65). The Thirteenth Amendment to the Constitution, ratified in 1865, formally abolished slavery in the United States.

Among the other major exporters of captive Africans, similar patterns occurred. In 1814 Spain agreed to stop the slave trade to everywhere except her own possessions, and in 1820 Spain extended the ban to all its possessions except Cuba. In 1880 Spain emancipated the Africans in all of its colonies except Cuba; Africans in slavery in Cuba were not emancipated until 1886. Portugal outlawed slavery in 1816 but continued shipping Africans to Brazil, its largest colony, whose sugar plantations absorbed the greatest number of Africans sent to the New World. The Portuguese did not emancipate Africans in Brazil until 1888.

In the Muslim world, the forced servitude of Africans persisted longer than in the Americas. The first Muslim ruler to outlaw slavery was the bey, or ruler, of the North African city of Tunis. In 1846 he ordered every African freed who desired it. Abolition was completed after the French occupation in the 1880s. The Ottoman Empire, which ruled EGYPT as a province from 1517 to 1789 from its capital at Istanbul (formerly Constantinople) in modern Turkey, began the process of emancipation in 1830, but only for Christian slaves. Those who had become Muslim remained in bondage.

In 1857, at the insistence of Britain, the Ottoman Empire outlawed the slave trade throughout the empire except in the Hijaz, the region along the Red Sea in western Saudi Arabia. However, African captives shipped from TRIPOLI and Benghazi in what is today LIBYA still reached the Ottoman Empire in large numbers well into the 1870s. The British occupation of Egypt in 1882 and later the Sudan curtailed the slave trade from Africa to Arabia and Iran and drove it underground until it finally ended between the two world wars (1914–18 and 1939–45).

After the period of enslavement came what historians call "the scramble for Africa"—the partitioning of Africa by the major Western powers. In a series of conquests consolidated at the Berlin Conference of 1884–85, the African continent was divided among the seven major European contenders. France and Britain built the largest colonial empires in Africa, but Spain, Portugal, Belgium, Germany, and Italy also had substantial African possessions.

The Human Cost Africa's greatest export from 1530 to 1830 was its people. Records indicate that at least 10 million Africans from West Africa and Central Africa were landed alive in North and South America and the Caribbean and sold as slaves to work in the plantation-based economies of the region during those years. If deaths in transit are calculated, an additional 2 million people can be added to that number. An average of 20,000 Africans per year were taken into chattel slavery during the 1600s, a number that leapt to between 50,000 and 100,000 Africans per year for much of the 1700s. Less conservative historians argue that much of the trade in slaves went unrecorded and that the actual total is twice or more the conservative estimate, or somewhere between 24 million and 50 million Africans.

Slavery in all its forms, however, took its human toll on Africa both before and after the European involvement in the slave trade. Between the seventh century and the late 19th century, roughly 14 million Africans were transported into the Islamic world and beyond in trans-Saharan trade or from ports along the Swahili Coast. Traditional forms of slavery also thrived in West African states throughout this period. When the Berber Almoravid empire of North Africa attacked the ancient Ghana Empire in the 11th century, the conquerors found thousands of African captives at the trans-Saharan trading town of Audaghost, which was then under Ghana's control. Ghana's successor states, the Mali Empire and the SONGHAI Empire, took thousands of captives in their wars of expansion. Historians believe that, during the 19th century, the SOKOTO CALIPHATE in what is now northwestern NIGERIA may have utilized the labor of as many as 2.5 million captives to produce the PALM OIL, cloves, and other products it sold to its European trading partners.

Nevertheless, the transatlantic slave trade significantly differed from the practice of slavery in other parts of the world, including earlier times in Africa. Never before had so many people been forcibly uprooted from their places of birth. The status and treatment of the abducted captives was extremely brutal, the single business of enterprise of the transatlantic slave trade all but dominated African life.

The Economic Cost The slave trade brought West Africa into the international economy not as a partner but as a market to exploit and a source of cheap labor to ensure the profita bility of enterprises elsewhere. Slavery deprived Africa of the productive labor of significant numbers of its youngest and healthiest people. In places where the Islamic slave trade across the Indian Ocean and the Red Sea was dominant, local populations often had their women and children carried off into bondage, often as concubines or menial laborers, to other parts of the Muslim world. The European slave trade deprived Africa of its strongest young males, who were carried off in chains to do productive labor in the Americas. Populations often became unbalanced, with a surplus of males existing in some areas and a surplus of females in others. The ability to develop a local, labor-intensive AGRICULTURE was thereby impaired.

Slavery and the slave trade also arrested the development of local industries. The availability of cheap European textiles undermined the local production of cloth, and the availability of cheap European manufactured goods caused local production of metal goods to dwindle, thus blocking the growth of a local ironworking industry.

See also: AGE OF DISCOVERY (Vol. II); AUDAGHOST (Vol. II); IRONWORKING (Vol. II); KINGDOMS AND EMPIRES OF WEST AFRICA (Vol. II); MIDDLE PASSAGE (Vol. III); PRINCE HENRY THE NAVIGATOR (Vol. II); SLAVERY (Vols. I, IV); SLAVERY, CULTURAL AND HISTORICAL ATTITUDES TOWARD (Vol. III); SLAVERY IN SOUTH AFRICA (Vol. III); SLAVE TRADE, EXPANSION OF EUROPEAN INVOLVEMENT IN (Vol. III); SLAVE TRADE ON THE SWAHILI COAST (Vol. III).

Further reading: Clifford Lindsey Alderman, *Rum, Slaves, and Molasses: The Story of New England's Triangular Trade* (New York: Crowell-Collier Press, 1972); Tom Feelings, *The Middle Passage: White Ships/Black Cargo* (New York: Dial Books, 1995); Willie F. Page, *The Dutch Triangle: The Netherlands and the Atlantic Slave Trade, 1621–1644* (New York: Garland Publishing Co., 1997); Rosemarie Robotham, ed., *Spirits of the Passage: The Transatlantic Slave Trade in the Seventeenth Century* (New York: Simon & Schuster, 1997); Junius P. Rodriguez, ed., *The Historical Encyclopedia of World Slavery* (Santa Barbara, Calif.: ABC-CLIO, Inc., 1997); Hugh Thomas, *The Slave Trade: The Story of the Atlantic Slave Trade, 1440–1870* (New York: Simon & Schuster, 1997); John Thornton, *Africa and Africans in the Making of the Atlantic World, 1400–1680* (New York: Cambridge University Press, 1992); Ehud R. Toledano, *Slavery and Abolition in the Ottoman Middle East* (Seattle, Wash.: University of Washington Press, 1998).

slavery, cultural and historical attitudes toward The earliest form of "slavery" in human history is sometimes called domestic servitude, to distinguish it from the chattel SLAVERY that characterized the Americas beginning in the 16th and 17th centuries. The institution of chattel slavery, by which human beings were legally considered property, was responsible for the wide-scale uprooting and enslavement of African peoples brought on by the transatlantic SLAVE TRADE of the 1500s to the 1800s. In domestic servitude, people were bought, sold, or kidnapped into bondage as a way to obtain LABOR. Captives were enslaved as spoils of war; debtors or the children of debtors were enslaved to settle debts. Criminals were bonded and sent to work at hard labor for a long period of time, even a lifetime. In the Middle East, families were known to sell a child into slavery, and adults even sold themselves into bondage if times were difficult.

In domestic servitude the bonded had whatever rights the owner decided to grant. Traditional servitude respected FAMILY bonds, allowing slaves to marry and not separating spouses from one another or from their children—but there was no obligation to do so. The children of bonded labor remained in servitude or were freed as local customs dictated. Owners often had the right to punish a bonded person without penalty.

The Widespread Acceptance of Servitude Servitude is not unique to Africa or the African experience but was commonly accepted in Europe, the Arab world, and the Mediterranean world before the 19th century. In the ancient world, the Greeks and Romans kept large numbers of bonded laborers for work both at home and in their overseas colonies in North Africa. These laborers were considered chattel, or the property of their owners, and had no legal rights. The Egyptians and Nubians also kept bonded laborers, although in these societies, their numbers were fewer and persons in slave status were not considered chattel. Domestic servitude was also practiced in Babylon and in Palestine, the ancient Jews were kept as bonded labor by the Egyptians and Babylonians, and the Old Testament indicates that the Jewish people themselves kept "slaves."

During the European Middle Ages, Europe was often a source of slaves for the Arab world. Viking raiders sailing from Scandinavia in the years 800 to 1050 often raided the coast of Britain and France for slaves that they sold as far east as Constantinople (now Istanbul). From the eighth to the 11th centuries Rouen in France was a major transfer point for Irish and Flemish slaves being shipped to the Arabian Peninsula.

Religious, political, and commercial rivalry and military conflict between Muslims and Christians, which started during the Crusades (1096–1272), expanded greatly during the 14th century. Attacks by the Muslim Ottoman Empire against Christian eastern Europe made the

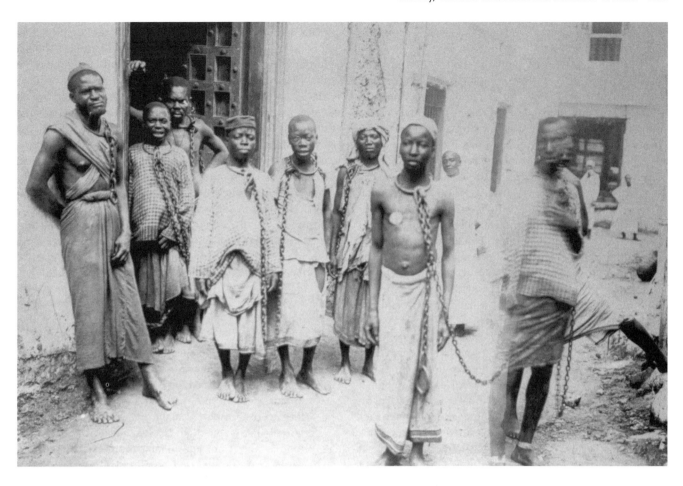

Captive Africans in chains in Zanzibar. Slavery was not abolished until 1873 on the island of Zanzibar, off the Swahili coast. This photograph was taken during the 19th century. © *Bojan Brecelj/Corbis*

Balkans and the Black Sea region an active source of slaves for the Ottoman slave markets in Constantinople, KAFFA in the Crimea, Tana-Azov on the Black Sea, and, in the 16th century, Alexandria and CAIRO in EGYPT. In the Ottoman Empire of the mid-1500s, bonded laborers from sources in Africa, Europe, and the Caucasus took part in both the military and civil service and served as craftspeople, bureaucrats, domestic servants, and concubines.

The English word *slave,* from Medieval Latin *sclavus* through Old French *esclave,* is derived from the word for Slav, an indication of the number of Slavic peoples of Europe who were enslaved by Muslim raiders in the Middle Ages.

Domestic servitude, that is, slavery not associated with the export slave trade, was also part of Saharan and sub-Saharan Africa before Europeans arrived. The no-

madic TUAREGS of the Sahara kept bonded labor, although the living conditions of laborers and masters may have differed very little. Among the peoples of West Africa and Central Africa, taking captives was an ordinary practice of war. Some of these captives remained in bondage locally and became incorporated in local lineages and kinship groups. Others were exchanged for trade goods and transported north across the Sahara along the caravan routes or sold to Arab merchants involved in the Red Sea and Indian Ocean trade. The Berber Massufa people who controlled the salt mines at Taghaza and the kings of the AKAN state of BONO, who controlled the Akan GOLD fields, often used the labor of captive Africans to mine the products that made Africa prosperous for centuries.

As with Muslim-Christian slave-taking, RELIGION and politics were intermeshed when Muslim states in Africa expanded into the lands where traditional African religion was practiced. The Muslim kingdoms and empires in West Africa, notably the early empires of Ghana, Mali and SONGHAI, and the later Muslim states such as FOUTA TORO, FOUTA DJALLON, and the SOKOTO CALIPHATE, which were established as a result of the FULANI JIHADS of the 18th and

19th centuries, took thousands of nonbelievers captive in their wars of conquest and expansion.

Religious Attitudes Toward Slavery Both the Old Testament and the New Testament of the Bible recognize and accept slavery, as it was practiced in biblical times, as a fact of life, and both insist on the need to treat slaves humanely because they are fellow human beings. Christianity's emphasis on salvation and its focus on the afterlife have been raised in defense of Scriptural tolerance of slavery. In this view all believers are equal in the eyes of God but not necessarily according to human law, which mattered less in the divine plan. Slaves were told to submit to their masters, and masters were enjoined to treat their slaves with consideration. These beliefs remained largely unexamined despite mounting evidence of the brutality of chattel slavery in the Americas. Local church authorities in the Spanish and Portuguese colonies in the Americas generally sided with the land owners and the status quo.

By the 19th century in the West, the horrors of chattel slavery made slavery of any kind no longer defensible. Protestant religious thinkers in the two dominant slave-trading states of the period led the movement to abolish it. These reformers included William Lloyd Garrison (1805–1879) and the liberal Congregationalist minister Henry Ward Beecher (1813–1887) in the United States and Thomas Clarkson (1760–1846) and the evangelical Christian activist William Wilberforce (1759–1833) in Britain.

The Quran condoned slavery but improved the position of slaves in Muslim society by considering them more than just the chattel, or property, of their owners but as human beings. Islam recognizes the social inequality of master and slave but gives persons in slavery, if they are Muslim, a certain religious and social status that makes them the religious equal of a freeborn Muslim and the superior of the freeborn nonbeliever. In practice, the enslavement of free Muslims was discouraged and, later, prohibited. Freeborn Muslims could no longer be sold or sell themselves into slavery, nor could they be reduced to slave status to pay a debt. However, a non-Muslim slave who converted to Islam did not have to be freed, and a Muslim child born to parents in bondage remained in slave status. The slave population could only grow by the addition of individuals born of slave parents or captured in war, and these were soon limited to nonbelievers captured in a jihad, or holy war. (In Africa, Muslim rulers sometimes proclaimed a jihad without looking too closely at a neighboring people's religion. In the Fulani jihads of the 19th century, backsliding Muslims were considered legitimate targets for attack.) Captives were often liberated as an act of piety, and children born of a mother in bondage were frequently freed and accepted as family members.

The downside of the Muslim position on the status of slaves was the constant need to replenish their numbers from markets in Europe, Asia, and Africa. The birth rate among people in slave status was low. Many males were imported as eunuchs (the Quran forbids mutilation, so the castration had to be done at the border). Military slaves, such as the MAMLUKS in Egypt or the elite Turkish corps of Janissaries, the main fighting force of the Ottoman Empire from the late 14th century to 1826, rose to positions of great prominence and won their freedom, making their children also free. Marriage between persons in slavery was discouraged, and casual procreation forbidden. The death rate from disease and epidemics was high, especially among imported Africans, who had no prior exposure to the diseases of the Mediterranean world. Thus, the need for the services of slaves in many capacities overwhelmed the Quran's humanitarian reforms; massive numbers of slaves had to be imported from the outside.

The main sources of slaves in the Arabic world were Africans and peoples from the Eurasian steppes and the Caucasus. Blacks from West and Central Africa entered the Islamic world from ports in MOROCCO, TUNISIA, and LIBYA. From East Africa, they were transported along the Nile to Egypt or ferried across the Red Sea or Indian Ocean to Arabia, Iraq, Iran, and other parts of the Muslim world. Later routes led from KANO by way of AGADES and Ghadames to TRIPOLI, and from WADAI and DARFUR in present-day Republic of the SUDAN via Bornu and Tibesti in CHAD to Kufra and Cyrenaica in Libya.

The abolition of slavery took longer in Islamic countries. Because slavery was sanctioned by the Quran and regulated by Islamic law, Muslim states believed that they could not abolish outright what Allah allowed any more than they could permit what Allah forbade. Thus conservative 19th-century Muslim scholars, especially in Mecca and Medina, who spoke out against abolition believed they were upholding the law of personal status, a key principal of Islam. In parts of the Arabian Peninsula, slavery persisted until the middle of the 20th century.

Slavery and Racism Slavery in Africa and in Islam was generally not based exclusively on race. Language, dress, name, religion, and customs were often the factors used to distinguish between master and slave, and it was a distinction by class. In South America, in the Caribbean, and in North America, however, discrimination by race separated Africans from other members of the population, and this form of discrimination affected the lives of Africans in the New World long after the institution of slavery was abolished.

Historically, in Africa, in Egypt, and in other societies where both slave and master were the same race, slaves were frequently released from bondage; when races differed, as in the plantation economies of the West Indies and the American South, freedom was granted rarely or not at all. Plantation owners imposed on enslaved Africans a heavy degree of social isolation that treated them in a dehumanizing manner. Fear of revolt further served to distance owners from those held in bondage. And even if slaves managed to win their freedom, the color of their skin often presented obstacles to their success and marginalized them in society

To justify the enslavement of Africans it became common in the 18th and 19th centuries among people of European background to assume that blacks both in Africa and in the New World were inferior in nature to Europeans and that they were better off Christianized and abducted from their homeland than left in an Africa depicted as "primitive" and "barbaric." To uphold this erroneous view, Africans in bondage were often stereotyped in ART and literature as little better than children—irresponsible, lazy, and unable to handle freedom and practical matters. Biblical justifications and arguments based on skull size, dental structure, and posture were also used as pseudo-scientific proofs of European superiority.

The Roots of European Racism Europe's sense of superiority has its roots in the 1500s. Europe at the start of the 16th century was finally free of the threat of Islam, its main religious, political, and commercial rival. After the expulsion of the Moors in 1492, the Christian kingdoms of Spain and the new kingdom of Portugal no longer shared the Iberian Peninsula with the kingdoms of Muslim Spain. In the East, the power of the Ottoman Empire was receding after its unsuccessful siege of Vienna in modern-day Austria in 1529. At the same time, European technology began to surpass what other civilizations offered and allowed it to expand (and defend) its commercial interests far beyond its borders. By that time, the exploration and exploitation of the Americas and the West African coast were well under way. The superiority of European technology, especially its firearms, over traditional societies led to a belief in the superiority of European peoples over all others.

The conversion of nonbelievers provided a religious motivation for conquest. Roman Catholic MISSIONARIES often accompanied the Spanish conquistadores on their voyages to the New World; their task was to Christianize the native peoples that the soldiers conquered. In Africa, the Portuguese generally baptized African captives before loading them aboard ship for the Americas. Although instruction was perfunctory and the captives had no understanding of what baptism meant, important to the Portuguese and the Spanish was the assumption that they were doing God's work by saving souls.

Forces within Christianity turned Christianity's focus from heresy and dogma to the exclusion of the human rights of others. The Protestant Reformation, led by the German theologian Martin Luther (1483–1546) and the French reformer John Calvin (1507–1574), plunged Europe into a long period of bitter religious intolerance and commercial rivalry between Protestants and Catholics. Often, in the Protestant view, material prosperity and commercial success were signs of divine favor. The Protestant countries of Europe, including England and Holland, developed strong, trade-based economies that soon involved them deeply in the slave trade. Protestant slave traders and slaveholders discouraged conversion because of church restrictions on enslaving and exploiting fellow Christians.

The first peoples enslaved in the Western Hemisphere were not Africans but Native American peoples in the newly explored lands of the Americas, whom the Spanish captured and put to work in fields and mines. The mission to Christianize these pagan peoples was used to justify seizure of their lands. Because their traditional lifestyles differed from European ways, the Native Americans were regarded as primitive, ignorant savages. When native populations dwindled from smallpox and other diseases to which they lacked immunity, these stereotypes were transferred to the African captives who were brought over in chains to take their places, with no hope of return to the land of their birth and a short life of hard labor ahead of them.

In the minds of the colonizers, the system of chattel slavery became a necessity to the ECONOMY in the Western Hemisphere. Forcibly imported Africans did jobs that whites from Europe were unwilling to do and for which the dwindling populations of Native Americans were insufficient. In the view of the plantation owners, the low cost of transporting Africans across the Atlantic into slavery made slavery attractive, and the use of slaves from African sources soon supplanted labor from other sources, including the poor white deportees, convicts, and indentured servants from Europe. Race replaced the prior tests of economic and social status to determine who lived in bondage and who was free. The transatlantic slave trade created a system of slavery that because of race, extensiveness, duration, the emphasis on profit, and the denial of human rights was different from any system of slavery that preceded it.

See also: OTTOMAN EMPIRE AND AFRICA (Vols. III, IV); RACE AND RACISM (Vol. IV); RELIGION, TRADITIONAL (Vol. I); SALT MINING (Vol. II); SLAVE TRADE, EXPANSION OF EUROPEAN INVOLVEMENT IN (Vol. III); SLAVERY IN SOUTH AFRICA (Vol. III); SLAVE TRADE ON THE SWAHILI COAST (Vol. III).

slavery in South Africa The Dutch farmers and pastoralists who laid claim to the KHOIKHOI people's lands at the southern tip of Africa, in what is now SOUTH AFRICA, did not practice the kind of large-scale plantation AGRICULTURE that occurred in other parts of the world. But both the CAPE COLONY and CAPE TOWN, its principal settlement, depended on the LABOR of enslaved Africans for their existence and prosperity during the years of Dutch rule. Following Dutch rule the Cape Colony was briefly in French hands, from 1781 to 1784. It was occupied by the British from 1795 to 1803, during the Napoleonic Wars in Europe (1792–1815), and then reverted to Dutch control until 1806, when it was formally ceded to Britain. In 1838, when Britain emancipated all slaves in South Africa, some 38,000 people, predominately Africans, lived in bondage in Cape Town.

Located roughly halfway between Europe and India, the Cape of Good Hope at the southern tip of Africa was a logical stopping point on the journey to the East Indies, where the Dutch, the Portuguese, and the British were building commercial empires in India and Southeast Asia. The nomadic-pastoralist Khoikhoi people inhabited the lands surrounding Table Bay; archaeological evidence indicates that their ancestors had been grazing sheep and cattle on the land for more than 1,500 years. Evidence of agriculture dates from at least the third century, if not earlier. Present in more isolated areas were small bands of hunter-gatherer SAN, who are distinguished from the Khoikhoi only by their occupation. To the north and the east, at the fringes of the region, were XHOSA and other Bantu-speaking peoples.

The Founding of the Cape Colony After Portuguese explorer Vasco da Gama (c. 1460–1524) first rounded the Cape of Good Hope in 1497, sailors would put ashore there to collect fresh FOOD and water and timber for masts and to make any needed repairs. Shipwrecked sailors waited for rescue or tried to make their way toward the SWAHILI COAST. The British government resisted the urging of its sea captains to establish a base at the Cape of Good Hope. Finally, in 1650, the directors of the DUTCH EAST INDIA COMPANY ordered the establishment of a garrison, a fort, and a small, self-sufficient supply station at the cape for Dutch ships.

The Dutch East India Company, founded in 1602, was chartered by the Dutch government to protect Dutch trading interests in the Indian Ocean and to maintain the Dutch commercial empire in the East Indies. Much of the Indonesian archipelago was under its control. It became corrupt, fell into debt, and had its charter revoked by the government in 1799.

In 1652 Jan van Riebeeck (1619–1677) arrived at Table Bay with a garrison of 80 men under contract with the company to establish the Cape Colony. They set up a garden and traded TOBACCO, copper, and other European goods with the Khoikhoi in exchange for sheep and cattle. The Khoikhoi were also expected to provide the heavy LABOR needed to build roads and erect buildings.

Because the Dutch needed Khoikhoi cattle to meet their own dietary needs and to sell to passing ships, van Riebeeck was originally under orders from the company to treat the Khoikhoi, whom the Dutch called *Hottentots*, with the respect due to free people. The Khoikhoi, however, were not willing to sell enough cattle and sheep to meet the growing demands of the Europeans or to work for poor pay under the harsh conditions imposed by the Europeans. Van Riebeeck accordingly encouraged the company to import slaves to undertake the most difficult work. Some thought was given to enslaving the Khoikhoi, but the suggestion was rejected as foolhardy on the grounds that the Khoikhoi outnumbered the 200 colonists almost 100 to 1.

Between 1652 and 1657 the company made a number of mostly unsuccessful attempts to obtain slaves from other Dutch territories. The only ones brought in were a handful of Malay people from Java in the East Indies who worked in bondage as domestic servants in van Riebeeck's house.

In 1657, to strengthen the colony after a shaky start, the Dutch East India Company released nine men from their contracts and gave them land along the Liesbeek River to cultivate as *freeburghers,* or free citizens. This action transformed the Cape from supply station to settlement and set the stage for the racially stratified society that characterized the Cape Colony thereafter.

Finally, in 1658, the Cape Colony was able to get its first shipments of African captives: 200 from DAHOMEY (present-day Republic of BENIN) and 200 taken from a Portuguese ship captured off the coast of ANGOLA. These were the only persons held as slaves in South Africa who were brought in from West Africa. The remainder of Africans in bondage came from East Africa, MOZAMBIQUE, and MADAGASCAR. Large numbers of non-Africans were brought from Dutch East India Company territories in India, Ceylon, and Indonesia to perform the agricultural and other menial tasks the colonists needed done. (Over time, the descendants of these racially diverse peoples intermarried and, with ex-slaves and Khoikhoi servants, formed the nucleus of what the white colonists of the 19th century called the Cape Coloured People.)

Records at the end of the 17th century indicate that a very large percentage of those in bondage were male and their numbers had to be replenished with constant imports to maintain and increase growth. Africans and others were imported at the rate of 200 to 300 per year; by 1700 the roughly 25,000 people in bondage outnumbered the 21,000 Europeans in the cape. Utilizing the labor of people in servitude became a symbol of status and wealth for white people. In the more arable areas near the coast, almost every colonist had someone in bondage to work the land, though few had more than ten people.

Between 1659 and 1676 the number of *freeburghers* increased, and their farms extended outward from Cape Colony. These farms encroached on the Khoikhoi's open pastures and led the colonists to engage in a number of skirmishes with the Khoikhoi. These armed conflicts ended in a treaty that granted the Dutch *freeburghers,* or BOERS (from the Dutch word *boer,* meaning "farmer"), sovereignty over the land they had settled. Khoikhoi society disintegrated: Some moved away from the cape; others found work as shepherds on Boer farms.

A smallpox epidemic in 1713, caused by infected blankets taken off a European ship, caused the deaths of many Africans and non-Africans in servitude and an estimated 90 percent of the indigenous Khoikhoi who lived closest to Cape Town. Neither group had natural immunity to this unfamiliar disease.

The Growth of the Colony   After 1700 the colony underwent a strong period of expansion inland. Earlier, farming had been limited to the fertile, well-watered valleys near Cape Town. However, after that land was bought up by the wealthier *freeburghers* and because few white immigrants were willing to work the land for others if they could own the land themselves, a new group of cattle-raising Boers arose. These colonial pastoralists, often called *Trekboers,* moved onto the arid, less desirable lands that belonged to the Khoikhoi because land there, except for the payment of a small fee to the Dutch East India Company, was treated as if it belonged to no one and was free for the taking. The farms that the Trekboers established inland averaged 6,000 acres (2,500 hectares). When the land was overgrazed, they simply bought more land from the company and moved on.

The Trekboers traveled by wagon, accompanied by their families and a few slaves. However, they often employed Khoikhoi servants from among the dispossessed children of the Khoikhoi that their local militia groups, called *commandos,* killed in large numbers. Such raids were mounted with great frequency, both to protect the colonists' farms and to enlarge their territory. These children worked as unpaid servants—"apprentices," according to some sources—well into adult life, whereupon they were released from service with nowhere to go. The hunter-gatherer San in the interior fared no better. They

were pushed back into less desirable areas where they were forced to survive by raiding the cattle herds of the Boers, an offense used to justify their systematic eradication as a conscious decision of the Dutch governors of the Cape Colony. The period of the Dutch-San Wars (1676–1795) was a time of brutal, though sporadic, conflict between the two peoples. San males who did not retreat into the inhospitable Kalahari Desert were captured and killed; women and children were enslaved.

Illustrating the unenlightened thinking of the times, debate persisted among the Boers about whether or not the Khoikhoi and San peoples were the same species as whites. As late as 1913, the Cape Synod of the Dutch Reformed Church had an intense debate on whether the San, whom they called *Bushmen,* should be considered human beings or animals.

Apartheid   The series of laws that the descendants of the Dutch colonists passed to formally establish the strict system of racial segregation known as *apartheid* (from AFRIKAANS, meaning "aparthood" or "separateness") did not come into being in South Africa until between 1910 and 1940. These rigid laws, which black South Africans openly resisted whenever possible, radically restricted the rights of native peoples and made them second-class citizens in their own land. The racial and political climate that led to the passage of these laws had its origins in the racial stratification of Cape Town society, the forced servitude and virtual enslavement of the Khoikhoi and San peoples in the 1700s and 1800s, and the feelings of racial superiority on the part of European South Africans over native South Africans, both free and in bondage.

See also: APARTHEID (Vols. IV, V); CAPE COLOURED PEOPLE (Vol. IV); RACE AND RACISM (Vol. IV); SLAVERY, CULTURAL AND HISTORICAL ATTITUDES TOWARD (Vol. III); SLAVE TRADE, EXPANSION OF EUROPEAN INVOLVEMENT IN (Vol. III); SLAVE TRADE ON THE SWAHILI COAST (Vol. III).

slave trade, expansion of European involvement in the Although records on African life before the 16th century are meager, it is known that various forms of servitude and bondage existed for hundreds of years both in North Africa and below the Sahara. In North Africa, SLAVERY originated in Roman times, before 300 CE, following customary practices in the Roman homeland in present-day Italy. The Arab peoples in North Africa before the rise of Islam in the seventh century also trafficked in slaves, who were sent to and from destinations in EGYPT, Europe, and the Near East. After North Africa was converted to Islam, a trans-Saharan slave trade arose in the 10th to the 14th centuries to bring captives, very often women, to Islamic markets in the north, where they would become agricultural laborers, household workers, and concubines.

The kind of servitude or bondage imposed by Africans on one another bore little resemblance to the chattel slavery imposed on Africans by Europeans. In Africa, warring peoples taking part in even small-scale skirmishes took captives, who were then kept in bondage. The females and children of these captives were used to provide field LABOR and to extend the kinship groups of the captors. In time, these newcomers were assimilated into the people and, very often, were emancipated. Bondage servants were a sign of a ruler's wealth and position and were often in evidence at the royal court. When Mansa Musa I (d. 1332) of the Mali Empire set out on his famous pilgrimage to Mecca, in 1324, 500 captive retainers carrying bars of GOLD accompanied the entourage of 60,000. Not every person in bondage status was African; captive Turks, Asians, and Europeans were known to be present at his court.

Among later states of the region, the Muslim SONG-HAI Empire (c. 1400–1591) held large numbers of war captives by virtue of expansion and conquest. To the east, a third of the population of Kanem and more than a third of Bornu lived in bondage status; most were acquired in war or by raiding neighboring peoples. Neither Arab nor European slavers ventured very far inland for fear of malaria and other diseases; instead, they armed coastal peoples and forced them to raid their neighbors and kidnap men, women, and children. These neighbors were often enemies of long standing, and often Europeans took advantage of this enmity and their own superior weaponry to coerce one neighbor to side with them.

Gold and salt were the two most important non-living commodities in trans-Saharan trade. The brutal work of MINING salt in the Berber-run mines at Idjil, in MAURITANIA, and Taghaza, in the desert near MOROCCO, was done by captives in bondage. Gold was a major source of West African wealth and a main reason why the Portuguese were initially attracted to Africa. Though strong even in the earlier days of Islam, the gold trade grew considerably in the 10th century with the rise of the Fatimid Caliphate and surged again in the 11th century when the Almoravid dynasty of Morocco united Muslim North Africa and Muslim Spain.

The major sources of gold in West Africa were the gold fields of Bambuk and Bure, the gold-bearing areas along the Black Volta River, and the AKAN gold fields, where most of the backbreaking labor was done by people in bondage. When, in the early 1480s. the Portuguese built their first trading fort in sub-Saharan Africa, they built it in Akan territory (present-day GHANA) and named

it São Jorge da Mina Castle, better known as ELMINA (The Mine) for its original use in the gold trade. Soon Elmina was used both as a holding station for West African captives shipped across the Atlantic and for captives (some 12,000 between 1500 and 1535) that the Portuguese sold to the Akan people to labor in the mines. The presence of this labor force allowed the Akan to expand operations from alluvial panning to below-surface mining and also to clear their land for farming.

Roots of European Involvement The kingdoms of Europe in the 15th century still faced a powerful and aggressive Muslim foe, the Ottoman Empire, which had a foothold in the Balkans as early as 1346. From their geographically advantageous position on both shores of the Mediterranean Sea, they controlled the sea and land trade routes to the Far East and grew rich on the high tariffs they charged on goods exported from Asia and Africa.

Starting in 1420 Prince Henry the Navigator (1394–1460) of Portugal sponsored a series of voyages along the Atlantic coast of Morocco that continued, after 1441, with voyages along the West African coast as far south as SIERRA LEONE. Navigational and shipbuilding advances enabled Portuguese sailors to sail further along the African coast than they earlier could. In 1441 Portuguese captain Antão Gonçalves landed at the Rio de Ouro (River of Gold) near what is now Villa Cisneros, in today's Mauritania, and returned home with a small number of captives for Prince Henry.

By 1448 more than 1,000 Africans had been abducted; the number rose to 1,000 per year in the 1450s, as a systematic trade in humans arose. Some of these Africans were taken in bondage to Portugal, where they undertook the most common tasks in traditional slavery. They were sent into the countryside to alleviate local agricultural labor shortages on the large estates that Christians had acquired from Portuguese Muslims during the late Middle Ages. In the cities and great houses, they worked as exotic domestic servants and became status symbols for their masters. In the Mediterranean region, more accustomed to diverse populations than Northern Europe was, persons in bondage were considered human and could buy their freedom.

Starting as early as 1502, Africans were kidnapped and transported across the Atlantic Ocean. This trade was based solely on commercial interests and paved the way for the development of the system of chattel slavery in plantation-based economies that became standard in the Americas. Unlike traditional forms of servitude, chattel slavery meant that these humans were, under law, considered the property of their masters. The Africans were transported in bondage to Portugal's newly acquired islands of the Azores and Madeira, located roughly half-way to the New World. There, far from home, they were forced to work on sugarcane plantations and in the sugar mills, where the cane was ground into raw granulated sugar.

Slavery and sugar have a long connection. The plantation system, which requires large tracts of land, originated in the kingdom of Palestine in the 12th and 13th centuries. Slaves, often of Syrian or Arab origin, were used in the 14th century to produce sugar plantations on Cyprus. Slave or coerced labor was also used on the plantations in Sicily, where use of the rolling mill, which increased productivity, was also introduced. The Sicilian plantations became the model for the Portuguese plantations on the Atlantic islands and later in Brazil.

Once primarily used as a MEDICINE, sugar, produced from sugarcane, was increasingly in demand as trade brought new products to Europe's tables: coffee from Africa, tea from China, and chocolate from the Americas. Sugar was now diffiicult to access in Palestine and Cyprus and other Mediterranean islands that were in Muslim hands. The plantation system that developed in the New World was highly profitable but also labor-intensive. Kidnapped Africans provided that labor.

At the same time these Portuguese voyages of EXPLORATION were happening in the West, Europe was being pressured once again from the East. In 1453 the Ottoman sultan, Mehmed II, captured Constantinople, the capital of the Byzantine Empire and one of the leading cities of Christendom. The church reacted strongly. The papal bull, or decree, *Romanus Pontifex* (1455), written by Pope Nicholas V (1397–1455), empowered the king of Portugal to enslave and seize the land and property of "all Saracens and pagans whatsoever and all other enemies of Christ." (Portugal and Spain later used the language of this bull to justify their conquests in the New World and justify kidnapping Africans.) The bull also gave Portugal a monopoly over Africa.

In about 1456, the Portuguese explorer Diogo Gomes (d. 1484) sailed beyond the Geba River in what is now GUINEA-BISSAU and on his return sailed 200 miles (322 km) inland up the Gambia River to Cantor (now Kuntaur in The GAMBIA), then under SONGHAI rule, where he met traders from TIMBUKTU. In 1461 the Portuguese built their first trading fort in the region on Arguin Bay, along the coast of present-day Mauritania. Arguin Island became the major conduit for the Portuguese slave trade, with captives from local Arab and indigenous sources being transported to the Portuguese homeland or to the sugar plantations on the Atlantic islands.

Built originally as a depot for the gold trade, Elmina became a major staging area for the trade in humans des-

tined for Portugal and the sugar plantations and, later, for the transatlantic SLAVE TRADE to the Americas. By 1500 Portugal had established sugar plantations on most of the Atlantic islands under their control: the Azores, Madeira, the Canary Islands, the Cape Verde Islands, the Bissagos Islands, SÃO TOMÉ AND PRÍNCIPE, and Bom.

As the 15th century came to a close Portugal and neighboring Spain were in the ascendancy. The fall of the kingdom of Grenada in Muslim Spain and the expulsion in 1492 of Muslims from the Iberian Peninsula (shared by Portugal and Spain) ended Muslim rule in western Europe and released Spain's and Portugal's energies for other conquests. By 1498 the Portuguese explorer Vasco da Gama (c. 1460–1524) had sailed around the Cape of Good Hope at the southern tip of Africa. This voyage and subsequent voyages around Africa to India in 1502–1503 and in 1524 opened up the sea route to India and the East and made Portugal a dominant power in world trade. The Ottoman Empire's unsuccessful siege of Vienna in 1529 ended the political and military threat of Islam to the kingdoms of continental Europe.

Portugal's purpose in Africa in the 1400s and the 1500s was not to establish colonies but to form secure trading links with coastal West Africa. The African coast provided few good harbors, so many of the early trading forts were built on islands. Kept from moving much past the coast by the power of the African rulers in the inland kingdoms, the Portuguese forced coastal peoples to act as their go-betweens and enforcers to trade European-made goods for ivory, gold, ostrich feathers, and gum Arabic from the interior. When captives could not be purchased for European goods, force was used to kidnap them and bring them to the coast. The European presence in West Africa also had repercussions in North Africa. It diverted the flow of trans-Saharan trade and weakened North Africa as a commercial center.

The large sugarcane plantations on the island of São Tomé in the Atlantic became, for a time in the 16th century, the world's largest producers of sugar. The production techniques used there provided the model for highly successful sugarcane plantations in Portuguese Brazil. Uninhabited when discovered by Portugal, probably in 1470, São Tomé was settled in the 1480s by men from Portugal, many of whom were *conversos,* or "new Christians," the name given to the newly baptized converts from Judaism expelled from Spain and Portugal by the Spanish Inquisition. The Africans they imported to do productive labor in the cane fields and sugar mills formed a majority of the population, and the ECONOMY of the island was fully based on forced labor. It has been argued that exporting African captives to São Tomé was the start of the transatlantic slave trade.

See also: GAMA, VASCO DA (Vol. III); GEBA RIVER (Vol. II); HENRY THE NAVIGATOR, PRINCE (Vol. II); RACE AND RACISM (Vol. IV); SLAVERY, CULTURAL AND HISTORICAL ATTI-

TUDES TOWARD (Vol. III); SLAVERY IN SOUTH AFRICA (Vol. III); SLAVE TRADE ON THE SWAHILI COAST (Vol. III).

slave trade, the transatlantic

slave trade, the transatlantic The transport of millions of Africans across the Atlantic Ocean by the Portuguese, the Spanish, the British, the Dutch and other European peoples. These Africans were kidnapped from their homelands, shipped in chains across the ocean, and then sold into servitude against their wills to buyers in European-founded colonies and settlements in North and South America and the Caribbean. There the captives lived and worked as the legal property of their masters. The system of enslavement they endured in the Americas had few, if any, parallels in the African experience.

Historians disagree about the extent of the transatlantic trade in humans. The most conservative estimates, based on shipping records and other documents, indicate that 10 million Africans were landed and sold into bondage; an additional 2 million died aboard ship. Less conservative estimates, based on the probability that many transactions went unrecorded, suggest that between 24 million and 50 million Africans were shipped to the Americas between the 1530s and the 1830s.

The transatlantic trade was not solely based in West Africa, although it began and first flourished there and many of the major ports of embarkation were located along that coast. Although ports along the East and North African coasts were generally associated with destinations in the Arabian Peninsula, these ports, too, were sometimes used for the TRANSPORTATION of Africans to the Americas.

When the Portuguese first landed on the SENEGAL coast, in 1441, the first Africans they captured were brought back to Portugal and other parts of Europe, where they became exotic domestic servants and field laborers. By the time that Columbus sailed to the Americas, in 1492, African workers were already producing much of Europe's sugar in plantations on the Portuguese-owned islands of Madeira and São Tomé, off the western coast of Africa, as well as on many other Portuguese-owned islands in the Atlantic.

In 1493 Pope Alexander VI (c. 1431–1504) sought to solve conflicting territorial claims between Spain and Portugal that had arisen following Columbus's first voyage to the Caribbean. Accordingly, he established a line of demarcation between the two countries' land claims. The Treaty of Tordesillas, based on this edict and signed in 1494, set up an imaginary north-south line at a point 1,185 miles (1,907 km) west of the Portuguese-owned Cape Verde Islands in the Atlantic Ocean. The line passed through the edge of Brazil roughly 800 miles (1,287 km) inland from present-day Recife. The treaty gave Portugal possession of any unclaimed territory to the east of that line and Spain similar rights to lands west of the line.

Portugal's monopoly over Africa was preserved, and, but for a small (later expanded) portion of Brazil, Spain received exclusive rights to the Americas.

In 1502 Spain began importing captive Africans into New Spain. Their primary goal was to alleviate LABOR shortages that had been caused by the deaths of the Native American populations, their original labor pool. These people died in huge numbers from diseases to which they lacked prior exposure and, hence, immunity. The first Africans in New Spain labored in the GOLD and silver mines. Soon, however, setting a pattern that remained true until the abolition of the slave trade, the captives' dominant occupation became the tending major cash crops. In the Caribbean islands, the crop was sugar; in Brazil, first sugar and then coffee; later, in North America, first TOBACCO and then COTTON. With less room for expansion because of the Treaty of Tordesillas, the Dutch, the British, and the French provided ships to transport Africans to the Americas. Before long, however, they established colonies and settlements of their own.

Competition for Control The Portuguese dominated the West African slave trade until the early 1600s, when Dutch competitors began to vie with them for control. The Dutch armed their ships and captured Portugal's trading forts along the coast. The government-sponsored DUTCH WEST INDIA COMPANY, chartered in Amsterdam in 1621, dedicated a 40-ship fleet exclusively to the coastal slave trade. To increase their wealth, the Dutch served as go-betweens for other European countries, exporting Africans to the British, French, and Spanish colonies in the New World, as well as to Dutch colonies in Brazil and elsewhere in the Americas. By the middle of the 1600s, the Dutch were in firm control of the West African trade in African captives.

Britain and France, however, contended with the Dutch for control, using tactics that the Dutch had used on the Portuguese. They built trading forts and established government-sponsored trading companies to oversee operations. The British were the main competitors of the Dutch in Lower Guinea, and they soon gained control of the entire Grain, Ivory, and Gold coasts, an area stretching from the Cestos River in LIBERIA through present-day GHANA. Founded in London in 1672, the ROYAL AFRICAN COMPANY held the monopoly on the trade in African captives until 1698, when all Englishmen were given the right to take part. Trade laws were also used to protect the British trade. The various Navigation Acts passed by the British Parliament in 1660 and subsequent years required that goods shipped to its colonies had to be carried in British ships. Such laws effectively excluded the Dutch and the French from selling Africans to British colonies in the New World. Jamaica was the single largest British market. In 1763 nearly 150 ships with a combined capacity for 40,000 captives, sailed from the British ports of London, Liverpool, and Bristol.

West Africa Every part of the Atlantic coast of West Africa from Senegal to southern ANGOLA was involved in the trafficking of captive Africans. SENEGAMBIA was the most important early source of captives. Ghana, known then as the GOLD COAST, had the greatest concentration of trading forts. Of the 42 forts built along the coast, 36 were in Ghana, including ELMINA, Cape Coast Castle, Fort Coromantine, and Fort Metal Cross. In addition to Ghana and the Senegambia, other major staging areas were SIERRA LEONE, the Bight of BENIN, and the Bight of Biafra, in southern NIGERIA.

At the same time that the English were contending with the Dutch in Lower Guinea, in the early 1600s, the French were active further up the coast. In 1638 the French established an outpost at the mouth of the Senegal River. They built Fort Saint-Louis in 1659 and, in 1677, took claim to GORÉE ISLAND, a trading fort that had previously belonged to the Portuguese and then the Dutch. The French exported Africans, gum arabic from Senegalese acacia trees, gold, and ivory from the Senegal coast until the late 1700s.

In 1673 the French founded the Senegal Company for the purpose of transporting Africans to the West Indies and to Guyana in South America. In 1684 the Senegal Company was replaced by the Guyana Company. In 1701 the French received the ASIENTO, or license, from Spain to be the exclusive supplier of African captives to the Spanish-controlled territories in the Americas. From then until 1713 the French transported cargoes of humans to Venezuela in exchange for cocoa.

During those years, Spain was preoccupied in Europe by the War of the Spanish Succession (1701–1714), which was motivated in part by competition for West African trade. This war had begun after the death of Charles II (1661–1700), who had died without an heir. By the terms of the Treaty of Utrecht (1714) that resolved Spain's conflicts with France and other European kingdoms, the Dutch were all but eliminated as a major trading power. The *asiento* passed to the British, who then dominated the slave trade until the British Parliament banned it in 1807.

Although they were relatively minor players, Sweden, Denmark, and Brandenburg, a state in what is today eastern Germany, followed the British, French, and Dutch model and between 1680 and 1700 established government-sponsored Africa companies for the slave trade. All had forts along the Gold Coast.

The British also dominated the area known as the SLAVE COAST, stretching from the Volta River to LAGOS across the modern countries of TOGO, Republic of BENIN, and Nigeria. SENEGAL alternated between French and British control until 1814, at which time it was awarded to France by the Treaty of Paris that ended the Napoleonic Wars (1792–1815) between France and Britain.

King George II of England, in 1750, took what had earlier been a royal monopoly and opened it to all, declaring, "It shall be lawful for all His Majesty's subjects to trade and traffic to and from any port or place in Africa, between the port of Sallee, in South Barbary [modern Salé on the Atlantic coast of Morocco], and the Cape of Good Hope."

Central Africa The majority of captives sold into slavery from Central Africa became part of the transat-

European slave merchant at Gorée. This 1796 illustration by Grasset de St. Sauveur and Labrousse shows a European man dealing with an African go-between for captives. © *Gianni Dagli/Corbis*

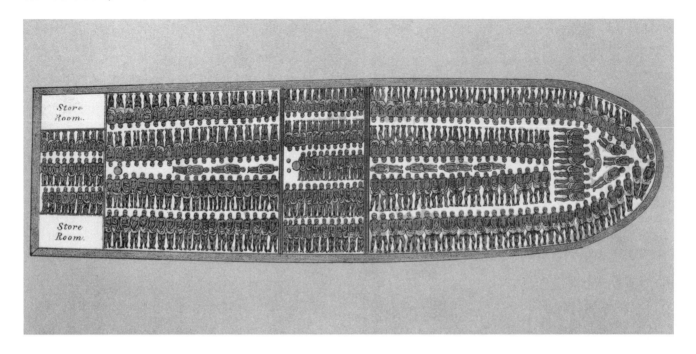

Nineteenth-century diagram of the lower deck of a ship used in the slave trade. This vessel carried captive Africans between Africa and the Americas before the U.S. Civil War (1860–65). © *Bettmann/Corbis*

lantic slave trade, although some were sent to the AKAN gold fields or to the Portuguese plantations on the islands in the Atlantic. In one of their rare incursions inland, Portuguese traders in search of precious metals gained a foothold at the royal court of the KONGO KINGDOM. There, for a time, they placed on the throne a convert who took the name AFONSO I (c. 1451–1543), who sent his army on raids to abduct captives from his neighbors. Popular rebellion against the Portuguese broke out after Afonso's death; it was quelled finally in the 1570s.

As the trade in humans grew in importance, the LUNDA EMPIRE became a commercial force in the southern savanna. Beginning in the middle of the 18th century, the Lunda, with their ancillary KASANJE kingdom in what is now Angola, effectively monopolized trade in Central Africa. The Lunda mercantile network eventually reached as far as the ZAMBEZI RIVER and the Indian Ocean. Much of the Lunda economy was based on the trade in kidnapped Africans, and the Lunda kingdom actively sent raiders through the countryside for the express purpose of capturing people for sale to the Portuguese.

The Triangular Trade   Africans shipped to and sold in the Americas sold for two or three times what they cost to purchase in Africa; thus, the trade in humans became one of the most important enterprises of the 17th century. In order to make each voyage as profitable as possible, a "triangular trade" was established between Europe, Africa, and the West Indies. The British colonies in North America sometimes added a fourth stopover, forming a "quadrilateral trade." Ships

left Europe laden with iron and copper bars, brass pots and kettles, cowrie shells, textiles, alcohol, and, in the 17th and 18th centuries, antiquated guns and gun powder. Landing in Africa, the ship captains met with the European agents at the trading forts along the African coast and representatives of the local kings and exchanged their goods for cargoes of captives. Two hundred to 600 captives per ship were loaded in chains below decks for the so-called MIDDLE PASSAGE to the Americas, during which many captives aboard died. On arrival in the West Indies, the Africans who survived the ordeal of the journey were traded for local agricultural products, especially sugar, to be sold in Europe after the third leg of the voyage. In the quadrilateral trade, West Indian molasses, a by-product of sugar production, was carried to the New England distilleries for the manufacture of rum. At every point along the route, large sums of money were made; a profit of at least 100 percent was expected.

Large-scale sugar plantations, established first in Brazil and, after 1645, in the Caribbean islands, were enormously profitable. Plantations in Cuba gave more than a 30 percent return on capital investment; those in Barbados returned 40 to 50 percent. These islands became societies whose economies relied heavily on the labor of African captives. In 1789, one-third of the population of Cuba was comprised of Africans. Between 1730 and 1834, up to 90 percent of the populations of Jamaica, Antigua, and Grenada were Africans. In Brazil in 1800, half the population was African.

As early as 1619 whites from England could pay their passage to the British colonies in North America by working as indentured servants for a period of four to seven years. By 1680, however, the system of indentured servitude had all but disappeared because planters realized that they could make more money using the labor of captives from Africa and because changes in the law made slave owning more attractive. At first the Africans tended the tobacco crops that grew along the Chesapeake Bay and the rice fields of South Carolina, which was the American colony—and, later, state—with the largest plantation-based economy. In the minds of the Carolina planters, the ideal African field laborer was a tall, healthy male from Senegambia between the ages of 14 and 18, free of blemishes, and as dark as possible. In the 18th century the cost of an African averaged between £100 and £200 sterling, equaling slightly more than $11,000 to $23,000 in today's money.

Most of the Africans in the southern United States were not imported directly from Africa. Instead they were transshipped from the West Indies, where most of them had labored on the sugar plantations. The American plantation owners thought that a period of prior bondage made them more docile and tractable. Unlike the British, French, and Dutch planters in the Caribbean, these American plant-ers generally came to the New World to build a new life rather than return some day to Europe with their wealth.

What sugar did to increase the number of captive Africans needed in the Caribbean islands, the cotton gin, invented in 1793 by American Eli Whitney (1765–1825), did for the plantations in the southern states. By 1850 nearly two-thirds of the field hands in the United States were working on cotton plantations. Over 60 percent of the population of South Carolina in 1720 were African. As the Civil War began in 1860, 55 percent of the people in Mississippi were African.

A cotton gin (short for *engine*) is a mechanical device to separate cotton fibers from the seeds. Previously this time-consuming task had been done by hand.

How Africans Were Obtained The fear of disease and the military power of kingdoms in the interior kept the European traders from mounting their own expeditions. Instead, they frequently coerced coastal peoples by the threat of force or the enticement of trade to become their go-betweens.

Although in Africa, some Africans in traditional forms of bondage were criminals and outcasts, many were captives taken in war. The supply of captives at the coast was usually related to the frequency and intensity of wars fought in the interior. When the kingdom of BENIN, for instance, was undergoing a period of expansion in the late 15th century, many captives were taken, and some became available for sale to the Portuguese; in the 16th century, however, the rulers of Benin refused to trade in captives. Similarly the FULANI JIHADS of the 18th century, during which the Muslim FULANI were expanding into the lands bordering the kingdoms of FOUTA DJALLON and FOUTA TORO, many prisoners of war became available along the coast. Wars waged by the expanding OYO and ASHANTI empires during the 17th and 18th centuries also added dramatically to the numbers of available captives. When captives were unavailable, men, women, and children were kidnapped from their homes and sent to the coast.

Historians record that a trickle of captives, some 20 or 30 at a time, generally reached the coast daily from road or river networks that stretched inland. At the coast, when the European traders arrived, the captives were examined for fitness for labor. Once a price was agreed on, the captives were loaded on the next available ship. On board they were chained below decks in inhumane conditions. In many ships the captives were secured to specially built platforms that allowed little room for movement but that maximized the cargo capacity of the ship. They sailed, often with insufficient food and water and the stench of their own excrement, for the weeks or months it took to reach their destinations. During that time they were rarely allowed above deck except in death, in which case their bodies were thrown overboard. Historians estimate that between 15 percent and 30 percent of the captive Africans died from disease, malnutrition, or mistreatment during these voyages.

When the passage was completed and the ships reached landfall in the West Indies, the captives again underwent the same kind of degrading inspection that had

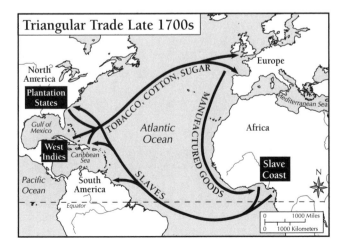

Triangular Trade Late 1700s

A cargo of Africans from a Dutch man-of-war being unloaded at Jamestown, Virginia. The painting is undated. © *Bettmann/Corbis*

occurred in Africa, followed by sale at auction to the highest bidder. Records show that in the harsh working conditions of the plantation system more than 30 percent of the Africans died within the first three years. Few survived past 10 years.

See also: SLAVERY, CULTURAL AND HISTORICAL ATTITUDES TOWARD (Vol. III); SLAVE TRADE, EXPANSION OF EUROPEAN INVOLVEMENT IN (Vol. III); SLAVERY IN SOUTH AFRICA (Vol. III); SLAVE TRADE ON THE SWAHILI COAST (Vol. III).

Further reading: Herbert S. Klein, *The Atlantic Slave Trade* (New York: Cambridge University Press, 1999).

slave trade on the Swahili Coast

The SWAHILI COAST, with its important market towns of MOGADISHU, Shanga, KILWA, and MOMBASA, was already an important center of commerce and the terminus of a large network of inland trade routes by the time the Portuguese explorer Vasco da Gama (c. 1460–1524) sailed around the Cape of Good Hope and landed there, in 1498. The cities were united by a common culture and RELIGION (Islam) and the Swahili language, which served as the common language of commerce and trade among the Arabs, Persians, and Africans who lived along the coast.

Although some persons in bondage in Muslim lands worked in the fields, a widespread system of forced servitude never took root among Arab peoples as it did in the Americas and the Caribbean as a result of the transatlantic SLAVE TRADE. Keeping slaves was a status symbol, a visible measure of an owner's wealth and prestige. A 10th-century caliph of Baghdad had over 10,000 servants at his palace. Rulers of the Muslim states in West Africa utilized captives taken in war in much the same way.

By 1510 the Portuguese were able to dominate portions of the East African coast from Kilwa, in what is now southern TANZANIA, to Mombasa, in present-day KENYA, and, with those cities, the trade routes to India. Threats from Ottoman Empire expeditions descending from the north and the need to protect their position in Mombasa led to the construction of FORT JESUS, the Portuguese stronghold there, in 1593–94. Despite some setbacks in the Persian Gulf islands of Hormuz and Muscat in the 1620s at the hands of the shah of Persia's forces, Portugal controlled trade in the western Indian Ocean until 1652, when the imam (religious leader) of Oman in the Arabian Peninsula in Muslim Asia began to foment resistance to Portuguese rule.

In 1696 a fleet and army from Oman lay siege to Mombassa, and by 1698 the Omani had successfully driven the Portuguese out. ZANZIBAR, south of Mombasa, fell to Omani forces a few years later. The Omani, however, became preoccupied by conflicts at home and for the next 100 years, despite minor resurgences of Portuguese power, the Swahili Coast was free of outside domination. During the 18th century Mombasa reached the height of its influence under the MASRUI dynasty of Mombasa. The Masrui had Omani roots but were rivals of the Sadian clan that ruled Oman. The Masrui were able to control rival factions in the cities along the coast and maintain good commercial relations with the Bantu-speaking NYIKA people inland.

The Arab Indian Ocean Slave Trade The Arab Indian Ocean slave trade dates back at least to the seventh century, when many slaves from Africa, Asia, and Europe were taken to work in bondage on the plantations of the Abbasid Caliphate (750–1278) in what is today Iraq. Slaves were also shipped as far as Muslim lands in India and Indonesia, where they worked as soldiers, household servants, and concubines. The trade in humans declined after the ninth century because Arab and Asian markets became more interested in African goods, especially ivory and GOLD, than humans.

The trade in humans revived as the 17th century ended. At this time the sultan of Oman needed laborers for his date plantations on the coastal plain of Al-Batinah along the Gulf of Oman, and the French needed workers for their sugar plantations on the Indian Ocean islands of Réunion and MAURITIUS. As many as 20,000 Africans annually were sold in the markets on Zanzibar and PEMBA ISLAND, off the coast of present-day Tanzania. The Arab trade in captives persisted in Zanzibar well into the 19th century, undeterred by British antislavery patrols in the Indian Ocean.

Contemporary accounts indicate that the Zanzibar slave trade was known for its brutality. Groups of captives, who were abducted from as far away as the present-day border of Tanzania and MALAWI, were marched to the coast in leg irons or carrying heavy wooden yokes. In some cases, they were forced to act as bearers for the ivory that the caravans also carried. After weeks or months of marching, the caravans arrived in Kilwa, Bagamoyo, and other ports along the coast. There, 200 to 600 captives at a time were packed into 100-foot (30-m)-long dhows and shipped to Zanzibar. Sold to the highest bidders, the captives were then brought to their final destinations in Zanzibar or the Indian Ocean islands.

European Involvement Mombasa, north of Zanzibar and the chief port of present-day KENYA, was founded by Arab traders in the 11th century. Vasco da Gama visited it in 1498, on his first voyage to India. Subsequently the superior military and naval strength of the Portuguese allowed them to dominate the poorly defended cities along the coast. In 1502 they forced the ruler of Kilwa to pay tribute. The following year they sacked Mombasa and Kilwa and soon built Fort Jesus in Mombasa and erected a customshouse on PATE ISLAND. By 1506 the Portuguese dominated the coast and the trade routes to India. Mombasa was at that point the chief city of the coast. What lured the Portuguese was trade in ambergris, gold, coral, and ivory.

Portuguese power was broken, in 1698, after Mombasa was besieged by the combined forces of the sultanates of Oman and Pate led by Seif bin Sultan Seif al-Yarubi (1649–1679) of Oman. When Oman placed garrisons in Kilwa, Zanzibar and Pemba, the Portuguese fled to MOZAMBIQUE, which, in the 18th century was a center of the East African slave trade.

Farther south along the coast, at what is now the town of MAPUTO, a Portuguese trader named Lourenço Marques reached the lower ZAMBEZI RIVER in 1544. This river, a major artery into the interior, rises in ZAMBIA and empties into the Indian Ocean at the 250-mile (402-km)-wide Mozambique Channel between MADAGASCAR and the African mainland. At the mouth of the Zambezi, Portuguese merchants exchanged trade goods, including firearms, for gold and ivory from the interior. Later a Portuguese trading fort, which was finally completed in 1787, was built at Maputo.

European slave traders did not begin operating in the Indian Ocean until the mid-17th century. When the French East India Company settled Réunion and Mauritius (collectively called the MASCARENE ISLANDS) in the Indian Ocean, the French established coffee and, later, sugarcane plantations there. Although some Africans were shipped around the Cape of Good Hope to the Caribbean, especially Saint-Domingue (present-day Haiti), the majority went to the Mascarene Islands, where slaves from Madagascar, India, and Malaysia also labored.

In the early 1700s the Bantu-speaking NGONI and YAO peoples moved into the region from the south and became the intermediaries between the Portuguese and Swahili traders along the coast and the CHEWA, the NYANZA, and other peoples in the Zumbo, MANYIKA, and TETE regions of the interior. Like the ZULU, the Ngoni practiced universal military conscription and divided their warriors into regiments by age set. They expanded by warring with their neighbors, taking many captives. The Ngoni incorporated some of the captives into their kinship groups; others were handed over to Swahili Coast traders. Because of their involvement in the coastal trade, the Islamized Yao became one of the most prosperous peoples in the region. By 1800 Yao trading networks reached as far inland as the tip of Lake Nyasa in what is now Malawi. There, traders from Portugal and Portuguese India had established semi-independent great estates, called *prazos*, along the Zambezi River in an attempt to colonize the region; these traders trafficked extensively in gold and captives along the coast.

In the early 1800s, when the supply of captives from West Africa began to dwindle because of British restrictions on the slave trade, the Indian Ocean slave trade intensified in order to supply labor for the Portuguese plantations in Brazil, the sugar plantations on Réunion and Mauritius, and the plantations of the sultan of Oman on Zanzibar. By the 1820s Mozambique had surpassed ANGOLA as a source of captives.

Captive African men, women, and children yoked together. Groups of captives were forced by their abductors to walk hundreds of miles from the interior to the Swahili coast. Illustrations like this one were often used to blame the enslavement of Africans on the complicity of other Africans. Undated lithograph.
© *Bettmann/Corbis*

See also: DHOW (Vol. II); GAMA, VASCO DA (Vol. III); SLAVERY, CULTURAL AND HISTORICAL ATTITUDES TOWARD (Vol. III); SLAVE TRADE, EXPANSION OF EUROPEAN INVOLVEMENT IN (Vol. III); SLAVERY IN SOUTH AFRICA (Vol. III); SLAVE TRADE, THE TRANSATLANTIC (Vol. III).
Further reading: Edward A. Alpers, *Ivory and Slaves: Changing Pattern of International Trade in East Central Africa to the Later Nineteenth Century* (Berkeley, Calif.: University of California Press, 1975).

Sofala Swahili city-state on the east coast of Africa. Located in what is now MOZAMBIQUE. At the mouth of the Sofala River, Sofala was the southernmost point of Islamic culture on the African coast and a center of the GOLD and ivory trades. The oldest harbor in southern Africa, Sofala was visited as early as 915 by Arabs in search of gold from the interior. During the 14th and 15th centuries it was an outpost of the sultanate of KILWA and the coastal depot for trade goods carried in from Great Zimbabwe and the other SHONA KINGDOMS located in what is now the Karanga Province of ZIMBABWE. Sofala's importance began to decline in the 1500s.

The Portuguese conquered local resistance in Sofala with cannons and crossbows. They razed the town before hunting down its Islamic leader, the blind Sheikh Yusuf (d. 1505). They beat him and cut off his head, which they fixed on a lance and displayed at their new fort as a warning to potential challengers.

Hearing tales of Sofala's "infinite gold," the Portuguese wrested the port city from its Swahili rulers in 1505. The Portuguese goal was to control the gold trade, which had been previously monopolized by the coastal city-state of Kilwa, in what is now TANZANIA.

Internal conflicts between inland Bantu groups and a thriving black market trade with the Arabs limited the amount of gold obtained by the Portuguese. What gold they did get, they rerouted south around the Cape of Good Hope for trade in Europe. Arab and African merchants, who had been doing business with each other for almost a thousand years, started to bypass Sofala in favor of trading posts at Kilwa and in the Zambezi valley. The leader of the MWENE MUTAPA kingdom set up markets in villages throughout the interior, where the Portuguese could not easily penetrate. The Sofala gold trade thus began to decline in importance, although the region continued to supply captives to the French and Portuguese for the next two centuries.

See also: IVORY TRADE (Vol. III); PORTUGAL AND AFRICA (Vol. III); SOFALA (Vol. II); SLAVE TRADE ON THE SWAHILI COAST (Vols. II, III, IV).
Further reading: T. H. Elkiss, *The Quest for an African Eldorado: Sofala, Southern Zambezia, and the Portuguese, 1500–1865* (Waltham, Mass.: Crossroads Press, 1981); Michael N. Pearson, *Port Cities and Intruders: The Swahili Coast, India, and Portugal in the Early Modern Era* (Baltimore, Md.: Johns Hopkins University Press, 1998).

Sokoto Caliphate Located in northeastern NIGERIA, the largest empire in 19th-century West Africa. Sokoto was formed from the HAUSA STATES and other territories conquered by the FULANI JIHADS led by USMAN DAN FODIO (1754–1817). In 1804 this FULANI scholar and cleric set out to convert the surrounding regions of West Africa to Islam. His instrument of conversion was a Muslim holy war, the headquarters of which was the town of Sokoto. Located along the Sokoto (KEBBI) River, a main tributary of the NIGER RIVER, Sokoto was situated on an important Saharan trade route.

Between 1804 and 1808 the *shehu* (chief) Fodio and his followers succeeded in defeating the seven main Hausa States, or Hausa Bakwai, made up of KANO, ZARIA, (formerly Zazzau) GOBIR, Rano, Daura, KATSINA, and Biram. These states, located between Lake CHAD and the NIGER RIVER, were then incorporated as emirates of the emerging caliphate. Meanwhile the Fulani jihad began to move to points southward, conquering the outlying Hausa states of ILORIN and NUPE. In time, it reached all the way to the northern borders of YORUBALAND, destroying such well-known kingdoms as Old Oyo. In 1809 the town of Sokoto became the official capital of the SOKOTO CALIPHATE, an empire that stretched over 181,468 square miles (470,000 sq km).

Within the caliphate, individual emirates retained their independent authority even though they were required to pay tribute to the capital at Sokoto. They also had to pledge their allegiance to the reigning religious leader, who was called the *amir al-muminin* (commander of the faithful). Usman dan Fodio remained *amir al-muminin* until his death, in 1817, at which time his son, MUHAMMAD BELLO (c. 1781–1837), assumed the title. The caliphate operated as a theocracy and in subsequent years became a center for religious learning in West Africa. Trade was a main source of income, with items such as salt, leather goods, kola nuts, cloth, brass, spice, and captives being the primary articles exchanged. During the 1820s Sokoto became known for the large mosques built to honor Usman dan Fodio and his son, called the Masallacin Shehu and Masallacin Bello.

The Sokoto Caliphate remained powerful throughout the 19th century. During this time it took the jihad in new directions, leading, for example, to the replace-

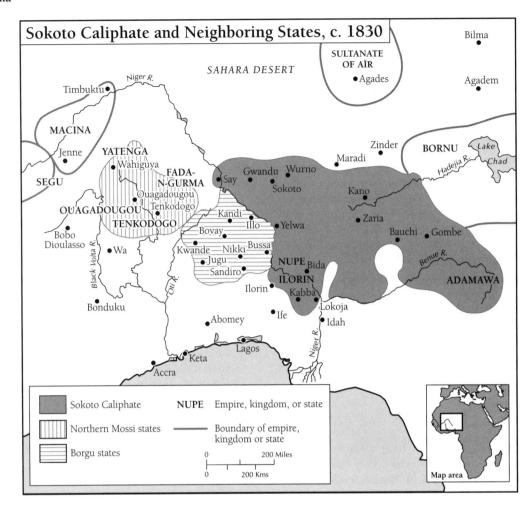

Sokoto Caliphate and Neighboring States, c. 1830

	Sokoto Caliphate	**NUPE** Empire, kingdom, or state
	Northern Mossi states	Boundary of empire, kingdom or state
	Borgu states	

0   200 Miles
0   200 Kms

Map area

ment of the SEFUWA dynasty of KANEM-BORNU in favor of the al-Kanemi dynasty. The solidarity of the caliphate was not tested until the last years of the 19th century, when the British, French, and German powers began to attack, breaking up the caliphate and putting it under European rule.

See also: BIRAM (Vol. II); DAURA (Vol. II); OYO EMPIRE (Vol. III); RANO (Vol. II); SOKOTO CALIPHATE (Vol. IV).

Further reading: Murray Last, *The Sokoto Caliphate* (New York: Humanities Press, 1967); Ibraheem Sulaiman, *The Islamic State and the Challenge of History: Ideals, Policies, and Operation of the Sokoto Caliphate* (New York: Mansell Pub., 1987).

Somalia Country measuring approximately 246,000 square miles (637,100 sq km) located in northeastern Africa. It is bordered by Republic of DJIBOUTI to the northwest, KENYA to the southwest, and ETHIOPIA to the west. Located north of the equator, between the Gulf of Aden and the Indian Ocean, Somalia occupies the coastal territory of what is called the Horn of Africa. MOGADISHU is the capital city and main port. At various times the country has also been known as Somaliland. The region was named after the Somali peoples, migrants from the Yemen in the Arabian Peninsula who occupied the territory as early as the 10th century. Other early inhabitants of Somalia included the OROMO, non-Muslim pastoralists who migrated into western Somaliland from Ethiopia prior to the 16th century, and the AFAR, a Cushitic-speaking ethnic group related to the Somali.

Historically, the six or seven major Somali clans that have dominated the region have been defined by their environment. Those living in the rugged interior regions practiced nomadic pastoralism, and those living along the coastal plains practiced trade, mostly with Arab merchants. Somalian cities that have figured prominently in history include the Indian Ocean ports of Mogadishu, Marka, and BRAVA, and the cities of ZEILA (now Seylac) and BERBERA on the Gulf of Aden, to the north.

Somaliland was crossed by several major trade routes that brought ivory from the African interior to the Red Sea and Indian Ocean ports for export to the Arabian and Indian markets. GOLD was brought north along the coast from southern ports, including ZANZIBAR off the coast of present-day TANZANIA and SOFALA in MOZAMBIQUE. Portuguese seamen first visited the coast of Somaliland as early as 1499. By 1505 they had made their way up the coast from their military outposts in Mozambique and occupied the trade town of Brava, south of Mogadishu. However, during the rest of the 16th century, the Portuguese were unable to control the trade in Somaliland's other coastal cities in their efforts to monopolize the lucrative gold and ivory trades.

In the early 16th century the Muslim state of ADAL, located in what is now northwest Somalia, rose to power under the leadership of AHMAD GRAŇ (c. 1506–1543). This cosmopolitan kingdom prospered largely because of the lucrative commerce in Zeila, a Somalian trading center on the Gulf of Aden. Zeila's merchants exchanged Arabian cloth, glass, and weapons for African goods, including ivory, hardwoods, and animal skins, that were brought by caravan from the interior, and Adal grew rich by taxing and regulating the trade.

By 1533 Adal had conquered many of the formerly Christian territories of neighboring Ethiopia. Graň was killed in battle in 1543, and Adal subsequently went into a rapid decline. The disintegration of Adal was accelerated by the arrival of waves of Oromo migrants, who had been moving into the region steadily, even prior to the 16th century.

In the 17th and 18th centuries various Somali groups, Arab clans, and Portuguese explorers, traders, and soldiers fought over the trading towns of Somalia's Indian Ocean coast, sometimes called the BENADIR COAST. At the same time, rival Somali and Oromo clans fought to control the hinterland and the important caravan routes there.

In the early 19th century Somaliland fell under the nominal rule of the Arab OMANI SULTANATE, whose East African center of power was Zanzibar, an island located south of Somaliland off the coast of modern Tanzania.

See also: ADEN, GULF OF (Vol. II); MARKA (Vol. II); SOMALI (Vol. II); SOMALIA (Vol. I, II, IV, V).

Songhai (Songhay) West African empire that reached its zenith in the 16th century, largely due to the leadership of its two greatest rulers, Sunni Ali (r. 1464–1492) and Askia MUHAMMAD TOURÉ (1493–1528). Even though it was under Sunni Ali that the Songhai kingdom underwent its greatest expansion, he was not favored by his

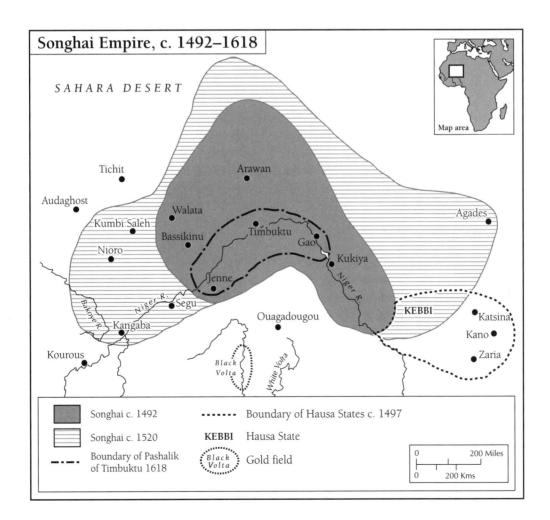

Songhai Empire, c. 1492–1618

SAHARA DESERT

Tichit
Audaghost
Arawan
Walata
Kumbi Saleh
Bassikinu
Agades
Nioro
Timbuktu
Gao
Jenne
Kukiya
Niger R.
Segu
KEBBI
Bakoye R.
Kangaba
Ouagadougou
Katsina
Kano
Kourous
Zaria
Black Volta
White Volta

Map area

Songhai c. 1492
Songhai c. 1520
Boundary of Pashalik of Timbuktu 1618
------- Boundary of Hausa States c. 1497
KEBBI Hausa State
Black Volta Gold field

0   200 Miles
0   200 Kms

Muslim contemporaries. His reputed pagan leanings, coupled with his seemingly weak support of his Islamic faith, made him many enemies within his own government. He also earned a reputation as a violent and merciless leader for his attacks on TIMBUKTU (1468) and on JENNE (1473). In his latter years, however, Sunni Ali apparently mellowed somewhat, even marrying the mother of the king of Timbuktu as an offering of peace for his past deeds. By the time of his death, in 1492, he had secured control over most of the Middle and Upper Niger.

Not long after Sunni Ali's death, a Muslim general in Sunni Ali's army, Muhammad Touré, later called Askia the Great, seized the throne and became the first in a line of kings known as the ASKIA DYNASTY. Early in his reign Askia Muhammad went on a two-year pilgrimage to Mecca. Although he led many expeditions that expanded the borders of Songhai, it was his reorganization of the state and his contributions to culture, RELIGION, and education that made him one of the most celebrated leaders of his time. In 1528 the elderly and ill Muhmmad Touré was deposed by his son, Askia Musa, which led to a series of skirmishes for control of the empire. Between 1528 and 1582 there were five *askias:* Muhammad Musa (r. 1528–1531), Muhammad Benkan (r. 1531–1537), Ismail (r. 1537–1539), Ishaq I (r. 1539–1549), and Askia DAUD (r. 1549–1582).

In the late 16th century Sultan ABD AL-MANSUR (c. 1549–1603) of MOROCCO set out to conquer the Songhai Empire. It took the Moroccan army of 4,000 troops six months to cross the Sahara, a feat that most believed impossible for such a large military force. Though al-Mansur's army was greatly reduced by the end of the journey, his men were equipped with guns, which put the Songhai soldiers at a serious disadvantage. The Moroccan army was victorious in the ensuing battle, winning a major victory in 1591. Songhai refused to submit, however, and conflict between Songhai and Morocco lasted well into the 17th century.

Meanwhile, descendants of the Askia dynasty continued to rule the area in what is now NIGER until 1660. Thereafter what remained of the Songhai Empire was divided into smaller principalities and chiefdoms. These remained independent, until 1898, when they were conquered by the French.

See also: ISLAM, INFLUENCE OF (Vol. III); FRANCE AND AFRICA (Vol. III); MUHAMMAD TOURÉ, ASKIA (Vol. II); SONGHAI (Vol. II); SUNNI ALI (Vol. II); WARFARE AND WEAPONS (Vol. III).

Songo Subgroup of the MBUNDU peoples that lived between the Kwango and Kwanza rivers in what is now northeastern ANGOLA. Songo are unique among the Mbundu in that they did not develop an extensive kingdom and preferred instead to organize as a segmentary society, ruled by geneaological ties. Because of their lack of a central power, invading rulers of the LUNDA EMPIRE, called *kinguri,* easily settled in Songo lands in the middle 16th century and eventually established a kingdom there. The Songo people were fishers, farmers, and hunters. They were also highly skilled sculptors and mask makers, and were well known for their craftsmanship.

Soninke (Sarakole, Serahhule, Marka, Wakore)

Mande-speaking people, mostly Muslims, inhabiting parts of what are now Republic of MALI, SENEGAL, The GAMBIA, and MAURITANIA. At one time the rulers of the powerful Ghana Empire, by the 16th century the Soninke people had dispersed over vast stretches and formed smaller states.

One such Soninke state was Gadiago, established along the upper Senegal River in what is now Senegal. Founded in the early to mid-17th century, Gadiago was the home of skilled traders who marketed their grain, kola nuts, and GOLD along north-south trade routes and traded captives and gold along the east-west routes. Soninke traders transported most of their goods to the coastline over the waterways of the Senegal River, but they also made use of the overland trade routes. In the Gambia region, they used land routes that were controlled by the DYAKANKE people.

By the 18th century many Soninke groups were involved in the trade of humans. Through their trading endeavors, Soninke men accumulated great wealth, even acquiring their own captive workforce to tend their lands while they traveled to other cities to conduct trade. During this time and into the 19th century, the Soninke were steadily coming under the influence of the French, who would later colonize Soninke territories as part of what became French West Africa.

See also: FRANCE AND AFRICA (Vols. III, IV); FRENCH WEST AFRICA (Vol. IV); SLAVERY (Vol. III); SONINKE (Vol. II) TRADE AND COMMERCE (Vol. III).

Sotho (Basotho, Suthu, Suto)

People of southern Africa who speak the Bantu language of Sesotho. The ancestors of the Sotho began migrating to their present-day locations during the 11th century. They settled in large, scattered villages, relying on AGRICULTURE and animal husbandry for their livelihood.

The Sotho people, also called the *Basotho,* are made up of three separate ethnic groupings: the Sotho proper, who live in present-day LESOTHO; the TSWANA of BOTSWANA; and the Sotho residing in Transvaal. The area that is present-day Lesotho was occupied by SAN hunter-gatherers as late as the 16th century. Toward the beginning of the 17th century, however, Bantu-speaking peoples began to migrate to the area and intermarry with the native San.

The Sotho identity was forged in the early to mid-1800s, when neighboring ZULU clans invaded the area, killing many of the San and Bantu speakers. The ruler MSHWESHWE (c. 1786–1870) gathered refugees from the remaining clans at the mountain stronghold of Butha Buthe. This eclectic mix of peoples formed the first Sotho nation. Conflicts with neighboring groups continued, and by July 1824 the Sotho were on the verge of defeat. Mshweshwe moved his people to a less vulnerable settlement at THABA BOSIU.

For the next 40 years the mountain settlement at Thaba Bosiu withstood attacks from the Ndebele, Griquas, BOERS, and British. In 1868 the Boers overtook the Sotho lands. Mshweshwe appealed to the British for help, and the country became a British protectorate in March of 1868. The Sotho nation was preserved, but the country remained under British control until it became an independent nation, in 1966.

The Sotho were traditionally ruled by a system of hereditary chieftains. Control began at the village level and rose through a series of district headmen, all of whom had ultimate responsibility to a paramount chief. The paramount chief was allowed to make provisional decrees, but the legal code was based primarily on custom. Today, Lesotho is a constitutional monarchy, but the traditional legal code is now published law applied by the court system.

The ECONOMY of the Sotho has always relied heavily on agriculture and animal husbandry. Grains and cereals have been important crops throughout the centuries, but corn is the primary staple crop today. Cattle, sheep, and goats also play an important role in the Sotho economy. Most families possess livestock that can be used for various subsistence and income-producing purposes.

The honoring of ancestors is the traditional religion practiced by the Sotho. Although there is a belief in a supreme being, and Christianity has greatly influenced religious belief, ancestral worship remains the practical religion of the people.

See also: ANCESTOR WORSHIP (Vol. I); BASUTOLAND (Vol. IV); CHRISTIANITY, INFLUENCE OF (Vols. III, IV); SOTHO (Vol. IV).

South Africa
Country measuring 470,700 square miles (1,219,100 sq km) bordered by the Atlantic Ocean to the west, the Indian Ocean to the south and east, NAMIBIA to the northwest, ZIMBABWE and BOTSWANA to the north, and MOZAMBIQUE and SWAZILAND to the northeast. South Africa completely surrounds LESOTHO, which is situated in the eastern central plain. Today South Africa's administrative capital is Pretoria, but it also has CAPE TOWN as the legislative center and Bloemfontein as the judicial center.

Prior to 1500, the southern and western regions of present-day South Africa were inhabited by Khoisan-speaking SAN and KHOIKHOI peoples. Khoikhoi subgroups included ORLAMS and NAMA herders who, by the 1600s, moved north and settled near Namibia north of the ORANGE RIVER. Bantu-speakers, who arrived after the Khoisan speakers, occupied the fertile valleys of the eastern regions stretching north to Mozambique. The Bantu-speaking groups were made up of the XHOSA and their subgroups, including the MPONDO, Thembu, Mpondomise, NGQIKA, NDLAMBE, GQUNUKWEBE, and ZULU. In the 17th century the Xhosa people migrated west and north from the Fish River area, incorporating some Khoikhoi into their villages. Xhosa pastoralists amassed wealth through cattle-raiding in the 17th and 18th centuries.

Europeans first reached the southern tip of South Africa when the Portuguese explorer Bartolomeu Dias (c. 1450–1500) sailed around the Cape of Good Hope in 1488. By the middle of the 16th century the Portuguese had begun trading in Indian Ocean coastal areas north of South Africa. The real impact of Europeans in the region was not felt until 1652, when the DUTCH EAST INDIA COMPANY established its trading station at Cape Town, on the southern Atlantic coast. Beginning in 1657 the company began assigning land to farmers so they could cultivate agricultural products. These, it was hoped, would supply the Dutch ships sailing to and from the Indian Ocean around the cape. The land had been occupied by Khoikhoi hunter-gatherers, who began peaceful trading relations with the BOERS that lasted until the late 18th century. During this time Khoikhoi hunters exchanged their meat, skins, and ivory for Dutch cloth and manufactured metal goods. Smallpox, introduced to the region by the Dutch, killed a great number of Khoikhoi, and their vacated land was then occupied by Dutch settlers. Some Khoikhoi women bore children by the Dutch men, and a mixed race called *Cape Coloureds* emerged by the middle of the 18th century.

Portuguese explorer Vasco da Gama (1460–1524) sailed past the southeastern coast of South Africa on Christmas Day, 1497. He named the land he saw beyond the coast *Terra Natalis*, or "Christmas Land." The term *Natal*, which is Portuguese for "Christmas," was later used to name the southeastern province of colonial South Africa.

Early Dutch settlers who moved into the interior were called *Boers*, or *Trekboers*. The Dutch came in relatively small numbers, so to work their land they imported forced LABOR from East Africa, MADAGASCAR, and Asia.

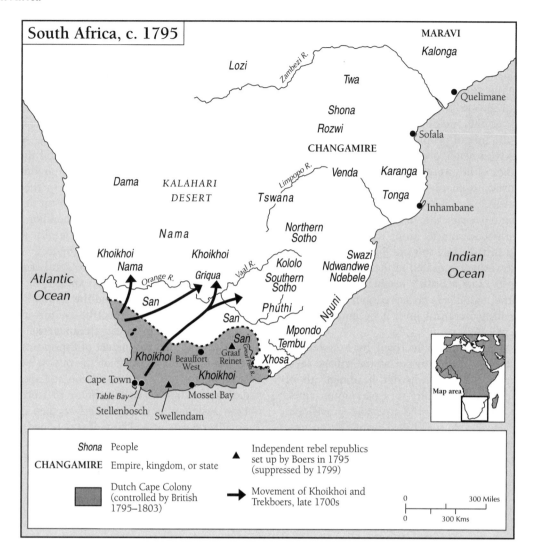

South Africa, c. 1795

MARAVI
Kalonga
Lozi
Twa
Zambezi R.
Quelimane
Shona
Rozwi
Sofala
CHANGAMIRE
Dama   KALAHARI
DESERT
Limpopo R.
Venda   Karanga
Tswana   Tonga
Inhambane
Nama   Northern
Sotho
Khoikhoi   Khoikhoi   Swazi
Nama   Griqua   Kololo   Ndwandwe
Orange R.   Vaal R.   Southern   Ndebele
Indian
Atlantic   Sotho   Ocean
Ocean   San   Phuthi   Nguni
San   Mpondo
San   Tembu
Khoikhoi   Graaf   Xhosa
Beauffort   Reinet   Great Fish R.
West   Khoikhoi
Cape Town   Map area
Table Bay   Mossel Bay
Stellenbosch   Swellendam

Shona   People   ▲   Independent rebel republics
set up by Boers in 1795
CHANGAMIRE   Empire, kingdom, or state   (suppressed by 1799)

Dutch Cape Colony   →   Movement of Khoikhoi and
(controlled by British   Trekboers, late 1700s
1795–1803)

0   300 Miles
0   300 Kms

These workers were incorporated into an increasingly diverse population.

After 1700 the TSWANA, a SOTHO subgroup, occupied the northern territories of modern South Africa, near the Botswana border. Agriculturalist Sotho groups inhabited the region between modern Pretoria and SWAZILAND and also the northern slope of the Drakensberg Mountains (in modern Lesotho), where they traded with Khoikhoi pastoralists.

Throughout the 17th century Xhosa groups and Boers traded peacefully in the southern regions of southern Africa. The Dutch traded beads, nails, glass, and metal items for cattle and ivory. But as the Xhosa expanded west and Trekboers moved east, they met near the Fish River by about 1770 and fought over scarce resources.

During the last quarter of the 18th century the southern region of the continent was threatened with the prospect of armed conflicts between Boers and various Xhosa groups. In 1779 violence erupted in the fertile Zuurveld region, marking the beginning of the CAPE

FRONTIER WARS. By the end of the 18th century the Dutch East India Company was in dire financial straits, and the British government assumed control of the Dutch Cape Town holdings. They returned the administrative duties of the CAPE COLONY to the Dutch, in 1803, but assumed them again, in 1806. The British did not fare much better than the Dutch in dealing with the Xhosa, and under British control the region continued to be wracked by violent armed conflicts until the late 1800s.

During the 1820s drought, famine, and scarce resources caused warrior NGUNI groups from southern Africa's eastern region to begin campaigns of territorial expansion. Among the groups involved in these migrations were the Nguni-speaking Ndwandwe, Ngwane, Mthethwa, and Zulu. Led by their storied chief SHAKA (1787–1828), the Zulu emerged victorious and forced the other groups to leave the region. The Ndwandwe moved north into Mozambique to found the Gaza state and the Ngwane were pushed west to found the Swazi kingdom. The powerful Ndebele kingdom was also founded at this time by MZILIKAZI (1790–1868), a Khumalo chief. This time of forced migration of people from southeast Africa was called MFECANE, or "The Crushing."

Throughout the 19th century the British controlled Cape Colony and adopted laws that restricted Boer movement and expansion. The Boers reacted by moving further inland, establishing permanent European settlements in the interior, which they defended tenaciously against attacks by Xhosa-speaking groups. The pattern of rule by the white European minority over the indigenous black majority led to the colonial race troubles that plagued South Africa into the late 20th century.

See also: CAPE COLOURED PEOPLE (Vol. IV); SLAVERY IN SOUTH AFRICA (Vol. III); SOUTH AFRICA (Vols. I, II, IV, V).

Further reading: Robert Ross, *A Concise History of South Africa* (New York: Cambridge University Press, 1999); Leonard Thompson, *A History of South Africa* (New Haven, Conn.: Yale University Press, 2001).

Soyo (Mbanza Soyo, Sonyo)

Kongo settlement, located on the African Atlantic coast just south of the Congo River, that declared its independence in the 17th century. By the 1600s, the town of Soyo, with a population of 30,000 by the end of the 17th century, was the largest in the Kongo after SÃO SALVADOR. An independent court consisting of a prince, his royal household, and other titled nobility ruled the region. The nobility owned large plantations outside the city and supported a powerful military force. Soyo was also an important trading center for ivory, cloth, copper, and animal skins from the interior. The city competed with LOANGO for control of these lucrative trade items.

After Soyo declared its independence from the KONGO KINGDOM, in 1636, the Kongo kings waged war with the province to try to bring it back under their control. Soyo was victorious with the help of firearms that they purchased from the Dutch, who traded heavily at the port of Mpinda. The English, Portuguese, and eventually the French also traded there. Along with LUANDA, Mpinda was the main port for shipping captives from the Kongo kingdom to the Americas during the 17th century.

By the 1640s Soyo's independence from the kingdom was reluctantly recognized by the Kongo kingdom. The province soon became a refuge for challengers to the sovereignty of São Salvador (formerly Mbanza Kongo), the capital of the Kongo kingdom, and its armies sacked that city during the succession disputes of the latter half of the 17th century. After the subsequent decline of São Salvador, the city of Soyo was the only large urban settlement in the Kongo region.

See also: MBANZA KONGO (Vol. II); PORTUGAL AND AFRICA (Vol. III).

Spain and Africa

Spanish activity in Africa throughout the 16th, 17th, and 18th centuries was limited. While Spain continued to battle various Muslim factions throughout North Africa, they were never able to gain more than a few coastal footholds in the region. Most of Spain's interest in Africa at this time lay in their need to supply a workforce for the plantations in their New World possessions. In 1580 Portugal became a holding of the Spanish Crown, so Spain was able to rely on Portuguese naval superiority to help feed their insatiable demand for captive LABOR. Consequently Spanish ports developed into leading centers of the trade in human beings.

Previously a Portuguese outpost, the town of CEUTA on the Mediterranean coast of MOROCCO became a Spanish holding in 1580 (and was still administered by Spain in the early 21st century). From Ceuta, Spain supplemented the Portuguese raids against Africans with raids of their own on North African Muslim populations. Spain's contributions to the era of European colonization in Africa in the 19th century were minimal.

See also: ANDALUS, AL- (Vol. II); ALMOHADS (Vol. II); ALMORAVIDS (Vol. II); CHARLES V, EMPEROR (Vol. III); CRUSADES, THE (Vol. II); PORTUGAL AND AFRICA (Vol. III); SPAIN AND AFRICA (Vol. IV).

Stuart, John

See CUGOANO, OTTABAH.

Suakin (Sawakin)

Trading port located on the Red Sea coast of present-day Republic of the SUDAN. Before 1500 Suakin served as trading center, especially for the export of Sudanese captives to Arabia and the Middle East. For nearly three centuries, Suakin competed with the nearby port of Aidhab, but Aidhab was destroyed in 1428. Suakin then flourished as the most important port on the Red Sea coast. It also became a major stopover point for African pilgrims heading across the Red Sea to Mecca, on the Arabian Peninsula. Suakin continued to prosper as Indian, Persian, Chinese, and Portuguese merchants met there to trade cloth, glass beads, and spices for humans, gum, incense, and ivory.

Beginning in the 16th century, Turks of the Ottoman Empire in EGYPT dominated commercial activity at Suakin. Throughout the 18th century FUNJ sultans from SENNAR, in present-day Republic of the Sudan, used Suakin as their main port. In the 19th century, however, Suakin lost much of its trade as a result of Sennar's decline, Red Sea PIRATES, and political pressure from the Turks.

See also: MECCA (Vol. II); RED SEA (Vol. I); RED SEA TRADE (Vol. II); SLAVERY (Vol. III).

Sudan, Republic of the

Country measuring 966,800 square miles (2,504,000 sq km) located in northeastern

Africa. It is bordered by EGYPT and LIBYA to the north; ETHIOPIA and ERITREA to the east; KENYA, UGANDA, and the Democratic Republic of the CONGO to the south; and CHAD and the CENTRAL AFRICAN REPUBLIC to the west. Sudan is the largest country in Africa. KHARTOUM is its largest city and capital.

By the end of the 15th century the armies of the MAMLUKS in Egypt had moved south and overtaken the Christian kingdom of Nubia. But in the early 1500s the Ottoman Empire conquered Egypt, driving the Mamluks into their northern Nubia stronghold. The Turks pursued the Mamluks and established Ottoman rule along the Nubian coast of the Red Sea. Ottoman power, however, did not effectively extend further inland, and the Turks relied on the conquered Mamluks to maintain peace in the interior.

Meanwhile, Amara Dunqas (fl. early 1500s) established the FUNJ kingdom farther south, in SENNAR, in 1504. During his reign Dunqas adopted Islam, which quickly spread throughout the region. The Funj gained control of the major trade routes that ran between West Africa, Ethiopia, and Egypt. Their prosperity allowed them to rule over much of present-day eastern Sudan into the 18th century.

In 1596 the independent DARFUR emerged to the west of the Funj kingdom. Darfur became a powerful and prosperous state by controlling the trans-Saharan trade routes to KANEM-BORNU, near Lake CHAD. Important trade goods included salt, ivory, and humans. Led by SULIMAN SOLONG (r. c. 1640–1680), the FUR sultanate established Islam as its official RELIGION in the 17th century, and by the 18th century most of the surrounding region also was Muslim.

See also: KASSALA (Vol. III); KORDOFAN (Vol. III); NUBIA, CHRISTIAN (Vol. II); SUDAN, REPUBLIC OF THE (Vols. I, II, IV, V); SUDAN, THE (Vol. II).

Sufism Religious movement within Islam that emphasizes mysticism and personal interaction with God. Sufism emerged in the Middle East during the seventh century and had spread to the African continent by the 12th century. It was a common Islamic movement by the 1800s. While some scholars consider Sufism to have non-Islamic roots, most modern historians attribute its development to ascetic Muslim sects.

The mystical component of Sufism is central to its followers, who believe that a personal connection with God is attainable through loyalty and a strict humility. The road to mystic enlightenment begins with repenting for one's sins. The Sufi would then follow the orders of a mystical guide (sheikh), who encourages meditation, abstinence, renunciation, and poverty.

The final stage of a Sufi's conversion to asceticism is *marifah* (interior knowledge), the union of God and his follower. A euphoric sensation reportedly follows, until ultimately the Sufi's whole self is transformed into a remembrance of God. In this final and ideal state (as a *shaykh*), the Sufi believes that meditation can transport him between the human and spiritual worlds, enabling him to perform miracles.

The sheikhs pass down their divine knowledge to other followers through a series of initiation rites. Followers can then begin the arduous process toward asceticism. The relationship between sheikh and pupil paralleled the relationships found in lineage societies, thus making Sufism particularly popular in these societies.

During the 1700s Sufism spread throughout sub-Saharan Africa. In the 19th century Sufism made its way through West Africa, where its stability and hierarchical structure made it popular among nomadic Muslims. Many of the leaders of the FULANI JIHADS of the 19th century in West Africa were members of Sufi brotherhoods. The purpose of these jihads was to convert the unbeliever and to restore the fervor and orthodoxy of Muslims whose observance of Islamic law had become lax. The founders of the Muslim state of FOUTA DJALLON, including the influential cleric Alfa Ba (fl. 1725), were members of the large, loosely organized QADIRIYYA Sufi brotherhood, the oldest Sufi order in Islam, which traces its origins to the preaching of 12th-century cleric Abd al-Qadir al-Jilani (1078–1166) in Baghdad. USMAN DAN FODIO (1754– 1817), the founder of the powerful SOKOTO CALIPHATE (1808–1903), was also a member of the Qadiriyya order. Ahamadu ibn Hammadi (c. 1745–1844), who preached the jihad that led to the foundation of the Muslim state of MACINA, near TIMBUKTU, and Umar Tal (c. 1797–1864), the founder of the vast Muslim TUKULOR empire, were both members of the fundamentalist Tijaniyya brotherhood, founded about 1781 in FEZ, MOROCCO, by Ahmad al-Tijani (1737–1815). The Tijaniyya order became the largest and most influential Sufi brotherhood in West Africa.

See also: ISLAM, INFLUENCE OF (Vols. III, IV, V); SUFISM (Vols. II, IV); UMAR TAL (Vol. IV).

Suliman Solong (Sulayman Solondungu) (r. c. 1640–1660) *First Muslim sultan of Darfur, in present-day Republic of the Sudan*

In the early 17th century Suliman Solong successfully conquered the TUNJUR peoples, a group that had ruled the kingdom of DARFUR since the 13th century. He proclaimed himself sultan about 1640, made Islam the official RELIGION, and successfully established Darfur as a Muslim sultanate. The FUR, after whom Darfur is named, have worn Arab dress and taken Arab names ever since Suliman Solong's reign.

Although Islamic influences had already become increasingly present in the western Sudan, Suliman Solong was credited with incorporating Muslim practices and giving the religion a strong foundation in the region. Known as a great warrior, he also carved larger boundaries for his sultanate by conducting battles, with the help of Arab nomads, around the territory of the Jebel Marra Mountains, the highest region of the Sudan. After his death, around 1660, his heirs created the beginnings of a powerful Islamic ruling family, known as the KAYRA DYNASTY, which ruled Darfur, with a brief interruption between 1874 and 1898, until 1916.

The son of an Arab woman, Suliman Solong brought Arabic dress and customs to Darfur, thereby earning him the nickname "The Arab."

See also: ARABS, INFLUENCE OF (Vol. II); ISLAM, INFLUENCE OF (Vol. III).

Sumbwa Ethnic group long residing in present-day TANZANIA. Although the Sumbwa have traditionally maintained that they originate from the Bantu-speaking Ha people, Sumbwa political and social structures are much more like those of the NYAMWEZI than those of the Ha. They practice traditional African RELIGION.

During the late 18th and early 19th centuries the Sumbwa became great traders, transporting the copper and copper products, for which they were well known, from present-day KATANGA Province in the Democratic Republic of the CONGO to western Tanzania. They also were early practitioners of the IVORY TRADE.

See also: COPPER (Vols. I, II); COPPER MINES (Vol. II).

Susu (Soso, Soussou, Soosoo) West African ethnic group located in present-day SIERRA LEONE, GUINEA, and SENEGAL. The Susu had migrated to the FOUTA DJALLON region of what is now Guinea in the 15th century, but they were soon displaced by waves of FULANI peoples moving into the area. During the early 16th century the Susu were mainly located on the coastal regions of Guinea and Sierra Leone, where they were involved with other coastal peoples in the trade of cloth, GOLD, salt, and iron. By the mid-16th century clashes with an inland group from Sierra Leone, known as Manes or Sumbas (meaning "cannibals"), led the Susu to begin trading northwards at the Rio Nuñez. Although the Susu were strongly tied to their animist RELIGION, many were converted to Islam during the FULANI JIHADS led by Ibrahim Sori (fl. 1725) and Karamoko Alfa (r. 1725–1750), which swept the Fouta Djallon and beyond beginning in 1727. By the late 18th century the Susu kings had all converted to Islam, and the Susu had become intermediaries in the growing trade in human beings.

See also: ISLAM, INFLUENCE OF (Vol. III); SUSU (Vol. II).

Swahili Coast Area along the East African shoreline on the Indian Ocean. Generally, the term refers to both the coastal area proper and to the adjacent islands, including the COMOROS and the LAMU archipelago and the islands of MOMBASA, PEMBA, ZANZIBAR, Mafia, and Kerimba.

When the Portuguese first sailed north along the Swahili Coast in 1498, after rounding the Cape of Good Hope, they were amazed at the wealth of the coastal cities and the extent of their trade. Determined to seize control of it, they sailed into the harbors of the important towns, their ships bristling with cannons, and threatened to bombard the shore if their demands for tribute were not met. The year 1505 saw even more determined attacks on the towns of the Swahili Coast. After pillaging the towns, the Portuguese established forts at KILWA, SOFALA, and MOZAMBIQUE, thus gaining control of the coastal GOLD trade between Sofala and the highland plateau of present-day ZIMBABWE.

History The Swahili Coast had its "golden age" some time after the 13th century, and this period lasted until approximately the 15th century. When the Portuguese arrived, around 1498, they found a thriving culture along the East African coast, one with learning, wealth, and power. Indeed, Swahili entrepreneurs had created a complex society successfully amalgamating African and Asian elements as well as the input and contributions of wave after wave of new immigrants.

Swahili power was essentially economic and cultural, not military, and the Swahili proved no match for the better-armed Portuguese, who were more interested in conquest and possession than in establishing trading relationships. After a brief period the Portuguese began capturing city after city, beginning with Kilwa, which fell to them in 1505. In their campaign, which was based on the notions of displacing Islam and taking possession of both the gold and spice trade, the Portuguese carried out a ruthless policy of looting towns, while selling some inhabitants into forced LABOR and massacring others.

In spite of this, Portuguese control was never very successful. The Portuguese lacked the numbers to enforce their system and authority over such a vast area. As a result, although they managed to collect tribute from local rulers and demand those rulers' declaration of fealty to the Portuguese king, they were unable to control smuggling and other activities that demonstrated Swahili independence. Beyond this, the Swahili, the MIJIKENDA, and others adopted, probably without planning, a policy of noncooperation that slowed the East African ECONOMY to the point that even the Sofala gold mines—which had produced vast fortunes—were barely profitable under Portuguese control.

By the late 17th century the Portuguese were losing influence in the region, and, with the help of the Omanis, the Swahili gradually took back control. By 1729 the Portuguese were gone, never—except for a brief revival a few years later—to return.

Unfortunately for the Africans the Omanis increasingly took control over East Africa themselves, so the resurgence of Swahili independence was short-lived. As a result the Swahili Coast became, in effect, part of the OMANI SULTANATE, a situation that lasted into the 19th century.

Some historians suggest that the decline of Swahili culture and power was caused by the Portuguese conquest, which they point to as having destroyed a thriving culture. Others, however, believe that Swahili culture was, for various reasons, already on the decline when the Portuguese arrived. Scholars taking this view point, for example, cite a widespread drought that affected the area before the arrival of the Portuguese in 1498. This, they note, forced people to dig canals for irrigation, to relocate, and to take other steps to provide themselves with the water they needed for survival. Ultimately, the drought led to a flight into the few usable lands that remained, creating a competition for land and water that resulted in increased conflict and, at times, open warfare. Instead of the peaceful competition between city-states that had dominated East Africa for centuries, by the beginning of the 16th century Pate was battling with Lamu, MALINDI was fighting against Mombasa, and Kilwa was in conflict with Sofala over the control of the gold and ivory trades.

Regardless of whether the Portuguese were solely responsible for the decline of the Swahili Coast or whether they ultimately accentuated and sped up a process that was already in progress, the result was the same. Trade declined, and the general prosperity that had long marked the region vanished. Local industries along the coast foundered to the point that even the once-thriving weaving industry of Pate, MOGADISHU, Mombasa, and Kilwa were destroyed, and the people of those cities were reduced to dependence upon textiles imported from India. Ironwork—once so important to Malindi, Sofala, and other city-states—also stopped. In time, the people of city-states like Mombasa, Barawa, and Sofala—once merchants and independent farmers—were reduced to making straw mats and baskets for sale to the Portuguese.

With the expulsion of the Portuguese in the early 18th century, and the arrival of the Omanis, the situation improved, and the coast revived. Although it never quite regained the levels that it had had before the 16th century, it once again became a commercial and cultural center.

See also: SWAHILI COAST (Vols. II, IV).

Further reading: Chapurukha M. Kusimba, *The Rise and Fall of the Swahili States* (Walnut Creek, Calif.: Altamira Press, 1999); John Middleton, *The World of the Swahili* (New Haven, Conn.: Yale University Press, 1992); Michael N. Pearson, *Port Cities and Intruders: The Swahili Coast, India, and Portugal in the Early Modern Era* (Baltimore, Md.: Johns Hopkins University Press, 1998).

Swazi Ethnic group living in SWAZILAND and in parts of SOUTH AFRICA. The Swazi descended from the Ngwane, a NGUNI subgroup. In the 19th century the Ngwane fled the MFECANE, an era of territorial expansion by the militant ZULU, led by SHAKA (1787–1828). The Ngwane ruler of the time, Sobhuza, wisely appeased Shaka and led his people to the central highlands of present-day Swaziland. Once there Sobhuza brought together a number of clans and began centralizing his power. By the 1840s Sobhuza's son and successor, MSWATI I (1820–1868), was recognized by his British allies as the rightful king of his people, the Swazi. Throughout the rest of the 19th century and into the era of European colonialism, Britain helped Mswati defend his kingdom against Zulu aggression. Today the Swazi number at least 1,000,000. They speak Sati, a Bantu language related to Zulu.

Swaziland Officially known as the Kingdom of Swaziland, country measuring approximately 6,700 square miles (17,400 sq km) located in southern Africa. It is bordered to the north, west and south by SOUTH AFRICA and to the east by MOZAMBIQUE.

In about 1750, people of the Ngwane clan left the MAPUTO area and settled in northern Zululand (present-day eastern South Africa). Unable to compete with the ZULU for territorial supremacy, they moved north and, in the 1800s, settled in present-day Swaziland. They were united under several strong leaders. Their most important leader was King MSWATI I (1820–1868), from whom they got their name. Mswati I ruled in the 1840s and expanded their kingdom to the north and south. In order to safeguard his kingdom against Zulu raids, Mswati asked the British authorities in South Africa for assistance. The subsequent agreements with the British in South Africa led to British claims on resources, and administrative authority. Boers, too, made claims on SWAZI territory until 1902, when Britain won the Anglo-Boer War and assumed control.

See also: SWAZILAND (Vols. I, II, IV, V).

Further reading: J. S. M. Matsebula, *A History of Swaziland* (Cape Town, South Africa: Longman Southern Africa, 1972).

Swellendam Third-oldest town in SOUTH AFRICA and former Boer republic located in present-day Western Cape

Province. Situated on the Breede River Valley, the town was first established in 1743 by the DUTCH EAST INDIA COMPANY and was named for Hendrik Swellengrebel— governor of CAPE TOW from 1739 to 1751—and his wife. In 1795 a local Boer revolt against the authority of the East India Company led to the dismissal of a company magistrate and the establishment of Swellendam as a Boer republic. The republic lasted three months, until the British occupied the Cape later that same year.

T

Tabora (Kazeh) Capital of the NYAMWEZI people; located in the west-central part of what is now TANZANIA. Officially founded in 1852, Tabora was an important part of the trade linking peoples of the Congo basin, to the west, with merchants on the SWAHILI COAST of East Africa. The Nyamwezi, also known as the Banyamwezi, brought iron, copper, salt, ivory, and captives from the interior to the coast. These items were exchanged for Arabian cloth, spices, tools, and firearms. In later centuries, this trade represented an important supplement to the primarily agricultural economy of the Bantu-speaking Nyamwezi.

See also: NYAMWEZI (Vols. III, IV); MIRAMBO (Vol. IV).

Tananarive (Antananarivo) City located in the central highlands of MADAGASCAR that was the capital of the MERINA empire. Formerly known as Analamanga, Tananarive is located on an isolated plateau near the Ikopa River. Its location allowed the local Merina to avoid the influence of the SAKALAVA people, who created an empire as they conquered most of the western half of the island of Madagascar in the 17th century. Tananarive became the official center of the Merina kingdom about the end of the 18th century, when King ANDRIANAMPOINIMERINA (r. c. 1782–1810) used the city as the location for his government, courts, and land administration. Under Andrianampoinimerina, the city was fortified and transformed into the center of a flourishing Merina culture.

Andrianampoinimerina was suspicious of foreign influence in the capital and didn't allow interested European powers, especially the French and British, to establish a presence there. However, under Radama I (r. 1810–1828), Andrianampoinimerina's successor, the Merina were more tolerant of foreign influence, and during the early 19th century the capital was home to several European MISSIONARIES, among them English Protestants and French Jesuits.

> The city, which is the capital of the modern Republic of Madagascar, was renamed Antanana-rivo in 1977, under the revolutionary socialist regime of Didier Ratsiraka (1936–   ).

Tangier Port city and capital of present-day MOROCCO and an important trading post for over 2,000 years. Situated on a limestone hill between the Atlantic Ocean and Mediterranean Sea, Tangier was founded by Phoenician traders in ancient times. Romans, Vandals, Byzantines, Visigoths, and Arabs subsequently ruled it. Under Arab rule, which lasted from 682 to 1471, Tangier became an important trade center and royal city.

In 1471 the Portuguese and Spanish battled for control of this strategically positioned town. The Portuguese were victorious and continued to rule Tangier until 1662, when the Portuguese princess Catherine of Braganza transferred control of Tangier to England upon her marriage to Charles II of England (r. 1660–1685). During their brief 25-year rule, the English built extensive forts around the ancient town.

The fall of Tangier in Morocco to a European army. The city was occupied by the Spanish and the Portuguese until 1662. The tapestry is from the 15th century. © *Archivo Iconogtafico, S.A./Corbis*

In 1684 the Moroccan sultan, MAWLAY ISMAIL (c. 1645–1727), staged a successful trade blockade, forcing the English to return Tangier to Morocco. Although British trade still dominated the Tangier economy, the city flourished under Moroccan control and became its capital, in the 19th century.

Morocco became a French protectorate, in 1912, but Tangier was spared French rule. It was granted special status as an international zone jointly governed by Britain, France, Spain, Portugal, Italy, Belgium, the Netherlands, and Sweden.

See also: ENGLAND AND AFRICA (Vols. III, IV, V); PORTUGAL AND AFRICA (Vols. III, IV, V).

Tanzania Country measuring approximately 342,100 square miles (886,000 sq km) that includes ZANZIBAR, PEMBA ISLAND, and Mafia Island, all located offshore, in the Indian Ocean. Mainland Tanzania borders UGANDA and KENYA to the north, the Indian Ocean to the east, MOZAMBIQUE, MALAWI, and ZAMBIA to the south, and the Democratic Republic of the CONGO, BURUNDI, and RWANDA to the west. DAR ES SALAAM is the capital and largest city.

The arrival of the Portuguese at the end of the 15th century undermined Arab dominance in the region. In contrast to the earlier Arab immigrants, who had developed an extensive trading network that reached into the interior, the Portuguese did not develop positive relations with the indigenous peoples. As a result Portuguese influence led to the disruption of both town life and trade and ultimately to a general decline.

At the end of the 16th century a group from southeastern Africa, the ZIMBA, began a violent incursion along the coast. This drove many groups into the interior, where they mingled with what was left of the older population as well as with new immigrants who were arriving from southern Arabia and the Persian Gulf. The exact makeup of such groups, however, including those living farther in the interior, is not precisely known. Indeed the only group specifically mentioned by the Portuguese were the Sageju, who were located near the city-state of MALINDI.

Many of the groups associated with Tanzania's interior—ranging from the Taita and CHAGGA to the SHAMBAA and KIKUYU—identify a town known as SHUNGWAYA as their origin. This common origin seems unlikely, however, since few of these people exhibit the traditions of centralized kingship and Islam associated with Shungwaya.

In 1698 the Portuguese were defeated by a combination of local forces and Arabs from the OMANI SULTANATE. This, except for a brief Portuguese revival around the year 1725, ushered in what amounted to a second period of Arab ascendancy, this time under the aegis of the sultans of Oman. Omani influence increased during the 18th century with the rise to power of the BUSAIDI dynasty, in Oman, and the appearance on the political scene of the MASRUI family, in ZANZIBAR. This reached its culmination during the reign of Sultan SAYYID SAID (1791–1856), who not only solidified Omani power in East Africa but eventually transferred his capital from Muscat to Zanzibar. This period saw the development of trade and the growth of wealth in many parts of the region, as new caravan routes began to cross the interior and commerce in GOLD, captives, and ivory increased. In fact it was the possibility of participating in this commerce that began to draw European colonial powers back to the region as the 19th century continued.

See also: ARABS, INFLUENCE OF (Vols. II, III); INDIAN OCEAN TRADE (Vol. II); SWAHILI COAST (Vols. II, III, IV); TANZANIA (Vols. I, II, IV, V).

Further reading: John Iliffe, et al., *A Modern History of Tanzania* (Cambridge, U.K.: Cambridge University Press, 1979).

Ta'rikh al-Fattash Narrative of the western Sudan region written in the 16th century. Although the work is attributed mostly to the Islamic scholar Mahmud Kati (b. 1468), it was actually completed by Kati's sons and grandsons. *Ta'rikh al-Fattash* means "history of the seeker of knowledge," and the book chronicles the history of the empires of Ghana (fl. ninth–11th centuries) and Mali (fl. 12th–15th centuries), both of which were located primarily in present-day Republic of MALI.

Kati was part of the entourage that accompanied Askia (King) Muhammad Touré (r. 1493–1528) of the SONGHAI Empire on his journey to Mecca. In his writing Kati details the life and reign of this influential ruler. He then goes on to relate the history of the Sudan, describing in detail how, in 1591, an invading Moroccan army used their European firearms to topple Songhai and take control of the crucial trading city of TIMBUKTU.

While the *Ta'rikh al-Fattash* was widely known throughout the Muslim world, it was not as accessible to Europeans as the *TA'RIKH AL-SUDAN*. This other 17th-century chronicle was written by the scholar Abd al-Rahman SADI (c. 1569–1655), who, like Mahmud Kati, was born in Timbuktu and educated at that city's famed institution of Islamic learning, SANKORE UNIVERSITY.

See also: MUHAMMAD TOURÉ, ASKIA (Vol II); HISTORICAL SCHOLARSHIP ON AFRICA (Vols. IV, V); SUDAN, THE (Vol. II).

Ta'rikh al-Sudan   Text written in the early to mid-17th century by the Muslim scholar Abd al-Rahman SADI (c. 1569–1655); its title means "History (or Chronicle) of the Sudan." The work eventually became the best-known historical reference to events taking place in the western Sudan region from the mid-15th to the late 17th centuries.

Dealing with the region that became present-day Republic of MALI and NIGER and focusing on events that occurred from about 1464 to well into the 17th century, *Ta'rikh al-Sudan* narrates the rise and fall of the SONGHAI Empire and its various rulers. The *Ta'rikh al-Sudan* also recounts the shaping of some of the major cities that came into contact with the Songhai, including the well-known trading towns of TIMBUKTU and JENNE, both of which were located in what is now the Rpublic of Mali. Indeed, since the *Ta'rikh al-Sudan* was popular in the Muslim areas of Africa and, later, became the basis of early European knowledge of the history of western Sudan, this chronicle represents the source for much of what we know about these two merchant centers.

Sadi himself was born in Timbuktu and attended the city's prestigious SANKORE UNIVERSITY, where he studied Islam before he began writing the *Ta'rikh al-Sudan*. These personal roots played an important part in Sadi's writing, since he claimed in his preface that his purpose for writing the *Ta'rikh al-Sudan* was to chronicle the life of his homeland in the wake of the devastation caused by the Moroccan invasion of Timbuktu, in 1591.

It is likely that many Europeans assumed the *Ta'rikh al-Sudan* was written by another well-known Muslim scholar, Ahmad Baba (b. 1556), who wrote texts that are still in use today. In 1853, however, the identity of the true author became known when the the German geographer and explorer Heinrich Barth found the original manuscript of Sadi's work in the city of Guandu, in present-day NIGERIA.

See also: HISTORICAL SCHOLARSHIP ON AFRICA (Vols. IV, V); SUDAN, THE (Vol. II); *TA'RIKH AL-FATTASH* (Vol. III).

Tegbesu (Tegbisu, Bossa Ahadee) (r. 1740–1774)
King of Dahomey

When King AGAJA (1708–1732) of DAHOMEY died, a bitter fight for succession ensued. King Tegbesu was elected to the throne in 1740. To secure his position, he assassinated or sold into SLAVERY all of his rivals and their followers, as well as anyone who had the potential to threaten his kingship. He changed the rules of succession, stating that only direct descendents of a ruler could be in line for the throne and that the king could choose which of his sons would succeed him. Tegbesu also implemented the *Ilari* system of the OYO EMPIRE into his government. *Ilaris* were messengers, easily recognizable because they shaved half their heads, who carried messages back and forth from the coast. In addition, they spied on the various Dahomey chiefs and reported their activities back to Tegbesu.

Tegbesu inherited an impoverished kingdom that continually suffered from attacks from Oyo for not paying its annual tribute. In 1748 Tegbesu signed a treaty with Oyo, which, according to oral tradition, stipulated that Dahomey owed a yearly tribute of "40 men, 40 women, 40 guns, and 400 loads of cowries and corals." Despite being tributary to Oyo, Dahomey still had some autonomy, especially in regards to its military. In an attempt to improve the economy of Dahomey, Tegbesu tried to expand his trade routes. He decided to attack the Mahi people, a FON subgroup living to the north, along what is now the border between TOGO and the Republic of BENIN, because the Mahi's heavy tariffs were cutting into Dahomey's profits from the slave trade. Though Tegbesu managed to conquer the Mahi, Dahomey's position in the slave trade continued to decline. By the time of Tegbesu's death, in 1774, the economic situation had reached a desperate point. Tegbesu was succeeded by his son KPENGLA (r. 1774–1789).

Teke (Bateke)   Bantu-speaking ethnic group that occupied the region north of the Malebo Pool, near Brazzaville in the modern Republic of the CONGO. The Teke, whose kingdom was called *Anziko*, are related to the neighboring KONGO, Woyo, Kunyi, Bembe, and Vili people. In the 16th century the Teke developed a reputation as a fractious and independent people, rebelling against the domination of LOANGO and the KONGO KINGDOMS.

With their independence secured, in the 17th century the Teke became influential traders. The coastal Loango kingdom to their west had established trading ties with Portuguese and Dutch merchants, who wanted ivory to bring back to Europe. (By that time, ivory was in short supply on the coast, since elephants had been hunted for centuries.) Loango employed the Teke as intermediaries between them and the ivory hunters from the interior, thereby exposing the Teke to European manufactured goods and bringing the Teke into the European trade circles. The Teke also supplied Loango with large amounts of copper, which they mined on the Teke Plateau using slave LABOR. During the era of European colonialism, in the 19th century, the Teke kingdom fell within a French protectorate.

See also: COPPER (Vols. I, II, IV); FRANCE AND AFRICA (Vols. III, IV, V); IVORY TRADE (Vol. III); PROTECTORATE (Vol. IV).

Tekla Haymonot (Takla Haymanot, Tekla Haimanot) (r. c. 1706–1708) *Ethiopian king*

Tekla Haymonot's father was known to his subjects as IYASU I (Iyasu the Great) and was the most celebrated Ethiopian king of his time. Iyasu I was a stellar military leader who often participated in expeditions that took him away from his capital at GONDAR. Upon arriving home from one of his campaigns, he was informed that his favorite concubine had died. Deeply saddened by the news, he fled to a remote island on Lake Tana.

Tekla Haymonot took advantage of his father's absence and enlisted the support of his mother, Malakotawit, to seize the throne. Upon hearing of his son's and wife's betrayal, Iyasu I tried to reclaim his throne but to no avail. Tekla Haymonot protected his position as emperor by having his father murdered. His reign was met with a great deal of hostility, and it marked the beginning of an unstable period in the Ethiopian monarchy that lasted several decades. Tekla Haymonot himself was killed in, 1708, by followers of Iyasu I.

See also: ETHIOPIA (Vol. III).

Tekyiman (Techiman, Takyiman) City and trading center of the AKAN people, located in the central Brong-Ahafo region of present-day GHANA. Tekyiman was a major trade destination along a route that led northwest from the kingdom of DENKYIRA. The lands around this kingdom produced large amounts of GOLD, which were then shipped on the northwest route to Tekyiman and BEGHO, another Akan trading city, to be traded for other African and European goods.

The FANTE people of the coastal regions of present-day Ghana are also linked to Tekyiman, as the city enters into part of their foundation legend. While the time frame of the legend is uncertain, ranging between the 15th to the 17th centuries, Fante oral tradition states that the warrior leaders Obrumankoma, Odapagyan, and Oson led their ancestors from Tekyiman to their present locations along the southern Ghanaian coast.

Beginning about 1698 OSEI TUTU (r. c. 1650–1717), the king of the ASHANTI EMPIRE, began a four-year war to conquer Denkyira. His purpose was to obtain the rights to the trade routes reaching Tekyiman and Begho, as well as to the lucrative Denkyira gold-producing lands. He also aimed to control another trade route running northeast to the city of Kafaba. While Osei Tutu's war destroyed the Denkyira kingdom, the city of Tekyiman did not come under Ashanti rule until it was conquered during the reign of OPOKUWARE II (r. 1720–1750).

Tenda (Tanda) Western Atlantic ethnic group native to eastern SENEGAL and the area along the Gambia River that they still inhabit. The agriculturalist Tenda are related to the Coniagui (Konagi), Bassari, Badyaranke, Bedik, and Jalonke peoples. The region of the Gambia beyond Barrakunda Falls in which they lived was sometimes known as DYULA country because of the large number of Muslim Dyula traders who settled there. From the 15th century on, a brisk trade in slaves, salt, wax, and animal skins existed along the coast.

The commerce of the region was heavily reliant on the fortunes of the SONGHAI Empire, its main trading partner, in what is now the Republic of MALI. In the 17th century, when this important trading state fell to musket-bearing armies from MOROCCO, the local trade routes were redirected to KANO, in what is now northern NIGERIA, and to WADAI, in present-day CHAD. The loss of these routes had a devastating impact on the Tenda economy.

For most of the 18th and 19th centuries the fundamentalist Muslim state of FOUTA DJALLON raided the animist Tenda, selling captives from these attacks into slavery. Subsequently many Tenda fled to mountainous regions in southeastern Senegal and GUINEA-BISSAU.

Tengella (r. c. 1490–c. 1512) *Fulani ruler and founder of the Denianke dynasty in Fouta Toro at the end of the 15th century*

Tengella and his son Koly Tengella (fl. c. 1530) were members of the pastoralist FULANI group that had been migrating southwards from the Termes since the 13th century in search of suitable grazing lands and water. For centuries, the Fulani, who settled in FOUTA TORO, BONDU, MACINA, and FOUTA DJALLON, lived under the rule of indigenous chiefs who generally fell under the sovereignty of the great Mali Empire. Eventually Tengella organized his army in an effort to conquer all of SENEGAL, moving northwards from Fouta Djallon.

Between 1481 and 1512 Tengella encountered opposition from Mande-speaking peoples as he expanded his Fulani territory. After crossing the Gambia River and occupying Bondu, Tengella and his son separated, with Koly continuing northward to conquer Fouta Toro. Tengella, on the other hand, traveled east toward the kingdom of Zara, which had been under siege by Umar Komzagho (fl. 1500), a prince of the SONGHAI Empire.

Tengella was killed in a confrontation with the Gao army, part of the Songhai forces, when invading Umar Komzagho's state. According to the TA'RIKH AL-SUDAN, Tengella died around 1511 or 1512; the TA'RIKH AL-FATTASH lists the date of his death as 1512 or 1513.

In an attempt to give the Denianke line of rulers a more legitimate history, Fulani peoples later claimed that Koly Tengella was actually a descendent of Sundiata Keita (d. 1255), the founder of the Mali Empire.

In Fouta Toro, Koly Tengella encountered lesser chiefs who, after freeing themselves from Mali, had become quarrelsome and divided. Taking advantage of these fractious chiefs, Koly invaded Fouta Toro, settling in the capital of Anyam Godo. Koly later attacked the Jolof kingdom, killing its king, and went on to conquer territories of the Moors and the WOLOF EMPIRE. The DENIANKE DYNASTY ruled over Fouta Toro until the first half of the 18th century.

See also: MALI EMPIRE (Vol. II); MANDE (Vols. I, II, IV); SUNDIATA (Vol. II).

Tete (Nhungue) Town on the banks of the ZAMBEZI RIVER, in present-day MOZAMBIQUE; it was established as a Portuguese trading center, in the 1530s. The town may have previously existed as a Zambezi settlement of Onhaquoro, though evidence is inconclusive.

The Portuguese, who began trading in southern East Africa shortly after their arrival at the beginning of the 16th century, settled in Tete in an effort to control the GOLD trade. They had previously attempted to dominate the market through their port in SOFALA, but Muslim and Swahili traders simply diverted their gold-trade routes to bypass that port city. Tete, located about 185 miles (298 km) up the Zambezi from its mouth on the Indian Ocean, was established to intercept this trade and to position the Portuguese closer to the gold sources, mostly in the kingdom of the MWENE MUTAPA. Goods brought to the Tete fairs were traded as far away as KALONGA territories, to the north, near Lake Malawi.

In 1575 the Portuguese established trade relations with the Mwene Mutapa, and they were subsequently granted exclusive gold-trade rights. Gold flowed freely along the Portuguese trade routes through Tete to the coast for export. However, the influence of the Portuguese seriously weakened the Mwene Mutapa kingdom, and toward the end of the 17th century the formerly glorious kingdom fell victim to the more militaristic ROZWI king-dom. The Rozwi also mounted a serious challenge to the Portuguese traders, eventually driving them from the region. This enabled the Rozwi to dominate the area and end Tete's importance as a gold port.

See also: PORTUGAL AND AFRICA (Vol. III).

Thaba Bosiu (Thaba Bosigo) Settlement in the Drakensberg Mountains of present-day LESOTHO, from which emerged the kingdom of SOTHO. During the MFECANE of the early 1820s, the ZULU drove thousands of Sotho people, also known as Basotho, from their homelands. MSHWESHWE (c. 1815–1870), leader of the Kwena clan, united these Sotho refugees and relocated them to Thaba Bosiu. Located on a mountaintop plateau, Thaba Bosiu proved to be unassailable by enemy forces. From this mountain fortress Mshweshwe was able to expand his kingdom to include all of present-day Lesotho and parts of the Orange Free State.

See also: BASUTOLAND (Vol. IV); ORANGE FREE STATE (Vol. IV).

Tibesti (Tibesti Mountains, Tibesti Massif) Mountainous region in the northern part of present-day CHAD and southern LIBYA, in the central part of the southern Sahara desert. Though there are no major trading centers in Tibesti, from the 16th through the 19th centuries the region was important because of the trading caravans that passed through it. Muslim Arab merchants brought cloth, salt, and glass beads from the northern FEZZAN region to the Saharan trading centers of the HAUSA STATES, near Lake CHAD, where they were traded for slaves, GOLD, pepper, kola nuts, and other items from sub-Saharan regions. Also passing through the Tibesti region was a popular trade route that was followed by Muslims from West Africa on their hajj, or pilgrimage, to the city of Mecca, in Saudi Arabia.

The land around the Tibesti Massif is arid and inhospitable, but the region is visually impressive. Emi Koussi, a dormant volcano located in the southern part of Tibesti, is the highest point in the Sahara.

The Tibesti region was the home of the Teda people, a Muslim group of desert warriors of mixed Arab and black descent who survived in the harsh Tibesti climate by herding and practicing limited AGRICULTURE. Their animals included goats and camels and they mostly cultivated DATE PALMS. The Teda also controlled the caravan routes that passed through their territory, raiding them with merciless efficiency and carrying off plunder and slaves.

See also: CARAVAN ROUTES (Vol. I); SAHARA DESERT (Vols. I, II); TEDA (Vol. II); TRANS-SAHARAN TRADE ROUTES (Vol. II).

Timbuktu (Timbuctu, Tombouctou)   Historic trading city and center of Muslim scholarship located along the NIGER RIVER in the central region of present-day Republic of MALI. Founded in the 12th century by nomadic TUAREGS, the city of Timbuktu came under the rule of the Mali Empire before falling to SONGHAI in the 15th century. A prominent feature of Timbuktu during this period was SANKORE UNIVERSITY, a mosque and center for Islamic learning that once accomodated as many as 25,000 Muslim scholars.

Although Timbuktu suffered a great deal of destruction during its conquest by Songhai's Sunni Ali (r. 1464–1492), it revived under succeeding rulers of the empire. Songhai continued to rule over Timbuktu until a powerful army from MOROCCO, led by the Sadid commander JUDAR PASHA (c. late 16th–early 17th centuries), invaded and conquered it, in 1591. By 1593 the city had fallen into decline, as the Moroccans arrested, killed, or expelled the residents who were assumed to be hostile toward their rule.

During the next two centuries trade was greatly reduced in the area, but Timbuktu nevertheless remained a valuable city, sacked and taken over by different groups who desired control of its markets. Timbuktu was ruled by FULANI peoples as well as by the BAMBARA ruler Mamari KULIBALI (r. 1712–1755), who conquered the city during his reign over the kingdom of SEGU. In 1737 the Tuaregs gained control of the city, holding it until the middle of the 19th century, when first the Fulani, and later the French came to dominate the region.

See also: ALI, SUNNI (Vol. II); ISLAMIC CENTERS OF LEARNING (Vol. II); PASHALIK OF TIMBUKTU (Vol. III); SADIAN DYNASTY (Vol. III); TIMBUKTU (Vol. II, IV).

Further reading: Richard L. Roberts, *Warriors, Merchants, and Slaves: The State and the Economy in the Middle Niger Valley, 1700–1914* (Stanford, Calif.: Stanford University Press, 1987).

Tlemcen (Tilimsan)   Important trading center located in ALGERIA, near the present-day border with MOROCCO. This one-time intellectual and artistic center in the MAGHRIB was known for its distinctive Muslim ARCHITECTURE. The city has more buildings built prior to the 15th century than any other city in Algeria.

From the 13th century to the 15th century the city was a religious and cultural center of Islam. It also served as the capital of the kingdom of Tlemcen under the Abd al-Wadid dynasty, becoming an important commercial center on the trade routes in coastal North Africa. After a period of decline that started in the late 1300s, the city was in Spanish hands for a time following 1510, when Spain ineffectively tried to control the North Africa coast in support of its commercial ventures. In 1559 Tlemcen fell to Ottoman Turks from Algeria. It remained in their hands until 1842, except for a brief period of rule by the sultan of Morocco. It finally was captured and fortified by the French in 1842.

See also: FRANCE AND AFRICA (Vols. III, IV); OTTOMAN EMPIRE AND AFRICA (Vol. III); TLEMCEN (Vol. II).

tobacco   Plant with coarse, large leaves grown in warm climates and traditionally cultivated for nicotine, the addictive substance found in its leaves. While tobacco was used mostly for smoking purposes, it was also sometimes used as a medicinal treatment for various maladies. First found and grown in North America, tobacco was brought to Africa in the late 16th century or early 17th century by Europeans involved in the transatlantic SLAVE TRADE. While the tobacco plant was initially an imported product, it was quickly adopted in Africa and became a cash crop by the latter half of the 17th century in regions of southern africa and portions of what are now ZIMBABWE and the Democratic Republic of the CONGO.

One of the major tobacco-producing states in the Central African region was Kuba, in the CONGO region. The Kuba people, known as Bakuba, began growing the crop in the 17th century after trade routes from the Atlantic coastline brought the plant to the interior. In the MWENE MUTAPA kingdom of present-day Zimbabwe, however, tobacco was not a cash crop but instead was used by local groups to pay tribute to the rulers of the CHANGAMIRE DYNASTY.

By the 18th century tobacco had become highly prized in many regions of Africa and was one of the most commonly traded commodities in West Africa. By this time the Dutch also had introduced the tobacco plant to the island of MAURITIUS, located east of MADAGASCAR, in the Indian Ocean, where it became a staple crop.

Tobacco was used as a form of currency during the slave-trade era. For instance, a female African slave could be bought in the Americas for 120 pounds (54 kg) of tobacco.

See also: AGRICULTURE (Vol. III); CASH CROPS (Vol. IV); MONEY AND CURRENCY (Vol. III); NETHERLANDS AND AFRICA (Vol. III).

Togo Present-day West African country measuring approximately 22,000 square miles (57,000 sq km) and bordered by BURKINA FASO and NIGER to the north, the Republic of BENIN to the east, the Gulf of Guinea to the south, and GHANA to the west. Togo's southern ancestors came from Benin and Ghana, while those in northern Togo came from Burkina Faso and Niger. The migration of these groups took place between the 16th century and the 19th century.

During the 15th and 16th centuries Portuguese explorers and traders visited what is now the Togo coast. For the next 200 years Europeans used the coastal region as a raiding area for captives, and Togo and its surrounding area became known as the SLAVE COAST. European influence was greater in the south of the country, nearer the coast. Lomé, the capital city, is situated in the southern part of the country. Today, most of the country's Christians live in the south. German traders and MISSIONARIES began arriving in Togo in the first half of the 19th century. In 1884 German diplomat Gustav Nachtigal signed a treaty with King Mlapa III of Togodo, which led to the creation of German Togoland. Togo then became a German protectorate.

See also: GERMANY AND AFRICA (Vols. IV, V); LOMÉ (Vol. V); PROTECTORATE (Vol. IV); TOGO (Vols. I, II, IV, V).

Togwa (Torwa, Toloa) Dynasty of the SHONA KINGDOMS that flourished between the 15th and 17th centuries in the BUTUA (Guruhuswa) region of present-day southwestern ZIMBABWE. The Togwa dynasty got its name from a ruler of the southern part of the state of MWENE MUTAPA. According to tradition, in the late 15th century Togwa (fl. 1490) and his contemporary, Changa, revolted against Matope, the ruler of the Mwene Mutapa. Changa took the throne, but he was soon vanquished. Togwa fled south and became the leader of a kingdom in Butua that controlled the area from Shangwe to the SABI RIVER, in the north, and as far as the Limpopo River, in the south. The kingdom's later rulers, who bore the title of *mambo*, named their dynasty after Togwa.

In Butua, especially in its capital of KHAMI, the Togwa continued the stone-building techniques of Great Zimbabwe. Terraced hillsides and dry stone walls were a hallmark of the kingdom. This apparently led Shona traditions to link the Togwa with Great Zimbabwe itself, although the city had ceased to be an important political center several centuries before.

The Togwa dynasty remained in effective control of Butua for some time, maintaining power until it was overthrown by the CHANGAMIRE DYNASTY. According to various sources, this took place some time between the end of the 16th and the end of the 17th centuries.

See also: CHANGAMIRE (Vol. II); GREAT ZIMBABWE (Vol. II); LIMPOPO RIVER (Vol. II); SHONA (Vol. I).

Tondibi, Battle of Clash that took place in 1591 between soldiers from MOROCCO and SONGHAI. The Battle of Tondibi led to the demise of the Songhai Empire. In the latter half of the 16th century, Sultan ABD AL-MANSUR (r. 1578–1603) of Morocco made several unsuccessful attempts to take control of the lucrative Taghaza salt mines. When he finally took the mines, in 1586, he found them deserted, as Askia al-Hajj Muhammad (r. 1582–1586), the Songhai king, had been warned of al-Mansur's impending attack. The *askia* refused to allow anyone to trade at Taghaza, and he opened the mines of Taodeni. Al-Mansur later sent a threatening letter to the new Songhai king, Askia Ishaq II (r. 1588–1591), who rebuffed the sultan. This enraged al-Mansur, and he immediately set his sights on the Songhai GOLD mines. Knowing that the Songhai Empire was in trouble from its civil war, al-Mansur organized an expedition that he hoped would force a resolution to the issue.

A Spanish commander by the name of JUDAR PASHA (c. 16th–17th centuries) was put in command of the 4,000 troops, 8,000 camels, and 1,000 horses that al-Mansur assigned to the mission. Judar's forces endured countless difficulties during the journey in the desert and lost many men. By the time they got across their numbers were significantly depleted, perhaps down to as few as 2,000 or even 1,000 troops. But the Moroccan army had firearms, and the Songhai did not. When Judar's forces reached Tondibi, they were met by a a Songhai army of vastly superior numbers. (Estimates range from anywhere from 20,000 or 30,000 to up to 100,000 Songhai.) Despite their numeric disadvantage, the Moroccans' weap-onry and military tactics made them a superior fighting force. As a result the Battle of Tondibi led to a decisive defeat of the Songhai.

Askia Ishaq II called a truce and began negotiations with Judar. Seeing little evidence of the vast riches that he had been led to expect, Judar demanded that the *askia* deliver 12,500 ounces of gold to stop the war and another 1,000 in exchange for Judar's evacuation of TIMBUKTU. When he was informed of all this, al-Mansur became so angry that he promptly replaced Judar with another pasha, Mahmud ibn Zergun (r. 1591–1618), also known as Mahmud Zarqun.

Mahmud was more ruthless than Judar had been. He hunted down Askia Ishaq and had him killed. Mahmud then slaughtered the succeeding *askia* and his court. He was unable, however, to deal so easily with the next *askia*, Nuh, who retreated to Dendi and escaped Mahmud's grasp. Mahmud continued his reign of terror, seizing the riches of Songhai's wealthy and driving out from Timbuktu the city's scholars and artists. Mahmud's ruthless attempts to subdue the Songhai ended only when he met his death while pursuing Nuh. It was left to Mahmud's successor, Mansur, to kill Nuh and put to an end the once-great Songhai Empire.

See also: ASKIA DYNASTY (Vol. III); TAGHAZA (Vol. II).

Torodbe   Clan of Muslim scholars and clerics who, starting in the late 17th century, established theocracies in FOUTA TORO and FOUTA DJALLON. The Torodbe, from the central provinces of Fouta Toro, served as counselors and administrators in nominally Muslim and non-Muslim states as far east as today's Republic of the SUDAN.

The Torodbe were heirs to the legacy of Nasir al-Din (fl. 1700s), a Muslim cleric who led the movement to supplant the DENIANKE DYNASTY—who were nominally Muslims—in BONDU in the 17th century. The Torodbe believed in the superiority of Islam and strictly adhered to Islamic law. Because of their strong beliefs, they resented serving non-Muslim overlords and paying taxes to them. Another source of frustration for them was military conscription, a policy that forced them to fight alongside non-Muslims against true believers.

Wishing to overthrow unjust regimes throughout the Fouta Toro region, the Torodbe initiated a revolution in the early 18th century, moving first on Fouta Djallon, in 1725. By 1776 they had conquered Fouta Djallon and had also taken Fouta Toro by pushing out the Denianke ruler. These Torodbe campaigns ultimately led to the establishment of small Islamic theocracies in Fouta Toro and Fouta Djallon. Despite the devoutness proclaimed by the Torodbe leaders, their theocratic states were Muslim more in name than in practice.

During the 18th century the Muslim theocracy in Fouta Toro lived on the most fertile lands and collected rents from the conquered Foutanke people. They implemented an aristocratic constitution by which descendants from the ranking Muslim families elected a weak central authority, the *almami*, into office. In the 19th century the French were able to expand into Torodbe-led territories in West Africa because of aristocratic divisions and the weak, fractious central government of the *almami*.

trade and commerce   See ASIENTO (Vol. III); BISA TRADING NETWORK (Vol. III); CAPE COLONY (Vol. III); CORSAIRS (Vol. III); DUTCH EAST INDIA COMPANY (Vol. III); DUTCH WEST INDIA COMPANY (Vol. III); DYULA (Vols. II, III); ENGLAND AND AFRICA (Vol. III); GOLD (Vol. III); IVORY TRADE (Vol. III); MALAGUETTA PEPPER (Vol. III); MONEY AND CURRENCY (Vol. III); NETHERLANDS AND AFRICA (Vol. III); PALM OIL (Vol. III); PIRATES (Vol. III); PORTUGAL AND AFRICA (Vol. III); ROYAL AFRICAN COMPANY (Vol. III); SLAVE TRADE, EXPANSION OF EUROPEAN INVOLVEMENT IN (Vol. III); SLAVE TRADE ON THE SWAHILI COAST (Vol. III); SLAVE TRADE, THE TRANSATLANTIC (Vol. III); SPAIN AND AFRICA (Vol. III); SWAHILI COAST (Vol. III); TRADE AND COMMERCE (Vols. I, II, IV, V); TRADING STATIONS, EUROPEAN (Vol. III).

trading stations, European   Commercial outposts located mostly along the African coastlines that were established by European powers in order to trade with indigenous African groups. In the 15th century the Portuguese were the first Europeans to begin establishing trading stations on West Africa's coast. They established outposts on islands off the coast—the Cape Verde Islands, SÃO TOMÉ AND PRÍNCIPE, and FERNANDO PO. Later, outposts were built on GORÉE ISLAND, Bolama, Îles de Loos, and other islands closer to the coast.

Usually, a local African ruler controlled the land and charged the Europeans rent, collected taxes from them, and offered protection in return for a share of the trading profits. The local rulers also helped establish ties to indigenous commercial networks located inland.

The Portuguese traders were soon joined by the Dutch, English, French, and Spanish. One of the most famous Portuguese trading stations was the fortress-castle of ELMINA, meaning "the mine," which was located along the coast of the GOLD-producing regions of present-day GHANA. Established in 1482, Elmina was probably the most important gold-trading station in the tropical areas of West Africa until 1637, when the Dutch gained control of it and used the castle to house captives awaiting transport overseas.

By the 16th century Europeans had built numerous trading stations near river mouths and at the ends of profitable caravan routes from the interior. Trade items that passed through the stations in West Africa included ivory, CLOTH AND TEXTILES, beeswax, GROUNDNUTS (peanuts), EBONY, weapons, PALM OIL, and human captives. The goods were either bartered at the trade station for other items or held until the next ship laden with goods and captives left for Europe.

On the Atlantic coast of Central Africa, in what is now GABON, outposts were built by the Dutch, French, and English at the mouth of the Ogooué River by the late 16th century. Until well into the 19th century, groups including the Vili and ORUNGU used waterways as well as land routes to transport captives and other goods down the river to the European trading stations.

East Africa, too, had its share of European trading stations and fairs. Early in the 16th century Portuguese seamen established outposts on MOZAMBIQUE ISLAND and in SOFALA on the southern coast. By 1599 they also built FORT JESUS in MOMBASA on the coast of present-day KENYA. By the middle of the 17th century the French had established Fort Dauphin, a small trading outpost on the Indian Ocean island of MADAGASCAR, and had begun trading in the nearby MASCARENE ISLANDS.

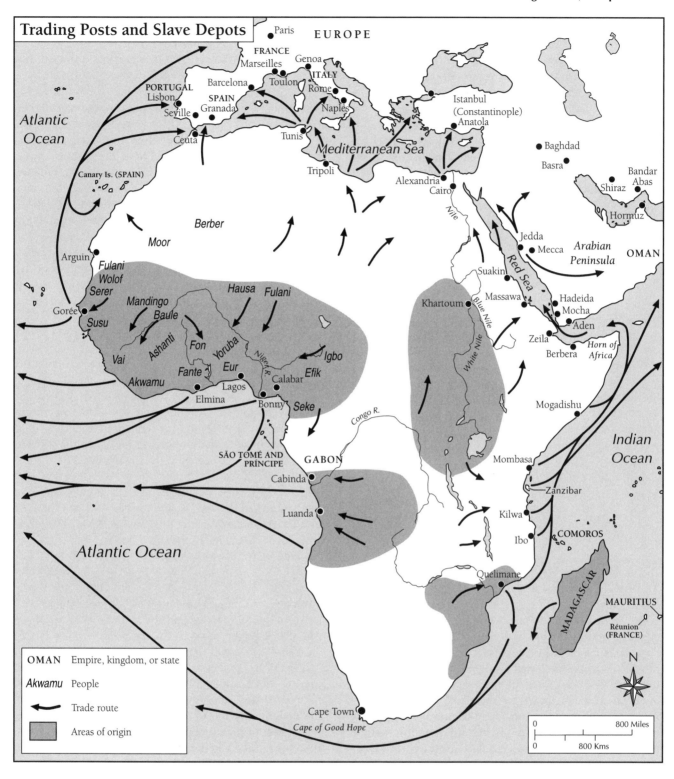

Trading Posts and Slave Depots

Factories The settlers, merchants, and soldiers who lived at the African trading outposts were hardy, sometimes lawless individuals—invariably men—who were able to survive far from the familiarity of their native Europe. The compounds they built were also called *factories,* with the heads of the stations called *factors.* Factors

acted as agents for the governments or the major European commercial firms that sent them to Africa. The factors employed a variety of sub-agents, some of whom were indigenous Africans.

Factories were typically made up of a trading station, simple residences, warehouses for goods, repair facilities for ships, and a barracoon, or corral, for holding captive African men, women, and children. The buildings often resembled military forts with gates and heavily fortified walls intended to protect the occupants from the hostile actions of any local populations that might object to the foreign intruders.

Some European traders—Portuguese *prazeros,* for instance—moved from the coastal outposts and settled on land in the African interior. Once establishing themselves on their PRAZOS, or royal land grants, they often married African women and started families. Though the living conditions at African trading stations were generally difficult and many Europeans died from tropical fevers, the trade was usually profitable enough to attract more traders. By the end of the 17th century the French, English, and Dutch had set up stations along the eastern coastline of Africa where regular trade fairs were conducted and ivory, gold, and captives were sent for export.

Whereas these trading stations were immensely profitable for the European powers that controlled them, their establishment also increased the wealth and importance of many smaller African states located on or near the coastal regions. Some groups capitalized on their ability to trade directly with the Europeans, while other groups, such as the FANTE of present-day Ghana, became powerful middlemen who brought the wares produced by the groups of the African interior to the trading stations.

See also: CAPE COLONY (Vol. III); ENGLAND AND AFRICA (Vol. II); FRANCE AND AFRICA (Vol. III); IVORY TRADE (Vol. III); NETHERLANDS AND AFRICA (Vol. III); POR-TUGAL AND AFRICA (Vol. III); SLAVERY (Vol. III); SPAIN AND AFRICA (Vol. III); TRADE AND COMMERCE (Vol. III).

Tripoli (Tarablus al-Gharb)
Capital of LIBYA, located along the Mediterranean coast. During the early 16th century the Christian-Muslim conflict that had characterized the Mediterranean area for centuries found its way to Tripoli. Christian Spain captured the port city in 1510, but its rule lasted a mere 40 years. In 1551 the Ottoman Empire gained indirect control of Tripoli; its reign would span nearly three and a half centuries.

Tripoli thrived due to Mediterranean trade. However, its wealth was derived from a unique source, since most of its assets were accumulated through the COR-SAIRS. Much of this wealth came from the booty they amassed from their attacks on Christian merchant ships. The corsairs also managed to do a thriving business in "protection," demanding payments for ensuring the safe passage of European vessels through corsair-infested waters.

The United States attacked Tripoli from 1801 to 1805 in an attempt to end assaults on American vessels that refused to pay the corsairs for protection. The cor-

sairs' profits soon declined, and the Ottoman Empire initiated a more direct control of the city.

See also: OTTOMAN EMPIRE AND AFRICA (Vols. III, IV).

Tsonga (Thonga)
Bantu-speaking people who inhabit present-day MOZAMBIQUE and northern SOUTH AFRICA. Prior to the 16th century the Tsonga migrated from the north, settling throughout the region between the SABI RIVER and St. Lucia Bay. They settled in independent clans, and for centuries they apparently considered themselves to be separate peoples rather than a single ethnic group. As a result the Tsonga were not unified for several centuries.

The Tsonga traditionally have been agriculturalists, growing cassava, corn, millet, and sorghum. They also have engaged in fishing and a limited amount of trade. By the late 18th century many Tsonga men worked as migrant laborers in ZIMBABWE and South Africa.

Tswana
Agro-pastoral people of present-day BOTSWANA, SOUTH AFRICA, and NAMIBIA. Ancestors of the Tswana migrated into the Tswapong Hill, near present-day Botswana, as early as the first century and settled in present-day Transvaal in the 11th or 12th century. By the early 1600s the Tswana had settled in Botswana and Bophuthatswana, where they established powerful chiefdoms. These settlements were disrupted during the MFECANE of the early 19th century, when Ndebele peoples, fleeing the ZULU conquest, attacked the Tswana and forced them into the Kalahari Desert and areas along the Limpopo River. The greatly weakened Tswana fell to the BOERS, in 1837.

See also: TSWANA (Vols. I, IV).

Tuaregs
Saharan group long associated with the AÏR MAS-SIF of present-day NIGER and the city of TIMBUKTU of present-day Republic of MALI. Tuaregs claim BERBERS as their ancestors and have enjoyed autonomy throughout their history by being successful traders. In the early 16th century the Tuareg capital of AGADES, situated at the south end of the Aïr Massif, was captured by the SONGHAI Empire. Still the Tuaregs were able to remain strong in the area by retaining control of the trade in salt and GOLD and the caravan routes that linked the Sahara with LIBYA and EGYPT.

By the early 17th century the nomadic Tuaregs migrated toward the Middle NIGER RIVER, becoming a prominent force in the trading activities of that region as well. Their ability to hold sway over the area's trade and pasture lands helped them to finally displace the Songhai Empire. In 1680 they conquered the Songhai city of Gao, located on the northern banks of the Niger, and used it as their base for the 1737 recapture of the original Tuareg settlement of Timbuktu.

For the Tuaregs who had remained in the Aïr Massif region, however, the 17th century brought conflict from the kingdom of KANEM-BORNU and its most powerful ruler, Mai IDRIS ALAWMA (r. c. 1580–1617). Conflicts with Kanem-Bornu continued for almost two centuries, with the Tuaregs slowly contributing to the decline of the powerful kingdom. Their greatest victory over Kanem-Bornu came around 1800, when the Tuaregs conquered and demolished the kingdom's important tributary state of Gaskeru.

The Tuaregs are known for a form of writing known as *tifinagh,* which is historically connected to ancient Libya and remains specific to their group of peoples.

See also: TUAREGS (Vols. I, II, IV).

Further reading: Johannes Nicolaisen and Ida Nicolaisen, *The Pastoral Tuareg: Ecology, Culture and Society* (New York: Thames and Hudson, 1997).

Tukulor (Toucouleur, Tukolor) Muslim peoples located mostly in the river valley of present-day SENEGAL, as well as parts of present-day Republic of MALI and MAURITANIA. The Tukulor are a FULANI subgroup closely related to the Wolof and Serer peoples and speak a Fulani language known as Fulfulde. The name *Tukulor* derives from their traditional 10th-century Islamic kingdom of Tekrur. This first Tukulor kingdom was superseded, in the mid-16th century, by a group comprised of both Fulani and non-Muslim Mandinka peoples who banded together and formed the DENIANKE DYNASTY in the former Tekrur region—now called FOUTA TORO—of Senegal. The Tukulor again became prominent in the latter half of the 18th century when Islam gained adherents in West Africa.

In 1776 the Tukulor conquered the reigning Denianke king and declared Suleyman Bal (fl. 1770), the sultan of their newly founded theocratic state in Fouta Toro. Later, in 1852, a Tukulor scholar named al-Hajj Umar Tal (1794–1864) rose to power and launched a widespread jihad that conquered kingdoms such as the BAMBARA states and MACINA and created the vast Tukulor empire.

See also: FULANI JIHADS (Vol. III); SERER (Vol. II); TUKULOR (Vol. II); TUKULOR EMPIRE (Vol. IV); WOLOF (Vols. II, IV).

Tumbuka Ethnic group living in ZAMBIA and MALAWI. Today the Tumbuka number approximately 150,000 and speak a Bantu language. The Tumbuka were traditional farmers, growing grains and raising livestock. In the 19th century they were largely conquered by the more militaristic NGONI, who came from the south.

Tunisia Country in North Africa measuring approximately 60,000 square miles (155,400 sq km) and bordered by the Mediterranean Sea to the north and east, LIBYA to the southeast, and ALGERIA to the west. Berber Hafsids succeeded the Almohads and ruled Tunisia from 1230 to 1574. During this period Tunisia prospered.

After consolidating his control of the central MAGHRIB, in 1534 the Turkish corsair Khayr ad-Din Barbarossa (d. 1546) successfully seized the coastal town of Tunis. The ruling Hafsids were forced to seek refuge in Spain. With the help of Emperor CHARLES V (1500–1558), the Hafsid sultan, Hassan, was restored to the throne when the Spanish recaptured Tunis, in 1535.

The Muslim Hafsids served as a crucial ally of Spain as it struggled with the Ottoman Empire for control of the Mediterranean Sea. Tunisia was often center stage in this conflict between the two powers. In 1569 the Turks regained control of Tunis for a brief time until the city fell, in 1573, to the military leader and illegitimate son of Charles V, Don Juan of Austria (1547–1578). However, in 1574, the Turks returned with a massive army and naval fleet. They ousted the Hafsids and Spanish from the city, and Tunisia became an Ottoman province.

Authority in Tunisia was placed in the hands of a pasha, or governor, who was appointed for a one-year term by the Ottoman sultan. Janissaries, Christian soldiers originally of Balkan peasant stock who were conscripted into a lifetime of military service, assisted the pasha. The Janissaries served as an elite self-governing military body that, in 1591, wrested control of the government away from the pasha. The Janissaries' own elected leader—or *dey*—became the head of government, and the pasha's role was reduced to that of a ceremonial figurehead.

Since the Barbary CORSAIRS generated the country's income through piracy, the Janissaries' role was simply to maintain order and collect taxes. The job of regulating the tribes living in the interior fell on a civilian official, or bey, who had the support of a private army made up of local Tunisian recruits. One of these officials, Corsican renegade Murad Bey (d. 1631), became so powerful in the Tunisian interior that he was also able to secure for himself and his heirs the role of pasha. Thus began a political struggle between the Janissaries and the bey-pashas that lasted throughout the 17th century.

During the mid-1660s the bey-pasha gradually overtook the *dey* and his Janissaries as the major power within the government. The bey-pasha had established an identity characterized by order and stability. While indirect Ottoman rule was restored to Tunisia, the country became, in effect, an independent state ruled by the heredity bey-pashas.

Amid the struggles between the Janissaries and the bey-pasha, during the 17th and 18th centuries Tunisia was also threatened by outside interference from ALGIERS, which sought to dominate the various Ottoman subgovernments of North Africa. Eventually, in 1702, an officer of the Janissaries, Ibrahim al Sharif (r. 1702–1705), murdered the bey-pasha and took control of the government. However, in 1705 Janissaries from Algiers removed Ibrahim from office and seized control of Tunis. The Algerian commander planned to reinstall Ibrahim in office as his puppet, but a Tunisian Janissary, Hussein ben Ali (d. 1715), was able to secure the Ottoman sultan's appointment as pasha. With Hussein ben Ali's death, the Ottoman government tried to install a pasha of its own choosing. However, the military and religious supporters of the Husseinid dynasty thwarted their plan. The HUSSEINID DYNASTY remained in power throughout the 18th century.

See also: OTTOMAN EMPIRE AND AFRICA (Vol. III, IV); TUNISIA (Vol. I, II, IV, V).

Tunjur Ethnic group that, during the early 16th century, established the WADAI kingdom, in what is now CHAD. The origin of the Tunjur is obscure. According to some sources, they are of mixed Arab and Nubian origin; other sources believe that the Tunjur originated in Nubia and were influenced by Arab nomads, whose language they adopted. Still other sources believe that the Tunjur originated in TUNISIA. The Tunjur apparently began migrating into the DARFUR area during the 14th century, gradually gaining economic and political power.

In the 16th century the Tunjur were ousted from Darfur and eventually migrated to the Wadai region, an inhospitable area east of Lake CHAD near the border of present-day Republic of the SUDAN. There the Tunjur established their own kingdom, which lasted until the early 17th century.

At that time the Muslim Maba people, headed by Abdel-Kerim (fl. 1610–1640), mounted a revolt against the Tunjur. This led to the installation of an Islamic leadership at Wadai, and the non-Muslim Tunjur migrated once again, this time farther west. The Tunjur finally arrived in the area of Kanem, where they defeated the BULALA kingdom and assumed a dominant role among the peoples of the region. The Tunjur allied themselves with Wadai in an attempt to maintain their independence, but it was not long before an invasion from Bornu subdued the Tunjur and brought Kanem back under the control of Bornu.

See also: BORNU (Vol. II); KANEM (Vol. II); KANEM-BORNU (Vol. II); SLAVERY, CULTURAL AND HISTORICAL ATTITUDES TOWARD (Vol. III).

Tutsi (Batusi, Batutsi, Tussi, Watusi, Watutsi, Hima) Nilotic pastoralists of East Africa in what are now BURUNDI and RWANDA; called Hima in other kingdoms in the region. Prior to 1500 the Tutsi began migrating south to the hills of the GREAT LAKES REGION. Most of these Tutsi were members of the cattle-owning Hima caste, although a small minority belonged to the agricultural Iru class. Over the next few centuries the Tutsi slowly established dominion over the HUTU and Twa agriculturalists who were living in the area.

During the early stages of their settlement, the Tutsi probably incorporated Hutu chiefs into their ethnic group. For some time Hutu who owned cattle or otherwise attained a high position in society continued to be absorbed into the Tutsi class. The Tutsi also adopted many aspects of Hutu culture, including the Bantu language and the institution of divine kingship.

In Rwanda the Tutsi served as patrons (*shebuja*) to Hutu clients (*guragu*), who tended their cattle in return for Tutsi patronage and protection. Gradually, the Tutsi almost exclusively came to occupy the positions of kings, chiefs, military officers, and court officials.

The late 18th century saw the Tutsi in firm control of the territory that would become Rwanda, transforming it into the largest and most powerful precolonial state in the southern Great Lakes region. The government was run by a king, or MWAMI, to whom regional rulers swore allegiance. The Tutsi government reached the pinnacle of its power under two kings, Mutara I (r. early 19th century) and Kigeri IV (r. 1853–1895), the latter of whom established a well-armed standing army for his country.

In Burundi the Tutsi also occupied a privileged economic status because they owned cattle, although they did not enjoy the overwhelming political power they possessed in Rwanda. In Burundi the Tutsi were subservient to the *ganwa*, or royal princes, who comprised the kingdom's ruling class.

See also: HIMA (Vol. II); IRU (Vol. II); TUTSI (Vol. II, IV, V).

U

Uganda Country in East Africa measuring approximately 91,100 square miles (236,000 sq km) bordered by the Republic of the SUDAN to the north, KENYA to the east, TANZANIA and RWANDA to the south, and the Democratic Republic of the CONGO to the west. Kampala is its largest city and capital. In precolonial East Africa, Uganda was occupied by the kingdoms of BUNYORO, BUGANDA, Toro, and NKOLE, among others.

In the 14th and 15th centuries the pastoralist Chwezi rulers conquered the Bantu-speaking farmers in the Kitara Complex of kingdoms. This Chwezi-controlled region represented Uganda's first unified state and had multiple capitals at Bigo, Mubende, Munsa, Kibengo, and Bugoma, in the western part of the country. Chwezi rule, which was responsible for developing the region's monarchical system of government, lasted in places into the early 16th century. However, in the early 15th century, in the northern part of Uganda, the Chwezi rulers were replaced by rulers of the BITO clan, Nilotic LUO-speaking pastoralists who invaded from the Sudan. They founded the kingdom of Bunyoro, in the north. According to some traditions, the Chwezi rulers moved south and gave rise to the HINDA states, which were controlled by TUTSI monarchs.

Throughout the 16th and 17th centuries the Bito clan founded several subsidiary states whose vulnerability to invasion ensured their allegiance to the Bito. These states included Bukoli, Bugabula, Bugwere, Bulamogi, Kiziba, and Toro. The Bito also allied themselves with the states of Nkole, Buganda, BUSOGA, Karagwe, and Rwanda. The Bito empire grew so large that it could barely sustain itself, with internal revolts substantially weakening the regime.

At the same time that Bunyoro-Kitara was declining, Buganda, the neighboring kingdom of the GANDA people,

was gradually expanding. By the 17th century its territory included a number of outlying kingdoms including Butambala, Gomba, Mawokota, and Singo. The people of Buganda, also called the Baganda, were a mix of Luo- and Bantu-speaking clans, many of whom migrated from Bunyoro-Kitara. Buganda's success was a result not only of its territorial conquests but also of its increased wealth through trade. This, in turn, produced loyal subjects and a strong military. By the 19th century Buganda surpassed Bunyoro-Kitara as the largest and most powerful kingdom in East Africa.

The Nkole kingdom, founded by Ruhinda (fl. late 15th century), was made up of Hima pastoralists, who became the ruling class, and Iru agriculturalists, who became their subjects. The dichotomy between these groups caused much internal strife and revolt. Nkole's problems worsened in the 17th century as Bunyoro-Kitara began to usurp portions of their territory. In the 18th century Bunyoro-Kitara removed Nkole's ruler, Ntare IV (1700–1725), the ninth *mugabe*, or king, from his throne. However, he soon reclaimed it and devoted his energy to strengthening his military. The Nkole kingdom continued to expand until the 19th century.

See also: BIGO (Vol. II); CHWEZI DYNASTY (Vol. II); KITARA COMPLEX (Vol. II); NKOLE (Vols. II, III); UGANDA (Vols. I, II, IV, V); TORO (Vol. II).

Further reading: Thomas P. Ofcansky, *Uganda: Tarnished Pearl of Africa* (New York: Westview Books, 1996).

Ughoton (Gwato) West African town located about 19 miles (30 km) from present-day BENIN CITY. In 1487 the Portuguese visited Ughoton and soon after set up a trading post in an attempt to reap the commercial benefits of the trades in both pepper and human captives from Ughoton's proximity to Benin City, the chief city of the kingdom of BENIN. To strengthen commercial ties, Esigie (1504–1550), the *oba* (ruler) under whom Benin attained its greatest splendor, sent a traditional priest of Olorun named Ohen-Okun from Ughoton to Portugal to ask the Portuguese king to send Christian priests to Benin.

Early in the 16th century the Portuguese abandoned Ughoton because trade was not proving to be as profitable as they had anticipated. English and Dutch merchants followed the Portuguese into the region, but by the 17th century the center of trade in Benin had been relocated from Ughoton to Arbo (Arogbo), in the neighboring Warri kingdom in the Niger Delta, where it was away from the control of the *oba*.

See also: ENGLAND AND AFRICA (Vol. III); PORTUGAL AND AFRICA (Vols. I, III); NETHERLANDS AND AFRICA (Vol. III); SLAVE TRADE, THE TRANSATLANTIC (Vol. III); WARRI (Vol. II).

Usman dan Fodio (Usuman or Uthman dan Fodio) (1754–1817) *Muslim mystic, cleric, and leader of the Fulani Jihads*

Fodio was born Usman ibn Muhammad Fudi ibn Usman ibn Salih, in the Hausa state of GOBIR, in present-day NIGERIA. He was educated in both Arabic and Fulfulde, the language of his native FULANI people. His parents were Islamic scholars, and his father was a religious leader, or imam, who taught Usman how to read as well as recite the Quran. The second major influence in his life was Jibril ibn Umar, a teacher from the city of AGADES who admitted Usman to the QADIRIYYA brotherhood and other Sufi orders.

At 20 years of age Usman dan Fodio (*Fodio* meaning either "learned man" or "jurist" in Fulfulde) began preaching a grassroots version of Islam and became successful in reaching the farmers, women, and other more isolated peoples of Gobir. His teachings earned him a great number of followers as well as a reputation as a scholar who spoke out against the elite of Hausaland who, as he said, broke the laws of Islam by adopting such practices as taxation. Many Hausa people identified Usman with the Mahdi, a long-awaited Muslim redeemer. Usman disavowed the identification but encouraged the righteous indignation of his followers against irreligion.

By the late 18th century Usman dan Fodio, who was also known by this time as the Shehu (Chief), had become the political enemy of the sultan of Gobir, the authority of the emirate. In 1802 Sultan Yunfa (r. 1780–1808) gave an order to suppress Fodio's followers. At this point the Fodio went on a hajj, or spiritual pilgrimage to Mecca, and was subsequently appointed by his fellow Muslims to the position of imam. Combined with his massive following of rural Hausa people also dissatisfied by the ruling classes of Hausaland, Usman dan Fodio launched a major jihad, in 1804. Over the next four years Usman's forces conquered the states of Hausaland, leading to the founding of the SOKOTO CALIPHATE.

Fodio ruled over the Sokoto Caliphate and its emirates until 1812, when he was succeeded by his son MUHAMMAD BELLO (c. 1781–1837), in the northern and eastern regions, and by his brother, Abdullahi dan Fodio, in the southern and western regions. Usman dan Fodio's later life was spent teaching and writing poetry and other works on the Islamic life and faith. By the time of his death, in 1817, Usman dan Fodio had 12 wives and possibly one concubine and had fathered 37 children, some of whom held positions of authority in the Sokoto Caliphate or followed in his footsteps as religious teachers and leaders.

See also: FULFULDE (Vol. I); FULANI JIHADS (Vol. III); ISLAM, INFLUENCE OF (Vols. II, III, IV); JIHAD (Vols. II, IV); MAHDI (Vol. II).

Further reading: Mervyn Hiskett, *The Sword of Truth: The Life and Times of the Shehu Usuman dan Fodio* (New York: Oxford University Press, 1973).

V

Vai (Vey, Vei, Gallinas) West African people mainly located in SIERRA LEONE and LIBERIA. The nickname *Gallinas,* meaning "chickens," was given to the Vai by the early Portuguese in reference to the indigenous breed which inhabited the region. Related to the Mandinka peoples, the Vai speak a Niger-Congo Mande language and are largely Muslims.

Vai society operates with the help of secret societies. Both the Sande women's society and the Poro men's society serve to help the group through various aspects of daily life, including the EDUCATION of young children and the reinforcing of laws through disciplinary actions. Generally an agrarian and fishing community, the Vai were also active in the transatlantic SLAVE TRADE, prior to its general abolition in the early 19th century.

The Vai are most notable, however, for their system of writing, which was invented in the early 19th century by Duala Bukere. This writing system, categorized by linguists as a *syllabary,* is now made up of 212 characters, which represent syllables rather than single sounds, as the English alphabet does. It was said to have come to Bukere in a dream. It has developed beyond its earliest pictographic origins. Vai script is used to record laws and traditional tales, to keep accounts, and to translate the Bible.

See also: ALPHABETS AND SCRIPTS (Vol. I); MANDE (Vols. I, II); LITERACY (Vol. IV); SECRET SOCIETIES (Vol. I).

Vassa, Gustavus See EQUIANO, OLAUDAH.

Venda (Bavenda) Bantu-speaking people of SOUTH AFRICA. The Venda have occupied the mountainous region south of the Limpopo River since the 13th century. In the early 18th century the Venda people, also known as the *Bavenda,* established fortified chiefdoms throughout their territory, allowing them to defend themselves against invaders from the south. Able to fend off even the powerful ZULU warriors, the Venda were one of the last groups in the region to fall under European control. It was not until the late 1800s that the Venda lost their independence and became a part of the Transvaal.

See also: LIMPOPO RIVER (Vols. I, II); TRANSVAAL (Vol. IV); VENDA (Vol. II).

Vili See LOANGO.

Volta basin Located in present-day central GHANA, between the Gambaga Scarp and the Konkori Scarp and between the Kwahu Plateau and TOGO. Today the Volta basin is sparsely populated with farmers, but at one time was a place of great activity and prosperity.

About the 15th century small bands of horse-mounted immigrants from the east peacefully conquered the Gur-speaking inhabitants of the Volta basin. The two groups assimilated, and by the 16th century they had established several independent kingdoms, including Dagbon (the kingdom of the DAGOMBA) and MAMPRUSI, and the MOSSI STATES of OUAGADOUGOU and YATENGA. Many of these kingdoms and states thrived economically from AGRICULTURE and from trading GOLD, kola nuts, and captives as well as livestock, grains, and other FOOD crops.

Despite suffering a severe blow at the hands of the SONGHAI Empire, Yatenga grew to become a powerful king-

293

dom by the latter half of the 17th century. The Yatenga nobility (*nakomse*) acquired a great amount of power at the beginning of the 18th century, surpassing that of the *naba* (Mossi chief). This caused dissension within the kingdom and led to various conflicts over the throne.

Throughout the 17th century, Dagbon was under increasing threat by Gbanya warriors of the GONJA state to the south. After almost a century of battling Gonja, the Dagomba were pushed out of their capital in 1700. In 1713 the Dagomba fought back and defeated Gonja and founded a new capital at Yendi. In the mid-18th century Dagbon and Gonja were subjugated by the growing ASHANTI EMPIRE. About the same time, Wattara mercenaries of Mande origin came to the Volta basin from the west. They were called *Chakossi* by the Dagomba and Mamprusi, and they assisted the Mamprusi in their conflicts with the Gurma of FADA-N-GURMA. The Volta basin region was colonized by the French in the 19th century.

See also: FRANCE AND AFRICA (Vol. IV); VOLTA LAKE (Vol. V); VOLTA RIVER (Vols. I, II).

W

Wadai Kingdom that was located in present-day eastern CHAD. Wadai reached its height as an independent power during the mid- to late 19th century. Founded in the 16th century, Wadai was initially ruled by the Daju dynasty, which had been forced out of DARFUR by the TUNJUR people. Later the Tunjur were themselves ousted from Darfur by the KAYRA DYNASTY. The Tunjur then migrated to Wadai, where they founded a kingdom that lasted until the early 17th century. It was then that the Muslim Maba people revolted against the non-Muslim Tunjur. About 1630 the Maba, led by Abd-el-Kerim (fl. 1610–1640), established a Muslim dynasty that remained in power for several centuries.

Wadai was situated at the crossroads of two major trade routes. One ran from the Upper Nile, in the east, to the western limits of KANEM-BORNU, near Lake Chad. The second route ran northward from Wadai to Banghazi, on the Mediterranean coast of present-day LIBYA. As a result Wadai quickly became a prosperous kingdom. By the 1790s Wadai was expanding into the Bornu kingdom, to the west. During this period Wadai was characterized by remarkable political stability, leading trade to increase even further, with caravans using the safer routes that ran through the Wadai region.

See also: TRANS-SAHARAN TRADE ROUTES (Vol. II).

Walata (Oualata) Town in present-day southeastern MAURITANIA that, between the 13th and 15th centuries, was a major commercial center on a trans-Saharan trade route. By the 14th century, however, as the trans-Saharan routes began to change, Walata started to lose its importance and, like TIMBUKTU, it was conquered by the TU-

AREGS. When the great SONGHAI ruler Sunni Ali (r. c. 1464–1492) conquered Timbuktu, in 1468, the Tuareg chief and many of the city's Sanhaja scholars took refuge in Walata. Although Sunni Ali never formally occupied the city, he took control of it in 1480. This prevented the Mossi from annexing the nearly ruined city. Among Sunni Ali's projects for the city was a plan to build a canal from Lake Faguibine to Walata, but he never completed the project. Walata eventually was subjugated by the Songhai in the 16th century.

See also: SANHAJA BERBERS (Vol. II); SUNNI ALI (Vol. II); TRANS-SAHARAN TRADE ROUTES (Vol. II); WALATA (Vol. II).

Walvis Bay Town on the Atlantic Ocean coast of west-central NAMIBIA. In the 1480s Portuguese explorers became the first Europeans to enter Walvis Bay. They originally called it Conception Bay, but after the 16th century it became known as Whale Bay, because of the constant presence of the large aquatic mammals in the area. In the 17th century Dutch expolrers sailed up from SOUTH AFRICA to explore the area and reported skirmishes with the local NAMA people. In addition to the Nama, the inhospitable Namib Desert made it impossible for European sailors to access the interior from Walvis Bay.

See also: WALVIS BAY (Vols. IV, V).

warfare and weapons Between the 15th and 19th centuries the ability to wage war in Africa was abetted by important changes in firepower and tactics. While spears and arrows were the primary weapons in earlier centuries, firearms reached Africa as early as 1432, when the MAMLUKS introduced the smoothbore harquebus, an early form of musket, into EGYPT. Such weapons changed the balance of power in every clash in which they were used.

Although battles rarely lasted more than a day and often less, the empires of the savanna, Mali and SONGHAI in particular, had for centuries fielded large armies of infantry and cavalry to achieve their commercial and territorial aims. By the start of the 19th century large and powerful indigenous armies were found elsewhere in Africa, as well. The ZULU of eastern southern Africa organized their young men into highly disciplined and structured regiments. Their confidence and physical preparedness made them a formidable fighting force against both indigenous armies and European colonial forces, who began arriving later in the 19th century.

A tradition of women warriors dates back in Africa to ancient times in EGYPT and Nubia. In more recent times, the notable Queen NZINGA (c. 1581–1663) was a fierce warrior who, through warfare and political intrigue, managed to fend off the hostile advances of the Portuguese for many years. She was assisted in this by a band of female warriors who became noted for their courage and tenacity on the battlefield.

The Introduction of Firearms Gunpowder is first mentioned in a Chinese manuscript dating from 1044. The Arabs received the formula for gunpowder by way of India and Persia. By 1304 the Arabs had made a gun that had an iron-reinforced bamboo barrel; in 1324 the Marinid rulers of MOROCCO used cannons at the siege of Huesca in Spain—the first recorded use of gunpowder in Europe.

Early firearms were heavy, slow to load and fire, relatively inaccurate beyond short distances, and capable of only a low sustained rate of fire. The sword and other edged weapons remained important in close-quarters fighting for many years. Firearms, however, gave the side that employed them a significant advantage in a battle when soldiers faced conventionally armed foes. Even so, their use was not always accepted without resistance. When the Mamluks introduced the harquebus into Egypt in 1432 and trained Sudanese infantry to fire them, the

Zulu soldiers running to the attack. The short thrusting spears, called *assagais,* that the soldiers carried were deadly at close quarters. © *Corbis*

weapon was not popular with the cavalry because it scared the horses and burned soldiers' hands and clothes.

Sometimes generically called muskets, early fire-arms were also known by specific names that indicated the means whereby the gunner ignited the gunpowder and discharged the weapon. This mechanism is called the lock, and there are various kinds. The most familiar is the flintlock, because it was used on the muskets carried by soldiers during the American Revolution. The lock of a flintlock strikes a piece of flint against steel to produce a spark that in subsequent steps sets off the explosion inside the gun barrel that propels a shot out of the barrel. Earlier forms of locks were matchlocks, which used a smoldering wick, or match, to ignite the powder, and wheel locks, which used a wheel much like the one in a modern disposable lighter to produce the spark. The harquebus is named for the metal hooks mounted below the barrel to absorb recoil; this weapon was so heavy it had to be fired from a support. All of these firearms were muzzle-loaded smoothbores, which means they lacked the grooves cut into the barrel of the modern rifle; without such rifling, these weapons were notoriously inaccurate. Muskets shot a round lead ball that could be as large as .75 inch (19 mm) in diameter.

Ship-mounted weapons also came into use in Africa at roughly this time. The squat two- and three-masted 35- to 90-ton (27- to 82-metric ton) caravels of the early Portuguese explorers mounted mostly small swivel cannons. When Antão Gonçalves (fl. 1440s) landed in SENEGAMBIA in 1444 to abduct Africans, his slow-firing guns had difficulty hitting the fast-moving canoes full of archers sent to chase him off. Larger guns called for larger ships. By the time Vasco da Gama (1460–1524) sailed around the Horn of Africa to reach the port of Calicut in India in 1502, his larger, full-rigged ships had broadside guns. On his way to India, in 1505, Portuguese admiral Francisco de Almeida (c. 1450–1510) led a fleet of 21 ships that explored the SWAHILI COAST of Africa. He captured KILWA in present-day TANZANIA, where he built a fort, and then sailed up the coast to bombard and destroy MOMBASA. In 1509 Almeida's cannons dominated the Muslim galleys at the battle of Diu off the southern coast of India in the Indian Ocean and won dominance over the spice trade for Portugal.

The Effect of Firearms The side that had firearms had a decisive advantage over the side that was armed only with traditional weapons. The kingdom of BENIN, in West Africa, and the KONGO KINGDOM, on the western coast of Central Africa, both had armed forces that were typical of the indigenous armies at the end of the 15th century. Portuguese merchants landing in BENIN CITY in 1485 later reported that the soldiers of the Edo people were armed with iron swords, wooden shields, and iron-tipped spears. In addition their archers used poisoned arrows. Members of the Leopard Hunters Guild, a military secret society, wore helmets and armor made from the skin of the scaly anteater, one of the few animals capable of resisting a leopard. This armor was thought to have magical properties.

In 1491 the Kongo kingdom boasted an army of 20,000 soldiers organized as infantry, musicians, and priests. They were armed with wooden clubs, buffalo-hide shields, bows with iron-tipped arrows, and metal-tipped spears. They wore uniforms of palm leaves, animal skins, and feathered headdresses; bells, rattles, and amulets offered wearers magical protection. Most battles were preceded by three days of dancing and chanting, in which soldiers focused their growing fury. Clashes were brief and relatively bloodless. Most battles lasted less than a day, with the loser retreating in disarray, the victor in full pursuit, taking captives. Casualties were few.

The soldiers of Benin and Kongo were probably armed and trained much like the soldiers of the SONGHAI Empire in what is today the Republic of MALI. Muslim Songhai traditionally dominated the trans-Saharan trade routes and the supply of GOLD that was sent north to Morocco and other states in North Africa. At the end of the 16th century, however, Songhai was torn by rivalries within its royal family. These encouraged the Sadian sultan of Morocco, Ahmad al-Mansur (1549–1603), to intervene. In order to improve its trading position with the Europeans, Morocco needed the trade routes and the gold that Songhai controlled.

After first trying to seize the salt mines at Taghaza, which were an important part of the gold-salt trade, al-Mansur decided, in 1591, to seize the important trading city of Gao. He dispatched an army under the command of JUDAR PASHA (c. 16th–17th centuries), a Spanish Muslim eunuch, to capture the city. Judar Pasha's army was made up of 4,000 Moroccan, Andalusian, and Turkish soldiers; they were armed with 2,500 muskets and transported and supplied by 10,000 camels. Later that year, the Moroccan forces met and decisively defeated a much larger army of about 20,000 Songhai infantry and cavalry at the battle of TONDIBI, near Gao. The firearms carried by Judar Pasha's army panicked the horses of the Songhai cavalry, which had never before encountered these weapons. This battle represents the first major use of firearms in West Africa savanna. Its major cities of Gao, TIMBUKTU, and Jenne-Jeno soon overrun, Songhai became a province of the sultanate of Morocco.

Firearms were even quicker to appear in the Horn of Africa, perhaps because of its proximity to the Ottoman Empire. By 1515 Swahili Coast traders were selling Turkish-made matchlocks in the interior of East Africa, but these firearms had little effect. Not many were sold, and gunpowder was scarce. Turkish-made weapons made an appearance again in 1541, when the Ottoman Turks sent 900 Arab, Turkish, and Albanian musketeers, plus some cannon, into Muslim SOMALIA to support the jihad led by the sultan AHMAD GRAÑ (c. 1506–1543) of ADAL against the Christians of ETHIOPIA. In response the Portuguese supplied a force of 400 matchlock-armed soldiers to help the Ethiopian emperor, LEBNA DENGEL (r. 1508–1530), regain control of the highlands, which had fallen into Muslim hands. Ethiopian craftsmen soon learned how to make copies of these Portuguese weapons, and within a century more than 100,000 of these matchlocks were manufactured in northeastern Ethiopia alone. Clumsy and slow to handle, they were easy to make and repair. Artillery was slower to be copied. The Ethiopians did not manufacture their own cannon until after 1850.

Improvements in Firearms   In the middle of the 16th century Dutch gunsmiths developed a simpler version of the expensive matchlock musket. It was called a *snaphaunce* (from a Low Dutch word meaning "pecking hen") for the way its hammer moved. Unlike the later flintlock, which had a closed flash pan, the hammer of the *snaphaunce* struck a piece of flint against a stationary piece of steel and dropped a spark into an open flash pan below, where a small charge of gunpowder lay exposed as a primer for the main charge inside the gun barrel.

In 1605 the Danes introduced *snaphaunce* muskets into West Africa and exchanged them for trade goods and captives. These muskets found their way into the hands of inland peoples and added a new element to West African warfare.

During the 17th century North Africa was developing its own firearm-manufacturing capabilities, using iron brought north along the caravan routes. Arabs and BERBERS in southeastern Morocco used *snaphaunce* muskets crafted by mostly Jewish gunsmiths who lived in the *kasars* (fortified towns) of the Tafilalt and Figuig regions. These muskets were highly ornate and of fine quality.

The flintlock, the next step in the evolution of the musket, had a covered flash pan that was exposed only when the flint struck a hinged steel plate called the *frizzen* and a spark dropped down. Various models of the flintlock musket, including British "Brown Bess" musket of 1682, became the standard infantry firearm in Europe and North America.

Flintlocks became obsolete in the mid-1800s, when the percussion cap replaced the flintlock mechanism. The percussion cap contains a chemical that explodes when struck, sending a jet of flame through a hole in the back of the gun barrel to ignite the gunpowder inside.

Large numbers of European muskets were sold in Morocco during the 18th and 19th centuries. Many were surplus military weapons, available after European armies adopted percussion cap rifles. Flintlocks were popular among the Arabs in Africa, but percussion cap muskets never were. The percussion caps were hard to buy and could not be manufactured locally.

Changes in Patterns of Warfare   Firearms gradually became a standard military weapon among African peoples, although traditional edged weapons and war clubs also remained in use. (This pattern is similar to military practices outside Africa, where the sword, bayonet, and lance remained in common use even into the 20th century.) By 1700 the ASHANTI EMPIRE, centered in the forests of southern GHANA, was arming its conscript soldiers with muskets.

Ashanti nobility carried richly decorated ceremonial swords (*afena*) as badges of rank. Common soldiers often fought using iron-tipped spears and poisoned arrows. Although formally Muslim, the Ashanti believed in protective magic and on their bodies wore charms to bewitch or confuse their enemies and amulets to defend them against injury and sickness. Many of these, including ones from traditional priests, contained verses from the Quran. They also believed in the magical power of ritual objects, sometimes called *fetishes,* which are contact points with the spirit world and to which devotees offer blood sacrifice.

Among the pastoralist MAASAI people, as with other peoples of East Africa, firearms were uncommon in the 17th and 18th centuries. The Maasai, who were reknowned for their fighting skills, continued to use their traditional weapons: the long spear; the *rungu,* a club which is both a striking and a throwing weapon and is lethal to 50 feet (15 m); and the knife, about 18 inches (46 cm) long and sharpened on both edges.

Their military training was handled in traditional ways. Maasai society is organized into age sets whose members pass together through the stages of junior warrior, senior warrior, junior elder, and senior elder, when they are finally entitled to make decisions for the whole people. As junior warriors (called *morans*) they live in isolation in the bush, developing the strength, courage, and endurance that characterize the Maasai warrior. When an age set undergoes the ritual to become elders, their long hair is shaved off and they are told: "Now that you are an elder, drop your weapons and use your head and wisdom instead."

The Bantu-speaking Zulu people of South Africa represent a major improvement in tactics and organization. The Zulu were originally one of a number of NGUNI clans. They were formed into a nation by SHAKA (c. 1787–1828), who gave the clan name to the new empire he founded. The changes in weaponry, organization, and tactics that Shaka instituted had a profound effect on the peace of southern Africa for the better part of the 18th century. Shaka's achievements have won him the title of "Black Napoleon," after his contemporary, the French general and tactician Napoleon Bonaparte (1769–1821).

Shaka changed the standard armament of his troops. He replaced the long, thin throwing spears that were suitable for conventional battles with the long-bladed, short shafted stabbing spear called an *assagai*. The *assagai* forced Zulu soldiers to fight at close quarters, where their weapon could inflict serious wounds. The *assagai* has been compared with the short Roman thrusting sword, or gladius, that made the Roman legionnaire a fearsome opponent in close combat. Soldiers also often carried a heavy club called a *knobkerrie* (from the AFRIKAANS *knopkierie,* meaning "knob club") and a long shield. Zulu battles were marked by many casualties.

Shaka then instituted a rigid regimental system based on age sets. Members of each regiment, or *impi*, were distinguishable by uniform markings on their shields and by headdresses and ornaments. They lived in separate military kraals, or villages, and were governed by strict rules regarding marriage. Soldiers had to remain celibate until they became elders; violations were punishable by death. Any soldier who showed signs of fear was also killed. Regiments were trained in fighting skills and in endurance, so that soldiers could run for 50 miles a day to reach the site of battle and begin combat without need to rest. On maneuvers they lived off the land, commandeering supplies and cattle from the villages they passed. A troop of boys carrying the soldiers' cooking pots and sleeping mats followed behind.

Shaka trained his soldiers in unit tactics and developed a basic strategy—a pincer, or buffalo horns, formation—that he employed with success in every battle. The regiments in the "chest," or center of the line of battle, attacked up the middle, while the regiments on each flank, or "horn," raced out to encircle the enemy and attack from behind. A final set of regiments, the "loins," stayed in reserve, to fill any gap in the line and to reinforce any part of the ring as it enclosed the foe. The reserves waited with their backs to the fighting so that they would not be caught up in the excitement of battle. Troop movements were indicated by officers called *indunas,* who used hand signals to direct flow of battle.

Shaka fought his opponents with ferocious brutality. By 1817 Zulu territory had expanded fourfold. His army helped him create the most powerful kingdom in the history of southern Africa. He is credited with saving the region from European domination during his lifetime.

See also: WARFARE AND WEAPONS (Vols. I, II, IV, V).

Wargla (Ouargla) North African market town in present-day north-central ALGERIA that was founded by BERBERS in the 11th century. Despite a brief period of occupation by the Ottoman Empire in the 16th century, Wargla was able to remain an independent Berber trade center throughout most of its history. Merchants in Wargla prepared caravans of luxury goods for shipment to regions of sub-Saharan Africa. North African horses, captives, copper, cowries, and foodstuffs were popular trade items. Berber merchant rule in the city ended in the second half of the 19th century, when the French captured Wargla.

See also: OTTOMAN EMPIRE AND AFRICA (Vol. III); TRANS-SAHARAN TRADE ROUTES (Vol. II).

Wassaw (Warshas, Wassa) Forested region located just north of GOLD COAST in West Africa. Wassaw was one of several AKAN chiefdoms established in the 16th century that, under pressure from the confederation of Akan ADANSI states, were forced to seek new territories. The Akan were drawn to Wassaw for both its own GOLD resources and its trade routes to the Gold Coast.

Although Wassaw was not a particularly aggressive nation, its efforts to protect its valuable gold resources led it to become involved in numerous conflicts. In the late 17th century the DENKYIRA, under the Agona dynasty, conquered Wassaw as well as Adom, Fetu, and the Sehwi states. For most of the 18th century Wassaw and the ASHANTI EMPIRE battled over Wassaw's trade routes. These conflicts were exacerbated by British interference. By the late 19th century Wassaw joined the FANTE confederacy of states previously dominated by the Ashanti.

Wegbaja (c. 1645–c. 1680) *King of Abomey and self-proclaimed first king of Dahomey, in West Africa*

Wegbaja, the grandson of Do-Aklin (fl. early 1600s), the founder of what was then the ABOMEY kingdom, is considered the first true leader of the kingdom of DAHOMEY. He is credited with strengthening Abomey, establishing its independence from the kingdom of ALLADA, expanding the kingdom's borders into the surrounding region, and transforming it into the larger, more powerful kingdom of Dahomey.

By reorganizing his various armies and introducing new training techniques and fighting tactics, Wegbaja was responsible for several innovations that enabled his kingdom to flourish. These led to decisive victories over invading armies and allowed Dahomey to expand its power along the coast. He also promoted the idea of a cohesive kingdom by reforming religious practices to focus on the idea of a sacred kingship rather than on ancestor worship.

See also: ANCESTOR WORSHIP (Vol. I); DIVINE RULE (Vols. I, II).

Western Sahara Country in North Africa measuring approximately 103,000 square miles (266,800 sq km) bordered by MOROCCO to the north, ALGERIA to the northeast, MAURITANIA to the southeast, and the Atlantic Ocean to the west. The capital and largest city is Laayoune. The Western Sahara has a small polulation of about 220,000 due to it environment. Much of the land is barren and rocky, and it gets little rainfall. The majority of the population, made up of BERBERS and Arabs, is nomadic.

Spain first claimed the area in 1509, but Morocco ruled it from 1524. Spain reclaimed it in 1860 and made it one of its provinces later known as the Province of Spanish Sahara. In 1884–85, at the Berlin Conference, Spain claimed the coastal stretch between Cape Bojador and Cape Blanc and called the mineral-rich region Río De Oro (Gold River). The regions of Río de Oro and La Aguera were merged to form the Spanish Sahara. Spain ruled the Western Sahara until 1976 when it gave control of the country to Morocco and Mauritania.

See also: SPAIN AND AFRICA (Vols. III, IV); SPANISH SAHARA (Vol. IV); WESTERN SAHARA (Vols. I, II, IV, V).

Wheatly, Phillis (Phillis Peters) (c. 1753–1784)
Senegalese captive and first published African-American poet

Phillis Wheatly was brought to America from her native SENEGAL in 1761 and was purchased by John and Susannah Wheatly of Boston. They quickly recognized her intellectual abilities and set about teaching her the Bible and classical literature at a time when it was rare for a woman, and especially a woman slave, to have a formal education. At 14 years of age she published her first poem in a Boston broadside, or newspaper, and achieved considerable renown.

Later, in 1770, the publication of her "Elegiac Poem," which commemorated the death of Reverend George Whitehead, caused a sensation. She followed up that poem with another entitled "On Being Brought from Africa to America," first published in 1773, in which she laments having lost her freedom. Unable to find an American publisher for a collection of her poetry, Wheatly sailed to England, where she found a London publisher for *Poems on Various Subjects, Religious and Moral.*

Back in America, in 1776 Wheatly wrote her poem, "To His Excellency General Washington," and the future first president subsequently met with her to thank her for her heartfelt work. Despite her early success, Phillis Wheatly died young in relative poverty.

See also: CUGOANO, OTTOBAH (Vol. III); EQUIANO, OLAUDAH (Vol. III).

Further reading: Phillis Wheatly, *Complete Writings,* Vincent Carretta, ed. (New York: Penguin, 2001).

Whydah (Ouidah) Port city and coastal kingdom located on the Gulf of Guinea that served as a European trading post for the transatlantic SLAVE TRADE. The kingdom of Whydah was founded by AJA peoples during the

16th century, about the same time as the neighboring kingdoms of PORTO NOVO and ABOMEY. It wasn't until the 17th century, however, that it gained in importance as a major trade center, with the most valuable trade items passing through the markets at Whydah being salt, European manufactured goods, and captives. Whydah's highly structured, centralized government and its proximity to the coast attracted Dutch, Portuguese, English, and French traders, all of whom established trading stations (called *factories*) and forts along its shore. The French East India Company was the first to build a factory there, in 1671. By the 1680s Whydah had won its independence from the kingdom of ALLADA, to which it had been paying tribute.

See also: TRADING STATIONS, EUROPEAN (Vol. III).

Wolamo (Ometo, Walamo, Welamo) Southern SIDAMO group that established a kingdom of the same name within what is now ETHIOPIA. The Wolamo speak Omotic, a Cushitic language written using the Ge'ez alphabet. They are also known as the Ometo for their proximity to the Omo River valley.

Although many Wolamo adopted Islam or Monophysite Christianity, many of their traditional beliefs and rites remained an important part of their culture. Traditionally agriculturalists, the Wolamo produced grains such as barley and teff, as well as COTTON, and coffee. They were also involved in cattle breeding and bee keeping.

The first king of Wolamo, Moti Lami (Motelemy), came from DAMOT and ruled during the latter half of the 13th century. A later ruling dynasty, the Wolaitamala, came from Mount Kucha and controlled not only Wolamo but also Kucha, Gamo, Kullo, and Boroda. In the 16th century, waves of OROMO immigrants began dominating the Sidamo groups, including Wolamo.

The most notable Wolamo rulers were Gazenja, an early 17th-century king who led his people to several victories over the Oromo, and Kawo Kote, who in the late 1700s made the Wolamo kingdom known throughout the region. By 1830 Wolamo and many other Oro states were subject to the king of KAFFA.

See also: CHRISTIANTIY, INFLUENCE OF (Vols. II, III); COFFEE (Vol. II); ISLAM, INFLUENCE OF (Vols. II, III).

Wolof Empire West African empire in present-day SENEGAL. By the 15th century, the Wolof Empire included the states of Jolof, KAYOR, Walo, BAULE, SERER, and Saloum in its extensive sphere of influence. Initially Jolof was the most important of all the Wolof states. Not only was it the founding state but it was the place from where the *burba jolof,* or Wolof ruler, reigned and where all Wolof tradition originated. When seafaring Portuguese traders arrived in West Africa, in the 15th century, Jolof's

disadvantage as a landlocked state became apparent. With the prospect of increased wealth from maritime trade with the Europeans, the Wolof coastal states felt little incentive to remain within the empire. This internal unrest, made worse by invasions by Mauritanian Moors and other enemies, severely strained the resources and power of the Wolof Empire and jeopardized the leadership of the *burba jolof.*

The most notable internal revolt occurred late in the 15th century when Burba Biram (r. c. 1481) named as his successor his full brother, Bemoy, over his half brothers. When Bemoy took the throne, Biram's half brothers led a rebellion that sent Bemoy to ask for protection from the Portuguese, bringing increasing political unrest. In 1556 Kayor, the largest of all the Wolof states, rose up against the *burba jolof* and declared itself independent. The kingdom chose its own ruler, whom they called *damel.* Confident of its military prowess, Kayor conquered Baule, thereby cutting Wolof off from its two largest centers of commerce.

Further turmoil marked the 17th century. In 1670 Mauritanian marabouts convinced the Wolof people to rebel against their leaders by promising that they would show them how to grow crops by magic, without the effort of planting. With the help of the Wolof people, the Mauritanians successfully defeated the leaders of Kayor and Walo and the *burba jolof.* However, when their crops failed to grow, the Wolof reinstated their royal families and banished the Mauritanians from the region.

See also: WOLOF (Vols. II, IV); WOLOF EMPIRE (Vol. II).

Further reading: Samba Diop, *The Oral History and Literature of the Wolof People of Waalo, Northern Senegal* (Lewiston, N.Y.: E. Mellen Press, 1995).

women in precolonial Africa

In the period between the end of the 15th and the beginning of the 19th centuries, the role of women in Africa varied by region. Among some groups whose cultures prized the matrilineal side of their families, women held positions of power and authority. In the predominantly Islamic areas of Africa, however, women were respected but considered socially inferior. Historically, most ideas of women in Africa prior to the 16th century came from legends and the reconstruction of historical findings. But the arrival of Europeans who traveled and wrote of their experiences in Africa left historians with a written record of how, in the eyes of the Europeans, women lived and were perceived by their families, villages, and peers.

Mother Figures, Helpers, and Healers In many parts of Africa, such as in YORUBALAND and the region around the CROSS RIVER in present-day NIGERIA, women of various ethnic groups were seen as an integral part of society and a counterpart to the male members of the village. Though not necessarily perceived as the social

equals of men, in these societies, including the Yoruba, women were respected as the producers of life and a continuation of the all-important FAMILY lineage, and they were therefore highly regarded. This notion of women being the source of life was common among groups that practiced more traditional religions. Among those groups, the female was linked with fertility and abundance and was often represented by symbols of the earth, moon, and water. In some regions of Africa, the birth of a daughter was cause for much celebration, since girls were able to reproduce and ensure the family's growth.

Fertility goddesses were worshiped with great reverence throughout most areas of sub-Saharan Africa. Two such goddesses were Atetie, of the OROMO people of East Africa, and Eka-Abassi, of the IGBO of West Africa.

Women were expected to help other women in their village during pregnancy and childbirth. For instance, among the MAASAI of present-day TANZANIA and KENYA, women used the art of massage to help ensure an unborn child was correctly positioned within the womb for a healthy birth. Midwifery was also practiced—among some groups, on a professional level—and midwives helped with all aspects of childbirth, from labor to the first few days of the infant's life. Healing the sick was also an important responsibility for women of many different ethnic groups. Some became the assistants to the chief priests, or medicine men, and assisted in diagnosing and treating the ailing. Among the MENDE peoples, located mostly in present-day SIERRA LEONE, the women of the female secret society assumed an important role during times of sickness in the village, consulting the oracle of healing, who answered questions of the victim's health and the likelihood of recovery.

Farmers, Gatherers, Artisans, and Merchants Whether Islamic, Christian, or practitioners of a traditional RELIGION, precolonial African women were hardworking and were more often than not involved in helping the men with various aspects of the daily workings of the household and village. This included collecting firewood and water, and, among peoples whose religion did not forbid women from handling animals, helping with the upkeep of livestock. In most groups, while the men were responsible for hunting prey and fishing, the women were responsible for cultivating crops and gathering roots and vegetables. Food preparation was possibly the most important domestic task, and women were expected to dry fruits and meats and pound out grain for the making of bread and beer. It was noted that many women performed their daily tasks with their infant children in animal-hide slings on their backs and often worked several hours longer per day than their male counterparts.

From an early age women were also taught the skills of basket weaving, pottery making, and the spinning and dyeing of cloth. Handcrafts were used both within the household and for trading purposes with other African groups, as well as with the European traders who began arriving in greater numbers in the 16th century. Women from West African ethnic groups such as the Mandinka and the Ashanti were particularly well known for their weaving and dyeing techniques to make elaborate cloths such as the Ashanti's royal *kente* cloth, which originated around the 17th century and was made from raffia strips and, later, from COTTON. These items, along with other goods produced by women—including jewelry, beads, leather objects, and storage jugs made from calabash gourds—were all sold at trading centers by both men and women to the benefit of their respective economies. In West Africa there also were women who participated in the GOLD trade by MINING gold dust for the Dutch and English during the 17th and 18th centuries. Despite the fact that they were only allowed to work for six weeks out of the year, these women succeeded in securing some income for themselves through the tedious and often disappointing work of gold mining.

Among the Yoruba, women known as *iyalode* were given the important responsibility of protecting women who sold goods in marketplaces.

In contrast to women in these societies, women occupied a much different social role among the Islamic groups of North Africa, the Sudan, and other parts of West and East Africa. Initially, little changed by way of women's complementary role to the men of their group and their duties outside the home. As Islam became more entrenched in some African societies, however, women were relegated to much less prestigious secondary roles in their society. Some personal freedoms, such as the right of a woman to leave her house without permission from her husband, were greatly diminished. Even as the tenets of Islam allowed for great advances in scholarship and commerce, the religion also called for a strong patriarchal society wherein women had few functions outside of the immediate household.

Warriors and Queens   African history has many legends and tales of women soldiers and warriors who fought with or without the company of men to great success and notoriety. Two such notable women were Queen NZINGA (c. 1581–1663), who ruled in present-day AN-

GOLA, and Queen AMINA (r. c. 15th or 16th century?), empress of the Hausa State of ZARIA, in Nigeria. Known for maintaining her people's freedom from the Portuguese, Queen Nzinga was also famous for her band of loyal and fierce female warriors, which helped her resist the Portuguese invaders until her death, in 1663. Amina, too, was reknowned for shrewd military and political tactics that helped extend her nation's boundaries all the way to the Atlantic coast.

Queens Nzinga and Amina were not the only noted female warriors in Africa. In the CONGO, for example, during the 1640s, Queen Llinga, armed with a sword, ax, and bow and arrows, led forces of women warriors against the Portuguese. Not long after, in the 18th century, the HERERO of modern-day NAMIBIA were led by the warrior queen Kaipkire, who successfully battled against British slavers.

Princesses, queens, and queen mothers also played a significant role in many kingdoms in Africa before the colonial era. European writers who visited some of the powerful African kingdoms during the 17th and 18th centuries described the role of favored women in the royal courts in great detail. In the WOLOF EMPIRE, located in what is now SENEGAL, for example, a number of women held high positions within the palace, with the Wolof queen apparently possessing virtually the same rights as the king himself. Beyond this, in many parts of Africa, the daughters of a chief or king possessed considerable amounts of wealth and had numerous opportunities open to them. Among the KONGO people, princesses had the right to force their husbands to remain monogamous during their marriage. Succession to positions of authority from the maternal line was a common practice in the empire of Mali and the ASHANTI EMPIRE in today's GHANA, where kingship was passed down to the son of the king's sister instead of the son of the king himself.

Nevertheless it was the queen and queen mother who were held in the highest regard throughout most African royal courts. In the Wolof Empire and in MWENE MUTAPA, for example, both women were regular advisers to the king. In the Congo region, queens frequently became regents or co-regents when a king died and his successor was considered too young to rule. Regarded as wise and powerful, Mwene Mutapa queen mothers held the title of "mother of all kings," and their opinions on royal matters carried much weight with the king and his council of advisers. Elsewhere some queens and queen mothers held the power to influence the choice of the king's successor. Queen mothers were also often able to

hold land, their own living quarters, and their own courts (sometimes protected by a standing army).

Europeans Bring Changes In the 19th century, with the various European powers establishing a more permanent presence in parts of Africa, the role of women slowly began to change. While the centuries prior had afforded women of most groups a chance to be productive in their communities, as well as their households and immediate families, colonialism brought about a more advanced network of commercial AGRICULTURE that became the exclusive domain of men. Chances at education, too, were curtailed as the women were generally made to stay and tend the homesteads. Regardless, for many women, the precolonial period was one of continued respect and opportunity that came with their roles both within the family as mothers, and also outside the home, as skilled artisans, farmers, healers, and warriors.

See also: QUEENS AND QUEEN MOTHERS (Vol. II); WOMEN IN ANCIENT AFRICA (Vol. I); WOMEN IN COLONIAL AFRICA (Vol. IV); WOMEN IN INDEPENDENT AFRICA (Vol. V); WOMEN IN MEDIEVEL AFRICA (Vol. II).

Further reading: Iris Berger and E. Francis White, eds. *Women in Sub-Saharan Africa* (Bloomington, Ind.: Indiana University Press, 1999); Elizabeth Isichei, *A History of African Societies to 1870* (New York: Cambridge University Press, 1997); Heinrich Loth, *Woman in Ancient Africa;* trans. Sheila Marnie (Westport, Conn.: Lawrence Hill, 1987).

X

Xhosa (Xosa, Kaffir) Subgroup of the NGUNI-speaking peoples of present-day SOUTH AFRICA. The Xhosa trace their foundation to a group of Bantu speakers—Nguni is a Bantu language—who migrated into the area as early as the third century, settling in agricultural and pastoral villages.

> According to oral history a king named Cirha forged the Xhosa kingdom out of the Bantu-speaking people who migrated to southern Africa. Cirha was later overthrown by his brother, Tshawe, who founded the dynasty to which all Xhosa kings trace their lineage.

Traditionally, Xhosa villages were organized into independent, patrilineal chiefdoms; polygamy was accepted. When the son of a chief reached a certain age, he was required to move from his village with his wife and family to start a new Xhosa settlement. In this way the Xhosa spread throughout southern Africa, becoming especially concentrated in the area between the Kei and Fish rivers, near the coast. For more than 1,000 years the Xhosa continued small-scale farming, hunted wild game, raised their herds of cattle, sheep, and goats, and mingled with the Khoisan-speaking pastoralist groups that had settled in the area prior to Bantu expansion (c. 500 BCE–1000 CE).

Dutch settlers began moving to South Africa in the middle of the 17th century, establishing a trading outpost and maritime resupply station at CAPE TOWN, near the Cape of Good Hope. By the late 1760s Dutch-African farmers known as BOERS, or Trekboers, had begun moving into the fertile Xhosa pasturelands in the Zuurveld region from their settlements on the southern tip of the continent. This infiltration of European settlers was initially tolerated by the Xhosa, but the Dutch began claiming larger and larger expanses of Xhosa land.

In 1779 a Xhosa herder was killed in a Boer cattle raid near the Fish River, triggering violent reactions among the Xhosa and leading to a series of armed conflicts called the CAPE FRONTIER WARS, or Boer-Xhosa Wars. The conflicts lasted until the late 1800s. While the Xhosa were able to fend off the Boers, they eventually succumbed to the British, who gained control of the Cape in 1806.

See also: XHOSA (Vols. II, IV, V).

Further reading: J. B. Peires, *The House of Phalo: A History of the Xhosa People in the Days of Their Independence* (Berkeley, Calif.: University of California Press, 1982).

Y

Yaka See IMBANGALA.

Yao Bantu-speaking people inhabiting MALAWI, TANZANIA, and MOZAMBIQUE. The Yao were subsistence farmers and ivory hunters until the 17th century, when they began to emerge as prosperous traders of ivory and human captives. Their increased trading activity curtailed Portuguese ivory collecting around the ZAMBEZI RIVER and also caused the decline of the MARAVI confederation, in the mid-18th century. Yao traders opened up routes between the African interior and Indian Ocean coastal ports including MOZAMBIQUE ISLAND, KILWA, and ZANZIBAR. In the 18th century Yao traders acted as intermediaries in the BISA TRADING NETWORK, which brought ivory through the heart of Yao territory from regions of present-day ZAMBIA and Democratic Republic of the CONGO.

Many Arab and European traders relied upon the Yao to meet their demand for captives as well as ivory. In the 18th century the Yao acquired firearms from Arab traders on the coast and invaded Malawi from western Mozambique. The people they did not kill they captured to sell into bondage.

See also: IVORY TRADE (Vol. III); SLAVE TRADE ON THE SWAHILI COAST (Vol. III); YAO (Vol. IV).

Yatenga (Wahiguya) One of the MOSSI STATES, located in present-day BURKINA FASO. Originally much of what became Yatenga was part of Zandoma, a state in the original Mossi kingdom founded about 1170. Yatenga became independent of Zandoma around 1540, under its chief, or *naba*, Yadega, who supplanted his tutor, Naba Swida, and declared himself chief of a small new state.

> Yatenga comes from *Yadega-tenga,* meaning "the land of Yadega."

Yadega's successors gradually expanded the realm. In the late 16th century Naba Lambwega held sway over the remnants of Zandoma and incorporated the kingdom of Lurum, to the east, into his territory. In the 17th and early 18th centuries Yatenga's expansion continued, generally by establishing Mossi chieftancies to replace local rulers. In the middle of the 18th century Yatenga became embroiled in a series of clashes with the neighboring state of Yako, today a province of Burkina Faso, which vied to control two local chiefdoms. These disputes lasted into the early 1800s.

Although they shared a number of cultural practices, the Mossi States never coalesced into a homogeneous society. By the end of the 18th century Yatenga society was made up of three groups: the Mossi themselves, Fulfulde-speaking FULANI peoples (who call themselves Fulbe), and a Silmi-Mossi group. The Fulani had the status of guests, since they grazed their herds on a broad strip of Mossi territory that was, since the 17th century, leased to them. The Silmi-Mossi were sedentary pastoralists, who resulted from the intermarriage of Mossi women and Fulbe men.

See also: FULFULDE (Vol. I); YATENGA (Vol. II).

Yejju Province in ETHIOPIA inhabited by the OROMO people during their mass migrations in the 16th century. The Oromo of this region were primarily Muslim and the name of their ruling family was Were Shaikh.

The leaders of Yejju superficially adopted Christianity late in the 18th century in order to secure their power over GONDAR. Ras Ali Gwangwil (unknown–1788), known as "Ali the Great," was the first to be baptized. After his death, in 1788, there was an intense battle for the throne. During this time the people of Yejju not only fought each other but also plundered Gondar and Begemdir, leaving a trail of death and destruction behind them. In 1803 Ras GUGSA (r. 1803–1825) took the throne, maintaining order through his strict and often violent rule. The battle for control of Yejju continued on into the 18th century, but rulers such as Faris Ali (r. 1831–1853) were able to prevent the many attempts by Ethiopia's emperors to absorb the region.

Yendi Dabari One-time capital of Dagbon, the kingdom of the DAGOMBA people, located near the contemporary village of Dapeli, in present-day GHANA; its name means "Ruins of Yendi." Although the exact origins of Yendi Dabari are not known, it was, according to oral tradition, founded by Nyagse, the first ruler, or *Ya Na,* of Dagbon. Archaeological excavations suggest that it predates the 17th century. These archaeological excavations also suggest that Dagbon was exposed to Islam sometime during the 16th century, long before the reign of its first Muslim king, Muhammadu Zangina (r. c. 1700–1714). The kingdom's introduction to the religion was most likely made through such Muslim traders as the DYULA.

Among the notable discoveries made at the Yendi Dabari excavations is a two-storied rectangular structure surrounded by a wall that was probably the residence of the Dagomba ruler. Other artifacts found include iron tools, pottery, pipes, and elaborately decorated bowls, jars, and pots.

Like many towns in northern Ghana, Yendi Dabari benefited from trade with AKAN kingdoms and the HAUSA STATES. Indeed it was in attempt to gain the riches from this trade that GONJA attacked Dagbon during the late 17th century. By the early 1700s the Dagomba capital was moved eastward to the site of modern-day Yendi. There Dagomba's twelfth king, Luro (r. c. 1715), attempted to hold off the Gonja invasion. The Gonja, however, proved too powerful, and the Dagomba were pushed out of the White Volta area.

Yishaq (Bahr-Negash Yeshaq) (c. 1540–1580)
Ruler of Eritrea

The title *bahr negash* means "lord of the sea." Appointed by the Ethiopian emperor, the *bahr negash* was the governor of central ERITREA and the coastal regions of Massawa and Zula, in present-day ERITREA. After the 1530s the *bahr negash's* rule became autonomous as a result of the jihad waged by the Muslim warrior AHMAD GRAÑ (c. 1506–1543), which cost Christian ETHIOPIA most of its territory.

In 1535 Ahmad had conquered Ethiopia, forcing the Christian emperor LEBNA DENGEL (r. c. 1508–1540) to hide within in his own country. During this time Yishaq's father, Bahr Nehash Degana, abandoned his position and joined the Muslim forces. Yishaq, however, remained loyal to Ethiopia and his fallen king, and he too spent the next few years in hiding. In 1541 the Portuguese, who were fellow Christians, finally answered Lebna Dengel's appeal for help. Christavão da Gama (fl. c. 1540s), the son of the explorer Vasco da Gama (c. 1460–1524), arrived at Massawa with 400 reinforcements. Yishaq joined in the campaign against Ahmad's army, defeating Ahmad Grañ at Akele Guzai. He also helped the new emperor, Galawdewos (r. 1540–1559), in the campaigns that, in 1543, threw back the Muslims and killed their celebrated leader.

In 1557 the Ottoman Empire helped Yishaq build a fort at Debarwa, his capital. For a time this prevented the Ethiopians from encroaching on his territory. However, the following year, the Ottomans invaded the Ethiopian highlands, only to be turned back by Yishaq. Despite this friction, Yishaq once again turned to the Ottomans for help in 1560–61, when he found himself at odds with Galawdewos's successor, Minas (r. c. 1559–1563). He also called on the Ottomans again for support against Minas's successor, Sarsa Dengel (r. c. 1563–1580). Despite their aid, however, in 1578 Yishaq and the leader of the ADAL state were defeated and killed by Sarsa Dengel in a battle at Adi Qoro, in Tigray. From this time on the power of the *bahr negash* was substantially limited.

See also: MASSAWA (Vol. II).

Yorubaland Located in southwestern NIGERIA, this region was home to several cities that were bound to one another through ethnicity, ancestral heritage, and RELIGION. In time these city-states developed into kingdoms and even empires. At different times, Ile-Ife, Oyo, IJEBU, and Benin were the largest and most powerful of these states. They managed to thrive for nearly 800 years.

Although Ile-Ife was the first state to emerge, and the place where all Yoruba religion and tradition originated, by the 15th century it had begun to lose its political importance to the rising kingdoms of Benin and Oyo.

The Yoruba states participated in a complex political system in which each was at once tributary to the *oni,* or ruler, of Ile-Ife and autonomous in its own right. Each city was ruled by its own *oba,* but on matters that affected or threatened the Yorubaland as a whole, Ile-Ife had the ultimate authority. As Yorubaland expanded economically and territorially, the various kingdoms started to become dissatisfied with such limitations on their power.

As the first state to break away, the kingdom of Benin owed its success to both a strong military and substantial economic wealth, the latter of which was based on trade with the Portuguese. Benin became a kingdom, forming a system of government that was more centralized than that of the other Yoruba states, although in terms of religious practices Benin remained loyal to the *oni* of Ife.

Many changes came about in the 15th century under Benin's Oba Ewuare (c. 1440–1480), who is said to have killed his younger brother in order to obtain the throne. With Ewuare as leader, the kingdom of Benin expanded substantially. By the 17th century, it held most of southeastern Yorubaland, the IGBO area on the western part of the NIGER RIVER, the northern EDO regions, the towns of Akure and Owo, and the areas in and around Ekiti.

In the mid-16th century Oyo was plundered by its NUPE and BORGU neighbors. It took Oyo nearly two centuries to recapture the lost territory. During the 17th and 18th centuries Oyo grew into a powerful empire, with its main source of wealth being the export of human captives. Between 1730 and 1750 Oyo overthrew DAHOMEY, whose interference with Oyo's trade routes was becoming an increasing threat to the stability of the empire. With Dahomey out of the way, Oyo focused on developing its relationship with the Europeans. Trade was conducted through Badagri, LAGOS, and Ajase, ports that came to be known collectively as the SLAVE COAST. By the 18th cen-

tury Oyo controlled a vast region in northern Yorubaland that extended from the Opara River to Sabe and from the Moshi River to Borgu. It also controlled a number of small kingdoms and tributary states. In the latter half of the 18th century Oyo's ruler, the *alafin*, moved the capital of Oyo from Igboho to Old Oyo.

The downfall of the OYO EMPIRE came with the breakdown of its political administration, which eventually collapsed due to internal strife and opposition to the central government. The *alafin's* wealth had corrupted his leadership, and many of the chiefs refused to accept his authority. To add to its problems, Oyo lost its trade routes. With a depleted economy, an unstable government, and a weakened military, Oyo became vulnerable to its enemies from abroad. The FON of Dahomey made a bid for power in the 18th century and inflicted a serious defeat on Oyo. In 1837 the FULANI seized what remained of the once mighty empire.

When the Oyo empire fell in the 18th century the rest of Yorubaland declined as well. What resulted was a series of civil wars that led to the dismantling of all the Yoruba states.

See also: *ALAFIN* (Vol. II); BENIN CITY (Vol. III); *OBA* (Vol. II); OLD OYO (Vol. II); *ONI OF IFE* (Vol. II); YORUBA (Vols. I, II, IV, V); YORUBALAND (Vol. II).

Further reading: G. J. Afolabi Ojo, *Yoruba Culture: A Geographical Analysis* (London: University of London Press, 1966); Robin Law, *The Oyo Empire, c.1600–c.1836: A West African Imperialism in the Era of the Atlantic Slave Trade* (Oxford, U.K.: Clarendon Press, 1977).

Z

Zaghawa Seminomadic people located throughout the central regions of the southern Sahara, especially around Lake CHAD. In the sixth or seventh century the Zaghawa helped to lay the foundations for the kingdom of Kanem, which came to be ruled by the KANURI people. Throughout their history the Zaghawa were active traders, using the numerous caravan routes that crossed their territory to transport goods across the Sahara into the northern reaches of Africa.

In the early 17th century the Zaghawa territories, including the states of Kobe and Dar Kimr, were contested by the two powerful Muslim sultanates of WADAI, in present-day CHAD, and DARFUR, in present-day Republic of the SUDAN. Also during the 17th century Abdullay Boru, from Kobe, became the first Zaghawa ruler to convert to Islam.

By the 18th century the leaders of the KAYRA DYNASTY of Darfur had aligned themselves with the Zaghawa through political maneuvering and marriage alliances. Thereafter, Zaghawa rulers, called sultans, were chosen by the sultan of Darfur.

See also: CARAVAN ROUTES (Vol. I); KANEM (Vol. II); TRANS-SAHARAN TRADE ROUTES (Vol. II).

Zaïre See Democratic Republic of the CONGO.

Zambezi River (Zambesi) River flowing from west to east across southern Africa before emptying into the Indian Ocean on the MOZAMBIQUE coast. Though it is exceedingly difficult to navigate because of its shallowness and its many gorges and falls, between the 16th and 19th centuries the Zambezi was an important means for the movement of people and trade goods, especially CLOTH AND TEXTILES, GOLD, and ivory.

East of the Barotse Plain, the Zambezi River passes over the dramatic 335-foot (102-m) Victoria Falls. The rumble and mist produced by the falling water inspired local Bantu speakers to name it *Mosi o tunya* (smoke that thunders). In 1855 the explorer David Livingstone named the falls in honor of the British queen. Victoria Falls is approximately twice as high and, at almost 1 mile (1.6 km), about twice as wide as the well-known Niagara Falls, on the United States–Canada border.

Before being dammed in the 20th century the Zambezi carried so much silt and sand to the shore that its several mouths could shift drastically in a very short amount of time. For example, the buildings at the trading port of QUELIMANE were used without incident one year only to be abandoned the next because of flooding caused by the drastically different flow of the river.

Despite its poor soil and dry climate, the region surrounding the lower Zambezi, known as Zambezia, was heavily populated by the end of the 15th century. A busy trading center had developed at INGOMBE ILEDE at the confluence of the Kafue and Zambezi rivers, and people from all over were attracted by the region's lucrative trade. The gold sources were controlled by the rulers of the MWENE MUTAPA kingdom, a Karanga state that established several trading markets, or fairs, at sites throughout the Zambezi valley, including Zumbo and possibly Onhaquoro (later the Portuguese town of TETE). These fairs were attended by Indian, Arab, and Muslim traders from the SWAHILI COAST who settled in the Zambezi valley and transported their trade goods to the fairs in canoes on the Zambezi waterway as well as by overland routes. The Muslim presence at the fairs was so strong that the Mwene Mutapa court even had a Muslim representative with jurisdiction over the disputes between Muslim traders. By taxing each transaction at their trade fairs, the Mwene Mutapa kingdom became very wealthy and powerful.

At the beginning of the 16th century, though, the Mwene Mutapa monopoly on the gold trade was being challenged by the newly arrived Portuguese. From the Mwene Mutapa the Portuguese acquired large landholdings, or PRAZOS, all along the Zambezi. The landholders, or *prazeros,* bought many African captives to defend their interests and cultivate their land. The *prazeros* also became heavily involved in the trading and the politics of the region. Their new arrangement disrupted the regular trading patterns that had been established by the coastal Swahili traders, and the Mwene Mutapa kingdom went into what would be a long, steady decline.

Gold remained the most important trade item in the Zambezi valley, but the Portuguese found that the IVORY TRADE was also quite lucrative. By 1530 they had established a trading station on the Indian Ocean coast at Quelimane, which at the time was at one of the mouths of the Zambezi. At the station the Portuguese processed substantial amounts of ivory from the African interior and prepared it for export to India.

Because of the decline of the Mwene Mutapa, the rise of the ivory trade, and the continuing importance of the gold trade, the Zambezi valley became the site of conflicts over the next 200 years. The power struggles that ensued involved not only the Mwene Mutapa kingdom, Portuguese traders, and Swahili traders, but also the CHANGAMIRE DYNASTY, MANYIKA, Tonga, and Barue peoples to the south, and the MARAVI, MAKUA, and YAO peoples to the north.

Trading fairs along the lower Zambezi continued throughout the 17th century, with the most important ones being the Portuguese settlements of Tete and SENA. Although the Portuguese were few in number—in 1633 there were only about 200 settlers in the region—they still were able to bar the Muslim Swahili traders from entering the Zambezi to participate in the trading fairs. Swahili merchants responded by simply using overland routes to bypass the Portuguese blockades, and their trading activities continued nearly unabated.

In the late 17th century the ROZWI rulers of the Changamire kingdom turned the tables on the Portuguese

and excluded them from trading in Manyika territory to the south of the Zambezi. The ban was short-lived—the Portuguese were able to reestablish trade in the region by the 1720s—but their influence in the area had been diminished.

By the middle of the 18th century the once-plentiful gold sources around the lower Zambezi were nearly unworkable and much of the MINING activity had moved to the untapped gold fields to the north. About the same time, the Portuguese established a new trade fair at Zumbo, near the confluence with the Luangwe River, in order to be closer to the new gold sources and to trade more directly with the groups living to the north and south of the river. By the end of the 18th century the Portuguese traders in Zumbo had developed trade contacts with the Bisa and with the expanding LUNDA EMPIRE to the northwest.

Early in the 19th century trade along the Zambezi was upset by the invasions of NGONI warriors, who were chased from their homelands south of the Zambezi by ZULU military campaigns and territorial expansion.

See also: LIVINGSTONE, DAVID (Vol. IV); PORTUGAL AND AFRICA (Vol. III); SLAVE TRADE ON THE SWAHILI COAST (Vol. III); ZAMBEZI RIVER (Vol. I).

Zambia Country in southern Africa measuring approximately 290,600 square miles (752,700 sq km). It is bordered by TANZANIA and the Democratic Republic of the CONGO to the north; MALAWI and MOZAMBIQUE to the east; ZIMBABWE, NAMIBIA, and BOTSWANA to the south; and ANGOLA to the west. Lusaka is its capital and largest city. The Zambia region is an elevated plateau that was home to Bantu-speaking groups that practiced AGRICULTURE, farming, and MINING. The town of INGOMBE ILEDE, located in southern Zambia, at the confluence of the Zambezi and Kafue rivers, was a popular trading center until it was abandoned in the 16th century. Early European contacts, which began in the 16th century, were primarily with Portuguese traders. Ivory and copper were the first items exchanged, but the trade in human captives soon came to define European-African relations for centuries to come.

In the 17th century Bantu speakers moved into Zambia from the kingdoms of the LUNDA EMPIRE to the north when land became scarce there. The Bisa people became renowned ivory traders, acting as intermediaries between Lunda traders and merchants in Mozambique and farther north along the SWAHILI COAST. The LOZI people, probably related to the people of the eastern Lunda kingdoms, migrated to the Zambezi floodplains, where they cultivated subsistence crops. In the 18th century the BEMBA people joined the Bisa and the Lozi in the region. Ivory hunters and warriors, the Bemba practiced some agriculture and moved when resources became scarce.

The 19th century was a pivotal period in the region's history. The Kololo people from the north and the NGONI from the south invaded and conquered large portions of the country.

See also: BISA TRADING NETWORK (Vol. III); IVORY TRADE (Vol. III); ZAMBIA (Vols. I, II, IV, V).

Further reading: Andrew Roberts, *A History of Zambia* (New York: African Publishing Co., 1976).

Zamfara One of the seven so-called illegitimate HAUSA STATES located in present-day NIGERIA between the NIGER RIVER and Lake CHAD. Possibly inhabited as early as the 11th century, the state of Zamfara only truly began to gain importance in the mid-14th to 15th centuries. Along with its sister states—which vary according to different sources but are generally thought to include ILORIN, Gwari, NUPE, KEBBI, KWARARAFA (also known as Jukun), and Yauri—Zamfara is considered one of the seven Banza Bakwai, or "bastard," states supposedly formed by Prince Bayajidda of Baghdad. According to oral tradition, the seven "true" Hausa States, or Hausa Bakwai, of Daura, Rano, KANO, Zazzau (later known as ZARIA), Biram, GOBIR, and KATSINA were established for the seven children born to the prince and a Hausa queen. According to that tradition, the Banza Bakwai were created to be ruled by Prince Bayajidda's seven illegitimate children born of concubines.

As the whole of Hausaland lacked a sense of unity, it was common for the states to wage war against one another for tribute as well as for rights to the profitable trans-Saharan trading routes. During the early 18th century Zamfara became a major force within the Hausa States, defeating the powerful state of Kano and becoming the chief rival of the equally strong Katsina. Throughout the century, Zamfara continued to be a dominant presence in Hausaland. However, this changed in the 19th century, when the state of Gobir gained control over the region. Constant battles had a debilitating effect, and ultimately Zamfara's weakness made it susceptible to a forcible takeover. This came through the FULANI jihad waged in 1804 by USMAN DAN FODIO (1754–1817). The Fulani scholar and religious leader sought to convert the peoples of Hausaland to a purer form of Islam than the mixture of Islam and traditional religious customs that they were practicing. With the success of the jihad, Zamfara and the other Hausa States were then incorporated as emirates into Usman dan Fodio's vast kingdom, which became known as the SOKOTO CALIPHATE.

Zanzibar Island and city off the East African coast. Although its history probably dates back to 1200 BCE or even earlier, little is known definitely about the early history of Zanzibar. Its name is believed to come from the Persian words *zanj* (meaning "black") and *bar* (coast), and the term *Zanzibar* was at one time used by Arab geographers to refer to all of the East African coast. Eventually, however, the term was reserved for only the island that is now known by that name.

From the second to the 15th centuries Zanzibar was essentially ruled by a network of Arab and Persian traders, who mixed with various local populations and under whom commerce expanded. During this period immigration from Arabia, Persia, and India brought in a host of new residents, who joined the long-standing Haidmu and Tumbatu inhabitants, both of whom apparently were of Shirazi origin.

The period known as the First Arab Period is described in the *Chronicle of Kilwa*, which tells how a Persian merchant set sail, along with his six sons, across the Indian Ocean for Zanzibar and PEMBA ISLAND. There, according to the chronicle, the Persians established Kizimkazi in 1107, a date that is generally accepted as the first firm timeframe in the history of Zanzibar.

The arrival of Portuguese explorers and soldiers, beginning in the last years of the 15th century, radically transformed Zanzibar. Vasco da Gama (c. 1460–1524) himself stopped at Zanzibar, in 1499, later attacking it, in 1503 and 1509, and destroying the main town. Using their superior military might, the Portuguese gained control of Zanzibar, forcing the local ruler to become a vassal of the king of Portugal. In time the Portuguese assumed power over much of East Africa, holding sway for 200 years. The Portuguese, however, were too thinly spread in the area to maintain firm control. Also, they encountered continued resistance from the local KISWAHILI-speaking inhabitants. As a result, by 1698 they had lost control of Zanzibar and other holdings in the region.

At this time the second period of Arab dominance began, and Zanzibar, as well as much of East Africa, came under the influence of the OMANI SULTANATE. The various city-states of the region, however, frequently fell back into their old habits of rivalry and warfare, especially between the BUSAIDI and MASRUI families, the two dominant dynasties battling for control of Zanzibar. This instability, along with continued resistance to Arab domination from local African people, kept the region in turmoil for much of this second Arab period.

Eventually the Busaidi family won out in the battle for supremacy among the Omanis, and the dynasty transformed Zanzibar into an important commercial entity. By the time of the powerful sultan SAYYID SAID (1791–1856),

An illustration from around 1815 of Stone Town, the old city of Zanzibar. The old city is the site of winding alleys, bazaars, old mosques, and large Arab houses, whose builders vied with one another in extravagance. Zanzibar was one of the most important centers of Indian Ocean trade. © *Bojan Brecelj/Corbis*

Zanzibar was the dominant state in the region, a position it continued to hold during the colonial period that followed.

See also: INDIAN OCEAN TRADE (Vol. II); PIRATES (Vol. III); SHIRAZI ARABS (Vol. III); ZANZIBAR (Vol. II, IV, V).

Further reading: Norman Robert Bennett, *Arab Versus European: Diplomacy and War in Nineteenth-Century East Central Africa* (New York: Africana Pub. Co., 1986).

Zaramo Largest ethnic group of DAR ES SALAAM in TANZANIA, on Africa's SWAHILI COAST. Historically, there are two main clans of Zaramo: the Shomvi, who live along the coast, and the Pazi, who live in the hills. Artistically, the Zaramo are noted for their wood carving and drums. For centuries their traditional culture has been intertwined with Islamic religion and law.

Further reading: I. N. Kimambo and A. J. Temu, *A History of Tanzania* (Nairobi, Kenya: East African Publishing House, 1969).

Zaria Capital city of Zazzau, one of the original HAUSA STATES, located in present-day NIGERIA. Founded as early as the 11th century, Zazzau, was one of the seven "true"

states of Hausaland known as Hausa Bakwai. Beginning in the 15th century the state's southern location made it the central region for the capture of people for the northern Hausa States during their involvement in the transatlantic SLAVE TRADE. Zazzau was also a trading market for other goods, such as animal hides and grains, with merchants from the Sahara.

Zazzau and other Hausa States were converted to Islam by the 15th century. The writings of Arab traveler LEO AFRICANUS (1485–1554) tell of Zazzau's conquest by SONGHAI ruler Askia MUHAMMAD TOURÉ (d. 1538). Perhaps the most notable ruler of Zazzau, however, was the legendary Queen AMINA (r. c. 15th century?). Famous for building defensive walls around the city of Zaria, Amina was a great warrior-queen and military strategist. Her successful conquest of neighboring Hausa States allowed her to extract tributes from even the influential states of KATSINA and KANO.

Near the end of the 16th century Zazzau, by then renamed Zaria, was conquered by KWARARAFA, a "bastard" Hausa state centered near Ibi. Zaria remained under Kwararafa rule until 1734, when it became a tributary state of KANEM-BORNU, located near Lake CHAD. In 1804 the fundamentalist FULANI leader USMAN DAN FODIO (1754–1817) launched a jihad and conquered the whole of Hausaland, incorporating it into the SOKOTO CALIPHATE. By the end of the jihad, in 1808, Zaria was under Fulani rule. In 1835 it became an emirate ruled by both the sultan of Sokoto and a local emir.

See also: ZAZZAU (Vol. II).

Zawaya Muslim Berber clerics of the central Sahara who wandered North Africa, studying at Islamic retreats called *zawiya*. By the beginning of the 16th century nomadic Zawaya clerics had attained positions of power in various cities throughout MOROCCO and the central Sahara.

The Zawaya were the spiritual descendants of the Almoravids, a reformist group of Islamic BERBERS from the Sanhaja confederation who ruled the MAGHRIB and much of southern Spain in the 11th and 12th centuries. The root of *Almoravid* is the Arabic word *ribat,* meaning "retreat," which has a meaning similar to the word *zawiya.*

Early in the 16th century the Sanhaja Berbers of Morocco actively resisted Arab influence by trying to preserve their own Berber language and by attempting to unify several of their clans under a single leader. Overwhelmed by the Arab migrations, though, a group of respected Sanhaja Berbers renounced their warrior status and instead pursued Islam as a means of gaining influence. Islam had been brought to North Africa by an early wave of Arab invaders starting in the seventh century. Ironically, the Zawaya of the 16th century used Islam as a political tool against a later wave of Arab immigrants in order to regain some power in the region.

Prior to their becoming holy men, the Zawaya adhered to the Berber custom of following matrilineal descent, but their new emphasis on Islam caused them to retrace their descent along patrilineal lines back to the prophet Muhammad.

By the beginning of the 17th century Zawaya retreats had become centers of political power as well as centers of Islamic learning. The SADIAN DYNASTY (1510–1613), a line of Zawaya clerics, led Moroccan efforts to end Portuguese occupation and called for resistance to the invasion of the Ottoman Empire. Their influence spread so that between 1640 and 1660 Berber forces, influenced by the teachings of Zawaya clerics, occupied most of the major cities of northern Morocco.

Toward the end of the 17th century the Zawaya sultan, Mawlay al-Rashid (d. c. 1672), established the Alawid ruling dynasty (1668–present). Rashid success-

fully repressed other Islamic clerical brotherhoods in Morocco and recaptured the Moroccan city of FEZ. After al-Rashid it was clear that the Zawaya movement would not evolve into a new Berber dynasty, as the Almoravid movement had done centuries earlier.

See also: ALMORAVIDS (Vol. II); ISLAM, INFLUENCE OF (Vols. II, III, IV); ISLAMIC CENTERS OF LEARNING (Vol. II); OTTOMAN EMPIRE AND AFRICA (Vol. III).

Zazzau See ZARIA.

Zeila (Saylac, Zayla) Chief port of the northern coast of present-day SOMALIA, along the Gulf of Aden, and capital of the Muslim kingdom of ADAL. Zeila was a walled town and the chief port for commerce between traders from the Ethiopian hinterland and sea merchants from Arabia and Persia. Items brought from the interior included ivory, human captives, coffee, animal skins, gums, incense, and ostrich feathers. These goods were traded for cloth, metalwork, dates, iron, pottery, and weapons. Firearms were first introduced into Somalia, in 1515, when Arabian traders brought them to Zeila.

Zeila became the target of European aggression in 1516 when Portuguese sea captains sacked the town in their attempts to control Red Sea and East African maritime trade. After the attack, the nearby port of BERBERA assumed the importance that Zeila had enjoyed until it, too, was pillaged. Between the middle of the 16th and the middle of the 17th centuries, Portuguese expeditions in ETHIOPIA periodically attacked Zeila, disrupting long-established trade relations in the region.

Seeking protection from the Portuguese, Zeila eventually swore allegiance to the sultan of Yemen, across the Gulf of Aden, late in the 16th century. By the 18th century the Ottoman Empire had replaced the Yemeni rulers in Zeila. The port would become critical during the European colonial era because of its strategic location near the Red Sea.

See also: OTTOMAN EMPIRE AND AFRICA (Vol. III); ZEILA (Vol. II).

Zemene Mesafint (Age of Princes) Period of anarchy and political unrest in ETHIOPIA that lasted from 1769 to 1855; known in English as the "Age of Princes." It was at this time that the central government collapsed and the provinces of Begemder, DAMOT, SIMIEN, SHOA, Tigray, and Wag-Lasta became autonomous.

The event that precipitated Ethiopia's fall into a period of anarchy happened when Ras Mikael Sehul (c. 1692–1794), the *ras,* or governor, of Tigray Province, helped the emperor resist a takeover of the government by the Muslim OROMO people. He occupied the capital by force and had himself proclaimed regent. He then orchestrated the assassination of the emperors Iyoas (r. 1755–1769) and Yohannes II (r. 1769). Mikael Sehul handpicked the next emperor, the ineffective Tekla Haymonot II (r. 1769–1777), whom he, as regent, was able to control and manipulate.

This dynamic between the Ethiopian emperor and his nobles, or regents, continued for nearly 100 years. As a result the emperor became a figure with no power or authority. During this period what was once the vast domain of the Christian empire became a region characterized by warfare and violence, bred not only by politics but also by conflicts within the Ethiopian Orthodox Church.

Ras GUGSA (r. 1800–1825), the regional lord of YEJJU stands out as having a successful reign at GONDAR. This was in part due to his having the foresight to reach out to the Christian lords. He did this by offering them his daughters' hands in marriage. Ras Gugsa's grandson Ali Alula (r. 1831–1853) became lord of Yejju, in 1831. His reign was as ineffectual as his father's and uncles' had been, although he managed to hold onto Begemder and GOJJAM during his leadership.

In 1853 Kassa Haylu, later crowned Téwodros II (1855–1868), conquered Ali Alula and put an end to the Age of Princes. Although his rule was met with a certain amount of instability, Téwodros II is credited with consolidating the empire and paving the way for the elimination of the feudal system that destroyed the Christian empire and its monarchy in the first place.

See also: TÉWODROS II (Vol. IV); TIGRAY (Vols. I, IV, V).

Zimba East African ethnic group indigenous to the region southwest of Lake Malawi in present-day MALAWI, ZAMBIA, and MOZAMBIQUE. The Zimba are probably related to the Karanga, the original Bantu-speaking settlers of the region to the west of Lake Malawi. In the 15th century Zimba territory was overrun by the groups that would come to constitute the MARAVI, a loosely organized confederation of peoples in and around Malawi that came to power in the 16th and 17th centuries. The Maravi group most closely associated with the Zimba are the Lundu peoples, who split from the KALONGA chiefdom in the middle of the 16th century, migrated south, and peacefully assimilated the Zimba into their chiefdom.

In the 16th century Portuguese spice traders had settled MOZAMBIQUE ISLAND, Angoche, and QUELIMANE, on East Africa's southern coast to the west of Zimba territory, but had not attempted to move into the inhospitable inland regions to the north of the ZAMBEZI RIVER. In the second half of the century, though, they attempted to monopolize the region's lucrative IVORY TRADE. In response a Lundu group, probably led by fierce Zimba warriors, pushed east into the coastal region between KILWA

and MOMBASA, disrupting the ivory trade and leaving death and destruction in their wake.

In 1592 the Portuguese attacked the Maravi groups who lived to the south of Lake Malawi. They were forcefully repelled by these Maravi, whom they called *mazimba,* and were subsequently routed from SENA, an important trading center on the Zambezi. Tales of Zimba fierceness kept the Portuguese from making further attempts to settle lands to the north and west of Mozambique Island until the middle of the 17th century.

By the middle of the 18th century the Portuguese, seeking to capitalize on the area's GOLD trade, had assumed control of most of the former Zimba territory. When slave trading became a force in the region, in the late 18th and early 19th centuries, the Zimba were subject to raids by Arab, YAO, and European traders from the east. Also during this period some of the Zimba were subjugated by the Macanga, a chiefdom ruled by the descendants of Portuguese Indian immigrants.

See also: KARANGA (Vol. II); PORTUGAL AND AFRICA (Vols. III, IV).

Zimbabwe Country in southern Africa measuring approximately 150,900 square miles (390,800 sq km) and bordered by ZAMBIA to the north, MOZAMBIQUE to the east, SOUTH AFRICA to the south, and BOTSWANA to the west. The present-day capital and largest city is Harare.

Bantu-speaking Shona people dominated the region that is Zimbabwe by the 10th century. As competition for the ivory and GOLD trades increased in the 14th century, distinct centralized SHONA KINGDOMS emerged throughout the region. The first major kingdoms, Great Zimbabwe and Torwa, emerged by the mid-1500s. Also around this time, the MWENE MUTAPA kingdom was established. This kingdom, which came to power in northeastern Zimbabwe, was built on the gold trade. In the late 17th century the kings of the ROZWI dynasty emerged, conquered the Mwene Mutapa, and seized control of the gold trade.

The MFECANE, or "The Crushing," a mass migration caused by ZULU expansion in the early 19th century, forced new peoples into Shona lands. The movement of people led to the establishment of the Ndebele kingdom but also eventually caused the disintegration of some Shona states—including the kingdom led by the Rozwi kings—that had been weakened by earlier NGONI assaults.

See also: GREAT ZIMBABWE (Vol. II); HARARE (Vol. V); IVORY TRADE (Vol. III); ZIMBABWE (Vols. I, II, IV, V).

Further reading: Martin Hall, *The Changing Past: Farmers, Kings and Traders in Southern Africa, 200–1860* (Cape Town, South Africa: D. Philip, 1987); Innocent Pikirayi, *The Zimbabwe Culture: Origins and Decline of Southern Zambezian States* (Walnut Creek, Calif.: AltaMira Press, 2001).

Zulu (AmaZulu) Clan of the Bantu-speaking NGUNI people of Natal, in SOUTH AFRICA. The Nguni were divided into the Mthethwa, Elangeni, Ndwandwe, and Zulu clans. These were part of a larger people, including the NDLAMBE, Gcaleka, Thembu, MPONDO, Mpondomise, Bhaca, and Hlubi clans, who inhabited much of southern Africa. Early in the 1800s the Zulu clan became predominant and gave its name to a new empire.

Each Zulu clan, which was highly patriarchal, had its own chief, who was the senior male. By virtue of patrilineal descent, he had both religious and political authority. The clan chief was its leader in war and its law giver and judge in peacetime. Most clan leaders were related by marriage to the local king.

Traditional Zulu religion was based on a belief in a supreme being and supernatural powers. The king performed seasonal rituals in the name of the people to propitiate his royal ancestors at planting time and in times of drought or famine.

The Zulu clans were both pastoral and agricultural. The women grew millet, and the men tended the cattle.

Marriages were generally arranged between clans, and cattle were used as *lobola*, or bride-wealth. Women moved to the villages of their mates. Polygamy was practiced, and wives were ranked by seniority, starting with the chief wife, who was the mother of the heir. In some circumstances widows married the dead husband's brother.

In 1807 DINGISWAYO (d. 1817) of the Mthethwa clan began the process of absorbing nearby Nguni clans into a larger centralized state. He also began a trade relationship with the Portuguese at MOZAMBIQUE. Dingiswayo was assassinated, in 1817, by the head of the rival Ndwandwe clan. For his heir, Dingiswayo had chosen SHAKA (1787–1828) of the Zulu clan. Shaka made the Zulu the dominant Nguni clan in the region and continued the process of expansion and conquest that Dingiswayo had begun.

Under Shaka, the Zulu nation developed into a military power, dominating the region for most of the 19th century and engaging in wars of expansion against its neighbors and the colonial powers. Zulu expansion led to the MFECANE of the 1820s and 1830s, which forced the

Zulu warriors, circa 1865, shown in traditional dress. Their distinctive headgear, the markings on their shields, and the ornaments on their clothing were used to distinguish members of different regiments in battle. © *Corbis*

migration of many peoples and permanently changed the social and political structure of southern Africa. The Zulu empire fell after of the Anglo-Zulu War of 1879. In that confrontation, Zulu armies effectively fought the British army to a standstill until the Zulu leader, Cetshwayo (c. 1826–1884), was defeated at Ulundi.

See also: ANGLO-ZULU WAR (Vol. IV); BRIDE-WEALTH (Vol. I); CETSHWAYO (Vol. IV); ZULU (Vols. IV, V).

Further reading: John Laband, *The Rise & Fall of the Zulu Nation* (New York: Sterling Publishing, 1997).

GLOSSARY

agriculturalists Sociological term for "farmers."

agro-pastoralists People who practice both farming and animal husbandry.

alafin Yoruba word for "ruler" or "king."

Allah Arabic for "God" or "Supreme Being."

Americo-Liberian Liberians of African-American ancestry.

ancestor worship Misnomer for the traditional practice of honoring and recognizing the memory and spirits of deceased family members.

al-Andalus Arabic term for Muslim Spain.

animism Belief that inanimate objects have a soul or life force.

anglophone English speaking.

apartheid Afrikaans word that means "separateness"; a formal system and policy of racial segregation and political and economic discrimination against South Africa's nonwhite majority.

aphrodesiac Food or other agent thought to arouse or increase sexual desire.

askia Arabic word meaning "general" that was applied to the Songhai kings. Capitalized, the word refers to a dynasty of Songhai rulers.

assimilados Portuguese word for Africans who had assimilated into the colonial culture.

Australopithicus africanus Hominid species that branched off into *Homo habilis* and *A. robustus*.

Australopithicus anamensis Second-oldest species of the hominid *Australopithicus*.

Australopithicus ramadus Oldest of the apelike, hominid species of *Australopithicus*.

Australopithicus robustus A sturdy species of *Australopithicus* that came after *A. africanus* and appears to have been an evolutionary dead end. *Australopithecus robustus* roamed the Earth at the same time as *Homo habilis*.

balkanization The breaking apart of regions or units into smaller groups.

barter Trading system in which goods are exchanged for items of equal value.

bey Governor in the Ottoman Empire.

Bilad al-Sudan Arabic for "Land of the Blacks."

bride price The payment made by a groom and his family to compensate the bride's father for the loss of her services because of marriage.

British Commonwealth Organization of sovereign states that were former colonies under the British Empire.

caliph Title for Muslim rulers who claim to be the secular and religious successors of the Prophet Muhammad.

caliphate Muslim state ruled by a caliph.

caravel A small, maneuverable ship used by the Portuguese during the Age of Discovery.

caste A division of society based on wealth, privilege, rank, or occupation.

circumcision The cutting of the clitoris (also called clitorectomy or clitoridectomy) or the prepuce of the penis; a rite of passage in many African societies.

cire perdu French for "lost wax," a technique used to cast metals.

clan A group that traces its descent from a common ancestor.

conflict diamonds Gems that are sold or traded extra-legally in order to fund wars.

conquistadores Spanish for "conquerors"; term used to describe the Spanish leaders of the conquest of the Americas during the 1500s.

constitutional monarchy State with a constitution that is ruled by a king or queen.

customary law Established traditions, customs, or practices that govern daily life and interaction.

degredados Portuguese criminals who were sent to Africa by the Portuguese king to perform hazardous duties related to exploration and colonization.

dhow Arabic word for a wooden sailing vessel with a triangular sail that was commonly used to transport trade goods.

diaspora Word used to describe a large, readily distinguishable group of people settled far from their ancestral homelands.

divination The interpretation of supernatural signs, usually done by a medicine man or priest.

djembe African drum, often called "the healing drum" because of its use in healing ceremonies.

emir A Muslim ruler or commander.

emirate A state ruled by an emir.

endogamy Marriage within one's ethnic group, as required by custom or law.

enset Another name for the "false banana" plant common in Africa.

ethnic group Term used to signify people who share a common culture.

ethno-linguistic Word used to describe a group whose individuals share racial characteristics and a common language.

eunuch A man who has been castrated (had his testicles removed), generally so that he might be trusted to watch over a ruler's wife or wives.

francophone French speaking.

government transparency Feature of an open society in which the decisions and the policy-making process of leaders are open to public scrutiny.

griot Storyteller, common in West African cultures, who preserves and relates the oral history of his people, often with musical accompaniment.

gross domestic product (GDP) Total value of goods and services produced by a nation's economy, within that nation. GDP is measured within a certain time frame, usually a year.

gross national product (GNP) Total value of goods and services produced by the residents of a nation, both within the nation as well as beyond its borders. Like GDP, GNP is measured within a certain time frame, usually a year.

hajj In Islam, a pilgrimage to Mecca.

hajjiyy "Pilgrim" in Arabic.

hegira Arabic for "flight" or "exodus"; generally used to describe the move of the Muslim prophet Muhammad from Mecca to Medina.

hominid Biological term used to describe the various branches of the Hominidae, the family from which modern humans descend according to evolutionary theory.

ideology A coherent or systematic way of looking at human life and culture.

imam A spiritual and political leader of a Muslim state.

imamate The region or state ruled by an imam.

indigénat Separate legal code used by France in its judicial dealings with the indigenous African population of its colonies.

infidel Term used as an epithet to describe one who is unfaithful or an unbeliever with respect to a particular religion .

infrastructure Basic physical, economic, and social facilities and institutions of a community or country .

Janissary From the Turkish for "new soldier," a member of an elite Ottoman military corps.

jebel "Mountain" in Arabic.

kabaka The word for "king" in Babito and Buganda cultures.

kemet Egyptian for "black earth."

kora Small percussion instrument played by some griots.

kraal Enclosure for cattle or a group of houses surrounding such an enclosure.

lineage A group whose individuals trace their descent from a common ancestor; usually a subgroup of a larger clan.

lingua franca Common language used by speakers of different languages.

Luso-African Word that describes the combined Portuguese and African cultures, especially the offspring of Portuguese settlers and indigenous African women. (The Latin name for the area of the Iberian Peninsula occupied by modern Portugal was Lusitania.)

madrasa Theological school for the interpretation of Islamic law.

Mahdi Arabic word for "enlightened one," or "righteous leader"; specifically, the Muslim savior who, in Islamic belief, is to arrive shortly before the end of time.

mamluk Arabic for "one who is owned"; capitalized, it is a member of an elite military unit made up of captives enslaved and used by Islamic rulers to serve in Middle Eastern and North African armies.

mansa Mande term for "king" or "emperor."

marabout A mystical Muslim spiritual leader.

massif A mountainous geological feature.

mastaba Arabic for an inscribed stone tomb.

matrilineal Relating to descent on the maternal, or mother's, side.

medina Arabic word for the old section of a city.

megaliths Archaeological term meaning "large rocks"; used to describe stelae and such features as cairns and tumuli that mark important places or events for many ancient cultures.

mestizo Adjective meaning "of mixed blood."

mfecane Zulu word meaning "the crushing." When capitalized, the word refers to the nineteenth-century Zulu conquests that caused the mass migration of peoples in southern Africa.

microliths Archaeological term meaning "small rocks"; used to describe sharpened stone blade tools of Stone Age cultures.

Monophysite Related to the Christian tradition that holds that Jesus Christ had only one (divine) nature.

Moor An Arab or Berber conqueror of al-Andalus (Muslim Spain).

mulatto The offspring of a Negroid (black) person and a Caucasoid (white) person.

mwami Head of the Tutsi political structure, believed to be of divine lineage.

negusa negast "King of kings" in Ethiopic; traditional title given to the ruler of Ethiopia.

neocolonialism Political or economic policies by which former colonial powers maintain their control of former colonies.

Nilotic Relating to peoples of the Nile, or Nile River basin, used especially to describe the languages spoken by these peoples.

Nsibidi Secret script of the Ekoi people of Nigeria.

oba Yoruba king or chieftain.

pasha A high-ranking official in the Ottoman Empire.

pashalik Territory or province of the Ottoman Empire governed by a pasha.

pass book A feature of apartheid-era South Africa, pass books were identification documents that black Africans, but not whites, were required by law to carry at all times.

pastoralists People whose livelihood and society center on raising livestock.

patriarch Male head of a family, organization, or society.

patrilineal Relating to descent through the paternal, or father's, side.

poll tax A tax of a fixed amount per person levied on adults.

polygyny The practice of having more than one wife or female mate at one time.

prazeros Portuguese settlers in Africa who held prazos.

prazos Similar to feudal estates, parcels of land in Africa that were leased to Portuguese settlers by the Portuguese king.

primogeniture A hereditary system common in Africa by which the eldest child, or more commonly, the eldest son, receives all of a family's inheritance.

proverb A short popular expression or adage. Proverbs are tools for passing on traditional wisdom orally.

pygmy Greek for "fist," a unit of measurement; used to describe the short-statured Mbuti people.

qadi Arabic for "judge."

Quran (also spelled Koran) Arabic for "recitation," and the name of the book of Muslim sacred writings.

ras A title meaning "regional ruler" in Ethiopia.

rondavel Small, round homes common in southern Africa.

salaam Arabic for "peace."

sarki Hausa word for "king."

scarification Symbolic markings made by pricking, scraping, or cutting the skin.

secret society Formal organizations united by an oath of secrecy and constituted for political or religious purposes.

shantytowns A town or part of a town consisting mostly of crudely built dwellings.

sharia Muslim law, which governs the civil and religious behavior of believers.

sharif In Islamic culture, one of noble ancestry.

sheikh (shaykh, sheik) Arabic word for patrilineal clan leaders.

sirocco Name given to a certain type of strong wind in the Sahara Desert.

souk Arabic word for "market."

stelae Large stone objects, usually phallus-shaped, whose markings generally contain information important to those who produced them.

stratified Arranged into sharply defined classes.

stratigraphy The study of sequences of sediments, soils, and rocks; used by archaeologists to determine the approximate age of a region.

sultan The king or sovereign of a Muslim state.

sultanate The lands or territory ruled by a sultan.

syncretism The combining of religious beliefs to form a new religion.

taboo (adj.) forbidden by custom, usually because of the fear of retribution by supernatural forces; (n.) a prohibition based on morality or social custom.

tafsir Arabic for "interpretation," especially as regards the Quran.

taqwa In Islam, the internal ability to determine right from wrong.

taro Another name for the cocoyam, an edible tuber common throughout Africa.

tauf Puddled mud that, when dried, serves as the foundation for some homes in sub-Saharan Africa.

teff A grass native to Africa that can be threshed to produce flour.

theocracy Government of a state by officials who are thought to be guided by God.

ulamaa Islamic learned men, the inheritors of the tradition of the prophet Muhammad.

vizier A high-ranking official in a Muslim state, esp. within the Ottoman Empire.

SUGGESTED READINGS FOR AFRICA, FROM CONQUEST TO COLONIZATION

Abir, Mordechai. *Ethiopia: The Era of the Princes: The Challenge of Islam and the Re-unification of the Christian Empire 1769–1855*. London and Harlow: Longmans, Green and Co., 1968.

Abun-Nasr, Jamil M. *A History of the Maghrib in the Islamic Period*. New York: Cambridge University Press, 1987.

Ajayi, J. F. Ade, ed. *UNESCO General History of Africa. Vol. VI, Africa in the Nineteenth Century until the 1880s*. Berkeley, Calif.: University of California Press, 1989.

Ajayi, J. F. Ade. *Christian Missions in Nigeria, 1841–1891; The Making of a New Elite*. London: Longmans, 1965.

Ajayi, J. F. Ade and Michael Crowder, eds. *History of West Africa*, Vol. 1. 3rd ed. Burnt Mill, Harlow, Essex, UK: Longman, 1985. Vol. 2, 2nd ed. Burnt Mill, Harlow, Essex, UK: Longman, 1987.

Alpern, Stanley B. *Amazons of Black Sparta: The Women Warriors of Dahomey*. New York: New York University Press, 1999.

Alpers, Edward A. *Ivory & Slaves in East Central Africa: Changing Patterns of International Trade to the Later Nineteenth Century*. London: Heinemann, 1975.

Anderson, Martha G., and Christine Mullen Kreamer. *Wild Spirits, Strong Medicine: African Art and the Wilderness*. New York: Basic Civitas Books, 1999.

Austen, Ralph A., and Jonathan Derrick. *Middlemen of the Cameroons Rivers: the Duala and their Hinterland, c.1600–c.1960*. New York: Cambridge University Press, 1999.

Awolalu, Omosade. *Yoruba Beliefs and Sacrificial Rites*. New York: Longman, 1979.

Barry, Boubacar. *Senegambia and the Atlantic Slave Trade*. New York: Cambridge University Press, 1998.

Baur, John. *2000 Years of Christianity in Africa: An African History, 62–1992*. Nairobi, Kenya: Paulines, 1994.

Bay, Edna G. *Wives of the Leopard: Gender, Politics, and Culture in the Kingdom of Dahomey*. Charlottesville, Vir.: University of Virginia Press, 1998.

Beach, David N. *The Shona and Zimbabwe, 900–1850: an Outline of Shona History*. Gwelo, Zimbabwe: Mambo Press, 1980.

Berens, Penny, Candy Malherbe, and Andy Smith. *The Cape Herders: A History of the Khoikhoi of Southern Africa*. Emile Boonzaier, ed. Athens: Ohio University Press, 1998.

Birmingham, David. *Trade and Conflict in Angola: The Mbundu and their Neighbours under the Influence of the Portuguese, 1483–1790*. Oxford, UK: Clarendon Press, 1966.

Birmingham, David and Phyllis M. Martin, eds. *History of Central Africa*. 2 vols. New York: Longman, 1983.

Bonner, Philip L. *Kings, Commoners, and Concessionaires: The Evolution and Dissolution of the Nineteenth-Century Swazi State*. Johannesburg: Ravan Press, 1983.

Brett, Michael, and Elizabeth Fentress. *The Berbers*. Malden, Mass.: Blackwell Publishing, 1997.

Brooks, George E. *Landlords and Strangers: Ecology, Society, and Trade in Western Africa, 1000–1630*. Boulder, Colo.: Westview Press, 1993.

Brooks, Miguel F., trans. and ed. *Kebra Nagast [The Glory of Kings]*. Lawrenceville, N.J.: Red Sea Press, 1998.

Burr, Sandra and Adam Potkay, eds. *Black Atlantic Writers of the Eighteenth Century: Living the New Exodus in England and the Americas: Selections from the Writings of Ukawsaw Gronniosaw, John Marrant, Quobna Ottobah Cuguano, and Olaudah Equiano.* Hampshire, UK.: Palgrave, 1995.

Buxton, David. *The Abysinnians.* New York: Praeger Publishers, 1970.

Clarke, Peter B. *West Africa and Christianity.* London: E. Arnold, 1986.

Cleaveland, Timothy. *Becoming Walata: A History of Saharan Social Formation and Transformation.* Portsmouth, N.H.: Heinemann, 2002.

Clifford, Mary Louise. *From Slavery to Freetown; Black Loyalists After the American Revolution.* Jefferson, N.C.: McFarland & Company, 1999.

Cohen, David William. *The Historical Tradition of Busoga, Mukama and Kintu.* Oxford: Clarendon Press, 1972.

Crais, Clifton C. *White Supremacy and Black resistance in Pre-industrial South Africa: The Making of the Colonial Order in the Eastern Cape, 1770–1865.* New York: Cambridge University Press, 1992.

Crummey, Donald. *Land and Society in the Christian Kingdom of Ethiopia: From the Thirteenth to the Twentieth Century.* Urbana, Ill.: University of Illinois Press, 2000.

Cugoano, Ottobah. *Thoughts and Sentiments on the Evil of Slavery and Other Writings.* Vincent Caretta, ed. New York: Penguin, 1999.

Curtin, Philip D. *The Atlantic Slave Trade: A Census.* Madison, Wisc.: University of Wisconsin Press, 1969.

_____. *Economic Change in Precolonial Africa; Senegambia in the Era of the Slave Trade.* Madison, Wisc.: University of Wisconsin Press, 1975.

_____. *The Rise and Fall of the Plantation Complex,* 2nd ed. New York: Cambridge University Press, 1998.

Daaku, Kwame Yeboah. *Trade and Politics on the Gold Coast, 1600-1720: A Study of the African Reaction to European Trade.* London: Clarendon Press, 1970.

DeCorse, Christopher R. *An Archaeology of Elmina: Africans and Europeans on the Gold Coast, 1400–1900.* Washington, D.C.: Smithsonian Institution Press, 2001.

Duffy, James. *Portuguese Africa.* Cambridge, Mass.: Harvard University Press, 1959.

Eldredge, Elizabeth A. *A South African Kingdom: The Pursuit of Security in Nineteenth-century Lesotho.* New York: Cambridge University Press, 1993.

Elleh, Nnamdi. *African Architecture: Evolution and Transformation.* New York: McGraw-Hill, 1996.

Elphick, Richard. *Kraal and Castle: Khoikoi and the Founding of White South Africa.* New Haven, Conn.: Yale University Press, 1977.

Elphick, Richard and Giliomee, Hermann, eds. *The Shaping of South African Society, 1652–1840.* Rev. ed. Middletown, Conn.: Wesleyan University Press, 1988.

Ephirim-Donkor, Anthony. *African Spirituality.* Trenton, N.J.: Africa World Press, 1998.

Equiano, Olaudah. *The Interesting Narrative of the Life of Olaudah Equiano, or Gustavus Vassa the African, Written by Himself.* Werner Sollors, ed. New York: Norton, 2000.

Esposito, John L., ed. *The Oxford History of Islam.* New York: Oxford University Press, 2000.

Etherington, Norman. *The Great Treks: The Transformation of Southern Africa, 1815–1854.* New York: Longman, 2001.

Falola, Toyin, ed. *Warfare and Diplomacy in Precolonial Nigeria.* Madison, Wisc.: African Studies Program, University of Wisconsin, 1992.

Feierman, Steven. *The Shambaa Kingdom: A History.* Madison, Wisc.: University of Wisconsin Press, 1974

Fisher, Robert B. *West African Religious Traditions.* Maryknoll, New York: Orbis Books, 1998.

Floyd, Samuel A., Jr. *The Power of Black Music.* New York: Oxford University Press, 1995.

Forester, C. S. *The Barbary Pirates.* Mattituck, New York: Amereon House, 1975.

Gailey, Harry A., Jr. *A History of the Gambia.* London: Routledge & Kegan Paul, 1964.

Garrard, Timothy F. *Akan Weights and the Gold Trade.* London: Longmans, 1980.

Hair, P. E. H., Adam Jones, and Robin Law, eds. *Barbot on Guinea: The Writings of Jean Barbot on West Africa 1678–1712*. London: The Hakluyt Society, 1992.

Hall, Martin. *Farmers, Kings, and Traders: The People of Southern Africa 200–1860*. Chicago: University of Chicago Press, 1990.

Hassan, Yusuf Fadl. *The Arabs and the Sudan*. Edinburgh: Edinburgh University Press, 1967.

Hassen, Mohammed. *The Oromo of Ethiopia: A History, 1570–1860*. New York: Cambridge University Press, 1990.

Hilton, Anne. *The Kingdom of Kongo*. Oxford, UK: Oxford Studies in African Affairs, 1985.

Hiskett, Mervyn. *The Development of Islam in West Africa*. New York: Longman, 1984.

_____. *The Sword of Truth: The Life and Times of the Shehu Usuman dan Fodio*. New York: Oxford University Press, 1973.

_____. *The Course of Islam in Africa*. Edinburgh: Edinburgh University Press, 1994.

Holt, Peter Malcolm, and M. W. Daly. *The History of the Sudan, from the Coming of Islam to the Present Day*, 4th ed. New York: Longman, 1988.

Ifeka, Caroline, and G. T. Stride. *Peoples and Empires of West Africa*. New York: Africana Publishing Co., 1971.

Inikori, Joseph E., ed. *Forced Migration: The Impact of the Export Slave Trade on African Societies*. London: Hutchinson, 1982.

Isaacman, Allen F. *Mozambique: The Africanization of a European Institution; the Zambesi Prazos, 1750–1902*. Madison, Wisc.: University of Wisconsin Press, 1972.

Isichei, Elizabeth Allo. *A History of the Igbo People*. New York: St. Martin's Press, 1976.

_____. *A History of Nigeria*. London: Longmans, 1983.

Johnson, Douglas H. *Nuer Prophets*. New York: Oxford University Press, 1994.

Karugire, Samwiri Rubaraza. *A History of the Kingdom of Nkore in Western Uganda to 1896*. Oxford, UK: Clarendon Press, 1971.

Kiple, Kenneth F., ed. *The African Exchange: Toward a Biological History of Black People*. Durham, N.C.: Duke University Press, 1988.

Klein, Herbert S. *The Atlantic Slave Trade*. New York: Cambridge University Press, 1999.

Kusimba, Chapurukha M. *The Rise and Fall of the Swahili States*. Walnut Creek, Calif.: Altamira Press, 1999.

Law, Robin. *The Horse in West African History: The Role of the Horse in the Societies of Pre-colonial West Africa*. New York: Oxford University Press, 1980.

_____. *The Oyo Empire 1600–1836: A West African Imperialism in the Era of the Atlantic Slave Trade*. Oxford: Clarendon Press, 1977.

_____. *The Slave Coast of West Africa 1550–1750: The Impact of the Atlantic Save Trade on an African Society*. New York: Oxford University Press, 1991.

Law, Robin, ed. *From Slave Trade to "Legitimate" Commerce: The Commercial Transition in Nineteenth-Century West Africa*. New York: Cambridge University Press, 1995.

Levtzion, Nehemia and Randall L. Pouwels, eds. *The History of Islam in Africa*. Athens: Ohio University Press, 2000.

Lovejoy, Paul E. *Salt of the Desert Sun: A History of Salt Production and Trade in the Central Sudan*. New York: Cambridge University Press, 1986.

Lovejoy, Paul E. *Transformations in Slavery: A History of Slavery in Africa*, 2nd ed. New York: Cambridge University Press, 2000.

Lynn, Martin. *Commerce and Economic Change in West Africa: The Palm Oil Trade in the Nineteenth Century*. New York: Cambridge University Press, 1997.

Manning, Patrick. *Slavery and African Life: Occidental, Oriental, and African Slave Trades*. New York: Cambridge University Press, 1990.

Marcus, Harold G. *A History of Ethiopia*. Berkeley, Calif.: University of California Press, 1994.

Martin, Bradford G. *Muslim Brotherhoods in Nineteenth Century Africa*. New York: Cambridge University Press, 1976.

McCann, James. *Green Land, Brown Land, Black Land: An Environmental History of Africa, 1800–1990.* Westport, Conn.: Heinemann, 1999.

McCarthy, Justin. *The Ottoman Turks: An Introductory History to 1923.* New York: Longman, 1997.

McCaskie, T. C. *State and Society in Pre-colonial Asante.* New York: Cambridge University Press, 1995.

Middleton, John. *The World of the Swahili.* New Haven, Conn.: Yale University Press, 1992.

Miers, Suzanne, and Igor Kopytoff, eds. *Slavery in Africa: Historical and Anthropological Perspectives.* Madison, Wisc.: University of Wisconsin Press, 1977.

Miller, Joseph C. *Kings and Kinsmen: Early Mbundu States in Angola.* Oxford, UK: Clarendon Press, 1976.

Miller, Joseph Calder. *Way of Death: Merchant Capitalism and the Angolan Slave Trade, 1730-1830.* Madison, Wisc.: University of Wisconsin Press, 1988.

Mudenge, S. I. G. *A Political history of Munhumutapa, c 1400–1902.* Harare: Zimbabwe Publishing House, 1988.

Northrup, David. *Africa's Discovery of Europe: 1450 to 1850.* New York: Oxford University Press, 2002.

Ogot, B. A., ed. *UNESCO General History of Africa. Vol. V, Africa from the Sixteenth to the Eighteenth Century.* Berkeley, Calif.: University of California Press, 1992.

Ojo, G. J. Afolabi. *Yoruba Culture: A Geographical Analysis.* London: University of London Press, 1966.

Page, Willie F. *The Dutch Triangle: The Netherlands and the Atlantic Slave Trade, 1621–1664.* New York: Garland, 1997.

Pankhurst, Richard. *The Ethiopian Borderlands.* Lawrenceville, N. J.: The Red Sea Press, 1997.

_____. *History of Ethiopian Towns from the Middle Ages to the Early 19th Century.* Philadelphia: Coronet Books, 1985.

Park, Mungo. *Travels in the Interior Districts of Africa.* Kate F. Marsters, ed. Durham: Duke Univ. Press, 2000.

Parry, J. H. *The Age of Reconnaissance.* Berkeley, Calif.: University of California Press, 1982.

Pearson, Michael N. *Port Cities and Intruders: The Swahili Coast, India, and Portugal in the Early Modern Era.* Baltimore, Md.: Johns Hopkins University Press, 1999.

Peires, Jeffrey B. *The House of Phalo: A History of the Xhosa People in the Days of their Independence.* Berkeley, Calif.: University of California Press, 1982.

Pennell, C.R. *Morocco since 1830: A History.* New York: New York University Press, 2000.

Peters, F. E. *The Hajj.* Princeton, N.J.: Princeton University Press, 1994.

Quataert, Donald *The Ottoman Empire, 1700–1922.* Cambridge, UK.: Cambridge University Press, 2000.

Reefe, Thomas Q. *The Rainbow and the Kings: A History of the Luba Empire to 1891.* Berkeley, Calif.: University of California Press, 1981.

Rodney, Walter. *A History of the Upper Guinea Coast, 1545–1800.* Oxford, UK: Clarendon Press, 1970.

_____. *How Europe Underdeveloped Africa.* rev. pbk. ed. Washington, D.C.: Howard University Press, 1981.

Ross, Robert. *Adam Kok's Griquas: A Study in the Development of Stratification in South Africa.* New York: Cambridge University Press, 1976.

Ruedy, John D. *Modern Algeria: The Origins and Development of a Nation.* Bloomington: Indiana Univ. Press, 1992.

Ryder, Alan Frederick Charles. *Benin and the Europeans, 1485–1897.* New York: Humanities Press, 1969.

Sayyid-Marsot, Afaf Lutfi. *Egypt in the Reign of Muhammad Ali.* (Cambridge, UK, Cambridge Univ. Press, 1984).

Scarr, Deryck. *Slaving and Slavery in the Indian Ocean.* Hampshire, UK.: Palgrave, 1998.

Schoffeleers, J. Matthew. *River of Blood: The Genesis of a Martyr Cult in Southern Malawi, c. A.D. 1600.* Madison, Wisc.: University of Wisconsin Press, 1992.

Searing, James F. *West African Slavery and Atlantic Commerce: The Senegal River Valley, 1700–1860.* New York: Cambridge University Press, 1993.

Shell, Robert Carl-Heinz. *Children of Bondage: A Social History of the Slave Society at the Cape of Good Hope, 1652–1838.* Hanover, N.H.: University Press of New England, 1994.

Sheriff, Abdul. *Slaves, Spices, & Iivory in Zanzibar: Integration of an East African Commercial Empire into the World Economy, 1770–1873.* Athens: Ohio Univ. Press, 1987.

Shick, Tom W. *Behold the Promised Land: A History of Afro-American Settler Society in Nineteenth-Century Liberia.* Baltimore, Md.: Johns Hopkins University Press, 1980.

Sweetman, David. *Women Leaders in African History.* Exeter, N.H.: Heinemann, 1984.

Thomas-Emeagwali, Gloria, ed. *Science and Technology in African History with Case Studies from Nigeria, Sierra Leone, Zimbabwe and Zambia.* Lewiston, N.Y.: The Edwin Mellen Press, 1992.

Thompson, Leonard Monteath. *A History of South Africa,* 3rd ed. New Haven, Conn.: Yale University Press, 2001.

_____. *Survival in Two Worlds: Moshoeshoe of Lesotho, 1786–1870.* Oxford: Clarendon Press, 1975.

Thornton, John Kelly. *Africa and Africans in the Making of the Atlantic World, 1400–1800,* 2nd ed. New York: Cambridge University Press, 1998.

_____. *The Kingdom of Kongo: Civil War and Transition, 1641–1718.* Madison, Wisc.: Univ. of Wisconsin Press, 1983.

_____. *The Kongolese Saint Anthony: Dona Beatriz Kimpa Vita and the Antonian Movement, 1684–1706.* New York: Cambridge University Press, 1998.

Valensi, Lucette. *Tunisian Peasants in the Eighteenth and Nineteenth Centuries.* Translated by Beth Archer. New York: Cambridge University Press, 1985.

_____. *On the Eve of Colonialism: North Africa before the French Conquest.* Translated by Kenneth J. Perkins. New York: Africana Pub. Co., 1977.

Vansina, Jan. *Paths in the Rainforests.* Madison, Wisc.: University of Wisconsin Press, 1990.

Vansina, Jan. *The Children of Woot: A History of the Kuba Peoples.* Madison: University of Wisconsin Press, 1978.

Webb, James L. A. *Desert Frontier: Ecological and Economic Change along the Western Sahel, 1600–1850.* Madison, Wisc.: University of Wisconsin Press, 1995.

Wilks, Ivor. *Asante in the Nineteenth Century: The Structure and Evolution of a Political Order.* New York: Cambridge University Press, 1989.

Worden, Nigel. *Slavery in Dutch South Africa.* New York: Cambridge University Press, 1985.

Wright, Donald R. *The World and a Very Small Place in Africa.* Armonk, N.Y.: M. E. Sharpe, 1997.

Wrigley, Christopher. *Kingship and State: The Buganda Dynasty.* New York: Cambridge University Press, 1996.

INDEX FOR THIS VOLUME

Bold page numbers indicate main entries. Page numbers followed by the letter *c* refer to a timeline; the letter *f* refers to illustrations; and the letter *m* indicates a map.